ALSO BY STEVEN SOLOMON

Small Business U.S.A.—
The Role of Small Companies in Sparking
America's Economic Transformation

THE CONFIDENCE GAME

HOW UNELECTED CENTRAL BANKERS ARE GOVERNING THE CHANGED GLOBAL ECONOMY

STEVEN SOLOMON

SIMON & SCHUSTER

New York London Toronto Sydney Tokyo Singapore

SIMON & SCHUSTER
ROCKEFELLER CENTER
1230 AVENUE OF THE AMERICAS
NEW YORK, NY 10020

DESIGNED BY IRVING PERKINS ASSOCIATES
MANUFACTURED IN THE UNITED STATES OF AMERICA

1   3   5   7   9   10   8   6   4   2

LIBRARY OF CONGRESS CATALOGING-IN-PUBLICATION DATA
SOLOMON, STEVEN.
THE CONFIDENCE GAME : HOW UNELECTED CENTRAL BANKERS ARE GOVERNING
THE CHANGED GLOBAL ECONOMY / STEVEN SOLOMON.
P.   CM.
INCLUDES BIBLIOGRAPHICAL REFERENCES AND INDEX.
1. BANKS AND BANKING, CENTRAL.   2. MONEY SUPPLY.   3. INTERNATIONAL
FINANCE.   4. BANKERS.   5. GOVERNMENT EXECUTIVES.   I. TITLE.
II. TITLE: CENTRAL BANKERS
HG1811.S65   1995
332.1'1—DC20   94-45734
CIP
ISBN 0-684-80182-5

Acknowledgments

This book could not have been written without the generous cooperation of many individuals. I would first like to express my gratitude to the two hundred fifty busy public and private officials around the world who consented to be interviewed, often at length and on more than one occasion, for the book. The project simply could not have been completed without them. Most of those interviewed were not quoted. Yet their contribution informs the author's voice throughout. Many were part of the unknown cadre of public technocrats who staff the world's central banks. I and my fellow citizens of the industrial democracies owe them a debt of thanks for their diligence, intelligence, and dedication to the public good of maintaining financial order throughout this trying era. They are too many to name here.

I owe an exceptional debt to Professor William Branson of Princeton's Woodrow Wilson School, who enlightened my understanding of international economics, as well as real-world economic politics, during long private tutorials over *pranzo* at a trattoria across from the Foro di Traiano in Rome. I am also grateful to Bill for helping me experience the lively circuit of academic conferences on international monetary economic issues. He is a great teacher. I also am indebted in a similar vein to Professor Alberto Giovannini of Columbia University and, more recently, of the Italian Treasury, and to Professor Neils Thygesen of the University of Copenhagen. I would be remiss not to acknowledge as well the generous education I received from three central bank economists, Kengo Inoue of the Bank of Japan, Hans Josef Düdler of the Bundesbank, and M. Akbar Akhtar of the Federal Reserve Bank of New York.

William P. Bray, Tag Murphy, and Ignacio Ponce de Leon read all or parts of early drafts and offered insightful observations that helped shape the final manuscript. My deepest appreciation as well to Professor Robert Heilbroner of the New School and Princeton Professor Peter Kenen for reviewing the final manuscript for comment.

Much of what is right about the book I owe in part to the above named individuals. All errors, of course, are mine.

I am especially grateful to the many persons who made introductions on my behalf. At the risk of offending those not mentioned, I would like to single out Alexandre Lamfalussy, Jerry Corrigan, Jeremy Morse, Walter Wriston, Mario Schimberni, Rob Johnson, Tim McNamar, and Jack Loughran.

Wherever I traveled, I was greatly assisted by the collegial help of fellow journalists. I owe double thanks to Yoichi Funabashi: once for sharing insights from his outstanding book *Managing the Dollar* and once for helping open important doors for me in Japan. I thank Karel G. van Wolferen for countless insights, hours of stimulating conversation, and generous help regarding many facets of the book's publication. Peter Norman took a beneficent interest at an early stage, as did Peter Kilborn. Mike Tharp helped make my visits to Japan far more productive by arranging guest membership privileges at the Foreign Correspondents' Club. The Japan Foreign Press Center was helpful. I wish to extend thanks to my friends Peter Koenig, Darrell Delamaide, Sharon Reier, Rick Smith, and Kevin McAuliffe, who in various ways helped me along the right track.

I benefited immeasurably from standout assistance from several public affairs officials, including Peter Bakstansky of the New York Fed, Joseph Coyne of the Federal Reserve Board, Philip Warland and his successor, John Footman, at the Bank of England, the Bundesbank's Manfred Körber, and Tetsuya Nishida of the Bank of Japan. I would also like to thank the exceptionally able former IMF public affairs officer Hellmut Hartmann.

My editor at Simon & Schuster, Bob Asahina, made my work a great deal easier with his patience, organizational suggestions, and intelligent observations throughout. His assistant, Sarah Pinckney, has been a model of competence and kindness.

I thank Melanie Jackson, my agent, for giving me support at key junctures as well as for her excellent representation.

The most special thanks of all goes to my dad, Lee Solomon, who read and discussed the manuscript at every stage with acumen and the solidarity of a best friend.

Finally, to *mio amore,* Claudine, who has lived the project with me in countless ways, I am eternally grateful for keeping me anchored in the really important things in life.

TO ALL MY GIRLS:
CLAUDINE, NOLA, CORDELIA, AURELIA, AND MY DEAR MOM

Contents

Dramatis Personae*

The Americas

Wayne Angell, governor Federal Reserve Board of Governors
James Baker, Reagan White House chief of staff, U.S. Treasury secretary, later secretary of state in Bush Administration
Howard Baker, Senate majority leader, Reagan White House chief of staff
Nicholas Brady, Dillon Read chairman and chairman of the Brady Report, U.S. Treasury secretary
Arthur Burns, chairman Federal Reserve Board
Richard Darman, deputy treasury secretary
C. Todd Conover, comptroller of the currency
E. Gerald Corrigan, president of the Federal Reserve Bank of New York
John Crow, governor of the Bank of Canada
Miguel de la Madrid, president of Mexico
George Gould, U.S. Treasury undersecretary for finance
Alan Greenspan, chairman Federal Reserve Board
Jesus Silva Herzog, finance minister of Mexico
Manuel Johnson Jr., vice chairman Federal Reserve Board of Governors
José Lopez Portillo, president of Mexico
R. T. (Tim) McNamar, U.S. deputy treasury secretary
G. William Miller, chairman Federal Reserve Board, U.S. Treasury secretary
David Mulford, U.S. Treasury assistant secretary and undersecretary for international affairs
Gustavo Petriocioli, finance minister of Mexico
John Phelan, New York Stock Exchange president
Lewis Preston, chairman J. P. Morgan, later president of the World Bank
Donald Regan, U.S. Treasury secretary, White House chief of staff
John Reed, chairman of Citibank
William Rhodes, senior executive at Citibank and chairman of the international bank advisory committees for many troubled LDC debtors

* Titles are listed according to those that are most germane to the book.

George Shultz, U.S. secretary of state

Anthony Solomon, undersecretary of the U.S. Treasury for monetary affairs and president of Federal Reserve Bank of New York

Beryl Sprinkel, undersecretary of the U.S. Treasury for monetary affairs, chairman White House council of economic advisers

William Taylor, director division of banking supervision and regulation, Federal Reserve Board

Edwin Truman, director division of international finance, Federal Reserve Board

Paul Volcker, chairman Federal Reserve Board

Walter Wriston, chairman Citibank

Europe

Edouard Balladur, French finance minister, later prime minister

George Blunden, deputy governor of the Bank of England

Michel Camdessus, Bank of France governor, IMF managing director

Carlo Azeglio Ciampi, governor of the Bank of Italy, later Italian prime minister

Peter Cooke, chairman of the G10 Committee on Banking Regulations and Supervisory Practices and Bank of England associate director

Jacques de Larosière, IMF managing director, governor of the Bank of France

Jacques Delors, president of the European Commission

Lamberto Dini, deputy governor Bank of Italy and chairman of the G10 deputies, later Italian Treasury Secretary, later Prime Minister

Otmar Emminger, president of the Bundesbank

Wilfried Guth, speaker of managing board, Deutsche Bank

Helmut Hesse, member of Bundesbank central bank council, Land central bank president in Lower Saxony

Erik Hoffmeyer, chairman Denmark National Bank

Helmut Kohl, German federal chancellor

Norbert Kloten, member of Bundesbank central bank council, president of Land central bank in Baden-Württemberg

Alexandre Lamfalussy, general manager Bank for International Settlements

Nigel Lawson, U.K. Chancellor of the Exchequer

Daniel Lebegue, director of French treasury, ministry of finance

Robin Leigh Pemberton, governor of the Bank of England

Fritz Leutwiler, president Swiss National Bank

Geoffrey Littler, second permanent secretary of the U.K. Treasury

Jeremy Morse, chairman Lloyds Bank Plc

Wilhelm Nölling, Bundesbank central bank council member and president
   of the Land Central Bank in Freien and Hansetadt
Karl Otto Pöhl, president of the Bundesbank
Brian Quinn, executive director in charge of supervision Bank of England
Gordon Richardson, governor of the Bank of England
Helmut Schlesinger, Bundesbank vice president and president
Helmut Schmidt, German federal chancellor
Gerhard Stoltenberg, German minister of finance
Margaret Thatcher, U.K. prime minister
Hans Tietmeyer, state secretary German finance ministry, vice president and
   president of the Bundesbank
Jean-Claude Trichet, director of French treasury of the ministry of finance,
   governor of the Bank of France

Asia

Tadao Chino, Japanese ministry of finance director general of banking bu-
   reau, later vice minister for international affairs
David Finch, IMF director of exchange and trade relations
Tsuneo Fujita, director general, securities bureau of the Japanese ministry
   of finance
Toyoo Gyohten, Japanese finance vice minister for international affairs
Takashi Hosomi, member of Nakasone's Advisory Friends Group and for-
   mer Japanese vice minister of finance for international affairs
Yusuke Kashiwagi, chairman Bank of Tokyo and former vice minister of fi-
   nance for international affairs
Haruo Maekawa, governor Bank of Japan
Yasushi Mieno, governor Bank of Japan
Kaneo Nakamura, president Industrial Bank of Japan
Kiichi Miyazawa, Japanese finance minister, later prime minister
Yasuhiro Nakasone, Japanese prime minister
Tomomitsu Oba, Japanese vice minister of finance for international affairs
Shijuro Ogata, Bank of Japan deputy governor for international relations
Takeshi Ohta, Bank of Japan deputy governor for international relations
Satoshi Sumita, governor Bank of Japan
Yoshio Suzuki, executive director Bank of Japan
Setsuya Tabuchi, chairman Nomura Securities Co.
Noboru Takeshita, Japanese finance minister, later prime minister
Makoto Utsumi, Japanese ministry of finance director general of interna-
   tional finance bureau, vice minister for international affairs

Introduction

"Follow the money!" I can still hear the voice of my first editor at *Forbes* magazine exhorting me years ago that it was the trail of money that would lead us to the core of any story. In writing this book, I have in a sense "followed the money" to its origins—into the secretive society of the central bankers who manage the democratic world's supply of money.

Central bankers' fingerprints are everywhere behind the daily financial headlines: the rise and fall of interest rates, the ups and downs of the dollar, the emergency rescue of a crashing stock market or a nation in crisis. But they themselves are rarely seen or understood except by an elite minority.

Through behind-the-scenes, dramatic narrative, I have attempted to report for the general audience who the central bankers are, how they have shaped the course of economic and political events in the past fifteen years, why their influence relative to elected political leaders has reached a historical zenith, and how it reveals one of the greatest pressing dangers facing free market democratic society. I believe the specialized reader as well will find inside these pages much heretofore unknown information that illuminates the public record.

The heart of the reporting is two hundred fifty personal interviews I conducted during two round-the-world trips with American, European, and Japanese central bankers; the finance ministers, bank chairmen, and senior political leaders with whom they consort; and the financial market investors and economists who scrutinize and react to their every move. (A list of those interviewed is at the back.)

International financial relations among nations, it has been said, are accorded privileges of secrecy second only to national security. With limited legal obligations to reveal their private deliberations and an aversion to publicity, central bankers in particular operate in the public half light. Only a few, such as the U.S. Federal Reserve Board's Paul Volcker and Alan Greenspan and the German Bundesbank's Karl Otto Pöhl, are well-known names; most citizens have never heard of the Bank of Japan's Yasushi Mieno, the Bundesbank's Hans Tietmeyer, or the Bank of England's Eddie George.

I found central bankers' reputation for being tight-lipped to be well deserved. Verbal parsimony is understandably inbred among individuals whose few words, or even casual "No comment," can set world financial markets into spasm and political leaders to ranting. Gradually, however, they accepted my questions and held forth.

The panorama that came into view from their unique position at the financial apex of the world economy was dramatic and disturbing: free market democracy was undergoing a historical transformation driven by an oceanic tide of "stateless" money that broke free from national borders in the 1980s financial revolution. Stateless money was surging unanchored through integrated private financial markets across sovereign borders at lightning-fast speed and volatility, altering national interest rate levels, currency values, employment, savings and investment patterns, growth rates, and everyday human lives as it came and went. Its great size and force overwhelmed all government efforts to control it. Its internally driven financial dynamics often collided with, and effectively vetoed, national economic policies. For lengthy periods, its trends also divorced from the underlying fundamentals of the real economy, producing the unprecedented exchange rate misalignments, economic imbalances, and financial booms and crashes that have marked the era.

As power shifted to financial markets and away from governments, more of the world's key governing economic decisions were falling to central bankers. Their unspoken role to straddle the uneasy marriage of convenience over money between free markets and democratic governments gave them unique tools to influence stateless capital flows and to contain the worst economic damage from the violent excesses to which it was prone. But maintaining confidence and order was growing more difficult as stateless money altered the workings of the postwar economy in novel ways that were dimly understood by economists and politicians.

Following the trail of money to central bankers led, in short, to a second, larger story about the global political economic transformations being wrought by the rise of stateless money of which central bankers' increased importance was but one manifestation. This dual story of central banker prominence and the advent of stateless money defines the book's structure.

Part One introduces the theme by narrating central bankers' role in containing the 1987 global stock market crash, which dramatically warned of the perils in the changed landscape. Part Two recounts central bankers' key role in postwar democracy's great economic success in the early 1980s in beating back inflation, which itself spurred and was fueled by the financial revolution. Part Three reports how central bankers engineered the unprecedented, multiyear rescue that saved the world from a likely depression when the Less Developed Countries (LDC) debt bubble burst in mid-1982. One of the largest and most needlessly painful disruptions in economic history was the astronomical rise and near collapse of the superdollar. Through the secret G5 and G7 Plaza, Louvre, and "Christmas" Accords, as revealed in Part Four, central bankers connived with, and at times against, finance ministers to bring down the dollar without a crash landing. Part Five narrates the unknown story behind central bankers' pioneering diplomatic achievement of the first worldwide regulatory standard for stateless money. When the warning message delivered by the 1987 stock market crash went unheeded, the record economic imbalances and financial excesses finally combined to throw America and the world into an unusual type of recession not experienced since the Great Depression. Part Six tells how central bankers steered the world away from a financial and economic precipice that was much closer than most people realize. The epilogue makes the case for the remarkable worldwide trend to upgrade central bank independence. It underlines that the great, unmet political challenge of the new post–Cold War era is to "civilize" stateless money with world rules and reforms before the productiveness of the free market economy and the stability of democratic society are damaged. Until then, the world's well-being will be uncomfortably dependent upon the judgment of a tiny cadre of unelected and secretive world central bankers.

Our stability is but balance, and conduct lies
in masterful administration of the unforeseen.
                    —From Robert Bridges, *The Testament of Beauty*

PART ONE

CRASH THAT SHOOK THE WORLD

Chapter 1

Black Monday

Alan Greenspan, newly appointed chairman of the Federal Reserve Board, disembarked from his airplane at the Dallas–Fort Worth Airport at 5 P.M. (eastern time) on Monday, October 19, 1987. "How did the stock market close?" he inquired.

"Five oh eight," Greenspan was told.

"What a recovery," he commented in his unexcitable soft voice, thinking 5.08 was meant. When he'd left the central bank's white marble headquarters overlooking Constitution Avenue in Washington, D.C., it had been down a record 250, but rallying.

"No, five *hundred* and eight!"

Greenspan's eyes widened incredulously behind his thick black frame eyeglasses. "Five hundred and eight?!"

Greenspan had come to Dallas to address America's leading bankers at the annual American Bankers Association convention. It was an important event on any Federal Reserve Board chairman's calendar. But it was especially so for Greenspan. This would be the first opportunity for the commercial banking fraternity to size up the kind of leadership to expect from the man who had replaced the legendary Paul Volcker on August 11 as head of America's politically independent central bank. By national opinion poll Volcker had ranked as the United States' second most powerful man after the president. In Washington he was feared and revered as the only man capable of standing up to Ronald Reagan's redoubtable political popularity. In U.S. and world financial capitals, he stood beside George Washington as the symbol of the U.S. dollar's integrity and unofficial leader of the world economy.

This mantle had now passed to Greenspan, sixty-one. The mild-mannered former professional jazz musician, self-made millionaire, and Wall Street economic forecaster with a passion for numbers crunching had been entrusted with one of the world's most awesome levers of political power: mo-

nopoly power to regulate the U.S. and world's money, the dollar. With it came
captaincy of world interest rate levels and financial system stability.

Five hundred and eight! Volume of 608 million shares, more than three
times normal! Sellers outnumbering buyers forty to one! About $700 mil-
lion in market value—Americans' wealth—wiped out! One and a half years
of stock market gains lost!

It was like a massive heart attack in the financial system. It worked out to
a fall in the New York Stock Exchange's (NYSE) Dow Jones Index of 22.6
percent, more precipitous than the 1929 Great Crash of Black Thursday, October 24, and Black Tuesday, October 29. The Great Crash had been associated with the subsequent collapses in the U.S. and world banking systems
and the 1930s Great Depression.

The failure to prevent that economic tragedy had been the central banking profession's darkest ignominy, a miserable failure to meet its raison
d'être. On Black Monday that collective memory informed the actions of
Greenspan and his fellow central bank governors from the leading capitalist
democracies, who had clubbed together for two days of fine cuisine and top-
secret discussions each month at the Bank for International Settlements
(BIS) in Basel, Switzerland, to discuss, and sometimes cooperate in steering,
world monetary and economic affairs.

The October 1987 crash stunned Greenspan, and everyone else, by knock-
ing over the world's stock markets like dominoes regardless of their level,
underlying business, or national economic prospects. The significance was
plain to the few, like central bankers, who sat at the financial apex of the
world economy: the dawning epoch of "stateless" money was even further
advanced than they had imagined.

The emergence of the new regime of mobile, stateless capital amounted
to a silent coup d'état in the capitalist democratic world. Large, volatile volumes of high-speed capital had broken free of sovereign political control to
roam freely across national borders and the financial compartments within
which governments tried to confine and manage them throughout the postwar era. Instead of passively following the ebbs and flows of real economic
activity, modulated by government policies, the "symbol economy" of finance had become the "flywheel of the world economy."[1]

Increasingly, and in as yet dimly understood ways, stateless money was
defining the policy options of elected democratic governments, reordering
the economic and political balances over which groups within democracies
had struggled for decades, altering the power balances among nations, and
governing the fortunes of individual human lives from Peoria, U.S.A., to
Nagoya, Japan, to Rennes, France, to São Paolo, Brazil. It was a financial revolution akin in importance to the Industrial Revolution two hundred years
before.

As power slipped away from governments to financial markets, more of the world's governing economic choices were falling to the shadowy club of unelected central bankers who managed the world's money. Central bankers' special ability to influence the growing flows of stateless money was rendering to them more of the key political decisions about growth and recession, national currency values, and financial regulation that determined who won and who lost within society. Frequently they were doing so as emergency firefighters to prevent the unprecedented economic imbalances and fragile financial system arising from the globalization of capital from ending in catastrophe—the global stock market crash of October 1987 was a warning flare of distress. From the mid-1980s Paul Volcker often privately confided his fear of a "catastrophic chain reaction" in the financial system.[2] On October 19 many wondered if the day of reckoning had finally arrived.

Even before taking office in August 1987, Greenspan fretted that the stratospheric rise in stock prices constituted a speculative bubble, divorced from any realistic expectation of future corporate profits or other underlying economic fundamentals. Bursting bubbles historically often triggered financial crises and sometimes economic disasters.

While stock prices gyrated on Black Monday before the final terrifying 250-point late afternoon free-fall, which occurred while he was airborne, Greenspan had conferred whether or not to go to Dallas with Treasury Undersecretary for Finance George Gould and Federal Reserve Vice Chairman Manuel ("Manley") Johnson Jr. Johnson advised against the trip. But Greenspan, a reflective and cautious man, didn't want to risk showing any sign of panic. If order was to be restored in the depths of a crisis, a central banker had to display an almost otherworldly aura of confidence and calm.

Imperious and enigmatic, behind half-explained thoughts and a swirl of cigar smoke, Volcker had had this aura in spades. "Almost surely the biggest mistake of the Reagan presidency was the failure to press for Paul Volcker's reappointment as Fed chairman," opined *The Wall Street Journal*.[3] Within hours Wall Street was rife with unfounded rumors that Volcker was returning to Washington as Treasury secretary.

To *not* make the speech to America's bankers, his first major address as Fed chairman, Greenspan felt, might suggest that things were really out of hand. Before departing, however, he told Manley Johnson, "Let's convene the group."[4]

The "group" was a Fed financial crisis management team Greenspan had organized upon assuming the chairmanship.[5] The crisis team convened in the special library near Greenspan's office. It opened communication links with the Securities and Exchange Commission (SEC), the Commodity Futures Trading Commission (CFTC), and the Federal Reserve Banks of New York and Chicago. It began gathering and coordinating information. When

Greenspan got to Dallas, his first call was to Johnson, who camped there overnight. He also conferred with New York Fed chief E. Gerald Corrigan and with Gould.

Hardly was Greenspan settled into his Dallas hotel room when he got an urgent call from Howard Baker, President Reagan's chief of staff. By his own admission Baker, a longtime Tennessee Republican senator who had been majority leader, was "no champion expert on economic and financial matters." On Black Monday Baker had found himself alone in the nation's capital without top-ranking U.S. financial officials. "I looked for [Treasury Secretary] Jim Baker, but he was in Sweden," Baker recalls. "I looked for Alan Greenspan, but he was in Texas." Secretary of State George Shultz, an ex–Treasury secretary, was in the Middle East.

"I need you to come back," Baker told Greenspan.

"I can't, I'm about to speak tomorrow to the American Bankers Association."

"I need you more than they do."

They reviewed the next day's airplane schedules. None got Greenspan back fast enough for Baker. "Look," Baker decided, "I'm going to send a White House airplane down to Dallas to stand by to get you."[6]

"It [the crash] was the most terrifying moment of my public life," Baker reflects now. "I mean it."

Throughout Black Monday Baker arranged for President Reagan to get hourly market updates. About every thirty minutes he briefed Reagan on developments. Sometimes the president couldn't wait even that long and would call Baker for news. In concert with Gould, he also conferred with U.S. financiers and businessmen as well as private leaders he knew in Japan and England.[7]

In the frantic search for a response to the losses and chaos mounting on Black Monday, the big question became whether to close the stock market. That prospect became headline speculation at 1:09 P.M., when a Dow Jones newswire report quoted SEC Chairman David S. Ruder as saying that "there is some point, and I don't know what that point is, that I would be interested in talking to the NYSE about a temporary, very temporary, halt in trading."[8] The market immediately nosedived. *Wall Street Journal* editorialists dubbed it the "200-point quote."[9]

Baker's staff discovered that the stock market could be shut down by executive order of the U.S. president or by the exchange. NYSE President John Phelan was under huge pressure to halt trading from members facing staggering losses. Phelan talked to Baker by 12:30 P.M. and was on the phone again to Baker, Gould, and the SEC throughout the day. He described the financial massacre and the disintegration of market mechanisms that were driving the world's preeminent stock market toward collapse. At a post-closing news conference at 4:20 P.M., an exhausted Phelan bravely maintained that the exchange would open on Tuesday. But he added that the experience "was as close to financial meltdown that I ever want to see."[10]

On Terrible Tuesday Phelan's pleas for White House acquiescence to close the stock market would grow absolutely desperate. Although he had the power to act alone, Phelan "wanted someone to take the heat with him because you could have had such unpleasant fallout. He wanted someone to hold his hand."[11]

At last Howard Baker took the decision to President Reagan.

"There was real anguish in the president's voice and eyes," recalls Baker of the Tuesday encounter. "At one point he said something like 'I don't want to intrude in the stock market more than is necessary.' Let's wait and see, was his attitude. But he was ready to do it."

Baker prepared the executive order to close the NYSE. It was entered into a White House word processor.[12]

No one believed closing the stock market was at best more than a temporary stopgap, a Band-Aid. Worse, it could backfire by driving the panic underground, where it would spread throughout the financial system.

The White House frantically wanted to avoid closure for political reasons as well. In the U.S. political psyche, Wall Street euphoria augured economic good times and electoral success. No one needed reminding that there'd been a Republican president during the Great Crash of 1929. Closure would also have represented the failure of the Reagan Revolution's promised renaissance of the U.S. economy and postwar political hegemony. Along with the kindred policies of Margaret Thatcher in the United Kingdom, Reaganism represented an effort to reassert the faltering primacy of the laissez-faire, Anglo-Saxon model of capitalism that had dominated the world political economy for two hundred years. But potent newer forms of capitalism, with cozier relationships among markets and government, had arisen to challenge it, especially among World's War II's vanquished West Germany and Japan.

No single institution more represented the quintessence of Anglo-Saxon capitalism than the stock market. The five-year worldwide bull market in stocks provided the first and most hopeful sign of the revitalization Reagan promised. From 777 on August 11, 1982, the NYSE more than tripled to the 2722 peak on August 25, 1987, ushering in along the way the 1980s global financial revolution.

If Wall Street boomed, the serious critics of Reagan's resurrected laissez-faire ideology could politically be ignored. The United States didn't need to heed the doomsayers who spoke of industrial policies, managed international trade, and overhaul of American education and labor-management practices. Good old American ingenuity, released from its government shackles, would once again generate such wealth and innovation to dwarf

foreign successes, quell self-doubts, and render moot the acrimony over unfair trade and record external imbalances threatening to topple the international liberal economic order.

But if the stock market collapsed—if markets were seen to fail—it would
shake the entire philosophical edifice upon which Reaganism was predicated
and deprive it of the self-fulfilling confidence and optimism essential to its
potential success.

Short of closing the stock market, top Reagan officials wondered as the
crisis unfolded on Black Monday, what could the president do to prevent a
catastrophe? Surely the most powerful man on earth could do *something!*
But what?

Should President Reagan make a statement? George Gould, one of the
few career Wall Street men in the Reagan administration, advised against it.
"It could be taken wrong, or *proven* wrong by events," he argued.

He explains, "For the first couple of days, we just didn't know what was
happening."

Nevertheless, as Black Monday grew bleaker and clamors to the White
House from Wall Street and Main Street grew more frantic, the political
pressure to say something grew irresistible. At a 3:45 P.M. meeting, Howard
Baker told a worried President Reagan that the market was down 350 points.
Several minutes later the staff slipped Baker a note: The market had closed
down 508. Reagan agreed that the White House should release a nonspecific,
soothing statement "that the underlying economy remains sound."[13]

It was a bust. R. W. Apple Jr. noted in next day's *New York Times:* "[W]hen
the market plunged in October 1929, President Herbert Hoover issued a
statement eerily similar to Mr. Reagan's: 'The fundamental business of the
country, that is production and distribution of commodities, is on a sound
and prosperous basis.' "[14]

Congress fell into a powerless silence. "I don't know what kind of legislative reaction you can have to a stock market decline," said House Majority
Leader Thomas Foley (D-Wash.).[15] A panicked, every-man-for-himself free-
for-all that could have only one disastrous, self-fulfilling conclusion gripped
U.S. and world financial markets. The dilemma was that neither Washington's elected politicians nor Wall Street's top financiers possessed the tools
for decisive, emergency leadership to forestall the crisis.

Only one institution, and one man, did—the U.S. central bank and its
chairman, Alan Greenspan. "A president can *say* something, but he can't *do*
anything," says Gould. "But the Fed has a well-established statutory position
and the ability to *do* something."

The godlike moment of the anonymity-seeking central banker came when
the smooth functioning of market mechanisms broke down, top financiers
were stampeding with the frightened herd to be first to the exit, cool heads

were befuddled with panic, and the financial system was heading for a total smash-up. It was then that he—and *only* he—had the capacity to call for a time-out, restore confidence, and then let play resume according to usual market mechanisms. Beyond him there was no last resort. He was the ultimate backstop in democratic capitalist society against the spreading degeneration of order in finance into economic and, ultimately, political life. With economies driven increasingly by the unpredictable, sometimes violently shifting expectations of stateless capital, unelected central bankers were emerging as leaders in a crucial political confidence game with global financial markets at the fulcrum of the changed world political economy.

On the evening of Black Monday, October 19, 1987, the most powerful leaders in Wall Street, Washington, and financial and political capitals throughout the world nervously awaited word of how the new Federal Reserve chairman would respond to the world's financial distress.

Chapter 2

Between Markets and Governments

The peculiar essence of the central banker's shadowy role in democratic society was revealed in a brief verbal exchange at a congressional hearing in June 1982 between Senator Edward Kennedy (D-Mass.) and Federal Reserve Board Chairman Paul Volcker. At the darkest moment of America's deepest recession since the 1930s, arising from the Fed's relentless campaign to break spiraling double-digit inflation through high interest rates, Kennedy vented his frustration: "If you were up here as a member of the Treasury, our relationship would be different."

"That's probably true," Volcker replied calmly behind a veil of smoke from his cigar. "But I believe it was intentionally designed this way."[1]

The elliptical reference of senator and central banker was to the occulted political struggle over the control of money, which had delivered to the Fed a unique status and power over the economy. Kennedy's voice was one of the angry congressional chorus demanding more growth on the threat of legislative curtailment of the Fed's independence. To critics, the fact that central bankers did not stand for election, deliberated in cloistered councils whose members were chosen partly by the private sector, operated almost exclusively behind the scenes at the pinnacles of high finance and politics, performed functions esoteric to most citizens, and enjoyed unique political freedom from the executive or Congress constituted an intolerable "democratic deficit." "Power without accountability simply does not fit into the American system of democracy," declares Rep. Lee Hamilton (D-Ind.).[2]

Volcker's mordant reply—in private he dismisses the "democratic deficit" charge as "wrong"—was an allusion to the fact that the U.S. Constitution rendered unto Congress the power to "coin Money, regulate the Value thereof, and of foreign Coin." It was Congress itself that saw fit to insulate the Fed as an independent agency.

The inherent tension between central bank and government was not exclusive to the United States. The German Bundesbank, railed Chancellor Konrad Adenauer in 1956, was "responsible to no one, neither to a Parliament nor to a government."[3]

Central bankers' power at times could make or break a presidency or prime ministership. Three of Adenauer's successors—Ludwig Erhard, Kurt Georg Kiesinger, and Helmut Schmidt—owed their political downfalls partly to the Bundesbank. Jimmy Carter putatively blamed two men above all for his 1980 presidential reelection defeat—Iran's Ayatollah Khomeini and Volcker. In 1992 President George Bush blamed the sluggish economy, which undermined his reelection bid, on Alan Greenspan, who had refused to bow to political arm-twisting for easier money. The new president, Bill Clinton, promptly signaled the importance he attached to the Fed by prominently seating Greenspan between the First Lady and vice-presidential wife Tipper Gore, in full view of TV cameras, for his February 1993 first State of the Union address outlining his new national economic agenda. No one had shaped the budget-deficit-cutting emphasis of that agenda more than Greenspan, whose lengthy explanations had persuaded the young president that without it bond markets would veto all his ambitious goals by spontaneously bidding up long-term interest rates.[4]

Notwithstanding differences in political autonomy, customary and legal authority, every major democratic capitalist nation had a central bank whose tasks and methods seemed, at first glance, to run against the grain of representative government. Their most important decisions were taken in secret by appointed councils or by a single governor with the help of advisers unknown to the public. The Bundesbank's deliberations were sealed for thirty years; the Bank of England's weren't fully available for one hundred years. The decisions of the Fed, the most open central bank, were kept secret for six weeks and only then released with a sterilized summary of the policy debate preceding it. Only a few central bankers were obliged to testify regularly before elected fora. Public press interviews were rare. Most central bankers were appointed for unrecallable terms and some, such as the governor of the Bank of Italy, effectively for life. A large number had statutory divorces from any obligation to finance their government's fiscal deficits. Budgetary autonomy by statute, and seigniorage profits from the monopoly production of money, further insulated them from the daily currents of democratic political pressure.

"I have no use for politicians," snaps Fritz Leutwiler, the ex-president of the privately owned, constitutionally independent Swiss National Bank. "They lack the judgment of central bankers."[5] Leutwiler's sentiments were shared by the heads of the world's other major central banks—Bank of England, Bank of Japan, Bank of Italy, Bank of Canada, Bank of France, Nederlandsche Bank, among them—who retreated ten times a year to their supranational second home, the BIS at Basel, in a cooperative ritual without parallel among policymakers. They were "international freemasons," possessing a natural second allegiance to the often lonely interest of international monetary order and sharing a sense of membership in an underappreciated, elite silent brotherhood unique in democratic capitalist society.

"Central bankers don't like governments," states Helmut Schmidt, ex–German chancellor. "The sheer existence of a government is a threat to the existence of the central bank."

"Central bankers tend to hang together," agrees Paul Volcker. "They feel disliked by their governments and misunderstood by the public."

High Priests of High Finance

Who were these enigmatic men whose special standing in democratic society caused powerful political leaders to fulminate and proud financiers to pay obeisance to their nods and winks? Why did taxpayers generally remunerate them more highly than their heads of state? What explained the contrast between central banks' physical splendor and the modesty of most government ministries striving to demonstrate frugality with public finances?

"No admittance, except on business" warned a sign near the two huge bronze front doors in the thirty-foot-high wall surrounding the Bank of England. Visitors to the three-acre complex of ornate masonry with grassy inner courtyards and laden with antique art were greeted by gatekeepers wearing the bank's historic livery of red waistcoats, pink tailcoats, and silk top hats. Rituals of bygone ages were carried out daily. Three floors below the "Old Lady of Threadneedle Street," the bank's moniker, was a gold vault holding the world's third largest store of bullion, a vestige of the era of British world hegemony at the heydey of the monetary gold standard.

The world's largest monetary gold holdings, 10,300 tons of non-U.S. gold, or one-third of official world reserves, had since accumulated in the fifth subbasement of the fourteen-story Italian Renaissance stone fortress of the Federal Reserve Bank of New York in Wall Street.[6] In the wood-paneled executive dining room on the tenth floor, important guests clipped their after-meal cigars with a golden cigar cutter.

The Bank of Italy and the Bank of France were literally former palaces, still replete with antique period furnishings, heavy draperies, and artwork. The stony elegance of the nineteenth-century Belgian architecture that distinguished the Bank of Japan, one of the few buildings to survive the Tokyo earthquake of 1923, stood in striking contrast with the shoddy, cramped offices of the powerful Ministry of Finance.

The culture inside these sumptuous environs likewise contrasted with the frenetic, partisan atmosphere of most democratic governing institutions. It was collegial, pensive, with an air of purpose higher than mundane politics. Ex–Fed Chairman Arthur Burns (1970–78), a lifelong Republican, was once interviewing Nancy Teeters for a potential board governorship, when Teeters suggested that he probably didn't want someone with her deep Democratic Party associations. Burns replied that it didn't matter. "In six months, everybody is a central banker."[7]

Central bankers' fingerprints were detectable in the stories behind the headlines they had quietly shaped over the past fifteen years: it was they who pulled the world back from the brink of spiraling inflation, saved it from the LDC (less developed countries) debt crisis and more financial distress than at any time since the Great Depression, and managed through currency crises, including the 1980s roller-coaster surge and near free-fall of the dollar; and it was they who were called upon to ride to the rescue on Black Monday. The Black Monday crash had been a warning shot by markets about unsustainable strains in the fragile financial system and unbalanced world economy. When it was ignored by political leaders, it would soon fall again to central bankers to rescue collapsing banking systems and to govern the world out of its first balance sheet recession since the 1930s—a "contained depression." Central bankers were the principals behind the world's first universal financial regulations. The Bundesbank was a central player in German reunification and European monetary union and economic integration. The Bank of Japan led the deflation of Japan's incredible bubble economy, which subjected that nation to its severest political and economic upheaval since World War II.

When economies were growing smoothly, central bankers were nearly invisible. This was as they preferred: not because they were men of shrinking egos, but because the delicacy of their anomalous political positions and the source of their influence with financial markets demanded it. Newspaper shorthand described them enigmatically as the bankers' bankers. On Wall Street they were " 'a financially celibate clergy' whose function is 'to guard us against ourselves.' The Federal Reserve is our economic conscience, and Paul Volcker was uniquely trained and temperamentally suited to be its high priest. Like our conscience, the Federal Reserve pinches and punishes us for our smaller sins, but its most important function is to prevent us from perpetrating the really big ones."[8] Most celebrated of all was the definition by one of their own, ex–Fed Chairman William McChesney Martin Jr. (1951–70): "To take away the punch bowl just when the party gets going."

Only in extraordinary times did the undesired notoriety fall on the reclusive central bankers. No mise-en-scène could obscure their paramount role in the crash that started on Black Monday in the United States and cascaded through world stock markets in Sydney, Hong Kong, Tokyo, Frankfurt, Milan, Paris, and London. Though spectacular, the global crash was only one of the series of events associated with the rise of stateless capital and the paralysis of constructive democratic world political response that was more often pushing Alan Greenspan and world central bankers into the unfamiliar glare of public spotlights. Increasingly, news media were reciting the names and deeds of Federal Reserve Chairmen Volcker and Greenspan; German Bundesbank Presidents Karl Otto Pöhl, Helmut Schlesinger, and Hans Tietmeyer; Bank of Japan Governors Haruo "Mike" Maekawa, Satoshi Sumita, and Yasushi Mieno; Swiss National Bank President Fritz Leutwiler; Bank of England Governors Gordon Richardson, Robin Leigh-Pemberton, and Eddie George; Bank of Italy Governors Carlo Azeglio Ciampi and Antonio Fazio; Governor John Crow of the Bank of Canada; Bank of France Governors Jacques de Larosière and Jean-Claude Trichet; and Bank for International Settlements General Manager Alexandre Lamfalussy. A new threshold was transcended in 1993 when Italy turned to Governor Ciampi to assume the prime ministership to rescue the country from one of its deepest political and economic crises since Mussolini.

Central bankers' unique power—the power that enabled Greenspan to act where even the president of the United States was powerless and caused the eyes of world leaders to be focused upon him on Black Monday—was exclusive control of the world's money: U.S. dollars, German deutsche marks, Japanese yen, British pounds, Swiss francs, French francs, Italian lire, Canadian dollars, Spanish pesetas, and Mexican pesos.

Money was a central organizing feature of civilization, a building block of economic society. In capitalist society money's role was paramount, carrying the DNA of economic life. It was the form in which wealth was measured, saved, traded, and recycled through the financial system to ever more productive investments—the core process of capitalism's fantastic historical capacity to produce wealth.

Central bankers regulated the supply of money in service of maximizing long-run economic production by striving to achieve two primary objectives: to steer the economy through the peaks and valleys of the business cycle in such a way as to maintain confidence in the currency; and to safeguard the orderly functioning of the financial system. Oversupply of money eventually led to ruinous hyperinflation, undersupply to unemployment, and recession.

Economic history was additionally littered with cases of depressions triggered and worsened by financial crises that abruptly severed the financial lifelines to all businesses without prejudice. To quell financial panics, such as Black Monday, central bankers stood ready like firefighters to inject emergency funds as "lenders of last resort." Supplementally, many possessed supervisory regulatory powers over banks, which supplied or backed up the bulk of the financial system's liquidity and were the main conduits for transferring payments from the accounts of buyer to seller whenever two parties made an economic transaction.

Recognition of money's vital economic role and the financial system's peculiar vulnerability to panic had induced even laissez-faire capitalism's most venerated theorist, Adam Smith, in *The Wealth of Nations* to advocate bank regulation by government as an exception to the general principle of natural liberty, much as party walls were erected to prevent the communication of fire. The essentiality of sound money in capitalist society was also comprehended by Lenin and expressed by economist John Maynard Keynes: "Lenin is said to have declared that the best way to destroy the capitalist system was to debauch the currency. By a continuing process of inflation, governments can confiscate, secretly and unobserved, an important part of the wealth of their citizens. By this method they can confiscate *arbitrarily.* . . . Lenin was certainly right. There is no subtler, no surer means of overturning the existing basis of society than to debauch the currency. The process engages all the hidden forces of economic law on the side of destruction, and does it in a manner which not one man in a million is able to diagnose."[9]

Democracy, too, rested on sound money. Noted Adenauer, "Safeguarding the currency forms the prime condition for maintaining a market economy and, ultimately, a free constitution for society and the State."[10]

Ever since President Richard Nixon unilaterally renounced America's pledge to convert paper dollars into gold on August 15, 1971, the world was being run on fiat money: no quantity of gold or silver restrained the amount of paper money that governments printed. With the final breakup of the postwar Bretton Woods monetary system of "fixed" exchange rates in 1973, de facto responsibility for governing the world's fiat money passed to the independent judgment of central bankers.

The Supreme Court of Money

How money was managed powerfully influenced interest rates, economic growth, employment, currency foreign exchange values, patterns of savings and investment, and society's long-term material living standards. Every po litical, economic, and social interest in the nation was favored or penalized by it. Its effects were transmitted not in the tailored-specific way of fiscal policy, its partner in governing the economy, where almost every line in the budget corresponded to a political constituency. Rather, money management did its work by bluntly raising or lowering the level of the tide over an uneven economic shoreline of sectors, classes, and demographic compositions: Creditors versus debtors. Savers versus borrowers. Wall Street versus Main Street. Domestic businesses versus exporters. Interest-rate-sensitive sectors versus those impinged by interest rates only indirectly. Rich versus middle class versus poor. Retirees versus middle-aged versus those just starting out.

Because citizens were simultaneously economic agents, how money was managed, quite simply, was one of democratic capitalist society's paramount political concerns. Governments exercised direct political control of the other main policy tools affecting growth and inflation, such as government spending, taxation, borrowing, and income policy. Why did democracy after democracy delegate responsibility for managing the state monopoly over money to unelected, institutionally separate, and increasingly independent central bankers?

Central banks arbitrated an unspoken marriage of convenience between the two disparate regimes that constituted democratic capitalism, the democratic nation-state polity and market capitalist economy, to make the rules of the game by which society's wealth was produced and managed. Since the sixteenth century these two overlapping, though at times opposing, forms of social organization evolved together through uneasy and shifting modus vivendi.[11]

The logic of capital was to maximize profit, regardless of national borders, political rights, social equity, or environmental consequences, and to seek to preserve the value of the capital it accumulated. The primary purpose of the democratic liberal state, by contrast, was to ensure liberty, equity, defense, and economic welfare for its citizenry. The disparate logics of capital and the democratic state converged on one crucial common goal—economic prosperity—and its prerequisite, a stable and friendly political economic environment for capitalist enterprise. Each of the main models of democratic capitalism—Anglo-American *laissez-faire,* European liberal social welfare, Japanese neomercantilist, "relationship" capitalism—provided this with varying divisions of responsibility and power between the market and governmental realms.

One of the main fulcrums of prosperity that had to be managed was the special role of money and finance. Governments naturally preferred to exercise the state monopoly over money freely itself. But private capitalists didn't trust them to and possessed a veto—abstention from lending. Central banks evolved as a medium of compromise from this historical tension, especially from the mid–nineteenth century, when the paper money and credit revolution had assisted "financial capitalism" to dominate the heights of the market economy.[12] "Central banking arose to impose control on the instability of credit," explains economic historian Charles Kindleberger. "The development of central banking from private banking, which is concerned to make money, is a remarkable achievement."[13]

Amid the daily shifting political currents and stalemates of democratic government and the economic gales of creative destruction, modern central bankers endeavored to supply the nonpartisan, technically competent continuity conducive to containing bouts of financial panic and inflation or deflation deleterious to the capitalist growth process in which all citizens and economic agents shared a long-term interest. They stood, in short, between markets and governments. They were hybrids, hermaphrodites: *in* the markets as bankers and *of* the government as appointed officials, coexisting in awkward tension with both. Their physical locations attested to their unspoken role. The Federal Reserve System was primarily a dual-headed institution: its political center, the board, had its place in Washington, D.C., alongside the executive, legislative, and judicial branches of government; its center of operations, the Federal Reserve Bank of New York, was on the market's front lines at Wall Street. The Deutsche Bundesbank was located in Germany's financial capital of Frankfurt, two hours' travel time from the government seat in Bonn. The Bank of Japan in Tokyo stood on the opposite side of the Imperial Palace from the Kasumigaseki Ministries and the Diet, abutting the Kabuto-cho financial hub. The Bank of England was "located not in Whitehall, but in the City, where the market is," notes Deputy Governor George Blunden. "Central banks bridge the gap. We represent Whitehall in the City and the City in Whitehall."

When selecting the first governors for the Federal Reserve Board in 1913, President Woodrow Wilson said: "I feel that is [sic] almost like constituting a whole Supreme Court. It's almost equal in importance."[14] The Supreme Court analogy stuck—and proved more apt than even Wilson expected. In democratic society the central bank effectively evolved into a semi-autonomous fourth branch of government, integrated within the system of checks and balances. Central bankers arbitrated the fierce competition for the political control of money on two dimensions: between markets and governments, and among partisan democratic rivals.[15]

Central bankers' specialized realm of operation, the financial system, could be visualized as a heart muscle that balanced on the tiny point of the central bank balance sheet. It had several compartments, which all supplied financing through an extensive circulatory network to businesses, individuals, and government in the surrounding economic body: the commercial banking system; the money and capital markets; and sundry financial services, including the financing arms of large corporations, insurers, and pension funds.

Central bankers sought to ensure an adequate and smooth flow of money through the financial heart and to the economic body by altering the capacity of the banking system to make loans. They did so by modifying bank liquidity regulations and, more frequently, by injecting or withdrawing central bank money reserves, known as "high-powered money" because of its financial leveraging effect, through two tiny auricular valves emanating from their balance sheet. One auricular valve was direct central bank lending to individual banks; this was most prominently done at the administratively set "discount rate." The second, and in most countries more important, auricular valve for managing bank reserves was through "open market" sales and purchases of government securities and other financial assets at market rates.

The central banker could not compel banks to finance, however—he could merely entice. The ultimate degree of money creation depended on the free market judgment of lenders and borrowers.[16] Central banking, as a result, was an art: it was as much about managing psychological market expectations as it was about the technical act of matching money supply with productive demand. This was illustrated most dramatically in a financial crisis like Black Monday, when panic destroyed the confidence necessary for free markets to function effectively.

The central banker's credibility with markets was thus his cardinal, if intangible, asset: credibility was what made him the feared and terrible unseen financial Wizard of Oz, able to leverage policy moves into fulfillment of his objectives instead of an exposed, cowering midget futilely pulling throttles behind a forbidding facade that spewed forth only fierce and terrible illusions. It was but a slight exaggeration to say that central bankers were adepts of a grand confidence trick—in lighter moments they said so themselves.

Yet credibility with markets wasn't enough. Monetary policy also had to be conducted within the political tolerances of democratic society. Despite their power, central bankers were always independent *within* government, never *of* it. "The most important constituency of the central bank is public opinion," explains the late ex–Bank of Italy Governor Guido Carli, "and the interpretation of public opinion by the politicians." Central bankers sought room to maneuver like other democratic political players by competing for credibility with the public through formidable PR, the public sector's best economic research, quiet legislative lobbying, and otherwise exploiting the public demoralization with partisan politics next to which their technocratic personae often appeared sterling pure. "Central banking is politics disguised as something technical," summarizes Professor Peter Kenen of Princeton University.

The finance minister (or Treasury secretary) was the central banker's main ambassador to his government. Finance ministers, in turn, counted upon central bankers to help sober the spending ministries within government and especially to manage the unruly financial market forces that could upset the government's political goals. The main tension between them arose because economic time and political time moved at different speeds. The economist's lag, policymakers joked sadly, was the politician's tragedy.

While central bankers inveigled politically guided governments to accept enough market logic for the economy to prosper in the long run, they also effectively presided over an inner club of the nation's core financiers, protecting and admonishing them in turn to temper their competitive quest for profit with due regard for the public good of financial order and political sensibilities. At the same time they entertained an ongoing, symbolical dialogue with bond markets, which independently determined the long-term interest rates central to economic investment and growth.

Central bankers' coziness with big bankers excited populist suspicions that they were ringleaders in an undemocratic financiers' cabal. Yet bankers often bridled that they were the long tentacles of government, invading their free market business realm. To ex–Citibank Chairman Walter Wriston, Paul Volcker was "the big nanny," who "believes very strongly that the Fed knows best and should control the world."[17]

From conflicting vantage points government and market leaders—as well as central bankers themselves—agreed on one thing: Central bankers were *different*.

The Evolving Independence of Central Banks

Central banks' peculiar role in democratic capitalist society developed gradually, and often unexpectedly, in reaction to changes in the economic and political environment. Until the recent rise of stateless money, independence had been confined mainly to the federal capitalist democracies.

Established after intense lobbying and close legislative vote in December 1913, the U.S. Federal Reserve System had evolved over many years into one of the world's most independent central banks. This was quite contrary to the intention of its original political framers. Its statutory independence as a federal agency reporting directly to Congress was made practicable by its budgetary autonomy, its freedom from obligation to finance U.S. government debt issues arising from federal budget deficits, the all but irrevocable terms of its policymakers, and its credibility with markets and the U.S. body politic. Its main policy-making body met in strictest secrecy roughly every six weeks to formulate policy. Its decisions, and a sanitized policy record summary of the meetings, were ultimately released to the public six weeks later. Not even the U.S. president or Treasury secretary had foreknowledge of its actions.[18] By virtue of the U.S. dollar's leading usage as an international currency, the Fed was the world's most influential central bank.

Even more independent than the Fed was the Deutsche Bundesbank, issuer of the world's second main currency, the deutsche mark (DM). That independence made credible the most rigorous anti-inflation reputation of any central bank. By virtue of the confidence markets placed in the DM, the Bundesbank effectively dictated monetary conditions for all Europe. The world's most independent central bank was the Swiss National Bank. The Dutch central bank, though nationalized in 1948, also enjoyed a practical independence almost on par with the Bundesbank. In the early 1990s the Bank of Italy gained full-fledged statutory independence to reflect its long de facto autonomy from its ostensible master, the Italian Treasury. Its authority derived from its being the most widely respected, impeccably professional, and consistent Italian public institution in a nation beset by chronically ungovernable and corrupt democratic governments.[19]

With the advent of global capital, upgrading central bank independence was evolving into a landslide worldwide trend. The pioneer in commonwealth nations was New Zealand, where an independent governor worked under an actual contract with the government to achieve a specified inflation rate of 0–2 percent—an earlier proposal to tie his salary to achieving low inflation was shelved as too politically inflammatory. Several years later, the first black majority democratic government in South Africa proclaimed the independence of its central bank. In 1989 Chile became the Latin American champion of upgrading central bank independence, followed soon by Mexico, Venezuela, and others. In 1993 Zambia and Pakistan took steps to join the parade.

In the former Soviet Union, Estonia made its central bank independent in June 1992, while de facto independence was being practiced by the Latvian and Lithuanian central banks. Going farther was Russia, which made its central bank *constitutionally* independent in its 1993 national constitutional referendum. Strong governors at the Bank of Canada and Bank of Japan, John Crow and Yasushi Mieno, boosted their nation's central banks' practical autonomy.

The most politically influential trend was in the European Community, where countries throughout the continent were upgrading the statutory independence of their central banks toward Bundesbank levels as a precondition for monetary union and a single pan-European central bank by the end of the 1990s. The 1991 Maastricht Treaty envisioned an independent "EuroFed": the first time in history that monetary union would precede—and serve as an external discipline to—political union. The EuroFed would not be directly accountable to any democratic national government.

Finally there was the anomaly of the supranational Bank for International Settlements in Basel, Switzerland, answerable to no government. All central bankers shared a collective independence through the BIS, which gave strength to their unique second allegiance to defending international monetary order.

Democratic governments were not transferring more monetary sovereignty to their central banks voluntarily. They were doing so mainly because stateless capital was *forcing* them to. Global investors who shopped among the world's nations for the safest, most profitable, and most liquid places to invest the world's savings were rewarding those with independent, credible central banks with lower interest rates and more capital. It was this fundamental power balance shift within the two electorates of democratic capitalism—the visible votes of citizens and the invisible ballots of global financial investors who spoke so violently on Black Monday—that was pushing reclusive central bankers reluctantly out of democratic capitalism's shadowy wings onto its governing center stage.

Capital Unbound

Two years before Black Monday, central bankers' growing prominence was captured in a newspaper photograph of representatives of the Group of Five (United States, Japan, Germany, United Kingdom, and France), gathered together to publicly announce completion of the September 22, 1985, "Plaza Agreement," calculated to drive down the dollar's value on currency markets. The photo showed Fed Chairman Paul Volcker, on stage with five finance ministers, being pushed front and center toward the TV camera lights by U.S. Treasury Secretary James Baker. Volcker "resisted and tried to hide, but to the amusement of all he was pushed on stage."[20]

"This is a central banker *smack* in the middle of the photograph—not the finance ministers!" exclaims Brookings Guest Scholar and veteran monetary expert Robert Solomon. "Central banking has become a very important function that everybody knows about, whereas you go back fifteen or twenty years and no one even knew what central banks were."

Several layers of central banker anonymity were peeled away in a single photo: it was a picture of a central banker literally positioned between government ministers and global financial markets. Volcker was pushed forward as the G5's ambassador because no government minister possessed as he did the confidence of dollar foreign exchange markets. Volcker's reluctance at being *pushed* to this task by politicians represented both central bankers' intuitive uneasiness with public exposure and their fear about political overburdening of monetary policy.

The most significant aspect of the Plaza photo was the unseen audience for whom all the actors were grandstanding—the huge, volatile, and high-speed global financial markets. The Plaza photo reflected government leaders groping for ways to influence the flows of stateless capital that more and more defined their national economic fates and the political options of their democratic constituencies. In this context, pushing central bankers to center stage symbolized their bankruptcy of genuine answers—the true "democratic deficit."

For some thirty years after World War II, national financial systems mostly recycled national savings within an imprisoned domestic loop. World finance, as designed at Bretton Woods, New Hampshire, in July 1944, consisted of segregated national islands with limited exchange among them to finance trade and direct investment and some financial asset investing. This arrangement created a buffer among nations that permitted each government great latitude to regulate how capital coursed through its financial system into its domestic economy. Internationally, governments managed the cross-currency exchange rates in defense of a free trade regime. This prosperous postwar order has been pithily summed up as "Keynes at home, Smith abroad."

But by the early 1970s growing international financial leakages caused the government-managed Bretton Woods system to collapse. The task of allocating international finance and governing economic adjustment was relegated entirely to private markets in which exchange rates floated daily. Speculative financial volumes, velocities, and price volatility increased in all markets throughout the 1970s. Financial innovations eroded the regulatory walls within and among national financial systems. Governments bowed to the financial market juggernaut with deregulations and liberalizations. Some, as in Japan and continental Europe, gave way grudgingly. In the United States and United Kingdom, clever free market–inclined politicians like Reagan and Thatcher made a political virtue of necessity by enthusiastically jumping aboard as its self-styled political conductors.

In the 1980s capital erupted free from its remaining national border confinements. On the wings of computer and telecommunications technologies, and transported by world-straddling financial institutions that traded and competed round-the-clock in an integrated, perpetually innovating financial market continuum spanning Asian, European, and U.S. time zones, a new regime of globally mobile capital was overturning the cornerstone compacts governing relations among markets and governments in postwar democratic capitalist society.

Capital was free to pursue its innate profit-expansive logic regardless of geographic boundary or political consequences. "For the first time," writes economic historian Robert L. Heilbroner, "the social formation of capitalism has succeeded in bringing into being a realm of capital seemingly beyond all political control."[21]

Global capital mobility caused government's sovereign control over national savings and national monetary policy to slip away—or, more specifically, to be pooled. George Shultz characterizes the new era as one in which the "court of the allocation of world savings" every day judges the economic policies of governments, rewarding those it favored with investment and strong currencies and punishing others by withholding capital and weak currencies.[22] "It used to be that political and economic follies played to a local audience, and their results could be contained. This is no longer true," adds Shultz's frequent interlocutor on the subject, Walter Wriston. "This state of affairs does not sit too well with many sovereign governments because they correctly perceive the new information standard as an attack on the very nature of sovereign power."[23]

The new regime of global capital was marked by an eruption in financial transactions and volatility out of line from historical trend lines across every sector of democratic capitalist society—within nations and internationally. Foreign currency exchange transactions catapulted in the decade from about $18 trillion a year to some $250 trillion a year ($1 trillion daily)—a fourteen-fold increase. World trade, by contrast, little more than doubled. As a result, the ratio of foreign exchange transactions to trade soared astoundingly from six to one to about thirty-five to one.

International bank lending also surged many times faster than economic activity. Outstanding international bank loans grew from 4 percent to 44 percent of the gross domestic product (GDP) of the twenty-four countries of the Organization for Economic Cooperation and Development (OECD) between 1980 and 1991.[24]

Securities transactions superseded banking as the main driving force behind the surge in global finance. Cross-border transactions in U.S. bonds and equities in the decade increased from 9.3 percent to 92.5 percent of U.S. economic activity; in Japan from 7 percent to 118.5 percent; in Germany from 7.5 percent to 57.5 percent.

Turnover within domestic securities markets likewise ballooned. From the start of the 1980s to the Black Monday global crash, U.S. securities transactions swelled from under 150 percent of GNP to 600 percent; in Japan from under 50 percent to 750 percent; in the United Kingdom from under 50 percent to about 200 percent; in Germany from under 10 percent to about 50 percent.[25]

At the start of the 1980s very few countries had established financial markets in Treasury bills, certificates of deposit, and commercial paper. A decade later only a few did not. Futures, options, swaps, and other financial derivative products were almost nonexistent in 1980. A decade later nearly $7 trillion worth were outstanding worldwide.[26] And the interaction of the parts was generating a disturbing leap in price volatility across the whole of the integrating global financial landscape.

Global finance seemed to take on a life of its own totally divorced from underlying economic fundamentals. Often financial prices snowballed and then snapped back in an abrupt adjustment. In classical economics, finance was supposed to be an unobtrusive veil following the lead of free market capitalist forces. But by the mid-1980s finance had become a self-propelling, volatile roller coaster, often visibly driving the determinants of real economic outcomes within and among nations. It was "Bretton Woods turned upside down."[27] To many experts, including Paul Volcker, the global capital regime of the post–Cold War world was reminiscent of the volatile, international private capital flows of the inter–world war period—though the sheer volumes and lightning-fast speeds at which it swung among countries and markets was brand-new.

The link between capital movements and trade "has become loose and, worse, unpredictable," notes Peter Drucker, professor at Claremont Graduate School.[28] "We . . . have no theory for an international economy that is fueled by world investment rather than world trade. As a result, we do not understand the world economy and cannot predict its behavior or anticipate its trends. . . . We also have no law for this new world economy. No country . . . has thought through the rules."[29]

When all was totted up, what did the volatile explosion in financial transactions relative to real economic activity portend? Did it signify the "invisible hand" at work, reshuffling assets in an as yet inscrutable way from the least to most capable hands that would one day yield greater productive bounty? Or was it creating a financial "casino society," as *BusinessWeek* wondered in 1985, that was distorting productive business investment and increasing financial fragility?[30]

One alarming sign was an associated pattern of unprecedented national and global economic imbalances, acute strains in the world financial system, and a worldwide debt explosion in all sectors—government, business, and households. The 50 percent surge in the dollar from 1980 to 1985, the largest appreciation until then of any major currency in modern history and well beyond everyone's realistic estimation of U.S. economic fundamentals, was associated with historic international imbalances.[31] U.S. current account deficits of $100 billion–plus annually from the mid-1980s reached a peak of 3.5 percent of GNP. Japan and Germany ran counterbalancing record surpluses. Formerly, developed nations normally couldn't attract enough foreign capital to run deficits beyond 1 percent to 2 percent of GNP; at that point market forces induced involuntary economic adjustments.

The advent of abundant global capital made possible unprecedented government profligacy. Borrowing at a record magnitude to finance its national deficits transformed the United States from the world's largest creditor to its largest debtor with astonishing speed, consuming in only three years the accumulation of three generations of Americans' net international savings. When market expectations turned abruptly, the dollar plunged back to, and then below, its original value. It was a completely unnecessary, disruptive round trip. It hindered growth, dislocated employment, left behind structural wounds, and helped trigger the stock market crash.

While the surge in U.S. federal government borrowing grabbed headlines, private indebtedness among businesses and households also exploded inexplicably in "a sharp departure from prior patterns of U.S. financial behaviour," to levels last seen just prior to the Great Depression.[32] U.S. company debt leaped from 36 percent to 49 percent of GNP in the decade and household debt from 75 percent to 97 percent of disposable income. Japanese company debt jumped from 86 percent to 135 percent of GNP and household debt from 59 percent to 96 percent of household income. U.K. company and household debt ratios both doubled. Only Germany and continental Europe kept debt growth to modest proportions.

Like the stock market boom and abrupt global crash on Black Monday, the LDC debt crisis was a manifestation of the dangerous debt explosions and revulsions unleashed by the global capital regime. So too were the real estate overlending booms and busts in Japan, the United States, and the United Kingdom, which contributed to the financial asset price deflation that made the 1990s "contained depression" unique in the postwar era.[33]

Global financial integration also diminished the national sovereign political autonomy. Large, high-speed international capital flows and exchange rate changes caused national economic policies and political economic structures to exert increasingly powerful mutual gravitational pulls. Even the United States, whose economic might and monopoly over the world's most widely used currency had in the past insulated it from developments in other countries, found its policy options increasingly constrained. "While [economic policy] instruments can still be used, the impact has changed enormously because of interdependence," elaborates Brookings Guest Scholar Robert Solomon. "It spills abroad. What effect it has depends on what policies and developments occur beyond the borders."[34]

Reluctant Captains

The mutation of global finance unbound from its national economic roots and from sovereign political control was rending the fabric of the capitalist economy and democratic society, jeopardizing the welfare of both. On Black Monday the political classes in the three major economies—the United States, Japan, and Germany—were largely paralyzed before the major structural, institutional reforms demanded by the rising power of financial markets relative to national governments. This was why more of the crucial political decisions were devolving into the hands of unelected central bankers, whose historical task was to manage existing systems, not to govern bootleg in substitute of decaying ones.

Five principal forces were propelling central bankers' heightened stature in the world economy. Foremost was their closeness to potent financial market forces. They were *in* the markets every day as bankers and traders: their ability to provide insight about financial market moods, trends, and expectations, and their indispensability in rapid and efficient policy execution, raised their influence within government chambers. This was evidenced dramatically on Black Monday, but also less vividly every day of the year. "The BOJ [Bank of Japan] is located on the front line; the Ministry of Finance [MOF] is strategy headquarters," explains Tsuneo Fujita, an MOF director general who headed its foreign exchange division in 1978–80. "The result is that without information from the BOJ, we couldn't do anything at all. We are very much influenced by BOJ opinion." As Bob Woodward has documented in *The Agenda,* President Clinton relied upon the arguments and quantitative judgment of Fed Chairman Alan Greenspan in deciding to subordinate his administration's other economic goals to credible budget-deficit cutting in a gambit to assuage financial markets that could otherwise undermine his entire economic agenda.

Second, the 1973 final collapse of the Bretton Woods world monetary system into unmanaged floating exchange rates gave central bankers far more authority over national monetary and exchange rate policies. Under Bretton Woods, all central banks save the U.S. Fed were effectively obliged to target interest rate policy on maintaining the currency exchange rate parities negotiated by their governments.[35] As a result, monetary policy could not simultaneously target domestic economic conditions. With floating, "the power to set exchange rates is still legally with governments, but it has become obsolete."[36]

"As long as the Bretton Woods institutions and the system of fixed but adjustable parities were the law of the world, then the role of the central bankers was a limited role," explains ex–German Chancellor Helmut Schmidt. "Since its fall, their freedom and independence to act has become enormous. Under the Bretton Woods system, it was the government's responsibility for the domestic economic policy mix and exchange values. Nowadays, more than formerly, it is in the central bankers' hands to determine the international fate of one's own currency."

The currency exchange rate was the single most important price signal governing a nation's economy. In one fell swoop the exchange rate raised or lowered national living standards, preferenced certain economic sectors over others, dominated trade and industrial policy, and set the fundamental conditions for labor negotiations. Through democratic government's passive acceptance of floating exchange rate changes by private market forces, more of the political responsibility inherent in exchange rate policy was deposited at the doorstep of central bankers.

To fulfill his role under the Bretton Woods system, Helmut Schmidt continues, "it wasn't necessary that the central banker understood the foreign policy of his own country or the complexities of foreign policy." Today, he says, he must. "We've been fortunate to have some outstanding personalities among central bankers with a broader scope of understanding of politics and foreign policy, men like Paul Volcker, Arthur Burns, Fritz Leutwiler, and Karl Klasen [Bundesbank president in the 1970s]."

The European Monetary System (EMS), established at the instigation of Schmidt and French President Valéry Giscard d'Estaing in 1978 to limit currency volatility and to promote intra-European trade and political integration, was an accord among central bankers. Their cooperation made the system operational and, in the 1980s, successful at helping European inflation to converge at low levels.

Central bankers' influence was also enhanced, third, by the public perception that inflation and inflation psychology had approached destabilizing levels by the late 1970s. It was central bankers' leadership in imposing painful economic austerity that broke the inflationary fever. "What we . . . discovered in the 1980s . . . is that at a certain point in the inflationary process, public opinion will support strong policies to restore stability even though those policies seem to entail a harsh short-term cost," reflected Paul Volcker in a 1990 speech, delivered before world financial leaders, entitled "The Triumph of Central Banking?"[37] That discovery encouraged the 1980s political turn in the leading liberal democracies toward liberating free market forces to reinvigorate capitalism's historic wealth-generation capacities at the expense of the previous emphasis on fairer wealth distribution.

Fourth, the world economy had been steered one-handed by central banker monetary policy through the 1980s since fiscal policies in the leading democracies were rigidly fixed by political stalemates—toward consolidation in Germany and Japan and toward massive expansion in the United States. "The problem that all central bankers face is that fiscal domestic policy doesn't work," explains William Branson, international economics professor of Princeton's Woodrow Wilson School. "It has gotten worse and worse, especially in the United States because we don't have a parliamentary system."

In nonunitary, and even some unitary, democracies, so many political hands were grasping for the tiller that fiscal policy was difficult to change—much less steer intelligently. The rarity of general electoral equilibrium "is why fiscal policy is a very good instrument that cannot be relied upon to any extent," notes a senior European Treasury official.

Monetary policy, in contrast, could be implemented flexibly, rapidly—even at times with informal coordination—and out of the political spotlight. Its theoretical efficacy in managing the economy remained strong, unlike fiscal policy. It had thus solidly replaced fiscal policy as the senior partner in macroeconomic policy-making. These same reasons, however, made it prone to overuse, even when suboptimal.

Finally and ominously, the global financial revolution was producing an unprecedented series of complex financial traumas that it was the central banker's raison d'être to contain. Until the global stock market crash on Black Monday, the most prominent included the world-shuddering fallout from the failure of Germany's Herstatt Bank in 1974, the LDC debt crisis from 1982, the collapse of the U.S.'s Continental Illinois in 1984, and two dollar crises in 1977–79 and 1986–87. Soon to come would be the U.S. S&L bailout, the EMS currency upheavals, the near meltdown of the core U.S. and Japanese banking systems, and the 1994–95 Mexican peso crisis.

Central bankers' improvised brinksmanship had deflected these and other financial traumas into near misses. They were little Dutch boys with their fingers plugging bursting holes in the world financial dikes to borrow time until the meandering processes of democratic government implemented fundamental political repairs. They even patched up some of the cracks with informal protocols and the first worldwide banking standards—the first collective effort to reconstruct the democratic capitalist compact eroded by global capital. But they lacked the political mandate and institutional scope themselves to hammer out more durable systemic remedies.

Paul Volcker, who plugged more holes than anyone else, privately predicted a contagious epidemic of financial fragility. "My fear of a financial crisis hasn't come to pass. We haven't had that catastrophic chain reaction," he would admit in 1989. "But I think the jury is still out."

Central bankers were uncomfortable with the added political responsibilities and technical challenges being thrust upon them. They spent many anguished nights worrying that the changed financial and economic landscape was jeopardizing financial stability, impairing the usability of monetary policy, weakening their power over money markets, and setting them up for a political backlash that could eclipse their independence and effectiveness if and when they stumbled. With economic fates more tied to the unpredictable course of volatile financial market expectations, central bankers increasingly felt reliant on maintaining confidence—with diminishing tangible power to back it up if and when they were challenged.

Central bankers' technical anxieties could be distilled into one essential problem: a heightened conflict between their twin goals of financial system stability and low inflation growth. Central bankers faced the no-win choice of bailing out fragile institutions with a loose monetary policy or permitting financial failures that could foment systemic crisis. As a consequence, markets perceived an ever-present inflationary bias in monetary policy. This tended to push up real interest rates, slow economic growth, keep inflation higher, and aggravate financial system fragility.

"The financial system on a national and international basis has become more fragile," worries Guido Carli, whose artifices as Bank of Italy governor helped hold together the world monetary system through the 1960s. "It is more fragile because it is harder to define what is money, because the correlation between money and prices is more difficult to assess, and because of the amount of capital movements. The system is adrift. There is no anchor—only central bankers. But the central bankers' two objectives—monetary stability and protecting the integrity of the financial system—are more in conflict."

"I see increasing fragility constraints on monetary policy," agrees Princeton Professor of International Finance Peter Kenen. "Central bankers face a new world. The system is more fragile in ways we don't fully understand. Central bankers don't like to talk about that."

So many economic conceptions had been turned inside out by the combined global financial and economic information technology revolutions that the main theoretical economic and monetary guideposts of the past had been toppled like golden calves.[38] Central bankers were uneasily piloting the economic ship into uncharted seas ad hoc, with only seat-of-the-pants professional intuition to tell them if they were drifting into treacherous waters.

With central bankers' growing importance came more political scrutiny—

and renewed charges of lack of democratic accountability. While their rising authority relative to governments merited upgrading methods and standards of accountability, most of the political criticism was a sublimated cry of frustration by elected leaders that they were losing power over the economy to global financial markets. Central bankers' dilemma was that while it increased their prominence, global capital was also making it harder for them to deliver the expected economic results.

"Central bankers are being forced to do too much," warns Paul Volcker. "It makes them politically exposed."

Chapter 3

Accident Waiting to Happen

Although shocked by the stock market crash's magnitude, speed, and global nature, Fed Chairman Alan Greenspan had long believed that "[s]omething had to snap. If it didn't happen in October, it would have happened soon thereafter. . . . The market plunge was an accident waiting to happen."[1]

Upon assuming his Fed post in August, Greenspan had set up a task force to make sure the Fed was prepared to deal with a stock market crash and half a dozen other potential crises that could strike the distressed U.S. financial system. The task force, led by Fed Vice Chairman Manuel Johnson, produced a large loose-leaf notebook divided into eight sections with a pink cover, widely known as the Pink Book.[2] In the case of a stock market calamity, it had hypothesized a 150-point plunge. No one imagined a crash of 508.

Greenspan had also begun studying the stock market crash dangers with Treasury Undersecretary George Gould, SEC Chairman David Ruder, and the CFTC. "We were one-quarter of the way through when it hit the fan," says Gould.

A specific anxiety was the widening gap between returns on U.S. shares and U.S. government bonds. Soaring stock prices in early 1987 caused yields to fall to 3 percent, while thirty-year U.S. government "long" bonds yielded over 7.5 percent. A late March attack on the dollar in foreign exchange markets precipitated a bond market crash. Yields—which reflected the inverse of price moves—leaped to about 9 percent by the end of May. This was the first vivid example of the new, close linkage between the fluctuations in the value of the dollar and long-term U.S. interest rates that would come to preoccupy Treasury Secretary Baker and Greenspan in the autumn leading up to Black Monday.

Many Wall Street veterans reckoned that the stock market was 25–40 percent overvalued versus the bond market. But the stock market, after a hiccup, then stunned everyone by resuming its upward march. By August prices were a soaring twenty-two times earnings versus sixteen at the start of 1987 and a more normal eleven in 1986. "I'd never seen the stock market go up after a bond crash before," says Gould, an affable investment banker of aristocratic bearing who had spent a lifetime on Wall Street before joining his friend, Jim Baker, at the U.S. Treasury as head of domestic finance.

One of the extraordinary forces that caused the U.S. stock market to continue to soar in the summer 1987 was an inflow of foreign capital, primarily from Japan, that shifted out of bonds into equities after the April bond market crash. In the first half of 1987 foreign institutions bought as many U.S. equities as domestic institutions did.[3]

A second force propelling U.S. stock prices after the spring was a huge wave of highly leveraged corporate takeovers, financed by the abundance of new funds produced by the global financial revolution. The takeover wave reduced net U.S. corporate equity by a stunning $456 billion between 1984 and the third quarter of 1987—helping push up corporate debt burdens to postwar record levels. Only once before in American history, during the merger wave in the trust era at the turn of the twentieth century, had there been a net reduction in equities.

"We'd been nervous most of the summer about the continued appreciation of the stock market relative to the bond market," says the Fed's Manley Johnson. "Our internal debate was that one market had to be proved wrong. Either the bond market would be proved wrong or the stock market would fall."

Just days after Greenspan moved into his new office in August, the bond market plunged again in coincidence with a falling dollar. The twin plunges followed the report of a larger than expected U.S. trade deficit, a portent that the United States would have difficulty to continue borrowing $15 billion a month from foreigners to avoid a decline—possibly sharp—in its economic activity.

This time the stock market began to correct. By the week before Black Monday it had lost over two hundred points from its August peak of 2722. Yet bond prices fell farther than equities. The extraordinary yield gap thus continued to widen.

Greenspan knew that his success as central banker hinged on establishing his credibility with Wall Street. He was aware that his personal credibility was suspect because he was a Republican appointed by a Republican administration rumored to have dumped Volcker for fear he was too independent for the 1988 presidential elections. Greenspan responded vigorously by engineering the first increase in the discount rate in three years. In the symbolic dialogue between the Fed and bond markets, the discount rate signified the Fed's strongest "announcement" of its policy intentions.

Greenspan's aim of calming market psychology would be achieved if long-term interest rates fell or remained unchanged. However, long-term bond yields rose. A key reason was that the German Bundesbank and the Bank of Japan, worried about rising inflation pressures at home, had also started in the summer to raise interest rates. One effect was to cause their currencies to appreciate by attracting global capital. This dampened imported inflation and expectations. But not all countries could strengthen their currencies simultaneously. Markets grew spooked at the prospect of a global interest rate spiral as the United States, Japan, and Germany each tried to snatch advantages from one another to fight inflation.

In each of the three main international currency countries the pattern in the autumn was the same: rising short-term interest rates pushed up the entire structure of interest rates. Between mid-August and mid-October U.S. bond yields backed up one percentage point to 9.5 percent; in Japan by 1.5 points to 5.5 percent; and in Germany by 0.75 points to 6.75 percent. Rising, and more volatile, world interest rates in 1987 marked the end of the long cycle of falling interest rates that had commenced in mid-1982.

The final countdown to the crash started with a jolting series of news reports on October 14. Word spread that the House Ways and Means Committee was preparing to introduce legislation to eliminate some key tax benefits driving the highly leveraged corporate takeovers. Early that morning the markets also learned that the German Bundesbank was nudging up its key short-term repurchase (Repo) interest rate from 3.75 percent to 3.85 percent. At 8:30 A.M. the Commerce Department announced a whopping August U.S. trade deficit of $15.7 billion.

As the news hit Tokyo, Japanese investors began to dump U.S. bonds and flee the dollar. The dollar sold off worldwide. As it did, U.S. long-term interest rates leaped forward, piercing the psychological threshold of 10 percent—en route to a 10.4 percent peak. The extraordinary gap between stock and bond yields suddenly became the feverish focus of U.S. financial markets.

Pandemonium erupted in the futures pits at the Chicago Board of Trade (CBOT) and the Chicago Mercantile Exchange (CME). Futures pits had historically been the markets of Main Street. Contracts for the future delivery of real goods like pork bellies, soybeans, and metals were made and traded. But in the 1980s futures were swept up by the financial revolution. Contracts were added on foreign currencies, Eurobonds, U.S. Treasury securities, and, since April 1982, indices on a basket of shares that represented the stock market.[4] By 1987 the soaring popularity of stock index futures had transformed the traditional self-contained and well-understood stock market into one component of a new single, integrated intermarket continuum of stocks, stock index futures, and stock and futures options.[5]

Led by dumping of stock index futures contracts in Chicago, the stock market dropped a huge 95 points on Wednesday. Overnight, in response to the triple fall in the U.S. dollar, bond market, and stock market, the Tokyo stock market, then at its historic peak, fell 218 points to 26,428. The London stock market fell 22 to 1812.

Two news items out of Washington aborted a Thursday morning stock market rally. The administration announced that "simple prudence" would be enough to meet its 1988 federal budget deficit reduction target. The rally fizzled. Wall Street believed that the mammoth $150 billion–level federal deficit—the deficit had not fallen below $145 billion since 1983 and had peaked at $220 billion in 1986—was the single main force behind the unsustainable U.S. and international imbalances hanging like a Damocles' sword over economic growth and dollar stability. Washington and Wall Street, the political and the economic U.S. capitals, were not on the same wavelength.

At 3:30 P.M. trading room newswires reported that Treasury Secretary James Baker had attacked the Bundesbank for raising interest rates. He suggested that the United States would not follow Germany into recession in order to defend the dollar by following suit. The stock market plunged. So did the dollar. It threatened DM 1.80, which foreign exchange traders presumed—erroneously—to be the secret dollar/DM floor of the dollar exchange rate range that the Group of Seven (G7) leading industrial countries had adopted at the Louvre Accord of February 22, 1987, in their cooperative effort to stabilize the falling dollar and unwind the international economic imbalances. Several times over the next days, Baker went out of his way to repeat his comments.

On Friday the dollar broke through its presumed Louvre DM/dollar floor. The stock market had one of its worst days in history, down 108 points on 338 million traded shares. In the three days from October 14 to 16, the Dow Jones index plunged over 250 points on record-shattering volume. The stage was set for Black Monday.

Jim Baker was scheduled to leave for Europe on Sunday evening to go hunting with the king of Sweden. En route he had scheduled a Monday, October 19, stopover at Frankfurt to meet with German Finance Minister Gerhard Stoltenberg and Bundesbank President Karl Otto Pöhl. On Friday he conferred with Greenspan about whether the trouble in the markets portended a financial crisis.

As a central banker, Greenspan's worry was *not* the plunge in stock prices per se. Loss was part of investor risk and a healthy part of the capitalist winnowing process. Greenspan's concern, rather, was that precipitous loss might ignite a financial panic. The financial system faced an unavoidable demand crunch for financing simply to settle the record trading volume and change in prices. But if fear of client failures seized markets, the demand for liquidity among those reliant on credit would multiply and set off an opposite impulse to retrench among those who lent it. Panicked lenders withdrawing credit lines and calling in their loans from businesses and consumers was the short cut to financial crisis and economic depression.

Greenspan's threshold question boiled down to this: At what point were the normally smoothly reequilibrating free market mechanisms in peril of snapping and transmitting a liquidity panic that would interrupt lending and cause interest rates to shoot up throughout credit markets?

The actual degree of risk hinged on the general robustness of the U.S. financial system. Greenspan possessed great faith in the resiliency of free markets. But he worried that "[r]igidities created by the rising debt burdens make the economy and financial system less shock resistant. Hence the risks to the economy are greater than at any time since the end of the war."[6]

Greenspan's concerns about financial fragility informed the Pink Book. The Pink Book's first focus was the distress in the core U.S. banking system, the financial system's main source of primary and backup liquidity in a crisis. As chief conduits of monetary policy, and as necessary allies in upholding financial system stability, the core banks' relationship with its central banker was inherently incestuous, even though central bankers also viewed bankers as congenitally prone to collective fits of bad lending judgment and self-destructive urges to cut and run in a crisis that required supervision and sometimes tutelage. In effect, central bankers brokered the unspoken democratic capitalist understanding between government and the nation's main banks that prevailed through the postwar era of highly regulated, segregated national banking systems. "The tacit offer from governments for about thirty years after 1945 was that they would allow banks a stable and high level of profit by ensuring that depositors had few other places than banks in which to put their liquid funds, and that borrowers would have few other places from which they could respectably borrow," explains *The Economist's* ex–deputy editor Norman Macrae. "In return for governments' blessing on these cartels, bankers agreed to become governments' poodles in nefarious ways."[7] Bankers, for instance, were attentive to political wishes in setting their lending rates, cooperative in government tax collection and its occasional imposition of foreign exchange controls.

Yet the competitive free market forces unleashed by the global financial revolution had overwhelmed the unspoken bank-government compact and depreciated the value of banking license that sealed it, "leaving only messes behind."[8] Banks' traditional turf was being invaded by fleet new competitors from neighboring securities and financial services sectors free of onerous regulations and expensive branch networks that were better able to exploit the innovative potential of information technology and electronic money transfer. Domestic banks were also under competitive assault from foreign banking institutions chasing the surge of global capital. Governments simply could no longer uphold their end of the compact by guaranteeing a stable, high level of profits for banks. Banks tried to compensate for their declining market share of the financing business by chasing less creditworthy borrowers and expanding into innovative kinds of "off balance sheet" businesses with hard to quantify, often volatile, risks.[9]

Banks were facing a worldwide shakeout and industry consolidation. At the top of the financial industry pyramid, the world's largest financial institutions of all types were battling each other for the few dozen profitable slots. How disruptive the process would be to the economy, no one could say. The Pink Book noted there were some 1,600—or one in eight—banks on the U.S. "problem" list. The postwar record one thousand failures in the second half of the 1980s had depleted to its lowest level in history the cover of the Federal Deposit Insurance Corporation (FDIC), the government guarantor of individual deposits created in the Depression to prevent banking system runs.

In addition to the huge LDC debt exposures, which were still solvency threatening enough to merit their own section in the Pink Book, the core U.S. banking system was at risk to the record indebtedness building up on corporate balance sheets and in commercial real estate. By 1987 many insiders regarded corporate indebtedness, not the celebrated federal budget deficit, to be the "King Kong of debt."[10] Debt service burdens had soared from $.16 per $1.00 of pretax (preinterest) earnings in 1950s and 1960s to $.33 in the 1970s, to an onerous $.56 in the 1980s.[11] Not surprisingly, corporate bankruptcies and defaults were running at postwar records.

Another time bomb was the savings and loan industry fiasco, which at the time both the Reagan administration and Congress were still pretending didn't exist. The government's quick-fix response to early 1980s distress in the S&L industry had been to deregulate the scope of its activities and to expand the government safety net guarantees for depositors. This deadly combination produced what Volcker called "kamikaze banking"—attracting government-guaranteed deposits by paying high interest rates in order to pursue high-risk lending to businesses the S&Ls had no experience in. The result, said the Pink Book, was that one-fourth of the entire S&L industry was basically insolvent. It estimated the bailout cost at $40 billion to $50 billion.[12] Other Pink Book nightmares included defaults in overtraded junk bonds and in national and international payments systems, and a currency crisis in the wobbly dollar.

With the Fed chairmanship, Greenspan inherited the excruciating dilemma of all central bankers whose words could set off financial stampedes. He could not risk ringing the alarm bells on specific problems too loudly. "There was the basic dilemma: if you jumped up and down, you would have precipitated it," Volcker explains.[13]

Despite his fears of financial fragility and the economic vulnerability, when Greenspan conferred with Treasury Secretary Baker on Friday, October 16, he judged that the critical thresholds of systemic risk had not yet been crossed for the Fed to be forced into emergency action. On Sunday evening, after one further incendiary parting shot at the Bundesbank and a dollar "talk-down" on the popular Sunday morning television show *Meet the Press*, Baker departed for Europe.

Over the weekend a big new leak sprang: the country's largest thrift, American Savings & Loan Association of California, with assets of over $25 billion, told regulators that the rise in interest rates the prior week had broken it. It would default on major obligations on Monday. It wasn't a huge surprise. Its default was specifically hypothesized in the Pink Book.

Fed Vice Chairman Manley Johnson and Treasury Undersecretary George Gould worked feverishly over the weekend with S&L regulators, trying unsuccessfully to line up a buyer.[14] Fortuitously, sharply falling interest rates starting Monday afternoon provided American S&L a brief second lease on life. It rescued the Fed from having to cope with a second crisis while the stock market was crashing.

Huge stock market selling pressure was mounting ahead of New York's Monday market opening. The Tokyo and London offices of big U.S. firms received massive sell orders from their Japanese and European clients throughout the world. The London Stock Exchange was inundated by sales of U.S. stocks that traded in London by investors trying to get a jump on the opening of U.S. markets.

Tokyo stocks had fallen only 2.5 percent. But that cloaked Japanese government pressure on large market participants. "An hour before their [Tokyo stock market] opening on Monday, they had a large number of sale orders— maybe two billion or three billion dollars, I don't recall—and then they all went away because they talked to the traders," recounts Dan Crippen, a top aide to White House Chief of Staff Howard Baker.[15]

The New York Stock Exchange's computerized trading system was loaded with $500 million of sell orders even before the market opened at 9:30 A.M. As the morning progressed, the pattern was similar to the prior week, though more intense: large institutions employing a recent computer-driven trading strategy called "portfolio insurance" led the selling charge by dumping stock index futures contracts in the pits of the CBOT and the CME. The selling was then transmitted back to the New York stock market by "program traders," who arbitraged between price differences in the futures index and the actual cash value of underlying shares in the stock market.[16]

Yet by late morning, with the market down two hundred points, the panic selling seemed to have spent itself. There was even a rally from about 11:00 A.M. to 11:45 A.M. The market gained back over sixty points. For a short while it looked as if the storm were winding down and market mechanisms self-equilibrating.

But then a new selling blitz in the futures market began to overwhelm the rally. The record selling volume began to swamp the technical capacities of the stock exchange. By 1 P.M. there was over an hour delay in the posting of trades and prices. This meant that program traders couldn't be sure of arbitrage positions. Rather than shoot blind, many simply quit trading starting around 2 P.M.

A disastrous gap in the intermarket continuum had been created: by dropping out, program traders had caused the futures and stock markets to become disconnected. Portfolio insurers lost their natural buyers. Futures prices plummeted. Equity buyers disappeared. The stock market was down about 175 points at 1 P.M. By 2 P.M., following the newswire report of SEC Chairman Ruder's comment about a possible closure, the market plunged to almost 300 points down. After a brief rally the market went into a terrifying 250-point free-fall in the final hour and a half.

Greenspan had left his office for the airport to address the American Bankers Association in Dallas just before the final plunge. He was airborne when things spiraled downward out of control. When Howard Baker reached him by telephone in Dallas, Greenspan had no doubt: the stock market crash had bounded in one great uncharted leap across the threshold to systemic risk.

Chapter 4

The Last Resort

By late afternoon on Black Monday an intense demand for liquidity was already sweeping the financial markets. Brokers, dealers, and others who relied on borrowing to meet their obligations across the integrated intermarket continuum were anxiously trying to line up huge amounts of additional credit from increasingly reluctant bankers. If the bankers failed to gratify them, the rational urge for liquidity would produce a self-fulfilling, irrational outcome: a chain reaction of failures to pay across the credit system that would eventually bring down even the soundest firms and banks.

Greenspan knew it was time to roll out the central bank's ultimate emergency weapon, lender of last resort. Its theoretical essence, expounded by Walter Bagehot in his 1873 classic, *Lombard Street,* in support of the already existing practice of last resort lending, was for the central bank to use its powers to pump money in a hurry to healthy entities within the financial system in the hope of restoring enough confidence to stanch the panicked urge for liquidity.

The essential strength of the bank credit system was its virtually infinite capacity to expand credit—promises to pay—from a small reserve of money. Its Achilles' heel was the obverse—an acute vulnerability to sudden shrinkage when doubts arose about the ability of the system as a whole to repay. Abrupt credit collapses that fomented financial panic and economic disruptions often afflicted capitalism in the nineteenth and early twentieth centuries until central bank lender of last resort practices were firmly established. Lending of last resort was necessitated by the fact that "markets generally work, but occasionally they break down. When they do, they require government intervention to provide the public good of stability."[1]

The purpose of last resort lending was not to fix anything per se. Rather, it was to restore enough confidence for the free market's self-equilibrating mechanisms to function normally again—until the next bout of instability.

The key to success in an incipient panic, Bagehot exhorted, was to "[e]ither shut the Bank at once, and say it will not lend more than it commonly lends, or lend freely, boldly, and so that the public may feel you mean to go on lending. To lend a great deal, and yet not give the public confidence that you will lend sufficiently and effectually, is the worst of all policies."[2]

To lend boldly in a panic made a paradox of banking maxims such as Gresham's law of not throwing good money after bad. When financial asset prices were plunging, forced selling due to illiquidity quickly begat insolvency. Sufficient liquidity to ride out the storm until prices recovered, conversely, could restore technical solvency.

A central bank could not succeed at last resort lending alone. It had to induce the inner club of core banks to suspend their natural state of competition, to stand visibly with it against the financial stampede by on-lending the central bank's high-powered reserve injections. Doing so was not easy: top bankers had often tried to organize emergency lending rescues by persuading colleagues to desist from the paradoxical behavior of retrenchment that was rational for each alone but destructive to all collectively. But they often failed because "[t]he short run warred with the long run, the private good with the public."[3]

Greenspan knew that to transform market expectations he'd have to bet the Federal Reserve's most preciously guarded asset, its credibility. He'd also personally have to demonstrate that he possessed the Jekyll-Hyde character of the adept central banker: the capacity to suddenly change skin from quietly defending the most cautious position to the last in normal times, to seizing command with rapid, radical improvisations as the crisis unfolded.

Greenspan also knew he was operating in the giant shadow of Paul Volcker, whose virtuosity as a crisis manager had been earned by experience in nearly every major financial trauma involving the rise of global capital, including the war on inflation, the LDC debt bomb, and the dollar crises of 1978 and 1987. The soft-spoken Greenspan, by contrast, had never been tried before under fire. His previous experience as a policy adviser to President Nixon in the early 1970s, Council of Economic Advisers chairman for President Ford, and head of President Reagan's Commission on Social Security Reform, and his personal predilection for trying to win consensus by intellectual argument rather than call of command, gave little reassurance that he could rise to the occasion. He disliked the tough personal diplomacy at which Volcker excelled. He was philosophically more averse to imposing government solutions on market problems. Yet he was keenly aware that the crash was likely to make or break his chairmanship.

The central bank had two main tools at its disposal to quell the panic: injections of high-powered money into the financial system and the announcement effect of what it intended to do. How the Fed broadcast its intention to inject lender of last resort liquidity, Greenspan quickly reckoned, held the key to avoiding Bagehot's worst case of lending a great deal without restoring public confidence.

The speech Greenspan was due to make next day to the American Bankers Association presented a ready opportunity to announce the Fed's intentions. On Black Monday evening he began the revisions. But he wasn't satisfied with the results.

"Why not cancel the speech and issue a statement instead?" he wondered.[4]

Ultimately, issuing a statement that declared the Fed's intention to lend freely and boldly, so that bankers felt confident that they could cover their own short-term funding needs at low cost if they requited those in the inter-market continuum clamoring for liquidity, was the heart of the high-visibility gamble upon which Greenspan staked all the Fed's credibility. It was akin to the strategy used by besieged bankers in the 1930s, who put all their cash in the bank's front window in the hope of staving off the run.

The decision to go with the statement strategy, however, was reached only after agonizing debate inside the Fed. One big concern was that issuing an extraordinary statement could backfire. The crisis would be worsened if it was ineffective or even interpreted by markets as a sign of panic at the central bank.

"Those who argued 'Yes' [to make a statement]," recalls Michael Bradfield, then Fed chief counsel, "argued that the damage was done already and now was the time to see what we could do. The others said 'Don't use up your credibility.'

"What tipped the balance? The situation was pretty desperate."

The Moral Hazard Dilemma

Another substantive concern was voiced by Governor Wayne Angell. On Black Monday afternoon Angell wandered in among the Fed crisis team. "Be careful before making any statement," he warned. "We don't want to give the impression that the Fed stands behind the equity market."

Angell's concern, deeply felt at the Fed, was "moral hazard." Moral hazard was a spreading cancer on the U.S. and world financial system. It arose when the market believed that public officials so feared financial failure that they would rescue even imprudent, troubled lenders or borrowers. This encouraged high-risk, high-reward lending. Prudent competitors were thus penalized. The financial system as a whole grew more fragile. Fragility fears, in turn, constrained the effectiveness of central bank monetary policy, as investors began to anticipate lax monetary policy and bailouts.

"To the extent that the market perceives that the central bank will bail out everyone, then real interest rates will go up," says Greenspan. "This affects the level of economic activity and reduces capital investment, growth, and standards of living."

"This [moral hazard] is *the* big problem of the Fed," adds Steven Roberts, Volcker's personal assistant from 1983 to 1987. "Everyone looks to the Fed to bail them out of every problem."

The most egregious case of moral hazard in the 1980s was the legislatively mandated expansion of federal deposit guarantees and deregulation that produced the S&L debacle. Another was the emergence of the "too big to fail" doctrine, epitomized by the $4.5 billion 1984 rescue of all depositors and the nationalization of banking Goliath Continental Illinois.

The financial integration wrought by the new regime of global capital made "too big to fail" a misnomer. Too "strategic" to fail was more accurate. Even small financial institutions, and often nonbanks, were frequently linchpins in the opaque web of cross-market, cross-border, counterparty linkages. The interlinked international network was more robust as a whole than the old rigidly compartmentalized national system, many believed, but problems could spread through it like inextinguishable brush fires that over time could do great damage. As a result, central bankers felt compelled to intervene frequently and early, within and outside banking, and involving institutions for which they had no prudential regulatory responsibility.

"Central bankers used to regard their task as standing behind banking systems and regarded banks as distinct from the rest of the financial system," explains London School of Economics Professor and ex–Bank of England high official Charles Goodhart. "But with banks doing capital markets business, and capital market institutions doing banking, central banks must go beyond banking and cover capital markets and financial intermediation of whatever type."[5]

Navigating the moral hazard dilemma was analogous to negotiating with terrorists: a public rescue might resolve the crisis at hand, but it encouraged more of the pernicious behavior in the future. On Black Monday Greenspan thus sought to carefully calibrate the Fed's lender of last resort statement and actions. He wanted them to be reassuring enough to quell the degenerating financial panic, but not so comforting as to leave a lasting presumption that the Fed's lender of last resort facilities would always be deployed to protect nonbank players in financial markets from punishing losses. In the event, Greenspan labored to skirt the moral hazard trap by refusing to inject funds directly to securities firms. Instead the Fed followed the clumsier procedure of liquefying the banks, which would in turn liquefy securities firms.[6]

Greenspan's moral hazard concerns were validated even while waves from the Black Monday crash were still rippling. NYSE President John Phelan began campaigning for explicit extension of last resort lending to the stock market: "What would have happened if the stock market went down another five hundred points? There's not enough money in the world from dealers to handle that. You'd need temporary capital from the Fed. That's the structural stuff we need to talk about. Plug in the lender of last resort. It's absolutely essential. The lender would have access to dealers in all systems—not just equities. It would be a safety valve—liquidity in times of stress."[7]

The first line of defense against the spread of moral hazard was a sound financial industry and regulatory structure. America's had grown woefully obsolete. "If we had the financial industry and supervisory structure all right and enough clear rules, we wouldn't run the risk of crossing the line on the safety net all the time," says Fed Vice Chairman Manley Johnson. "Politicians are less and less flexible to adjust to the changes in the world, and it forces us to get involved in it."

The U.S.'s idiosyncratic and vulnerable financial structure was a relic of Great Depression–era legislation. It was based upon financial segment compartmentalization anchored by a heavily regulated core banking industry. But compartmentalization had degenerated into fragmentation in the global financial revolution that was instead undermining bank stability. America was the only nation without a true national banking system, and it defied the worldwide trend toward "universal banking," where banks did both securities and commercial banking business. It was also the only major country without consolidated supervision of its principal banking and financial institutions, and it possessed a convoluted bank supervisory network. To heap absurdity on top of inanity, what American banks were prohibited from doing at home in the name of bank safety, they were able to pursue vigorously in the international Euromarkets beyond the reach of U.S. law.

"[T]he U.S. banking system is simply out of step with the rest of the world and, more important, it is out of step with the realities of the marketplace," New York Fed President Jerry Corrigan warned. "Even more important, the system as now configured may be risk and accident prone, rather than risk averse." As a result, the "U.S. banking and financial system [is] characterized by the dual conditions of recurring bouts of instability and competitive slippage both at home and abroad."[8]

Lending Boldly

On Monday evening in Dallas, Greenspan still hadn't made up his mind whether or not to issue a lender of last resort statement. Whether it would be more propitious to issue the prospective statement that night or the next morning, he discussed by phone with the New York Fed's Corrigan and the Washington crisis group headed by Johnson. Both thought that an early Tuesday morning statement would be more dramatic. It lessened the risk of the dreaded popgun effect, where the Fed played all its cards and nothing happened.

Greenspan wanted to sleep on it before committing to the statement. In the morning he would know what market signals had come from Tokyo and Europe.

Strangely, Greenspan slept soundly that night.

When he awoke he learned that the market vote was a landslide: the Wall Street crash had rippled worldwide. Tokyo had fallen a record 14.9 percent. The Hong Kong stock market had collapsed; it would be shut the remainder of the week. At midday London was down 14 percent, en route to a two-day fall of 21 percent. The Frankfurt stock market was headed to a forty-eight-hour decline of 11 percent. The story in Paris, Milan, Sydney, and Singapore was similar: huge losses, panicked conditions. The smaller screen-based exchanges like the OTC had gone virtually blank. The "Eurobond" markets had all but dried up.

Greenspan decided to launch a statement. George Gould at Treasury had no objections. Fed General Counsel Mike Bradfield worked up a draft. At around 7:30 A.M. Manley Johnson read it to Greenspan over the phone. Jerry Corrigan, who was hooked in by phone patch, thought it was too long. He suggested cutting it down to a single, simple sentence. The others agreed.

At 8:41 A.M. Greenspan gave final approval to release the one-sentence statement: "The Federal Reserve, consistent with its responsibilities as the nation's central bank, affirmed today its readiness to serve as a source of liquidity to support the economic and financial system."

Not relying on the classic last resort approach of lending to individual banks that came forward to the discount window, the Fed backed up the statement with nearly two weeks of highly visible, large injections of liquidity through the New York Fed's open market desk.[9] In the first twenty-four hours the Fed helped guide down three-month interest rates from 6.75 percent to just over 5 percent. The yield curve steepened to a postwar record, a 3.74-percentage-point gap between short- and long-term interest rates.

One worry was that the large liquidity injections might cause the wobbly dollar and the bond market to nosedive. Chiefly to mitigate that possibility, Fed Vice Chairman Johnson informed the Bank of Japan and Bundesbank on Black Monday evening of the Fed's intended actions in the hope that they would act similarly. Since Monday afternoon, long-term interest rates had been falling and the dollar holding steady. Fortunately that favorable trend held up through the worst of the crisis.[10]

Statement issued, Greenspan boarded the jet that the White House had sent to Dallas to transport him back to Washington. Once again he would be airborne while his lieutenants fought the war. It was to be the worst day of the crash, with markets coming unglued, the infrastructure of the payments system breaking down, and the financial system coming within a whisker of devastation.

After the dust had settled, market participants and the postcrash studies all concurred: the Federal Reserve, Alan Greenspan, had saved the day. The Brady Report concluded that "had decisive action not been taken by the Federal Reserve, it appears that far worse consequences would have been a very real possibility."[11]

Greenspan arrived in Washington around 12:45 P.M. After stopping at his office, he headed to the Treasury. Chief of Staff Howard Baker's pithy greeting summed up the relief most political leaders felt about the Fed's statement: "Those are the best lines I've read since Shakespeare." Then they went into meetings with Treasury Secretary Jim Baker, George Gould, and Counsel of Economic Advisers Chairman Beryl Sprinkel and later, at the White House, with President Reagan, to formulate the government's main political response to the crash.

When Black Monday dawned in New York, Jim Baker had been in Frankfurt, patching over his public differences with Bundesbank President Karl Otto Pöhl and German Finance Minister Gerhard Stoltenberg. He learned of the crash after his arrival in Sweden and promptly made plans to return home. Dillon, Read Chairman Nicholas Brady, one of the Ivy League Republican circle of friends around Baker's best friend, Vice President George Bush, joined him on the Concorde next day. Baker invited Brady to stay on for the Tuesday afternoon meeting at the Treasury, when all the top U.S. financial officials finally assembled together for the first time.

Most of the meeting was spent discussing what President Reagan could do and say to demonstrate steadying leadership in a crisis—something that wouldn't later be proved wrong by events. "We had a long discussion whether to have a press conference and what the president should say," recounts Gould. "The president hadn't had a press conference in a long time. He'd be sure to be asked about the Iran-contra affair, and we were very afraid he'd blow his cool. What we didn't want in that environment was a messy press conference." But they finally decided that a press conference was necessary, though "we weren't sure what he could say."[12]

One uncontroversial thing the president could say was that he was announcing a study of the causes for the crash. Who ought to do it?

They looked around the room and "saw poor Nick sitting there." Brady offered, "I'll do anything the president asks."[13] Thus the Brady Task Force, announced at President Reagan's Thursday, October 22, 1987, press conference, was born.

Far more difficult was what of substance could be done to assuage markets. They finally drafted a paragraph declaring the administration's readiness to enter a budget-deficit reduction summit with Congress, where "everything"—including politically despised tax hikes—would be on the table. They took it to the White House. With some reluctance, President Reagan approved it.

Late on Tuesday afternoon Greenspan returned to the Fed to assume personal charge of the crisis team.[14] Yet once the lender of last resort statement was launched, he knew that success hinged on the actions of Fed officials beyond Washington in the front lines—in the markets.

Chapter 5

In the Markets

The Fed's "eyes and ears on the markets" was the Federal Reserve Bank of
New York, located in the heart of Wall Street, just a stone's throw from the
New York Stock Exchange. The New York Fed president was the second
most important official in the Federal Reserve System; his roughly $250,000
annual salary, though humble by Wall Street standards, was double that of
the Fed chairman's and on par with the president of the United States among
American public officials.

The New York Fed's special position in the system derived from its loca-
tion and activities in the heart of the U.S.'s main financial center. Its regular
contact with key financial players and sense of market developments provided the system's dialectical counterpoint to the more government-oriented
administrative center in Washington in shaping policy and tactics. The system consisted of a seven-man board of governors in Washington and twelve
regional Federal Reserve Banks in Boston, Buffalo, New York, Cleveland,
Richmond, Atlanta, Chicago, St. Louis, Minneapolis, Denver, Dallas, and San
Francisco. The seven governors were nominated by the U.S. president and
approved by the Senate for unrecallable fourteen-year terms, each expiring
every two years. They were supposed to hail from different regions and reflect a cross section of financial, agricultural, and business interests. A chairman and vice chairman, each serving for four-year renewable terms, were
selected among them. The Reserve Bank presidents, by contrast, were chosen mostly by the private sector: they were nominated by its nine private directors—six of whom were selected by its member commercial banks.

Although the board managed the Fed's regulatory authority, set the minimum reserve requirements, and voted on requests from the Reserve Banks
to alter the discount rate, the true power center was the Federal Open Market Committee (FOMC), which decided open market policy. Alone among
the Reserve Bank presidents, the New York Fed president held a permanent

voting place on the FOMC along with the seven board governors; the other eleven reserve bank presidents rotated the four remaining voting seats among themselves annually. By majority vote, the FOMC issued monetary policy instructions, called the "directive," which were then implemented by the open market desk on the eighth floor at the New York Fed. The FOMC also decided on a foreign exchange market intervention directive, which was likewise implemented by the foreign exchange desk at the New York Fed in coordination with the Treasury. As bankers New York Fed officials operated in the market physically, taking credit risk and running the country's main payments system, Fedwire. The New York Fed was also a main communication portal for international central bankers.

In the aftermath of the Great Crash of 1929, division between the then semiautonomous New York Fed and the board in Washington contributed to the Fed's gross policy failure to mitigate the Great Depression. This time there was unanimity in purpose and execution between Greenspan and the New York Fed president, forty-six-year-old E. Gerald Corrigan. A six-foot-three-inch, 220-pound, Jesuit-educated native of the factory town of Waterbury, Connecticut, the ruddy-complexioned Jerry Corrigan had joined the New York Fed in 1968 and become Paul Volcker's prize protégé when Volcker became its president in 1975. After stints in Washington and at the Minneapolis Fed, Corrigan acceded to the New York Fed presidency in 1985.

Corrigan had served as Volcker's point man for handling many of the U.S.'s financial flash points in the 1980s. In the process he learned more about what made markets tick than anyone else. By 1987 he'd become one of the world's leading pragmatic thinkers about the transformations and risks posed by the global financial revolution. "Corrigan is even better on the nuts and bolts of the [financial] system than Volcker," Lewis Preston, chairman of J. P. Morgan, says admiringly. With Volcker's retirement Corrigan was really the only senior official in the Federal Reserve System who could get down into the mechanisms of the marketplace, roll up his sleeves, make sure that the Fed's policy intentions were understood—and hold the pieces together if it started to blow up.

On Black Monday morning Corrigan was in Venezuela, where he'd been meeting with that nation's president on LDC debt. That afternoon, during the four-hour flight to New York, Corrigan contemplated the hot spots where market mechanisms were most likely to break down.

Financial markets' first defense against selling frenzies were market-making firms, which bought unwanted shares, futures contracts, and options in order to provide an orderly market environment. But the defense line was only as deep as market makers' capital cushion against bankrupting loss. When market prices actually crashed, as on Black Monday, it was often quickly blown away.

What worried Corrigan as much as the price declines was the massive trading volume. More shares traded meant more payments had to change hands. Huge additional financing would be required to bridge temporary cash gaps in the payments chain. If it wasn't readily forthcoming, it could unleash a fresh wave of panic stock selling to obtain liquidity. The liquidity squeeze would spread the crisis beyond the equity-futures-options continuum through all financial markets—and to the economy.

Corrigan's focus was on what he called the "plumbing" of the financial system—the interconnected clearing, settlement, and payments mechanisms that ran underneath all financial markets and the economy the way arteries and veins ran through the human body. In normal conditions they were out of sight and mind to everyone but the central banker. "There is no question that payments and clearing systems are the mechanisms through which a problem can spread very rapidly," Corrigan says.[1]

Clearing and settlement occurred whenever anyone cashed a paycheck or wrote a check to pay a bill: the bank receiving the check verified, or "cleared," the sum with the payee's bank. Fund transfer, or "settlement," between the two banks was then effected through an electronic payment network, which was basically a bank debt and credit accounting scoreboard.

A similar process occurred whenever a share, futures contract, or option was traded: the trade was processed by broker-dealers and then matched, or "cleared," within a "clearinghouse." After clearing came settlement—the delivery of the financial asset by the seller and the payment by the buyer. Most deliveries by 1987 were done simply by computer registry of ownership changes—no paper actually changed hands. Payment moved along bank channels: the buyer's clearinghouse member agent instructed its bank to transfer funds to the clearinghouse. The clearinghouse then paid the representative member of the seller. The member settled with its client.

The hydraulics of this plumbing system were dependent upon short-term bank financing at every stage. The heaviest borrowers were broker-dealers. Their financing needs were elevated when the clearinghouse called upon them to post additional net margin to cover the losing positions of their clients as the market moved up and down each day and at the date they had to settle final positions with their counterparts. Yet a fast-moving crash, when losses were mounting so rapidly that no one could readily tell who was only temporarily illiquid and who had crossed the line into insolvency, was when the lenders' panic instinct to pull back was strongest. "If word goes out that a stockbroker is in trouble, banks can pull credit lines just like that!" describes Bank of England Executive Director Brian Quinn, snapping his fingers.

If financing evaporated, clearinghouse members couldn't settle their trades—first the clearinghouse, then the financial market itself, would fall apart. Corrigan's ultimate nightmare was gridlock—the point when funds stopped flowing through the plumbing network altogether because no one would release payments or make loans until they received covering funds first. Gridlock would back up the plumbing network until the the entire financial credit system imploded. At that point healthy industry companies might not be able to receive financing for business operations or make routine business payments. Payroll check cashing might be disrupted.[2]

The first thing Corrigan wanted to do on Black Monday was to "limit the market's instinct to cut back on counterparties that may be at risk but that fundamentally are really sound." His greatest enemy was uncertainty. No one in his right mind would trade or lend with a failed firm or if he himself feared being caught short of liquidity.

One big problem on Black Monday was that the design of the plumbing system had not kept pace with the rapid financial market transformation in the 1980s. Surging financial transaction volumes created a commensurate increase in the overall financing pressures within payment system plumbing. The stock, futures, and options markets, moreover, each had their own clearing and settlement mechanisms with disparate rules, even though together they functioned effectively as a single market continuum linked by broker-dealers and investors who operated across each simultaneously. The inchoate design made it harder for creditors to get a global view of the solvency of a broker-dealer, who often did risk arbitrage, block trading, foreign exchange trading, and clearing across various U.S. and foreign markets. It also created numerous bottlenecks as sellers in one market awaited payment to be able to pay for their purchases in another market. This unnecessarily further inflated financing demand to bridge the gaps.[3] Simply, the intermarket continuum was so new, and had never been tested under duress, that no one could be sure how well it would hold up under the extraordinary pressures.[4]

Black Monday

Corrigan was met at New York's Kennedy Airport with a briefcase of papers summarizing Black Monday's developments. On the ride to Wall Street he learned that the situation was worse than he'd anticipated.

It was obvious that because of the record-shattering volume in the stock and futures markets, the demand for liquidity was going to be unprecedented. NYSE market makers were already trying to line up the increased financing for settlement five days hence on the three-times-normal volume of equity transactions. Stock index futures contract transactions, swelled by twice normal volume, had to be settled next day. In anticipation, the futures market clearinghouse was calling for additional margin from its members of $2.1 billion, on the order of ten times normal. Clearinghouse members in turn were raising margin calls on their clients by up to eightfold and refusing to clear for some of them at all. While options market volume was only three-quarters normal, that suggested the plumbing mechanisms were already buckling. And margin calls of $1 billion were due to the clearinghouse next day.

Arriving at his mahogany-paneled tenth-floor office at the New York Fed, where a half-dozen-man crisis team headed by Executive Vice President Stephen Thieke had established its headquarters, Corrigan took his own quick inventory of what was happening by telephoning senior executives throughout Wall Street: What are your funding needs like? What is your level of pain? Where were the big hits taken? Where are tomorrow's trouble spots?

Corrigan spoke under a rule of confidence and, for fear of spreading panic, was careful to talk around the names of firms that might be in danger of failing. At the same time, calls were flooding in and bringing more information in an undifferentiated torrent of sometimes contradictory facts, market perceptions, anxieties, rumors, and rumor planting. Corrigan sifted through them, relying on his instincts and personal relationships to read between the lines of the messages he was receiving.

Rumors were rife that many of the market-making stock exchange specialists had exhausted their capital and faced bankruptcy. Prestigious securities houses like E. F. Hutton and L. F. Rothschild were rumored to be on the ropes. The troubled firms, predictably enough, denied it. Hutton would survive the crash but six weeks later be forced to sell itself to Shearson Lehman. Rothschild would soon fail. Massive foreign selling was another frightening rumor sweeping the markets.

At around 5:30 P.M. Corrigan dialed John Phelan, president of the New York Stock Exchange, who had called earlier to open lines with the Fed.

"We got through today, but another one like it tomorrow and the whole system is gonna have a problem," Phelan told him.[5] The two fears preoccupying the big market players were the absence of buyers and the difficulty in obtaining financing at reasonable costs. A liquidity squeeze now, he said, would doom the stock market.

Corrigan assured him that the Fed understood that.

Not yet fully apparent on Monday was how fast bankers were already pulling back from undercapitalized NYSE specialists as well as other securities firms rumored to be in trouble. Postcrash markets studies revealed that over 60 percent of the buying power of the specialists was obliterated on Black Monday. By midafternoon Monday many had stopped buying shares despite their obligation to do so. The three hundred Chicago locals who normally provided liquidity by making markets in the S&P 500 futures index contract pit had also ceased doing so around 2:30 P.M. Even the big firms that did block trading began to drop out.

The crunch time for financing decisions was only beginning that evening. Peak intensity would start next morning with margin postings and settlements in futures and options. It would last at least a week, when stocks settled. How severe it got depended on whether crashing market prices could be stabilized.

Over the next hours one of the big "money center" banks, Bankers Trust, told Wall Street firms that it would no longer extend unsecured credit. Specialist A. B. Tompane, which had survived the 1929 crash, was denied financing by Bankers Trust; with the help of a middle-of-the-night rule change by the NYSE, it sold out at 3:00 A.M. to Merrill Lynch. The chairman of one of the biggest and best-capitalized specialists, Henderson Brothers, called Bankers Trust five times beween 11:00 P.M. and 12:30 A.M. to seek additional financing to meet payments due the following Monday. But Bankers Trust refused to make any commitments.

Bankers Trust also refused to make an overnight yen payment to troubled Hutton since it would receive the covering dollar amount fourteen hours later—and thus would have a fourteen-hour credit exposure—although this contravened foreign exchange market practice of delivery during the business hours of the country whose currency was being traded. Other banks eventually stepped forward to cover Hutton's position, but not before the world's foreign exchange markets shuddered. As the SEC later reported, "Because the settlement of foreign exchange trades involves interrelated transactions, any significant departure from convention could have frozen the foreign exchange market and precipitated a widespread credit constriction. . . ."[6]

Other U.S. banks tested borrowers, especially the risk arbitrage speculators, by calling for intraday deposits on their loans. If the borrower met the call, the bank usually resumed lending. Medium-size U.S. regional banks and foreign banks were fastest to cut back their exposures. Foreign banks cut back to U.S. securities' firms in all global markets, not just in New York.

Rumors were fever pitched that Japanese banks were cutting and running. Corrigan met with the chief of the BOJ's representative office in Wall Street. Senior officials in Tokyo were also queried. "The Japanese banks are saying that the U.S. money center banks are closing their lines of credit," the BOJ officials reported to Corrigan. "These U.S. banks have very good analysts and long, long experience in this market. Japanese banks are just following."

Like many Europeans, the Japanese raised their lending rates to test borrowers they didn't know well. When the securities firms took the money, they interpreted it as a sign of weakness. Some cut lending—one sharply. Others kept lending at still higher rates. At least one exploited the rare opportunity to expand its business substantially. Overall, the Japanese did not desert the market more than most foreigners.

All in all, thought Corrigan on Monday evening as he headed home to suburban Westchester around 9:30 P.M., the situation was grim but not yet disintegrating to zero-point gridlock. When he got home Corrigan consulted with Alan Greenspan in Dallas for the first time. They agreed to wait and see how foreign stock markets reacted before releasing the Fed's lender of last resort statement.

Terrible Tuesday

Corrigan arrived at his office Tuesday at 6:00 A.M. Far East markets had plunged. London and the European bourses were plummeting. U.S. firms were selling stocks worldwide to obtain cash. U.S. corporations listed on foreign exchanges were being sold until their liquidity was exhausted. Psychological contagion fueled the selling charge. "The linkages among markets were extreme and unexpected," says Stephen Thieke of the New York Fed. "Each market set the tone day to day for the next."

Around 6:30 A.M. Corrigan telephoned George Blunden, deputy governor of the Bank of England, to begin opening foreign central banker channels.[7] Each had set up a task force; the forces collaborated throughout the crash. During the crisis, Corrigan and Blunden conferred twice a day, at New York's opening and London's close.

At 7:00 A.M. Corrigan received a call from John Crow, the tall, fifty-year-old governor of the Bank of Canada, where the stock market had fallen 11.3 percent on Monday. "We talked less than five minutes," says Crow. "We can describe what we're each doing in very brief words since we understand each other. He had a lot of calls to make."

Corrigan told Crow that the Fed might make a statement. Crow, like most other central bankers, did not follow this lead. But he began calling bankers to let them know that the Bank of Canada was making liquidity available in order to "grease the shift in volume and positions without forcing further selling and avoiding panic."[8]

Corrigan also talked to Bank of Japan Deputy Governor for International Relations Takeshi Ohta. "We were in close contact with our central bank brethren in Europe, the Far East, and Canada," says Corrigan. "Mostly we were just comparing notes to be sure we all understood what was going on in the others' markets. Everyone was basically on the same wavelength. We all knew what had to be done."

When Greenspan decided later that morning to make the lender of last resort statement, Corrigan suggested that he call around to be sure that the banks understood the Fed's intentions. Greenspan agreed.

This "moral suasion" was one of the most nuanced of central banker's arts, since it trod directly upon the fragile paradoxes governing the relationship between markets and governments. It sprang from central bankers' unspoken role as bank club leader to rally concerted action that protected the best long-run interest of all members and to shield them from hostile democratic political forces. Now and then the lavishly paid financiers were invited in behind the central banks' closed doors to receive elliptical, informal guidance on how to behave. Most often they accepted the hint. Moral suasion traditions were most developed in England, where the semaphoric raising of the governor's eyebrows and his subtle "nods and winks" elicited seemingly spontaneous, harmonious behavior among the inner bankers' club. This fostered both the public good of financial order and the stabilizing illusion that markets had reequilibrated largely on their own. Moral suasion was practiced with pragmatic delicacy: enough force to halt the self-destructive market urge to cut and run, but so couched to be able to deny moral or legal responsibility for any resulting losses.

"There is a very fine line that has to be drawn between telling someone what you think should be done and reminding them of the broader implications [of their actions]," explains Corrigan. Final lending responsibility was "subject always to their own prudent credit judgment."

Moral suasion, however, worked better in the more regulated, less competitive world of banking's past, when central bankers had more direct administrative discretion over the carrots and sticks that conditioned banks' profit opportunities. Easier profits afforded big bank chairmen the luxury of acting as gentlemanly statesmen, not solely profit-driven "players"—the protective wink of the central banker assured them that their gentlemanly behavior wouldn't be taken advantage of by competitors. "We look to the Fed to get the other guy to behave properly," quips one senior U.S. banker.

As soon as the Fed's statement was released at 8:41 A.M., Corrigan began telephoning the chairmen of America's leading banks, securities firms, insurers, and other institutional investors. One of the things he told them was that two floors below him, the manager of the New York Fed's open market desk was pumping liquidity into the markets as fast as firemen at a towering inferno.

The conversations were brief, two-way, and laced with code, "like the language of diplomacy," explains ex–Citibank Chairman Walt Wriston. "They use terms like 'must give due consideration to.' But we all understand it."

Decoded, Corrigan's message was simple: Keep lending as you would under normal conditions, and we'll all pull through. The strategy was for the Fed to liquefy the banks and the banks to liquefy the securities firms and the rest of the financial system.

America's financial bosses were receptive to the Fed's taking command. Some needed comforting words or hand-holding. But none of the major bankers argued with him or required arm-twisting. That included Charles Sanford Jr., chief executive of Bankers Trust, which had been cutting back fast. "Corrigan really chewed Charlie's ass," confides one banker close to Sanford.

"Our job was to assess the credit of our customers in a crisis and not to worry about whether we were going to run out of dough," Sanford himself reported of Corrigan's message. "He made it clear we didn't have to worry."[9]

Bankers Trust quickly got back into step with the other money center banks.

By lunchtime, when Corrigan finished his main battery of calls, credit was beginning to flow more freely from the New York banks. Only later, when the weekly lending data came in, did Corrigan discover that the ten large New York banks had increased their loans to securities firms by nearly $5.5 billion—82 percent higher than the previous week. The big Chicago banks increased their lending by 21 percent.[10] While the large foreign banks cut back, they didn't do so as much as the smaller U.S. banks. Thus the hierarchy of cooperativeness was based more on size than on nationality.

The increased liquidity flow proved crucial to averting a near collapse in the intermarket plumbing network on Terrible Tuesday. In the morning rumors were rampant that the clearing and settlements mechanisms of the Chicago futures and options markets were on the verge of collapse. If Chicago plumbing collapsed, the securities giants that took positions across all markets simultaneously would not be paid for their winning positions. In turn they might default on their stock payments. That could drive the NYSE to closure.

The most serious bottleneck was the intersection of the futures and options plumbing. Investors who had written put options—that is, undertaken obligations before the crash to buy shares or futures at a specific, now much higher, price—were suffering geometrically soaring losses. As their loss exposures mounted, so did their margin owed to the options clearinghouse.

Where could they raise the extra funds necessary to prevent the options clearinghouse from collapsing? Most were depending upon receiving payments from their winning short position hedges in the falling futures market.[11] Yet as prices plunged, the writers of put options were aggressively increasing the size of their futures hedges. This was placing considerable additional downward pressure on futures prices—and pushing futures losers closer to default and the futures market clearinghouse closer to collapse.

The futures market plumbing was already buckling from other crash pressures. The huge margin calls of $2.1 billion were due to be paid to the CME (Merc) clearinghouse by each clearing member's Chicago "settlement" bank by 7 A.M. (CST). When the margin payments were in hand, the clearinghouse would then authorize payout on all the winning positions from Monday. But the large size of the morning margin payments exceeded the funds that several large New York–based clearing members kept at the four designated Chicago settlement banks. The Chicago bankers were nervous about lending them the excess. Amid Monday's losses and all the confusion and rumors of firms in trouble, the bankers fretted that the clearinghouse might not be able to collect all its margin calls. It might thus be unable to pay in full the amount owed to clearing members.

Chicago bankers wanted reassurance from the clearing members' New York banks that if they extended overdrafts to enable margin commitments to be met, they'd receive covering fund transfers within the day. But early on Terrible Tuesday morning, two and a half hours before the Fed's statement would be released, the skittish New York bankers weren't taking their phone calls.

Nevertheless, three of the four settlement banks extended their overdraft credits by 7:20 A.M. and confirmed to the CME clearinghouse that there were sufficient funds to meet margin calls. The fourth did so an hour later.

But the actual payouts to futures winners were effected with agonizing slowness throughout the day. Chicago banks waited for the covering funds from the New York bankers—some of whom were only then receiving their call from Corrigan—which were agonizingly slow in coming. The covering payments also were delayed by two breakdowns in Chicago in the overloaded Fedwire payments system between the crucial hours of 10:00 A.M. and 12:30 P.M.

A further complication was that Goldman Sachs, among others, released some of the roughly $600 million it was owed in winning futures positions to its own institutional customers before receiving payment from the clearinghouse. This worsened Goldman's liquidity shortfall in covering the overdrafts advanced by its Chicago settlement bank.

When noon passed and the clearinghouse still had not paid out the winnings to Goldman or Shearson Lehman, another firm with big gross (but not net) winning positions, rumors began to intensify that these two giants—and the futures market clearinghouse itself—were on the ropes. Fears were further inflamed because Goldman and Shearson, along with Morgan Stanley and Salomon Brothers, were facing losses running into the hundreds of millions of dollars from their underwriting commitments for the unpropitiously timed £7.2 billion ($12 billion) British Petroleum privatization in London. The size of their losses depended upon how far BP shares ultimately fell.[12]

Rumors that the Merc's clearinghouse was on the verge of collapse drove the futures markets into a virtual free-fall. Panicked customers withdrew all excess funds deposited with clearing members, further exacerbating their liquidity squeeze. Speculation that the options market clearinghouse was about to colapse fueled the panic. Certain banks likewise pulled back credit lines, imposed new loan restrictions, and "declined to transfer funds for a customer until they received covering funds for that customer's account from another source."[13] The dribbling flow of payments began to dry up in gridlock.

The attention of America's senior financiers became riveted on their accounts receivable. "You had very senior people talk about what they were owed and by whom, and asking regularly whether they'd been paid," says the New York Fed's Steve Thieke. "On normal days these people never think of it."

With the plumbing threatening to come apart, the big market players refused to take advantage of once-in-a-lifetime profit windows. Buyers disappeared. After the crash, Treasury Undersecretary George Gould asked the chief of trading for Goldman Sachs why Goldman hadn't leaped through the huge index arbitrage window when the futures market free-fell 27 percent in the morning and was trading at the equivalent of Dow 1400, a mind-boggling three hundred-plus-point discount to the Dow's 1700 level.

"What good is arbitraging if you can't get paid?" was the reply.

With the futures markets pointing to sharply lower stock prices, institutions dumped all stocks still capable of being traded. The selling avalanche overwhelmed the last pockets of speculative buyers. By late Tuesday morning, after an initial rebound in futures and stock prices collapsed, the stock/futures/options market continuum was disintegrating. Market price relationships disconnected and became haphazard.

Recalls Thieke, "I was in the trading room when the S&P 500 contract started falling through the cash [stock] market. I had the ominous feeling that things were falling apart. Things were happening that we all felt *couldn't* exist—but on the screen it was telling the truth. There were completely irrational relationships. The sad fact is that there was nothing we could do." Gloomily, U.S. central bankers began to anticipate closure of the U.S. capital markets—and to wonder how to get them reopened.

NYSE President John Phelan had been frantically calling top White House and Treasury officials throughout Terrible Tuesday morning. All morning they persuaded him to postpone the dire action of halting trading on the NYSE. Yet around midday, with markets in many of the biggest, most liquid stocks on earth collapsing and NYSE members pleading for relief from their massive losses, Phelan apparently decided that the most sacred symbol of U.S. free market capitalism had to be officially shut down. The directors of the stock exchange were to convene at 12:30 P.M. to confirm the decision that had been all but made.

Phelan called the people who had to know in the market and in Washington. Howard Baker was entering an official White House luncheon in the second-floor "family dining room" when one of the ushers informed him, "A Mr. Phelan is on the phone for you." They had already talked nearly hourly that morning.

Baker detected a special anguish in Phelan's voice this time. "I don't think I can hold it," Phelan said. "The specialist system is breaking down, and the 'upstairs people' "—Baker never understood who precisely these were— "are clamoring. . . . You've got to get the president to issue the executive order to close it."[14]

"Can't the specialists hold out just a little bit longer?"

Baker suddenly caught sight of John Whitehead, deputy secretary of state and a former head of Goldman, Sachs, entering the luncheon. Baker signaled furiously for him to come over. Clasping his hand over the telephone receiver, he informed Whitehead what was transpiring. "Can you talk to him?" he asked.

Whitehead took the phone.

Fed, Treasury, and political White House officials all the way up to President Reagan desperately did not want the stock market to close. "All my instincts told me that if we closed the market, we might have a hell of a time getting it open again," Baker explains. "Hong Kong had already closed. In Tokyo something like only twenty percent of the listed shares had traded. If New York closed, we feared London would not open. What happens when the world's capital markets are closed?"

Whitehead reasoned with Phelan as one Wall Street veteran to another. He finally persuaded him to hang on just a bit longer—one hour at a time.

"Okay," Phelan said to Baker when he took the phone back from Whitehead. "But please have the executive order [to shut the exchange] ready."[15]

With President Reagan's agreement, the executive order was drafted.

Yet the NYSE had already communicated its probable closing to the SEC. "The New York Stock Exchange told us they were clearly inclined to close during the next ten minutes," recalls SEC Director of the Division of Market Regulation Richard Ketchum. "We informed Chicago."

Chicago cut and ran to be first to the exits. Facing a huge new wave of losses that would come as selling pressure transferred to Chicago once New York stock trading stopped, the Chicago Mercantile Exchange, at 12:15 P.M., terminated trading in the most important stock futures index, the S&P 500. The Chicago Board of Options, with many options closed since the underlying stocks were not trading, had shut down a half hour earlier at 11:45 A.M.

At that point widespread credit breakdown seemed likely, and, concluded the Brady Task Force, "the financial system came close to gridlock."[16]

At 12:15 P.M. Phelan told Corrigan that unless there was a miracle the stock exchange would close.

The U.S. stock market almost surely would have collapsed had not the unexplained "miracle" occurred. First, a mysterious rally, which raised suspicions of deliberate manipulation, broke out at 12:20 P.M. in a minor futures contract, the Major Market Index, on the Chicago Board of Trade, which had refused to close. Next, shortly before 1:00 P.M. and gathering force through the afternoon, blue chip corporations began announcing plans to make $6 billion worth of stock repurchases. By that time the Fed's lender of last resort rescue was paying off: security firms were receiving enough pledges of support from the big New York banks that they were willing to execute trading orders. The liquidity panic was further eased by a sharp fall in long-term interest rates. Payments began to flow. Shortly after 1:00 P.M. the Merc resumed trading in the S&P 500. Market spirits were buoyed by the midafternoon news of the $1.5 billion payment of Monday futures winnings to Goldman and Shearson.

The day was wild. The stock market rallied 125 points between 12:20 and 1:00 P.M., then soon fell back 100 points within a half hour; from 2:00 P.M. to 3:30 P.M. rallied 170 points, then fell over 50 points in the final half hour. For the day, the market had a historic gain of 102 points. Volume was also a record 608 million shares. On Wednesday the stock market soared 187 points more.

Why did the market rally mysteriously? Was the announcement of corporate stock repurchases a spontaneous market bandwagon or was it prompted by a concerted effort that in normal times might be considered collusive? None of the postcrash studies investigated it. Why not?

"There may be a reluctance to probe it," says Treasury's Gould. "You don't want to find something untoward, so it would be closed if it happened again."

White House Chief of Staff Howard Baker and Gould himself, in the course of consultations with America's business and financial leaders as the panic worsened, had raised the question "Where could buyers be found?" Corporations had plenty of cash. As their share prices plummeted well below the companies' fundamental value, they also had incentives to buy back their shares.[17] If many started to do so, the stock market possibly could be turned.

"Did I cross-pollinate [this idea]?" Baker asks rhetorically. "Probably. In the course of conversation, a few volunteered some ideas and said that they'd do what they could. I told them who I'd talked to." The SEC helped by giving "comfort" to Merrill Lynch that soliciting corporate repurchases under these conditions would not be construed as market manipulation.

Even if market meltdown had been reached, Corrigan avers that he had "a few more ideas I could try."

What were they?

"I won't tell," he answers, eyes twinkling. "I might need them again in the future."

For most of the world, the stock market drama seemed to be over. Not so for central bankers. "Most people don't realize the stock market crisis didn't end on Tuesday," Corrigan says. "It lasted two solid weeks."

First Options

A fresh crash was threatened by lasting doubts about the survivability of the options clearinghouse, the Options Clearing Corporation (OCC). The deadliest problem was the near failure of First Options of Chicago Inc., by far the largest of the clearinghouse's nineteen members. Washington politics was right in the middle of it.

First Options' owner was Continental Illinois, the same bank that had been rescued by the U.S. government in 1984. In late 1986 its new management wanted to acquire First Options as part of its strategy to seek profits in the booming capital markets. It held informal discussions with the Fed about doing so through its holding company, for which the Fed was the lead federal regulator. Under Volcker the Fed was unsympathetic to banks' engaging in securities and derivatives activities. Rather than be denied by the Fed, Continental sought approval to buy First Options through Continental Bank, which was federally regulated by the deregulation-minded Reagan Office of the Comptroller.[18] It was a classic case of what ex–Fed Chairman Arthur Burns called the "competition in laxity" in America's convoluted bank supervisory network.[19]

The Comptroller's consent was forthcoming, provided that Continental adhered to certain limitations on the bank's total exposure to its First Options subsidiary—in effect, that it would treat it as an independent entity. This caveat confirmed the Reagan administration's political argument for financial industry reform wherein potential contagion from securities losses could be contained by building "firewalls" between a bank and its securities operations.

During the week of October 19, First Options suffered $92 million in losses. In an illustration of how the negligence of one intermediary in assessing the risk position of its customers in globalizing financial markets could endanger the entire system, $52 million of the losses resulted from the bankruptcy of a single Taiwanese options speculator, Hwalin Lee.[20]

First Options needed a large infusion of funds immediately to meet the big jump in margin calls to the OCC and the timing disparity of settlement

dates—one day for options and five days for equities—in the markets between which it hedged, and to remain in compliance with the SEC's minimum net capital requirements. Failure to obtain sufficient financing would
prompt forced liquidations of First Options' options positions. This could
trigger a new options market crash. Continental Illinois stared at a corporate
tragedy of $400 million to $600 million in losses if First Options failed.
Worse, the failure of First Options, which cleared for 1,200 option specialists, among many others, was likely to bring down the options clearinghouse—setting off a domino chain reaction across the intermarket
continuum.

Who would lend First Options the large sums needed to stave off disaster? Under crash conditions the only source was Continental itself. On Black
Monday Continental Bank loaned First Options $102 million. But First Op-
tions needed $138 million more on Terrible Tuesday. If Continental provided
it, it would violate the firewall limit it had promised to respect.[21]

The Office of the Comptroller resolutely refused to relax its firewall
limit—and thus tacitly confess that firewalls were a political sham. Using the
fig leaf of a dubious legal interpretation, Continental executives decided to
make the $138 million unsecured loan to First Options anyway.

Furious Comptroller officials informed Continental they were likely to
resort to formal legal enforcement action.

The next day, Wednesday, Continental withdrew the loan from the bank.
They replaced it with a loan from the holding company—*without* Fed approval.

The market panicked at news of the Comptroller's rigidity about the firewalls. A run broke out on First Options, exacerbating its liquidity squeeze.
On Wednesday its customers pulled out $157 million in deposits. First Op-
tions' New York bankers, who in all had lent it about $1 billion, also hit the
panic button.

By Thursday the prospect of massive selling of First Options' options positions threatened to drive the collateral value of the options below the face
value of the bank loans they supported. One bank, with a $250 million credit
line to First Options, demanded better collateral—or it wanted out.

Fed officials, although enraged by the Office of the Comptroller's subor-
dination of financial system safety and soundness to political face-saving,
were forced to act. Manley Johnson recounts, "The Comptroller decided to
force the issue. We all knew they needed funds from somewhere or the option market would shut down."

The matter was decided within minutes on Thursday as the run on First
Options reached massive proportions. Suppressing their urge to force the
Comptroller's Office to face up to its reckless disregard for financial system
safety, Fed officials moved urgently to approve the loan from the holding

company and to "deal with the Comptroller later."[22] Later, Alan Greenspan dealt personally with the Comptroller of the Currency.

In New York, meanwhile, Jerry Corrigan was letting the big banks know that the Fed was going to approve the loan from the holding company.

The panic fever broke. Lending to First Options became a minor worry, says J. P. Morgan Chairman Lewis Preston, "once we knew it wouldn't shut down the clearing corporation."

Plugging the First Options hole, however, spread moral hazard. "It demonstrated that the federal safety net extends beyond banking and covers securities firms," observes ex–Senate Banking Committee staff chief Kenneth McLean.

The First Options drama, incredibly, didn't end there.

The Office of the Comptroller decided to press ahead with its formal enforcement action. This reignited the client run on First Options.[23]

The First Options drama finally reached its climax with the clearing and settlement of Black Monday's and Terrible Tuesday's stock trades on Monday and Tuesday, October 26 and 27. First Options' financing needs would shrink substantially after that, since its liquidity strain was caused partly by the lag between the one-day settlement in options (where it was a net loser and had to pay out) and the five-day settlement in stocks (where it was a net winner).

Would the stock trading system clear? Corrigan had been working all week and into the start of the next to make sure that it would.

It did. "As we got Friday of the first week and Monday and Tuesday of the second week under our belt, my comfort level began to rise," says Corrigan. "I wasn't yet dancing in the aisles."

The most perplexing lingering question about the First Options episode was, What possessed the Office of the Comptroller, in the midst of such an obvious threat to financial system stability as the stock market crash, to persist in its tunnel-vision adherence to maintenance of First Options firewalls?

The answer, it seemed, lay in the gulf between government and markets. "They followed through with the formal cease and desist order because their attitude was 'We better protect our tails—this will be well publicized,' " says the Treasury's George Gould, to whom the Comptroller's Office failed to report on Terrible Tuesday. "For a couple of years we'd been trying to change Glass-Steagall [the act segregating banking from securities activities] on the basis that securities losses can't get into bank capital. They didn't want to ruin the whole legislation."[24]

An ironic postscript: Two years later Continental's brass decided its foray into options hadn't been such a good idea after all. It announced it would get out of the market and scale back its other capital market operations.[25]

The Treasury Auction

Hardly had New York stock trades settled from Black Monday than a new flame flared. Lingering fear about financial damage somewhere that hadn't yet surfaced was making U.S. government securities primary dealers reluctant to take positions in the when-issued (WI) trading for the huge quarterly refunding of U.S. Treasury debt that would begin on Wednesday, October 28. WI trading was done blind over brokers' screens with anonymous counterparties. Since settlement would not occur for two to three weeks, "you could be dealing hundreds of millions of dollars with a failed firm."[26]

The U.S. government securities market was the fulcrum of the interlinked global financial marketplace. Trouble in WI trading could cause U.S. interest rates to spike, interfere with the sale of government bonds, and ignite a global currency crisis in the wobbly dollar. As a result, Corrigan says, "it was imperative that the when-issued trading got off to a good start."

When early WI trading started badly, a meeting was convened on Wednesday among representatives from the primary government dealers, the interdealer brokers, the Treasury, and the Fed. The primary dealers wanted the Fed to guarantee their trades with a listed group of firms. They were in effect requesting an official subsidy—it was the moral hazard dilemma all over again.

Fed officials refused. "There's nothing in our charter that permits us to do it."

"Then we can't trade. Only you can stabilize the trading."

An impasse was averted through a classic central banker "wink and nod" understanding: the Fed agreed to institute daily monitoring of dealer positions. Any firm whose survival seemed to be imperiled would be told, in effect: "Stop trading."[27]

"We did introduce some rather extraordinary monitoring procedures of dealer positions," admits Corrigan, "and we made them know we were watching."

That was enough. When-issued trading got off well enough for a successful quarterly refunding of the U.S. debt. The stock market crisis was over.

Chapter 6

In the Realm of the Establishment

On Terrible Tuesday night, long after the stock market had closed, an exhausted George Gould sat in his office at the U.S. Treasury, wondering if the chaotic rally that afternoon would hold up.

The telephone rang. It was White House Chief of Staff Howard Baker. "Why don't you go home and get some sleep?" Baker suggested.

"I will," Gould said, eyeing his financial market computer screen. "But first I would like to see how Tokyo opens. In this global market that will set the tone for New York."

Sometime later Baker called Gould back. "George, if I told you we were in a 'hold harmless' situation, would you go home and get some sleep?"[1]

"Howard, I've heard of 'hold harmless' as a legal term. But I don't know how it applies to the stock market."

"What if I told you we've just talked to Japan and they said the Ministry of Finance is calling in the Big Four [securities firms] and big investors? Would that take care of it?"

"I suppose it would." Gould soon went home to bed. The next day he discovered, "Sure enough, they'd taken care of it."[2]

Baker explains his sanguineness. His unofficial Japanese interlocutors "were convinced that the Establishment was taking care of it. . . . And the Establishment in Japan means more than in most any place."

Foreigners had a record of unsurpassable misjudgment about the Tokyo stock market—and about much in Japan generally. Prior to Black Monday, many of the world financial cognoscenti, including Basel central bankers, feared that Tokyo would be the first of the world's high-flying stock markets to crash.

As Pacific anchor of the twenty-four-hour global financial market, Tokyo had defied virtually every Western concept of investment fundamentals to become the stellar performer of the global bull market that started in mid-1982 and ended abruptly with the stock market crash. By late 1987 the Tokyo stock market's total value to GNP was four times greater than it had been in 1983. In the process, Tokyo surpassed New York as the world's most largely capitalized stock market.[3] After the NYSE peaked out in August 1987, Tokyo kept soaring right up until Black Monday. Sensing that the market was in the grip of a speculative frenzy, foreign investors had been unremitting net sellers—and big losers—throughout its 1986–87 surge.

"Those who knew the incestuousness of Tokyo knew that it would be different," says Tatsuya Tamura, executive director at the Bank of Japan, of the global crash. "Day by day people were learning about the stock market in Tokyo."

The first phase of the Tokyo stock market's stratospheric rise in the early 1980s was fueled by Japan's large trade surpluses and a surfeit of business cash flow due to a slowing national growth rate. Reduced business loan demand forced banks to seek alternative types of business. But what? Through unofficial guidance, the Ministry of Finance (MOF) and Bank of Japan (BOJ) whispered "real estate." "In the early 1980s, when there was a recession in Japan, housing was encouraged," says Bank of Tokyo Chairman Yusuke Kashiwagi. "It became a fad."

Real estate lending and prices soared. The hidden value of Japanese companies that owned land increased, as did their share prices. This set in motion the reinforcing upward spiral between rising land and stock prices that marked soaring Japanese financial asset markets in the 1980s.

The second and most spectacular phase of this *zaiteku,* or speculative "financial engineering," started with the high yen shock of 1985–87, when the yen's value doubled against the dollar. To offset the recessionary impact, and to help prevent a catastrophic collapse of the dollar, the BOJ slashed its discount rate to a postwar low of 2.5 percent and added some $60 billion to its foreign exchange reserves through intervention. This easy money policy failed to stimulate much domestic capital investment. But it did fire up *zaiteku* to new heights. Japan was awash in liquidity, and its huge "weight of money" was concentrated upon the country's few attractive domestic financial investment options. Extravagant real estate speculation—banks loaned over 100 percent of the collateral value on the expectation of rising land prices—made the property frenzy in the United States and United Kingdom pale by comparison. As real estate values soared, so did stock prices.

The rising value of property and equities accounted for the lion's share of bank profits and artificially inflated their capital base. Security firms thrived. Businesses raised capital at virtually no cost and plowed much of it into financial speculation. Lower capital costs and financial profits helped business offset the decline in export earnings from the soaring yen. Employment was maintained. Free-flowing financial profits were an unexpected bonanza for Japan's extravagant "money politics." Almost everyone in Japan's close-knit Establishment, in short, was content and increasingly bewitched by the narcotic effects of *zaiteku*.

While a few Japanese expressed concern about a bursting of the nascent "bubble economy" of the late 1980s or a spillover from financial asset to goods inflation, most retained confidence in the ability of Japan's Establishment to manage it—a concept alien to most Western capitalisms. The euphoria infected the Japanese man in the street, much as it had Americans in the 1920s. Summed up one stock market investor, "The Nikkei average may fall, but the Japanese market is controlled by the government. Why worry?"[4]

Japanese confidence was reinforced by the belief that soaring stock prices reflected the competitive advantage of their "relationship capitalism" in the world free trade order—ironically, an inverse echo of the unfair competition charges fueling Western threats of protectionism. Business relationships often took priority over price among families of cross-share-owned corporations, or *keiretsu*. An inefficient, archaic distribution sector provided an additional buffer against easy penetration by foreign imports. "The success of Japan versus the United States is that Japan has long-term relationships with implicit contracts, while the United States is a spot market. When Japanese come to the United States they can benefit immediately, but it is much harder when U.S. firms come to Japan in goods and in finance," explains Hirohiko Okumura, Nomura Research Institute's chief economist. "This is reflected in Japanese asset prices. It is an explosive situation."

Black Tuesday

The first account Wall Street received that New York's Black Monday crash had spilled over to Tokyo on what became known as "Black Tuesday" came at slightly past 8 P.M. on Monday evening. At a New York Japan Society dinner honoring Setsuya Tabuchi, the silver-haired chairman of Nomura Securities, the world's largest security firm, he told the audience, "I've been informed that in the first thirty-five minutes of trading on the Tokyo exchange, there have been only six trades."[5]

On Black Tuesday 95 percent of stocks in Tokyo were unable to open because of the overwhelming selling pressure, versus about 30 percent of stocks in New York. By midday only about 10 percent of the leading stocks had been traded at all. Volume was so light that whenever a trade was done, hundreds of floor dealers in their white shirts and blue suits burst into spontaneous applause. The Nikkei 225 closed the morning session down 7.5 percent and for the day down 14.9 percent, or a 3,836-point fall to 21,910.

Despite the record fall in prices, the Tokyo Establishment remained calm. "We had very little concern for the Tokyo stock market and were one hundred percent sure it would recover and beat the worldwide markets," recalls Tsuneo Fujita, director general of the MOF's securities bureau, the Japanese counterpart of the SEC.

Why were the Japanese authorities so composed? The main reason was confidence in their ability to guide Japan's highly regulated domestic financial markets. In contrast with the United States and United Kingdom, deregulation and innovation were being introduced at a very measured pace so as not to upset MOF's supreme influence. Tokyo simply did not have the portfolio insurance and index arbitrage program trading that overwhelmed U.S. market mechanisms. Nor were Tokyo's Big Four brokers—Nomura, Daiwa, Nikko, and Yamaichi—which with their affiliates accounted for over three-quarters of trading, required to make markets by stepping forward as buyers. Thanks to the huge profits they had amassed from oligopolistic broker commissions (five to ten times greater than in the United States) and underwriting fees, they were so well capitalized that it would take almost unthinkable losses to put them in jeopardy.[6]

The only unruly force that the Japanese Establishment couldn't control very well was the one that led the Black Tuesday selling charge—foreigners. Despite the unfounded rumors about Japanese flight from the New York market, it was only in Tokyo of the three major stock markets that foreign selling actually led the crash.[7] Net foreign selling continued every week through December 7 for a total of ¥2.9 trillion ($22 billion). One-third was concentrated during the crash week. The foreign selling might have been more dangerous, but foreign penetration of Japan's stock market had been allowed to reach only 5 percent of ownership and 10 percent of trading.

The main Establishment stabilization on Black Tuesday came during a previously scheduled, routine hour-long monthly luncheon meeting between one of Fujita's underlings, Takashi Matsukawa, director of the MOF's secondary markets division, and the equity division managers of the Big Four. The main agenda topic was to reach a Japanese-style "consensus" on how to act in everyone's best interests. The obvious thing was not to sell—and to discourage selling pressure from clients.

"The decision not to sell [stocks] was made by the securities firms," says Fujita, a warm, slender man with a dark complexion and a bubbly laugh. "It was not the result of the strong recommendation by the MOF, but the MOF was strongly involved in the decision-making process. We made a 'consensus.' It's not hard, since we have close relations." With a smile he adds, "We are *still* concerned about the dominant presence of the major four—the major one—securities houses. But in a crisis, this means there is no need for us to talk to the other securities firms. We are quite lucky in this regard!"[8]

Forging a consensus to buy was more difficult. The Big Four weren't eager to risk losses by buying into such huge selling pressure themselves. Instead they agreed to call upon their "armies" to drum up buy orders from individuals by making "more advertisements to stress the sound fundamentals of the Japanese economy. They made an agreement among themselves in the attendance of MOF officials."[9]

To get the ball rolling on Black Tuesday, the Big Four themselves agreed to buy shares of the market's psychological bellwether, the partly privatized supergiant Nippon Telegraph and Telephone (NTT), of which the government was scheduled to sell 12.5 percent more to the public in mid-November. NTT had ceased to be quoted in the morning session. In the afternoon the Big Four fueled an NTT buying blitz.

One potential flash point of concern was the margin calls that would be triggered if the market fell below 21,000. In contrast with the panicked raising of margin requirements by the futures exchange in Chicago, the Tokyo Stock Exchange, in consultation with MOF, *eased* margin requirements in an effort to facilitate buying.

The Bank of Japan assisted by modestly easing credit conditions and through daily monitoring of securities firms to make sure no one was cheating on the consensus.[10] "The Japanese have knowledge *who* is selling [stocks]," marvels Brian Quinn, Bank of England executive director. "In the crash we couldn't tell who was selling until we got the stock exchange data that came later."

So confident were Japanese monetary authorities in the robustness of the Japanese economy and financial system to sustain a crash that they didn't immediately grasp what Fed Vice Chairman Manley Johnson's concerns were when he telephoned them Black Monday afternoon (U.S. time). Johnson suggested that the BOJ move with the Fed in easing credit and issuing a lender of last resort statement in order to amplify the calming message to the global markets. "I called [BOJ Deputy Governor for International Relations Takeshi] Ohta first because the Eastern markets would be the next to open and I wanted Japan to move before their Tuesday opening," Johnson says. "If a comforting statement came out of there before the market opened, it might minimize the pressure. We didn't try to twist anyone's arm. You don't get anything by demanding action. We simply told them what we were doing in our domestic market and requested that they do something of an equivalent nature in their markets."

Johnson's related anxiety was that if the Fed eased aggressively to fight the crisis, but Japan and Germany stood pat, the wobbly dollar might plunge—pushing U.S. bond interest rates *higher.* "We'd have a real mess on our hands if all markets caved in at the same time," he explains. "There were some initial fears in the weeks before and during the crash that if the dollar were to collapse, we'd get a symmetrical movement in bonds. The dollar held up amazingly well, in the event."

Though sympathetic to Johnson's concerns, Ohta expressed little willingness for the BOJ to comply. The BOJ resented having been arm-twisted over two years of international politics to prop up the dollar by slashing domestic interest rates to levels that were overinflating Japan's money supply. Baker's renewed dollar "talk-down" at the weekend, although aimed at the Bundesbank, initially reinforced BOJ suspicions that the United States was again trying to make other nations adjust their policies to avoid disagreeable budget-deficit cutting at home—until they grasped the full dimensions of the U.S. crash. A second reason, which Ohta did not tell Johnson, was that the BOJ was laying the groundwork for an imminent discount rate *increase* through quiet discussion with MOF officials. By some accounts it was close to reaching a consensus.

Having little success with Ohta, Johnson communicated his concerns to the MOF's Makoto Utsumi. Utsumi was a personal friend and the MOF's leading activist in manipulating Japanese policy to stabilize the dollar. Throughout the period, Japanese officials were in fact more worried about a crash in the dollar than in their stock market.

On Tuesday morning Johnson called back Ohta and Utsumi to say that the Fed's statement had been issued. "We were uncertain whether we should do so or not," says Ohta.

The Bank of Japan

How Japanese monetary policy was made was one of the enigmas of global financial politics. Like so many things in Japan, apparent and real power diverged greatly. Under the law, the BOJ had exclusive power over discount rate and open market policies. Any change in bank reserve ratios required the MOF's approval.

Interest rate policy was made formally by the seven-man BOJ policy board. It was composed of the BOJ governor, two private-sector representatives from finance, one from industry, one from agriculture, and one non-voting member each from MOF and the Economic Planning Agency. The board, which met every Tuesday and Friday from 10:00 A.M. to 12:30 P.M., was popularly known as the "sleeping board" since it merely ratified decisions taken elsewhere. "Only one member ever raised his hand against an action, and that was twenty years ago," says the MOF's Tsuneo Fujita, a policy board member in 1985–86.

The "sleeping board" ratified the recommendations made by the BOJ's executive board, which met every day for one hour except Wednesday.[11] The executive board, however, rarely recommended action until consensus emerged from an opaque web of economic argument and political negotiation between the BOJ and the MOF. The process often started with policy proposals drafted by BOJ departments. At the pinnacle, the negotiations were conducted among the governor, deputy governor, and executive director for policy planning on the side of the BOJ and in the monetary affairs office at the MOF. Occasionally the prime minister got involved. "We and the MOF have a love-hate relationship," says one high BOJ official. "They say that they decide and we execute."

Although 45 percent of the BOJ's shares were still owned by private stockholders and a special nongovernmental juridical entity, the BOJ since its founding in 1882 had been closely supervised by the MOF, Japan's most powerful ministry.[12] The BOJ's subservience and Japan's stellar economic performance were sometimes cited by critics of central bank independence as proof that democratically elected government was capable of responsibly managing monetary policy. The analogy, however, was spurious. MOF dominance did not translate into political control. MOF's elite career technocrats themselves made policy largely independently of Japan's elected leaders. In Japan, idiom declared that "politicians reign, bureaucrats rule." Nevertheless, the MOF-BOJ nexus was well integrated into the web of overlapping public- and private-sector hierarchies, without a true governing center, of bureaucrats, politicians, industrialists, and other cliques that marked the Japanese Establishment.[13]

The BOJ governor and the senior deputy governor were formally appointed by the government cabinet for a five-year renewable term. Protocol over the last two decades was for BOJ governors to be career BOJ and MOF men in alternation—in Japan one's original bureaucratic association determined one's lifelong loyalties.

The BOJ relied more on direct, nonprice operating methods for guiding monetary policy than any other leading central bank. Discount "window guidance" provided an informal ceiling on bank lending growth for the coming three-month period, while moral suasion steered banks on specific types of lending.

Yoshio Suzuki, former executive director of the BOJ, explains, "Window

guidance is to prevent too much competition among banks. There is guidance on the amount of lending to all banks equally. There is moral suasion,
but no sectoral ceilings. But we do say 'not' real estate."[14]

Myriad written and unwritten rules, or administrative guidelines, many
known only by the regulators and regulated, also strongly conditioned Japanese finance. Bank of Tokyo Chairman Yusuke Kashiwagi, a former vice minister at the MOF, expands: "MOF issues letters of instruction. The BOJ is
more oral. . . . Periodically they make their comments and ask us to show
them our lending and investment plans. They say, 'This is a little too big, do
more of that, et cetera. More on exports, or less on imports. How much are
you doing in international lending?' It is more direct [than MOF]. Here you
have very good cooperation between the central bank and the banks. It is
quite different from the United States, where everything is done not by talking it over, but by open market operations."

The relationship was solidified by the fact that the BOJ's administratively
controlled discount window was the main, and an effectively subsidized,
funding source for Japan's "city" banks. "The BOJ is quite different from any
Western central bank," says Akio Mikuni, president of bank credit rating
agency Mikuni & Co. "In the rest of the world there are two systems. The
Bank of England doesn't discourage discount borrowing, but the rate is high.
The Fed's discount rate is usually lower than market rates, but discount window borrowing is discouraged. Here in Japan they have both goodies—rates
are low and lending is not discouraged."

He adds, "At home the MOF and the BOJ serve as player-managers, cap-
tains of the Japan Inc. financial team on the field. The notion that they should
be referees—à la Bank of England or the Fed—is wholly foreign to us!"[15]

Through most of the postwar era, Japanese monetary authorities had managed the financial system to promote high savings and to ration perpetually
scarce credit through banks, which acted as financial "queen bees" to Japanese businesses. This was a key linchpin of the state-capital compact that governed "Japan Inc." The BOJ governor was known informally as "the Pope,"
and the discount rate underpinned the structure of all interest rates. Bank
prices were legally cartelized.

The global financial revolution and the surfeit of domestic savings that
had to be recycled abroad and that accompanied the maturation of Japan's
fantastic postwar economic success, however, was causing the BOJ and MOF
slowly to recalibrate their control methods. More price-driven techniques,
such as indirect steerage of money market interest rates, were being employed. Many career BOJ men believed that more market-oriented operating
procedures in liberalized financial markets could increase the BOJ's monetary policy autonomy from the MOF. Why? Because knowledge was power:
as free market forces, rather than government fiat, determined financial con-

ditions, those closest to the markets gained influence. It was easier for the BOJ autonomously to influence ever-shifting money market interest rates than to alter the highly politically visible discount rate. The BOJ's stature was also being recast by Japan's meteoric rise as the world's banker in the 1980s. How Japan managed the yen, quite simply, significantly influenced world money supply, interest and currency exchange rates, and trade balances.

It was concern over the dollar that informed the BOJ's response to Manley Johnson's solicitations on Black Monday and Terrible Tuesday. At the close of the worst day in Tokyo's stock market since its near collapse in the 1960s, BOJ Governor Satoshi Sumita issued a compromise statement of cooperation from the BOJ. Rather than echo Greenspan's statement of liquidity support, Sumita emphasized his support for the October 19 U.S.-German joint statement of Baker, Stoltenberg, and Pöhl, stressing dollar stability: "The Bank of Japan is determined to continue to pursue firmly the cooperative framework of the Louvre Agreement."[16] To head off a sharp dollar decline, Japan intervened over the next days in foreign exchange markets.

"U.S. security firms lacked liquidity, so the Fed had to make an announcement," explains then Deputy Governor Yasushi Mieno. "In Japan there were no such problems for liquidity support. We didn't make an announcement of liquidity support. But we did monitor the firms and their daily operations."

"It took twenty-four hours for them to make the statement," Johnson says. "Ohta was very apologetic about it. Once the Japanese realized the severity, they moved."

Aftershocks

When markets opened on Wednesday morning in Tokyo, the world witnessed just how stunningly well the Establishment had taken care of the stock market crash. On the conviction that the MOF and Big Four had colluded to support the market, individual investors reversed their year-long caution and piled into the market in record numbers. The psychological turnaround was so dramatic that there was again a serious shortage of liquidity—but this time because there weren't enough *sellers!* The Tokyo stock market closed up a record 2037, or 9.3 percent. "We had a record number of bills cut that day from individual investors buying shares," recalls Nomura Chairman Setsuya Tabuchi.[17]

Genuine market stability, however, was not achieved until the following week, when institutional investors became forceful buyers. Tokyo opened the week badly, plummeting 4.7 percent. At one point it fell below Black

Tuesday's bottom. Fresh plunges in London and New York followed. If Tokyo fell farther, it was feared, a new round of global crashes would be set off.

Once again the Establishment swung into action. "People said Tokyo would trigger a further crash," says MOF Director General Fujita. "So we expressed our [MOF's] serious concern to the institutional investors."

On Tuesday morning, October 28, MOF's securities bureau invited in eight leading institutions to exchange views on the market and their buying plans. "We had four life insurers and four trust banks," Fujita recalls. "We said: 'The world is looking at Tokyo.' Frankly I wished they would reach a consensus. But we left it to them to reach a consensus. I didn't know if they reached a consensus or not. Very officially, no consensus. There was no official or private report to me saying so. Journalists say they made a consensus to buy."

A rally, sparked by buying by trust banks and other institutions, promptly erupted. Heavy net institutional buying sustained the Tokyo stock market through a second volatile spasm in mid-November. That was set off by the combination of a renewed dollar plunge and frayed nerves about whether the privatization of a 12.5 percent tranche of NTT for ¥5 trillion ($40 billion) would drain so much liquidity that there mightn't be enough buying power to hold up share prices in the rest of the market.

BOJ and MOF officials had been initially perplexed, and much relieved, about the dollar's strength in the week after Black Monday. In hindsight the dollar gained because of the U.S. investor–led flight into the safest and most liquid assets in a crisis—still epitomized by U.S. government securities. Once the crisis atmosphere abated, the more fundamental concerns that had been undermining the dollar in 1987 prevailed.

The plunging dollar was the kind of external shock that the Establishment could at best buffer, not control. Despite its economic might, Japan retained the soul of an island rice farmer who felt acutely vulnerable to external forces like earthquakes, typhoons, Commodore Matthew Perry's "black ships," oil shocks, and foreign protectionism. Now the falling dollar haunted the stock market with specters of further collapsing export profits, unemployment, expropriation through devaluation of Japan's huge investment in U.S. government securities, and international economic disorder.

The second part of the Japanese stock market's woe, however, was the purely homemade NTT problem. Selling at three hundred times earnings, NTT shares were worth more than IBM, AT&T, GE, Exxon, and GM combined! To ordinary Japanese, owning a share of NTT symbolized faith in the almost mystical strength of postindustrial Japan. To the MOF, and in particular its budget bureau, NTT represented a golden chance to achieve its 1980s goal of balancing Japan's budget. Thus when MOF directors general, securities house executives, NTT managers, and the main banker, Industrial Bank of Japan (IBJ), discussed postponing the NTT offering to 1988, reports IBJ President Kaneo Nakamura, "the MOF said: 'It's already included in the fiscal budget.'"

The MOF budget bureau also refused to reduce what many considered to be an inflated share offering price—an unkinder interpretation was price ramping. The day after NTT first went on sale, November 11, the market plunged to below Black Tuesday closing levels. It was rescued by a relaxation of margin lending restrictions and Big Four buying. But over the ensuing months NTT sank far below its offering price, hurting shareholders and undermining confidence in the market.

"I always stressed that unnecessary manipulation of equities price should not be made," says MOF's Fujita. "But the budget bureau strongly wanted a high equity price to generate higher revenues for the budget. The price level of NTT remained higher than other stock prices. It was not a result of manipulation of price levels, but of the *belief* that the government supported the price and would never let it fall down. NTT fell later. We can't explain why it went up or down. What we can say is that the auction price of ¥2.55 million [about $20,000 a share] was too high. During the decline, securities houses tried to sustain it but couldn't against the selling pressure."

The conjuncture of this weakening confidence, due to NTT and the dollar's near collapse at the end of 1987, finally pushed Tokyo to its closest brush with genuine crisis, as narrated in Part Five.

The ability of the Establishment to manage Japan's financial asset markets almost as economic policy tools played a propitious role in stabilizing the world economy at critical junctures during the 1980s. It also provided a powerful competitive edge that highlighted the politically explosive incompatibility of Japan's relationship capitalism with prevailing norms of the international political economic order.

"We do open market operations, they force institutions to the sidelines," says the Fed's Manley Johnson of the differing American and Japanese responses to financial crises. "Their system is more interventionist on the stock market than ours."

Yoshio Terasawa, who headed Nomura Securities' international business and was known as "Terry" on Wall Street, expounds, "Wrongly or rightly, the Japanese capital market has been guided by the Japanese government. The government tends to stick their big noses into management of the securities houses. There are so many unwritten rules, called administrative guidance. Even Nomura Tokyo, a giant, must send people to the MOF before we do anything different. Because we don't want to receive a long sermon from mother, 'You didn't behave.' Then the ball bounces differently."

The quid pro quo for playing ball was an implicit share of the regulatory profits and knowledge that the full resources of the Establishment stood behind its financial institutions. No bank had ever been allowed to fail in modern Japan. "Our banking system is protected," states Bank of Tokyo Chairman Yusuke Kashiwagi.

In contrast with the Fed, the BOJ stood openly ready to bail out any major security firm.[18] The moral hazard concern that governed the stance of the Fed and other main central banks was simply moot in the web of Establishment relationships, where, according to an acclaimed analysis of Japanese power, it was "not possible to separate the realms of public and private business."[19]

Even as the sun set on Japan's successful market turnaround after Black Tuesday, and rose on London, the third and most innovative leg of the twenty-four-hour, global financial "golden triangle," the dark cloud of another ill-starred megaprivatization, that of British Petroleum, threatened to set the world's stock markets crashing anew.

Chapter 7

When Markets and Governments Collide

The regime of stateless capital sprang from the womb of London's unregulated, freewheeling Euromarkets, which flourished from the early 1960s by dealing in the swelling pool of internationally circulating dollars produced by the Bretton Woods monetary system. Banks and financial firms from around the world expanded their presence in London to conduct business that was banned at home. From a sovereign state point of view, the United Kingdom's nurturing of the Euromarkets within the City was piracy of entire chunks of their financial industry through global competition in regulatory laxity. From the viewpoint of capital, it was deliverance from the imprisonment within national borders imposed by the postwar financial order.

With the rise of global finance, London became the booming financial capital for the entire European time zone. Although the German DM was effectively the anchor for all Europe's money, and the Bundesbank its central bank, some 80 percent of trading in German government bonds took place in London's telephone line–based, over-the-counter Euromarkets. London's 1980s financial boom was both engine and brightest validating symbol of free market "Thatcherism," which in 1987 was being hailed for having produced a miraculous British economic revival.

The London stock market, in fact, had been in a bull market since October 1974. In 1987 it soared 48 percent more to its peak on July 16. The City's jubilation at Margaret "Iron Lady" Thatcher's Conservative Party election victory helped the stock market overcome signs of reviving inflation, a crash in the bond market, and nervousness that there might be insufficient liquidity to absorb the privatization of the final 31.5 percent tranche of the United Kingdom's largest company, British Petroleum. As in the United States, stocks traded at a historic yield gap with bonds, over 7 percent. Foreign money contributed, especially from Japan. By October 5 stocks were within 1 percent of the July high.

Yet also as in the United States, the London bulls were hard-pressed to explain what sustainable economic fundamentals had actually changed to merit such euphoria. Then, in reaction to the U.S. financial turmoil that started on October 14, the bottom caved in. Even before New York opened on Black Monday, the London stock market had crashed 10.1 percent. Following Tokyo's overnight crash, after the United States's Black Monday, London crashed again on Terrible Tuesday, 11.6 percent.

Bank of England Deputy Governor George Blunden had been in the futures pits of the Chicago Merc when bedlam broke out at the bad U.S. trade deficit figure on Wednesday morning, October 14. He returned to London the next day. Governor Robin Leigh-Pemberton was embarked on a long-planned diplomatic visit to three Eastern European countries, so Blunden was in charge during the crash. A stern-visaged career central banker, Blunden had been enticed out of retirement by the deputy governorship in order to bring unassailable central banking skills to complement the oft maligned, genial banker-aristocrat Leigh-Pemberton, whom Thatcher had hand-picked to be governor in 1983, after several conflictual years with his strong-willed, internationally renowned predecessor Gordon Richardson.

Despite its illustrious pedigree, the bank's actual independence had been a seesaw struggle over its three-century existence. Its early prestige among capitalists was tarnished at the close of the eighteenth century, when, under the duress of government pressure to more cheaply finance England's military defense against Napoléon, it temporarily severed convertibility of its banknotes into gold. Gold convertibility, the capitalists' check on government confiscation through inflation, was eventually restored and the gold standard championed by the bank during Britain's heyday.

Within the bank, the governor's power was supreme. His actual authority over financial affairs, however, rested upon his stature with City financiers and government officials. By long-established tradition, Britain's mightiest financiers could be assembled rapidly, often within an hour, in the governor's parlor whenever a crisis brewed to find out what the governor expected of them. By tradition begun before World War II, the governor met once a week with senior Treasury officials as well.

The bank's independent power reached a zenith under the long interwar governorship of the gold standard's ardent champion, the eccentric Montagu Norman. With nationalization in 1946, the bank's monetary independence plunged. Its influence revived in the 1970s, thanks to the strong leadership of

Gordon Richardson, who supplied Labour with much-needed market credibility during the mid-1970s sterling crisis.

Independence fell to an all-time low under the prime ministership of Tory Margaret Thatcher, who came to power in 1979 with strong monetarist convictions and a political priority to dominate the central bank. So abject had BOE independence become under Leigh-Pemberton that one Basel central banker remarked, shaking his head sadly, "I've been in meetings when Leigh-Pemberton had to go out to take a phone call and be informed of a discount rate change. It was embarrassing."

On Friday, October 16, a freak hurricane, like a warning storm before the cataclysm in a Wagnerian opera, prevented all but a few City financiers from reaching their offices. Blunden informed Chancellor of the Exchequer Nigel Lawson that despite uncertain legal authority, he was going to declare a bank holiday, thereby effectively closing the City, since no financial settlements would be executed.

The stock market closure left a huge overhang of unrequited selling pressure over the weekend. On Monday the stock market opened down 137 points, or 6 percent.[1]

Blunden set up a six-member interdisciplinary crisis team headed by Brian Quinn, the BOE's executive director for supervision. Quinn was fifteen minutes into a forty-minute training speech for bank supervisors at the BIS in Basel, Switzerland, when he was slipped the note instructing him to take the first plane back to London.

Governor Robin Leigh-Pemberton was alerted in Eastern Europe. He elected not to return to London because "it's not good advertising to those countries on the virtues of capitalism to have to run home in a crisis."[2]

Blunden also began opening channels to international central bankers. In addition to Corrigan, Blunden talked over the ten days of the crisis's height to Governor Jacques de Larosière at the Bank of France; President Karl Otto Pöhl and Leonhard Gleske, the directorate member in charge of international at the Bundesbank; Tatsuya Tamura, the BOJ's London-based chief representative for Europe; Bank of Canada Governor John Crow; and the central monetary authorities in other parts of the commonwealth, Australia, and Hong Kong. He was also called by the Fed's Manley Johnson. Although Johnson did not suggest that the BOE make a statement of readiness to inject liquidity, doing so was discussed at Threadneedle Street.

"If we put out an announcement, it would be a message that the system is breaking down," explains Blunden, who recommended to Chancellor Lawson that no statement be made. Indeed, most foreign central bankers concluded with Blunden that a statement could counterproductively incite panic.

The BOE's lender of last resort tradition was sufficient to calm City financiers with the expectation that the bank would inject liquidity. In concert with its masters at the Treasury, it did. Over the crash period it made three one-half-percentage-point interest rate cuts.[3]

One special concern was how well the U.K.'s financial "big bang" deregulation of October 27, 1986, would meet its first severe test. Overnight, traditional British financial practices and institutional arrangements had been radically restructured to create the British vision of the financial center of the future. Would it stand up?

The results were mixed. One strength proved to be big bang's creation of "universal banking," the co-joining of banking and securities in one entity, which was so politically controversial in the United States. "We have no firewalls like Glass-Steagall," says BOE's Brian Quinn. "Thus the larger banks could recapitalize their brokers. Though the brokers were losing a lot and quickly, it contrasted with New York, where the banks didn't lend and there were rumors day after day of a U.S. house in trouble."

Bankers and brokers were calling, and being called in, by Blunden and Quinn. As in New York, rumors, some planted, were flying everywhere. "The worst thing is you don't know what the hell is going on," says Quinn. "We got a very good picture of it, it turns out, but we didn't know that until after the fact."

Each day Quinn's team tried to learn (1) the worldwide trading positions of U.K. banks and securities firms; (2) the London position of non-U.K. firms; and (3) the worldwide lending exposure of U.K. banks to various global securities firms. One scary blind spot proved to be the inadequacy of universal banks' risk control systems to keep pace with evolving worldwide financial interlinkages. "[T]he risk of counterparty default in the broker community seems not to have been analyzed or controlled," Governor Leigh-Pemberton later scolded bankers. "[W]hile most banking groups active in market making knew what was going on in their own home markets in the period immediately following 19 October, they were not so well equipped to know what their position was in the more far-flung markets. . . . [I]t is just as important to know what your exposure is to a securities firm's Tokyo office as it is to their London office."[4]

While volume on the over-the-counter stock market was greater than usual on Black Monday, liquidity deteriorated rapidly on Tuesday. Market makers answered their telephones, but they reduced the number of shares they were willing to trade to one-fourth of average. Liquidity in London's seven hundred listed foreign equities dried up badly. The foreign share segment all but shut down. While the prevailing view in the London markets at the time was that foreigners led the London sell-off—foreign selling was ten times heavier than normal—domestic selling was later found to be the main factor.[5]

One illustration that global financial markets had a life of their own occurred when the Chicago Board of Trade halted trading in U.S. Treasury bond futures. Traders rushed next day to the London International Financial Futures Exchange, where trading volume in the U.S. contract was eight times Chicago's previous day.[6]

Despite disappointment at London's illiquidity, there were no major failures. "The crash put us in unknown territory," Quinn says. "With a fall like twenty-five percent in two days you'd think someone would surely catch a cold. But security houses had enough capital, and banks maintained their lines. No one panicked. There were some nervous moments on Tuesday, a couple of forced recapitalizations. Big enough to trigger rumors, but not giants."

Governor Leigh-Pemberton adds, "We had accurate daily figures of positions. If a collapse of a counterparty had occurred, we could have acted to avoid it."

The shaky rebound in New York on Terrible Tuesday, and the more solid stabilization in Tokyo, brought some relief to London. But something else profound was troubling the London market. "The New York stabilization was a great relief, but it was not enough to say, 'Phew, that was a close call!' " remembers Quinn. "The big question here was always 'What is going to happen to BP?' "

The Global BP Shock

Rolling back the state's ownership of British Petroleum (BP) to under 50 percent had been one of Margaret Thatcher's first actions upon becoming PM in 1979. Selling the remaining 31.5 percent to private citizens would underpin the consolidation of U.K. finances with windfall revenue of £7.26 billion ($12 billion) and politically crown Thatcher's ambitious revival of British free enterprise. The global crash, however, transformed BP into an allegorical tragicomedy of global markets and national governments that, for a moment, held up to the spotlight the contradictions within the edifice of democratic capitalism.

The BP privatizaton was so huge, it was planned that one-quarter of BP shares would be sold outside the United Kingdom.[7] Merchant banker N. M. Rothschild was chosen to manage the sale. Rothschild formed an underwriting group with sixteen other U.K. firms and four sets of foreign underwriters from the United States, Japan, Europe, and Canada. The underwriters would commit to buy all the BP shares from the British government at a negotiated price. They'd then sell them to the public at a profitable markup.

By unlucky coincidence, the underwriting group and U.K. Treasury negotiators were closeted away, finalizing the deal on October 14, totally oblivious that the U.S. futures and stock markets were erupting in turmoil. The underwriters agreed to pay 330 pence per BP share. The previous day's close had been 362p. It seemed reasonable that under normal conditions the margin would hold up until October 30, when dealing was to begin. In case normal underwriting risk was transformed by force majeure—providential interventions such as natural disasters and war—the contract provided that the U.K. underwriters could ask the U.K. chancellor of the exchequer to cancel the issue. If he didn't agree, he was obliged to ask for a Bank of England recommendation, which would carry significant public weight, before making his final decision.

On Thursday, October 15, BP shares fell to 347p. On Friday the freak hurricane closed the London stock market. A further bad omen arrived from New York, where the stock market had fallen a record 108 points more.

London woke up to the full-blown nightmare on Black Monday. BP shares fell 33 pence to 317p, well below the underwriting price. On Terrible Tuesday BP fell 32 pence more to 285p. Instead of easy profits, the underwriters faced a £1.5 billion ($2.5 billion) bloodbath. Unless the crash was halted, some could be driven to bankruptcy.

The losses were spread unevenly among underwriters. Heaviest hit were the foreigners. The U.K. underwriters had already syndicated much of their risk to subunderwriters on October 15. Grimmest were the £330 million ($554 million) losses faced by the four U.S. underwriters, Goldman Sachs; Salomon Brothers; Shearson Lehman; and Morgan Stanley. SEC regulations effectively prohibited subunderwriting until the end of October, revealing one of the hazards of incongruous national regulations in an era of global financial markets. U.S. firms stressed this prohibition in lobbying for a bailout.

According to U.S. Treasury Undersecretary and career Wall Street man George Gould, their lament was specious. "The U.S. firms were greedy. They didn't want to syndicate anyway. The risk of underwriting is overstated, but once in a while you see it. This was one of those times. Then they came crying into our office."

Although the Canadian underwriting group centered around Wood Gundy faced losses of only £75 million ($126 million), Wood Gundy's smaller capital base made the situation there even more desperate. When the market fell, the nine dealers who'd agreed to subunderwrite walked away from their nonbinding commitments.[8]

The £110 million or $184.4 million losses facing the Japanese group headed by Daiwa Securities was larger in absolute terms but would hardly make a dent in the Japanese giants' capital base. The Continental European underwriters were likewise sufficiently capitalized to take the hit implied by Terrible Tuesday's price.

But what would be the level of underwriter losses if the market fell another 25 percent? Quinn's crisis team, which conferred with the New York Fed team, tried to calculate "what would bring you to the dire situation when a house failed."

On Terrible Tuesday George Blunden exchanged a few words with Nigel Lawson about BP. To avoid compounding the market trouble with a political mess, they agreed that the BOE, which might be called upon to fulfill an arbiter's role between government and market, should maintain an arm's length distance from the Treasury. Thus, during the most tempestuous period in the stock market in decades, the bank and the Treasury could not confer intimately. "BP forced us to cut ourselves off more from the Treasury than we would have liked," says Blunden.

The bottom-line question was, Should the BP privatization be suspended or canceled as force majeure? Many underwriters, their view colored by their own predicament, pleaded that it was a case of force majeure. For central bankers the overriding consideration was BP's impact on the world's convulsing capital markets. On Tuesday the U.S. markets' plumbing problems had been aggravated by the rumors that the BP losses had put Goldman and Shearson in jeopardy. The losses didn't have to be enough to drive an underwriter into bankruptcy to wreak havoc. All they had to do was cause it to fall below its SEC regulatory minimum net capital requirements. It would then have to dump shares to raise capital—a new wave of selling would be on!

"We were conscious on day two about the BP problem," says the New York Fed's Jerry Corrigan. "It's not the losses—that's the risk they run by being in business. The key question is: Could the [selling] overhang unleash another round of instability? You can never make this judgment with great precision."

What to do about BP was a devilish political dilemma for Thatcher and Lawson, ardent champions of free market capitalism. The British government promptly terminated its advertisements of BP shares, lest it be accused of conning widows out of their pensions. But did the crash constitute force majeure?[9]

Obviously not. It was not a manifestation of providence. It was straightforward underwriting risk and free market capitalism at its purest. To bail the underwriters out of their losses by pulling the issue would be to cheat the British taxpayer of some good—or fortuitous—government management. More concretely, it would add credence to the political allegations that Thatcherism was biased in favor of fat cat financiers and big business. Even the "public good" argument of pulling the issue to avoid setting off a new wave of financial crashes exposed the democratic capitalist ambiguity normally handled discreetly in the political half-light by central bankers. The path of responsibly resolving the BP crisis and that of following the espoused free market principles of Thatcher and Lawson were asymptotes. Principle led to likely ruin. Pragmatism knocked liberal principle off its political pedestal.

Sensing the political dilemma, Lawson declared outspokenly that the BP offering had to go ahead. Yet a campaign soon mounted from the markets and foreign governments to pull the issue. Goldman sent its partner in charge of equity markets from New York to a meeting at the Exchequer in London on Thursday, October 22, to plead its case. Led by the United States and Canada, foreign underwriters turned up the heat on their domestic authorities to lobby for them.

The New York Fed's Corrigan, Takeshi Ohta of the BOJ, and European central bankers from France and Germany argued to the Bank of England that financial stability had to take priority, even if that meant putting off the issue. Lawson was also directly besieged by calls from fellow finance ministers, especially in North America.

"I had calls from [Canada's Michael] Wilson and [U.S.'s James] Baker," says Lawson. "The point they put to me was this: Considering the fragility of the situation, the issue should be pulled. I made it clear I was *not* prepared to do it, but understood their concern. The U.S. pressure was very, very considerable."

"We pushed hard," acknowledges the Treasury's Gould. "Baker to Lawson. Once we contemplated to have the president call Thatcher. Word came back they didn't want to have Thatcher receive such a call." The U.S. lobbying effort, however, did not satisfy the U.S. underwriters, who thought there was an opportunity for postponement.

To Lawson's irritation, Canadian Finance Minister Michael Wilson went beyond private channels and appealed publicly for a postponement because of the dire straits facing Wood Gundy. (Wood Gundy was eventually sold in June 1988.) The Japanese MOF politely asked for a postponement in a letter to the Treasury.

On Friday, October 23, the U.K. underwriters convened to decide whether to invoke their legal privilege to ask Lawson to postpone the issue. Market conditions were increasingly skittish. The NYSE had fallen seventy-seven points the prior day. Even while their meeting was taking place, word arrived from Canada that if the BP issue went ahead, the Toronto stock market might not be able to open on Monday morning, October 26—the same day NYSE trades from Black Monday were to settle. The world was at the precipice of a new round of global crashes. BP could push it over the edge.

Yet many of the British underwriters were reluctant to run the long-term business consequences of provoking Lawson's wrath by challenging him publicly to postpone, as long as their own losses were manageable. The losses of the foreign underwriters, who did not share the right to ask for force majeure, were a secondary concern. Their final vote was eight to eight. But that was impossible. There were seventeen persons present. The Kleinwort Benson representative confessed that he had been the abstention.

They reconvened on Monday. By *undisclosed* tally, they voted to ask Lawson to invoke force majeure.

Lawson was furious. He chose not to attend the formal presentation of the City's case for postponement at the Exchequer on Wednesday night, October 28. The meeting, which went on into the small hours, ended in deadlock. That put the case in the court of the Bank of England to render an independent recommendation.

Rarely did central banks ever so explicitly arbitrate among governments and markets. After hearing first the underwriters' case, then the Treasury's, the BOE was to make its recommendation by 4 P.M. Thursday. Governor Leigh-Pemberton decided to cut short his East European trip by a couple of days to conduct the Thursday meetings personally. Upon his return to London from Sofia, Bulgaria, on Wednesday night, he endorsed the strategy presented by George Blunden: if it was not possible to terminate the issue, then a safety net should be fashioned, in the form of a floor price at which the underwriters could put their shares to the bank. It was a classic, pragmatic, conservative, and politically nonconfrontational central banker compromise.

At 11:30 A.M. on Thursday the underwriter representatives arrived at an elegant upstairs parlor called the Treasury Room, with a view overlooking the bank's quiet inner courtyard, for the extraordinary arbitration hearing. A senior Treasury official, Peter Middleton, followed.

In the end, the bank decided to go for the safety net. But its deliberations dragged on past the 4 P.M. deadline because its arguments had to be rationalized by legal logic and because the actual floor price had to be decided upon.

The BOE decided in favor of a strong safety net—so strong, in fact, that the bank would end up buying most of BP's shares. In effect, the bank proposed socializing the losses in what had been hailed as one of the world's greatest privatizations!

Lawson was growing impatient with the bank's delay because he had to render his final decision to the House of Commons that evening. Finally, at 6 P.M., the BOE's recommendation came over the fax machine. He was relieved that the bank had not recommended to terminate the issue. But he could not live with the government-owned BOE ending up as buyer of all the government shares to bail out the underwriters.

Lawson, who himself had been thinking in terms of the safety net compromise, accepted the bank's recommendation. But he decided to lower its floor to a level that would be painful to the underwriters. Ideally it would not be so painful that it would destabilize financial markets. This ten-degree difference between the central bank and Treasury view reflected the inherent salutary institutional tension in the democratic capitalist compact over money between technocratic defenders of financial stability and elected representatives of democratic political sensibility.

With the imposition of a safety net after October 29, 1987, the BP cloud lifted. The underwriters' final losses totaled £750 million ($1.3 billion). This was enough to wipe out all the profits made by U.K. underwriters from all previous privatizations and deliver serious pain to foreign underwriters. But it was less than previously feared. Most important, the markets took it in stride. The crisis phase of the global crash of October 1987 had been weathered.

The Thatcher government's free market principles received one last tweaking over BP. On November 4 it became apparent that someone was buying large amounts of BP stock at bargain prices just above the safety net floor.

On November 18 the London-based Kuwaiti Investment Office, which managed some of the $100 billion in foreign assets owned by oil-rich Kuwait, announced that it was the mystery buyer and owned 10 percent of BP. Through the spring 1988, repulsing quiet British overtures for a diplomatic compromise, it enlarged its stake to 21.7 percent. It was the largest hostile raid in U.K. history! Kuwait became distressingly well placed to pressure BP to transact business advantageous to Kuwait's oil interests.

Signals had gotten crossed in an event whose details still remain murky. The KIO, it seemed, felt invited in by BP management and the U.K. Treasury as a logical long-term investor for a piece of the huge privatization. Behind the decision to proceed with the hostile raid was the powerful oil minister, Sheikh Ali Khalifa al-Sabah, a member of the emir's ruling family, who was also involved in an internecine Kuwaiti power struggle over control of the KIO.

When the dust settled it was clear that two-thirds of the BP privatization tranche, and with it control of the United Kingdom's strategic oil assets, had been sold at bargain prices, under free market conditions, to a foreign country. Free market principle and national sovereign interest were in head-to-head clash.

Although Kuwait denied any political intent, the U.K. government ordered it, in January 1989, to reduce its BP holding to 9.9 percent. The Kuwaitis did so, at a handsome profit made possible by a huge British tax break derived from the sovereign tax immunity enjoyed by the KIO's state fund, which Kuwaiti officials testified was the true owner of the BP shares. But two years after British troops in the Gulf War helped reinstall the al-Sabah family to power, the *Financial Times* reported that the KIO may have lied: the BP shares apparently had been held beneficially for the Kuwaiti Petroleum Corporation, a taxable, nonsovereign entity.[10] If so, Kuwait owed U.K. taxpayers a £600 million ($900 million) refund. By late 1993 the British government was still dithering whether to risk offending a longtime, oil-rich ally with many post–Gulf War state business contracts to award by officially pressing for repayment.

Other International Tremors

Following Black Monday, the Bank of England also took the lead in league with the international central banker network by dispatching a rescue team to resurrect the closed Hong Kong stock and futures markets. Hong Kong was the only other world market outside the United States in 1987 with extensive trading of stock index futures. Its week-long closure locked several major international firms into positions they wanted to liquidate. It also illustrated the potential for cross-border liquidity backup and international plumbing gridlock from discordant national clearing and settlements mechanisms in the interlinked, global financial landscape. Two U.S. securities firms, Salomon and Merrill Lynch, were especially big players in Hong Kong. Over the weekend of October 24–25, the New York Fed's Jerry Corrigan helped persuade a reluctant Merrill Lynch to participate in the $256 million funding (which ultimately had to be supplemented by another $256 million) rescue package to reopen the futures clearinghouse and the futures and stock markets.

Incongruities in the international plumbing network also punished the efficiency of the small Frankfurt stock market. Frankfurt experienced an intense foreign selling wave of DM 8 billion ($4.4 billion) because its two-day settlement system made it one of the fastest sources of equity liquidity in the world.

Yet the greater import of Germany in the global crash was in the foreign exchange market. It was fear for the dollar that prompted Fed Vice Chairman Johnson to call the Bundesbank after hanging up with the BOJ on Black Monday. Bundesbank President Karl Otto Pöhl was away at a state dinner in Bonn for French president François Mitterrand, so Johnson talked with Vice President Helmut Schlesinger.

Schlesinger assured Johnson that the Bundesbank would act as emergency lender of last resort—if necessary. "But I don't see any need at the moment." He reiterated the Bundesbank's rigorous test of genuine systemic risk to prompt action.

In the event, Germany's universal banking system, in which the country's big commercial banks were also the largest securities dealers, obviated the risk of a liquidity crisis. Banks simply financed all the liquidity needs of their securities arms. The Bundesbank's liquidity injections at the height of the crisis were meager.

A statement paralleling that of the Fed was never seriously entertained by the Bundesbank. Fed Chairman Greenspan did not ask President Pöhl to make such a statement when they talked on October 20. Making a statement was never discussed at the October 22 meeting of the Bundesbank's main decision-making body, the Central Bank Council.

Bundesbank monetary policy soon became a heated focus of central banker and finance minister efforts to contain the second phase of the global financial crisis, which began with renewed plunges in the dollar. By year end the dollar came close to the long dreaded "free-fall." A new global financial crisis was averted only by a spectacular dollar rescue by central bankers, described in Part Five, who remained nervously vigilant about the financial markets until the spring of 1988.

"All through the weeks [after Black Monday] we kept hearing that in 1929 the crash had been followed by a technical recovery, then a new collapse," says Brian Quinn. "That we hadn't seen the worst of it yet. All the commentators were comparing the situation to 1929."

Chapter 8

Why the Crash?

Why the crash?

That was what Setsuya Tabuchi, chairman of Nomura Securities, asked himself, as did everybody else in the world's political and financial capitals, on Black Monday. Unlike all others, Tabuchi, who was in New York at the start of a week-long U.S. tour, had the opportunity at 4 P.M. Black Monday afternoon to put the question to the single individual on earth everyone else most wanted to ask—Greenspan's predecessor, Paul Volcker. Volcker was early into a Fed retirement that would eventually lead him to a second career divided between a professorship at the Woodrow Wilson School at Princeton University and investment banking for James D. Wolfensohn Inc. at a reported twentyfold annual salary increase to about $2 million.

When Tabuchi, accompanied by Nomura's international chief, Yoshio "Terry" Terasawa, arrived at Volcker's Manhattan office for their appointment, the ex–Federal Reserve Board chairman was caught up in a whirlwind of incoming telephone calls, rumors that he was about to return to Washington as Treasury secretary, and preparations for the arrival of TV news cameras.

Upon inviting Volcker to participate in Nomura's annual Tokyo Forum on world finance, Tabuchi posed his question: "What caused the crash?"[1]

The most celebrated of the postcrash studies, Nicholas Brady's Presidential Task Force on Market Mechanisms, highlighted technical failures to keep pace with the global capital revolution: "Institutional and regulatory structures designed for separate marketplaces were incapable of dealing with a precipitate intermarket decline which brought the financial system to the brink."[2]

Greater velocity, volumes, volatility, concentration, and a one-way shift in expectations simply overwhelmed market mechanisms designed for a by-gone world. When a strong selling turning point was reached, all the big players, employing the same computer-driven trading strategies, tried to sell at once. Stock and derivatives market mechanisms were inadequate to supply sufficient buying power and plumbing liquidity to requite them across the intermarket continuum. Professional investors had woefully misjudged the liquidity and other risks of integrated financial markets.

Initially puzzling was why the New York crash spread worldwide. The direct volume of cross-border flows out of foreign equity markets were too small to account for it. What did, experts later realized, was a homogeneous, psychological reaction of world-straddling players linked by instantaneous communications across all markets. All lost confidence and panicked together.

The global break highlighted that *expectations* were becoming a far more powerful determinant of financial prices. Yet unchecked, expectations were wont to be volatile and to stampede unpredictably far out of line with real economic fundamentals—and then to adjust spasmodically as on Black Monday.

"The market went up thirty percent this year and it's gone back down thirty percent," Volcker noted after Black Monday. "Nothing has happened in the economy to drive stocks down. Did anything happen between January and August, I can ask, to justify thirty percent higher stock prices?"[3]

The overtrading and revulsions characteristic of global capital also highlighted the second, fundamental explanation for the crash. It was the one to which Volcker's mind turned in formulating his answer to Tabuchi—the plunging dollar in 1987. "The Japanese had been buying a lot of [U.S.] Treasury paper, but I noticed that in the last few months they've been buying less. This could be one of the reasons for the crash." Because of the United States' unhealthy dependence on Japanese money, he added, between numerous phone calls, the slowdown in Japanese capital flows may have weakened the dollar and pushed up U.S. interest rates, possibly triggering the crash.[4]

The meeting was cut short by the arrival of a television crew. When Tabuchi returned to Tokyo the following week, he checked up on Volcker's leads. Volcker was right: "From July there was a rather huge reduction of the [capital] inflow."

Tabuchi found that whereas the Japanese had been net purchasers of U.S. bonds and equities of $10 billion to $14 billion every quarter from mid-1985 and had bought $8 billion in June 1987 alone, those fell sharply to $4.1 billion in July, $2.8 billion in August, $839 million in September, and to net *sales* of $39 million in October.[5]

Six months after the crash, Nick Brady, speaking to institutional investors, also cut past the technical reasons for the crash on which his task force so voluminously dwelled and zeroed in on the same trail of Japanese money that Volcker had fingered on Black Monday: "People ask me: What was it that blew it off on the nineteenth of October—was it the twin deficits, was it the Rostenkowski [Ways and Means Committee] legislation, what was it? The real trigger was that the Japanese came in for their own reasons and sold an enormous amount of U.S. government bonds and drove the thirty-year government up through ten percent. And when it got through ten percent, that got a lot of people thinking, 'Gee, that's four times the return you can get on equity. Here we go, inflation again.' That, to me, is what really started the nineteenth—a worry by the Japanese about the U.S. currency."[6]

Indeed, Japanese money left footprints through all 1987's financial upheavals: the falling dollar, two U.S. bond market crashes, and the stock market crash. A rush of Japanese bond selling in late March 1987 when the dollar knifed below ¥150—the floor Japanese investors erroneously believed had been guaranteed by the February 1987 Group of Seven (G7) Louvre Accord—helped trigger the U.S. spring bond crash; the homeward flight of Japanese capital was reflected in a mirror opposite the Japanese bond market boom. The preference shift of remaining Japanese money for shares fueled the unprecedented subsequent surge in equities following a bond crash.

The second U.S. bond crash from August to Black Monday likewise tracked the slowdown in Japanese buying of U.S. financial assets following the unexpectedly bad trade report on August 14. That set the stage for the Japanese selling that drove the U.S. long bond over 10 percent and lit the fuse to the stock market crash. That bout of selling was set off by the disappointing U.S. trade deficit figure of October 14, the Bundesbank's bump-up of interest rates, and Treasury Secretary Jim Baker's angry response with renewed dollar "talk-down." Volcker also mentioned Baker's comments to Tabuchi as a hair trigger to the crash.

The trail of Japanese money was clear. But what did it signify?

Volcker's citation of Japanese capital flows was a shorthand allusion to the failure of the leading countries to adjust their national policies to correct the source of the record world economic imbalances of U.S. current account deficits and Japanese and German surpluses, as well as to the dragging anchorage of the fully-floating, privatized international monetary "nonsystem" that fostered them. Global flows of Japanese money so closely correlated to movements in U.S. financial prices in 1987 because Japan had become the world's top banker nation and thus the major player in determining when those imbalances would become insupportable.

The law of market economics dictated that these global imbalances eventually had to adjust—softly or with a bang. Without voluntary changes in national economic policies, the dollar could fall precipitously, setting off financial market turmoil and market-induced adjustment through recession. From late 1984, dollar "free-fall" had been one of Volcker's paramount worries. It was to borrow time for a smooth global economic adjustment that the G7 had made the Louvre Accord, that non-U.S. central banks held interest rates at record low levels and acquired a stunning $120 billion worth of dollars on foreign exchange markets—enough to finance three-quarters of U.S. foreign borrowing needs in 1987. But when governments failed to implement fundamental policy changes, the borrowed time ran out. Japan's still not fully explained willingness to stay with dollar assets when virtually all other foreign creditors had fled U.S. assets by the end of 1986, in fact, probably saved the world from a financial crisis much earlier. "The most desirable thing for world economic interest was for the people of the United States to reduce the budget deficit by hard work," says Tomomitsu Oba, ex–Japanese MOF vice finance minister for international affairs. "When the government would not do so, the invisible hand of God appeared in the market and the invisible hand of God reduced equity prices."

The postwar monetary order had been designed to prevent a recurrence of the destabilizing international capital flows of the 1920s and 1930s that had fed the spiral of competitive currency devaluations, trade protectionism, cross-border spread of banking crises, and ultimately degeneration into economic depression and war. To manage the inherent tension between economic autarky and international order, they created the government-run Bretton Woods system anchored in fixed but adjustable currency exchange rate pegs around the dollar, which in turn was convertible into gold at a fixed price. National restrictions on private international capital movements in many countries, always an untidy corner, supported the regime. Temporary balance of payment disequilibria were financed with loans from the multilateral International Monetary Fund (IMF) while nations took corrective adjustment policies. Only when payment imbalances were deemed to reflect a change in underlying economic fundamentals were the fixed exchange rate parities renegotiated. The United States effectively enforced the rules by supplying the world's money, the dollar, and by using its world hegemonic position to discipline excessive cheaters.

The system was remarkably successful in its first fifteen years at promoting a fast worldwide recovery from the ruins of World War II. But its success altered fundamental national economic competitive balances to which governments adapted too slowly. The leakage of excess dollars into an unregulated and growing shadow international financial system called the Euromarkets provided fuel for growing private speculative attacks on the increasingly misaligned, pegged exchange rates. Cooperative central banker efforts to preserve the system were not enough to offset the sharp acceleration of U.S. inflation from the late 1960s. Inflation undermined the value of the system's monetary linchpin, the dollar. Governments were finally forced to face the unpleasant choice: adjust their national economic policies—the United States to deflate through possible recession or the other countries to inflate to U.S. levels—or radically realign exchange rate parities. When they did neither, the Bretton Woods system collapsed in a torrent of private market currency speculation into floating exchange rates.[7]

Floating failed to provide its promised domestic policy autonomy when free markets were no wiser than governments in efficiently adjusting exchange rates in line with underlying economic fundamentals. Instead of inducing basic economic adjustments as a well-functioning international monetary regime ought, unmanaged floating exchange rates sometimes imparted financial distortions that further painfully destabilized national economies. "It not infrequently happens that the floating exchange rate does not reflect fundamentals. Yet we cannot go back to the fixed rate system," declares OECD chief economist Kumiharu Shigehara.

With free-flowing international capital movements, the national structural political economic biases bred by the postwar order compounded the economic policy incompatibilities behind the record world imbalances. The U.S. bias toward low national savings, overconsumption, underinvestment, and trade deficits was expressed by its uncontrolled federal budget deficits. As Japan grew into an economic giant, its lopsided political economy that featured the export torso of a sumo wrestler and the spindly, underdeveloped domestic limbs of a ninety-eight-pound weakling generated huge amounts of surplus capital that its narrow financial system propelled abroad to feed the voracious appetite of the U.S. budget deficits. Similarly, Germany's labor market rigidities and subsidy excesses, like a runner with ankle weights, slowed its and all Europe's growth potential and aggravated the world imbalances.

To soundly reanchor the world democratic capitalist economy required three major reforms. As a first step, leading nations had to cooperate and perhaps coordinate their national economic policies while simultaneously restructuring deeply rooted relationships within their political economies, which had grown globally incompatible. Second, international monetary reforms were needed to reduce excess financial volatility so that adjustment-inducing signals of international competitiveness based on real productivity could be restored to clarity. The third reform was to overhaul obsolete and fragmented national financial market structures, regulations, and supervisory regimes so that they were able to accommodate global capital mobility without major accident or regulatory distortion.

Twice before in the twentieth century democratic capitalist society had remade its basic marriage of convenience when economic developments threatened political and economic balances—the era of trustification at the turn of the century and the Great Depression. Yet many experts noted sadly that until a cataclysmic event actually struck, democratic leaders normally lacked the political incentives or vision to tackle such major reform. On Black Monday many wondered if the stock market crash heralded just such a cataclysm.

The crash, to summarize, was a warning shot: it was the product of global capital flows surging through financial structures too obsolete to handle them, as well as democratic governments' failures to fundamentally alter national macroeconomic and structural incompatibilities. "If this crisis serves as a catalyst for constructive action, it will have served a useful purpose," Paul Volcker warned a few weeks after the Black Monday crash. "If it doesn't, it's a warning that went unheeded."[8]

Renewed dollar plunges in November and December 1987, which nearly triggered a new round of bond and stock market crashes, added an urgent exclamation point to Volcker's warning. Nervous Japanese private investors decided to keep their money at home for several months. They even threatened to recall their loans to America unless the dollar was stabilized. "In January 1987, the chairman of one of the big life insurance companies said, 'If the U.S. dollar continues to decline, we'll stop buying U.S. bonds,' " recalls ex–MOF Vice Minister Tomomitsu Oba. "In February 1988 the chairman of another big life insurer said, 'If the dollar continues to decline, we'll *sell* bonds.' That was the feeling."

When Greenspan and his fellow central bank governors gathered together for the first time since the crash at Basel on November 8, 1987, the dollar was in a tailspin and bond and stock markets in renewed turmoil. They stood precariously near the vortex of dollar free-fall and possible depression.

Chapter 9

International Freemasons

On Sunday, November 8, 1987, in shell-shocked state, central bankers from the G10 and European Community began checking into the old world Hotels Euler and Schweizerhof overlooking the Centralbahnplatz in front of the Basel, Switzerland, train station.[1] Just behind the Schweizerhof was an eighteen-story, dark glass, nuclear reactor–shaped tower that was their collective second home—the Bank for International Settlements (BIS). At the top of the tower was an exclusive dining room with a panoramic view of the Rhine River intersecting three countries—Switzerland, France, and Germany. There were also four floors of fully archived, technologically ultra-modern private offices that stood empty except for the central bankers' monthly visits, several simultaneous translation conference rooms, twenty miles of underground archives, and a nuclear bomb shelter; outside of town was the BIS's health club.

The central bankers were gathering together for their monthly "Basel weekend." It would be their first face-to-face encounter since Black Monday. Collectively they'd been stunned and puzzled by the crash's size, speed, and global reach as well as by the awesome violence of the shift in market expectations. They had been much more aware of the global linkages developing among bond markets. The stock market crash "was an event some thought impossible in our era," says Alan Greenspan. "It exposed gaps in our understanding of market processes."[2]

Haunting their collective search for comprehension was their profession's historic bogeyman, depression. "We were all terrified about making the mistakes of 1929," recalls Anthony Loehnis, Bank of England executive director of the overseas division. "It was a time when we instinctively came together and did similar things."

The governors of all the main central banks were there, including the Fed's Alan Greenspan and the BOJ's Satoshi Sumita, who made the transoceanic journey to Basel only a few times each year. Also crowding into Basel were some fifty journalists. Normally only half a dozen showed up. The BIS and press were like oil and water: journalists were normally excluded from BIS offices. Instead they hung around the fringes, outside the BIS building and in hotel lobbies, hoping for a few comments on currencies from passing central bankers.

The journalists had trekked to the sleepy international central banker capital, where central bankers had been convening in seclusion since 1930, because of the shudders the dollar's plunging in early November was sending through world stock, bond, and currency markets. A few days earlier, U.S. Treasury Secretary Jim Baker had fueled the turmoil by suggesting that the United States would let the dollar fall through its secret Louvre target ranges—which it in fact had done by the time the central bankers assembled in Basel—rather than risk recession by raising interest rates. In the next days the OECD would issue an unusually gloomy report echoing many private forecasts about the depressive consequences of the $1.2 trillion in lost wealth from the crash. The journalists asked what most everyone in markets and governments were clamoring to know: Would G7 cooperation be resurrected with an emergency meeting? What were the central bankers planning to do to save the day?

The Central Bankers' Central Bank

The BIS was one of the world's unique and most mysterious institutions. Central bankers owned and ran it. Sixteen percent of the BIS's shares floated over the counter—and fell on Black Monday.[3] It was run by a central banker–chosen general manager; in the second half of the 1980s he was a Hungarian-born Belgian professor, Alexandre Lamfalussy. Special exemption from taxation under the Hague Treaty of 1930 and self-financing through its banking activities made the BIS independent of any government, though absent any true power beyond that collectively extended by central bankers.

Interwar-era Bank of England Governor Montagu Norman used to dream that the BIS would one day foster a core of central bankers entirely autonomous of governments. That dream was translated into a loose credo of independence, sound money, international financial stability, pragmatism, and mutual support against government pressure that the governors imbibed ten times a year, from Sunday night through Tuesday at the start of the second week of each month. "The governors in Basel meet on trust; it is the meeting of a club," said the late Renaud de la Genière, governor of the Bank

of France in the early 1980s. "Outside of the official meetings there are dinners without secretaries, all in confidence."

The international freemasonry that flourished in Basel for over half a century reinforced central bankers' sense of unique supranational identity. "We
are clubby. It is related to the fact that we feel inferior about being unelected," explains one European governor. "I think there is an international
voice, a constituency, we represent. We must defend monetary policy even
against Treasury ministers—we need allies to mitigate the disadvantage of
not being elected."

Until May 1977 BIS headquarters was an anonymous, converted six-story
hotel across from the Basel train station. The address was so obscure that
visitors were told to look for Frey's chocolate shop next door. Only a small
plaque indicated the entrance. To the chagrin of many central bankers, their
increased world prominence with the rise of stateless capital then became
visible in a new eighteen-story office tower.

Although its founding task in 1930 to collect and disperse German World
War I reparations was soon aborted by a moratorium, central bankers found
the BIS to be a desirable venue for discussions and cooperation through the
troubled 1930s. Even during World War II, central bankers from the belliger-
ent countries often continued to meet. During the 1944 Bretton Woods conference, the United States pressed for the BIS's abolition on the grounds that
it had no place in the new (U.S.-dominated) monetary order. The United
States' relationship with the BIS had been uneasy since its founding when
America's isolationist streak prevented the Fed from officially taking up its
shares or board seat—it did so only in September 1994.[4] The BIS survived
only at the insistence of European delegations.

Over the years the BIS had come to perform four main functions with a
political anonymity prized by central bankers. It managed one-tenth of the
world's foreign exchange reserves on behalf of eighty central banks and multilateral institutions like the IMF. Second, it served as financial agent for several international agreements. Third, it collected and analyzed international
economic and monetary data that helped central bankers stay abreast of the
swiftly changing trends in global finance. But by far its most important function was the fourth: providing an international forum for central bankers to
confidentially discuss and sometimes coordinate policies. "The greatest part
of our work is the exchange of information of one [central banker] to the
other so they can hammer out understandings on what is going on in other
countries and can adapt their postures accordingly," explains General Manager Alexandre Lamfalussy, who served as an intellectual catalyst by raising
poignant questions on trends and policy issues.

The Basel weekend normally started with a Sunday night G10 governors-
only dinner, attended also by Lamfalussy and sometimes the managing

director of the IMF. It ended on Tuesday afternoon with the European Community meeting. Agendas were few, discussions informal. Fine food and wine washed it all down.[5] "Two full days each month, twenty working days a year, with four full meals permits an exchange of an enormous amount of knowledge," says Lamfalussy. Although voting and concrete decision making was very rare, consensus somehow formed out of each central banker's explanation of the problems he was having and what he wanted to achieve. What occurred was "some sort of monetary cooperation by intellectual osmosis. How these decisions get made no one really knows."

Kindred professional and personal feelings flourished among central bankers, who often felt that only in Basel were they truly understood. Summer evenings on the porches of the Hotels Euler and Schweitzerhof was the one place in the world where central bankers could be seen laughing freely. The Basel weekends were almost group therapy sessions that "provided not only a quiet testing ground for new ideas and approaches, but also an early warning system when things were beginning to go wrong. More generally, the BIS weekends were what the French would call *sérieux*. However much money was involved, no agreements were ever signed nor memoranda of understanding ever initialed. The word of each official was sufficient, and there were never any disappointments."[6]

Though easily overglorified or exaggerated into conspiracy theories, central bankers' cooperation was far more advanced than that among any other government officials. Many European central banks and the BIS even fielded sports teams against one another in competitions ranging from soccer to badminton to chess. At Basel, the governors "talk about their families. They are almost a family club."[7] Fritz Leutwiler of Switzerland and the Bundesbank's Karl Otto Pöhl took skiing holidays together. Bank of Italy Governor Carlo Azeglio Ciampi spent weekends with Pöhl, Bank of France Governor Jacques de Larosière, and Bank of Spain Governor Mariano Rubio. Alan Greenspan and Satoshi Sumita of the BOJ golfed together; so did Fed Vice Chairman Manley Johnson and Pöhl.

Oddly enough, although he was the undisputed stellar giant of the 1980s central banking universe, Paul Volcker always remained delphic, a lone wolf among the governors. "Volcker liked to swoop in" on BIS meetings, says one central banker. "When he did, everyone knew something big was up. It was not a meeting to be taken lightly." Notes Volcker sardonically, "It amazed me, the determination of the European central bankers to go to Basel each month. Sure it's only a one-hour plane ride. Beyond all that there is a sense in which they like to be together—they feel strong."

The BIS stood on two main legs—the first European, the second global. The technical negotiations creating the 1979 European Monetary System— established as an agreement among central bankers—were conducted in

Basel. So was the practical, often secret operative cooperation of the European governors that governed it. From the latter 1980s EMS would become a hub for Europe's monetary union ambitions.

The global leg of BIS cooperation, anchored in the G10 governors, revived in the 1960s when Basel became the center for patching the first serious cracks in the Bretton Woods monetary system with foreign exchange swap lines and gold pool schemes. The Fed and BOJ began attending meetings regularly. BIS weekends were focal points for concerted intervention and monetary policy cooperation throughout the currency turmoil of the 1970s and 1980s. They also became a fulcrum for coping with the recurrent international financial traumas presented by the emergence of global capital.

The lurching from financial crisis to crisis transformed BIS culture. Fritz Leutwiler, Swiss National Bank president and BIS president during the LDC debt crisis, describes, "The BIS people are international civil servants coming in at nine or nine-thirty and leaving early in the afternoon with a nap between two and three P.M. They never took any risk before. They wanted a low profile. Gradually they came to love their new role."

The BIS was becoming an increasingly important governing epicenter of world democratic capitalist society. This represented another discreet step in the remarkable evolution of central banks from their humble origins in the historical tension between private capital and the state. Most early central banks had started life as overtly private institutions, even when at the instigation of governments desiring ready and cheap forms of financing and orderly systems of payment and note issue.[8] Suspicious capitalists provided the central bank with the right to handle the government's accounts and a share in the sovereign's profitable monopoly over currency issue. The archetypal example was the three-hundred-year-old Bank of England, founded in 1694.[9]

For centuries the state's opportunity for abuse of its sovereign money monopoly, short of outright confiscation and debauchment through coin shaving, was restrained by a neutral, if arbitrarily nature-bound, international monetary system based on gold and silver money. Inflows and outflows of bullion dictated domestic economic conditions and induced involuntary adjustments by business enterprises and government policies.

The transformative financial innovation two centuries ago of paper money and bank credit allowed governments to temporarily finance through the printing press and issuing more credit rather than reflexively adjust to international capital movements. But the new bank credit system, which provided almost unlimited financial elasticity to a small, precious metal–linked monetary base, was prone to sharp contractions that fomented frequent financial panics and economic disruptions.

Central bankers evolved to maintain financial order. Their familiar, modern monetary policy responsibility evolved as governments began to exploit their new power to influence economic growth, especially following the 1930s Keynesian revolution. Governments tended to want to print too much money for short-run political gain. Capitalists tended to want to produce too little to preserve their capital's value. Central banks discreetly arbitrated the tension.

With the financial revolution and the rise of stateless capital beyond national political control, central bankers were acquiring still new dimensions of governing responsibility. In a world in which national monetary policy changes and financial crises, such as Black Monday, rippled swiftly across borders through the inflows and outflows of global capital, arbitraging the extensive disharmonies in national regulations, economic policies, and financial market structures, the democratic self-interest was increasingly best served by delegating monetary responsibility to an independent, nonpartisan cadre of internationally minded technocrats dedicated to continuity and financial order rather than relying on the right thing being done by foreign governments prone to political expedience, bouts of paralysis, and incompetence. As it did so, the supranational BIS began more to resemble the fulfillment of Montagu Norman's dream of central bankers autonomous of governments and perhaps even a transitional prototype for a world central bank.

International Lenders of Last Resort

All that was remote from thoughts on the Basel weekend of November 8 to 10, 1987. Grimly, central bankers asked themselves: Was there any reason to fear systemic fallout from the crash? Lamfalussy conducted a country-by-country damage report. Outside of some problems in Sweden, the system seemed to have held up remarkably well. Each central banker reported on how solid his banks and securities firms were. Many had questions about the novelties of options and futures markets.

Next the central bankers debated three main questions: How much would the crash alter the flow of global capital? If international capital flows through securities markets, the main channel of international finance in the 1980s, suddenly dried up, that could send the dollar and stock and bond markets into a new tailspin. Central bankers affirmed their responsibility to stand ready to fill any world financing shortfalls. Abrupt global capital movements, says London School of Economics Professor Charles Goodhart, were imposing a rarer form of lender of last resort upon central bankers: "What a central bank has to do is to recycle back to the original banks any large and destabilizing movement of funds."[10]

Would the crash cause another Great Depression? That was the central bankers' second question. The U.S. and German economies both appeared sluggish going into the crash. Many economists had been predicting a recession even before Black Monday. A key variable the central bankers pondered was how much investors would likely cut back their spending as a result of their stock market losses.[11]

The third and most pressing question that preoccupied the central bankers over the Basel weekend was really the linchpin of the other two: How to stabilize the plummeting dollar? For a week the dollar had remained steady as global capital flowed to the safe haven of U.S. government securities. But dollar assets became less attractive as the panic eased and further dollar devaluation seemed again a likely prospect.

The Fed's strategy for averting renewed financial market upheaval and recession hinged on keeping interest rates low. But at some point the plunging dollar was likely to force U.S. long-term interest rates higher, as it had earlier in 1987. The Fed's policy freedom would be perilously constricted. The falling dollar, Volcker admits, "creates a limitation on what the Fed can do in terms of providing liquidity."[12]

Volcker had pushed the Bundesbank and BOJ to cut interest rates whenever the dollar was weak. At Basel that weekend, Greenspan did not push Pöhl and Sumita. By late 1987 doing so was futile: central bankers felt they'd already taken too many chances with inflation by easing monetary policy to underpin the dollar. They strongly felt it was time for governments, particularly the United States, to take the lead by attacking the source of the unsustainable international economic imbalances.

The crisis atmosphere of the November 1987 Basel weekend instilled memories of the summer of 1974 when the Basel governors struggled to cope with the first international systemic shock of the nascent global financial era—the collapse on June 26, 1974, of a private German bank, I. D. Herstatt. Herstatt had bet wrong in the newly floating foreign exchange markets. The German authorities reacted promptly, as they would to any domestic bank problem. The federal bank supervisor revoked Herstatt's banking license, and the Bundesbank stopped clearing payments for Herstatt's accounts at the end of the day, 4 P.M. But that was only 10 A.M. in New York. It left $620 billion in partly completed Herstatt foreign exchange transactions in the international pipeline: the DM leg of the transactions had been transferred to Herstatt in Germany, but the corresponding dollar portions were still unsettled in New York.

This "Herstatt risk," as it ever after became known, shook confidence in the international foreign exchange and interbank markets—the lifelines of the newly privatized, floating monetary order. Herstatt's U.S. correspondent bank, Chase Manhattan, refused to pay claims against Herstatt in the Clearinghouse Interbank Payment System (CHIPS), the world's main private plumbing artery for clearing large dollar payments among banks. The German authorities also refused to stand behind Herstatt's debts. A panicked chain reaction of nonpayments backed up throughout CHIPS, threatening global plumbing gridlock. For several months international lending fell drastically, maturities shortened, and interest rate risk premiums were demanded from some banks. It took a year for counterparties to disentangle who owed what to whom.

"After Herstatt," remembers BOE Deputy Governor George Blunden, "something had happened—an international bank failure. Panic set in. 'Can the international interbank market survive?' That was the question."

At Basel in July 1974, the central bankers wondered whether the fall of Herstatt "was going to be the first in a series of failures."[13] Even as they did, the United States' Franklin National Bank was collapsing from foreign exchange speculation losses and fraud.

The Herstatt failure forced central bankers to confront the issue: Did the world need an international lender of last resort? Chapter and verse could be recited on the prewar cases in which national crises spread internationally— the banking crises of the 1930s stood out—when no last resort lender stepped forward to take responsibility for restoring confidence and order to the world financial system.

To prevent the Herstatt shock from becoming a full-blown world crisis, the Basel central bankers in July 1974 agreed in principle among themselves to supply lender of last resort liquidity to troubled Eurobanks.[14] In September they took the extraordinary step of issuing a reassuring, terse, and now celebrated communiqué: "The governors had an exchange of views on the problem of lender of last resort in the Euromarkets. They recognized that it would not be practical to lay down in advance detailed rules and procedures for the provision of temporary liquidity. But they were satisfied that means are available for that purpose and will be used if and when necessary."

The statement was classic central bankerspeak: delphic, noncommittal, "a real central bank confidence trick," admits George Blunden. "A major part of keeping order is to maintain confidence. Central bank governors were saying they stood behind the Euromarkets in that they would be lenders of last resort to the whole system. That turned the whole trick."

The Herstatt-induced panic began to ebb. But what specifically had the central bankers agreed?

The privacy of Basel was so inviolate that the substance of the pregnant 1974 statement remained a public enigma to the present day. The center, it turns out, was remarkably hollow. "We didn't know what we'd do," confesses

Swiss National Bank President Fritz Leutwiler.[15] The governors knew only that act they would, if necessary. A genuine confidence trick.

International lender of last resort support could be provided in two ways: by the creation of a true world central bank or by ad hoc cooperation among central bankers. Only the second was politically feasible: all international money originated in national money supplies managed by national central banks. All financial transactions also took place within an earthbound network of financial markets. If protocols for lender of last responsibility could be established, the closed international network could be safeguarded by the existing club of central bankers.

At the instigation of Governor Gordon Richardson of the Bank of England, which as host to the world's largest concentration of international banks had the keenest concern, the Basel central bankers in the autumn 1974 formed a standing supervisors committee to work out the substance for safeguarding the stability of the newly internationalized banking system. The Basel committee's first work was an urgent who-does-what agreement among central bankers of home and host countries to assign supervisory responsibilities for banks' international activities.

In December 1975 the governors approved the first Basel Concordat. Its content was kept secret until March 1981.[16] Responsibility for foreign banks was to be co-joint: primary responsibility for the supervision of liquidity—the adequacy of money and credit flows to solvent institutions—was with the host authority. Supervision of solvency was primarily the host country's responsibility for foreign bank subsidiaries and primarily the parent authority's for foreign branches.[17] Formally this was purely a supervisory agreement, not a lender of last resort responsibility accord, although, a high IMF official clucks, "it takes a central banker to believe the difference." To provide the transparency to make the concordat practicable, the committee in 1978 adopted the principle of worldwide consolidated financial reporting for banking groups.

One obvious problem was that this informal, ad hoc concordat would work only if all central bankers were capable and willing expeditiously to execute it. Yet in reality some were more aggressive and better prepared to fulfill it than others. The global network was only as strong as its weakest national link.[18]

The deficiencies were exposed in July 1982 with the scandal-ridden collapse of Italy's largest private bank, Banco Ambrosiano. When neither the Luxembourg nor the Italian authorities came to the rescue of its Luxembourg holding company subsidiary, eighty-eight international banks were left holding the bag for about $600 million. Technically Ambrosiano Holding fell through the cracks between Italy and Luxembourg because it was a holding company and not a bank.[19]

In response, the Basel supervisors drew up an amended second concordat in 1983. It emphasized the spirit of shared responsibility and cross evaluation by parent and host country of the adequacy of each other's supervision.

But it too hadn't been enough to keep pace.

The Basel weekend of November 1987 had long been circled on the governors' calendars. It was the date they'd planned to put the triumphant finishing touches on a landmark agreement—their attainment, related in Part Six, of the first worldwide banking standard. The Basel committee's two concordats and principle of consolidated reporting had been defensive measures. They were intended to give early warning signs of trouble and to outline responsibilities. The committee's multiyear effort to produce minimum and upgraded worldwide capital adequacy standards for international banks, by contrast, represented democratic society's first success in reasserting some political control over stateless money. It proactively sought to reduce the likelihood of systemic disruption from an international banking crisis and to roll back the steady stretching of the lender of last resort safety net.

The global stock market crash postponed the governors' initialing of their accord until December. It also muted any self-congratulations by demonstrating emphatically that just as they were catching up with the 1970s internationalization of banking, they and other supervisors had fallen far behind the huge, more complex minefield of systemic risks arising from the 1980s globalization of securities markets. The futures and options feedback in the crash was only the tip of the swelling, $8 trillion derivatives iceberg that would surface to give regulators headaches in the 1990s. Future-dated transactions, options, and currency and interest rate swaps constructed long and complex transaction chains, involving many parties, across national borders. A single obscure failure could cascade in incalculable permutations throughout the chain. Ever since a central bank study group report in April 1986, central bankers had been worrying aloud that market participants might be underestimating the risks of financial innovations and that the spiderweb of global interdependencies made all nations' financial institutions vulnerable in the event of a big counterparty failure or market unraveling.[20]

In one thunderous stroke the global crash warned that central bankers' nightmares were real. The world payments network was vulnerable to a big security firm failure just as it was to a big bank collapse. "These large dollar payment systems link all major institutions—but especially the large banks and large securities houses in ways that create operational, liquidity, and credit interdependencies that stagger the imagination," says New York Fed President Jerry Corrigan.[21]

Yet securities were less stringently and coherently regulated than banking. Every U.S. plumbing problem experienced in the crash existed on multiple dimensions abroad. New bank payments systems were budding up everywhere. Yet as a whole the global network was an incompatibly linked hodgepodge of facilities, equipment, software, and controls with often inadequate operational reliability to meet the pace and volume of transactions racing through world financial markets.[22] "The potential for defaults in the payments system is greater now. Those things keep me awake at night," confesses Fed Vice Chairman Manley Johnson. "There is no final settlement unless we stand behind the banks. It is our fear of being lender of last resort to the entire world that is forcing us to catch up with innovation in the financial system."

One large anxiety in a global world of intraday price volatility and mushrooming volumes was the time differentials between entering a transaction and final payment completion. Chase Manhattan Bank in Tokyo ran a global dollar clearing service in which dollar transactions were prenetted in Tokyo, cleared into Europe when markets there opened, and then settled and paid through CHIPS in New York. That left a gaping fourteen-hour window for a counterparty to fail the global marketplace—the very window that caused Bankers Trust to pull away from E. F. Hutton in the foreign exchange market on Black Monday. The result could be massive "Herstatt risk." "If something goes wrong and a British firm goes down, who will bail it out—the Bank of England, the Federal Reserve, or the Bank of Japan?" wonders the BIS's Lamfalussy. Such issues raised lender of last resort "questions about the fabric of central banking that really haven't been answered," says ex–German Chancellor Helmut Schmidt.

Concordats notwithstanding, global financial stability and containment of the unsettlingly large number of cases with international spillover potential depended upon the adequacy of national prudential supervision and the good judgment and cooperative spirit of national lenders of last resort.[23] "I must leave it to the Bank of Japan and the Ministry of Finance if a Japanese bank fails and it reverberates on Italian banks," explains Lamberto Dini, director general of the Bank of Italy. "And they must leave it to me if it's an Italian bank that fails. It can't be written. It must be dealt with case by case."

Yet by any frank assessment it was doubtful that central bankers possessed the ability ever to catch up with the new risks posed by perpetually innovating global financial markets and by unscrupulous financiers, through present ad hoc cooperative arrangements.[24] Only political reform could provide the compatibility of world financial playing rules, equity of competition, and the centralized oversight for all major banks, financial institutions, and plumbing networks necessary to deliver a safe circuit for global capital. Until reform was made, central bank monetary policy too would be increasingly compromised by the need to protect against financial fragility.

Containing the Crisis after the Crash

The November 1987 Basel weekend, informed by the deteriorating global financial conditions, created an osmotic consensus toward easier monetary policy. Over the next weeks, in a sympathetic—but definitely uncoordinated—way, central bankers governed the world economy toward easier monetary policy.

The financial turmoil and scrutiny of so many journalists, the governors also agreed, demanded an immediate and extraordinary issuance of a rare public statement, à la Herstatt. "Issuing a communiqué is an exceptional thing for us to do, but something needed to be said," explains the BIS's Lamfalussy. "There were many journalists present, and the G10 chairman had to say something. It was better to write it up in advance than to make it up in response to a question."

The central bankers easily agreed on the communiqué's message: Government fiscal policies were at fault for the world economic imbalances and financial instabilities. If remedial fiscal actions were taken, they'd be willing to support them with monetary policy. Late in the afternoon on November 9 and entertaining no questions, Bundesbank President Pöhl, as chairman of the G10 governors, issued the communiqué to the press.[25] After expressing "satisfaction" with their measures to ease the crash, it said, "They [the governors] stressed the importance of moves by governments of major industrial countries to adopt fiscal policies with the objectives of reducing existing payments imbalances, promoting exchange rate stability, and sustaining noninflationary growth.

"They are ready to support these objectives with appropriate monetary policies."

"The message of the communiqué was that we were all together and we knew what we were doing," sums up Bank of Canada Governor John Crow.

The global financial markets weren't assuaged. The New York stock market plunged 3 percent. On November 10 the dollar, bond market, and stock market all fell in tandem for the first time since just before the crash. In reaction the Tokyo stock market fell sharply to below its October 20 low. The White House showed its alarm when President Reagan, at Treasury Secretary Jim Baker's behest, publicly declared on November 10 that he did not want to see any further dollar decline.

Central bankers left Basel with foreboding. "On the eleventh of November," recalls Lamfalussy, "there was an uneasy feeling that the story wasn't over."

As the dollar continued to lurch downward through November and December, Greenspan and the central bankers grew increasingly alarmed that time was running out. A new round of financial market crashes and the risk of global depression seemed to be drawing closer. Everything hinged on decisively turning market expectations on the dollar. "There was a sense that if you could stop the dollar falling, you could prevent the stock market and financial markets from tumbling," recalls Ted Truman, head of the Fed's international finance division.

Central bankers didn't yet know that the moment of truth, in which they would make a last-ditch stand to save the dollar from collapse, was only six weeks away.

The plunging dollar evoked memories of the late 1970s inflationary crisis that had come close to undermining democratic capitalist society. Beating back inflation in the 1980s had been the central bankers' finest hour. Yet the central bankers left Basel on Tuesday disturbed by a gnawing question: Would they, to avert a rupture in the fragile financial system and a global depression, have to flood the financial markets with so much money that their painful gains against inflation would be lost?

PART TWO

SOUND MONEY

Chapter 10

The War on Inflation

On Sunday, September 30, 1979, in Belgrade, Yugoslavia, just before the start of the IMF/World Bank annual meetings, the world's financial leaders gathered to listen to seventy-five-year-old Arthur F. Burns, Federal Reserve Board chairman from 1970 to 1978, deliver his swan-song speech, the distillation of a lifetime of lessons learned at the apex of U.S. and world political economic policy-making. His topic was the main economic disease of the era—inexorably accelerating inflation.

Even as Burns spoke, the world economy was on the verge of chaos. The dollar was in its most perilous rout in history. Investors were fleeing into gold, silver, real estate, artwork, racing horses, wine, and any other asset that speculated on future greenback debauchment. A series of failed dollar defense packages over two years lay strewn in its wake. Oil-rich Saudi and Kuwaiti sheiks had put U.S. President Jimmy Carter on notice that unless he stabilized the dollar, they'd raise oil prices (priced in depreciating dollars) and diversify their portfolios away from the U.S. currency. Even Americans were fleeing their own national money.

Markets had lost confidence in political leadership. The unwritten marriage of convenience between markets and governments that underpinned democratic capitalist society was crumbling. Capital was exercising its veto to withhold productive investment and its growing mobility to flee the sovereign borders of inflating nations. There was no other fiat currency to replace the dollar as monetary anchor of the free world economy. Panicky investors thus took refuge in the "barbarous" monetary relics of the past, gold and silver. Gold had started 1979 at just over $200 an ounce. By midyear it surpassed $300. In the single month before the start of the IMF meetings it leaped, by spasms, 28 percent to $411. Silver prices vaulted a spectacular 53 percent to $16.89 an ounce.

In March, in a resounding expression of no confidence in the dollar and

American policy, European leaders inaugurated the European Monetary System (EMS) with the avowed purpose of creating an "island of stability" for Europe against the disruptive effects of the sinking dollar.[1]

The reason for the run on the dollar was inflation. From 1958 to 1964 the United States had virtually zero inflation. From 1964 to 1968 wholesale prices rose 2 percent; from 1968 to 1972, 4 percent; from 1972 to 1978, 10 percent. By the Belgrade meetings inflation was roaring at 14 percent a year. The pattern was similar in other countries. G10 inflation rose from about 2.5 percent in the 1950s, to 3.5 percent in the 1960s, to 9 percent in the first half of the 1970s. After dipping in the 1974 recession, inflation was again accelerating as the decade closed.

The cardinal logic of capitalism was sabotaged by inflation that often exceeded interest rates. When such "real" interest rates were negative, the monetary value of capital was debased. Creditors lost money by lending it. Debtors profited by borrowing and repaying in devalued dollars. Any saver who thought he was investing safely by buying ten-year U.S. government bonds at 5 percent in 1967 discovered that he'd *lost* about one-quarter of his real buying power because of inflation.

By the end of the 1970s this perverse logic had become embedded in the psychology of debtors and creditors. An unsustainable borrowing spree was under way among LDCs, farmers, corporations, and financial speculators betting that tangible assets would outstrip the value of money. For a while inflation created a financial illusion of robustness since it made reported profits nominally higher. But in real replacement cost terms, net worth was eroding. So was the faith necessary for making long-term economic commitments. As more capital went to speculation, less went to productive investment. U.S. productivity fell from a 3 percent a year average between 1947 and 1973 to 0.8 percent from 1973 to 1979. Simultaneous high unemployment and high inflation, which many policymakers until then believed impossible, began to be reported publicly as the "misery index." Real economic growth was increasingly anemic.

The extraordinary wealth-producing mechanism at the heart of capitalism—the transmutation of money into economic goods and back into still more money—was breaking down. Inflation, it was said, was the long-run accumulation of short-run expediences. By 1979 the long run had overtaken the short run. Lenin's observation, seconded by Keynes, that currency debauchment was the best way to destroy capitalist society, was coming true. The specter of the German hyperinflation of 1923, in which German citizens used wheelbarrows to transport their rapidly depreciating currency and which paved the way for Hitlerism, was increasingly imaginable.

Inflation psychology was the obverse face of the lost confidence that marked the Great Depression. Both inflation and depression, instability upward and instability downward, could destroy capitalist society—and with it, the economic prosperity and transparency conducive to democracy. Inflation "allows the politician to make promises that cannot be met in real terms. . . . [It] becomes the means of promoting changes in our economic, social, and political institutions that circumvents the democratic process."[2]

Like so many forces in economics that were benign up to a certain point, inflation psychology by the late 1970s had achieved sufficient critical mass to become a malignant cancer. Its international manifestation, as many of the financial experts gathered in Belgrade understood, was the panicked flight from the dollar.

Few in Belgrade felt more culpable for what was happening than Arthur Burns. Despite the many forces that propelled inflation, at the end of the day he knew that inflation could not get severely out of hand unless the central banker succumbed to pressures to accommodate it by consistently overproducing money. "Why, in particular, have central bankers, whose main business one might suppose is to fight inflation, been so ineffective in dealing with this worldwide problem?" posited Burns in his Belgrade address, "The Anguish of Central Banking."[3]

Gloomily Burns alluded to the familiar analysis of inflation's sources: inflation pressures arose from financing the Vietnam War through government borrowing and lax monetary policy instead of higher taxes and spending cuts. Inflation accelerated through dollar devaluations in 1971 and 1973 and then again more sharply under floating exchange rates when U.S. politicians refused to introduce austerity. More inflationary momentum was generated by the worldwide economic boom of 1972–73, which got the foreign world trade multipliers ratcheting higher than anticipated, and the ensuing surge in food and oil prices, which were multiplied by worldwide crop failures and the OPEC oil cartel. Finally, inflation became self-accelerating as the expectation of inflation induced preemptive behavior by economic agents to stay ahead of the rising inflation curve.

Yet, Burns expounded, "I believe that such analyses overlook a more fundamental factor: the persistent inflationary bias that has emerged from the philosophic and political currents that have been transforming economic life in the United States and elsewhere since the 1930s." Modern capitalist society, in which the government played such an ever-increasing role in the name of political equity and safeguarding productive market processes, bred a chronic upward pressure on prices. Ever larger budget deficits were one visible symptom of this inflationary illness.

Despite the central banker's theoretical independent power to end inflation, Burns said, getting to the heart of his speech, in practice he quickly ran into strong political constraints against raising interest rates. "As the Federal Reserve, for example, kept testing and probing the limits of its freedom to undernourish the inflation, it repeatedly evoked violent criticism from both the executive establishment and the Congress and therefore had to devote much of its energy to warding off legislation that could destroy any hope of ending inflation." This reference was to the 1970s attacks on the Fed's autonomy, which mounted with its failure to control inflation painlessly.

"If the United States and other industrial countries are to make real headway in the fight against inflation, it will first be necessary to rout inflationary psychology—that is, to make people feel that inflation can be, and probably will be, brought under control. . . . I have therefore reluctantly come to believe that fairly drastic therapy will be needed." He concluded glumly that victory would not come "until new currents of thought create a political environment in which the difficult adjustments required to end inflation can be undertaken."

Burns's audience departed with an impression of doom. "Burns's speech was a lament," recalls one disappointed Bundesbank official. "Burns had a reputation as the inflation fighter par excellence, and all he was telling us was the constraints he had. I would have expected more from Burns."

The Coming of Volcker

Nor did Burns's speech favorably impress its single most important listener in the audience—the man in whose hands now lay the task of battling the formidable inflation dragon, the newly appointed fifty-two-year-old Fed chairman, Paul Volcker. As the six-foot-eight-inch Volcker left the hall, he grumbled sarcastically in his booming voice, "I see, I must be doing things wrong."[4] Volcker, who had not known what topic Burns was going to address, today allows of the speech, "It was very long and very gloomy."

Even as he sat through the speech, Volcker was working on a plan for just such drastic therapy as Burns prescribed. He had been so intent to march ahead on implementing it that his staff had had to dissuade him from forgoing the Belgrade meetings altogether by stressing the panic that could seize markets if the chairman of the Fed failed to make his customary appearance. That plan was finally implemented six days later. On the strength of that plan, wrote former Bundesbank President Otmar Emminger, "Paul Volcker refuted conclusively a basic theory of central bank policy which . . . Arthur Burns had advanced only a few days earlier in Belgrade."[5]

As the ascension of Winston Churchill as U.K. Prime Minister was to Adolf Hitler and Nazi power, so was the appointment of Volcker as Fed chairman to the inflation menace in democratic capitalism. Like Churchill, that Volcker was chosen at all was due only to the deficit in democratic leadership that failed to prevent the problem from reaching crisis proportions. He was not known to President Jimmy Carter or trusted to be a "team player" by the White House inner circle that recommended him.

Paul Volcker "was *born* to be chairman of the Fed," states Albert Wojnilower, First Boston economist. "It was as though somebody had trained all his life to play the piano and now was finally allowed to play the best instrument in the world."[6]

His résumé was impeccable: His Princeton undergraduate senior thesis in 1949 was entitled "The Problems of Federal Reserve Policy Since World War II." After a Harvard master's degree in political economy and postgraduate study at the London School of Economics, he began his professional career as an economist at the New York Fed. He later worked at Chase Manhattan Bank. He then served in the U.S. Treasury under Presidents Kennedy, Johnson, and Nixon. Between 1969 and 1974 he circumnavigated the globe as the U.S. government's point man in the last-ditch negotiations to preserve the Bretton Woods international monetary order. Until Carter's call he served in the Fed's second-ranking post in the markets as president of the New York Fed, where he battled the 1977–79 dollar crisis.

Volcker's qualifications included an old-fashioned ideal of government service that placed the public good ahead of partisan politics, which had been instilled in him since childhood in Teaneck, New Jersey, where his father was city manager. His utter disinterest in personal wealth made ideal public relations for the leader about to impose drastic economic austerity on the nation. His personal life was spartan. The cloud of cigar smoke at congressional hearings that became his media image was made by a $1.45-per-six-pack brand. He dined off homemade spaghetti and cheap Chinese food. His $58,500 Fed chairman's salary was a fraction of what he could have commanded on Wall Street. "What's the subject of life—to get rich?" he asked dismissively. "All of those fellows out there getting rich could be dancing around the real subject of life."[7]

Oddly for capitalism's top monetary official, Volcker was fundamentally skeptical that left to their own devices, financiers and markets would produce best results for the public good. "Volcker is a fascinating individual," comments Treasury Undersecretary George Gould. "He brought almost moral precepts, totally Calvinistic, to the job: those who've sinned [speculated on inflation] should be punished. He liked the idea of earlier times when life was simpler and people were paid less. To him money was a corrupting influence. He doesn't spend a dime on himself. So to him, if a guy was making a lot of money on Wall Street, something was wrong. Bring up Glass-Steagall or the S and L problems, and Paul would start out moralizing that what had gone wrong with the world since the 1950s was that we had gotten too much too soon, people in finance today were paid too much, we were giving wrong incentives to the economy with all these bonuses tied to deals and yuppies running risks with innovative products that senior management didn't understand. He had almost contempt for the financial establishment. When he held forth, people shut up. Then he'd go on about fishing stories and he'd say: 'You can't tell me the quality of life has improved even if quantity has. When I was a boy in New Jersey you could find good trout fishing fifty miles away from my home. Now you have to charter a plane and go all the way to Montana and Wyoming.'

"He saw himself as the last responsible man on earth. He had to hold the fort against political appointees like myself, free market excess, anyone who didn't see the long term as he did. The 'pernicious effects of inflation and inflation psychology'—he always talked about it. It is sometimes hard to have a discussion with an individual like that. I must admit it took an unusual man to squeeze out inflation so singlemindedly."

Volcker had a native distrust of financial activity that didn't clearly serve the productive economy. "He'd say that it was not good that finance was the determinant of economic activity," says Gould. "He favored the real economy."

Volcker was also dismissive of Ph.D. economists, many of whom staffed the Fed. "Volcker is simply skeptical of analysis," says Princeton Professor William Branson, who co-taught a course with him after his retirement from the Fed. "He always sees the counterargument."

Volcker's genius for monetary policy was intuitive, unteachable. It was as if he had a model of the economy sitting in his consciousness that sensed how much production capacity there was in different sectors of the economy at any given time. The more unused capacity, the greater leeway he had to push for growth through financial stimulus without the risk of igniting inflation. Few individuals in the world understood better the international political economy of the dollar. Volcker was a quintessential central bank brooder, quick to see potential disaster lurking around each corner. When a financial crisis did erupt, he improvised a plan and presented it with the usually fulfilled expectation that everyone would jump on board unquestioningly. Then he manipulated the tools of power for all they were worth to implement it. Finally, Volcker possessed the crucial qualification of a sound money reputation with bond markets, whose ups and downs so powerfully conditioned the real economic environment.

Volcker, in short, was a one-man central bank. With a natural genius for the job and the presence of a natural leader, he didn't need much of a staff. He worked mainly through a few trusted confidants, many of whom adopted his crusty and cynical tone.[8]

At Belgrade in September 1979, however, there was little disagreement: disaster loomed dead ahead unless inflation was brought under control.

The plunging dollar was propelling inflation and inflation expectations more than most experts then realized. The economic dynamics were still too novel under floating exchange rates, and the symptoms occurred in such slow motion as to obscure clear causal linkages. "The lesson of the 1970s was that the exchange rate was a bigger channel of inflation than expected at the time," explains Ted Truman, Fed International Finance Division chief. "People said imports were only seven percent of GNP, so the effects [through higher import prices] couldn't be that great. They were off by a factor of two or three due to the indirect effects [on prices of competing goods and wage pressures]." Under fixed exchange rates, easing monetary policy first stimulated growth. Inflation arrived with a lag. Under floating, lower rates led to currency depreciation and rapid inflation effects, offsetting the growth stimulus.

The dollar had been under worldwide assault since June 24, 1977, when Treasury Secretary W. Michael Blumenthal, hoping to pressure Germany and Japan to speed up their economic growth (and implicitly raise their inflation rates toward U.S. levels) to stimulate U.S. exports, adopted the unorthodox tactic of talking down the dollar following a contentious OECD meeting at Paris. Blumenthal's talk-down spooked the foreign exchange markets. Between September 1977 and October 1978 the dollar fell 17 percent, a stunning downswing by postwar standards.

The dollar run overwhelmed the world's unique successful example of fiscal policy coordination—Germany and Japan to expand and the United States to belt-tighten—undertaken at the Bonn head of state summit of July 16–17, 1978. Only temporary respite came from the most massive, top-secret, concerted intervention and dollar rescue package in history on November 1, 1978.[9]

The Federal Reserve Board chairman at the time was G. William Miller, who had succeeded Burns in early 1978. Miller never won financial markets' confidence or that of Fed professionals. An ex-chairman of conglomerate Textron, Miller retained a Main Street manager's view of the world. He tried to transform the Fed's culture of open-ended, collegial policy debates into crisply focused business boardroom decision making. He was more tolerant of inflation than Wall Street financiers or central bankers. Miller swiftly compounded the inflationary policy errors he'd inherited from Burns. By spring 1979 even Carter's advisers wanted Miller to tighten. It was the only episode in memory in which the government pushed harder money upon a central bank.

In July 1979 President Carter retreated to the mountaintop at Camp David, Maryland, to reflect on the dismal condition of the economy and his government. When he came down, he made his famous "malaise" speech and overhauled his cabinet. Miller became the new Treasury secretary. "We all thought Miller was not up to the job," recalls his counterpart, then German Finance Minister Manfred Lahnstein. Neither did Wall Street. The dollar plunged. Gold leapt above $300 an ounce.

When A. W. "Tom" Clausen, president of the Bank of America, turned down the Fed chairmanship, Carter turned to Paul Adolph Volcker. It was destined to be the most important appointment of Carter's presidency and probably the most important anywhere in the capitalist democracies in the 1980s. The financial markets cheered. Equity and bond prices rose. The dollar surged. Gold eased $2.50 an ounce.

Practical Monetarism

When Volcker took office on August 6, 1979, inflation was 14 percent, inflation expectations were running riot, money supply was exploding three times faster than the Fed's annual target. Money growth that regularly exceeded productive economic potential was likely to turn into inflation over the next six to twenty-four months.

Money was the lifeblood pumping through the financial system heart muscle to nourish activity in the economic body. But the supply of money and the capacity of the economic body had to be proportionate, lest the end result be unsustainable overexertion or underproductive sluggishness. This was why central bankers normally tried to take something off booms by supplying less money than demanded, raising the cost of money in the process. In sluggish periods they tried to perk things up with more money than demanded, pushing interest rates down. In ex–Fed Chairman William McChesney Martin's memorable characterization: "Our purpose is to lean against the winds of deflation and inflation, whichever way they are blowing."[10]

The difficulty lay in knowing how *hard* to lean one way or the other and *when.* "The magic of money," explains Volcker, "is that the implications for the long term are often substantially different from the implications for the short term." Yet the short-run and long-run appearances of money working in the economy were often hard to distinguish. By the time signs of divergence became clear, economic forces and expectations had been set in motion that usually made it too late to catch up painlessly. Monetary oversupply often revved up economic activity in the short run, for instance, but bred long-run inflation. As a result, central bankers tried constantly to gauge and adjust policy to how much of the demand for money was going to wealth-enhancing investment and how much to inflationary excess or, worse, as in 1979, to the self-fulfilling speculation of outright currency debauchment.

Because a monetary policy move worked its way through the financial system to the economy with a long lag, the adept central banker also had to be a kind of seer who looked past current conditions to formulate a monetary stance appropriate for a year or so into the future. Whether the impact would be slight or dramatic, intended or unexpected, he could never reliably predict, however, in an economy of perpetually changing nature, with uneven expansive and contractive tendencies across sectors and geographical regions, and shifting expectations of growth and inflation.

The alchemy of central banking could be characterized epigrammatically: if there were only one tomato and one dollar bill in the world, the tomato's price would be $1. The central banker's art was to supply a second dollar bill through the financial system into the economy in such a way that it stimulated the production of two tomatoes at $1, rather than merely inflating the price of one tomato to $2.

The secret to doing so went beyond mere technical proficiency—above all, it hinged upon creating and constantly renewing confidence in money's long-term soundness. This was achieved by persuading markets and governments that they were producing only so much money as society needed, but not quite so much as it usually wanted.

Money was one of civilization's atavistic mysteries. Its value was symbolic, animated only through universal acceptance and faith. An ordinary metal or piece of paper became accepted throughout society as representing goods and concepts of stored value; yet if shaved or shredded, it became a worthless artifact once again. The entire financial credit system edifice underpinning modern capitalist society rested on faith in credit's ultimate transferability into money. But on what faith did money rest?

In ancient times money was often minted of precious metals in temples and consecrated by priest kings to imbue it with man's deepest religious faith. It was not coincidental that central bankers, like their black-cloaked Supreme Court legal brethren in camera, practiced their secretive art with an abundance of ritualistic cant from inside huge stone templelike edifices that subconsciously conferred safety, confidence, and faith.[11]

Ancient temple priests, such as at Delphi or Eleusis, safeguarded a sacred mystery of death and rebirth. So, too, in a sense, did central bankers. Their mystery was the transmutation of monetary dross into economic gold. Their task was to assist the cycle of money's transformation into economic production, back into liquid or money form, and again into still greater production. This unending circuit of accumulation was the essence of capitalism.[12]

The Federal Reserve sought to regulate the supply of money and credit from the banking system to the economy by managing bank reserves, or "high-powered money." Minimum reserve requirements compelled banks to hold back a fraction of their deposits, in the form of vault cash or reserve deposits at the central bank, to ensure they had enough liquidity on hand to redeem depositors' claims.[13] Banks could make loans or financial investments only within a defined multiple of the excess reserves they held.

In order to expand or reduce the lending capacity of the banking system, the Fed occasionally altered the minimum reserve requirements. Ordinarily, however, it injected or withdrew reserves by buying or selling government securities in the open market from among three dozen designated "primary dealers." When it bought securities, it paid for them by crediting the dealer's bank account with newly created central bank reserves. Selling securities caused reserves to be debited from the dealer's bank. When reserves were injected, the nation's money supply usually swelled; interest rates—money's price—fell. Lending and economic activity was stimulated. The currency exchange rate often declined, too, boosting exports but causing imports to cost more. Withdrawing reserves had the opposite effects.

Each of the main measures of the money supply had its own reserve requirement. The U.S. money supply aggregate M1, covering the most spendable money such as cash and checking account funds, carried a minimum requirement of 12 percent. Since every time a dollar was lent, deposited, and lent again a minimum of $.12 had to be held back, the maximum potential mathematical creation of new money was $8.33 per dollar of injected reserves.[14] The progressively broader definitions of money, which included money more likely to be spent slowly and saved, such as M2 and M3, had different minimum requirements and associated rates of money creation.

Although a central bank could not compel banks to lend and create money, the leverage worked obligatorily downward when enough high-powered reserves were withdrawn. Banks that were short of the minimum reserve requirement tried to borrow from other banks with excess reserves in the short-term Fed Funds market. Their borrowing pushed up Fed Fund interest rates. A bank unable to obtain sufficient reserves in the Fed Funds market—perhaps because of a rumor it was in trouble—could as a last resort try to borrow them from the central bank's discount window.

Central bankers normally injected and withdrew reserves to try to achieve some intermediate financial target—such as the growth of a money supply aggregate, the level of interest rates, or an exchange rate value—which they believed in turn would produce its desired final economic effects. The monetary process thus resembled a loose Rube Goldberg contraption: the small auricular valve of central bank reserves pumped financial heart valves, which pumped the still larger valves of the economy. But because the valve openings and closings were unsynchronized and guided by other changeable relationships, the central banker's influence over the economy was always loose and at two removes. His single sure grip was the ability to manage reserves to guide Fed Funds interest rates in the present. After that, short- and long-term financial and economic market forces took over. The "animal spirits" might be so low that businessmen could not be induced to borrow and invest even if the central bank pushed interest rates down to the lowest levels, as in a depression—in such cases injecting more reserves would be as futile as pushing on a string. Banks might be so fearful of losses from their exposure to bad debt that they refused to lend despite Fed stimulus—resulting in a bank-induced credit crunch. Alternatively, as in 1979, the demand from speculators, who doubted society's will to control inflation, could be so lusty that borrowing accelerated even faster than interest rates rose.

Winning credibility with financial markets was the central bankers' philosophers' stone, the catalytic key to creating a favorable power curve of market expectations so that his small manipulations of short-term Fed Funds interest rates leveraged big, desired changes in the market-driven, real long-term bond interest rates that most influenced economic activity. But market credibility had to be earned within democratic political tolerances.

Although at his second board meeting as chairman Volcker persuaded the seven board governors to unanimously raise the discount rate from 10 percent to 10.5 percent—the highest level in Fed history—he swiftly ran into the same political obstacles that Burns had lamented at Belgrade. Despite the signals of rampaging inflation, the governors and Federal Reserve Bank presidents were hesitant to push up interest rates very far. "The art of central banking lies in large part in approaching the right answer from a sense of experience and successive approximation," Volcker explains. "But it is also a psychological fact of life that the risks almost always seem greater in raising interest rates than in lowering them. After all, no one likes to risk recession, and that is when the political flak ordinarily hits."[15]

On September 18 Volcker convinced a majority to bump up the discount rate to 11 percent—but the vote was only four to three. Politicians promptly took to their soapboxes to decry the increase. Markets, on the other hand, immediately panicked for precisely the opposite reason. "The four-to-three vote didn't bother me much," says Volcker. "I knew I had the votes to raise it again. But still, that was *not* the way the market took it. 'Jesus, he had only four votes—next time he won't have a majority,' they said."

On September 19 the dollar dropped 2 percent against the Swiss franc and DM. Gold and silver prices spasmed to all-time highs. The Fed was trapped impotently between the divergent expectations of markets and governments. Its credibility was at its lowest point since the Great Depression.

In late August Volcker secretly began working on his plan for administering drastic anti-inflation therapy. For any program to work, it had to meet three necessary conditions: It had to convince both markets and governments that from that point forward the Fed was going to cut off the free-flowing money spigot. It had to be credible within existing political tolerances. Finally, it also had to restore a common anti-inflationary spirit among demoralized Fed policymakers themselves.

Volcker, an experienced Washington hand, knew that the short-term political constituency that favored the low interest rates was as huge as Burns had portrayed. "The short-run interest of everyone is in having the lowest possible interest rate," explains ex–Senate Banking Committee Chairman William Proxmire (D-Wis.). "It puts people to work. It makes debtors and borrowers happy. Even rich people are more in favor of low interest rates in the short term since they get the benefits in higher bond and stock prices. Yet in the long run interest rates should be high enough to encourage savings and discourage borrowing and to restrain inflation. We obviously failed to do this."

Yet by 1979 Americans were growing frightened about inflation. Few politicians were bold enough to lead the anti-inflationary struggle that would entail economic hardship and uproot cozy relationships in the political economy that had grown up over fifty years and that had come to be viewed as cornerstones of U.S. democratic capitalism.

Many were privately relieved to transfer the responsibility to do political dirty work to Paul Volcker and the Fed. Volcker had no illusions that disinflation therapy could be administered without a painful recession. He also knew that the first casualty of failure would almost certainly be the Fed's institutional independence. But that was worth little if democratic capitalist society was degenerating from runaway inflation.

Reestablishing central bank credibility required imposing discipline on the burgeoning, innovative global financial markets. Banks were no longer waiting for people to make deposits or for the Fed to inject high-powered reserves before making new loans. In a phenomenon known as "managed liabilities," they extended the loans first and then borrowed the required covering funds from the reservoir of international Eurodollars and through innovations that were liquefying balance sheets. In the summer of 1979 liability management fueled about half of U.S. bank credit expansion.[16]

The Euromarket functioned like a parallel financial universe. It flourished from the same basic root, the central bank monetary reserve, as the regulated domestic financial market. But it created money according to the forces of the free market, unregulated by central bank minimum reserves liquidity ratios. Throughout the 1970s ever larger volumes of global capital sloshed back and forth between these two financial universes. From 1973 to 1987 the gross sum of Eurocurrency accounts multiplied from $315 billion to nearly $4 trillion.[17]

As a result, borrowers and lenders weren't nearly as restrained when the

Fed raised interest rates as they had been when alternative sources of funding were limited and regulated interest rate ceilings choked off lending at lower and more predictable interest rate levels. This made it harder for the Fed to gauge the impact of any monetary tightening.

The chronic dilemma of central banking was that one never knew for certain what was motivating the demand for money—rising inflation expectations or productive investment. Fed operating policy in the 1970s was to inject and withdraw enough reserves to keep Fed Fund interest rates at a level it believed consistent with maximum productive investment at lowest inflation. As inflation expectations rose, interest rates had to go higher to be restrictive. But how high? At Belgrade Burns confessed that the Fed's consistent underestimation of market inflation expectations had "often taken the sting out of interest rates."

Volcker's drastic therapy solution was "practical monetarism." Practical monetarism had been adopted in Switzerland, Germany, and England in the mid-1970s to control inflation expectations. At the New York Fed, Volcker had conducted informal, ad hoc seminars on its uses in his office and around the lunch table. "I was getting frustrated, so I was fooling around with a more monetarist approach," he remembers. "Sitting around with the staff in New York, I was brainstorming: Why doesn't this approach work? I was thinking operationally, not theoretically. But I wasn't ready to crusade for it. . . . I didn't arrive [in Washington] with a plan."

Monetarism shifted the main intermediate focus of central bank policy from interest rate levels to a desired growth path for the money supply. Central bankers could manipulate central bank reserves to try to ration the amount of money supplied by the financial system to the economy indirectly through interest rates—money's price—or by targeting money supply directly. In the first case, interest rates were likely to be stable and the supply of money to fluctuate with shifts in loan demand by businesses, consumers, and financial speculators. In the second, the money supply would be stable, but interest rates would shift up and down.

The underlying rationale for practical monetarism was closely related to classic central banker good housekeeping—inflation could rise only as far as excess money was supplied over time to nourish it. Central bankers' problem in the inflationary 1970s was that their focus on short-term interest rates had caused them to drift off course from the long-term lighthouse of money supply. Practical monetarism was intended to restore the long-term lighthouse more prominently to view.

Central bankers' practical monetarism was distinct from academic monetarism championed by Nobel Prize–winner Milton Friedman. Volcker and most central bankers vigorously disputed academics' prescription of an automatic rule to expand money supply at a constant and predictable annual rate between 2 percent and 5 percent to replace central bankers' discretion to "lean against the wind" of inflation and deflation. What made them "practical" was that while they gave prominence to targeting money supply measures as a guidepost, they did reality checks against other factors they believed affected growth and inflation. "You can't do monetary policy just by reading Milton Friedman," declares one of its most celebrated practitioners, former head of the Swiss National Bank Fritz Leutwiler, from whom monetarist-minded U.K. Prime Minister Margaret Thatcher sometimes sought private consultations. "You don't go to the office and blindly follow a rule. You've got to keep your eyes open. You have to look at the exchange rate. This is true in Germany as well."

Volcker and his fellow Basel central bankers doubted the robustness of the short-term linkage between money growth and inflation. They didn't believe that the velocity of money circulation—the number of times money turned over each year to generate a given level of economic output—was as predictable as the academic monetarists alleged. This was a serious qualification: if money was spent faster than expected—that is, if velocity increased—then even modest growth in the money supply aggregates could flood the economy with inflationary excess. Just defining a measure of money that would remain stable in a deregulatory and innovative environment could also be difficult.

Volcker was aware that the uncertainties about monetarist theory raised the danger of a rule trap: the Fed's credibility to influence inflation expectations might become tied to a monetary rule that proved faulty. Yet it was in Volcker's nature to be supremely confident of his ability to manage that risk if it arose.

Despite its drawbacks and uncertainties, practical monetarism held several overriding attractions for Volcker. First, it offered a clear, objective method of communication to financial markets, businesses, labor unions, Congress, and the administration by which the Fed could frontally assault inflation expectations.

"How to sell monetary policy to the market? We central bankers discussed it often," says Leutwiler. "People don't care if the money supply target is 2 percent or 3 percent. The important thing is to *tell* people that this is what is needed to bring down inflation. Except for a few professors no one listens to anyway, no one knows whether it is sufficient to lower inflation. If people trust you, you can tell them that 2 percent or 3 percent is fine and they'll believe you. Then you destroy inflationary expectations—that's the really important thing."[18]

A second overriding advantage of practical monetarism was that it permitted interest rates to move automatically and sharply higher to inflict punishing financial losses upon inflation speculators. This built credibility. "The new operating techniques were supposed to explicitly inject greater uncertainty into the system so they had better watch out," Volcker explains.

In a flash of political genius, Volcker realized that practical monetarism also delivered into the Fed's hands a precious political shield to drastically hike interest rates. Failure to control inflation despite high nominal rates had subjected the Fed to vigorous attacks in Congress. By the late 1970s an odd alliance of conservative monetarists and soft-money populists had united around the idea of binding the Fed's autonomy with monetary targets—though for incompatible motives.[19] If interest rates rose while the Fed was holding monetary growth along a predefined, targeted path, Volcker could answer critics that market forces, not the Fed, were responsible—and all according to Congress's own bidding!

"Volcker valued the political shield aspect very highly," says Anthony Solomon, Carter's Treasury undersecretary for monetary affairs and Volcker's successor at the New York Fed. "He could say, 'We're not controlling interest rates—we're just controlling the money supply.' Yet there was also sufficient concern in Congress about inflation to accept such high rates. Without it, the shield wouldn't have been worth nearly as much."

Finally, practical monetarism offered a needed self-discipline and a way to coalesce support among a fractious FOMC united only in its disillusionment with gradualist interest rate targeting. "Some board members were reluctant to take overt moves to raise interest rates," Volcker recalls. "So I asked myself: 'Is there a way to get more unanimity?' "

There were some strong objections at first. The traditional hard money dean among the governors, Henry Wallich, feared that monetary targetry would produce volatile swings in interest rates that might undermine financial markets and the economy. He worried that the technique might cause interest rates to fall too quickly before inflation psychology was expunged from the economy.

Others objected that by voting on a technically esoteric path for money growth, whose meaning had to be translated for them into its rough interest rate equivalent, more de facto operational discretion slipped into Volcker's hands as chairman. In the end, Volcker's personal diplomacy overcame each individual dissent by eliciting a collective willingness to unite behind the new experiment if the others did.

Volcker crafted a semiautomatic monetary targetry approach centered around supply of a controlled amount of "nonborrowed reserves"—high-powered money the Fed injected through the open market—that was associated with a desired target for money supply growth in the financial system. Whenever speculative demand caused the money supply to grow beyond the Fed's announced target, interest rates would automatically be forced up by the Fed's withdrawal of "nonborrowed reserves." When money supply fell,

so would interest rates. Volcker set the Fed's main focus on the M1 aggregate. M1 was money that was immediately spendable—the total of all cash
and checking accounts in the country—and thus most likely to turn into inflation.[20]

In actuality, Volcker's approach was more automatic in appearance than
in fact.[21] Milton Friedman later charged, "If somebody had wanted to deliberately adopt a policy to discredit monetarism, they would have done what
Volcker did."[22] Yet by the mid-1980s monetarist techniques had been abandoned as unworkable in Thatcher's United Kingdom, Leutwiler's Switzerland, and almost everywhere else it was tried. By the late 1980s even the
Bundesbank's leading monetarist, Helmut Schlesinger, was plagued by increasing doubts.[23]

Many have debated whether Volcker's use of the monetarist technique
was an "act of skillful hypocrisy" to get higher interest rates, as one admir-
ing European central banker thinks, or whether, as Solomon says, "Volcker
had a semiconverted attitude toward practical monetarism." Yet the distinction tended to blur when looked at from Volcker's pragmatic viewpoint:
"We've got a market that will seize upon markers of one kind or another. It
is fair to say that my style—more than most others—is to search out some
rule or indicator to supply discipline."

Volcker had moved so stealthily that the day before departing for the
IMF/World Bank annual meetings in Belgrade, not even all of the twelve
Federal Reserve Bank presidents, and very few of the staff, were aware of
the historic policy turn that was about to be engineered. Nor had Volcker informed the Carter administration of his thinking.

Volcker told Carter's men for the first time on the Treasury secretary's airplane en route to Belgrade. Treasury Secretary Miller and Charles Schultze,
chairman of the Council of Economic Advisers, immediately opposed it. The
monetary rule was almost sure to lead to a recession—in a presidential election year.

Volcker promised to think over their objections and talk again before
acting.

Before Belgrade, the entourage stopped briefly in Hamburg to try to persuade top German policymakers and Chancellor Helmut Schmidt to do more
to defend the plummeting dollar.[24] The dollar's weakness stemmed from lack
of confidence in Carter policies, Schmidt said in rejecting their proposal.
The remedy was tougher U.S. monetary policy.

"Are you perhaps of the opinion that the American interest rates are not
yet high enough?" Volcker teased, referring to Schmidt's complaints about
the adverse pressure of high U.S. interest rates on Germany.

Bundesbank President Otmar Emminger interjected that "money was indeed expensive but plentiful." The problem wasn't interest rates, but oversupply of money.

Volcker, to Emminger's surprise, quickly agreed. "Yes, the money supply is what really matters."[25]

The depressing Hamburg meeting reinforced Volcker's conviction that drastic therapy was needed. That same afternoon the U.S. delegation left for Belgrade. State Secretary of Finance Manfred Lahnstein and Bundesbank Vice President Karl Otto Pöhl hitched an airplane ride with them.

On Monday evening, October 1, in the presence of Tony Solomon, his only confidant within the Carter government, Volcker briefed Emminger and Pöhl of his practical monetarist plans.[26] Volcker estimated that it would take him about a week to get the support of his Fed colleagues and the White House.

Next day, Tuesday, October 2—prior to the conclusion of the IMF meetings—Volcker departed Belgrade. Panic hit world financial markets at the news. Gold shot up $25 an ounce. Rumors circulated that Volcker had resigned or died.

Why did Volcker leave early? "I had this [the new policy] on my mind, and I wanted to get to it."

When top Carter economic officials returned to Washington on Thursday, they promptly tried to dissuade Volcker from acting. They urged he raise the discount rate by two percentage points with a stronger majority instead. At an impromptu meeting among Volcker, Solomon, Schultze, and Miller in Solomon's office, Solomon suggested that the four of them go to President Carter so Volcker could discuss his idea.

Miller said he'd talk to the president.

Soon thereafter Miller informed Solomon, "By the way, Tony, I mentioned it to the president with Charlie [Schultze] present. The president said he didn't like to."

Solomon answered, "That was unfair of you. You should have given Volcker the chance to present his case himself."

Upon hearing the news, Volcker wondered to Solomon, "What do I do now?"

"Try to make a good-faith effort to get a substantial majority for a substantial rise in the discount rate. If you can't get it, then just give us notice if you make the switch."[27]

Volcker did not consider raising the discount rate by two points sufficient, since it lacked staying power. He knew there wasn't much support for the idea among the board. So he never pressed it seriously.

Instead he made the momentous decision without the White House's support. In utmost secrecy, and taking advantage of the media hoopla on the coincidental visit of Pope John Paul II to Washington on October 6, he summoned the Federal Reserve Bank presidents to Washington for a highly unusual Saturday FOMC meeting.[28]

The main question discussed at the all-day meeting: "Will it work?"

Volcker had already prepared the ground with one-on-one meetings with key FOMC members before taking his seat at the huge oval table in the wood-paneled boardroom at the top of the Fed's twin marble staircases. He outlined the proposal in detail and gave everyone a chance to comment. Without advocating, he went over the merits and drawbacks, all the while subtly orchestrating the analysis toward his own inexorable conclusion. The vote for adoption was unanimous.

As the meeting was breaking up in the late afternoon, the Fed's public affairs director, Joseph Coyne, summoned the press to come within two hours to a press conference. One TV man, whose cameras were occupied covering the pope, asked if it would really be worth it. "Let me put it to you this way," replied Coyne. "Long after the pope is gone, you'll remember this."[29]

The press release outlined three actions: first, a one-point discount rate increase from 11 percent to 12 percent; second, the imposition of an 8 percent reserve requirement on increases in Eurodollar borrowings, large CD issuance, and other managed liabilities; third and last, the really big news—the change in operating procedures. Volcker insisted on calling it an "experiment." Why put the big news last? "To say there'd been a change in operating procedure sounded like gobbledy-gook to the normal reporter or person," explains Volcker. "You could hardly lead with it. People understood the meaning of a discount rate increase. At least they recognized the other."

Volcker soon called his first foreign central banker, the Bundesbank's Otmar Emminger, whom he awakened around midnight (European time), at the Yugoslavian resort of Opatija. "I did it, and I wanted you to be the first to know," he told him.[30]

Henry Wallich telephoned Japan Sunday morning. He explained the Fed's thinking to the BOJ's Deputy Governor for International Relations Shijuro Ogata. "I understood their strategy," Ogata says. "Using apparently objective indicators to impose generally unpopular measures on the public."

"Ah," Wallich quipped to Ogata, "but which 'M' to use?"[31]

President Carter put the best face on Volcker's action. Having just appointed Volcker, and with his administration's economic policies in disarray, Carter felt he could neither object nor afford a bruising public battle with the Fed. Declaring inflation to be the number one threat to the national economy, Carter endorsed it.

At that point political responsibility for the U.S. economic agenda had shifted from the government to the central bank. To some this was a corruption of democratic principles. To others it was checks and balances—a healthy safeguard against ungovernability.

The Lost Year

It took a while for the significance of Volcker's "Saturday night special" to be understood by much of Washington. Wall Street reacted more promptly, but with cynicism: although the Fed Funds rate jumped from 11.5 percent to 14 percent, the speculative lending boom continued at an *accelerated* pace. Inside the Fed, Volcker fumed.

By January 1980 inflation was galloping at an annual 17 percent rate. The markets were steamrolling right over the Fed's drastic practical monetarist therapy.

What happened?

Salomon Brothers' Henry Kaufman, who earned the moniker *Dr. Gloom* for his accurately bearish bond market forecasts, had an answer: The 1980s global financial revolution would result in much higher and more volatile interest rates before inflation was cooled than most people thought. Practical monetarism, he explains, "occurred against the backdrop of a market that now had floating rates in it and adjustable rate mortgages, a prime loan rate that was floating, the advent of floating rate financing in the Euromarket, the beginning of leakages of funds—that is, from one national border through another national border; if you couldn't finance here, you could go to the Euromarket, and so on. All of that meant a substantial escalation in the rate structure."[32]

At the FOMC debate of October 6, no one had contemplated that banks' prime interest rate would soon rise to over 20 percent or that long-term interest rates would become so volatile. Nor did anyone fully expect "the velocity of circulation to shift so much or that deregulation would screw it up," reports Tony Solomon.

Throughout the postwar era of closed and tightly regulated national financial systems, more by accident than design, whenever interest rates edged above regulated bank deposit ceilings, depositors switched funds out of banks and thrifts into higher-yielding assets such as government securities. Loan money dried up. Like an early-braking mechanism against overheating, housing and consumer durable goods sales fell. This had a fortuitous economic logic since these were postponable items. It was also convenient for central bank monetary policy because, explains Volcker, it "made the economy sensitive to what we now think of as small policy adjustments."[33]

With the brake now off, lending sprees were free to go farther. The monetary brake worked eventually, but interest rates had to move higher and more swiftly than in the past. Restraint finally came not through an artificially induced credit crunch, but through inflicting of actual wounds on business borrowers and financial speculators. But what if monetary restraint killed before it chastened them? That was the fast road to financial crisis, depression, and early abortion of the disinflation campaign.

Volcker had a close brush with the no-win clash between monetary stability and financial system fragility in early 1980, when his slamming on of the monetary brakes caused the silver bubble to burst. Between February and April Fed Funds interest rates were pushed up from 14 percent to beyond 18 percent. Banks responded by lifting their benchmark prime lending rates above 20 percent.

Silver had soared from $6 an ounce in early 1979 to $18.77 by the end of November. Then it rocketed, in tandem with gold, to a $52.50 peak in mid-January. The silver bubble was driven by an audacious speculation by the fabulously wealthy Texas oil barons Bunker and Herbert Hunt, in league with some Saudi Arabians. The Hunts had started buying silver in 1973, but their big push began in early 1979. Their apparent objective, though they denied it, was to corner the world market for silver—one safe haven where money was likely to flee as the dollar's worth depreciated with inflation. The Hunts became the world's heaviest bettors that inflation wouldn't be beaten back. The biggest obstacle in their path was Paul Volcker.

The Hunts ended up controlling some two-thirds of all silver in the United States. In doing so, they borrowed nearly $1.8 billion from banks and brokerage firms to buy silver futures contracts on margins as low as 5 percent. The collateral for the loans was the loftily priced silver assets themselves. In February and March 1980, Hunt borrowings accounted for an astonishing 9 percent of all new U.S. bank credit.

The record interest rates in early 1980s added enormously to the Hunts' debt service burden and finally broke the silver fever. Silver prices crashed to $16 by late March. The Hunts suddenly lacked enough cash to meet their futures margin and contract obligations. When their default threatened to bring down the Hunts' main broker, Bache Halsey Stuart Shields, and possibly the troubled giant bank First National of Chicago with as much as $300 million at risk with it, Volcker blinked. He put the central banker's primary concern, financial stability, ahead of his wish to see the market's stern exemplary justice of bloody losses on inflation speculators play itself out.

On Silver Thursday, March 27, silver prices plunged to $10.40 as Bache began liquidating Hunt silver futures contracts and dumping shares on the stock market to raise cash. The stock market fell thirty-two points. On Friday, fortunately, silver prices held above the $7–$10 range that could have inflicted losses large enough to drive Bache to default on its bank loans. Over the weekend, Volcker's personal intervention helped seal a countertrade deal with Engelhard Mineral and Chemicals Corp. in lieu of the $665 million in cash the Hunts owed them on Monday but couldn't pay. Volcker's most important involvement came soon thereafter when he gave his blessing as godfather to a thirteen-bank consortium for a new $1.1 billion ten-year loan to enable the Hunts to repay their short-term bank debts.

Volcker's action averted a financial crisis. But as a by-product it also spared the Hunts' creditors and the Hunts themselves the full penalty of their entrepreneurial error. Although the Hunts' personal losses probably exceeded $2 billion, and the restrictive terms of the rescue loan tied up their other assets, indignant congressmen charged Volcker with "bailing out" the Hunts. Their charge touched a raw nerve in the bosom of democratic capitalism that politicians were only too glad to deflect onto central bankers. It was hard to explain to the democratic body politic why rescuing big financial institutions, because of their unique ability to spread contagion, served the public good while the government failed to intervene to save ordinary businesses employing thousands. In the United States this tension always threatened to reawaken the barely dormant, passionate political divisions fought over money since the founding of the republic.

Economic observers were troubled by the Hunt "bailout" for its moral hazardous broadening of the lender of last resort safety net. "The Hunts was an odd instance where the lender of last resort intervened not at the conventional point to protect the banks, but elsewhere to head off the pressures before they got to the banks," Princeton Professor Peter Kenen explains. "The Fed knocked heads while holding their noses. One major brokerage house was in trouble, and there may have been Eurocurrency and Saudi involvement where they didn't know what the vulnerability was."

Volcker's willingness to brook the political and moral hazards in the Hunt case reflected his fear that widespread financial fragility might prematurely curtail his war on inflation. "Volcker knew that his monetary policy would have a big effect on business conditions and in turn on banks," says Michael Bradfield, Fed chief counsel. "He knew the impact it would have on the S&Ls. He saw that the speculative boom, when wrung out, would have important effects on stability. He used to tell us in 1981: 'We ain't seen nothing yet.' "

Volcker was "frustrated, to say the least, that the weakest link in the chain was the banking system, which was supposed to be the most prudent."[34] How much anti-inflation therapy could the system stand? Volcker was never sure.

•   •   •

While the Hunt debacle was unfolding in the markets, Volcker's practical monetarist therapy was knocked askew by a thrust from the political front: the imposition of the Carter administration's credit control program on March 14, 1980. Through credit controls, Carter hoped to seize the political initiative for national economic policy back from Volcker and boost his electoral prospects in November.

Awkwardly, it was the Fed alone that was empowered to implement controls proposed by a president. Volcker opposed controls. Nixon's credit controls had convinced him that they didn't attack the root problem, merely suppressed its symptoms temporarily. But a direct request from the White House was a political limitation, Fed statutory independence notwithstanding, that the central bank had to respect, just as it could not disregard the financial limitations imposed by the bond market. "It was an impossible clash with the president," says Solomon, who acted as intermediary. "If the Fed wouldn't administer it, if we were one hundred percent serious, we'd have to resign."

Although the credit control "program was designed not to be harsh by us," says the Fed's monetary policy staff chief Stephen Axilrod, the effects were unexpectedly dramatic. The economy, which had begun to falter, abruptly collapsed. In the second quarter, real GNP declined at a terrifying 9.4 percent rate. Unemployment leapt from 6.1 percent to 7.5 percent. The M1 money supply, whose annual target growth path was 4 percent to 6.5 percent, *shrank* by nearly 15 percent in April. All at once people were paying off their loans. As loan assets were struck from the banks' balance sheets, so too were the corresponding checking account deposit liabilities counted in M1.

If Volcker wished to remain faithful to the semiautomatic practical monetarist operating technique—and possibly to avert a full-fledged depression—the Fed had to allow interest rates to plummet in reaction. "Pragmatist" Henry Wallich and new New York Fed President Tony Solomon wanted to ease less than the amount indicated by the monetary rule to ensure that interest rates stayed high enough to suppress inflation expectations. But Volcker and the majority stuck to the rule.

As a result, the Fed Funds rate plunged wildly. In two months it fell an astounding nine percentage points to below 9 percent. Both short- and long-term interest rates dropped far below the 11 percent inflation rate—the Fed had lost control and unintentionally again engineered negative real interest rates!

By mid-May Volcker realized that the easing was going too far. The Fed began to backpedal on its new monetarist guidelines by injecting slightly fewer reserves than called for by the monetary rule. Finally, in June, credit controls were abandoned. In midsummer 1980 the central bankers witnessed the economy roar back in the quickest reversal in postwar history. But it was a terrible blow to Volcker's war on inflation. By August 1980 money growth was exploding at 22.8 percent—twice the inflation rate.

Precious credibility had been squandered. Volcker's first year had been lost. Volcker "never forgave himself for the quick easing in 1980."[35] We lost some psychological ground," Volcker concedes.[36]

The Breakthrough

From the fall of 1980 and the summer of 1982, Volcker relaunched the Fed's attack on inflation with a relentless, single-minded shock therapy treatment. His success would reshape U.S. and world political economy. But there were many victims.

The most prominent was President Carter. Normally central bankers strived to keep their profiles low during presidential election campaigns. But from September 1980 the Fed tightened sharply. On September 25 it raised the discount rate from 10 percent to 11 percent. By election day Fed Funds cost 14 percent—a rise of nearly four percentage points in the eight weeks Americans were making their presidential choice. President Carter fumed. He took public potshots at the Federal Reserve, to no avail.

Carter's defeat opened a rare lame duck window until Ronald Reagan's inauguration in January. Volcker exploited it by twice hiking the discount rate, to 13 percent. This loudly signaled the Fed's tough anti-inflation determination and helped push up Fed Funds to almost 20 percent. Banks' prime lending rate soared with it to a record 21.5 percent. The yield curve grew steeply inverted in November and would remain so for ten successive months—the harbinger of a classic Fed-induced recession.

The Fed's first major breakthrough in the war against inflation came on the exchange rate front—the dollar. The dollar took off when Volcker started his second assault on inflation. Interest rates concurrently were being lowered by the Bundesbank and Bank of Japan. Between July 1980 and mid-August 1981 the effective dollar exchange rate soared a record 34 percent.

The soaring dollar crushed inflation by reducing the cost of imported goods and by influencing psychological expectations about future inflation. These expectations became self-fulfilling as they encouraged more moderate wage settlements and business pricing decisions. Fed officials operated under the rule of thumb that a 10 percent increase in the dollar translated into a 1.5-percentage-point reduction in inflation, half directly through import prices and half indirectly, over three years.

The 34 percent rise in the dollar thus accounted for about a five-percentage-point fall in inflation. From 1980 through 1982 the U.S. inflation rate declined from 13.5 percent to 6.1 percent—or 7.4 percentage points. Over two-thirds of the fall in inflation, in other words, could be attributed initially to the rise of the dollar.

Volcker knew, however, that most disinflation dividends from dollar appreciation were borrowed. Economic laws dictated that most of the gains would be paid back automatically when the dollar fell. The dividends were permanent only to the extent that inflation expectations were reversed in the meantime.

U.S. central bankers were less fully cognizant until later that dollar appreciation had provided them as well with political borrowed time to press their war on inflation. This was a by-product of the new ways in which the global financial revolution caused monetary policy to affect the economy. As deregulated interest rates oscillated over a wider range, the fulcrum of monetary policy was shifting away from its heavy concentration on housing and consumer durables toward sectors exposed to international competition. Whenever the Fed pushed up interest rates to slow domestic growth, the tightening effect was partially offset by global capital inflows attracted by the higher interest rates. The dollar rose. U.S. exporters and import-competitors shouldered a heavier brunt of the monetary restraint through lost sales.

Over many previous postwar business cycles, the housing sector had become politically well organized. It quickly began lobbying whenever rising interest rates started to bite. The tradables sector, by contrast, had to organize its political lobbying campaign from the ground up. It became effective only in October 1982, when Caterpillar Chairman Lee Morgan, acting as head of the Business Roundtable, began pressing high government officials for policy relief for battered U.S. manufacturing exporters.

"We might have gotten more time, since monetary policy falls on a broader range of the economy," Volcker agrees. "It helped. Home builders got annoyed less quickly."

Volcker's war to uproot inflation psychology was hindered by two unpleasant surprises. The first was the huge Reagan budget deficits. Wall Street began to show signs of uneasiness with the new Republican government soon after Ronald Reagan took office in 1981. At first glance this seemed odd. Reagan was personally one of the most pro-business, fiscally conservative presidents in history. Having been tutored personally by Milton Friedman, he was a strong supporter of monetarist policies. Like Volcker, the new president had a stern, Calvinist attitude that past inflationary excesses had to be paid for with a painful period of cure. During the election campaign he'd even argued that the Fed hadn't been tough enough.

But to Wall Street there was an unreconcilable gap between the president's rhetoric and his concrete programs. Above all, Wall Street was conservative. It could do its math. The Reagan fiscal program was a hydra-headed mix of incompatible economic philosophies—supply-siders, monetarists, and traditional pragmatists. It called for tax cuts and increased defense spending—yet forecast a balanced budget. It predicted monetary restraint leading to falling inflation and buoyant economic growth simultaneously. To traditional economists all this looked like pie in the sky.

The circle could be squared only by faith in supply-side ideology that tax cuts would unshackle boundless entrepreneurial enterprise and growth. Reagan's main Republican primary challenger, new Vice President George Bush, had derisively labeled the supply-side prescription "voodoo economics." Wall Street agreed. Even Budget Director David Stockman soon distanced himself publicly from his own "rosy scenario" forecasts: "Our original forecast was not an exercise in economic analysis. It was a statistical argument between the various doctrinal sects. The numbers became the medium by which those contradictory doctrines were harnessed together."[37]

Wall Street foresaw huge federal budget deficits that in turn would lead to a titanic clash with the Federal Reserve's anti-inflation goals. Two outcomes seemed possible, both negative: either the Fed would back down and monetize the government deficits; or interest rates would soar as record government borrowing clashed with the Fed's tight monetary policy. Recession would ensue.

In the event, the second occurred. The U.S. and world economy of the 1980s was molded by the Olympian struggle between massive $200 billion U.S. fiscal deficits and Volcker's relentless struggle to break the inflationary spiral through monetary policy. That policy mix helped generate record high real interest rates, world recession, the LDC debt crisis, U.S. financial fragility, the superdollar, record external imbalances, and numerous innovations of the financial revolution.

Volcker's second unpleasant surprise was the fundamental flaws that emerged in the practical monetarist prescription. Volcker began to suspect that something was amiss following an abrupt surge in the March and April 1981 money supply figures. Financial deregulation and innovation—specifically the nationwide introduction of interest-bearing NOW checking accounts—was artificially swelling M1. Not all the money pouring into NOW accounts was going to be used for immediate transactions. Some was for savings and thus might not portend future inflation at all. If a given monetary aggregate couldn't be consistently defined, it confounded any prescriptive policy formula that was based upon it. From late 1980 to January 1983 the interest-bearing component of M1—a strong determinant of the public's willingness to hold M1—more than tripled from 6.5 percent to 22 percent.[38]

Wall Street, however, reacted to the money supply deviation by zealously bidding long-term interest rates sharply higher. Volcker had to choose between softening his commitment to the flawed monetary rule or sticking hard to it in order to demonstrate his anti-inflationary resolve to market cynics.

In May 1981 Volcker chose the latter course. The Fed tightened sharply. Fed Funds rate soared over three percentage points, surpassing 19 percent. Money supply growth from May to October 1981 fell to zero.

The tightening that started in May 1981 was the decisive turn in the inflation war. High positive real interest rates—the mechanism for punishing inflation speculators—emerged in the summer. When long-term interest rates hit 15 percent in October, inflation expectations punctured suddenly. Measured inflation collapsed faster than anyone anticipated, to about 5 percent. That meant real interest rates were suddenly an astonishingly high 10 percent. Savers enjoyed windfall profits. Borrowers, obversely, were driven to their knees by soaring debt burdens.

The crushing high real interest rates came as a massive shock to the U.S and world economy. In the fourth quarter of 1981 and first quarter of 1982, the U.S. GNP fell by over 5 percent. Unemployment rose to 8.6 percent. Instead of the widely predicted short recession, the unusual coincidence of U.S. recession and high real dollar interest rates dragged the rest of the world into its deepest downturn since the Great Depression.

Inflation fears were nevertheless rekindled by another unexpected 14 percent jump in the money supply from November 1981 to January 1982. In retrospect the money supply rebound turned out to be not a sign of overexpansion at all, but an unanticipated plunge in the velocity of money. In the recession, money was being spent more slowly than usual. When all the statistics were counted later, Volcker saw that the velocity of money circulation had abruptly departed from its postwar trend line and *declined* in 1982 by about 3 percent. In 1983 it fell 5 percent. This meant that more money was needed to sustain growth levels than the monetary rule prescribed. By trying to hold money supply within its targeted ranges, the Fed was accidentally starving the economy of the money it needed to pull out of the recession.

In early 1982 Volcker had to choose between the unexplained divergence in the signals emitted by the monetary rule and his practical reality checks. He was frustrated by the resiliency of inflation expectations in financial markets and the economy. Long-term interest rates had backed up by one percentage point at the jump in money supply. Wages, business's main variable cost, were still rising at a 7.1 percent annual rate, or a two-percentage-point premium over inflation.

One Monday afternoon at Basel, Volcker complained to fellow central bankers about the failure of inflation expectations to respond favorably to the Fed's monetary targetry. "Look at my money supply figures," he said.

"They are more stable than [Swiss National Bank President] Leutwiler's. Why do markets trust Leutwiler and not me?!"

Leutwiler assured him, "Eventually they will."[39]

In February 1982 Volcker decided to make sure: the FOMC set an M1 annual growth target of 2.5 percent to 5 percent. To achieve it, it aimed at 0 percent growth in the first quarter.[40]

In the next few weeks Fed Funds surged three percentage points. It was highly unusual for interest rates to rise sharply in a recession. It evoked screams of economic pain and political outrage. Yet it delivered the death blow for inflation and inflation expectations. But had it also killed the economy?

Chapter 11

Escape from the Abyss

Adherence to the flawed monetary rule nearly caused the Fed to accidentally engineer a full-fledged depression. U.S. manufacturers, already battered by the strong dollar, faced lasting structural damage. Unemployment soared past forecasts to 10.8 percent. The Reagan supply-side miracle never materialized. Instead it was deformed into the most radical Keynesian deficit-spending experiment in history.

Throughout the spring of 1982 Fed officials, like most economists, erringly believed the recovery to be much closer at hand and inflation more persistent than it actually was. The money-supply aggregates were still growing at the upper tolerances of their ranges, "yet everything else was telling you that this was no time to be tight."[1] In mid-May Volcker persuaded the FOMC to hang tough just a little while longer.

"There was an anguished intellectual struggle going on at the Fed in 1982 as the aggregates grew, and with every passing month the recession wore on," recalls Volcker's assistant at the time, Neal Soss.

One thing telling Fed Reserve Bank presidents and board governors not to be tight was the outcry from small-business people, home builders, auto dealers, retailers, farmers, manufacturing exporters, and unions. Businesses failed at a record pace. Farmers were doubly hurt: the strong dollar priced them out of many of their large export markets, while high real interest rates caused foreclosures on the land they had bought with inflation-cheapened debt in the 1970s. Home builders printed "Wanted" posters of the Fed's seven governors. Nasty and threatening letters arrived at the Fed. In December 1981 a frantic man armed with a sawed-off shotgun, revolver, and knife burst into the Fed and was stopped by guards just outside the boardroom of convened Fed governors, whom he intended to take hostage to publicize the agony they were inflicting on the country. Volcker reluctantly accepted Secret Service protection.

Congress echoed the outcry. Volcker tried to shield the Fed by pointing out that it was following the monetary rule Congress itself had urged. But as the 1982 midterm elections drew nearer, fewer congressmen cared about the market logic of M1 or their own theoretical consistency. They wanted just one thing—lower interest rates.

"Volcker's got his foot on our neck. And we've got to make him take it off," declared Senate Majority Leader Howard Baker (R-Tenn.) to Republican congressional leaders anxious about losing control of the Senate.[2]

Over the next several months, and reaching a zenith of intensity in the summer, Baker initiated a series of meetings with Volcker to communicate the importance of lower interest rates. "I smell danger," Baker warned Volcker.

"There was open hostility toward the Fed and Volcker in Congress," Baker says. "The system can stand only so much. The Fed was in danger of repeal of Fed independence. It was implicit that if the country goes into a depression, you lose your autonomy. As majority leader you have two special tools. You can get recognized on the floor before anyone else. More important, you can schedule legislation—what will go first and what will go last—to the Senate for a vote. There was enough legislation being drafted that I only had to stand out of the way. He pushed it to the very edge."

Supply-side Republican Representative Jack Kemp and liberal Democrat Henry Gonzalez led calls for Volcker's resignation. By August senior Democrat Robert Byrd introduced legislation commanding the Fed to reduce real interest rates to below 4 percent.

To Reagan Budget Director David Stockman, such castigation was demagogic cover-up. The failure of Congress and the administration to cut the budget deficits was the main culprit for the high real interest rates. "Politics is truly the art of indicting the innocent and rewarding the guilty. Baker and most of the Republican rank and file were hotly accusing the Fed for the traumatic disinflation now under way."[3]

While listening to Baker, Volcker conducted his own personal diplomacy with Congress. He knew the Fed had two key defenders in Republican Jake Garn and Democrat William Proxmire, ranking Senate Banking Committee members. By the time Byrd's legislation was introduced, the Fed had been easing for a month. The political steam dissipated. "Volcker would come up to talk to Proxmire five or six times a year," says Proxmire's top staffer, Kenneth McLean. "In 1982 Proxmire was a big supporter of tight money and defending Volcker against the unwashed populists. Volcker didn't shift until the summer of 1982. The Fed read the tea leaves in Congress correctly."

Although they strained to portray themselves as nonthreatening, nonpartisan technician-managers of the status quo, central bankers, like proverbial Supreme Court justices reading election returns, used their acute political antennae to intuit how far they could lean against the popular democratic winds. "Chairmen of the Federal Reserve," observes ex–Citibank Chairman Walter Wriston, "have traditionally been the best politicians in Washington. The Fed serves a wonderful function. They get beat up on by Congress and the administration. Everyone knows the game and everyone plays it. But no one wants their responsibility."

Democratic leaders tolerated central bankers' special unspoken role because they welcomed the depoliticization of money questions. Why? First, simply, money was too powerful a political tool ever to entrust entirely to an opposition party. However tempting it was to an ascendant Democratic political party to manipulate money for electoral interests, that temptation was partly counterbalanced by the fear of ever allowing its political opponents the same opportunity. A second reason that "[t]he Fed exists in a twilight zone of political accountability [is] because its role is to make choices that others deem necessary but don't wish to make publicly."[4] Such choices arose whenever political and economic logic clashed, notably when monetary policy had to be seriously tightened or a failing bank required a taxpayer bailout. For most politicians it was easier to leave the thankless, necessary decisions to the technocrats at the central bank—and then join in the popular outrage against them.

Nevertheless there existed a genuine threshold of political tolerance, which if breached would result in legislative abrogation of central bank autonomy. Such oversight constituted the ultimate mechanism of democratic accountability for central bankers. The political hue and cry exchanged through the press and the Fed chairman's regular legislative testimony were thus part of the ongoing dialogue between government and central bank that defined the range of acceptable monetary policies. When the main governing forces—legislative and executive branches, opposition and governing parties—were largely agreed, no central bank, however independent in statute, could go its own way. "The Federal Reserve has a loose kind of independence," describes ex–Secretary of State George Shultz. "It works well."

More worrisome to Volcker than Congress was pressure from the White House. "There is a check on congressional willingness to take interest rate responsibility from the Fed—it's a thankless job, and they know it," explains Tony Solomon. "Congressmen know if there were high interest rates and they were responsible, they'd be voted out of office or blamed for inflation. The real danger is that some stupid president and secretary of the Treasury would reach farther."

Volcker appreciated that through most of the disinflation campaign President Reagan refrained from personally attacking the Fed. Although the two men usually met very infrequently, Volcker sensed that "unlike some of his predecessors, he had a visceral aversion to inflation and an instinct that, whatever some of his advisers might have thought, it wasn't a good idea to tamper with the independence of the Federal Reserve, which, after all was said and done, was trying to restore stability."[5] Don Regan's Treasury, a hotbed of ideological supply-siders and monetarists, as well as bombastic personalities, wasn't similarly restrained.

Between Treasury and central bank there were natural institutional alliances. The two often joined in arguing for budgetary spending restraint and in representing the case to modify national policy for internationally agreed reasons.

Yet their disparate missions also caused them naturally to differ over whether interest rate policy should be tilted toward controlling inflation or spurring short-term growth, over how cheaply the government's debt should be financed, and over the currency exchange rate trade-off between inflation and exports. Finance ministers routinely wanted ten degrees more monetary ease than central bankers, urgently so at election time. They were usually ten degrees less sympathetic about undertaking politically unpopular financial rescues. "We [central bankers] are a fortunate group," says Bank of England Governor Robin Leigh-Pemberton. "We're not under the same steady gaze or pressure as politicians are. This allows us to make more objective appraisals than politicians."

Volcker and Regan, an ex–Merrill Lynch chairman who possessed an outsized ego to match Volcker's own, "met weekly for breakfast one on one." Says Regan, "We went over the economy, politics. We talked about our views on fiscal management, and he gave us his views on monetary policy. There were never any secret agreements between us. More often than not, surprisingly, we agreed. Only in public did we not always get along."

Regan was no ideologue. But his arguments shifted between the competing camps within the administration and Reagan's sometimes contradictory sentiments. "The splits in the administration ran deep," says Volcker. "They'd use three inconsistent arguments against you at the same time."[6]

President Reagan was consistent about one thing: he desired a *gradual* reduction in the money supply. This reflected the academic monetarist complaint that the Fed's futile efforts to "fine-tune" the economy by leaning against the wind were responsible for the needless busts and booms of the past.

When the recession deepened and the money supply continued on its volatile, zigzag route downward, the first public tangles between the administration and the Fed erupted.[7] Don Regan publicly likened the Fed to a golfer who sliced from one side of the fairway to the other yet managed to make par.[8] He dismissed Volcker's contention that deregulation, innovations, and unpredictable velocity shifts were responsible for the erratic swings in money supply as "seventy percent excuse and thirty percent reality."

Regan began to make thinly veiled threats to reform the Fed's independence by giving the Treasury secretary a place on the board. "The ultimate threat to the Fed independence is to have its budget integrated with the federal budget like all other agencies. But in the period we're talking about, no one talked about it," he says remorsefully.

On January 19, 1982, President Reagan criticized the Fed for the first time. Reagan suggested at a press conference that "stop-go" money growth was adding an inflation-uncertainty premium to interest rates and was retarding the long awaited capital spending boom predicted by his administration's supply-side tax cuts.

Volcker shot back a week later. He blamed the financing pressures from the first $100 billion–plus fiscal deficits for driving up real interest rates. The political battle for control of the nation's economic agenda—between disinflationary monetary policy and superstimulatory fiscal policy—had been joined.

Volcker employed to full effect the Fed's formidable public relations machine—one of the best in Washington. Through congressional testimony and the media, he so masterfully pounded away at the theme that the budget deficit was the main source of the nation's suffering that it became ingrained as a cardinal truth on editorial pages across America and on Capitol Hill. The Fed's army of Ph.D.s routed the Treasury's few research troops with technical scholarship that bolstered Volcker's political position. It was a vivid use of the Fed's technocratic persona for political advantage, an art once described by Fed Chairman William McChesney Martin Jr. as using staff research the way a drunk uses a lamppost—not for illumination, but for support.

The result was a hands-down Fed victory. "In a town like Washington, where everyone either has a white hat or a black hat, Volcker was a white hat," Regan says, sighing. "On the Hill there was such a great mismatch of Volcker's performance against the quality of the questions asked of him. It became accepted that he was a guru on economic policy."

Volcker's shock therapy prescription triumphed politically over its administration and congressional critics who called for a less painful, gradualist inflation cure. "Gradualism is usually a semantic excuse for doing nothing," Volcker says dismissively. "And politically, no one would have believed it if it was going on forever."

Even gradualist Milton Friedman conceded that gradualism rarely could be implemented rigorously enough in democracies: "[T]he balance of recent evidence, I must confess, is rather on the side of those who favor a shock treatment."[9] Wall Street veterans like Treasury Undersecretary George Gould likewise believed that to exorcise inflation expectations, "you had to hit them with a sledgehammer, especially for a cynical bunch like Wall Street."

The most important political support for Volcker's harsh policies came from an apparently surprising source. "It was the middle class in the United States who saved our asses on monetary policy in the 1982 recession," says one of Volcker's closest Fed associates. In a 1983 poll, 64 percent of Americans said they were willing to endure tighter Fed monetary policy and slower economic growth again if necessary to contain inflation.[10] The Fed, though unelected, was able to reach beyond its government critics, to win the endorsement of the broad middle-class democratic electorate. Why?

Simply put, the central bank was perceived as honestly doing the distasteful work of imposing the necessary austerity to rectify America's foremost economic problem while the administration and Congress stalemated in fantastic economic theories and ever grander fiscal profligacy. "It's the middle class who lose real wealth when there is inflation," explains a Volcker associate. "The rich can protect themselves. Forget the poor, they're murdered in all cases, it's hopeless. It was the rich who were after our heads in 1981–82."

This view ran contrary to the conventional wisdom, which saw inflation as rewarding the borrower class at the expense of savers. But that was true only up to the point that inflation psychology took root. At that moment savers, using and inspiring financial innovations, began to find investment strategies, such as inflation-indexed instruments, that enabled them to protect the real value of their assets from rising prices. The best opportunities accrued to the wealthiest. The smallest savers—the vast middle class—were hardest hit. This threshold was crossed during the late 1970s.

The popular support for Volcker's harsh disinflation campaign refuted central bankers' alleged lack of democratic accountability. "Central bankers, by taking unpopular measures, become popular with the man in the street," says former Swiss National Bank President Fritz Leutwiler. "The people *hate* inflation. I was popular because the public knew that I knew what I was talking about—something you can't always say about politicians. Independence was what gave me and [Bundesbank President] Pöhl and Volcker such a strong position."

"Generally the Fed cannot win a public confrontation with the government," says Volcker. "Although the Fed could have won battles during the Reagan years on particular issues."

As the recession deepened in early 1982, Volcker began to sense that the Fed was reaching the political limits of its drastic disinflation therapy. The White House was angrily "blaming Volcker for the recession," remembers Don Regan. "I was not happy because they stayed tight for too long. They should have eased in early 1982. Stockman claimed he was undone by this—the Fed prolonged the recession, which reduced tax income, and that's why his [deficit] projections were wrong. On a number of occasions I thought I had indications from Volcker that they were going to ease. This caused me to report this to the president and that we'd get more growth sooner."

As the election drew closer, White House Chief of Staff Jim Baker and Senate Majority Leader Howard Baker tried to entice Volcker to cut interest rates by promising strong steps, including tax increases, to cut the budget deficit. Volcker listened, hinted, but promised nothing.

In the event, the budget deficit reduction package hammered out in mid-August by Congress and the White House was a momentous juncture in U.S. economic policy. Republicans felt swindled by the Democrats, who didn't deliver on their promised spending cuts. U.S. fiscal policy became effectively paralyzed by partisan politics for the rest of the 1980s. It was political failure on a grand scale. Yet national politics went on as usual, revealing the democratic political deficit behind the fiscal one.

Responsibility for governing the economy fell totally to the Fed. With power came blame. As the misery unfolded on a scale not experienced since the Depression, the inequities embedded in the political economy were more painfully exposed. But monetary policy was a blunt instrument, incapable of targeting compensation for one group or another. It was an imperfect substitute for fiscal immobility.

As the political limits of the monetary austerity were approached, congressional and administration voices came together in chorus to demand that the Fed abandon practical monetarism and free itself to lower interest rates. Included among them was Don Regan. "I told him [Volcker] over the summer and before to get more consistency—in terms of *interest rates*. I wanted them way down. I said, 'I don't care what you use as a guide.' My fear was that I saw $200 billion deficits coming."

By that time Volcker had already eased—but primarily for a different reason. Starting in the spring of 1982, a series of financial tremors revealed that the system's tolerance for austerity was fracturing.

At the Edge of Financial Fragility

The first big crack came on May 17, 1982. A small government bond dealer, Drysdale Government Securities, was unable to pay $160 million in interest due on government securities it had borrowed from Chase Manhattan and other big banks. Chase had borrowed the securities in turn from others. When Drysdale failed to pay back, Chase claimed it was merely a middleman with no responsibility itself to pay the $160 million to the original dealers.

The market panicked. Bond and bank share prices fell sharply. Rumors swirled about the viability of some major securities dealers. Clearing and settlements of U.S. government securities began to seize up.

Volcker dispatched Jerry Corrigan to New York from an FOMC meeting. Corrigan persuaded Chase to pay the disputed interest and to litigate the case later. The Fed helped restore normalcy with lender of last resort support.

A more dire crisis erupted a month later with the collapse of small "go-go" Penn Square Bank, whose loans were riddled with fraud and concentrated heavily in the Oklahoma energy business that went sour in the recession. Penn Square mattered because it was enmeshed with the mushrooming U.S. and global bank network of managed liabilities and off-balance-sheet risk. Penn Square had grown fast by selling participations in $2 billion of its loans to some of the nation's largest banks. Continental Illinois, the nation's seventh largest bank, had over $1 billion in Penn Square loan participations. Seattle First National Bank had $400 million. Chase Manhattan had $212 million. Each had relied primarily on Penn Square's credit judgment. If Penn Square went bust, these banks would take huge losses. They would have to retrench their lending and perhaps might themselves fail.

The crisis broke ahead of the July 4, 1982, weekend, when Penn Square ran out of money. The three main U.S. federal bank regulators—the Comptroller, the Federal Deposit Insurance Corporation, and the Fed—huddled to try to understand the problem's dimensions and what to do about it. Volcker argued for exploring bailout options, such as an FDIC capital infusion, against the others' instincts to close the bank. His main fear was Continental Illinois. Continental held $6 billion of the deposit base of 2,300 small banks that made loans from the Appalachians to the Rockies. A Continental failure would push the Midwest, perhaps the entire country, into depression.

Continental was also dependent on borrowing billions of dollars each day from global money markets to fund its loan portfolio. Rumors of imminent failure could dry up that funding overnight and become self-fulfilling.

Treasury Deputy Secretary Tim McNamar got a firsthand taste that weekend, as news of Penn Square's trouble circulated. At 10:00 P.M. he received a phone call from the U.S. Treasury attaché in Tokyo: "The Japanese are passing on Chase Manhattan CDs [certificates of deposit] due to some oil loans. They have questions if Chase is in trouble." In the middle of the night McNamar was awakened by a call from the U.S. embassy in Saudi Arabia: "We understand that Chase has collapsed. Is that true?" Soon came the Treasury attaché in Germany: "What's this we hear about Seafirst and Chase? No one wants their CDs. They have to pay up on the going rate." Next on the line was London. "By that time," says McNamar, "they had all three names."

He observes, "You put all these kids who trade on the money and foreign exchange desks together with CNN and you understand the world. This is the kind of world we live in. It was *not* that kind of world at the start of the 1980s. It means that central bankers are more important—but they have less influence because global capital markets take it away."

An FDIC bailout was rejected by its chairman, William Isaac, who didn't want the FDIC to foot the bill. He also wanted to teach the bankers and institutional investors a lesson in free market accountability. If they lost money on Penn Square, then next time they'd be more careful. Volcker, of course, agreed with this principle. He simply felt the stakes were too great to apply it. In the end, however, Volcker could find no viable way to save the bank.

Treasury Secretary Don Regan rendered the final decision in Volcker's office on July 5. Penn Square would be allowed to fail.

Through the summer 1982 top U.S. officials watched nervously as Continental Illinois was forced to offer up to one percentage point more on its CDs. In early August its chairman flew to Wyoming to explain to Volcker, who was on a fishing holiday, that Continental needed urgent Fed support. Continental ultimately survived until 1984. Seafirst lasted only until 1983.[11]

Volcker's anxieties about Penn Square paled before his fears about the brewing debt crisis in Mexico. About $30 billion of Mexico's $80 billion in foreign loans was owed to U.S. banks. If Mexico defaulted, the nine largest U.S. banks could lose nearly *half* their total capital—the cushion separating them from insolvency—and be forced to sharply retrench their lending. Brazil, Argentina, and other heavy Latin American debtors could be in trouble, too, although even Volcker in July 1982 was not fully cognizant of their parlous conditions.

The $540 billion LDC debt crisis, reported in Part Three, would for the next five years tax Volcker's energies and skills. It threatened to bankrupt the U.S.'s largest banks and toss the world economy into depression. Mexico made even free marketeer Don Regan blanch. "The last thing we needed to pull ourselves out of a recession was a banking crisis. That would have happened if Mexico defaulted."

The 1982 financial crisis, in part an inevitable by-product of Volcker's disinflation shock therapy, was the tip of an iceberg of chronic financial fragility that menaced economic growth and the Fed's disinflation gains throughout the decade. "It is true and undeniable that Volcker's single-minded policy to break inflationary psychology caused more problems in the banking system, with the LDCs, not to mention the S&Ls, than the Fed realized," says the Treasury's George Gould.

Senior Fed and Treasury officials became accustomed to making policy always looking over their shoulders for financial distress. In early 1982 Deputy Treasury Secretary Tim McNamar spurred the setting up of a top secret interagency task force, on which Volcker participated personally, that examined what would happen if oil prices fell sharply. It produced a classi- fied May 23, 1983, study entitled "Impacts of Declining Oil Prices." So ex- plosive were its conclusions—it very accurately predicted the *order* in which big energy-lending Texas banks would fail during the 1986 crisis, as well as the collapse of the Soviet economy—that its very existence was long denied. "It has been like a war here with the LDCs, the Texas banks, Penn Square, Continental, Crocker, Dome Petroleum, and the S&Ls," said the late William Taylor, Fed staff director for banking supervision and regulation.

On June 30 in the midst of the Penn Square crisis and on the very same day the Fed made its second secret overnight loan to Mexico, the FOMC con- vened for a two-day meeting in an atmosphere of pessimism and gloom. De- spite the continuing deep slide of the U.S. economy and evidence of fragility, the key monetary aggregates were still rising at the upper end of their long- run ranges.

With every intuition and real economic indicator telling him that the United States was on the edge of an economic catastrophe, Volcker at last ig- nored the monetary rule. The FOMC voted for a major easing. "[B]y the summer of 1982 the financial fabric of the United States itself was showing clear signs of strain," Volcker explains. "All that contributed to the timing of our decision to ease policy."[12]

The harsh disinflation squeeze was over. The Fed Funds rate plunged from 14 percent to 11 percent by the end of July. By mid-December 1982 it was down to 8.8 percent. Between July and December the Fed cut the dis- count rate seven times.

Yet the economy failed to rebound. In the third quarter it contracted 3.2 percent. With unemployment and business and bank failures running at a post-1930s peak, the Fed's December 15, 1982, "Green Book" economic analysis, prepared for each FOMC meeting, concluded that the economy was continuing to sink in the fourth quarter.[13]

Volcker desperately wanted growth. Growth was the tonic that could heal financial fragility, restore business confidence, create jobs and income for the unemployed, expand productive economic capacity, build national sav- ings, and reduce the federal budget deficit.

By the October 5 FOMC meeting, Volcker could no longer finesse the di- vergence between the real economy and the monetarist operating technique. From August, M1 had again exploded. Over the next three quarters it rose at a 15 percent annual growth rate. Volcker, however, didn't want to appear to be abandoning the monetary rule altogether for fear of reviving inflationary market psychology and of disuniting the FOMC: "There was more rigidity [in the monetarist approach] than I wanted in the first place. Not only by the market, which followed every turn in the M's, but also by board members who became holier than the pope."

Volcker now faced one of the most artful challenges in the central banking confidence game: having elucidated a policy everyone believed was antiinflationary, to credibly explain why it was impossible to follow it precisely at any given moment.

On October 5, 1982, Volcker proposed, and the FOMC accepted, his solution: The Fed would temporarily deemphasize the M1 target because of the unpredictable impact of $36 billion in maturing all-savers certificates and the introduction of bank money market deposit accounts in December 1982. This conjunctional technical explanation was valid. But it disguised the historic abandonment of the Fed's practical monetarist experiment. It was a typical central banker ploy of falling back on a technical explanation few would understand—or, among those who did, would wish to challenge.

Volcker vetoed the suggestion of Fed public affairs director Joseph Coyne that the Fed call a press conference to announce its policy change. Instead it was downplayed as a purely procedural change.

Wall Street celebrated with a huge bond and equity market rally. Inflation expectations remained quiescent: long-term interest rates continued to track the decline in the Fed Funds rate—falling 3.5 percentage points to about 10.5 percent in the second half of the year. Inflation for 1982 fell to 6.1 percent. In 1983 it would be only 3.2 percent.

Wall Street's rally from mid-August was the kickoff to the great global bull market run that lifted the New York Stock Exchange 200 percent until Black Monday, October 19, 1987. It inaugurated the worldwide securities market boom that moved the financial revolution into high gear.

In hindsight it signaled too the bottoming out of the recession in the fourth quarter. Only in looking back to the depths of late 1982, with the economy flat on its back and the U.S. and world financial system teetering, could one appreciate how close to the edge Volcker had pushed his disinflation campaign before pulling back.

Wall Street's celebratory reaction represented a crucial restoration of central bank credibility and a remarkable personal apotheosis of Paul Volcker. From that day on, faith in Paul Volcker's personal judgment became the new standard of anti-inflation credibility with world financial markets. Volcker acquired a political stature unparalleled for a central banker. A 1982 survey by *U.S. News & World Report* ranked Volcker behind only President Reagan as the second most influential American.[14] Even that was too low for economic commentator Robert J. Samuelson: "For the past eighteen months, Paul Volcker has been the most important man in the world."[15]

The prevailing historical view on Wall Street and Washington was that

Volcker was responsible for much of what went right economically for the first Reagan administration. "What economic success there was had almost nothing to do with our original supply-side doctrine," admits Budget Director Stockman. "Instead Paul Volcker and the business cycle had brought inflation down and economic activity surging back. . . . Paul Volcker will surely go down as the greatest Federal Reserve chairman in history for the masterful and courageous way he purged the American and world economy of runaway inflation. This success turned out to require the traditional, painful, costly cure of a deep recession, but it took all that Volcker brought to the task—a strong will, an incisive mind, and a towering personal credibility—to see it through."[16]

The U.S. central bank now stood at the apex of an evolving power and independence unanticipated by its framers and wholly unimaginable to America's founding fathers. The Fed's forerunners, the First Bank of the United States (1791–1811), and the Second Bank of the United States (1816–1836) had been the objects of a divisive controversy between the Federalists and the decentralist Jeffersonians and Jacksonians over the political control of money. For three-quarters of a century the United States did without a central bank. Private banks issued their own currencies; some, known as "wildcat" banks, made their paper notes redeemable into gold or silver only at arduously reached remote locations. State and federal government currencies were issued, too.

But money did not manage itself—at least not well. The economy suffered from the inelasticity of the money supply: the rigid linkage between the quantity of money and the limited stock of gold, silver, or government bonds caused wide interest rate swings with seasonal farm and business cycle borrowing demand increases. Western agrarian populists raged that hard-money eastern bankers were nailing them to a "cross of gold." Finally, a series of financial panics and recessions, culminating in the banking Panic of 1907, became intolerable to both government and markets.

The creation of a central bank was advocated by both parties in the 1912 presidential election—although whether it should be controlled by private interests or by the government was fiercely argued. The Populists feared that the Fed was a bankers' conspiracy for hard money. They wanted a decentralized central bank firmly under government control. The bankers feared such a central bank would subject them to unwanted political control and end in the debasement of money. They wanted a strongly centralized central bank controlled by the private sector.

When Woodrow Wilson defeated William Taft, firm federal government control seemed assured. Under Wilson, the Federal Reserve was constituted as a system of twelve semiprivate Reserve Banks overseen by the government-controlled seven-person board, which set the discount rate. The Trea-

sury secretary chaired the Federal Reserve Board meetings. No sooner had
the Fed first convened in 1914 than the hard-money banker minority on the
board began to complain about political control.

While these Washington political machinations took center stage, the
practical issue of Fed independence was being quietly shaped elsewhere—in
the Federal Reserve Banks closest to the financial markets and especially at
the New York Fed, whose regional banks held the lion's share of the nation's
deposits. When the Federal Reserve Bank presidents began trading in Treasury securities in order to earn a profit for their member banks and to support the World War I effort, they saw that they could alter financial
conditions—accelerating or slowing economic growth in the process. Open
market operations were thus inadvertently discovered.

Soon the Federal Reserve Bank presidents formed a committee to help
coordinate their trading, the forerunner of the FOMC. In late 1923, the Reserve Bank presidents mitigated a recession by buying government securities to expand the money supply and reduce interest rates. For the first time
contracyclical monetary policy—the hallmark of twentieth-century central
banking—was employed in America. The Board's role became secondary. It
was a palace coup by the private sector, which held the majority in nominat-
ing the Reserve Bank presidents.

Conflicts between Federal Reserve Bank open market operations and the
Board's discount rate policies undermined the Fed's effectiveness in managing the late 1920s speculative stock exchange bubble and in averting the ensuing banking crisis and Great Depression. The depression precipitated a
political overhaul of the banking system and a reform aimed at reasserting
greater Washington control of the Fed. The 1935 Banking Act created the
FOMC in its present form, which gave the voting majority to the Board governors. As balm for bankers, the Treasury secretary, the strongest symbol of
political control, was entirely dissociated from the Fed.

The 1935 reform triggered a fifteen-year power struggle for great monetary policy autonomy from the Treasury by Fed chairmen. From October
1936 an uneasy truce was maintained through informal weekly lunchtime
economic discussions between the Fed chairman and Treasury secretary—
by now a half-century-old custom. De facto Fed independence started with
the famous Treasury–Federal Reserve Accord of 1951, which freed the Fed
from the presumed obligation to finance the government debt at the Trea-
sury-set interest rates. The accord was negotiated following a remarkable
confrontation between President Harry Truman and the entire FOMC at the
White House on January 31, 1951. The day after the meeting, Truman announced that the FOMC had agreed to support all Treasury debt financings.
FOMC members were livid—they had agreed to no such thing. They considered mass resignation. Instead they responded with a Washington guerrilla

campaign of press leaks and backroom lobbying, which, with congressional support, finally produced the accord.

The man who negotiated the accord for the Treasury's side, William Mc-Chesney Martin Jr., soon took over as Fed chairman. He nurtured the Fed's independence until it became the accepted political norm. In December 1965, Martin, suspecting that the White Huose was hiding a spiral in Vietnam War costs, brooked a confrontation with President Lyndon Johnson by engineering a Fed discount rate increase, In hindsight, Martin failed to tighten monetary policy enough to offset Johnson's fiscal spending excesses. This set the stage for the breakout of inflation in the 1970s. Under Martin's successors Arthur Burns and William Miller, the Fed failed to prevent inflation from accelerating. Failure undercut the Fed's best justification for independence.

Volcker's successful crusade against inflation, by contrast, elevated the independent stature of the Fed and all central banks. Volcker reigned almost as a second sovereign power. He was even solicited for meetings by foreign heads of state, among them British Prime Minister Margaret Thatcher.[17]

Consolidating the Gains

Volcker's triumph over inflation may have redounded to the popularity of the Reagan government, but the Fed chairman's hero status also made him a potential political danger to the White House. In spring 1983 Reagan officials debated whether a powerful and independent Fed chairman could be trusted to manage monetary policy to maximize growth through the 1984 presidential election. At issue was whether to renominate Volcker as Fed chairman when his term expired in August.

Treasury Secretary Don Regan led the naysayers, supported by monetarists and antitax ideologues from the Republican right wing who regarded Volcker as the bogeyman who had undermined the Reagan Revolution's supply-side promises. Volcker's less influential supporters were mostly from the pragmatic mainstream.[18]

But Volcker had an ace in the hole—financial markets. In May 1983 fully 77 percent of 702 Wall Street investors polled affirmed him as their first choice; the runner-up, mainstream Wall Street economist Alan Greenspan, got less than 6 percent.[19] Throughout the spring, the nation's most influential financiers bent the ears of senior Reagan administration officials lobbying on behalf of Volcker.

Reagan's men were unable to propose an alternative who was satisfactory politically both to them and to Wall Street. Following a one-on-one meeting with President Reagan on June 6, Volcker won the key endorsement of White House Chief of Staff James Baker. Baker had grown to think that the supply-siders and monetarists opposing Volcker were too ideological to be trusted politically. Baker also feared that the LDC debt crisis that Volcker was then managing might explode if he was replaced. Volcker's gloomy nature colored his economic judgment, Baker thought, but he was at bottom a pragmatic man with whom he, Baker, could work. That tipped the balance.

On June 18 Reagan announced Volcker's reappointment. "We didn't reappoint Volcker," complained a Treasury official. "The markets reappointed Volcker."[20]

At the FOMC meeting of May 24, Volcker acted to restrain the recovery by nudging up interest rates. Having deflated inflation and inflation expectations at such a painful cost, he was determined to achieve the second phase of his disinflation goal—consolidation. In the past the Fed had always waited until it could see the whites of inflation's eyes before tightening up. Volcker believed this was what had caused the Fed to chronically slip behind the inflation expectations power curve. Although the FOMC's decision to tighten was made two weeks prior to Volcker's meeting with Reagan, Volcker was able to avert negative fallout at the White House by exploiting the six-week lag until the FOMC's decision became public.

Most economic forecasts for 1983 had predicted a modest recovery. But Volcker was intuitively uneasy about how much extra kick might come from the Reagan tax cuts and huge budget deficits. Volcker narrowly overcame opposition to the tightening from FOMC members who feared it might prematurely abort the recovery, as well as from inflation hawks such as Henry Wallich and Tony Solomon, who worried that adding to the record high real interest rates of 6 percent to 8 percent could detonate the LDC debt crisis and worsen the crushing toll the soaring dollar was taking on U.S. manufacturing. In the next two months interest rates were nudged up by one percentage point.

Why were real interest rates so high? Wall Street offered three main explanations: First were anxieties about the inflationary consequences of the $200 billion federal budget deficit forecast for 1983. Second were uncertainties about the widespread financial fragility, which could compel an inflationary bailout. Third was increased volatility, one of the main defining characteristics of the new deregulated, fully-floating global financial marketplace. To protect themselves, market investors demanded a larger safety cushion.

In the event, Volcker's intuitions proved correct. Data later confirmed that the economy had been exploding far faster than anyone forecast. Notwithstanding the record high real interest rates, growth in the second quarter was an astonishing 9.3 percent!

After cooling in the latter half of 1983, the economy began to rev up at a torrid pace in early 1984. Now the political fishbowl of presidential electoral politics complicated Volcker's work. On February 15, 1984, Volcker was summoned to the White House to meet President Reagan. The message was that the administration wanted uninterrupted growth for the election, even if that meant erring on the side of easy money. Democrats, meanwhile, insisted just as forcefully that Volcker resist the White House pressure. To show they meant business, congressional Democrats blocked legislation by Republican Jack Kemp (N.Y.) to rein in Fed independence.

The main culprit for the overheating and lopsided recovery was the swollen federal budget deficits. In 1983 it was $203 billion or 5.6 percent of GNP. When the divided government failed to reduce the rate of national debt growth below that of GNP growth during the cyclical recovery, the huge budget deficits became structural. In 1984, 1985, and 1986, the deficit continued to average $200 billion or above 5 percent of GNP.

Such deficits made a travesty of the Reagan Revolution and were a source of embarrassment to a president who had spent a career calling for balanced budgets. They also worsened two U.S. economic weaknesses. They consumed too much of the low national savings and left too little for the productivity-lifting business investment needed to create the next generation of American's wealth. Between 1983 and 1988 America's net national savings rate fell to an average 2.5 percent from the 6.5 percent that prevailed over the previous fifteen years. About 70 percent of the decline was the result of dissavings represented by the federal budget deficit.[21] With lower net savings on which to draw, U.S. net investment, which had averaged 7 percent of GNP annually since World War II, was squeezed down to only 5 percent from 1983 to 1988. Reagan supply-siders had promised that their program would raise U.S. savings and boost investment.

To compensate for the dearth of U.S. savings without cutting living standards, America borrowed 14 percent of the total net savings of foreign industrial countries between 1983 to 1988. Such borrowing transformed the United States from the world's largest creditor nation to its largest debtor with astonishing speed. It occurred through the record sale of U.S. financial assets, companies, and real estate to foreigners as well as foreign asset sales by Americans. The huge foreign capital inflows boosted the dollar and gave a huge fillip to the sale of imported goods in the United States. This was reflected in the swing in the U.S. international current account balance from a small surplus in 1980 to a deficit well over $100 billion from 1984 for the rest of the decade—a huge 3 percent of GNP. "[T]he 'miracle' of supply-side economics has now been revealed: foreigners supplied many of the goods and most of the money," commented one critic. "If the policies of the 1960s and 1970s were 'spend and tax,' the policies of the 1980s were 'spend and borrow.' "[22]

In early 1984 Volcker gloomily warned Congress that "we simply can't afford to become addicted to drawing on increasing amounts of foreign savings to help finance our domestic economy. Part of our domestic economy—that part dependent on exports or competing with imports—would be sacrificed.

"The stability of the dollar and our domestic financial markets would become hostage to events abroad. If recovery is to proceed elsewhere, as we want, other countries will increasingly need their own savings. While we don't know when, at some point the process would break down."[23]

Fiscal paralysis confronted the Fed with a big policy dilemma. The overheating economy had pushed inflation up from 6 percent to 6.5 percent and was threatening to reignite inflation expectations. Wall Street's nervousness was reflected in the one-percentage-point rise in long-term interest rates in six weeks. But if the Fed tried to cool inflation by further raising interest rates, it would drive up the superdollar, whose earlier boon to disinflation was becoming a depression for the U.S. manufacturing and farm economy.

At the March 26–27, 1984, FOMC meeting, Volcker determined that the incipient inflation risk had to take precedence: "I thought it was destructive that the dollar went up so much. But I couldn't do anything that wouldn't require me to loosen monetary policy to such a degree that it would risk being excessive. That was too high a price to pay."[24]

Yet financial fragility made Volcker unwilling to tighten as hard as some FOMC members desired. Even in a recovery, banks were failing at post-Depression records. At Volcker's suggestion the FOMC raised the Fed Funds ceiling guideline from 10 percent to 11.5 percent—indicating a willingness for interest rates to rise gradually by 1.5 percentage points. Short-term interest rates rose immediately by one-half percentage point. On April 6 the board bumped up the discount rate to 9 percent.

Reagan's men were furious. At a private dinner James Baker exploded that Paul Volcker was "double-crossing" him. In Baker's mind there'd been a bargain: "down payment" on a meaningful deficit reduction package in exchange for easy money. The fact that the White House's modest proposal was not yet enacted, and would be scaled back sharply when it was, didn't blunt Baker's fiercely expressed sentiment.[25]

In early May the administration began to jawbone Volcker on interest rates with anonymously sourced newspaper stories. On May 9 Treasury Secretary Regan publicly attacked the Fed for risking to toss the United States back into recession. "I knew that if they didn't ease up soon, we could get a recession," he explains. "Amid all the fragility, it would have caused another recession, in my opinion. By October 1984 we would end up with the worst of all worlds politically since Ronald Reagan was up for reelection."

While Regan and Volcker didn't discuss politics, "we did debate the economic issues, which was between having the economy slow down and hyperinflation, which was Volcker's worry. Volcker was looking at our deficits, and he didn't like our tax package. We almost choked off the recovery before it spread internationally and before it had a chance to reach all the sectors of our economy. We just squeezed by."

The administration's attacks proved ill timed. At just that moment, U.S. and world financial markets were rocked by a large crack in $40 billion Continental Illinois bank. Fears of systemic financial fragility broke to the surface. Exacerbated by the political attack on the Fed, interest rates lurched up sharply. The stock market fell.

The political implications of a financial crisis were ominous. The White House quickly called off its Fed bashing.

The Continental Illinois crisis was triggered by a global electronic run on its deposits. The run began in Tokyo on Wednesday, May 9, while it was nighttime at Continental's Chicago headquarters. It started with groundless rumors of Continental's imminent bankruptcy, reported over the Reuters newswire on Tuesday. Next day Commodity News Service filed a report of rumors that a major Japanese bank might buy Continental in a rescue. JiJi Press, one of Japan's two big wire services, picked up the story. But it mistranslated the word *rumors* as "disclosure." When Japanese money managers read the mistranslated story in the *Nihon Keizai Shimbun,* Japan's large financial newspaper, they concluded that Continental was failing.[26] What started as untrue that morning quite nearly became a self-fulfilling expectation by evening.

Large Japanese institutions began to dump Continental certificates of deposit before Japanese regulatory authorities and senior bank executives knew what was happening. Panicked traders on the money desk simply stampeded—until no one dared buck the momentum. The run proceeded with furious force when the European financial markets opened. By the time Continental executives got to their offices on Thursday morning, they discovered that their bank was hemorrhaging funds. They were powerless to stop it. Without those funds they would have to default on financial obligations due that day.

Volcker's nightmare in the July 1982 Penn Square debacle was coming true. About half the $1.1 billion in problem loans with which Penn Square had saddled Continental turned out to be a total loss. In addition, Continental had $1.2 billion in other problem loans and more than $1 billion exposure

to troubled LDC debtors that U.S. regulators didn't dare "classify" as problematic for fear of puncturing one of the accounting myths needed to sustain
management of the debt crisis. For a long time banking industry lore had it
that Continental was a paragon "go-go" bank, cunningly exploiting the
growth opportunities opened up by the financial revolution. The revealed reality was that its fast growth and superior book profitability had been
achieved by taking higher, even reckless risks. Instead of acting like a
paragon, Continental demonstrated what could go wrong in the new world
of unregulated global finance.

By May 1984 Continental depended heavily on the international interbank market to meet its daily $8 billion funding needs. Within three days of
the global run, half its funding vanished. And Continental was paying up to
one percentage point more than other banks for the other half, which cut into
its profit. To compensate for the lost funds, Continental increased its borrowing from the discount window at the Chicago Fed from $850 million to $3.6
billion. By May 16 it rose to $4.7 billion.

To try to halt the run, Comptroller of the Currency C. Todd Conover issued a carefully worded statement on Thursday denying the JiJi report. But
the statement carried little credibility with markets. The last time the government had issued such a statement was a decade earlier, with Franklin National Bank. Franklin had soon failed.

On Friday, May 11, the FDIC's William Isaac and Todd Conover huddled
in Paul Volcker's office to contemplate their options. Besieged by the 1980s'
financial distress, America's top regulators had already worked out a general
contingency approach to a major crisis. The FDIC would infuse capital into
the bank on an interim basis until a lasting rescue could be fashioned. All
depositors, not just those covered by the FDIC insurance ceiling, would be
protected. If things got really bad, the Fed would flood the markets with
money. The FDIC even had the documents prepared. The names simply had
to be filled in.[27]

Unlike Penn Square, where only the insured depositors were protected,
Continental seemed far too dangerous to Isaac and Conover for them to dare
enforce the free market implications of the deposit insurance regulations. In
addition to triggering a midwestern banking crisis and depression, a Continental failure could cause domestic and international interbank markets, the
lifeline of bank management liability operations, to dry up for all but the tiny
handful of the world's blue chip banks. That could trigger a worldwide liquidity panic. "The whole thing would implode as interbank transactions
halted," Alan Greenspan explained. "Treasury bill rates would fall sharply as
depositors rushed to more secure assets. Rates on bank CDs would rise
sharply. As the cost of money to the banks went up, so would the prime rate.
Borrowing would slow. Long-term bond yields would rise. . . . We could run

a scenario that we haven't seen for fifty years, an old-fashioned banking crisis."[28]

One last-ditch effort to avert a regulatory bailout was tried on May 14, when sixteen leading U.S. banks, which shared an enlightened self-interest in arresting the spread of Continental's instability, extended the bank a jumbo $4.5 billion, thirty-day credit line. The credit line was facilitated by Volcker's comforting wink and nod that the Fed held $17 billion in assets from Continental as collateral to secure its discount window borrowing.

But the global run on Continental continued. Volcker and the other government regulators, with the cooperation of the private banks, crafted the largest banking bailout in U.S. history. Announced on Thursday, May 17, it featured a $2 billion capital infusion into Continental by the government and private banks and, most controversially, an extension of the FDIC's limited deposit guarantee to *all* Continental depositors and general creditors.[29]

FDIC insurance, created in the 1930s, was intended to prevent banking runs by protecting small domestic depositors. But safety concepts that had been designed largely to prevent the banking panics among ordinary people had become obsolete in the high-speed, institutional panics that marked twenty-four-hour electronic, integrated financial markets. Some 85 percent of Continental's deposits exceeded the official $100,000 FDIC insurance ceiling. Unless the large and foreign depositors were covered by the U.S. taxpayer guarantee, they'd flee Continental—and every other big U.S. bank rumored to be in trouble. The result would be a U.S. and global liquidity crisis.

The Continental bailout ridiculed the Reagan government's free market beliefs. But the first victim of sticking to principle would likely be Reagan's own reelection just a few months away. "On Continental Illinois I backed him [Volcker] and he backed me," explains Don Regan. "There was nothing we could do. Continental had relationships with downstate Illinois banks and all through the neighboring Midwest. The heartland would have been affected had Continental gone down. I didn't think the banking system could stand it, though it was against my political and economic instincts."

Yet even the largest bailout guarantee in history wasn't enough to stop the ebb from Continental. Worse, the flight began to infect other major banks. On May 24 Manufacturers Hanover Trust Co., the nation's fourth largest bank, was besieged by rumors started in Europe that it was in trouble. With $6.5 billion in loans to the four largest Latin American LDCs, equal to a hair-raising 284 percent of its equity, Manny Hanny was the tip of an iceberg of fears about the exposure of the big U.S. banks to the LDC crisis. Manny Hanny too had to pay more to raise interbank money. Its stock price plunged 10 percent in a single day, leading the fall among all bank stocks. A generalized fright was taking hold in the financial markets: bond and equity prices skidded sharply in the United States and London. The dollar plunged. Other

American banks, including Bank of America, Chase Manhattan, First National Bank of Dallas, First Chicago, Crocker, Chemical Bank, and American Savings & Loan Association all had to pay over one percentage point more in the ensuing weeks to attract deposits.

To prevent financial markets from convulsing into one of their occasional historical bouts of destabilization, it was imperative to resolve the Continental crisis expeditiously. The bailout package had been approved only to borrow time until a buyer could be found. None could. Reluctantly regulators squared up to the fact that there only one purchaser was left—the U.S. government.

No free market American government wanted to be seen nationalizing a bank outright. In the thinly disguised plan announced on July 26, 1984, the U.S. taxpayer–owned FDIC would buy $4.5 billion of Continental's troubled loans—"socializing" the losses. Continental would use $3.5 billion to pay down its Fed discount window borrowings. The remaining $1 billion would go into Continental's capital, for which the FDIC would gain effective control of 80 percent of the common stock. This would leave a healthy bank that could later be "privatized" through a public share offering.

The Continental bailout came none too soon. The financial contagion was spreading to the S&Ls. A run had already broken out on Financial Corporation of America (FCA), the holding company of the nation's largest thrift, American Savings and Loan Association—the same thrift that announced its imminent failure to authorities on the weekend before the Black Monday 1987 crash. In the end, American S&L too required a mammoth government-assisted bailout to prolong its existence.

The Continental nationalization became the most celebrated case of the spreading moral hazard cancer in the American financial system. Comptroller Todd Conover soon conceded that any failing bank larger than Continental had an unspoken government safety net. This became dignified as the doctrine "too big to fail."

An unexpected by-product of the Continental failure nearly induced a disastrous Fed monetary policy error in summer 1984. To avoid being perceived by the market as fragile like Continental, U.S. banks suddenly stayed away from the Fed's discount window en masse. Instead they paid a premium to borrow the funds they required in the open market. As a result, the Fed, which "took out [reserves] through the open market and expected those who needed to borrow to do so through the discount window," saw Fed Fund interest rates rise one full point higher than it had intended.[30]

On August 21, 1984, Volcker urged the FOMC to ease. But the majority feared forfeiting some of the gains against inflation expectations. Volcker says, "I got worried that the committee would not ease as fast as necessary. They were always one meeting too late."

Although he voted with the majority to issue a directive to the open market desk at the New York Fed not to change reserve pressures, Volcker angered New York Fed President Tony Solomon and other FOMC members by guiding interest rates lower anyway through the discretion left to the chairman between FOMC meetings.

Volcker's economic intuitions again were right. The economy was slumping faster than expected. Fourth-quarter growth was only 1.5 percent. At its next meeting the FOMC voted to relax monetary policy. It was the first of three successive easings. The Fed Funds rate, assisted by two discount rate cuts, fell about three percentage points from late August through December. Long-term interest rates declined in tandem—indicating that the Fed was still ahead of the inflation expectations power curve.

Falling interest rates and low inflation prospects fomented another burst of euphoria on Wall Street. Turnover in the newly deregulated, innovative capital markets exploded amid a new wave of highly leveraged takeovers, venture capital financings, junk bonds, mortgage-backed securities, swaps, financial futures, and options. Stock prices erupted on the second leg of the 1982–87 bull market run. If Wall Street was "go-go," could the revival of Main Street and the promises of the Reagan Revolution be far behind?

Chapter 12

A New Global
Financial Landscape

One pause for doubt was the soaring superdollar. The unpredicted 50 percent real appreciation of the dollar between 1980 and early 1985 was the fastest rise until then of any major currency in modern history. It stretched the credulity of all but the most politically partisan that America's fundamental economic prospects had improved so much compared to the rest of the world in such a short time span. It was the new global capital regime's most spectacular example yet of how far, and unpredictably, a purely financial phenomenon could diverge from economic reality.

Theoretically mystifying was the dollar's 20 percent surge from July 1984 to February 1985. The Fed's 1984 tightening, by sharply widening the real interest rate differential over German and Japanese securities, had pushed up the dollar from DM 2.52 to almost DM 2.90 and from ¥220 to above ¥240. But when the interest rate differential was more than reversed after the summer, the dollar *continued* to soar. By February 26, 1985, the dollar capped a wild one-way market run to DM 3.47 and through ¥263.

"During this period all measurable fundamentals—not just real interest differentials, but also money growth rates, real growth rates, the current account, and the country risk premium versus the Eurodollar market—were, if anything, moving in the wrong direction," observes U.C. Berkeley Professor Jeffrey Frankel. "The dollar appears to have overshot the overshooting equilibrium."[1] In financial market lore it became known as the speculative dollar bubble.

The superdollar shock devastated America's internationally competitive manufacturing, agricultural, and mining industries by pricing them out of foreign and U.S. markets. Factories were shut down. American workers were laid off en masse. Long-term capital investment programs in the United States were aborted. In 1983 to 1984, U.S. export growth was only half as fast as in past recoveries; imports, by contrast, skipped ahead at double the historic average rate. While the overall U.S. economy expanded by a robust average annual 5 percent, U.S. manufacturing employment hardly increased from its low recession levels. U.S. capacity utilization actually fell in 1985 and 1986, another break with past recoveries. America's core industrial economy, with all the decades of business, social, and political relationships that underpinned it, was in increasingly visible jeopardy of long-term structural damage. The dollar's subsequent plunge to below 1980 levels proved it to be one of the world's most *needlessly* disruptive round trips in history, like the traumatic rise and fall of oil prices in the 1970s.

"None of us thought the dollar could go so high," says Treasury Secretary Don Regan. "The administration did not see the destructive side of the dollar's rise until late 1984." For the White House, and President Reagan personally, the strong dollar dangled a simplistic, self-vindicating message that was politically irresistible, especially in a presidential election year: a free market ratification of administration economic policies. Foreign capital was flooding into the U.S. dollar because American economic prospects were the world's brightest.

"Americans have two souls in their breasts when they talk about exchange rates," observes Kurt Richebacher, former chief economist of Germany's Dresdner Bank. "A strong exchange rate is good for Wall Street. In 1983–84, American politicians didn't care for the real economy. Wall Street was goal number one for them. If it booms, it creates an appearance of economic strength that politicians want."

With the election uppermost in mind, the Treasury solicited even larger foreign capital inflows in 1984 by marketing for foreign buyers a special new bearer bond that combined the enticement of tax anonymity with the elimination of the 30 percent U.S. withholding tax. In September 1984 Treasury Undersecretary Beryl Sprinkel traveled to Tokyo, and Assistant Secretary for International Affairs David Mulford left for Europe, on a successful selling trip. It was a "beggar thy neighbor" policy in global capital.

Secretary Regan desired capital inflows to dilute the effect of Volcker's spring tightening and to prevent any preelection dollar fall. "In 1984 we didn't want to do anything to undermine the recovery," he explains. "A drastic fall in the level of the dollar would certainly be disruptive to prosperity. We were aware it [foreign inflows] would lower interest rates in the United States. In hindsight it probably contributed to the dollar's rise."

The strategy succeeded. In 1984 foreign purchases of U.S. fixed income securities—mostly Treasuries to finance the U.S. budget deficit—tripled to $37.4 billion. In the fourth quarter 1984 Japanese purchases of foreign securities leaped to $13.6 billion; for the year, total capital outflow from Japan was an astonishing $50 billion.

In retrospect 1984 was a watershed in the shifting axes of global capital flows: first from banks to securities markets, second from transatlantic to transpacific inflows to the United States. In 1984 balances of payments developments in Japan were broadly "the mirror image of those in the United States."[2] The unprecedented inflow of capital from Japan may have been President Reagan's most important campaign contribution.

Even as the economic damage on manufacturing became visible, President Reagan continued to extol the dollar's strength. "Everyone at Treasury cringed every time the president said that a 'strong dollar is a strong country,' " says then Deputy Treasury Secretary Tim McNamar. "We couldn't get him off it."

Most mainstream economists saw that the driving force behind the superdollar was not America's bright prospects at all, but its huge structural federal budget deficits. Among them was Reagan's own CEA Chairman Martin Feldstein, who provoked the ire of Reagan's political handlers by stating bluntly that "the basic reason for the high dollar and our competitive problems is the prospect of large future budget deficits."[3]

The titanic clash between the expansive budget deficits and Volcker's anti-inflationary monetary policy produced real-dollar interest rates that were often five percentage points higher than outside the United States. Capital was sucked in from all over the world. That propelled the dollar and the U.S.'s foreign deficits.

"We financed our budget deficit through borrowing abroad, and it showed up on our trade deficit," explains Princeton Professor William Branson, adding a quip: "It is said that America found its comparative advantage in the 1980s—to sell Treasury bills!"

Without the record foreign borrowing, U.S. growth would have been anemic. U.S. net borrowing equaled fully *two-thirds* of U.S. GNP growth between 1983 and 1989. With most of that borrowing being consumed upon arrival rather than invested in wealth-producing assets, America's financial euphoria seemed destined for an eventual collision with economic reality.

Although an early Cassandra, Paul Volcker was nonetheless among the many who "didn't expect the dollar to go up as far as it did. He didn't believe we could get to $100 billion current account deficits because he didn't believe the foreigners would finance them," says Fed International Finance Division chief Ted Truman. "The first time we presented our projections, he said it would never happen. He said it was impossible to conceive borrowing so much in one year from foreigners. Remember, only a few years before we had seen current account deficits of at most $14 billion."

Volcker's misjudgment that foreigners would deviate from historical pattern to lend so much of their savings explained why his warnings that the U.S. fiscal deficits would drag down the economy were constantly overgloomy. "Volcker was surprised that the short-run effects didn't bite more and sooner," says his aide Steven Roberts.

Volcker's misreading of the superdollar signified how difficult it was even for the cognoscenti to comprehend the full dimensions of the financial revolution unfolding before their eyes. The changed world economy driven by swelling and fast-moving, volatile volumes of global capital at floating exchange rates allowed financial binges to go on longer and deviate farther from underlying fundamentals—and rendered the inevitable corrective adjustments potentially more violent. That increased the governing responsibility and pressures on unelected central bankers to maintain order.

The Financial Revolution

Paul Volcker began to grow exceedingly alarmed about the aberrantly soaring dollar in late 1984 when the U.S. current account deficit headed toward eclipsing the century level he had believed unsurpassable. Unlike the spring of 1984, when rising inflation risks conflicted with taming the superdollar, Volcker was now free to try to remedy faltering growth, financial system fragility, and the misvalued dollar with a single, easier monetary policy. Yet as the Fed eased sharply, the M1 money supply again surged beyond the Fed's public targets from spring 1985. Volcker ignored it. To avoid public repudiation of the monetary rule, he simply widened the Fed's target money supply growth range and raised the base on which it was calculated.

With interest rates falling, Washington didn't mind. Nor did financial markets frighten. By 1985 Wall Street trusted Volcker that the financial revolution had overthrown the reliability of past policy indicators, including domestic money supply. In the event, the 4.4 percent inflation in 1984 fell to 3.5 percent in 1985 and 2 percent in 1986.

In 1985 it grew evident that much of the increase in money supply balances was being used not to support real economic activity, but for financial transactions in Wall Street's mid-1980s boom. Falling interest rates, deregulation, and innovation helped trigger an explosion of financial transactions relative to real economic activity, which created a surge in the demand for money and credit, including M1, to support them. For many years the ratio of stock exchange dollar volume to GNP varied narrowly between 8 percent and 20 percent; by 1986 the ratio had climbed to 100 percent.[4]

Financial excess made central bankers instinctively nervous. In and of itself it was not harmful. But it became so if it seduced businessmen into making investments divorced from long-term economic reality or if chunks of the financial system collapsed when prices corrected.

Volcker was disturbed by the startling extent to which the financial boom was debt-driven. For many years the total debt held by individuals, non-financial businesses, and government had been remarkably stable at $1.40 per dollar of GNP. From the early 1980s to mid-1985, however, the ratio suddenly broke—to $1.65—en route to higher levels in the late 1980s not seen since just before the Great Depression.[5] The surge in business debt service burdens, fueled partly by a boom in highly leveraged takeovers that induced an extraordinary net substitution of equity for debt, was more alarming to experts than even the decried government debt buildup. Many fretted that at the height of a recovery more businesses were going bankrupt than at any time since the 1930s.

The financial boom was concentrated in the integrating, globalizing capital markets. To avoid being bypassed, banks sought ways to participate. They moved heavily into mushrooming "off balance sheet" activity—including interest rate and currency swaps, credit guarantees, lines of credit, and futures and options. Comforted by the liquidity of being able to sell their loans to other entities in innovative financial markets, and by the spread of variable interest rate loans (which transferred traditional bank interest rate risk to the borrower), bankers relaxed credit standards.

Yet Volcker and other central bankers worried that bankers were unwittingly increasing their overall credit risk exposure if overleveraged borrowers went belly-up. With the old early braking mechanism of regulated interest rate ceilings blown away by innovation and deregulation, there were no longer any effective artificial early restraints on overlending. "Unfortunately the bankers will never stop lending until they're bust," laments Volcker. "You don't operate any longer through the availability of credit, but by bankruptcy." To slow the economy, central bankers had to be ready to push interest rates up farther and more swiftly until borrower losses curtailed lending. But the central banker never knew when rising interest rates would unexpectedly pull the trip wire on some unseen pocket of fragility. At that point renewed inflationary monetary policy might be the only way to stave off a systemwide financial disruption.

Because of the financial revolution, financial risk was no longer concentrated only in the segregated, core banking system, but was spread around in far-flung ways that were difficult to assess. Cross-border and intermarket daisy chains among key banks, securities firms, and other financial intermediaries meant that destabilizing traumas emanating from obscure or poorly supervised locations could spread quickly. Increased volatility, volume, and velocity of transactions demanded instantaneous reaction when trouble started. Privately Volcker began to confide his fear that the U.S. financial system was being set up for a "catastrophic chain reaction." He believed that through counterparty linkages "[T]he mistakes made by some can spread financial stress to many others through ever more complex financial interrelationships."[6]

Central bankers were also uneasy how the global financial landscape in which liquidity was almost always available someplace beyond the control of national authorities was transforming the way monetary policy worked through the banking system and on the economy. "The feedback channels are getting so diffuse that you can't keep track of them—it is much more complex now to understand the trade-offs," says Charles Lucas, New York Fed senior vice president. "The macrodiscipline is still there, but it is more volatile, diffused, and not well understood politically."

Interest rates that swung over a wider spectrum stimulated international capital flows that produced bigger changes in currency exchange rates. This was shifting the main economic fulcrum for monetary policy from traditional housing and consumer durables to sectors exposed to international competition. Yet it also caused monetary policy to directly affect a broader political constituency than ever before. Millions of homeowners, businesses, and credit card debtors now had adjustable interest rate loans and thus were sensitive to every uptick in interest rates. Labor unions and tradable goods producers were becoming more keenly aware of the impact on them of fluctuations in the dollar.

The proliferation of nonbank substitutes for bank deposits and the dwindling share of total financing that took place within the banking system—the traditional transmission belt of central bank monetary policy—was loosening central bankers' grip on the money supply. It even raised the specter of a day when central bankers might lose all meaningful monetary control. Central bankers' ability to manage money was more difficult because the very definitions of money—what congeries of assets were counted within each monetary aggregate M1, M2, M3—had become conceptually slippery owing to innovations, rapid capital movements, and surging financial transactions.

At the same time, the new landscape was making market expectations a more potent, and often capricious, constraint on each central banker's policy latitude. Global capital mobility limited his scope to alter domestic interest rates much from world trends—regardless of his own goals or national political aspirations. "Global money limits the possibility to have interest rate changes—central bankers have lost freedom in this regard," says Wilfried Guth, former chief of Germany's banking powerhouse, Deutsche Bank, and a world monetary expert. "Central bankers aren't any more in a position to control the volume of national monies with exact velocities. They'll lose power even more. But it won't diminish their importance."

Scott Pardee, Yamaichi International chairman and ex–U.S. central banker, explains the transformation metaphorically: "The central banker is like a cop at an intersection directing traffic. In the old days you used to be able to tell this one to go there, and the next one to go there, and everyone more or less obeyed you. Now there are no road barriers or road maps. Everyone just goes their own way whenever they want. Central bankers are screaming bloody murder to influence people. *If* they are heard, they can provide some help in straightening out the mess. But the removal of road barriers means there is a greater need for persuasion and more difficulty reading the signals."

Politics of Deregulation

Ironically, by injecting greater interest rate volatility, Volcker's war on inflation spurred the financial transformation. Volcker was powerless to replug the bottle. He did, however, use his leverage as Fed chairman to try to slow the momentum added by Reagan's deregulatory agenda. Many of the political battles were fought in the five-man Depository Institutions Deregulation Committee (DIDC), upon which Volcker had a seat but whose majority was controlled by an unsympathetic Secretary Regan.[7]

"DIDC was a very painful process for him [Volcker]," remembers then Fed counsel Michael Bradfield. "Deregulation made it much more difficult to operate monetary policy. He worried about the destabilizing effects of deregulation."

Volcker anguished over the shift in 1982 of $230 billion in deposits—a sizable chunk of the money supply—out of the banks and into securities industry money market accounts at floating market interest rates. To help prevent money from fleeing the banking system, says then Comptroller of the Currency C. Todd Conover, "the bank money market deposit account [which allowed banks to offer unregulated interest on accounts of at least $2,500] was designed, principally by Volcker, on the back of an envelope."

Volcker also brooked political pique by employing the Fed's regulatory fiat power to try to arrest the expansion of nonfinancial corporations through regulatory loopholes into some activities that mimicked banking, to curb the use of junk bonds in corporate takeovers, and to allow some banks to fight back by entering a limited range of profitable underwriting niches. But Volcker's was an inevitably losing battle before the deregulatory political enthusiasm of the Reagan administration and, even more, the market forces of global capital.

Volcker and the first Reagan administration also clashed in a bruising behind-the-scenes fourteen-month battle when Reagan's men proposed streamlining America's tortured bank supervisory structure in a way that would strip the Fed of its supervisory powers—and thus its authority to hinder Reagan's deregulation agenda. The task force, chaired by Vice President George Bush, sought to concentrate all the Fed's existing supervisory power under the office of the comptroller, a Treasury domain.

Volcker rebelled. Often the lone nay vote, he refused to acquiesce in month after month of meetings at the Woodrow Wilson Room at the White House and at the vice president's residence. Although the battle was mostly about political control over money, the deregulatory agenda, and bureaucratic turf, Volcker had one intellectual argument that won some sympathy from some of those aligned against him. "The Fed said that if they no longer had power over the largest fifty bank holding companies, then they couldn't carry out their function as protector of the financial system," recalls Todd Conover. "One has to be sympathetic to that."

The Fed's use of its regulatory muscle from mid-1982 to keep recalcitrant banks involuntarily engaged in the Volcker-led LDC debt strategy put a politically forceful exclamation point on Volcker's argument at the time. Simply put, a central bank's supervisory powers provided important carrots and sticks to influence banks' profits—and thus their behavior. It also gave them the means to protect bankers against periodic political expressions of latent democratic hostility. This made it a key fulcrum for exercising political control over money. Supervisory oversight gave teeth to central banker moral suasions. "Fear is what makes the bank's powers so acceptable," explains Bank of England Deputy Governor George Blunden. "The bank is able to exert its influence when people are dependent on us and fear losing their privileges or when they are frightened and have no other friends."[8]

The spreading fragility constraints on monetary policy made the intimacy gleaned from front-line supervisory responsibility important for the formulation and timing of monetary policy moves as well. Sensitivity to financial fragility informed Fed monetary policy moves during Volcker's disinflation war; it would continue to do so through the early 1990s downturn, as told in Part Six.

The close political relationship that often evolved between supervised banks and the supervisor translated into enhanced protection for the central bank within the government. In the U.S. political culture, the Fed's position with Congress was enhanced by the support of the many small, but cumulatively influential, banks it regulated. Supervisory authority, in short, represented one of the hidden yet politically unmentionable foundations of central bank power in democratic society. Bank supervision was also a politically thankless task: good regulation was unpraised, yet the political fallout could be large when a wayward supervisory charge was perceived to injure citizens' pocketbooks. For this reason Federal Reserve central bankers didn't want *too much* front-line responsibility.[9]

Volcker's trump card in the 1984 confrontation was his towering political standing with Congress. "The vote was always thirteen to one against Volcker," says Volcker assistant Steven Roberts. "He said to them: 'Go ahead and issue the report. But I'll fight you in Congress.' " Because 1984 was an election year, the administration decided to compromise. "I remember a discussion where we said, 'Oh, God, everyone is going to say that we set up Volcker,' " says Deputy Treasury Secretary Tim McNamar.

In the end, "Regan and Volcker made a deal," says Todd Conover. "We changed the whole thing so the recommendations didn't strip the Fed's power and Volcker supported the Bank Holding Company Act, which the Treasury was pushing hard and needed Volcker's support on. It was a sad thing. We labored for fourteen months and nothing happened." As so often occurred in Washington, the political battle would be refought—a decade later it was the Democratic Clinton administration that proposed supervisory reform that stripped the Fed's powers.

Troubling Legacies

Paul Volcker's reservations about the freewheeling new global financial landscape went deeper than the technical difficulties it presented for central bankers. They sprang from the fabric of his Puritan work and public service ethics and a skepticism that an economy driven by unregulated financial markets would produce financial system stability and maximize long-term economic growth. In a reflective, unusually personal speech in June 1985, Volcker donned the priestly mantle of the conscientious central banker to remind his audience that certain core social and economic values were necessary to underpin the prosperous marriage between a capitalist economy and a democratic polity.[10]

Somehow amidst the prosperity of the postwar years "we . . . los[t] sight of the critical importance of some fixed principles to help guide the conduct of economic policy," he lamented. The painful wringing out of inflation had created the best opportunity in a generation to reestablish the virtuous principles upon which a new era of world prosperity could be built. Yet markets and governments were failing to do so responsibly: "The pressures of government finance on our capital markets are tolerable only because we have been able freely to draw upon massive amounts of capital from abroad—a significant drain on *their* savings. Even so, our interest rates remain historically high, and the capital inflow is necessarily matched by an enormous flow of imports, squeezing our manufacturers, miners, and farmers.

"We continue to build more new offices than we can occupy; we've become expert in trading all kinds of financial assets and companies . . . but all the while productivity still lags.

"We spend our days issuing debt and retiring equity—both in record volume—and then we spend our evenings raising each other's eyebrows with gossip about signs of stress in the financial system.

"We rail at government inefficiency and intrusion in our markets—while we call upon the same government to protect our interests, our industry, and our financial institutions. . . .

"These days we have a market for taking a financial position one way or another almost instantaneously on practically anything, all justified on the basis of sophisticated arguments about facilitating preferred investment strategies or hedging risks. But it all raises the question of whether in the process we haven't lost sight of some of the basic qualities that must underlie the stability and continuity of any market."

Too much of the burden of financial stability had shifted from market players to government regulators and central bankers, spreading the risk of moral hazard. "There has to be a better way than counting on bureaucrats to do so much of the job. . . .

"It's a problem of the governing process," Volcker synthesized. "It's the challenge of reconciling our individual interests into a coherent whole. It's recognizing that we need strong and consistent signals from government—in effect, clear and enforced rules of the road—for the marketplace to produce its magic in the form of stability and growth."

The Wall Street boom and strong dollar helped carry President Reagan to a landslide reelection victory in November 1984. Although the Fed remained meticulously nonpartisan, Paul Volcker's imprint on the outcome was profound. Had he been less successful in restoring faith in the U.S. dollar, subduing inflation, and nurturing economic growth despite serious structural budget deficits and financial fragilities, it was improbable that Wall Street would have boomed or that foreign investors would have lent so much of their savings to allow Americans to postpone the economic accounting day that Reagan's Democratic Party opponent, Walter Mondale, drearily insisted lay ahead.

"You and I, as individuals can, by borrowing, live beyond our means, but only for a limited period of time. Why, then, should we think that collectively, as a nation, we're not bound by the same limitations?" The message was Mondale's but the words were Reagan's. Delivered soon after he took office in 1981, they were destined to become an ironic self-indictment of his presidential legacy and symbol of the paralyzing deficit of U.S. government leadership. The egregious incapacity to restore government finance to a sound, long-term basis was just one element of a greater political challenge: to viably convert the principles and mechanisms of an increasingly obsolete national democratic capitalist marriage of convenience to the new world political economy driven by unrestrainable global flows of investment capital.

The failure to do so was inimical both to capitalist health and its political democratic ideals. Wealth production suffered when profit signals were distorted by financial excess. Volatile interest and exchange rates reoriented business success away from basic productive enterprise and toward financial acumen. Inflation had harmed productivity by bailing out inefficient entrepreneurs in the 1970s. One disease, it seemed, had been traded for another.

The U.S. government's passive decision not to buffer the social and economic impact of the 50 percent real appreciation of the dollar broke political faith with both businesses and individual citizens whose livelihoods were built upon America's postwar compact between markets and government. Viable factories were closed. Thousands of American citizens were abruptly thrown out of work. Organized labor was decimated as a political force as union membership collapsed by 2.5 million in the first half of the 1980s. Disemboweled were the social communities built up over many generations around local industries. Left behind was a big unhealed wound of unemployed middle-aged workers, untrained for new jobs, unable in depressed, deindustrialized regions to sell homes that represented their life savings, and unwilling to abandon a lifetime of family, friends, and ethnic roots to migrate in search of new work. Global capital was rendering national governments less able to defend its citizens' political interests, too. At a stroke, and with remarkably little public debate, political economic balances were being reordered. It was an economically painful, and politically explosive, substitute for the government-regulated buffer mechanisms of the "Keynes at home, Smith abroad" Bretton Woods monetary order. It put people's lives—their incomes and the nature, location, and stability of their jobs—more at the mercy of high-speed and volatile private financial flows driven by the global search for financial profit. Daily human lives, social economies, and political institutions adjusted more gradually than financial prices and were of course governed by many social, religious, political, and personal concerns beyond profit.

"Volatile exchange rates affect the real economy and lives in a strong way," explains Princeton Professor William Branson. "Look at the rise of the dollar from 1980 to 1985. One-third of total steel employment was cut. Autos and machine tools cut plants and lines of production. When the dollar comes down, the reexpansion is in different places. It comes in small new firms in nonunion towns in the South, using new technology, minimills, or the auto plants taken over by the Japanese in Tennessee and California. There is a dislocation of unemployment. Look at the layoff rate of people over forty. It is very high. It is long-term. Eventually the U.S. exports will be back to the 1980 level, but they will be different kinds of exports. You can think of it as speeding up a process that would have happened anyway—but the pain of adjustment for the people affected is left out of the equation."

The displaced workers, bankrupted manufacturers, and failed farmers were, of course, citizens of the political democracy as well as producers in the economy. With finance having broken free of democratic nation-state boundaries, some of the political control over the terms upon which wealth was produced and distributed within national borders was slipping away. Elected representatives were becoming less relevant to governing the economic environment of their constituents. What was conventionally explained as the consequences of unalterable free market forces was, at bottom, also a political democratic deficit. Democracies that arose within the nation-state and over the decades had developed a political economic structure geared chiefly to balancing the competing claims of domestic constituencies. If democratic governments were to continue to fulfill the political principles bred within the nation-state, maintain international political harmony among nations, and protect borderless capital against its inherent occasional instability, then new global rules of the game and operating mechanisms had to be devised.

Another disguised political decision was implicit in America's unprecedented debt accumulation: a historically perverse intergenerational wealth transfer from children to parents, from future to present generations. The high U.S. real interest rates rewarded savers at the expense of borrowers. The rich, who saved the most and were generally older and better educated, grew disproportionately much richer in the 1980s for the first time since the 1920s.[11]

For generations, the idea that hard work would yield personal economic progress was a motivational cornerstone of the U.S. political economy. Yet with upward economic mobility having stalled for all but a small elite, that faith was under stress. Its manifestations could be found in almost every U.S. economic and social ill. The wealth transfer was not simply between generations and economic classes, but also across national borders. America's new net international debtor status, which by 1993 would reach an estimated $600 billion, signified that America's children and grandchildren would have to sacrifice part of their living standards in order to pay back foreigners.[12]

Extraordinarily, all that foreign debt was in America's own currency, dollars. Thus if America failed to earn enough to pay back foreigners with political comfort, there was always an expedient way out—inflation. Inflation required no legal default action, no political repudiation. It could be done without telling foreign creditors or even American citizens. It required merely pressuring an independent Federal Reserve—or ordering one that had been subordinated to political dependence—to pump the money creation process into high gear, all in the politically appealing name of growth. Foreigners would be repaid with worthless, inflated dollars. Although the long-run consequences would be destructive for the U.S. economy and the international political economic order that would be deprived of its monetary spinal cord, the political temptations would plainly become great if America's trajectory of underinvestment, slow productivity growth, excessive consumption, and foreign borrowing dependence was not altered.

Ronald Reagan was dead right about one thing: America's ability to live beyond its means could not go on forever. A day of repayment, economically and politically, lay ahead. How it was divided within the society could be actively influenced by the political authorities. Absent political leadership, the adjustment would come anyway. But the burden sharing and timing of the repayment would be determined by the sometimes violent, always socially indifferent, logic of market forces. It could happen gradually without an abrupt economic and political wrenching, or all at once with a sudden financial crisis, economic depression, and political upheaval. Again, it would be the challenge of central bankers to fill the void left by derelict political leaders.

Volcker's nearly single-handed gains against inflation turned the gloom of the late 1970s into a cautious confidence that it was possible to muster the political gumption to tackle the formidable economic problems of the times. "Ten or fifteen years ago we were not sure we *could* fight inflation," says Wilfried Guth, former head of Deutsche Bank. "Now we believe it is possible. That is a tremendous achievement."

Remarkably, in the leading democracies the central banker–led war on inflation became the vanguard of a new political environment conducive to sound money whose absence Arthur Burns had lamented in his Belgrade address, "The Anguish of Central Banking." Thatcherism in the United Kingdom, the Socialist U-turn in France, Italy's wage deindexation, Germany's medium-term fiscal program, the European Community's drive for economic and monetary integration, Japan's fiscal consolidation: all in various ways placed renewed emphasis on wealth production and away from wealth's equitable distribution, toward smaller government and reducing structural supply-side impediments to private sector growth. This current enabled the seven major industrial nations to reduce inflation by 1985 to 4 percent—the lowest level since 1967. By the 1990s the political and economic success of disinflation would fuel a worldwide trend toward upgrading the independence of central banks with the explicit priority on price stability, not growth.[13] The ironic exception was in Volcker's America.

Yet Volcker's domination of U.S. economic policy invited a review whether democracy was best served by leaving the government of monetary policy to independent, unelected central bankers rather than to political leaders held directly accountable at the polls. National economic policy coherence could suffer from hiving off monetary policy, as demonstrated by the clash between Reagan's budget deficits and Volcker's monetary stringency. Some critics, overlooking the decade-long divided government and blame-gaming between Republicans and Democrats, even suggested that central bank independence encouraged fiscal irresponsibility, since politicians knew that central bankers were there to clean up their expediencies with tight money.

The principal lesson of the 1980s, however, was that an independent central bank protected capitalist economic and democratic political well-being from divided government and the political temptation to achieve goals through inflationary deception. Would the United States have been better off with a submissive Fed that monetized the Reagan deficits? Or was U.S. democracy better served by an independent Fed that was able to give checks-and-balance resistance—and thus evoke a public debate about economic strategies and goals—to the attempt of a small, organized fringe of supply-siders (a minority even within the Reagan government) to impose its radical gamble with America's economic patrimony on a largely ignorant body politic?

When the debate was joined, fighting inflation through traditional monetary austerity proved to be the priority of the two electorates of democratic capitalist society—the voting citizenry and global investors. Had it not been, a mere congressional majority would have rapidly forced Volcker and the Fed to political heel.

"People now seem to prefer price stabilty to full employment," observes veteran central bank Governor Erik Hoffmeyer of Denmark, with some surprise. "The choice has been made not by the politicians, but by the people."[14] Seconding the vote for sound money, and indeed driving the 1990s world-wide trend for upgraded central bank independence, was the increasingly potent veto power global investors in the "Court of World Savings" held over national sovereign economic policies.

Although Volcker's reputation as an inflation fighter was forever etched in the public and political consciousness, the second half of his tenure as Fed chairman was hallmarked by a preoccupation with growth. In actuality, the two objectives of growth and consolidating U.S. inflation gains were symbiotically reinforcing: growth expanded productive economic capacity and thus eased inflationary pressures, repaired financial fragilities, and eased the global economic imbalances threatening a hard economic adjustment that might reignite inflationary expectations of a monetary bailout.

Growth was also imperative to soothing the political wounds that could quickly strike Fed independence at any stumble. Senate leader Howard Baker explains that the Fed exhausted much of its political goodwill in the disinflation war: "After the recovery, the criticism of the Fed became less shrill and less relevant. As interest rates and unemployment came down, the pressure to overhaul the Fed subsided. But images were fixed then—if there is another recession and a run-up in interest rates like that again, they will come out *quickly* with pressure to overhaul the Fed.

"You don't need a 21.5 percent prime. If the economy is chugging along and interest rates are 12 percent or less, the Fed is okay. But the images of 1979–80 are fixed in the minds of so many people. Two-thirds of the discontent was about interest rates [not the budget deficit]. The era of Fed untouchability ended in 1979–80."

"The Fed operated for years and years without any knowledge on the part of American people as to what the Fed did: frankly, without any interest in the Fed. In recent years, the Fed has become a more visible participant in the conduct of economic policy, and many of us think the Fed may even be the chief actor," Rep. Lee Hamilton (D-Ind.) warned Paul Volcker in 1985. "People are coming to realize that what that board of yours does has a very profound impact on their pocketbooks, and yet it is a group of people basically inaccessible to them and unaccountable to them.

"I think the pressures on the Fed are going to build and the people are going to become more aware of the enormous economic power that you have. I would urge you to take the steps necessary so that you head off some of those pressures." Central bank independence, echoed Republican supply-sider and presidential hopeful Rep. Jack Kemp (R–N.Y.), "ought to be one of the great debates of the late 1980s."[15]

Volcker's great hope for consolidating his inflation gains was that disinflation had cleared the economic ground for a long period of growth. Although imbalanced, debt-driven, and often menaced by financial instability, GNP growth for the decade returned to an above average annual 3 percent. Unemployment halved to 5.2 percent by 1990.

Yet noting in a 1990 address entitled "The Triumph of Central Banking?" that inflation was again creeping up in the English-speaking world to between 4 percent and 10 percent, Volcker warned publicly of the threat of renewed inflation set off by the clash between monetary policy and financial stability and the unanswered challenges of global capital: "[E]ven the partial victory over inflation is not secure. At the same time, it is clear that the past decade has seen volatility in domestic and international financial markets, and strains on financial institutions, entirely out of keeping with earlier post-war experience. Indeed, nothing like it has been seen since the end of the 1920s and the 1930s. . . ."[16]

Volcker himself prevented a resurrection of accelerating inflation, and possible world depression, by stepping forward with a second remarkable performance of personal leadership to contain an epic, international free market financial breakdown from the LDC debt crisis that erupted in mid-1982.

PART THREE

LDC DEBT SHOCK

Chapter 13

Financial Armageddon

At the gloomiest hour of the U.S. and world recession in the summer of 1982, Paul Volcker took a short trout fishing holiday on the Snake River in Wyoming. Trouble pursued him. Continental Illinois Chairman Roger Anderson flew out in his corporate jet to inform Volcker personally that Continental was teetering from the Penn Square failure. It needed Fed help to prevent a collapse. The next day Volcker's office called him. Mexico was out of foreign reserves and couldn't meet payments due on its $80 billion in foreign debts. Mexican Finance Minister Jesus Silva Herzog and Bank of Mexico Director Miguel Mancera were flying to Washington the next day. Volcker aborted his holiday and returned to Washington.

On Friday, August 13, Volcker met with the Mexican officials at the Fed building from 10 A.M. through lunchtime. Earlier, the Mexicans had met briefly with IMF Managing Director Jacques de Larosière; afterward they conferred with Treasury Secretary Donald Regan and Deputy Secretary R. T. "Tim" McNamar. Late that evening de Larosière visited Volcker to discuss Silva Herzog's message: Mexico needed lots of money—and fast. If it didn't get it, President José Lopez Portillo was prepared to call world heads of state to announce that Mexico was defaulting on its debt.

What followed was forty-eight nonstop hours of frantic negotiation. By dawn Monday, a $3.5 billion emergency transfusion had been pledged for Mexico. "We had no real idea how far the money would go," says the Treasury's Tim McNamar. "The idea was that if their banks didn't open Monday morning, then our banks wouldn't open on Tuesday."

The "Mexican weekend," as it became known, was the start of the 1980s LDC debt crisis. Within weeks Mexico was again breathing fire about default, and the crisis spread in a chain reaction throughout Latin America, engulfing superdebtors Brazil, Argentina, and Venezuela. It also threatened to overwhelm large debtors in Eastern Europe, where the world debt shock had begun the year before, and even some struggling Asian debtors. Sub-Sahara African debtors were hopelessly swamped. In 1982 the total external debt of troubled Third World debtors was about $540 billion.[1]

The LDC debt crisis threatened to cause the world financial edifice to collapse, fomenting global depression and inestimable political turmoil. The greatest peril was the overexposure of commercial banks, which held roughly 70 percent of the troubled LDC debt. The rest was owed to government bodies. Default by the three biggest Latin debtors—Brazil ($87 billion in debt), Mexico ($80 billion), Argentina ($43 billion)—and perhaps either of the first two alone could inflict catastrophic loss on the world's largest banks.[2]

At gravest risk were the core U.S. banks, because of their paucity of capital to cushion them against bankrupting loss. The top nine U.S. banks had non-OPEC, LDC debt totaling 233 percent of their primary capital in late 1982. Their 140 percent exposure to the Big Three Latin debtors alone was technically enough to bankrupt them in the event of default.[3] Catastrophe could strike much earlier if fears of serious loss triggered a panicked run from endangered banks in world money markets, inducing a bank credit contraction.

Although the American banks were worst off, "probably no bank had adequate reserves," says Swiss central banker Fritz Leutwiler. London's big four clearing banks—above all Lloyds and Midland—had a significant portion of their capital at risk in the Big Three Latin debtors.[4] One of the big early shocks was that Japanese banks' exposure to Mexico was two and a half times greater than the Ministry of Finance had thought.[5] In Brazil, Japanese banks had over $10 billion at risk.[6] For the Bank of Tokyo, Japan's traditional main banking window to the world, "LDC loans were three times their equity."[7] Even German banks, which kept large publicly undisclosed or "hidden" reserves against loss, had greater direct exposure than portrayed initially. Conservative blue chip Deutsche Bank "had *substantial* engagements in Argentina, Brazil, and Mexico," reports its chief, Wilfried Guth.

Of greater danger to most non-U.S. lenders than direct LDC default was the losses they would incur from any major U.S. bank collapse in the globally linked market. "If a U.S. bank failed, the whole system would fail," says Deutsche Bank's Guth from his office in the clouds atop one of the two glass towers, nicknamed Debit and Credit, which dominated the Frankfurt skyline. "We examined all our correspondents in the United States and elsewhere."

Without confidence in the solvency of bank counterparties at the other end of a transaction, world payments systems—the international interbank "plumbing" networks through which money transfers were made—would freeze up in global gridlock. World trade and finance would come to a crashing full stop. Another major peril was the feedback upon the industrialized world if LDCs trying to husband foreign exchange reserves to service debt were forced to make draconian cutbacks in imports.[8]

There was no blueprint, no previous experience, how to cope with a problem of such complexity and magnitude as the world debt crisis. "If some small bank failed, we'd have said, 'Sorry, but go to hell,' " says Fritz Leutwiler. "If a major bank like Deutsche Bank, Union Bank of Switzerland, or Citibank crashes, we'd have had some second thoughts. But five hundred banks? It was beyond thinking about."

Into the Valley of Debt

The LDC debt crisis was a quintessential manifestation of what could go wrong from the rise of global capital. The lending boom to LDCs beyond any prudent assessment of underlying economic fundamentals, and the abrupt bust later on, was characteristic of the same financial overlending and revulsion that marked the inflation speculation, the superdollar, soaring stock prices, and, later, commercial real estate.

The sudden quadrupling of oil prices by the OPEC (Organization of Petroleum Exporting Countries) cartel in 1973–74 was a huge global economic and financial shock. In just one year OPEC current account surpluses multiplied tenfold to $68 billion. The rest of the world, especially non-oil LDCs, suddenly had commensurate balance of payments deficits. Unless those deficits were financed through international borrowing, the LDCs would be hit by a sharp, recessionary adjustment that could destabilize their fragile political economies.

Industrial democratic world governments had no appetite to supply such large financing. Even if they did, the public sector seldom could move fast enough. Instead government leaders looked to—and many encouraged—private bankers to recycle the surplus petrodollars that the OPEC countries deposited with them in the Euromarkets.

Bankers flung petrodollars at the LDCs. From 1974 to 1982 net international bank lending jumped fivefold to over $1 trillion; lending to LDCs set the pace. "The private sector showed they are completely unreliable," says Mike Bradfield, assistant to then Treasury Undersecretary Volcker. "They stop only when they're bankrupt."

Why did bankers, in hindsight, lend so much so imprudently? The short answer: profit. Between 1970 and 1982 the profits on international operations (mostly LDC loans) of America's largest seven banks soared from 22 percent to 60 percent of total earnings.[9] Bankers' headlong stampede into LDC lending was also whetted by two innovations of the global financial marketplace—syndicated lending and floating interest rate loans. Lending syndicates of dozens of banks led by the banking world's most prestigious names appealed to bankers' worst uncritical herding instincts. By the early 1980s even small U.S. regional and German mortgage banks, with absolutely no expertise in international lending, were pouring into the syndicates purely on the faith that their bigger brethren had done their homework. Floating interest rate loans, meanwhile, assuaged bankers' occupational anxiety about managing interest rate risk by passing it on to the creditor. The debt crisis illustrated their tragic misjudgment how floating interest rate loans transformed interest rate risk into borrower solvency risk.

The new international banking era's avatar was Citicorp Chairman Walter Wriston. A charismatic leader with a gift for metaphoric eloquence, Wriston had built Citibank into America's largest bank by pursuing a 15 percent annual earnings growth goal. His assertive free market postures that volunteered little to the old boy banking establishment often rankled fellow bank chairmen and Fed officials. With Volcker he had a personal rivalry that sometimes impeded professional collaboration.

Wriston dismissed critics who cited the long, sorry history of sovereign defaults in arguing that it was foolhardy for private banks to do what was in effect balance of payments financing to sovereign LDC borrowers over whom they lacked political and juridical means of forcing repayment.[10] "Countries don't go broke," Wriston rejoined. A country, unlike a company, could not declare bankruptcy and disappear. Its infrastructure and the productivity of its people survived. Though it could have cash-flow difficulties, it could—*if* it had the political will—eventually repay its obligations.

Where Wriston led, most big banks followed. Privately Volcker derided him for having led them down the primrose path: "I heard quite a few speeches when Wriston said, 'My Latin loans are as good as a T-bill.' "

LDC overlending was a world-class example as well of both private bankers and LDC borrowers being deceived by the illusions of inflation: current investment returns were overstated. Debt loads appeared manageable. Negative real (inflation-adjusted) interest rates enticed LDCs, just as they did speculative domestic U.S. borrowers—borrow now and pay back with depreciated dollars later. The same facile hope that bewitched industrial countries, that they could painlessly grow their way out of the OPEC oil shock through abundant financing, ensnared LDCs and their bankers.

The LDCs did grow exceedingly fast following the OPEC shock—but only half as fast as their foreign debts piled up.[11] Too much of the foreign borrowing was wasted on uneconomic, and often corrupt, investments. Much was never invested at all: private LDC borrowers simply reinvested their borrowed dollars in the United States to speculate against local currency devaluation stemming from runaway inflation at home. By one reputable estimate, up to *half* of the increased borrowing of ten major Latin American countries in the decade from 1975 left as flight capital.[12]

Rapid borrowing got many LDCs into a classic structural overindebtedness trap—debt service outstripped potential income growth. Two outside shocks finally sprang the trap. First was the second oil shock starting in late 1978, which substantially increased LDC financing requirements. Second, and most important, was the launch of Volcker's war on inflation and its clash with Reagan's megabudget deficits. Real interest rates suddenly became sharply positive: each percentage-point rise in long-term U.S. interest rates added $3.5 to $4 billion to LDC debt interest charges; the five-percentage-point increase between summer 1980 and fall 1981 thus added close to $20 billion to the LDC debt service burden. The soaring dollar, the currency in which the loans were denominated, compounded the blow. Disinflation produced the industrial world recession, which killed demand for commodities, the LDCs' main export.

"What nobody knew was that Volcker was going to lock the wheels of the world," says an embittered Wriston. "And when he threw the United States into the deepest recession since 1933, it spread to the whole world. And that's what started the 'international debt crisis': export ratios that looked very good the month before he took office looked like a disaster a year later."[13]

Others stressed the gross failure of bank supervision in the new, privatized, international landscape. "The debt crisis could have occurred only through the total negligence of central banks in the Western world," declares ex–German Chancellor Helmut Schmidt. "Governments didn't understand the danger, either. But it should have been clear before central bankers' eyes, even more than to finance ministers, who have no instruments to see it. Therefore it is only too obvious that someone responsible like Volcker, who saw it from hindsight, should be the person to correct it."

Central bankers' effete warnings, including a September 1977 international prudential "checklist" exercise instigated by Fed Chairman Arthur Burns and a rare G10 communiqué in April 1980 by Basel central bankers, were brushed aside disdainfully by bankers. "I guess we could be faulted for not pushing hard enough to sound the alarm on LDC debt," concedes BIS General Manager Alexandre Lamfalussy.[14]

In the United States, Volcker admits that "I was basically reassuring," in his elliptical March 1980 warning on the rapid buildup of LDC debt following the second oil shock. His aim was "to square the circle by raising [bank capital] standards without unduly impairing the flow. We leaned over backward to try to avoid that. Maybe too far."[15] By the time the incipient LDC crisis became clearly discernible, it was too late for the central bankers because "a warning to the bankers would have triggered it," explains Shijuro Ogata, BOJ deputy governor for international relations.

When the debt crisis struck in mid-1982, banks slammed on their lending brakes. To prevent the world economy from being thrown through the windshield, a rescue plan had to be invented expeditiously. It required an acceptable international burden-sharing compact among debtors and private and public creditors: Who pays? Who adjusts? The defunct Bretton Woods monetary order of "Keynes at home, Smith abroad" had provided a common vision for organizing the international political economy and a resolution mechanism for allocating burden sharing. But no such democratic capitalist compact yet existed for the fully-floating, privatized, global capital regime.

"Governments abdicated or couldn't deal with it," says Volcker. "Central bankers stepped into the breach and took over."

Debt Tremors in Eastern Europe

Central bankers had been quietly engaged since 1981 in containing the first tremor of the world debt crisis in Eastern Europe. Private bankers had fled all Eastern European countries after Reagan hard-liners, to the anger of Western Europeans with large financial and political investments in the East, rejected rescheduling Poland's foreign debts, especially after the suppression of Solidarity and the martial law declaration of December 11, 1981, in order to add pressure on the Soviet empire.

Among those driven to crisis was Hungary, the most market reform–minded of all the Soviet bloc countries. Desperate for financing, Hungary drew plans to apply for IMF membership and loans. To bridge the waiting period, its central banker, Janos Fekete, approached BIS Chairman and Swiss National Bank President Fritz Leutwiler. Private bankers had informed Leutwiler that if the BIS would go first with a bridge loan, they'd resume lending.

A bridge loan for a debtor caught in the middle of a political tempest, however, was repugnant to the culture of BIS central bankers. Leutwiler decided to press Hungary's cause only after Soviet visitors urged him to refuse the Hungarian bridge loan because bankruptcy "will show that their reformed system is all wrong."

With the influential assistance of Bank of England Governor Gordon

Richardson, Leutwiler rallied support within the BIS and among governments.[16] Fed Chairman Volcker used his contacts within the administration to urge a neutral stance toward Hungary in opposition to strident Reagan Cold Warriors. He facilitated two meetings between Leutwiler and Treasury Secretary Don Regan in Zurich and Washington.

Volcker's message was echoed by Citibank's Walter Wriston, who served as chairman of Reagan's Economic Advisory Council. Wriston wanted cooperative relations with European banks. In March 1982 he explained to visiting Lloyds Bank Chairman Jeremy Morse that America shouldn't "make trouble because we're about to have a problem in Latin America."[17]

Reluctantly the White House assented: the United States would not contribute—but would not oppose—a central bank bridge loan to Hungary. In keeping with the BIS's stealthiness, the loans were made without a press release.[18]

The Hungarian process, says then high State Department official Robert Hormats, "was designed to be handled through central bank channels to keep low political visibility." The use of central bankers' technical financial costume to depoliticize the crisis proved fortuitous when the Mexican debt crisis soon erupted on top of it.

Mexico Erupts

Mexico began to seriously worry world officials in February 1982. Huge capital flight caused the peso to fall by 60 percent and drained the nation's foreign exchange reserves. For President Lopez Portillo it was a humiliating finish to his final year in office. Under his tenure the Mexican economy had recovered on the strength of its oil wealth. But when oil prices plunged in the 1981–82 recession, Mexico's budget and external deficits soared. Inflation leapt to 35 percent. The rampant government corruption became debilitating.

Foreign observers had been relieved in September 1981 when Lopez Portillo nominated Miguel de la Madrid Hurtado, an orthodox economic liberal (and ex–central banker), to be the next presidential candidate for the PRI (Pardido Revolucionario Institucionale). That was tantamount to a virtual annunciation in single party–dominated Mexico. But as Mexico's economic condition deteriorated, worries revived that the left-leaning Lopez Portillo might still reverse himself and dump de la Madrid for a radical before the official election on July 4, 1982.

On March 17 Lopez Portillo replaced his finance minister and central banker with two liberal allies of de la Madrid, Jesus Silva Herzog and Miguel Mancera. Silva Herzog, whom everyone called by his nickname, "Chucho," began visiting Washington every three weeks to confer with Volcker, Regan, and, unofficially, IMF Managing Director de Larosière. All urged him to undertake austerity measures and an IMF adjustment program. Although Silva Herzog was sympathetic, he says, "instructions from the president prohibited me to talk to the Fund. Just talking to the Fund for the Mexican government was a formal recognition of failure." A domestic austerity program introduced in mid-April by Silva Herzog was too painful for Lopez Portillo, and "implementation was really mild. We didn't know the degree of the problem," he admits. "We were not aware what we'd face in a few months."

Nor was Mexico's imminent threat to the world financial system yet fully apparent to top U.S. officials. "Even by early 1982 no one understood the scale that the thing had taken on," says Ted Truman, chief of the Federal Reserve Board's International Finance Division. "Mexican debt was spread all over the place."

With an IMF rescue ruled out politically, Volcker, Regan, and Silva Herzog instead devised a confidence trick strategy of dressing up Mexico's deteriorating financial reports. Their aim was to dissuade capital flight to buy time until the de la Madrid presidency was secured and serious IMF-sponsored austerity measures could be undertaken. The first critical date was July 4, the presidential election. The next was September 1, the last annual report of the president to the nation. On September 10 de la Madrid would be declared president-elect by the Mexican Congress. On December 1 he would take office.

To build its dollar reserves and to try to satiate the panicked flight from the peso, Mexico borrowed as much as it could from foreign bankers. On April 30 and on June 30 the Fed, with Treasury Secretary Regan's approval, helped artificially swell Mexico's reported dollar reserves by extending several hundred million dollars in overnight currency swaps to the Bank of Mexico. The dollars were repaid the next day.

"These were phony swaps before the Mexican election," explains Volcker. "It created a moral dilemma. It was window dressing. They didn't want it collapsing before the election and wanted the accounts to look good." From a foreign policy perspective, it was clandestine manipulation of a foreign nation's election.

The first part of the confidence trick worked. De la Madrid's victory on July 4 went smoothly. But the aftershock of the Falklands-Malvinas War of March–May 1982 knocked the strategy awry. By triggering a U.K. freeze of the $1 billion in Argentine assets held in U.K. banks, and an Argentine counterfreeze on debt payments due to British banks, the war awakened banker fears about an Argentine debt moratorium. It soon infected all Latin American debt. Bank loans for Latin America dried up suddenly.

In 1981 Mexico had borrowed $15 billion; from June 1982, nothing. On orders of its government, the New York branches of six Mexican banks drew down their credit lines and borrowed some $6.5 billion in very short term money from the interbank market in order to finance Mexico's swelling budget deficits.

"By July it was clear we were going to the precipice," says Silva Herzog. At this point Lopez Portillo softened. Silva Herzog received "authority from the president to send a message to the Fund." On July 23 Silva Herzog requested a secret unofficial IMF mission. A week later a senior IMF man visited Mexico.

Despite the announcement of a new austerity package on August 1, another devaluation panic engulfed Mexico. Volcker offered an emergency $700 million three-month swap—a genuine Fed loan this time. "The swap was to get them to the IMF," says Volcker. "They said, 'We can't announce it until after September 1,' which was when the outgoing president made some big speech in the country. I remember Silva Herzog saying, 'I can assure you. I am the finance minister, a friend of de la Madrid.' " Mexico's commitment to negotiate an IMF adjustment program that would be announced in September was spelled out, albeit "elliptically," in an exchange of correspondences.

With the $700 million swap, Mexico was able to keep up interest payments due to U.S. banks. U.S. accounting rules required that loans upon which interest payments were ninety days overdue be classified as "nonaccruing." Unless appearances were kept, the public would be alerted to the crisis facing Mexico and the U.S. banking system.

The ability to create $700 million at a computer keystroke without protracted legislative political debate was one reason central bankers were so much faster on their feet than governments in a crisis. It was also why democratic governments were so often tempted to use discreet central banker channels to treat politically sensitive problems. This posed an uneasy dilemma to central bankers about their democratic accountability responsibilities.

To try to stem the peso attack, Mexico instituted a two-tier foreign exchange rate on August 5. But confidence was gone. The $700 million Fed loan disappeared in the tide of flight capital from Mexico. On August 12 the peso exchange markets were shut down. Just *before* the historic Mexican weekend meetings in Washington, Volcker telephoned "to the Bundesbank, the Bank of England, and to Leutwiler" to alert them to the impending problems. "Mexican troubles are worse than feared," he told them. "I warned you they were bad, and maybe we'd need a bridge [loan]."[19]

Quiet Crisis Management

Until the Mexican weekend, the Mexican debt problem was being stage-managed alone by Volcker with U.S. Treasury acquiescence. But once Mexico agreed to apply for an IMF program and the dire dimensions of the crisis became apparent, it was "only a matter of days before he [IMF chief de Larosière] was brought in and we developed a strategy," says Volcker. "You didn't need a genius to know you needed the Fund on board." Over the next weeks de Larosière and Volcker began to forge the close working alliance that became the strategic fulcrum for managing the debt crisis.

On Friday, August 13, Volcker outlined to Silva Herzog a scheme for ferrying Mexico to safety: international central bankers and the U.S. government might be able to provide a large emergency financing package to bridge Mexico over its political calendar and to an IMF adjustment program by late September. IMF financing would provide Mexico about $4.5 billion over three years and unlock private and government creditor debt reschedulings to alleviate Mexico's debt burden.

In the interim, Mexico's foreign bankers would have to be persuaded to grant a temporary moratorium on its debt principal repayments. Supplying the telephone numbers where America's top bankers, including Citibank's Wriston and Bank of America's Tom Clausen, could be reached even on weekends or vacation, Volcker urged Silva Herzog to set up a meeting with Mexico's 580 major bank creditors.

He soon did so at the New York Fed, for the following Friday, August 20.

After Silva Herzog left, Volcker began phoning key G10 central bank governors to advocate a $1.5 billion bridge loan to an IMF program for Mexico. The United States, he said, would contribute half of the total. He reached BIS President Fritz Leutwiler in the Swiss mountain town of Grison. Gordon Richardson of the Bank of England was away, so he talked to Deputy Governor Kit McMahon. BOJ Governor Haruo "Mike" Maekawa was out on the golf course when he received his call from the Fed chairman.

The intimacy of the Basel club, and its second allegiance to international monetary stability, obviated the need for long explanations about the nature of the crisis and cut through suspicions about hidden political agendas. Within forty-eight hours the central bankers reached an agreement in principle to proceed.

"The international debt thing was the high point for the central bank network," says Volcker. "I'd call them up to suggest something, and they could say 'yes' over the phone without entering into long negotiations or explanations. Over the weekend we could make a multibillion-dollar loan."

Securing $2 billion in emergency financing from the U.S. government, by contrast, was more arduous. Treasury Secretary Regan was departing for a weekend at Camp David with President Reagan to try to formulate a budget compromise with Congress, so he placed Deputy Secretary Tim McNamar, an energetic Californian in his mid-forties, in charge. He stayed in telephone contact. Throughout the hot summer weekend, representatives from State, Defense, Energy, Office of Management and Budget, and the National Security Council shuttled through the Treasury building. Top officials napped on couches and ate in as they worked forty-eight nonstop hours. Although the protocol was government to government, Volcker stalked the Treasury hallways and stayed in close touch by phone.

The first $1 billion, in Commodity Credit Corporation loan guarantees for U.S. crop purchases, was obtained by McNamar during a Saturday morning jog along Washington's C&O Canal with Agriculture Secretary John Block. A second $1 billion was sought by purchasing Mexican oil for the U.S. Strategic Petroleum Reserve. In order to justify spending $1 billion without congressional authorization, McNamar and Regan decided that they needed a bargain price. But the Mexicans had exactly the opposite political need—any perception that Mexico's patrimony was being sold at a discount to resented America could blow up in a nationalist backlash.

When Lopez Portillo was informed during his tennis game about the impasse, he ordered Silva Herzog to return to Mexico. "Let Rome burn," he snarled.[20]

To Volcker, the notion of jeopardizing the world financial system over a picayune price differential was madness. "I don't give a damn what you pay for oil," Volcker thundered at one point at U.S. negotiators. "If you *don't* do it, the whole thing is going to come crashing down—and it'll be your fault!"[21]

When McNamar proposed halving the U.S.'s discount, a "shouting match" broke out with Budget Director David Stockman, who objected vehemently. Regan finally overruled Stockman when he returned late Sunday afternoon. Silva Herzog, who had purposely dallied at the Mexican embassy, accepted the compromise. In hindsight, the $50 million front-end fee worked out to the equivalent of a hefty 15 percent price discount on the oil. As the final details of the deal were being worked out Sunday night, the exhausted McNamar turned to Volcker. "Paul, you've got to close it."

Volcker closed the deal. The world financial system inched back from the abyss.

Contrary to a cherished piece of financial folklore, rarely corrected by central bankers, the Basel governors' approval of the Mexican bridge loan was *not* finalized with merely a few harmonious weekend phone calls. "It was *not* so easy to raise the money," says Fritz Leutwiler.

Leutwiler summoned an emergency meeting of G10 deputy governors at the BIS for Wednesday, August 18, to concretize the governors' agreement in principle. The Germans, seconded by the Belgians, expressed skepticism that Mexico would conclude an adjustment program with the IMF—thus leaving central bank money at risk. Bowing to "heavy pressure from the Americans," however, the deputies approved the bridge pending review by the governors and Mexico's pledging adequate collateral in case the IMF negotiations failed.[22]

Among the governors, the strongest opposition came from Bundesbank President Karl Otto Pöhl. He expressed strong philosophical antipathy to prefinancing IMF agreements unless there was a clear and overriding systemic financial risk. Looking exclusively at German banks, the Bundesbank didn't see any: "I was never as convinced as my colleagues about the risk."[23] Says Don Regan, "I don't think Karl Otto [Pöhl] understood the weakness of the American banks."

A second problem was the personal competitiveness between Pöhl and Volcker. "There was no love lost between Paul Volcker and Karl Otto Pöhl," says one European governor. "I don't know if it is because Paul is so tall and Karl Otto is so short and round. But the American attitude *was* difficult to take: in the first case of Eastern Europe they say, 'It's you're problem, we won't help.' With Mexico they say, 'Our banking system's in danger and you *have* to help us.' So the personal tension between the two was a problem."[24] Since 1972 their careers had closely interweaved. When Volcker headed monetary policy and international affairs at the U.S. Treasury at the time of the breakup of the Bretton Woods system, Pöhl negotiated opposite him at the German Finance Ministry. Volcker's move to the New York Fed presidency in 1975 and chairmanship of the board in 1979 preceded Pöhl's parallel moves to Bundesbank vice president in 1977 and president in 1980.

Their personal contrasts were striking. Volcker was self-denying, puritanical in morality, introverted, intellectually soul-searching even though single-mindedly driven in pursuit of his concrete objectives, at times just plain rude. He'd had a close-knit family life as a child. Pöhl was a self-described "political animal": charming, humorous, and ebullient; he wore his emotions on his sleeve even when occasionally melancholic and was a natural consensus builder who shrewdly played economic political diplomacy on several dimensions. Despite a troubled childhood family life, he developed a personal bon vivant spirit that made him an atypical German: "A man who works to live, not lives to work."[25] Pöhl resented Volcker's imperious manipulations to achieve Fed goals. Pöhl was viewed by colleagues as frustrated by never quite being able to attain Volcker's stardom. Volcker, it seemed to one central banker, "rarely attended BIS meetings so as not to have his aura diminished by Pöhl."

The main task of mediating between Volcker and Pöhl during the debt crisis was undertaken by Leutwiler and Bank of England Governor Gordon Richardson. That August, in an early Sunday morning phone call, Leutwiler impressed upon Pöhl that the global crisis was real, not merely a Volcker political ploy to get others to pay for U.S. bank problems. "Goddammit, Fritz, okay," Pöhl finally relented at the end of the day. "But not a dollar or DM more."[26]

On Sunday, August 29, the BIS issued a terse communiqué announcing that the G10 governors had approved a $1.85 billion bridge loan for Mexico.[27] Final approval was facilitated by news that Mexico and an IMF team were making faster than expected progress toward agreement on an IMF program.

Engaging the private bankers was to prove the most vexing, though least publicized, dimension of preventing a calamitous detonation of the debt crisis. The task began in earnest on Thursday, August 19, when Silva Herzog called on a few top New York bankers to outline Mexico's plight. That evening he, his top financial assistant, Angel Gurria, Volcker, McNamar, New York Fed President Tony Solomon, Executive Vice President Sam Cross, and Ted Truman, the board's international finance chief, gathered in Solomon's tenth-floor office to discuss strategy for the big August 20 meeting with Mexico's international bankers.

Volcker and McNamar's trip had been declared a presidential mission so they could use one of the government's Lockheed Jetstars, says McNamar, because "Volcker and I didn't want anyone to know we were there. We were trying to ho-hum it because we were scared." The press had been slow to catch on to the scale of the impending crisis, which was "just how we wanted it."

Dinner was ordered in. Until 1 A.M. the group discussed "what kind of pitch to make to the assembled creditors. There weren't very many alternatives open. We wrote it out."[28] A failure to get the bankers to go along with a temporary suspension of principal repayments would torpedo the chances of ferrying Mexico to safety. They decided to display the Fed's blessing by having Solomon introduce Silva Herzog. He'd then recede as an observer while the Mexicans and bankers talked face-to-face.

The idea of creating an informal bank advisory committee composed of thirteen major international banks to overcome the logistical problem of negotiating with some six hundred creditors simultaneously jelled at this meeting. Volcker telephoned Walt Wriston of Citibank and Tom Clausen of Bank of America. They agreed to cooperate with Silva Herzog's request to provide two of the three advisory committee co-chairmen.

Wriston promptly dispatched a Citicorp jet to recall Senior Vice President

William Rhodes from his vacation in St. Martin's. In short order Bill Rhodes, a dogged negotiator who got on with everybody, became one of the heroes of the debt crisis as the world bankers' point man on debt for virtually every major debtor country. He worked intimately with Volcker and de Larosière.

Deutsche Bank, however, refused to serve as third co-chair on the grounds that it was turning into a U.S.-dominated process. Its slot was soon filled by Swiss Bank Corporation. "We had to put *some* European on it," explains Silva Herzog.

The next morning at 11 A.M. Tony Solomon addressed the 115 assembled bank representatives at the New York Fed. After explaining the official support actions that were in the works, including the Basel bridge loan, he turned the meeting over to Silva Herzog. Silva Herzog portrayed Mexico's problems as a foreign exchange liquidity squeeze caused by capital flight, the world recession, a bunching of debt repayments, and the sudden slamming shut of private bank doors on Mexico. He asked for a ninety-day "standstill," which sounded less menacing than "moratorium," on about $10 billion in principal repayments falling due over the coming three months. Interest payments would continue to be met. The additional time, he promised, would be used to tie up an IMF economic adjustment program with $4.5 billion financing over three years. At the end of the ninety days he intended to offer a plan to restructure Mexico's debts.

Bankers departed believing that they'd be asked to pony up $500 million to $1 billion to help Mexico get through.[29] They were still unaware of the full force of the LDC debt tempest that lay dead ahead. They believed they were dealing just with Mexico and perhaps Argentina. Mexico, they thought, was a short-term liquidity problem that would be solved with falling U.S. interest rates, economic recovery, and a little creditor forbearance. "Bankers felt Brazil wouldn't get into this mess," says Tony Solomon. "It was a shock later on. Only in hindsight is it easy to see the chain reaction effect."

On the afternoon of August 20 the new bank advisory committee started its first tedious weekend of totting up debt amounts and loan maturity dates and soliciting rollovers from banks with repayments that were coming due immediately. When there was a problem, the central bankers helped out. A few medium-size banks refused to roll over their interbank credits. But all major banks cooperated.[30]

By the end of August hopes were high that Mexico could announce an IMF adjustment program by the start of IMF/World Bank annual meetings in Toronto on September 6. And it might have been so had not the rug suddenly been pulled out from under everyone by the mercurial President Lopez Portillo.

The Crisis Explodes

In his final State of the Union address on September 1, Lopez Portillo stunned the world by defiantly announcing the nationalization of Mexico's banks to end the "looting" of Mexico. Private banks had "betrayed us" by encouraging flight capital. He also swiped at the IMF, whose medicine was to "deprive the patient of food."

Lopez Portillo regaled in the nationalistic adulations that ensued. Sycophants called it the most important act in Mexican history since nationalization of foreign oil companies in 1938. It represented a stunning eleventh-hour political victory for the radicals and defeat for the orthodox economic liberals. Silva Herzog hadn't been informed until the night before. Miguel Mancera was forced out of the central bank and replaced by a radical, Carlos Tellos.

The IMF solution anchoring the Mexican rescue was suddenly adrift. There were doubts that President-elect de la Madrid would make it to office on December 1. Rumors abounded about troop movements, assassinations, coups d'état. The radical urge would tempt LDCs throughout the debt crisis: that on balance the country might be better off spurning the rules of the international liberal economic order and instead turning inward toward autarky by renouncing its debts.

A few days later, under a vapor of confusion, gloom, and incipient panic, some ten thousand bankers, government financial policymakers, and journalists streamed into Toronto from all over the world for the 1982 IMF/World Bank joint annual meetings and events around it. The only silver lining in Lopez Portillo's shock was that it occurred when the world's financial leadership were gathering in one place and could react together.

Since the demise of the Bretton Woods monetary system, the fringes of the IMF/World Bank meetings had evolved into a sort of floating private marketplace, where OPEC surpluses were recycled from oil producers to LDC debtors. Bankers mobbed in like conventioneers, throwing ever more lavish parties in concert halls, museums, historic buildings, and boats, as they competed with each other to solicit OPEC deposits from Middle Eastern sheiks and to "sell" loans to LDC finance ministers. The hard-driving revelers of 1982, however, were consumed by a single alien preoccupation: how would they get their money back?

Even Silva Herzog could not assure them what Lopez Portillo would do, because he himself didn't honestly know. Argentina, rattled by the Falklands-Malvinas War, looked increasingly problematic. Anxious gossip was exchanged about Brazil and other Latin debtors. Citibank's Walt Wriston sardonically described the scene in Toronto as "150-odd finance ministers, 50-odd central bankers, 1000 journalists, 1000 commercial bankers, a large supply of whiskey and a reasonably small city that produced an enormous head of steam driving the engine called 'the end of the world is coming.' "[31] He adds, "That's a hell of a story. Everyone wants it."[32]

"The bankers were there a couple of days before the ministers," recalls German Finance Minister Manfred Lahnstein. "They were running around as if the world were coming to an end! We had other issues in Toronto, but when we got there it was Mexico, Mexico, Mexico! The Mexicans were lost, but absolutely relaxed. I had a ten A.M. appointment with Silva Herzog, and he showed up at eleven-fifteen. He said, 'I went to play tennis and I forgot. Sorry.' "

Volcker, Bank of England Governor Gordon Richardson, and Swiss National Bank President Fritz Leutwiler, backed by the quiet, stalwart financial support of Bank of Japan Governor Haruo "Mike" Maekawa, began naturally to take charge when they arrived in Toronto. They quickly linked up with the IMF's de Larosière. It was from the Toronto meetings that the world financial community's image of the LDC debt strategy's "Big Four" heroes—Volcker, Richardson, Leutwiler, and de Larosière—was first cast. "The first alarm was with the banks and the central banks," says Lahnstein. "They defined the scope and depth of the problem, not the governments. Governments are always slower to respond in these matters."[33]

At Toronto a loose routine was established whereby the Big Four met over breakfast in Leutwiler's room. Throughout the day they held court in Richardson's suite, which became the informal command and control center and clearinghouse for the most reliable available information. All day long LDC finance ministers and world bank chiefs shuttled in to present their problems and concerns, or at least as much as they were willing to reveal. "Banks, international organizations like the IMF, the politicians," says Fritz Leutwiler, "we all got acquainted with the debt problem in Toronto. The dimensions were previously unknown. Argentina, Chile, Venezuela—all said they were essentially broke." Secretly seeking help, "the countries promised us everything, of course."

Even though "it was clear in Toronto that you'd be in trouble with the other countries," Volcker and his fellow central bankers found it in their interest not to dispute the public assertions by the LDC ministers that their countries would be able to muddle through, lest all hope be consumed by a panicked stampede of fleeing bankers.[34] Above all that included the largest LDC debtor, Brazil, which confidently insisted that it was different and would rebound unaided with the world economic recovery. In the coming months, bankers morbidly tittered that Brazil was indeed different—*worse!*

As the terrifying dimensions unfolded, the Big Four somberly devised the course of action. "I was personally worried," says Leutwiler. "Richardson was worried. Volcker was worried. We were even depressed. We thought we were more than colleagues in the eye of a hurricane."

First on the agenda was ascertaining what was happening with Mexico. Early on during the "hours and hours" of discussions with Silva Herzog, Richardson asked whether Silva Herzog was still empowered to speak for Mexico. "That is a fair question," responded Silva Herzog. "If I'm not, then you'll be talking to someone less flexible." The central bankers insisted Silva Herzog check before they undertook any salvage operation. Upon calling Mexico City, he discovered that he was.[35]

With LDC debtors, Mexico included, so far not daring to utter the "default" word, the gravest immediate peril to the world financial order was that panicked bankers would try to cut separate deals with LDC debtors to salvage what they could and flee—setting off a self-destructive banker stampede to be first to the exits. Banker cohesion thus became a cardinal condition to avert catastrophe.

Some U.S. bankers tried to organize a bankers' solution. It quickly broke up on the shoals of clashing short-run competitive interests, mutual suspicion of motives, and divergent national bank regulatory incentives among banks. "There was a cacophony," recalls high Mexican policymaker Gustavo Petricioli, who later became finance minister. "It was almost impossible to have a solution without the participation of the central banks due to the short-term views of the commercial banks."

When the interbank markets reopened on Tuesday, September 7, following the Labor Day holiday, bankers panicked. They demanded that the New York branches of Mexican banks refund the roughly $6.5 billion they'd deposited with them. On September 2 the bank advisory committee had agreed that Mexico's interbank deposits should be rolled over temporarily; yet only five days later the bankers were trampling over each other to flee Mexico. It was a bank run on an entire country.

By day's end Mexican bank branches had ordered their CHIPS (Clearinghouse Interbank Payment System) representatives, Chemical and Manufacturers Hanover, to repay $70 million more than they could cover. CHIPS was run by America's biggest banks, which executed payment transfers on behalf of correspondent banks around the world. At the end of the day they netted out the transactions to be settled between them. Each bank collected what it was owed from its own correspondents.[36] But if all the netted CHIPS transactions could not be settled, then *no* CHIPS payments were made. Thus if Manufacturers and Chemical refused to cover the Mexicans' $70 million shortfall, all CHIPS transactions would unwind. In short order the world's dollar payment system would freeze up.

The international interbank market was already quaking from the teetering of Continental Illinois and other U.S. banks and the June 1982 collapse of Italy's Banco Ambrosiano. Ever since the 1974 fall of Herstatt Bank, central bankers had fretted that the international interbank market, which had grown twentyfold since the Bretton Woods demise, was an Achilles' heel of the world financial system since through it trouble could rapidly cascade worldwide. "The interbank market is like one of those electronic air route maps," says Brian Quinn, the Bank of England's point man for LDC debt. "It lit up all at once and you saw the myriad interconnections spanning the globe."

On September 7 in Toronto, a tragic end grew nigh. "I'm convinced that the international payments clearing system was on the brink," says Leutwiler. "New York interbank clearing would have broken down and after that spilled over to London and Switzerland. So we were all on the spot together. It was an unthinkable disaster if it happened." Volcker, Richardson, and Leutwiler improvised an unusual kind of lender of last resort operation. First they deposited $70 million of the Basel Mexican bridge loan funds in the Federal Reserve accounts of Chemical and Manufacturers so that they could meet their commitments to CHIPS. Over the next few days the central bankers "injected money every day, $50 to $70 million, whatever was needed, to keep the New York clearing system going."[37]

But unless the hemorrhaging was stanched at the source, the entire first tranche of the $1.85 billion bridge loan to Mexico could be drained away paying fleeing banks their interbank deposits, while the contagion spread to other types of Mexican debt. Since the classic approach of pouring in liquidity to stop a run would not work in this case, Silva Herzog, at the central bankers' exhortation, asked the Mexican banks *not* to honor any repayment demands. If they did try to repay, he told them, they'd face the virtual impossibility of finding the dollars themselves. Mexico's central bank would not exchange its dollar reserves for their pesos to help them.

Volcker, Richardson, Leutwiler, and de Larosière, meanwhile, applied moral suasion to curtail repayment demands from banks. In a rare, transparent demonstration of the central bankers' role as leader of the inner-core banking club, they summoned the major bank chiefs to a meeting and delivered a jarringly blunt message: If you press repayment demands for your short-term interbank credits, you'll precipitate a collapse of Mexico; the much larger amount of your longer-term outstanding Mexican loans will never be repaid. To give teeth to their message, they announced that any further drawings on the Basel central bank $1.85 billion bridge loan was contingent upon firm progress of an IMF accord for Mexico. "De Larosière, Richardson, Volcker, and myself, we four, said: 'If you don't put money in, these countries will be bankrupt and the world system will collapse,' " narrates Leutwiler. "Everyone was frightened. But the banks needed a leader to organize them. We were masters—teachers, really."

The central bankers' message awakened the bankers to the larger stakes. "Until that meeting," says J. P. Morgan Chairman Lewis Preston, "the commercial banks didn't realize their vulnerability."

Although Mexican interbank outpayment leakage to smaller banks continued, the heavy hemorrhaging ended. Sums up Volcker: "There was a narrow missing of an unraveling of the crisis at the IMF meetings in Toronto. There was panic in the banking system. We had a run on Mexico. We ended it by the skin of our teeth. It was a grievous way to stop a run, but we'd dole it [the Basel bridge money] out by the spoonfuls. There were ten- or fifteen-minute telephone calls [to dissuade fleeing bankers]. Finally we got a promise not to pay it out [from Mexico]. It was a continuous negotiation for a few days."

Chapter 14

Buying Time

The corking up of the incipient interbank run at Toronto was a decisive juncture in management of the debt crisis. A cohesive view of the problem was starting to jell. Strategic leadership was being asserted by the Big Four under Volcker. Creditor nation finance ministers were falling into line behind them. Bankers and LDC debtors were becoming aware of the stakes and aware that extraordinary sacrifices would be demanded.

The crisis containment goals of the nascent LDC debt strategy were two: first and foremost, to save the world financial system from crashing; second, to restore sufficient confidence to resurrect a functioning private market in LDC lending.

As experienced central bankers, Volcker, Richardson, and Leutwiler understood that success hinged on inventing an artificial mechanism to provide sufficient financing to borrow time for LDCs to adjust to the sharply altered conditions. "The more orderly and effective the adjustment," Volcker said a couple of months after the Toronto meetings, "the more readily growth in the developing world can be restored and sustained, the more our own export markets and those of other industrialized countries will expand, and the more promptly any questions about the possible impact on the earnings of international banks can be put to rest. It is precisely for these reasons that there exists the strongest kind of community of interest among borrowers and lenders, among governments and private businesses, and among the developing and industrialized countries, in working together to find effective answers to the evident problems."[1]

Free markets always adjusted to disequilibrating economic shocks—without adequate financing, however, they could so with an abrupt crash. A depression threatened to set off debt renunciations and a worldwide crisis. Volcker's attitude was informed by "an instinctive understanding that in the twenties and thirties it had fallen apart because there'd not been collective

action" to maintain an orderly international mix of financing and adjustment.[2] "In the end, adjustment in debtor countries had to be made," Gordon
Richardson of the Bank of England explains. "But it would have been a brutal adjustment without the financing. We wanted to make it as smooth as possible."

At Toronto the Big Four began to formulate what would become known
as the "buying time," case-by-case strategy. Its essence was to maintain systemic confidence by generating a financing flow to LDCs in support of economic adjustment under IMF aegis. "What we central bankers did before,
during, and after was to buy time," says Fritz Leutwiler. "The hope was to
buy time, by which I mean a couple of years, for the IMF and the countries
to elaborate a more durable solution to the LDC debt problem."

As the years went on, some critics faulted the "buying time" strategy for
misdiagnosing the LDC debt crisis as a short-term liquidity problem instead
of a long-term structural or solvency problem. But practical central bankers
trying to defuse an imminent world economic and political catastrophe "did
not use hackneyed phrases like liquidity or solvency," snaps New York Fed
President Tony Solomon.

"[T]he distinction between insolvency and lack of liquidity is easier to
make in a textbook than in the real world," elaborates Volcker. "After serving
for a while as a central banker, I'm not sure I've ever seen a pure liquidity
problem. Typically, significant liquidity problems arise because there is some
question of solvency, or there would be no lack of willing lenders."[3] Whether
the cause of a potential LDC crash landing was illiquidity or insolvency, crisis management required the same prescription—additional financing. If the
LDC debt problem turned out to be primarily a liquidity squeeze brought on
by unique external conditions, as most experts then thought, the financing
provided by the buying time strategy might alone be enough to ferry the
debtor countries and world banking system through. If it turned out to be a
deeper, longer-term structural problem, financing bought time to develop
better, more enduring strategies.

Simultaneously, the buying time strategy allowed bankers gradually to reduce their exposure to LDCs through growth in other areas and by building
capital against eventual LDC loan write-offs. "They knew they were buying
time for the banks to strengthen their balance sheets," says Lloyds Chairman
Jeremy Morse.

An often overlooked third goal of the strategy was to preserve the entrepreneurial Latin American middle class that had emerged in the 1970s.
"Volcker was worried about a private-sector collapse in Mexico and these
countries if the adjustment was too sudden," says Citibank's Bill Rhodes.
Politically the middle class was the backbone of support for democratic government. Economically it facilitated early restoration of voluntary market

finance. "Paul was a man who didn't talk only of interest and exchange rate policies," says Mexico's Silva Herzog. "He had a wide vision of the realpolitik. In this sense he was not a central banker but a politician."

Volcker's many uncommon central banker skills proved to be fortuitous in formulating the world's response to the debt crisis. His wider political vision, strength as a strategic thinker, proclivity for active leadership, skepticism that free market mechanisms always produced results consonant with the best public interest, acumen in sensing when negotiating parties had reached their limits, and talent for exploring the complexities of problems helped compensate for the fact that central banks institutionally were *not* optimally suited to govern a problem with such global political economic dimensions, as soon became evident when the debt strategy became entangled with trade, the dollar, and the future of Latin American democracy.

The fulcrum of the buying time, case-by-case LDC debt strategy was the IMF. Scaled down from John Maynard Keynes's grand vision as a proto–world central bank that could issue a world monetary reserve asset, the IMF was born from the 1944 Bretton Woods conference to supply short-term balance of payments financing to member countries that cut spending and undertook other adjustment policies in support of the fixed exchange rate parity regime. With floating exchange rates, the IMF's central purpose disappeared. It spent the 1970s trying unsuccessfully to discover a new mission. Thus when Volcker turned to Managing Director Jacques de Larosière for the Fund to take a central role in the debt crisis, the Frenchman leapt at the opportunity.

The IMF provided a common meeting ground for LDC debtors, private bankers, and creditor governments to negotiate the "burden-sharing" allocations—who paid—for the buying time debt strategy. "If a company is in trouble, the first thing you do is try to get all the people with problems into a room. The multiple negotiation surrounding an IMF agreement for an adjustment program does something like that," explains Gordon Richardson.

The LDC's share of the burden was the austere economic adjustment it undertook: a typical IMF program consisted of currency devaluation to enhance export competitiveness, tight monetary policy and wage restraint to control inflation, and sharp deficit reduction to give more scope to private enterprise. Achieving specific IMF adjustment targets was the condition for financing relief. Financing came from the multilateral IMF, the Paris Club of national government creditors, and from the private banks. Central bankers provided emergency bridge loans. "The debtors didn't doubt your sincerity even if they thought you were primarily interested in saving the banks and the financial structure," says one of the debt strategy's senior architects. "We were, of course. We didn't say it. But the debtors were better off if the system worked—that was their best chance."

Although the negotiation between the LDC debtor and the IMF received the most press attention, the negotiation among creditors over division of the financing burden was tougher. The first set of creditor negotiations was between governments and private bankers. A second set was among government creditors. The third, and most complex, pitted different nationalities and classes of private bankers against one another.

At Toronto, Volcker, de Larosière, Richardson, and Leutwiler began to tackle the problem of "how to engage those with money to contribute it for the process."[4] Finance ministers commenced the process by negotiating over how much to increase government financing for the IMF. Working on what for them was an expedited basis, they agreed within several months to boost IMF funding by $45 billion.

More difficult to engage were the bankers. "The banks, of course, just wanted the Fund to pay them the money," remembers the U.S. Treasury's Tim McNamar. "That was a nonstarter with all the governments and central banks. Just to show how rudimentary we all were in dealing with it, there was some discussion that surely there couldn't be any new bank money until the IMF was fully dispersed, that maybe after the third tranche the banks could come in with the fourth. The banks weren't organized yet."

Bankers argued that governments should assume most of the financial burden on the grounds that they had encouraged them to recycle the OPEC surpluses to the LDCs. "Could you show me the press release or speech where the government said this?!" retorted McNamar. Even though there was little doubt that many government leaders *had* tacitly encouraged lending, arguments over who should be responsible carried little weight when it came to hard-nosed bargaining over money.[5] The bottom line was that the cost of financing the LDCs was simply more than governments were alone willing to bear, above all when citizens' taxes would subsidize fleeing bankers.

For the first time, and only among themselves, Volcker, Richardson, Leutwiler, and de Larosière articulated the need for bankers to contribute far more amounts of new money (in addition to rescheduling LDC loans) than most bankers yet imagined. Extraordinary measures would be needed to compel all banks to pony up their share. Standard practice was for IMF financing to go first and banks to fulfill their tacit understanding to follow in good time. "The feeling among us was that the magnitude of the problem was so great that it couldn't follow the traditional issuing of an IMF program and expect the banks to follow," recalls New York Fed President Tony Solomon.

At a two-day seminar at Annapolis, Maryland, in late July 1982, top IMF officials wrestled with the problem of how to avoid sticking the IMF with all the financing burden on Mexico. "There was no question in anybody's mind that Fund money had to be linked to bank money," says its organizer, senior IMF executive David Finch. "The only problem was the exact tactics. How much time pressure to put on the banks was one question. De Larosière was probing on the strategy to be followed."

De Larosière's ultimate solution, worked out two months later, would become one of the milestones of the debt strategy. At Toronto Finch informally bounced the formula off Citibank's Walt Wriston that banks come in with new money equal to half Mexico's total annual interest payments—or about $6 billion. "We had the figures more or less," Finch says. "It was a political judgment to get half."

Wriston shrugged. He seemed favorable but didn't promise anything.

A second problem was that the IMF would have to work much faster than usual. This was emphatically impressed upon de Larosière one midnight at Toronto by the Treasury's Tim McNamar at a meeting of top U.S. and IMF officials. McNamar lost his temper when he heard that Fund officials hoped to put together an initial Mexican adjustment program within two months and have it ready for IMF board approval " 'sometime, on an expedited basis, this winter.' "

"This winter!" he shouted. "You are out of your goddamned minds! By then you'll have Argentina and Brazil in there as well! Continental Illinois is collapsing, too! We're going to have a crisis in the whole fucking financial system by this winter if we don't have a Mexican program!"

McNamar's tirade was greeted first with a stunned silence, then with a "traditional 'just because you're our largest shareholder you can't tell us what to do' kind of reaction."[6] David Finch, who was responsible for IMF economic adjustment programs and was especially distressed at the political pressure to force a quick program on the IMF, at one point retorted, "If you put the arm on us, any failure of the program will be the U.S.'s fault!"[7] He explains, "If we acted too quickly, without really doing our homework, the banks would see it as a fraudulent program. So we wanted more time."

Overriding the objections of Finch and most top IMF staff, de Larosière decided to greatly accelerate the Fund's pace. It was the first of his several courageous gambles to transform the IMF into an institution capable of crisis management. From that point on, "he moved into high gear and increasingly higher gear."[8] Says McNamar, "Jacques de Larosière responded not just magnificently, but superlatively."

Yet, as Finch predicted, IMF program credibility *did* suffer. Major debtor adjustment programs and financing needs were regularly worked out with Fed, and later Treasury, officials in order to strike a balance between what was economically desirable and what was politically feasible. The IMF's numbers became regarded by all parties as politically prostituted. "The Fund was the Fund—I don't need to say any more," says Volcker. "We don't have to discuss what kinds of programs they put in. Those are negotiated numbers. But they're the only ones in town."

Ironically, while the IMF's tilt over the years toward accommodating LDC debtors upset bankers, it also became a lightning rod for political discontent in LDCs that constantly threatened upheaval. "At times you wish it weren't there," Volcker says. "But we had no substitute."

Launching the Debt Strategy

The indispensable start of the debt crisis management process was getting the LDC debtor to accept an IMF adjustment program. Lopez Portillo hadn't expressly ruled out the IMF in his speech. But banker gloom was spreading at Toronto that an IMF package for Mexico couldn't be attained before the three-month standstill expired on November 23. Without the prospect of an IMF agreement, bankers would be tempted to break ranks to try to flee Mexico. All would be lost.

De Larosière worked fast. At breakfast on September 5, Silva Herzog asked de Larosière for a memorandum to take to Lopez Portillo to keep the negotiations alive. A politically inoffensive memorandum of flexible definitions, and without a single number, was prepared. De Larosière signed it on September 8.[9]

To the puzzlement of many, Silva Herzog delayed a day before returning to Mexico. He explains, "I wanted to get to Mexico as close to the official declaration of de la Madrid [as president-elect on September 10]. I wasn't sure the president would accept it. I saw him the day after and presented a carefully prepared memo of alternatives." To Silva Herzog's relief, Lopez Portillo agreed to resume IMF negotiations. Silva Herzog telephoned the good news to de Larosière and Volcker. They were at dinner in a Canadian resort to which Volcker had invited de Larosière for a brief, working fly-fishing holiday after the IMF meetings ended. That evening Silva Herzog rushed to the hospital with appendicitis. For several weeks he dropped out of sight. Bankers on the advisory committee grew anxious. Citibank's Bill Rhodes flew to Mexico on September 26 but for three days couldn't find him. Then, finally, Silva Herzog called. "He knew the reports that I'd had appendicitis," says Silva Herzog. "He wanted to check that I actually had it. There were rumors I'd been shot or kidnapped."

Reassured, Rhodes returned home. He looked for signs of progress in the IMF negotiations with the radicalized Lopez Portillo government.

• • •

Before leaving Toronto, the central bankers also managed one back-channel deal to alleviate the Argentine debt cloud that threatened to break on top of the Mexican crisis. At issue was the reciprocal U.K.-Argentine asset freeze. Even though Argentina withheld debt service payments to its international bank lending syndicate by the amount due U.K. banks, U.K. banks continued to invoke their legal rights to a full share of the Argentine repayments received by syndicate. The result was that the entire international banking community shared the penalty aimed at British banks. Argentine arrearages had accumulated to about $2 billion. At Toronto, Argentina made secret overtures to the Big Four for help. But international bankers refused to negotiate long-term rescheduling relief until Argentina settled its dispute with the United Kingdom. Without the banks, the IMF was unwilling to make an emergency loan.

When U.S. Deputy Treasury Secretary Tim McNamar first suggested seeking a U.K.-Argentine rapprochement to break the impasse, U.K. Chancellor of the Exchequer Geoffrey Howe rejected it. British casualties in the Falklands-Malvinas War made it an uncompromisable political issue for Prime Minister Margaret Thatcher.

At that point Bank of England Governor Gordon Richardson intervened. "Well, now, what if we thought about another way of phrasing it? Of course, it would be imperative that the Argentines went first. *If* they went first, and *if* it was something we could do through central banks rather than government to government, *then* perhaps we could have a constructive response."

Over the next few days McNamar shuttled between the several crowded floors separating the Argentine and U.K. offices until the two sides, never having spoken to each other, were pretty close. But each time Mrs. Thatcher was consulted by Howe, the U.K. position hardened. Finally it was agreed that an accord could be constructed as a technical exchange by telex between their two nominally nonpolitical central banks.

"Not only did Gordon have a global perspective, but he could do something that a chancellor could not do since he was independent from the government. So could [Argentine central bank Governor] Julio Gonzalez del Solar," explains McNamar of the utility of the central bank channel to depoliticize international financial problems. "We used the time differential so that the Argentines could say the British had gone first and the British could say the Argentines had gone first. We had to call an airline because no one knew the time differentials between London and Buenos Aires."

The final details were worked out via telephone with McNamar as intermediary during the week following the Toronto meetings. In mid-September the two sides unfroze each other's assets. That unlocked the door for an eventual IMF emergency financing package, a BIS bridge loan, and a private bank debt rescheduling.

Clearing the deck of the Argentine debt problem characterized the case-by-case approach of trying to deal with each major debtor separately. While the case-by-case approach evolved originally from timing disparities between the outbreak of each debtor's problem and the insistence of each that its debt problems were different from those of its neighbors, Volcker and the Big Four translated it into a divide-and-conquer tactic that reduced the chance of a debtors' cartel and alleviated the practical danger of being overwhelmed by having too much on the plate at any one time. "The case-by-case strategy has been very intelligent politically," admits Mexico's Silva Herzog.

Crisis Managers

If a debtors' cartel was anathema, forging a bank creditors' cartel was an absolute imperative of the unfolding buying time, case-by-case strategy. Unless bankers stuck together, explains Volcker, "they'd all have been running to the exits ahead of each other, and there'd be carnage at the exit." No bank would lend to an LDC debtor so that its noncooperating competitors could hitch a free ride and be paid back. "In Toronto we all knew that the solution for one had to be the solution for all," says Walt Wriston.

In the weeks following the Toronto meetings, the central bankers worked feverishly behind the scenes to maintain discipline among six hundred fractious international bank creditors, their governments—and the Basel club itself—while Mexico inched its way to an IMF program. They conferred everywhere from Basel to Tokyo, where there were several days of festivities in October to celebrate the Bank of Japan's one-hundredth anniversary. Richardson and Volcker, who grew especially close, secretly air-commuted back and forth by Concorde for dinner and one-day rendezvous.

The cross-default clause in the syndicated LDC lending agreements meant that any single bank that sued for debt repayment could trigger the avalanche of defaults that would pull down the rescue rope linking all banks. Unnaturally, a creditors' cartel required that banks suspend indefinitely the capitalist market forces that animated competition between them. German and Swiss banks, which had been more conservative in LDC lending, "had their noses out of joint because the American banks had profited so much from the oil recycling," recalls U.S. Treasury Secretary Don Regan. "They were crying that the American banks had overextended themselves."

The two deepest fault lines dividing bankers were size and national origin: between the international banks and the smaller, regional banks on the one hand and the vulnerable giant U.S. money center banks and the rest of the world on the other.[10] Central bankers also struggled constantly to bridge accounting regimes that were as incompatible as Beta and VHS video recorder formats. "Accounting rules of various sides of the Atlantic have been a curiosity until the advent of the global marketplace," notes Wriston.

Since any U.S. loan upon which interest payments were over ninety days late was automatically classified as "nonaccruing" and subtracted from reported profits until collected, big U.S. banks insisted that any debt strategy keep interest payments current. "Wriston's number one concern and that of the American banks was to maintain their profitability," says Regan. Yet German, Swiss, and other continental European bankers preferred to exploit the favorable tax and nondisclosure treatment of their nations' accounting regimes to build large bad-debt reserves and get the LDC problem behind them quickly. They had no motivation to keep up pro forma interest payments.

"On the creditor side, nothing was uniform," Volcker sums up. "Central banks did not operate in the same way, tax policies and accounting rules were different, and so was the supervisory treatment. There wasn't much we could do. We tried to avoid even more inconsistencies."

The singular incentive for the world's banks to join a creditors' cartel was the prospect that LDC defaults would cause big bank counterparty failures that toppled the world financial system. Volcker, Richardson, Leutwiler, and de Larosière tried to exploit the central banker's position as national banking club leader to persuade sophisticated, strong-willed bankers that the systemic jeopardy was real and that yielding their autonomy to the banking cartel was the best hope of salvation.

In the weeks after Toronto they coached the bankers to remain calm. In October 1982 Lloyds Chairman Jeremy Morse invited Richardson to address a gathering of bankers at London's Guildhall because "we were worried the banks wouldn't hold together. The French banks had just been nationalized, and they changed all the chairmen. It was a miracle getting four hundred banks to act together."

For about a month the central bankers also took the active lead in managing the bank advisory committee's Mexican interbank book "due to the ignorance of the commercial banks," says J. P. Morgan Chairman Lewis Preston. Each day the amounts due from the Mexican bank branches in New York and London were identified and creditors persuaded to roll over their credits and above all not to sue for repayments. Chairmen of recalcitrant banks were telephoned frequently. Calling upon its moral suasion tradition, Bank of England brass summoned stubborn chairmen to Threadneedle Street up to three times to impress upon them that systemic stability required their cooperation. When a foreign bank demanded repayment, the Bank of England and the Fed called their fellow central bankers in the Basel club for assistance.[11]

At critical moments in the months and years following, central bankers, led by the Fed and Bank of England, served as behind-the-scenes last-resort enforcers when the bankers and their chairmen could not make progress with a stubborn peer. In doing so, they often operated beyond the traditional political boundaries of central banking. "It was stepping quite far out of line for a central bank to ask each counterparty not to sue," acknowledges Bank of England Executive Director Brian Quinn.[12]

Some wouldn't. The Bundesbank eschewed trying to exert any moral suasion with small German mortgage banks, which just wanted out of the tiny $10 million participations they'd bought from bigger banks. "There was not much you could do to lean on them," says a Bank of England official. Even Fed intervention wasn't enough to dissuade the repayment demands of some determined U.S. banks, such as New Jersey's Mid-Atlantic, Florida's Flagship Bank, and European-American of New York.[13]

Mexican interbank outpayment leakage, and "topping up" fund injections into CHIPS by CHIPS members, remained problematic enough in the weeks after Toronto that many bank advisory committee members wanted formally to reschedule the interbank debt along with Mexico's medium- and long-term debt, as part of the Mexican rescue package. The showdown debate came on November 12, just days before the August standstill was to elapse. Cognizant that the Bank of England strongly opposed rescheduling interbank debt, committee chairman Bill Rhodes of Citibank invited Brian Quinn and the New York Fed's Sam Cross to address the meeting at the New York offices of the Shearman and Sterling law firm.[14] Although central bankers were regular fixtures at advisory committee meetings, this was the first time they would speak. Flying the Concorde, Quinn arrived while the meeting was already in session. Rhodes warned him and Cross privately that he "could sense the crumbling going on around the table." Quinn, a personable Scotsman, argued as persuasively as he could that rescheduling Mexican interbank debt could induce banks to flee from other suspect Euromarket interbank borrowers, such as Turkey and Korea. Their otherwise manageable liquidity problems would become full-fledged crises.

The advisory committee acquiesced. The ad hoc rollovers were continued. A very subtle—more gentleman's than legal—agreement was reached between bankers and Mexico, whereby the aggregate value of Mexican interbank debt (without specific single bank obligations) had to remain above $5.2 billion. If not, all Mexican debt would be considered in default. It was effectively a line in the sand to delineate the minimum threshold for holding together the creditors' cartel that anchored the Mexican rescue.

As the central bankers struggled to resolve the Mexican crisis, they also worked on their own national contingency plans in the event the LDC crisis exploded. In Switzerland Fritz Leutwiler developed a strategy to funnel all the country's dollar reserves in an effort to save the Big Three Swiss banks—Union Bank of Switzerland, Swiss Bank Corporation, and Credit Suisse—and *only* them. "We couldn't save a hundred banks," says Leutwiler. "Nor four or five or a dozen—just the Big Three of Switzerland. The bankers knew it at the time, though of course I never guaranteed them."

In the United States there was no formal contingency plan for fear of leaks. But there was a general understanding among the regulators about what would be done: "The approach on a bailout would have been for the Fed to pump in liquidity and the FDIC to buy capital notes [from the banks]—in effect, you nationalize the banking system for some time," explains C. Todd Conover, then U.S. comptroller.[15]

International central bankers discussed doomsday scenarios in private, but "there was no [international] plan how to cope with this," reports Leutwiler.

Near Disaster

The November 12 decision by the advisory committee to keep rolling over interbank debt was conditioned by the breakthrough signing on November 10 of a Mexican letter of intent for an IMF adjustment program. By niggardly rationing of the Basel central bankers' bridge money, Volcker had allowed the continuing attrition of Mexico's dollar reserves to push President Lopez Portillo into the IMF's embrace.

The actual breakthrough had come earlier in Washington on Friday, October 22, when the new radical Bank of Mexico chief, Carlos Tello, Silva Herzog, and Carlos Salinas (later Mexican president) met separately with Volcker and Bill Rhodes of the bank advisory committee. Tello demanded large concessions, an "anti-IMF" agreement. Volcker and Rhodes's steadfast refusals backed him down. In addition to IMF financing, the way was cleared for negotiations to restructure Mexico's private bank debt. The basic terms of Mexico's IMF adjustment program were similar to those in train before Lopez Portillo's defiant speech on September 1: cutting Mexico's budget deficit in half, reducing foreign borrowing by three-quarters, halving the 100 percent inflation rate, reducing subsidies and wages. In short, drastic austerity—but better than the upheaval Mexico faced without international help.

Only a handful of people to this day knew how narrowly the Mexican rescue came to being undone in the three weeks between the October 22 breakthrough and the November letter of intent's signing. The near disaster came not from Mexico, but from another quarter that had seemed safely harbored for the moment: Brazil.

Ever since the Toronto meetings, bankers' retreat from Brazilian bank branches in the interbank market had accelerated.[16] In nine months foreign interbank credit for Brazil had shrunk by over $1 billion. With a national election coming up on November 15, Brazilian officials continued to insist that their troubles didn't require IMF assistance or even rescheduling the $87 billion debt (then publicly estimated by Brazil at $72 billion). But in October Brazil entered secret negotiations with private bankers headed by J. P. Morgan for a bridge of up to $3 billion to get through the elections and into an IMF program. As soon as Morgan began to study Brazil's finances, the alarms sounded.

Recalls J. P. Morgan Chairman Lewis Preston, "Our view was that Brazil was a very different problem from Mexico. There was no capital flight. It had strong export capacity. [Brazil Planning Minister Antonio] Delfim [Netto] and [central bank president] Carlos Langoni came in for lunch and revealed their liquidity position as reported to the Fund [about $4.5 billion]. It was a much more serious problem than we had expected. They had counted in their international reserves credits from Iraq, Poland, et cetera. So their true liquid reserves were one-half of what we all assumed they were."[17]

Upon discovering Brazil's true financial state, Preston called Volcker. "I told Paul, and he agreed, that if the numbers were as they said, we were headed for trouble. The reason for my call was that I thought that the Fed didn't realize the seriousness."[18]

Political Cover

For Volcker, the news that the Brazilian problem was about to break contained an important political signal. "You could deal with Mexico ad hoc," he explains, "but you couldn't leave it to the Federal Reserve to manage the whole impending debt crisis this way. We didn't have the political base to run the debt strategy on our own."

Volcker decided that he had to go to the White House to seek democratic political "legitimacy" for launching a broader-based debt strategy. Fed International Finance Division chief Ted Truman articulated Volcker's plan in a memo dated October 23, 1982. It proposed treating the LDC debt crisis primarily as a financial problem through the IMF and the central banks. The political strategy was to focus mainly on four debtors—the Big Three Latin debtors Mexico, Brazil, and Argentina, which alone could threaten world financial stability, and politically sensitive Yugoslavia. The memo outlined the basic burden-sharing mechanics: new private banker financing, BIS and other bridge loans to IMF financing, and a debtor adjustment package. It urged rapid government ratification of a large IMF quota increase.

The inclusion of non–Soviet bloc communist Yugoslavia, whose debt did not pose a systemic menace, was an interesting footnote to the political atmospherics of the debt crisis. It was a gesture to the Europeans, who bridled at the American tilt of the debt strategy, as well as to top State Department officer Lawrence Eagleburger, who took a godfatherly interest in the country to which he had been ambassador.

Yugoslavia had already approached BIS Chairman Fritz Leutwiler for a $500 million bridge loan. It claimed to need it to avoid falling into Soviet arms; the Soviets pressed Leutwiler to refuse the loan. Leutwiler proposed the trade to Volcker: "We [Europeans] bring in Yugoslavia, and you [United States] bring in the Latin Americans."

A couple of days later, armed with Truman's memo, Volcker went to the White House with Don Regan. Chief of Staff James Baker assembled the key foreign and economic policy officials. Volcker describes, "First I got Regan on board and we went to the White House. We talked to everyone short of the president. The White House was not terribly excited by it. It was not a long meeting. I presented this case. 'Should the American government get so involved?' was the question. Generally their concerns are money and, more important, the commitment of the prestige of the United States. 'Are we sure we want to do this? Or is the Federal Reserve getting our ass out on a limb?' It was an issue they were not eager to take to the president. Baker said okay."

Regan's account of the White House visit was refracted through a political prism, but similar: "The administration didn't want to deal with the debt crisis. If it had been a more internationally minded president like Nixon, it might have been different. Autumn 1982 was a bad political season for the administration. The Republicans were losing seats in the House and Senate in the election due to the recession. Baker, [Presidential Counselor Edwin] Meese, [Baker's deputy Richard] Darman, and [Budget Director David] Stockman—I don't think [Deputy Chief of Staff Michael] Deaver even thought of it—were all blaming the Federal Reserve for the recession and blaming Paul Volcker. So for Paul Volcker to present this, and the problems in Argentina, Mexico, and Brazil, was viewed by them as his presenting them with yet another problem. Their problem at the time was to get ready for the new budget. Baker and Darman are fast learners, but frankly they could have cared less about international problems. They were content therefore to leave it to us. Volcker was the guru to everyone at that time, and I was an international finance Wall Street type, so it seemed logical."

Meddling in high-profile politics that could backlash upon the Fed made Volcker anxious. Any hint of bailing out the bankers was politically suicidal. Using national taxpayer money—especially at a time of record budget deficits—to ease a nominally "foreign" crisis likewise irked voters and raised awkward questions why Mexicans should receive preference over overindebted domestic farmers and other U.S. citizens. As a result, Volcker says, over the years "I kept going back [to the White House] for reassurance of support. They were willing to leave it to us, and we had their basic sympathy and occasional diplomatic help. My concern was: 'Would that support be durable?' I always wanted to reaffirm it."[19] Volcker found one key political ally in Secretary of State George Shultz, who met with him once every three weeks on debt.[20]

The prevailing view since 1982 has been that the Regan Treasury was also asleep at the switch, and that it was the heroics of Volcker and the Fed alone riding in with the Basel club cavalry that saved the world from the LDC debt crisis. Yet Volcker and high Fed officials believed this view was unfairly exaggerated and that "the Treasury has gotten a bum rap on handling of the debt crisis."[21]

Rather, the picture that emerged in hindsight was that although top Treasury officers were caught flat-footed, they quickly rallied behind Volcker's leadership once awakened to the scale of the potential catastrophe. They provided much of the political support Volcker needed to implement the strategy.[22]

One reason for the perception of Treasury negligence was Regan's decision, articulated over the Mexican weekend, to maintain a zero public profile. "My Wall Street background taught me that in the middle of a horrible market move you downplay the event and try to be reassuring," he explains. "What you shouldn't do is wring your hands and add fuel to the fire."

Many top bankers rejected Regan's contention that he consciously downplayed the crisis. "That's revisionist history. I'm not sure anyone in the Reagan administration understood," snaps Lewis Preston, chairman of Morgan. "They were ideologues, free marketeers. They were trapped in their own ideology."[23]

The bankers' resentment was fueled partly by the U.S. government's refusal to shoulder a larger share of the financial burden. But that didn't detract from the substantive criticism, echoed worldwide: the U.S. government's shirking of leadership for a world-class political and economic problem precluded more comprehensive political solutions than those that central bankers, with limited resources and mandates, could administer. Tim McNamar admits, "We were hoisted on our own petard by trying to soft-sell this thing. But by not yelling fire, no one brought any water."

Armed with White House political endorsement of his debt plan, Volcker promptly solidified support with the inner circle of central bankers. On Friday, October 29, 1982, Volcker dined with Richardson and Leutwiler at

Richardson's home at St. Anselm's Place, London. Leutwiler describes it as "small, like a doll's house—Paul Volcker was too big for the house."[24]

Richardson and Leutwiler supported the strategy on the three Latin debtors and Yugoslavia. Most of the dinner talk was "how to get coordinated. We weren't well enough coordinated internationally." They explored tactical options, above all how to bring along the private bankers. They also reaffirmed their resolution not to get sucked into the political trap of themselves providing long-term loans to the debtors—in effect, an inflationary promise to create more money—to alleviate the crisis. "We tried to keep the central banks out of it," says Leutwiler. "I said, 'We can do bridging loans and that's it.' "

To win international political endorsement, Volcker circled his calendar for December 9. That was when the secretive Group of Five (United States, Germany, Japan, United Kingdom, and France) was scheduled to convene near Frankfurt, Germany, to negotiate an agreement for an accelerated IMF quota increase. In the event, that negotiation was postponed because the Brazilian crisis had erupted.

The White House's endorsement of Volcker's debt strategy had kept alive the secret negotiations between Brazil and the big U.S. banks. On November 10—the very day that the IMF and Mexico signed their letter of intent—word of Brazil's dire straits hit the newspapers, along with news that six U.S. banks were ready to make a $600 million emergency bridge loan. The implicit caveats were that Brazil apply for an IMF financing and adjustment package. Another was that the U.S. government make a large emergency loan to Brazil—a $1.23 billion loan was announced by Reagan during a December 1 visit to Brazil. In late November bankers led by Morgan and Citibank began secretly working out a detailed, four-part long-term rescue plan with Brazil. Nevertheless, the interbank run on Brazilian bank branches became a hemorrhage at news of the troubles, threatening to capsize the country into default.

Not surprisingly, talk of Brazil and forming a common posture to manage the debt crisis dominated the agenda when the G5 finance ministers, their deputies, and central bank governors convened at the old palace in Kronberg, near Frankfurt, on Thursday, December 9. Volcker—speaking now for the United States since "Regan was on board by then and we could talk to the G5 as part of the government"—outlined the problems and debt issues confronting them.

Meeting chairman, new German Finance Minister Gerhard Stoltenberg, reports, "Volcker gave a very realistic assessment of the international debt crisis. It was only obvious that the leading industrial countries had to cooperate to solve it."

But how? "Should it be only Paris Club, OECD, or BIS? We'd been doing it all ad hoc," explains Don Regan. "We had to be very candid. What were we prepared to do and not prepared to do." The G5 ministers agreed they didn't want to treat the debt crisis as a political matter directly themselves. After some initial German dissension, with Stoltenberg "very influenced by Karl Otto Pöhl" of the Bundesbank, about the buying time strategy, they endorsed Volcker's Big Three Latin debtors plus Yugoslavia strategy.[25] They concurred that IMF conditionality should run through every debt program, including Paris Club reschedulings of creditor government debt. All in all, says Volcker, "[t]here was an international consensus that that meeting provided."

A huge funding increase for the IMF to meet the debt crisis was also urgent. To make it more politically palatable to a U.S. Congress deadlocked over its megabudget deficits, the G5 agreed to consider a U.S. compromise for a smaller IMF quota increase to be offset by a tripling to $20 billion of the sum provided by the lower-profile G10 under an enlarged version of its 1962 General Agreement to Borrow (GAB).[26] A month later, on January 18, 1983, the enlarged GAB plan was approved. On February 12 the ministers at an emergency IMF interim committee meeting agreed in principle to increase IMF funding by 47.4 percent, or $32.5 billion. Together the new funds allocated to fight the debt crisis totaled $45 billion.

This financial obligation represented the major burden-sharing responsibility assumed by the industrial democratic governments. The rest, including the complex foreign policy dimensions, were de facto left mainly to Volcker and the Big Four. The debt crisis "was treated as a financial crisis to be settled without governments," says Switzerland's Fritz Leutwiler. "The governments were very happy when we said, 'Leave it to us for a few months.' They thought it would be a three- to six-month problem and then maybe go away. We asked them to supply long-term money. We would supply short term. There were some political discussions, but disappointingly few. I was shocked by the lack of political vision."

Dissension in Basel

The political responsibility central bankers inherited by treating the LDC debt crisis as a purely short-term financial problem stirred discontent in the Basel club when the BIS soon debated the bridge loan requests from Argentina, Brazil, and Yugoslavia. Bundesbank President Karl Otto Pöhl maintained that the debt problem was long term and fundamentally political. It was thus inappropriate for the BIS to tie up its liquid central banker assets. Pöhl's nightmare, shared by other Basel central bankers, was entrapment into acting as a long-term lender of last resort—and, in the end, getting stuck with the bad LDC loans and compromising BIS sound money goals. Yet if they did nothing, the world financial system would collapse. Central bankers were caught in a global conflict between monetary stability and financial fragility. The only way out was to induce their governments to step up to take more responsibility, Pöhl argued.

While admitting that in the short run the central bankers were compelled to act in order to avert major chaos, veteran Danish central bank Governor Erik Hoffmeyer condemned the longer-run failure of the prevailing strategy to engage the politicians in the debt crisis's larger dimensions: "The Anglo-Saxon-led central banks and the IMF solved it in a way that was too easy for the politicians. Politicians, after a while, find it useful to have the IMF and the central banks with their short horizons buying time to save financial institutions in the industrial countries while the long-run problem was not discussed."

Over the years Hoffmeyer and other restive European central bankers commiserated privately but effetely about Volcker's handling of the debt problem. "Volcker was very consistent," says Hoffmeyer. "He had a strong conviction, and he didn't change his opinion. When you embark on a solution you don't discuss the horizon very much. You say, 'We see improvements here and there,' and, 'We expect markets to take over if we fulfill our role.' "

Yugoslavia had inflamed central banker nightmares in the autumn by making a request for a three-year loan—a term that was turned down flat. Private bankers made their $1.1 billion emergency loan to Argentina contingent upon a BIS bridge—conniving implicitly to make the BIS the de facto guarantor of their loans. And the governors had a nervous eye on a long line of troubled debtors getting ready to queue up at Basel if the floodgates opened. Central bankers, says Volcker, "were fully ready to act on Mexico, but we didn't want to make it permanent. Pöhl was the head character who was reluctant, dragging his feet, frankly. He cooperated, but he was not sympathetic."

The main task of selling the Brazilian, Argentine, and Yugoslav bridge loans was done by Leutwiler, as BIS chairman, with important assistance from Richardson. "I called around Europe to get support for the bridges," Leutwiler reports. "I was on excellent terms with [Dutch central banker Wim] Duisenberg, an independent central bank. [Bank of Belgium Governor Jean] Godeaux did what he could, which was limited [because he was not independent]. [Bank of France Governor Renaud] de la Genière was discreet. He had some political interest in Eastern Europe, less in Latin America. The French supported the loans, but he wasn't that cooperative."

Leutwiler reiterated to colleagues time and again that BIS loans were merely bridges to longer-term IMF and commercial bank money and would be made only if solidly collateralized and guaranteed. "The question was: a bridge to what?" he recalls, admitting, "I couldn't always see whether the rope was well fixed on the other side." In the case of the $500 million Argentine bridge, granted only three days after the IMF executive board approved a $1.65 billion Argentine standby loan on January 24, 1983, Leutwiler later discovered that the collateralizing Argentine gold held in the vaults at the New York Fed had already been pledged to another lender. "The Argentinians didn't tell us. Fortunately, they never used our credit."

In the end, all the Big Three plus Yugoslavia bridge loans were granted.[27] All were repaid in timely fashion except for that of Brazil, which became an incubus for the BIS, and Leutwiler personally, during 1983. Leutwiler "didn't sleep well at that time. I had promised to my colleagues that we'd get our money back." In early 1983 Leutwiler signaled an end to BIS emergency bridge loan operations. Although many other countries' troubles soon became unmanageable, none applied to the BIS. They knew they wouldn't be approved.

Involuntary Lending

One factor that helped persuade BIS central bankers to grant the bridge loans in winter 1982–83 was a sense that the debt strategy was working. Mexico had agreed to an IMF program. Also crucially, a bold gambit by de Larosière, backed by Volcker, tackled the huge problem of how to forge a bank creditors' cartel.

That gambit, put into play on November 16, 1982, came to be called "involuntary lending." Acting secretly within the IMF, de Larosière resolved to make IMF financing contingent upon prior commitment of new private bank loans—and in an amount dictated by the IMF. The departure from traditional voluntary linkage was resisted by top IMF staff, who feared making the IMF "morally" responsible for loan losses, and feared future noncooperation from banks if its adjustment program failed.

But de Larosière simply saw no other way to ensure enough financing in a way that protected IMF funds from being used to pay back private bankers, while LDC debt to the IMF piled up. Prior to acting, de Larosière sounded out Volcker, who "was on the same wavelength." He likewise received endorsement from the U.S. Treasury and assurances from the inner central banking circle that it would provide behind-the-scenes support for the IMF's leadership in involuntary bank lending.

Volcker reviewed the final details, along with a complementary strategy of his own, when he visited de Larosière at his home a few days before the IMF managing director was to spring the involuntary lending surprise upon international bank chiefs at the New York Fed on the afternoon of November 16.[28] At New York, de Larosière first detailed for the bankers the IMF austerity measures to which incoming President de la Madrid was committed. For 1983 he estimated Mexico's new financing need at $8.3 billion. The IMF could supply $1.3 billion. The U.S. and other governments could come up with $2 billion. That left a gap of $5 billion, which he expected the bankers to fill.

Then came the coup de grace: unless the bankers provided the $5 billion, he wouldn't recommend acceptance of the Mexican program to the IMF directors at their December 23 board meeting. He required the bankers' written financing commitments by December 15—only one month hence.

"It was a fait accompli," recalls Yusuke Kashiwagi, Bank of Tokyo chairman. "It was very much resented by us. The Fund made the analysis, and it was up to the bankers to come up with the money. People were saying: 'Should we go along or not?' " Nearly all bankers instinctively rebelled against this dictatorial incursion by government into the realm of private capital. Yet, insists Volcker, "[b]anks on their own initiative were not willing to lend new money. If you needed new money, you had to push them." Concurs Fritz Leutwiler, "We and the IMF blackmailed the banks. We cast over them responsibility for the financial system. But I don't feel bad. They would have lost much more had we not done it."

The November 16 gambit revealed the essence of the political compact for governing the debt crisis: the IMF, an institution with little independent authority, would provide the high-profile, high-risk operating mechanisms to be co-jointly managed with central bankers, whose occult political power, endorsed specifically by G5 governments, drove the process. "The Fund was the formal vehicle to keep the banks together," explains Volcker, who calls its role "maybe indispensable."[29]

Pushing the banks to lend was a thankless task fraught with moral, legal, and political hazards. From the beginning, says Deputy Treasury Secretary Tim McNamar, the Treasury made a decision never to "ask the banks to put another nickel into these countries because the minute the Treasury does that, they're our loans." Instead the Treasury left the dirty work to the Fed because "the Fed is not part of the government."

Volcker and the Basel central bankers, in turn, were relieved to have the IMF provide a political shield for them by going out front. "De Larosière was better placed to do some things," elaborates one high Fed official. "He got quite active in sending out telexes to banks. That's something that the Fed couldn't do. He could *demand* cooperation from the financial community. De Larosière is an international civil servant, and his role as the 'heavy' further depoliticized the process."[30]

"It was consciously exposing the institution, yes," acknowledges de Larosière of his involuntary lending ultimatum. "But without an agreement on financing, adjustment couldn't be done. I thought it was in the best interest of the world financial system, debtors and creditors. So I did it. The bankers were lost, they needed leadership. The November meeting might have been a shock to many, but it was also a relief."

One banker who supported de Larosière's bold involuntary lending ultimatum, but rose at the November 16 meeting to object to the 60 percent share of the financing burden being allotted to them—even though it was a lesser proportion than their three-quarter share of outstanding Mexican debt—was the co-speaker of Deutsche Bank, Wilfried Guth. "I was not surprised that Fund money was contingent upon ours," says Guth, who had been debating with de Larosière before November 16. "De Larosière's way of pressuring the banks was necessary. I felt the countries had to be provided with new financing. But I was disappointed, and said so at that meeting, at the lack of pressure he [de Larosière] could put on governments for money."

That evening, a few hours after bankers were still reeling from de Larosière's clubbing, Paul Volcker offered U.S. bankers a carrot. New bank loans in support of an IMF adjustment program, he signaled in a speech in Boston, would be treated by U.S. bank regulators with leniency.[31]

Volcker's pronouncement amounted to a blessing that new loans to troubled LDCs did not violate the cardinal banking maxim, Gresham's law, of not throwing good money after bad. The bad loans could be *made* good, Volcker argued, if the new lending facilitated economic adjustment—or at least good enough to avert a world bank crisis. The "fiction of good loans" was how Deutsche Bank Chairperson Wilfried Guth derided Volcker's inversion of Gresham's law. Yet Sam Cross of the New York Fed insists, "If we thought it was money down a rathole, we wouldn't have encouraged it."

New private lending, in actuality, allowed creditors to promptly receive even larger sums from debtors in interest repayments. The bottom-line logic of "new lending," explains William Taylor, chief of the Fed supervision, was that "if you put in one dollar, you get four or five dollars back; if you don't put in one dollar, you get nothing back."

New money bought U.S. bankers uninterrupted high reported profits plus time to "reduc[e] ratios of outstanding [LDC] loans relative to their capital or assets."[32] Volcker wanted bankers to build their capital by 15 percent a year.[33]

The LDC rescue epitomized the novel lender of last resort actions that could be demanded under the new regime of global capital in which contagion spread speedily among interlinked financial players and across national borders. It called attention to the world's absence of a reliable, standing international lender of last resort and how crucial it was to have central bankers who were sufficiently independent to be able to cooperate swiftly to prevent mayhem breaking out in the frontiers where global financial markets were racing ahead of the reach of any democratic government.[34] Oddly enough, it was Treasury Secretary Donald Regan who ingenuously called attention to this when he proposed a new international institution at the December 1982 G5 meeting. "My worry was that there were so many strings you had to pull to get the puppets to move up and down in the right way that maybe you needed a centralizing institution to coordinate it," he explains. "You have the Federal Reserve to solve the problems in the United States if there are bad loans. There is no such international institution. There was the IMF, but that's an institution no one gives any authority to. You have the Paris Club and some bilateral-based negotiations. You get political interference, though. The BIS was too fragmented, and it was informal, not quite ad hoc, but no ironclad agreements. . . . I was groping for an honest-to-goodness international central bank."[35]

The buying time strategy articulated on November 16, 1982, required that the bank creditors' cartel move in convoy to protect its most vulnerable ship— the big U.S. banks. As U.S. central banker, Volcker made sure the debt strategy also protected U.S. banks' competitive position. Yet although involuntary lending conformed to U.S. financial norms, it was contralogical elsewhere. As a result, banks in Canada and the United Kingdom were eventually forced into the absurd position of having immediately to make bad-debt provisions against every new involuntary loan. German bankers had to go before their boards of directors to justify new loans to countries already provisioned against. Foreign bankers, already irritated by the U.S. domination of the Mexican bank advisory committee, bridled that they were being forced to make sacrifices for a debt process that protected their U.S. bank competitors from the full, harsh justice of capitalist market forces. "There was much dissatisfaction that the IMF and the U.S. authorities decided what happens to non-U.S. banks," reports Bank of Tokyo's Kashiwagi.

Volcker inadvertently compounded the offense felt by foreign bankers by participating in a meeting held at the IMF with de Larosière and fourteen U.S. big bank chiefs, led by Citibank's Walter Wriston, aimed at organizing

U.S. banking system compliance with the forced lending cartel. At issue was the formidable problem of how to deal with "free riders"—those mostly small banks that refused to put up new money yet were still entitled to be paid back through the international lending syndicate.

Wriston and the bank CEOs were ready personally to explain to the chiefs of recalcitrant banks how free ridership could injure the financial system—and damage their vital correspondent links with the money centers. But they wanted to know that if the going got tough, the Fed would call in the holdouts for some tough moral suasion.

Through coded verbal and body language—everything short of an unambiguous commitment—Volcker indicated he would. "I doubt that I said the Federal Reserve would call," Volcker says. "Typically in the meeting they'd say that they can't do it: 'We're just the private sector, so the Federal Reserve must.' We'd say, 'We can't.' Then they'd say, 'We'll do what we can, but will you be there in the end?' " He concludes, "They may have taken my position to mean that we would."

Indeed they did. "Paul was obviously cautious," says Morgan's Lewis Preston. "But he left the impression with Walt [Wriston] that he'd been persuaded to help with the recalcitrant banks." News of "the American meeting," Preston adds, inflamed sore foreign banker feelings and "got Volcker into trouble with the Europeans."

The creditors' cartel might well have foundered at that juncture had it not been for the agile financial diplomacy of Bank of England Governor Gordon Richardson, an adept central bank practitioner of the art of raised eyebrow and backstage manipulator so that events played out publicly as he desired. Richardson's international stature was high because of his leadership of many Basel club responses to the multiple financial shocks that marked the rise of global capital. It was mainly Richardson, assisted by Fritz Leutwiler, who persuaded the private foreign bankers and central bankers that the debt crisis was not simply an American problem. Volcker says, "I would just marvel over Richardson's patience and the deliberate care in getting the Europeans on board." He says, "My style is to walk into a room and say, 'Here's the problem and here are some solutions,' and expect everyone to get on board in two minutes. He understood it took two hours of explanation over dinner to get them on board."

Aware of the dissension among non-U.S. bankers, Richardson arranged an intimate dinner for top world banking leaders, without Volcker present, to rally support for the new involuntary lending strategy unveiled on November 16. It was held at New Change, the Bank of England governor's official apartment near St. Paul's on November 22. To avoid panicky speculation should the dinner become public, the bankers arrived stealthily through the back entrance.

Those attending were Richardson, de Larosière, Leutwiler, and the Bank of England's overseas director, Anthony Loehnis, from the official sector, and one leading private banker from each major country: Wilfried Guth of Deutsche Bank, Yusuke Kashiwagi of Bank of Tokyo, Jeremy Morse of Lloyds, Jean-Yves Haberer of Crédit Lyonnais, Franz Lutolf from Swiss Bank Corp., and J. P. Morgan's Lewis Preston. "What I wanted was to ensure that the heads of the major institutions were involved," explains Richardson, "so they would know about what we were engaged in trying to do and would expose their own point of view. You can't tell people to do something contrary to their interests. But you can differentiate between their shorter- and longer-term interests. You have to make the arguments speak persuasively— and to very experienced people."

Everyone agreed that the key man to persuade was Deutsche Bank's Wilfried Guth. Guth, who had declined Chancellor Helmut Schmidt's offer of the Bundesbank presidency before it was offered to Pöhl, was a nephew of ex-Chancellor Ludwig Erhard and a former IMF executive director with a renowned international political economic *weltansicht*. He was unquestionably Europe's foremost banker-statesman.

Guth's views on LDC debt stood in intellectual counterpoint to Walt Wriston's; there was furthermore a professional and personal rivalry between the two men. At one bankers' gathering, when Wriston said, "Countries don't go broke," Guth snapped back, "I'm doubtful of that."[36] Despite Wriston's prestige among American bankers, it was Guth who commanded more respect internationally. "Wilfried's grasp of the international scene is better than Wriston's," states one European banker friendly to both. Guth "ran his bank as I'd have run mine—conservatively," adds one European governor. Wriston, by contrast, was viewed by central bankers as embodying "Citibank opportunism," which went awry on LDC lending.

Deutsche Bank had been among the most cautious LDC lenders. If any world-class banker had a parochial competitive incentive to turn his back on the international creditors' cartel, it was Guth. Guth saw the LDC debt problem as structural, linked to the political economic limitations of overindebted developing nations and global flows of capital and trade. It required a treatment with a long-term horizon. It was not the temporary liquidity squeeze purported by Wriston and implicit in Volcker's buying time debt strategy. Thus where Wriston advocated the short-term, muddle-through buying time approach that could be reassessed in a couple of years, and with some luck might get Latin flight capital to return and cause the problem to recede, Guth insisted on seeing the road map ahead: How will it work out? Is there an exit? How specifically will banks get the problem behind them? "From the beginning there were philosophical and analytical differences between Deutsche Bank and the other bankers. Deutsche Bank was more skep-

tical about the chances of getting these countries back to market," explained
the late Horst Schulmann, a former high German official who headed the Institute for International Finance, formed by 153 banks to represent their interests in the debt process. "It is the reason why they never joined this
organization."

Guth's view eventually prevailed years later, but it had few supporters at
the time. "It is only with the benefit of hindsight that all these issues [dollar,
debt, financial fragility, anti-inflation policies] are interrelated," says Lew
Preston. "Wilfried, and only he, due to his training, understood the structural
nature of the problem. No one else had any concept of it."

Guth feared that the involuntary new lending would merely build up more
debt without treating the long-term problems. He favored capitalization of
interest—the conversion of interest due into principal—and emphasis on
building up bank loan loss reserves. Only when bankers could gauge their
probable losses could they intelligently devise strategies to put the problem
behind them, he argued.

At dinner Richardson turned the floor over to de Larosière to review the
status of the debt problem and his rationale for linking IMF and new bank
money. From this common base they discussed, under Richardson's orchestration, the systemic implications of failing to act together. The dinner discussion included "attempts to educate Guth and Lutolf that the whole
banking system was at risk," reports Preston.

Guth, of course, had no trouble grasping the abstract systemic threat.
But the realistic degree of systemic risk depended upon accepting the
premise that the U.S. government would permit the U.S. banking system
to collapse without riding to the rescue. It seemed more plausible that
the Reagan government, abetted by Volcker, was making a huge poker
bluff to get the rest of the world's banks and economies to pay disproportionately for a primarily American problem. Preston explains, "If
you thought at the end of the day the U.S. government would come through,
then you *could* believe that the whole banking system wouldn't be at risk.
The Continentals could never accept that the U.S. government *wasn't* going
to come in and put in more money. But the reality is that they weren't going
to do it."

Part of the perception gap stemmed from incongruities in the unspoken
bank-state compact anchoring each nation's variety of democratic capitalism. In the bank finance–dominated European social welfare capitalist
model, the relationship between government and big banks was more intimate than in the more laissez-faire, populist U.S. democratic capitalism in
which capital markets played a bigger financial role. It was inconceivable to
Europeans that their governments would let their major banks go down in
the LDC debt crisis because of the social, economic, and political catastro-

phe that would result. In Japan's bank-centered "relationship capitalism," the bank-state relationship was even closer.

After a short discussion whether the debt crisis was fundamentally a liquidity or structural phenomenon, Guth relented. He put in abeyance his preferred approach to work for what he believed was an analytically flawed strategy. Without cohesion in the creditors' cartel, he knew, any strategy was foredoomed.

The rest of the dinner discussion centered on the two most formidable obstacles to the buying time strategy. First was how to ensure genuine adjustment among debtors without applying so much pressure that it would break their will for reform. The bankers wanted to keep the debtors on a short leash. "If you're going to use pressure on us, then you should use it on the countries, too," they told the central bankers and de Larosière. "These countries must do what they say."[37]

Next the bankers tackled the "free rider" problem. Guth was especially worried. "It was a discussion about how to save the situation and to support de Larosière," he recalls of the dinner, "and what to do with those who wanted to step outside."

Trading on the consensus forged at Richardson's dinner, Guth, Morse, Preston, and Kashiwagi each took the lead in organizing the banks in their respective countries. "Guth was the most helpful in Germany," Volcker praises warmly.

The momentum from Richardson's top-level dinner helped the bank advisory committee to agree a week later to fill the $5 billion financing "gap" with which de Larosière had presented them by soliciting a 7 percent lending increase from each Mexican creditor.[38] Negotiations on the terms for the new $5 billion loan opened the day after Miguel de la Madrid was sworn in as Mexican president on December 1. Less than a week later they were completed. At 2.25 percent over LIBOR (London Interbank Offered Rate), the six-year loan with a three-year grace period was priced very attractively for bankers. Some $20 billion in loans due in 1983 and 1984 were also restructured with a markup of half a point. As a result, banks' reported profits actually *rose*.

Yet the fatter spreads counterproductively worsened Mexico's debt burden. As debtor weariness grew through the decade, the loan spreads would be steadily shaved back. But at the time, the bankers insisted that the higher spreads were warranted to induce Mexico's creditors to join the involuntary lending drive.

The Mexican new money drive was kicked off with a de Larosière telex to the world's central bankers, urging them to "line up the troops."[39] De

Larosière showed this telex to the bank advisory committee representatives who visited him on November 30. At their behest, the text, expurgated of its central banker orientation, was telexed on December 1 to Mexico's international bankers over de Larosière's "Regards."[40]

Then began the committee's grueling hard sell of round-the-clock phone calls and periodic telex reports to raise the $5 billion from some six hundred banks worldwide. At first the entire banking systems of Japan, France, and Switzerland objected to the categories of loans that made up the 7 percent baseline. Numerous regional banks in the United States and mortgage banks in Germany simply wanted out regardless of the systemic consequences. Mexican Finance Ministry officials traveled to big lenders in Kuwait and Saudi Arabia and tiny ones in remote parts of the United States.

Finance Minister Silva Herzog himself solicited a small Miami banker with only $1 million in Mexican loans; the banker's emotional objection, that his original short-term less-than-one-year loan was becoming converted into an inappropriate and unwanted long-term commitment, was both reasonable and typical of the problems encountered. The common refrain of refusers: "It's throwing good money after bad."

Hard cases were identified and referred to bank chairmen and then, if needed, to the central bankers. "The Fed was very active in leaning on people all over the world," applauds Wriston. Although he routinely preached the importance of new money and debt reschedulings, Volcker never made coercive phone calls personally. Coming from a chief bank regulator, that would represent an egregious conflict of interest. Rather, the phone calls at the Fed were usually made by three of his trusted senior allies—Legal Counsel Michael Bradfield, New York Fed foreign operations chief Sam Cross, and Jerry Corrigan. Low-key inquiries were made whether bankers reached an "informed decision"—a phrase that resonated with intimidating innuendo. The central bankers walked bankers through some of the potential implications, systemic and for their individual institutions, of not cooperating. Direct orders to lend, however, were taboo. At least once one of the Fed's phone callers was warned to ease his tone to be sure he was staying on the safe side of the narrow moral hazard line.

"We don't want to be in a position of telling the banks what to do," Volcker explains, then confesses, "I violated it enough to inquire if they were lending or not."

Among the central bankers, "the heavy arm-twisting was done by Volcker and Richardson."[41] When the going got rough in Britain, Lloyds Bank Chairman Jeremy Morse, working in conjunction with Richardson, invited Mexico's fifty-three U.K. bank creditors to a meeting at the Bank of England. When they arrived on December 14, 1982—the day before the "drop dead" $5 billion commitment date set by de Larosière—the bankers were asked to cooperate by Deputy Governor Christopher "Kit" McMahon.[42] Then Morse, himself a former senior Bank of England official, passed the hat in what one described as a church charity drive.

In Japan, BOJ Governor "Mike" Maekawa, in collaboration with the MOF, had a few private meetings with senior bankers to ensure their participation in the creditors' convoy. Japanese banks' compliance was more thorough than anywhere else in part because the moral suasion Western central bankers employed ad hoc in emergencies was done routinely by the Japanese Establishment in guiding Japan's financial system.

On the European continent, by contrast, the central bankers were warier. Says Leutwiler, "It was a delicate problem. De Larosière wanted the central bankers to talk to the commercial bankers. Paul Volcker did, of course. We on the European continent decided to lie very low because we didn't want to be held responsible for further losses if it turned out to be good money after bad. In Switzerland I was careful to explain the global implications of what could happen, but I stressed, " 'It's your money, not mine.' "

In Germany, says Volcker, "the Bundesbank never wanted to get that involved. They wanted to wash their hands of it. They didn't even want to know what the problems were." In France "we called in the banks," reports then Governor Renaud de la Genière. "It was difficult to convince them to put up new money. They said 'no.' " De Larosière's own good political contacts helped facilitate cooperation in Paris.

However elliptical or artfully phrased, the meaning of the moral suasion was plain enough to bankers: they would either cooperate or face the consequences that their central bankers could mete out. While the profit-seeking horizon of capital was supranational, no banker could afford strained relations with his main political patron. "What the Anglo-Saxon central bankers did was to keep the banks together and put pressure on them to act in a uniform way," says Erik Hoffmeyer, chairman of the Denmark National Bank. "No one was allowed to cheat without being punished."

Central bankers had various means to "punish" recalcitrants. How? "By using the heavy eyebrows," suggests Fed Chief Counsel Mike Bradfield. "Tell them to cut back on their dividends. Make them dilute their shareholders: all the chairman must do is say that a bank is not sufficiently capitalized and the market makes them raise capital. If they're selling below book [value], every time they sell new capital they are watering down shareholders. That's hard. Actually, you don't need to make the statement, but just be credible enough that people think you might. How hard to push them, that was the issue. . . . One of my great regrets is that we didn't lean heavily enough on bankers to do more." The Fed could employ its discretionary authority powers to "screw up a bank's next [regulatory] application."[43]

"The power of the central bank is awesome," says Walt Wriston. "Although inside you might feel powerless and frustrated, when you're on the outside looking in you feel intimidated." The Fed's ultimate threat, he adds, was to unleash the latent democratic hostility against banks by publicly singling out a defiant bank for criticism. "If you say 'no,' well then, they can let it be known that these greedy bastards destroyed the world financial system. The Fed *has* played hardball sometimes—and will do so again."

There were two categories of miscreant bankers. First, the delinquents, who refused to put up new money. Second, the capital offenders, who threatened to file a lawsuit for repayment—and thus trigger the chain reaction of cross-default clauses in syndicated lending contracts. Although allowed to ride free, those who threatened lawsuits were placed on an informal blacklist. One Florida banker who refused bank entreaties to contribute to the Mexican package says he erred when he made noises about a lawsuit: "The threats came to the attention of the Federal Reserve Board. The Fed is our main regulator, and in fact we need approval for a merger. The bank examiners came around and started asking questions. That was enough for us. We dropped the suit, but in the end we didn't subscribe to the request for new money."[44]

The Mexican new money drive, describes Wriston, was "like filling up a tub, inch by inch. The last buck from the last bank is always the hardest."[45]

Indeed, the bankers *didn't* meet de Larosière's drop dead date. So de Larosière moved the goalposts closer. He declared that a "critical mass" of 90 percent or $4.5 billion would be enough for him to recommend approval to the IMF executive board on December 23. It took until March 23, 1983, and "topping up" contributions by major banks, to attain the $5 billion goal from 526 banks.

Brazil Bursts

De Larosière's early declaration of victory in the Mexican new money campaign was taken with a prudent eye fixed on Brazil, whose woes had grown acute. On Friday afternoon, December 20, Brazil's bespectacled thirty-eight-year-old central bank chief, Carlos Langoni, announced to 125 international bankers at New York's Plaza Hotel that Brazil needed $4.4 billion in involuntary new loans, a restructuring of $4 billion of 1983 debt, new trade credits, and restoration of Brazilian banks' international interbank deposits to about $9 billion from the $6 billion level to which they had shrunk. Furthermore, he declared, he wanted an in principle agreement from them by December 31—only eleven days away, including Christmas! Before year-end Langoni would add that Brazil was suspending principal repayments for the first two months of 1983 on the expectation that the rescheduling agreement would be completed by March 1. If it wasn't, he implied, Brazil might declare a unilateral debt moratorium.

Most bankers, not being privy to the rescue plan secretly being hatched with the New York bankers, had merely expected news that an advisory committee was to be formed. Langoni's haughty manner compounded their shock. Describes one central banker present, "Langoni got up and said in effect, 'Take it or leave it.' Then he left the platform without giving a chance for questions. That got a lot of people angry."

Volcker, de Larosière, and the governmental authorities developing the three big Latin countries plus Yugoslavia political strategy, of course, were involved in Brazil's demand for a new financing package agreement by December 31.[46] A day after the Plaza meeting, the U.S. Treasury advanced another $300 million to Brazil. The $1.45 billion BIS and Saudi bridge loans were in train; so was an additional $1.4 billion in bridge money from the biggest international banks. At the Plaza, de Larosière endorsed Brazil's economic program, a tip-off that a tentative $6 billion IMF adjustment package had already been agreed upon. In mid-January de Larosière formally linked IMF financing for Brazil to prior new money commitments from banks. He set the February 28 IMF board meeting as a deadline. Once again de Larosière and Volcker turned to the central bank network to crank up the pressure on recalcitrants.

From the outset, the ill-starred four-part Brazilian rescue—later derogatorily known as "Brazil Phase One"—was hindered by personality conflicts within the bank advisory committee, structural complexity, and Brazilian disingenuousness. Most problematic was the interbank debt Project IV, managed by Bankers Trust. The serious retrenchment by Brazil's 450 interbank lenders that had begun in late September remained at hemorrhage proportions through November, December, and January. The sudden December 14 pulling of interbank lines by France's Société Générale, in particular, triggered a wave of big bank flight.[47] Money markets shivered when one of the Brazilian banks, Banco do Brasil, seemed to run short of dollars to settle its CHIPS payments at day's end. Once again the world interbank clearing and payments system was teetering at the brink.

The central bankers tried but failed to end the run with moral suasion. Indeed, some of the central banks who had deposits with Brazil *themselves* fled—bankers mention SAMA of Saudi Arabia as one of the fleetest escapees. To prevent CHIPS from ending up short of cash and creating a chain reaction of unwinding transactions and possible world plumbing gridlock, CHIPS member banks made up the shortfall each night by passing around the hat in what became a $500 million safety net.

The situation grew so dire by late January that the bank coordinating committee and the Brazilians, with Volcker's knowledge, decided to play hardball—they went *public* with the names and amounts of the delinquent banks. Each week from February 2, Bankers Trust's computers produced lists of the interbank deposits of each of some five hundred banks and totals by nationality. De Larosière sent telexes to the delinquent banks and asked their central bankers to twist arms. The fleetest to cut and run were regional banks everywhere and international banks from Germany, Italy, Spain, and Japan. French and Swiss banks also cut back sharply.[48] All of the top ten that added interbank funds to offset their brethren's retreat were major U.S. and U.K. banks.

Bankers, and many central bankers, were furious at the hardball tactics. But they worked. By February 20 interbank deposits with Brazil rose to $7.5 billion.

By February 25 the Brazilian rescue package was signed: some 169 banks agreed to provide $4.4 billion in new loans, and 672 banks would reschedule $4 billion in 1983 Brazilian debt. Instead of $9 billion, Brazil said it needed only $7.5 billion in interbank deposits after all. In contrast with the gentleman's agreement on Mexico, each bank had to sign individually to maintain its interbank deposit lines. On Monday, February 28, the IMF approved its $6 billion credit package to Brazil.

The Brazilian rescue, however, was short-lived. The first portentous sign came at a Waldorf-Astoria "thank you" dinner the evening before the rescue package was signed, when the forty big bank guests who had extended the bridge loans were told by their Brazilian hosts that loan repayment would be delayed.[49] Soon thereafter the Brazilians requested another $400 million in emergency funds from the United States. They also tried to postpone the March 1 repayment date of their BIS loan. The Basel central bankers granted only a two-week extension.

By mid-April, only six weeks after the Brazilian package was signed, it was clear that the rescue had failed. Riots broke out in São Paolo. Economic targets agreed upon with the IMF were already being seriously missed. Brazil asked bankers to pony up an additional $3 billion by June. To bankers it looked like good money after bad, after all.

De Larosière had to decide whether to disburse the next $411 million tranche of IMF credits on May 31. At stake was the credibility of the IMF and the viability of the buying time LDC debt strategy. If the IMF was too lenient, debtor countries would lose political motivation to press austere economic adjustment and bankers would lose incentive for future cooperation. If de Larosière was too tough, destabilizing social and political unrest, and possible unilateral defaults, could result.

Bankers' skittishness was again reflected in the interbank market. Many simply never lived up to their February commitments. Others took flight at the first new signs of trouble. By April 12, interbank deposits had plunged back to $6 billion.

Each night that CHIPS had a payments shortfall, the question arose among member banks whether to "top up" themselves or let CHIPS unwind: when the amounts were small, the big U.S. bankers stood ready to pay through. But their reluctance mounted when the amounts sometimes reached $75 million to $125 million.[50] "We were tired of paying [fleeing] German bank CDs with our money," says Citibank's Walt Wriston. Nor did the U.S. bankers believe the Brazilians' claim of having no dollars available to cover their CHIPS debts. And they were frustrated that the Reagan government was not stepping forward to help with the burden sharing.

The bankers became so fed up that an informal meeting was held at the home of New York Fed President Anthony Solomon. Wriston and Willard Butcher of Chase Manhattan proposed rolling back their short-term credit lines to Brazil, says Wriston, by "$100 million a day—and see if the free world's markets can stand it." Lew Preston of J. P. Morgan stared at Wriston and Butcher in silent disapproval. "I was irritated with my colleagues," he says. "They were trying to play hardball to encourage the official side into the game. There was not much response from the U.S. Treasury."[51]

The nightmare of an unwind in CHIPS once came within a hairbreadth of occurring when the Brazilians had a large interest payment to make. "[Brazilian central banker] Langoni was telling Volcker it had been sent. Volcker was saying, 'I'm not sure we're going to get it.' He was twisting arms to be sure that the payment got done."

When CHIPS clearing time arrived without the payment, Volcker called McNamar. "We don't have it yet. You've got to keep CHIPS open."

McNamar contemplated the terrible consequences if CHIPS couldn't clear: "If you can't close all interbank transactions, you can't close any interbank transaction. It meant if we weren't going to close the New York clearing banks that night, what the hell were they going to do when they opened in Tokyo or London? What positions did they have? It would be absolute chaos. That CHIPS system was one of the greatest Achilles' heels of the world financial system and few people understood it." McNamar was informed by Treasury counsel, however, that he had no legal authority to order CHIPS to stay open. McNamar instructed the Treasury attorney to excuse himself. He then called Preston, whose Morgan bank then held the revolving chairmanship of CHIPS. He asked him to delay CHIPS closing.

As the hours passed, McNamar called the White House. "You better alert the president that it may hit the fan tonight," he told them.

What was the White House's reaction? "Of course the White House didn't know what it was, how it worked, or why it was important," McNamar relates sarcastically. "They said, 'Why don't you do something about that? It'd look bad in the press.' "

Frantic calls kept going back and forth to Brazil. Langoni claimed to be having a technical problem. Lew Preston remembers, "We *hoped* Langoni was telling the truth. It would have been an unwind if they hadn't paid. Brazil unwisely was not paying up. Everyone talked to Langoni. But it still didn't show up."

Finally, with dawn visible over the Pacific, the Brazilian payment came through, although "no one knew from where."[52]

The debt crisis was in its darkest period. In spring 1983 fifteen countries were engaged in jumbo debt rescheduling negotiations for over $90 billion in bank debt. Brazil would set precedent for all of them. Thus the bankers dug in for harder terms. With arrearages building, it was growing hard to prevent the U.S.'s Interagency Credit Exposure Review Committee (ICERC) from "classifying" Brazil as a problem debtor under U.S. accounting rules.[53] As the stalemate continued, the creditors' cartel was buckling from banker impulses to stampede for the exits.

Volcker looked worried. One European central banker remembers him muttering, "We badly need a victory." Any sign of despair from Volcker, the psychological anchor and strategic leader of the debt strategy, unnerved those working around him.[54]

When the May 31 showdown arrived, Volcker, de Larosière, and the inner circle resolved that whatever Brazil's special social and political strains, the IMF would not disburse any more financing until the country adopted new austerity measures. Bankers immediately froze their lending. Brazil was cut off.

Volcker meanwhile arranged for the restructuring of the fractious Brazilian bank coordinating committee. He wanted Bill Rhodes, who headed the Mexican and Argentinian committees, to take sole charge. Everything was accomplished at a secret meeting of U.S. and visiting foreign bank chiefs at the New York Fed on May 31 with Volcker and New York Fed President Tony Solomon. If news of the meeting leaked, says Solomon, "[Y]ou could imagine the press: 'Financial System Breaking Down,' etc.' " Rhodes recalls, "The bank chairmen saw the [interbank] outflow continuing. It was falling apart. It was a desperate feeling. It was the domino theory. The last in line was the Philippines in 1983, but there was also Peru, Uruguay, Venezuela, and Chile."[55]

Rhodes collaborated with de Larosière and Volcker on how a compromise Brazilian program could be worked out. The substantive economic differences were complicated by the fact that for Brazilians the IMF had become a political symbol of foreign exploitation and economic suffering. Grafitti said, "IMF out!" General strikes and looting of supermarkets plagued Rio de Janeiro and São Paulo. The Treasury attaché in Brazil warned U.S. officials that the military junta might seize upon the inflamed nationalist passions to short-circuit the country's fragile transition to democracy.

When Brazil used the IMF's cutoff as an excuse to suspend, in turn, repayment of its BIS bridge loan, an angry BIS President Fritz Leutwiler insisted to de Larosière that the IMF should guarantee repayment. Leutwiler also campaigned through political channels to influence the appointed IMF executive directors, without much success.[56]

Still the Brazilians refused to repay. In mid-August Leutwiler burst forth in frustration. "Things just cannot continue as they have been. These [debt] problems will never be solved . . . with money and more money. . . . To say that these [debtor] countries should not be treated with toughness is absolutely grotesque."[57]

The breakthrough with Brazil came in late August in a flurry of high-level secret meetings. Bank advisory committee chairman Bill Rhodes met with Brazil's top financial officials at the Rio de Janeiro home of Brazil's finance minister. De Larosière met secretly in Paris with Brazil's economic éminence grise, Delfim Netto. For a reluctant minister, Volcker drew a stark picture of the total cutoff of vital food and other imports if Brazil became a financial pariah by refusing to come to terms with the IMF.

Citing the progress in the IMF-Brazil negotiations, the BIS announced on August 29 that it would grant an extension on its next Brazilian bridge loan tranche due on August 31. In the event, it took until the end of November to finalize the IMF-Brazil compromise agreement. At that point the IMF disbursements resumed and all outstanding Brazilian BIS bridge loans were repaid.

Brazil remained in a state of perpetual distress, however. Even before the compromise agreement was finalized, a new $11 billion rescue plan for 1984 was being put forth. At a four-hour meeting on September 26 at the twelfth-floor IMF boardroom, de Larosière, with Volcker at his side, informed the chairmen of the world's twenty largest banks, including Wriston of Citibank, Guth of Deutsche, Morse of Lloyds, John McGillicuddy of Manufacturers Hanover Trust, and Willard Butcher of Chase Manhattan that they would be required to come up with an additional $6.5 billion.

The new $6.5 billion "gap" angered bankers. They thought it gave Brazil a $1 billion longer leash than necessary. "One thing was very troubling about the early [IMF] packages: if you increased their international reserves, the countries lost any incentive for discipline," says Morgan's Preston. "The IMF view was to rebuild reserves. We felt they should pay back."

The bankers were furious that the loan terms were to be *easier* than the February 1983 package—notwithstanding Brazil's deteriorated reputation. But Volcker and de Larosière were calling the shots in the artificial market for LDC bank loans. Short of detonating the debt bomb, the bankers had little alternative than to fall into line.

Nonetheless, to the annual American Bankers Association convention in Honolulu, Volcker made the unflinching confession that the LDC debt strategy would take "years, not months. And we had better recognize the stakes are too high to fail."[58]

Close Encounter with Congress

While the Brazilian crisis stalked the world financial system, the debt strategy nearly came undone on yet another front—the delay and uncertainty in procuring the U.S.'s $8.4 billion share of the IMF funding increase from America's elected congressional representatives. The IMF funding shortage grew so constraining that on September 14, de Larosière, with some political hyperbole, warned his board that the IMF soon would have to terminate negotiations with debtors for lack of funds.

In a patchwork compromise, the leading non-U.S. industrial nations, plus Saudi Arabia, pledged $6 billion in emergency loans to the IMF. But the loans wouldn't be disbursed until Congress approved the U.S.'s $8.4 billion contribution.

By November 10, only a few weeks from adjournment, the U.S. Congress still hadn't acted. De Larosière trekked to Basel to appeal for an emergency bridge loan from the G10 central bankers. But the governors were increasingly persuaded that LDC debt was a long-term quagmire that required a political solution. After listening to de Larosière's review, Governor Erik Hoffmeyer of Denmark said, "Frankly speaking, the numbers are impossible."

De Larosière bravely maintained there was "marginal improvement."[59] But the governors insisted on waiting for the U.S. Congress before granting the IMF bridge.

The U.S.'s IMF funding debate united right-wing neo-isolationists with left-leaning antibank populists, and domestically oriented Black Caucus Democrats with supply-side Republicans. Across the political spectrum it became hostage to the most shameless pork barreling of Congress. "Congress gave out a shrill cry to let bankers eat their own credits. All of them were stupid, and they were taking the nation down with them, was the attitude," describes then Senate Majority Leader Howard Baker.

Congressional outcries of a banker bailout were countered by Regan and

Volcker arguments that IMF quota increases, on the contrary, "bailed in" banks to involuntary lending. Banks' special role and the overlapping boundaries of the political and economic realms of democratic capitalist society meant that both sides were right: the buying time debt strategy bailed banks out of the worst free market costs of their folly; but it also bailed them into involuntarily following a public sector–led burden-sharing strategy aimed at serving the best democratic public good. Some "socialization" of the losses was inevitable: if congressmen refused the $8.4 billion IMF funding or inflicted punishing losses on banks, the fallout would ripple throughout the economy at far greater cost as bankers scaled back their lending, foreign and domestic, to restore healthy balance sheet ratios. The hidden ways in which the general public paid for the debt crisis were discussed in winter 1983–84 in Copenhagen by Lloyds Bank Chairman Jeremy Morse and the governor of the Danish central bank, Erik Hoffmeyer.

"I suppose the domestic bank customers will pay for whatever bad debt results through higher spreads between deposits and lending rates," Hoffmeyer reflected presciently. "It's a nonpolitical tax on the system. It's not a bad solution in a way."[60]

For weeks Democratic congressmen blocked the IMF legislation from coming to the floor for a vote, until President Reagan, after much agonizing debate, apologized in writing to each of twenty congressmen accused of "supporting communism" because they opposed Texas Republican Phil Gramm's amendment to prohibit IMF loans to communist countries. Final passage, achieved just before Congress adjourned at Thanksgiving, came only with buying off several key congressmen who didn't hesitate to risk a worldwide financial collapse to extract rapacious political profits—the sort of blinkered, special-interest politics that illustrated why the federal budget deficit was chronically out of control. For his support, House Banking Chairman Ferdinand St. Germain (D-R. I.) demanded a $15.4 billion low-income housing bill. "It passed as an amendment to a housing bill, which was not further amendable," remembers Senator Howard Baker. "It was an unusual parliamentary action. We had to do it that way—that was Freddie St. Germain's price."

Adds the Treasury's Tim McNamar, "It cost me three years of tobacco price supports to get [Republican Senator] Jesse Helms to not only not filibuster, but to not talk against it. And it cost me a couple of appointments I had to make that should go unnamed. . . . It only passed by six or eight votes, a hair. And that was only after I'd done damned near unconscionable things and Volcker called and said it was a world crisis!"

•   •   •

Volcker could gloat over one little-publicized component of the IMF funding legislation—an enhanced bank supervision provision called the International Lending Supervision Act (ILSA). ILSA was born as the Fed's alternative to remedial legislation proposed by Senator William Proxmire (D-Wisc.) that would have imposed tough bank lending limits to any single country and automatic write-offs of delinquent loans. "The Fed was trying to look the other way on classifying Third World loans in return for banks' participation," says Ken McLean, Proxmire's top staffer. "Their primary objective was to have enough flexibility to decide when loans should be put in value-impaired categories. In the end, [Fed Chief Counsel Michael] Bradfield and I negotiated. He had the votes, not I."

"Our primary concern was in soothing the savage beast [Congress]," Bradfield says, chuckling. "We came up with the proposal they adopted: increased supervision; value-impaired system; and international negotiations. With the criteria we got in, you really have to *work* at it to get someone value-impaired. Volcker played a leading role in organizing the regulators."

In addition to enhanced discretionary power over "classification," ILSA gave the Fed an explicit mandate to upgrade bank capital standards and the authority to pursue international negotiations to level the competitive world playing field. "ILSA made it crystal clear we had the authority on capital requirements," says Volcker. "We did try to take advantage of the movement in Congress to meet our needs and bolster our position. It did have that effect."

By riding the angry political currents set in motion by the debt crisis, the Fed effectively wrote the legislation it long desired. ILSA enhanced Volcker's authority to make sure U.S. bankers used the time bought with the debt strategy to augment their capital, as well as his leverage to steer U.S. banks and LDC debtors along desired paths in the debt negotiations. Ultimately ILSA helped catalyze the landmark common worldwide guidelines for bank capital adequacy standards negotiated by central bankers, as recounted in Part Five.

Chapter 15

Debt Fatigue

With the IMF funding increase, the emergency firefighting phase of the LDC debt crisis gave way to a more routine process and with it a reevaluation of the road ahead. The long-term structural nature of the debt problem dominated the new collective perspective. Less and less it looked like a temporary liquidity crisis that would correct itself with the industrial world business cycle.

As a result, all sides began to lose heart to stay engaged in the buying time strategy. Debtors began to despair that no amount of politically painful adjustment would restore growth. Banks bridled at forced lending without a clear end in sight. Except for the Fed and Bank of England, the crisis-weary central bankers retreated. "After 1983, only when the house was on fire did we intervene," remembers Bank of France Governor Renaud de la Genière.

The first big debtor problem in 1984 was Argentina. With $44 billion in debt, it did not pose the same overwhelming systemic threat as Brazil and Mexico. But uniquely being self-sufficient in food, it was more ready to contemplate breaking with the world community. The return of democratic civilian government to Argentina agitated upon newly elected President Raúl Alfonsín to do so unless the IMF relaxed its economic adjustment demands in its ongoing negotiation for a new Argentine package.

The IMF refused. When the end of the United States' first quarter accounting approached on March 31, 1984, with $500 million in overdue Argentine interest payments, it looked as if U.S. banks would be forced for the first time to take the dreaded big accounting hit against earnings. An early showdown was averted when the Fed, the U.S. Treasury, and the principal Latin debtors, led by Silva Herzog (who feared an Argentine crisis might disrupt Mexico's concurrent debt negotiations), cobbled together an unusual $500 million emergency loan package. Although floated publicly as a Latin initiative, it was backed secretly by informal U.S. guarantees, which permitted Argentina to pay its overdue interest by March 31.[1] When the second quarter accounting deadline also elapsed without an IMF agreement, a second artificial lending package was arranged.

Exacerbating LDC tensions was the Fed's spring 1984 monetary tightening to consolidate its gains against inflation. The 1.5-percentage-point spike in the U.S. prime interest rate added about $6 billion to the LDC's debt service burden. On June 21, 1984, eleven Latin debtors met conspicuously in the Colombian resort of Cartagena in order to feed speculation about the formation of a LDC debtors' cartel.

Yet, admits Mexico's Silva Herzog, "there was never any real talk of a debtors cartel" because the Big Three debtors were never in crisis simultaneously. Volcker nevertheless found the debt cartel specter useful to goad bankers to come to negotiating terms with debtors. "Get your act together or they will," he often warned.[2]

From the outset one of the most debatable propositions of the debt strategy was that the debtors' best chance lay in cooperation rather than uniting to renounce their debts. "It still amazes me the degree to which the countries played the game," Volcker admits. "I sure tried to sell it to them [that the IMF was their best chance]. Some went off the program and came back, so maybe that was right."

"We always feared the emulation effect to the extent you had a bad debtor who succeeded," elaborates the Fed's Mike Bradfield. That was why "it always was the technique to isolate the bad debtors."

In part to isolate Argentina in 1984, Volcker and de Larosière embarked on a strategy of rewarding the cooperative debtor, Mexico. Mexico had made significant adjustments since de la Madrid had come to power. It was willing "to play the good boy in the classroom to the resentment of all the other boys [Latin debtors] in the school" for a price—a multiyear restructuring agreement (MYRA) at reduced interest rates.

To non-U.S. bankers the surreal concoction of the financing packages on March 31 and June 30 to keep Argentina's interest payments technically current signified everything that was askew with the U.S.-tilted debt strategy.[3] It made many of them more determined to change it—or to find an exit from the creditors' cartel.

Since the debt crisis erupted, the continental European banks in particular had built up their bad-debt reserves and diminished their LDC exposures through growth elsewhere.[4] They were angry that the U.S. banks had done scarcely any bad-debt provisioning. "How to get new money while wanting them to expand their reserving was a dichotomy we could never resolve," admits Volcker. "We never pressed the banks to do more on reserving because

it would have been the end of the new money program. We could never resolve it."

Bankers and financial experts worldwide increasingly wondered: What
useful purpose was the buying time strategy still serving? Financial markets
had begun to catch on to the "fiction" of good loans. Despite high reported
earnings, U.S. bank stock prices were falling. In May 1984 jittery global
money managers had started to run from highly LDC-exposed Manufacturers Hanover following the Continental Illinois collapse. Only ordinary small
bank depositors seemed to remain calm in the blissful ignorance of deposit
insurance and the morally hazardous conviction that big banks were too crucial for the government to let fail.

The geodivisions between continental European and U.S. bankers came
to a head at the three-day International Monetary Conference starting June
3, 1984, at the Bellevue Stratford Hotel in Philadelphia. The IMC was the
apex of the world commercial banking pyramid: only the chief executives of
the world's top one hundred banks, and an elite few others, were invited and
lavished with designer gifts, chocolates, chauffeur-driven limousines, sumptuous buffets, and special evening arts and music entertainment. Central
bankers participated in a special panel on the third day.

The 1984 event, chaired by Bank of Tokyo's Yusuke Kashiwagi, was the
last hurrah of the debt strategy's Big Four. Fritz Leutwiler was set to retire.
Gordon Richardson had been replaced in 1983 by Prime Minister Thatcher's
hand-picked choice, Robin Leigh-Pemberton, who promptly demonstrated
his callowness as a central banker by pronouncing that "the international
debt crisis is over."[5] Richardson and de Larosière would speak as special invited guests.

Before the IMC convened, senior bank debt negotiator Bill Rhodes of
Citibank gleaned the coming conflict at lunch when Union Bank of Switzerland executive Guido Hanselmann and several European bankers said that
they thought the time had come for "new lending" to be superseded by "capitalization" of interest—adding overdue interest to principal—as the basis
for the bankers' cooperation with the debt strategy. Volcker and de Larosière
strongly opposed interest capitalization. It gutted the new financing for IMF-
sanctioned adjustment trade-off at the core of the buying time strategy to the
debtors' advantage. "The problem with capitalization is that it switches the
leverage from the creditors to the debtors," explains the Fed's Mike Bradfield. "Once you start on the road to capitalization it becomes too simple for
it to be extended at the initiative of the debtor." At the end of the line was
disengagement by bankers or debt repudiation by debtors—and a U.S. banking system crisis.

Interest capitalization was debated periodically at Basel. The Bundesbank
and Bank of Italy invited New York Fed President Jerry Corrigan to make
the case against it for top German and Italian bankers. "Jerry [Corrigan] and

Paul [Volcker] were very persuasive in the BIS as to the danger of capitalization," says J. P. Morgan Chairman Lew Preston. "[Bank of Japan Governor Haruo] Maekawa was strongly against capitalization. But the capitalization of interest issue would not die."

At the IMC, open fencing broke out between Deutsche Bank's Wilfried Guth and Citibank's Walter Wriston. Guth laid down the challenge in a carefully calibrated speech at the start: "The financial support arrangements must change from mere damage control to more forward-looking, longer-term strategies." Overindebted LDCs were simply having their debt burdens piled impossibly higher by new lending. The main focus of the debt strategy should be shifted to the debtors' "repayment capacity." In a jab at the Americans, he said, "To me, the mere fact of whether or not they pay on time interest falling due is not a valid indicator in this regard." For hopelessly overindebted LDCs, banks "have to face the fact that the problem can no longer be solved by the method of rescheduling and new financing as practiced up to this time."

Near the end of his speech, Guth threw down the gauntlet to Wriston. He declared that although countries don't disappear like bankrupt companies, "a sovereign state may very well, however, 'go bankrupt' in the sense of not being able to service and repay its debt. . . . Thus, in the final analysis, the results for bank creditors would be very similar to those which occur if a corporate debtor goes into default: in both cases a good part of their claims will have to be written off." He then warned bankers to prepare themselves for the inevitability of such write-offs with larger provisioning. He also urged de Larosière to solicit governments to contribute more toward a necessary political solution.[6]

In his speech Wriston retorted that interest capitalization merely hid, not cured, the debt problem. The clash between the two banking titans spilled over from the oratorical to the interlocutory when Guth rose from the floor during a panel discussion. He charged that it was the capital and bad debt provisioning inadequacies of U.S. banks that were creditors' main problem in getting the debt crisis behind them.

Panel chairman Lew Preston called on Wriston to respond. Wriston's team worked through the night to produce a statistical refutation. Wriston "got up and delineated it" the next day.

Guth was incredulous. "There is only one guy who sees the real balance sheets of all the banks in the world, and that's Paul Volcker." Turning to the Fed chairman, he asked point-blank, "Does this have any relationship to reality? Are the American banks undercapitalized?"

"Volcker drew himself up," recounts Wriston, "and Lord love him, said, 'It's true I see the real balance sheets of all the banks. . . . They all seem about the same to me.'

"It nearly blew Guth's mind!" Wriston says, chortling.

Recollecting the same incident, Guth reports dryly, "Paul—and I admired him for it—never once put the blame on his banks."

Whether dissent would break the ranks of the world bankers' cartel was finally put to the test when de Larosière and Volcker bluntly exhorted the bank chiefs to accept the long-term MYRA for "good debtor" Mexico. Gordon Richardson appealed that "to keep getting solutions, we had to steer a line that was sufficiently tough to ensure continued adjustment and sufficiently sensitive not to put the debtors in an impossible position."

Bankers were used to having the amount of the financing "gap" dictated to them—but not the loan's duration. Many opposed the MYRA.[7] Significantly, Guth did not.

"There was a very bad atmosphere," remembers Swiss central banker Fritz Leutwiler. "There was undiplomatic language by both Paul Volcker and de Larosière. It was really blackmail. The bankers objected. Their questions were partly answered, but mostly not. The conclusion was that they were told, 'You *have* to do the MYRA.' "

In the end, the dissident bankers backed down. The bankers' cartel, and the new money buying time strategy, survived. To assuage European restiveness, Volcker in the years following devised a "menu of options" of ways for bankers to cooperate financially with the debt strategy. Gradually, too, long-term LDC growth was accentuated over short-term austerity.[8]

The world economic recovery in mid-1984 was the optimistic peak of the debt crisis. With the Mexican MYRA completed by late summer, the world financial community expected to be able to do the same for Brazil and possibly Venezuela.[9] In late September Argentina finally reached a conditional IMF agreement. A wave of self-congratulation swept over the banking community—in the event, prematurely.

"During the 1984 IMF annual meetings there was a sense of complacency about the debt problem," says Mexico's Jesus Silva Herzog. "The speeches referred to it as if it were solved." In early February 1985 *The New York Times* ran a story headlined DEBT CRISIS SEEN AS ENDING.[10] Two weeks later *Fortune* proclaimed THIRD WORLD DEBT: THE BOMB IS DEFUSED.[11]

Ironically, the outburst of press optimism came at a time when to insiders the debt problem began again to bleaken. On February 15, 1985, the IMF suspended lending to Brazil, which had fallen out of compliance with its IMF program. Privately Volcker and de Larosière were negotiating with the economically liberal team of seventy-four-year-old President-elect Tancredo Neves, who had won a resounding victory in Brazil's first democratic election since 1964. But Neves died on the eve of his inauguration. His weak successor, José Sarney, was incapable of making any hard economic decisions.

"Who could have known he [Neves] would die, and we'd get a major change in policy?" bemoans Bill Rhodes. "It would take us years to work out a debt settlement between the banks and Brazil." Argentina fell out of compliance with its IMF program, delaying the final accord with bankers to the summer of 1985. The ensuing economic adjustment was also unsatisfactory.

One irony of the debt crisis was that while its onset helped catalyze the Western political goal of Latin American democracy, once they were achieved, the fear of toppling these fragile democracies limited the pressure the West could apply for adjustment. Of the Big Three debtors, only Mexico achieved any significant economic restructuring. "[Argentine President Raúl] Alfonsín was weak at first. The [Brazilian President José] Sarney government was fragile," explains Silva Herzog. "That made it difficult for them to implement the adjustment policies. The results prove the need to have a political answer to do adjustment." Despite harsh cuts in social welfare and education, the elite interests were untouchable. "Deprivation of the population they were prepared to do," says Morgan's Lewis Preston, who later became World Bank president, "but not to privatize [industries] because it upset all those who were on the inside. They failed to deal with the structural problems that were fundamental to the relationships in those countries." Adjustment was diluted by inflationary monetary policies, which all but destroyed the middle class in Venezuela and injured it in Mexico. In the abject, sub-Sahara African LDCs, structural overindebtedness went beyond political ineffectuality to the level of human and moral tragedy, as described by Tanzanian leader Julius Nyerere: "Should we let our people starve so that we can pay our own debts?"[12]

By mid-1985 evidence of "debt fatigue" was breaking out everywhere. Peru crossed a new threshold of debtor militancy by declaring unilaterally that it would limit its debt service payments to no more than 10 percent of its export earnings. As U.S. Treasury Secretary James Baker (who'd replaced Don Regan in early 1985) listened to heads of state demand a "political solution" on a summer 1985 trip through Latin America, he grew afraid of "some political actions like a [debtors'] cartel." Baker also fretted about the "transfer of risk on a subterranean basis from the bankers to the international institutions" that was going on as bank resistance to new lending stiffened.[13]

Debt fatigue also catalyzed momentum for a "global solution" alternative to Volcker's buying time strategy.[14] Most proposals were based on debt or interest rate forgiveness by bankers in exchange for creditor government guarantees on the remaining debt.

Volcker fought them all. None would have worked, he believed. A global solution would immediately kill new bank lending. It also raised moral hazard and political problems of discouraging good debtors, foreign and domestic. "How do you maintain the belief that if you borrow money, you should pay it back?" explains New York Fed President Jerry Corrigan. "What do you say to the farmers or oil men in Texas when things there went south?"

The major flaw in all global solutions, however, was even more basic. Simply, they posited a political willingness to assume a level of financial responsibility for the LDC debt crisis that democratic governments, led by the United States, were conspicuously *not* willing to take. Nevertheless, global debt plans became popular in Congress—especially with the 1986 midterm elections on the horizon. "I was plenty worried those guys would go off the reservation with a global solution," says Volcker. "I remember one debate in the office of [House Speaker] Tip O'Neill [D-Mass.], who hardly ever got involved in these matters. He was getting so much heat from some members for a global solution that he got me up in his office to talk to them."

Even Jim Baker expressed uneasiness with the buying time strategy during one of his first talks on debt with Volcker after becoming Treasury secretary. "You know, this doesn't look right. The banks ought to be taking some loss here."[15]

Yet each alternative approach Baker explored with Treasury staff violated his political bottom lines. Either they increased the government's share of the financial burden or they made the Treasury's role so visible that it conferred moral hazard responsibility for bankers' loans and invited formation of a debtors' cartel to "descend on us to negotiate a political solution to the debt crisis."[16] Insuring banks against their LDC loan losses was discarded because "you'd blow the insurance industry out of the water, too. You couldn't get private insurance for LDC debt unless the government guaranteed it," says Treasury Undersecretary George Gould. "Baker felt very strongly that there had to be no contingent liability for the government." Government-backed debt reduction schemes, such as those adopted later in the 1989 Brady Plan, were also excluded because Baker wasn't willing "to write down the debt on his watch," says David Mulford, who'd become the new Treasury point man on debt.

Bereft of alternatives, Baker stuck with Volcker and the buying time strategy. "Baker's view was that Volcker was good at it and liked doing it, so why change?" elaborates Mulford. "If there was to be a visible face, it should be the Fed."

Baker's political instincts, however, were strong that he needed some initiative on debt that would appear to address the depression in Latin America harming U.S. exports, employment, and, with it, Republican electoral prospects in November 1986. Facing "debt fatigue," Volcker was already searching for new ways to give "the whole process a creative kick in the pants. There must be a way to give the banks a kick, I thought. How to do it?"

• • •

The result was the Baker Plan. Proposed formally on October 8 at the IMF/World Bank Annual Meetings in Seoul, it was in fact cobbled together over a series of summer 1985 breakfast meetings between Volcker and Baker and their staffs, with input from Secretary of State George Shultz. Preparation was hasty because the Treasury staff was also busy working on the proposals that led to the September 22, 1985, G5 Plaza Accord on the dollar. The main draft was written on the airplane across the Pacific Ocean. When the penultimate version of the speech didn't feel right to him, Volcker stayed up until three A.M. one night in Seoul reworking the nuances.[17]

The plan, entitled a "Program for Sustained Growth," called for a $20 billion hike over three years in new bank money supplemented by $9 billion from multilateral institutions. It accented growth over austerity and promoted the role of the World Bank. "It laid out what we were already doing with renewed emphasis," says Volcker.[18]

The reaction of insiders at Seoul was underwhelming. To bankers it was the buying time strategy—with mostly their money—warmed over. To debtors "the Baker Plan never existed. It was just a political maneuver to avoid confrontation."[19]

Yet the press, captivated by Baker's panache in staging the Plaza Accord two weeks earlier, lavished the Baker Plan with headlines. Hoping to capitalize on the media momentum, Volcker and Baker pressed bankers to pony up their $20 billion.[20] De Larosière too chaired a Washington dinner for top bankers.

Abroad, ex–Bank of England Governor Gordon Richardson suggested to Lloyds Chairman Jeremy Morse that Morse host an intimate, consensus-building dinner like the one in November 1982. "Look here, Jeremy, it's getting a bit sticky," Richardson said. "There are some new people. [Alfred] Herrhausen is replacing Guth [at Deutsche Bank]. [John] Reed is replacing Wriston [at Citibank]. Why not call a dinner?"[21]

"The 1985 meetings were to bring Reed and Herrhausen up to speed," reports Morgan Chairman Lewis Preston, who attended the dinner. "I don't think Alfred had understood as well as Wilfried [Guth] the systematic problem."[22] Herrhausen never fully accepted that Deutsche should hold its banking strategy in indefinite abeyance in order to allow less prudent banks time to rebuild their capital. From 1987 until his assassination by terrorist car bombing in November 1989, Herrhausen waged a private campaign to persuade IBJ's Kaneo Nakamura and Morgan's Lew Preston, chairmen of the most prestigious and strongest banks in Japan and the United States, to break from the buying time creditors' cartel by jointly supporting a debt reduction scheme that would finally put the debt problem behind them.

In the end, the Baker Plan fell flat on its face. Bankers simply would not put up the new money. Another impasse arose with Argentina. The 40 percent plunge in oil prices in early 1986 undid big oil producer Mexico. Instead of becoming the model Baker Plan debtor as planned in Seoul, it again rocked the world financial system. "From October 1985 to July 1986," says a Fed official regarding the Baker Plan, "nothing happened."

Chapter 16

From Buying Time to Debt Relief

Until 1985 Mexico looked liked the world's paragon debtor. Under IMF tutelage, the current account balance had swung from a $6 billion deficit in 1982 to a $4 billion surplus in 1984. Growth was 5 percent. Many bankers believed that Mexico was on course to "break away from the pack" and overcome its debt crisis.[1]

But hidden political and economic riptides intruded. Government spending surged in regions where there was electoral competition. The budget deficit soared toward 13 percent of GDP, far beyond its IMF target of 5 percent. Inflation climbed. Then came the devastating Mexico City earthquake on September 19, 1985, which killed ten thousand. "The earthquake was a beautiful excuse from the macroeconomic point of view to justify the excess expenditures and for going off the IMF program," says Silva Herzog. The 40 percent collapse in oil prices in winter 1985–86 chopped oil export revenues. The budget math required by the IMF became impossible.

In a Friday, February 21, 1986, speech, President de la Madrid signaled Mexico's readiness to default on its debt unless it received relief in line with its "repayment capacity." He had in mind concessional interest rates, interest capitalization, or debt forgiveness. He also demanded direct talks with the U.S. government—to bypass the IMF—to seek a political solution.

On Monday, February 24, Finance Minister Silva Herzog and central bank Governor Miguel Mancera arrived in Washington. They told Volcker, Baker, George Shultz, and de Larosière that Mexico wanted a financial package worth about $9 billion—$7 billion in new lending and a $2.2 billion cut in interest payments—for which it was willing to trim its budget deficit within IMF compliance. "We explained that we'd lose six billion in revenues from the oil price fall and that we required another financing package," says Silva

Herzog. "On February 24 we made estimates of the money needed, but it varied depending on how much the price of oil was. They wanted us to cut expenditures. I felt more could be done. But there was political resistance conducted by Mr. [Budget Minister Carlos] Salinas, who said we couldn't do more."

Volcker and Baker's reception was cool. From March to May the negotiations went nowhere. Bank creditors and de Larosière remained adamant that Mexico stick to its IMF adjustment targets. Mexico's new financial projections didn't inspire much confidence at either the Treasury or the Fed. Too, the political maneuvering in Mexico—Carlos Salinas, among others, was trying to knock off the popular Silva Herzog as presidential heir apparent in 1988—was inscrutable.

Unknown to the Americans, pressures were building toward the outbreak of the second Mexican crisis at the end of May. To Silva Herzog's growing despair, "The U.S. Treasury was not moving."

Mexican Debt Crisis Phase Two

At the May 31 inauguration of the 1986 World Cup soccer championship, which Mexico was proudly hosting, three hundred million television viewers around the world witnessed one hundred thousand Mexican citizens in Azteca Stadium humiliate President de la Madrid by jeering his opening speech into inaudibility. In anticipation of a militant populist response, a huge wave of capital fled Mexico. Within a week the peso plunged 30 percent. Mexico's foreign exchange reserves dwindled rapidly.

The Azteca incident pushed de la Madrid over the edge. Although he had not yet given final approval, he seemed certain to announce Mexico's unilateral debt default during a June 10 televised speech. Even Silva Herzog "had decided to go the hard-line route. We had the mechanisms in place. Foreign exchange controls were ready at the central banks. I had a telex prepared and an internal memorandum how to implement it."

Yet in one final act of brinksmanship to avoid the rupture with the world economic community, Silva Herzog—acting without the knowledge of de la Madrid—leaked the story of the impending moratorium to one of the newswire services.[2] As intended, it got picked up by the Mexican press and *The Wall Street Journal*.

Silva Herzog then telephoned Volcker. He told him "they'd made their decision to withdraw from the process and were about to make it public," Volcker says.[3]

The Mexicans had derived a new bottom line: how much default would save in interest repayments versus how much net new money they could get through the debt process. With $10 billion in annual interest repayments on one side, and all new lending being repaid immediately to service existing debt on the other, the simple math seemed overwhelmingly to favor default. Sensing Silva Herzog's earnestness, Volcker made plans to rush secretly to Mexico City to try to forestall the default.

Volcker's judgment of the gravity of the Mexican default risk was also colored by his growing fear "in 1986 that the whole world economy would stall."[4] Although the big U.S. banks had reduced their debt exposures to Mexico from half to one-third of their primary capital, a Mexican default was still likely to trigger a bank lending squeeze that could push the U.S. and world economy over the edge into a sharp recession or worse. The only way to avert it might be the monetary printing press—renewed inflation.

On Sunday, June 8, Volcker flew to Houston. A Mexican government airplane stealthily transported him to Mexico City. A station wagon with polarized windows shuttled him to the home of the minister of tourism, a friend of Silva Herzog's, for the night. Next morning Volcker and Silva Herzog called on President de la Madrid for breakfast. Bank of Mexico Governor Miguel Mancera was also there.

"Whatever you do, don't break with the debt process," Volcker urged.

"We don't want to do this," de la Madrid responded. "Please don't push me into a political and economic corner where we have to take this road."[5]

Volcker assured him that the United States, and he personally, stood ready to assist Mexico to avert that outcome. But Mexico had to be ready to do something itself.

They reviewed the Mexican debt calculations of the apparent savings of debt moratorium. "It's not so simple as that," Volcker reminded them. "There are hidden costs. Trade finance will dry up. There'll be a run on the peso. Be realistic!" These were references to the Mexicans' two great worries in breaking with the world financial community—the country's dependence on food imports and its vulnerability to massive capital flight. Estimates were that Mexicans over the years had pirated $55 billion out of the country— equivalent to over three-fifths of the nation's total foreign debt.

Volcker was probably the only person in the world capable of dissuading the Mexicans at this late date. A former central banker himself, de la Madrid had collaborated with Volcker before. He trusted him to follow through on his word. Above all, Volcker alone was in a position to broker a deal with both governments and markets. "No one else knew the limits on both sides," says Gustavo Petricioli, a close adviser to de la Madrid. "Paul had a very clear idea of what was possible and how to go forward, not just for the moment, but for the longer term. The banks were not prepared to manage these problems. The Bretton Woods institutions were not prepared in mental attitude—including de Larosière. We needed his credibility to push this."[6]

The group explored the parameters of a possible package. The Mexicans outlined what economic adjustments they could undertake. Politically, de la Madrid said he simply could not be seen as knuckling under to the IMF. Economically, the oil price plunge, over which they had no control, had to be taken into account. They also wanted a package credible enough to induce flight capital to return. "The specific figure of $6 billion was not discussed," says Silva Herzog, "but it was in everyone's mind."[7]

A general understanding was reached: Mexico would stay within the debt process; Volcker promised to try to work out something with the IMF, the banks, and creditor governments. That Monday afternoon Volcker quietly returned to Washington. At his televised address on June 10, de la Madrid announced that negotiations were under way to adjust Mexico's debt burden in accordance with the country's ability to pay. The first dividend came immediately—the peso rebounded.

One political casualty was Silva Herzog, who resigned as finance minister under duress a week later. His replacement, Gustavo Petricioli, promptly flew to the United States to work on the $6 billion package with Volcker and Jim Baker.[8]

The first hurdle was to arrange an IMF standby agreement. With that in hand, Petricioli could go to the banks. Volcker and Baker campaigned to get de Larosière to compromise on Mexico's wayward budget deficit. "Volcker, Darman, and Baker were very concerned about the danger of Mexico," de Larosière recalls. "In 1986 the Mexican problem was less systemic, but it was extremely delicate."

One proposed compromise was for the IMF to adopt an "inflation-adjusted" budget deficit, which deducted inflation-influenced domestic interest costs. Doing so reduced Mexico comfortably under the IMF's 5 percent target. Yet as a fiscal expert de Larosière found it hard to countenance such an accounting gimmick. What remained of the IMF's tarnished credibility was at stake. "In 1982 de Larosière gave a more optimistic account of Mexico's problems," explains senior IMF man David Finch. "But by 1986 it hadn't worked well. The banks were pretty skeptical. The Fund had gotten them into it, and they felt trapped. The tension was building over what to do."

De Larosière finally yielded at a July Saturday meeting with Petricioli at the IMF. He added an oil contingency allowing Mexico to borrow more if oil prices fell below $9 a barrel and givebacks if they rose above $14. "De Larosière was a politician, too," says Finch. "He said, 'I need the United States.' "

The $1.5 billion IMF standby agreement announced on July 22, 1986, was intended to leverage $7.7 billion more in involuntary lending by banks, $1 billion in trade-linked funds from Japan, and $3 billion from multilateral agencies and governments. To tide Mexico over until IMF monies could be disbursed, a new $1.6 billion bridge loan package from the United States, private banks, the BIS, and foreign central banks was assembled in August.[9]

De Larosière gave the bankers and Mexicans until September 29 to reach their financing accord. After that the IMF standby would be nullified. Jim Baker joined Volcker and de Larosière in urging top bankers to cooperate. As soon as the IMF standby was signed, the Treasury also telexed to the monetary authorities of industrial democracies, saying, in effect, that "banks are expected to supply money to Mexico."[10]

The bankers were outraged. They objected to a $7.7 billion financing "gap" that was twice as large as necessary and to Mexico's insistence on long-term rescheduling of existing debt—including the 1984 MYRA. They were livid that interest rate concessions were expected, even though Mexico had missed its IMF targets. Foreign bankers' strong resistance was exacerbated by the plunging dollar of 1986, which further diminished to relative insignificance their direct exposure to dollar-denominated LDC debt. Even banks on the normally compliant advisory committee held out for various special conditions from the Mexicans. Most contentious of all, advisory committee chairman Bill Rhodes and Minister Petricioli had "hundreds of hours" of brutal negotiations over the interest rate on the new and rescheduled debt—the bottom line in profit for banks and in political symbolism for the Mexican government.[11]

At de Larosière's decreed September 29 deadline, nearly all the principals were gathered in Washington for the 1986 IMF/World Bank annual meetings. Yet the intensity of that environment did not produce a breakthrough as in the past.

With the debt process hanging in the balance, de Larosière and Volcker, under IMF aegis, summoned the chairmen or most senior representatives from the thirteen advisory committee banks to an afternoon head-banging meeting at the IMF building. World Bank President Barber Conable was also present. "Volcker was invited, and he naturally took over the chair," reports a high IMF official. "It was a very tense meeting. It went on until two A.M." Volcker and de Larosière urged the bank chiefs to accept the proposed agreement without significant modification. They admonished them to consider the consequences for the debt crisis if the Mexican agreement collapsed.

Citibank Chairman John Reed and some European bankers continued to argue for an expanded menu of options, including exit options, in structuring their loans and for dictating how their credits could be used by Mexico. Reed rejected the oil price contingency concept. He also "sprang a whole raft of new ideas on everyone," recounts Volcker, who became even more suspicious than usual that Reed was opportunistically trying to cut a deal that had special benefits for Citibank. "No one was ready for it. He was more or less isolated."

In the wee hours the bank chiefs relented on the amount and the structure of the financing package. But they could *not* agree on the price—the interest rate. All they could agree on was to reconvene the next morning to try again.

Originally the banks had offered 1 1/8 percentage points over LIBOR and the Mexicans' 3/8. The two sides moved together by eighths until the bankers were steadfast at 7/8 and the Mexicans at 3/4. There they stood at impasse.

The one-eighth difference was economically insignificant. It represented a mere $10 million spread over five hundred banks. Rather, it was almost wholly political symbolism. Each side was negotiating for much more than this one deal. Each was setting precedents for all future LDC deals—and who would psychologically dominate the debt process.

The next morning Mexican Finance Minister Petricioli sent an ultimatum "to the bankers through Paul [Volcker] and Jacques [de Larosière]" that he'd split the difference and settle for thirteen-sixteenths over LIBOR. Take it or leave it. "I used technical analysis, historical, *anything* to justify it," Petricioli relates. "I said I didn't want to talk to anyone who couldn't make the final decision—and by tonight!"[12]

At the outset of the reconvened Tuesday morning chairmen-only meeting at the Washington Sheraton Hotel, de Larosière declared, "No one leaves this room until we get an agreement!"

Volcker thundered, "Get all the hangers-on outta the room!"

By "hangers-on," Volcker meant all nonchairmen in general and bank debt maven Bill Rhodes of Citibank in particular. Volcker was annoyed at Rhodes's vocal support of John Reed, Rhodes's boss, at the first meeting. It was a brutal treatment of Rhodes, who had worked so indefatigably for the debt process over the years.

Jeremy Morse of Lloyds rose. "I'd like to have Bill stay," he objected. "He is the one who knows all the numbers."

When de Larosière seconded Morse, Volcker retreated: Rhodes could stay—but with the understanding that he couldn't speak.

Volcker then demanded that the bank chiefs accept Petricioli's compromise. " 'Settle it!' I said," recounts Volcker. "That was my overriding concern. They were only one-eighth of a point apart. The [Monday night] meeting at the IMF had dragged on interminably. I tried to get the damned thing settled. It was just a difference of bridging the one-eighth. Reed was holding out like crazy."

"Reed was trying a different line," recalls a non-U.S. banker. "De Larosière and Volcker really banged heads. Afterward I met three or four colleagues and had to repeat what had been said. It was worse secondhand."[13]

In the end, Volcker resorted to the hardest of central banker hardball. He commanded the chairmen of the world's most powerful private banks to drop their objections and to accept the thirteen-sixteenths. Otherwise, he suggested, focusing upon Reed, he would see to it that the world knew who was responsible for the collapse of the Mexican deal and the chunks of the financial system that might fall with it.

The bank chairmen capitulated.

"Volcker may have implied that the shortsightedness of the banks would result in the collapse," says Morgan's Lewis Preston. "The one-sixteenth was the difference between saving it and letting it go. John [Reed] felt that Herrhausen and the others let him down in capitulating on the one-sixteenth." Reed was "purple in the face" and "foaming at the mouth when he exited," described two eyewitnesses.

The bank chiefs still had to decide whether to apply the thirteen-sixteenths rate to both the rescheduled and the new loans or to mix them to achieve that average. The mix chosen was important in setting precedent for future debt deals. Volcker urged them to settle it themselves on the spot. But they turned it back to the bank advisory committee. When the advisory committee bogged down again, the agreement nearly unraveled.

"Instead of doing it themselves, they said, 'We're big chiefs—we don't do these things. We'll send it to our deputies,' " relates Volcker. "I begged them not to do it. They did it. The deputies reported back two hours later that they couldn't break the stalemate." The chairmen finally decided themselves on thirteen-sixteenths for all Mexican debt.

"Volcker and I had to get very tough," states de Larosière in hindsight. "What was it really about? They didn't like to be *told*. But we had to solve the problem. The Fund was accustomed to fixing the amount, but not the price. It was Volcker who was decisive on the price."

"Paul was wrong when he squeezed the bank chairmen to accept the interest rate concession," says one banker participant. "It went hard with the Europeans and John Reed. He should've let it go for a couple of days—cooled off—we would've gotten it. It was a 'Made in Washington' deal."[14]

With the second Mexican rescue, the authorities were effectively undertaking *all* the major decisions that sustained the artificial LDC debt market: since the first Mexican rescue in 1982, de Larosière with Volcker set the "gap" or *amount* of involuntary new bank lending; with the 1984 MYRA they began to set the *term* or duration; by 1986 they'd set the effective *price*

of those loans. Amount, term, price—there wasn't that much left for the
bankers to do but pay up. But such conditions also disengaged them. The unspoken democratic capitalist compact between private banks and governments over the LDC debt process had reached the breaking point. "Paul,
you've won the battle but lost the war," one bank chairman said vitupera-
tively to Volcker as the meeting broke up.[15]

The consequences of Volcker's autocratic intervention were felt in the her-
culean difficulty of the "dialing for dollars" exercise among Mexico's five
hundred-plus bankers. The first mass defections from the creditors' cartel,
and a rupture of the national divisions among creditors, forced de Larosière's
original one-month deadline to reach the 90 percent "critical mass" commitments on the $7.7 billion to be extended to six months—and still quite nearly
was missed. "Not [even] all of the steering committee banks contributed [at
first]," says Finance Minister Petricioli, who kicked off the worldwide campaign of "road shows"—sales presentations for bankers—in Washington on
October 10.

Bankers protested at everything that had galled the advisory committee
chairmen. Many wanted to bypass the advisory committee process and negotiate separately with Mexico themselves. Others wanted to take the write-
offs and forget about LDC debt forever. The defections were led by regional
and superregional banks in Germany, France, and the United States.

By 1987 the Fed had all but exhausted its moral suasion authority with
less exposed banks. In 1984–85 regionals had started to "talk back." In the
Mexican drive one regional bank chairman purportedly turned on his Fed
interlocutor: "Are you *telling* me that I have to lend to Mexico?" No central
banker could answer "Yes" and still operate within the customary bounds of
propriety between markets and governments. "That question quickly got
around," reports an advisory committee banker. "That ended the Fed pressure."

The Fed adopted the "two chairmen" rule: "We'll call [recalcitrant banks]
only if the [advisory committee] bankers can prove that at least two money
center bank chairmen tried and couldn't do it."[16] At each meeting of the advisory committee, Bill Rhodes would ask, "How'd your calls go?" then decide, "We talked enough to him. Have your chairman call his chairman."[17]
The process escalated until the Fed was asked for help. The Mexicans assisted by lobbying interested parties with leverage on recalcitrant bankers,
such as U.S. exporters to Mexico, congressmen from border states, and some
institutional money managers. "They would have erected statues to the regional bank presidents in the town square as heroes for defying the New
York banks," remembers the Treasury's Gould. "I saw this problem of rais-

ing money through Volcker's eyes. 'I'm having trouble,' he said. He always referred to it as 'I.' "

Foreign central bankers and finance ministers helped with an obstinate foreign bank at the prodding of Volcker or Baker, who conferred regularly with Petricioli. Often the money came through with word that "Baker talked to my boss."[18]

The main excuse of all foot draggers was the dramatic attrition of U.S. banks. The nonparticipation of the resurrected Continental Illinois especially "infuriated the Europeans."[19] Continental claimed that its old LDC loan obligations belonged to the FDIC. The FDIC said no. Because the FDIC was Continental's controlling shareholder, foreigners viewed it as a nationalized bank. Other national banking systems also lagged. The stellar performers, as usual, were the Japanese and British banks.

But with so many U.S. bank free riders, the four big U.K. clearing banks demanded that new money contributions be calculated on the basis of "national shares" for each banking system, rather than on a universal increase from the 1982 base. The French, although not fully subscribed themselves, quickly seconded the U.K. demand. A couple of Canadian banks dug in their heels. Even the normally compliant Japanese banks, which had grown into global leviathans for whom the debt crisis was almost a moot concern because of the stunning 80 percent appreciation of the yen against the dollar in two years, joined the rebellion. "We felt national shares would be better because we were angry with U.S. banks dropping out," says Yusuke Kashiwagi of Bank of Tokyo. "But we didn't want to stress this *too* much since the rise of the yen had made us stronger."[20] The most strident rebel, Industrial Bank of Japan Deputy Chairman Yoh Kurosawa, demanded a long-term exit option.

International central bankers rallied one last time to prevent the creditors' cartel from collapsing. "National shares" was discussed in Basel. New York Fed President Jerry Corrigan countered the renewed calls for interest capitalization, including having words with the Swiss National Bank to mute Franz Lutolf of Swiss Bank Corp.

"The British banks in particular were peeved on the Mexican issue," says Volcker. "I talked to [Bank of England Governor] Robin [Leigh-Pemberton] to talk to them." Jim Baker talked to his counterpart, Chancellor of the Exchequer Nigel Lawson. Mexican Finance Minister Petricioli spoke to both Leigh-Pemberton and Lawson. Bank advisory committee chairman Bill Rhodes spoke with Anthony Loehnis, the Bank of England's overseas executive director. "It was one of the last times in the debt crisis that the Bank of England leaned on the banks," says Rhodes. "It took several weeks. It was a crisis if we couldn't get it together."

Ultimately the "national shares" rebellion was put down after Citibank

Chairman John Reed flew to London. His first, late evening stop was with Bank of England Deputy Governor George Blunden. "He was going around the next day to talk to the bank chairmen here," Blunden recalls. "I gave him advice on what the sentiments were. The [U.S.] money centers were not taking enough themselves, was what people felt." The next day Reed persuaded his British counterparts to accept a "topping up" by big U.S. banks to compensate and participation by at least the top fifty-two U.S. lenders to Mexico. If not achieved, the U.K. bankers would cut their own contribution by 10 percent.

Recalls Morgan's Lew Preston: "It was John's [Reed] idea to top up. Reluctantly we all went along, except [Chase Manhattan Chairman Willard] Butcher. His relationship with Reed was not good. Jerry [Corrigan] may have had a few words with everyone, I'm not sure." Continental Illinois also contributed, though less than its full share, after its chairman, Thomas Theobold, got an earful from the Treasury and the banking club. The Treasury also talked to the FDIC.

In the end, the British banks acquiesced. IBJ's rebellion in Japan ended when "Fuji and Sumitomo didn't go along—that stopped [IBJ Deputy Chairman Yoh] Kurosawa's bandwagon."[21] The two recalcitrant Canadian banks were brought to heel with the help of Bank of Canada Governor John Crow. One by one the other major bank holdouts, including two Italians and one French, fell into line.

On March 20 some 360 banks signed commitments to lend $7.7 billion to Mexico. An unprecedented one-quarter of Mexico's lenders, over half of them from the United States, had refused to participate. The end for involuntary lending was nigh.

No More New Money

As in 1982, the Mexican package was nearly sabotaged by Brazil. Again overtaken by serious trouble, Brazil declared in January 1987 that it would unilaterally stop paying interest unless bankers agreed to a radical new debt package. Its demands included a MYRA, an interest rate at or below thirteen-sixteenths over LIBOR—and no supervisory IMF program. It amounted to a naked bid to seize control of the debt process.

Volcker, who says, "I was worried about them [Brazil] not paying," reacted with an unprecedented step: he engineered a rupture of the sacrosanct bond beween an IMF program and Paris Club debt rescheduling by creditor governments.[22] Volcker was able to persuade Baker and George Shultz, one of whose State Department officials was the U.S.'s Paris Club representative, to consent to this breach of Paris Club rules because the Brazilians had signaled him that as a quid pro quo they would call off their threatened halt in bank interest payments. "Volcker played an immense role—it shows that when he wanted to have influence at the Paris Club, he certainly could," reports a U.S. insider. "Almost everyone involved in that decision regrets it now."

The precedent was violated on January 21, 1987, at a rancorous, fifteen-hour session from 3 P.M. to 6 A.M. of the Paris Club. It required telephone calls through the night from U.S. Treasury Secretary Baker to persuade reluctant Europeans and Japanese members to reschedule over $4 billion in official Brazil debt arrears without the IMF seal of approval.[23]

Despite the extraordinary gesture, it soon became clear that the Brazilians intended to proceed with their private bank debt moratorium anyway. Two days before its February 20 moratorium, Volcker and Jerry Corrigan summoned key money center and large regional bank chairmen to the New York Fed. The showdown with Brazil was imminent, they said. They urged the bankers to expedite settlement of all outstanding LDC negotiations so that the deck would be cleared of potential falling dominoes.[24]

Bankers swiftly withdrew their objection against other debtors' getting terms as favorable as Mexico's. Deals were concluded in a flurry with Chile, the Philippines, and Venezuela. On February 26 the United States arranged a $500 million bridge loan for Argentina to facilitate an April debt rescheduling at thirteen-sixteenths over LIBOR. Within a week of Brazil's moratorium, the March 20 signing date for the Mexican package was announced.

The world financial system weathered Brazil's moratorium without upheaval. But it was a death throe for the buying time debt strategy. When Lloyds Bank Chairman Jeremy Morse visited Lew Preston at J. P. Morgan in New York soon afterward, he "was gloomy and pessimistic how things were going, particularly in Brazil."

Preston then surprised Morse: "The real risk is not south of the border, but at 399 Park."[25] Three ninety-nine Park was Citibank headquarters. Preston's allusion was to forty-eight-year-old Reed, who since the Brazilian moratorium had been pacing like a caged lion calculating actions to free Citibank from the LDC debt process and Volcker decrees. "We must do *something!*" he declared to Citi executives.[26]

On May 19, 1987, Reed acted—dramatically: Citibank added $3 billion to its bad-debt reserves, raising them to 25 percent of its total LDC loans. Although generating a $2.5 billion loss for the quarter, the action sent a defiant message to LDC debtors like Brazil, as well as to Volcker, that Citibank believed it was out of mortal danger from the debt crisis and would no longer be pushed around. Through such large provisioning—a prudent action Reed knew that no central banker could criticize openly—Reed was declaring his readiness to take a 25 percent loss on Citibank's LDC debt. This undercut Volcker's leverage to impose any involuntary new lending solutions. Reed noted that it cleared the path for Citibank to pursue other debt options. "There's some element of machismo in it," says the Fed's Mike Bradfield. "Who's going to run the system? Citi says, 'We run it.' "

Citi's share price rose by 5 percent; the shares of most unprovisioned money center banks fell. It was a surprising market reaction, almost as if the stock market sighed with relief that its darkest LDC debt fears were unfounded. Reed soon exploited it by stealing a march on his weaker bank competitors with a large equity financing.

Most of Citi's competitors were not well enough capitalized to follow. As if to underline this point to financial markets, Reed noted in his press conference afterward that he'd prenotified the chairmen of Manufacturers Hanover and BankAmerica, two weaker big banks whose survival was still threatened by their LDC debt.

"Many bankers were furious," recalls a top U.S. Treasury official. "They said of Reed, 'He's not playing the game, he's not part of the club.' His attitude was, 'I'll get control of my destiny, and if it screws BankAmerica, too bad.' " Reed's move characterized the generational transformation that was occurring in banking because of the global financial revolution. Formerly "gentlemen" banker-statesmen, responsive under the old national state-bank compacts to make short-term sacrifices in the enlightened systemic self-interest of the central banker–led banking club, were being replaced by "players" more focused on their own short-term advantages. "We were always brought up to believe in the responsibility of the central bank to the system, and that we were part of it and should do our utmost to cooperate with them. Other banks don't always have that feeling," says gentleman Lewis Preston, whose very strong J. P. Morgan could have provisioned years earlier and left the pack, including Citibank, stranded behind. "I thought it [Reed's move] was an unwise decision. It had the potential effect of weakening those banks named. That was why we didn't do it."[27]

In Washington "the John Reed move was a big surprise," says the Treasury's George Gould. "He told us on a Saturday and did it on a Tuesday. So one reaction was, 'How could he do it with so little advance notice?' " At the Fed, one visiting foreign central banker recalls, "It was regarded as a preemptive strike."[28]

Actually Volcker had learned about a month earlier, through a signal Reed had sent to New York Fed President Jerry Corrigan, that Reed was contemplating some such action. But he had taken no preparatory action.

Now the Fed and other bank regulators had to act. But how?

One high-level meeting was convened with Volcker, Baker, the Fed's Mike Bradfield, and the Treasury's David Mulford and Charles Dallara in a small conference room at the Treasury. "Reed's move was a source of real concern that it could put other American banks in difficulty," reports Dallara. "One concern was that we not send a signal that the move by Citi was Fed-instigated. That could force other banks to follow." These concerns were explored again at a large meeting of U.S. bank regulators and other Fed and Treasury officials held at the second-floor boardroom of the Federal Reserve at an "odd hour."[29]

"The problem is credibility," elaborates Gould. "If Citi does it, the perception is they must have a reason. How would the markets react to the others? Would the Fed and regulators look like they were wallpapering over a problem? The integrity of the Fed was at stake." The regulators debated whether to actively dissuade other bankers from imitating Reed or to sit back and watch how they and markets reacted. Their ultimate decision was to downplay the significance of Reed's action. The Fed put out a press statement emphasizing that Citibank's move simply reallocated its capital without fundamentally strengthening its balance sheet. Privately top Fed officials told chairmen from the weakest banks that they need not feel compelled by regulators to emulate Citibank. "What you didn't want was that people *thought* that something had happened when it was just bookkeeping," elaborates the Fed's head of supervision, William Taylor.

The Citibank provisioning sounded the death knell of the buying time new lending debt strategy. By siding with the foreign bankers who wanted out of the debt process, Reed shattered what was left of the creditors' cartel. His signal that Citibank itself reckoned its LDC debt at only 75 percent of face value exploded the "fiction of good loans" for all other American banks as well. Market forces were set in train whose inexorable logic favored debt reduction and forgiveness. Soon after Reed's announcement, "secondary market values [for LDC loans] fell like a stone. What Citi's action did was to fundamentally undermine the value of the debt in the eyes of banks and debtors. As soon as that happened, debtors claimed the benefit of the market discount [in negotiations], which reaches its logical conclusion in debt reduction."[30]

Despite the desire of bank regulators, market pressures forced big U.S. LDC lenders into line behind Citibank. Chase provisioned a week later. Within three weeks BankAmerica bit the bullet. Soon nearly every major U.S. bank had followed suit.

Central bankers grew alarmed when stronger U.S. regionals and foreign banks raised the stakes through "macho provisioning" of 50 percent of LDC debt and by year-end 1987 through actual LDC debt write-offs. If weaker U.S. money centers, including Citibank, were forced to match the macho provisioning, it could trigger a bank credit crunch that crippled economic growth and a cascade of LDC debt repudiations that caused debt crisis to end with a bang. The Bank of England's Robin Leigh-Pemberton and the New York Fed's Corrigan cautioned publicly against excessive provisioning.

The Fed's attention focused on the few U.S. money centers, especially J. P. Morgan and Bankers Trust, who were strong enough to provision 50 percent. To the Fed's great relief, they repressed the temptation to strike back at Citibank. Morgan moved only in September 1989, when the official strategy had changed to debt reduction under the March 1989 Brady Plan—and then, spectacularly, to 100 percent provisioning.

Totting Up

With Volcker's resignation from the Fed in mid-1987, and with the Brady Plan, total responsibility for managing the LDC debt process passed from central bankers to their governments.[31] The Brady Plan was essentially a global solution in which banks granted debt reduction to LDCs in exchange for creditor government guarantees to secure the remaining debt. "The Brady Plan shows you can get debt relief but no new money," says Volcker, noting the paucity of private funding that greeted the Brady Plan over its first couple of years.[32]

The final balance sheet of LDC burden-sharing costs came into sharper focus: banks took losses on roughly one-quarter to one-third of their debt. The remaining direct exposure to LDCs was passed on to the taxpaying citizens of leading democratic nations. "The IMF has a lot of debt out there that it won't be able to collect," warns George Shultz. The gradual, subterranean flow of exposure from the private to the public sector accelerated. At the start of the debt crisis, government creditors held 15 percent of all exposure to "Baker 15" heavily indebted countries. A decade later, they held 40 percent.[33]

Democratic citizens paid in hidden ways, too. Banks sought to recoup their LDC losses through higher spreads on other lending. Their retreat from LDCs encouraged overlending in other areas, such as commercial real estate, whose bursting bubble helped sink the S&Ls and induce the bank credit crunch and the balance sheet recession of the early 1990s.

• • •

As the LDC debt crisis wound down, the success of the buying time strategy in ferrying the world banking system away from the brink also became clearer. For the world's top one hundred banks, net Latin debt exposure to equity dropped from 125 percent to 57 percent between 1982 and 1987.[34] For the largest nine U.S. money center banks, exposure to primary capital fell from 233 percent to 106 percent; for thirteen large regional banks, exposure declined from 154 percent to 55 percent.[35] Stronger balance sheets allowed bankers to stare down Brazil, which abandoned its moratorium a year later. Capitalist financial markets, given the time bought by the debt strategy, had adjusted to the debt threat nonconvulsively.

A less noted success was that world financial crisis was averted without compromising the war on inflation. Volcker could have alleviated the debt service burden on LDCs, as well as fattened up bank profits and capital, by cutting short-term U.S. interest rates more sharply. Instead he steered through the tight passage between sound monetary policy and financial fragility to achieve the central bankers' two primary goals of low inflation growth and financial system stability.

The buying time debt strategy was less successful in its two other goals: rebuilding enough confidence to rapidly restore the voluntary private bank LDC lending market and instilling good growth prospects among debtors. It took nine years after the crisis broke for meaningful voluntary net private global financing to begin to return to Latin America. Living standards tumbled in what became known as the "lost decade." "We made a wrong assumption," says Swiss central banker Fritz Leutwiler. "We had the illusion that the time we bought would bring a more durable solution to the LDC problem."

In retrospect, Deutsche Bank chief Wilfried Guth had been right: the debt problem had long-term, international political economic structural adjustment dimensions that were not adequately addressed by treating it as a temporary financial crisis to be muddled through with new lending.

Making a virtue of necessity demanded by "stateless" capital, Mexico and some other big Latin debtors by the early 1990s were finally inducing a return of flight capital and inflows of foreign investment by pursuing a "hard currency" policy, buttressed by a more independent central bank and free market–oriented structural reform. An early reward was some restored growth, falling inflation, a more robust middle class, and political popularity. Yet despite the improved political economic atmospherics, most LDCs remained beset with heavy long-term debt burdens and considerable economic problems. Nor was it clear that the new capital inflows, much of which substituted rather than supplemented national savings, would be stable. They weren't—as Mexico learned at great pain in its 1994–95 peso crisis.

Treating the political aspects of LDC debt as a financial problem to be solved with temporary liquidity and economic austerity, argues Princeton Professor and early global solution advocate Peter Kenen, "was a central banker kind of solution. The main concern was for the banking system." Kenen's arguments echoed those of Basel dissenters that Volcker bailed out the politicians from what was essentially a political problem by seizing leadership responsibility too quickly and sustaining it for too long.

While admitting that the debt strategy was "less successful for borrowers," Volcker adds, "I'm not sure there was any other way to do it. Now [after Brazil] we know that not paying doesn't solve their problem." His fellow Big Four central bankers agreed. "The adjustments have taken longer than we'd hoped," says Bank of England Governor Gordon Richardson. "But what else was there to do?" Concurs Leutwiler emphatically, "We couldn't have done otherwise."

Given the scope of the threat to the world financial order, even Peter Kenen concedes, "You can't fault the strategy at the beginning. It was tactically reasonable to say it was a liquidity crisis and give them time to get their house in order and to ease the adjustment. Overstaying the strategy that was right for one time was the mistake. In 1984 they should have switched. The Brady Plan should have come along when the Baker Plan came along. I criticized it in 1983, in retrospect, prematurely."

Yet was there a *realistic* alternative to leaving government of the LDC debt crisis and its effect on hundreds of millions of lives in LDCs and industrial democracies to unelected central bankers when the Reagan government adamantly refused to step forward to take responsibility? Political and economic logics did not always converge, even in a crisis. A corollary question was whether politically controlled central banks would have been able to act so swiftly and coherently across competing national interests to fashion a successful [even if imperfect] last-resort rescue.[36] Central bank independence was no ironclad guarantee, but it did provide a welcome checks-and-balances backup when democratic political leadership did not rise to the challenges of global capital mobility.

"There is an enormous distance between the politicians who created the Bretton Woods institutions and the Marshall Plan, and the level of present-day thinking," laments Danish central banker Erik Hoffmeyer. "Our political systems will probably let things develop as best they can under the semi-political leadership of the monetary authorities."[37]

Global financial and economic phenomena were frequently, if often obscurely, interrelated. A third dimension of Volcker's containment of the debt crisis, and completion of his war on inflation, was to engineer a soft landing for the superdollar and the record world economic imbalances associated with it.

PART FOUR

SOFT LANDING FOR THE SUPERDOLLAR

Chapter 17

Overshooting Markets

What goes up, must come down. But how fast? How hard would it land?

Those questions haunted Federal Reserve Board Chairman Paul Volcker from 1984 as the superdollar soared far beyond all levels he'd believed possible on the tide of global capital inflows to the U.S. within the new integrating global financial landscape. Central bankers often said that although they couldn't define the "right" currency exchange rate, they sure could recognize a wrong one: at a peak of DM 3.47 and ¥263 in early 1985, the superdollar, by any reasonable measure of the underlying international competitiveness of the U.S. economy, was very, very wrong.

The misaligned dollar was both messenger and agent-saboteur of the unprecedented international economic imbalances: the U.S. balance of payment deficit on current account was soaring toward its eventual peak of $160 billion or 3.6 percent of GNP; Japan's and Germany's record-breaking surpluses were rising to over 4.3 percent of GNP. The foreign borrowing that financed the U.S. deficits transformed the U.S. in only half a decade from the world's largest creditor nation, and financial pillar of the postwar world, to its largest debtor.[1]

The laws of market capitalism guaranteed that the superdollar would eventually fall back to more rational levels. The crucial questions of how far, how fast, and when it fell would be dictated primarily by global currency market forces. "We are in a real sense living on borrowed money and time," Volcker warned in early 1985.[2]

Merely reversing the dollar's previous rise was insufficient to restore the world economy to healthy balance. Too many other economic relationships had been altered by it; they had to readjust. Simply taking away the original superdollar shock was the economic equivalent of trying to revive a pedestrian who had been run over by an automobile by running over him again in reverse.

"The worry, and a *big* one, was that when the dollar fell, would it collapse?" says ex–Fed monetary policy staff chief, Stephen Axilrod, who shared Volcker's preoccupation that the $100 billion–plus of annual foreign capital inflows propping up the dollar might dry up *abruptly* once the correction process started. A lightning-fast dollar plunge could cause the world economic imbalances to adjust with a convulsive, hard landing. A sharp spike in U.S. interest rates, to lure global investors back into the dollar, could trigger a recession and, given the financial fragilities from the LDC debt crisis and wounds of domestic disinflation, possibly a full-fledged systemic financial crisis.[3] The Fed would then be forced to pump in emergency liquidity to stave off depression—the war against inflation would be lost.

An orderly dollar decline would allow time for synchronized adjustments in the slower-changing, real economy of business investment and employee and consumer behavior. In summer 1984 Volcker had Fed staffers explore free market scenarios under which foreign investors might sell their depreciating dollar assets gradually, instead of all at once. But it "was hard to have much confidence in the answers."[4]

Government policy could facilitate the coming economic adjustment. Of foremost importance was to trim the outsized budget deficits that devoured U.S. savings. Until the 1980s the United States usually saved just enough to finance all its domestic spending on productive investment and consumption. Had the global capital not flowed in, the United States would have faced the unhappy prospect of trying to finance itself, per force, from insufficient national savings. Much higher real interest rates would have rebalanced U.S. national savings and investment through an involuntary cut in national spending—a recession.

To avert a hard landing, nasty timing cross-currents also had to be navigated. The dollar had to be falling for roughly eighteen months ahead of major budget deficit cuts because of the long lag before a devalued dollar yielded higher exports.[5] If the budget deficit was eliminated before U.S. net exports rose, there was likely to be a recession.

But if the United States failed to cut its budget deficit—the more likely scenario—as U.S. exporters expanded their investment, the competition for scarce labor, goods, and capital resources would push up prices. Renewed cost inflation would cancel out the competitive benefit of the lower dollar. The current account imbalances would persist.

Some inflation giveback was inescapable as the dollar fell simply because the anti-inflation dividend earned from lower-dollar import costs would be reversed. The greatest danger, says Volcker, was the potential "effects on inflation psychology. Revived inflation expectations could trigger the hardest of hard landings: interest rates could rise whenever the dollar was weak, producing inflation and recession simultaneously. "Then there can be a cataclysm when the foreign-dollar investors leave," says Fed Vice Chairman Manley Johnson.

Truly massive resources had to be transferred to the tradable goods sectors from the rest of the economy to bring the current account into balance. Manufacturing capacity, by expert estimate, had to be expanded by 30 percent. That would require five years of huge leaps in capital investment.[6] It also required mirror-opposite adjustments in Japan and Europe.

To the puzzlement of many, the dollar did plunge—but the landing was only bumpy. "If you told people that the dollar would fall as far and as fast as it did, they would have told you that it would be a hard landing. But it wasn't," says a Fed staffer. "The October 1987 stock market crash was the fallout." Comments U.S. Treasury Undersecretary David Mulford, "Volcker was always nervous about a free-fall of the dollar and rising interest rates. He was always wrong on it. From a market standpoint, there was plenty of dollar support. To worry about a dollar collapse was to take a page out of the past."

Did the absence of a hard economic landing from the dollar's fall herald, as some free market partisans maintained, that the virtually frictionless flow of global capital made national current account imbalances fundamentally smoother to finance than in the past? Or were special factors at work?

One key reason there was no dollar free-fall was that the world's new banker nation, Japan, maintained a level of investment that seemed to defy free market logic. Alone among major international investor groups, save the Saudis, who had a dollar-based oil economy, Japanese kept on buying dollar assets most of the time that the dollar fell, and their currency losses accumulated astronomically. Why they did so was one of the great enigmas of international finance of the latter 1980s.

"I must admit that the dollar went down more rapidly without the inflation and inflation psychology repercussions that I'd feared," Volcker confesses. "I still don't understand the force of foreign, especially Japanese, desire to invest in the dollar. Although they did *not* do so in 1987. I would like to see some analysis to explain it that wasn't so mathematical I couldn't understand it or so turgid I wouldn't want to."

The World's Problem

A problem in the dollar was a problem for the world. Even after the disintegration of the dollar-centered Bretton Woods monetary system, the U.S. currency remained the world's main monetary medium for international commerce, savings, and finance.[7] The dollar exchange rate remained the

most potent single price signal for allocating investment among nations, and
for influencing inflation, growth, and employment.

To foreigners, the stunning ascent of the dollar from 1980 hit like a "third
oil shock."[8] The same borrowed foreign capital inflows that drove up the dollar and permitted Americans to live so far beyond their means had its counterpart in capital outflows from other nations that forced their citizens to live
below theirs. It also fueled inflation through currency depreciation. The international capital flows into the superdollar thus effectively imposed a policy straitjacket that compelled foreign governments to hold domestic interest
rates higher than they wished. This exported the U.S. recession worldwide.
At its depth in 1982, there were thirty million unemployed in OECD countries. Europe went through four consecutive years of economic slump,
sixteen million unemployed, and a psychological gloom called "Europes-
simism." Japan endured a "growth recession," which meant subpar growth
below 3 percent. LDCs suffered the debt crisis. As a result, foreign leaders
grumbled bitterly about the dollar's strength, as they had a few years earlier
about its weakness.

The superdollar shock caused foreign policymakers to tighten monetary
and fiscal policies that had already been tightened in response to the inflationary pressures of the second oil shock of 1978–79. In the early 1980s
Japan and Germany moved toward fiscal restraint by the same degree that
the United States expanded its budget deficits. This enormous fiscal policy
clash was a powerful causal force of the superdollar and world economic imbalances.[9]

In Japan the austerity was led by Bank of Japan Governor Haruo "Mike"
Maekawa, who broke a taboo of the Japanese Establishment by raising the
official discount rate (ODR) from 6 percent to 7 percent on February 19,
1980, while the Diet was still debating the budget.[10] A career BOJ man loyal
to the Basel ideal of central bank independence, the first governor fluent in
English and a champion of reforming Japan's lopsided political economic
structure within international economic norms, Maekawa demonstrated the
influence a strong governor could have. He circumvented the Ministry of Finance (MOF) and political protocol by using his personal connections to "directly approach Prime Minister Ohira and, with his consent, break through
all possible opposition. He did it at the risk of his job," relates Deputy BOJ
Governor Shijuro Ogata. "He'd only been governor for two months."

The next month Maekawa boosted the discount rate again—this time by a
stunning 1.75 percentage points. In one month the cost of money in Japan
leapt 2.75 points. Maekawa's squeeze rallied the beleaguered yen and ended
the oil shock threat to inflation, which peaked at just under 9 percent.[11]

On August 20, 1980, Maekawa began reversing the BOJ's earlier tightening steps. This coincided with Volcker's relaunch of the Fed's practical mon-

etarist assault on inflation after the missteps of the lost first year. Yen–dollar interest rate differentials suddenly widened to 5–6 percent, "causing a capital outflow from Japan to the United States."[12]

Japan's swelling domestic savings and trade surpluses, which in the 1980s made Japan the world's largest net creditor nation, were propelled abroad by the comparative shortage of attractive financial and economic investments in Japan's highly regulated and underdeveloped domestic economy. They became concentrated upon the voracious U.S. appetite for capital generated by the massive U.S. budget deficits. The dollar soared. So did Japan's exports to the United States.

Japan had been generating current account surpluses since the late 1960s. But they were obscured by the two oil shocks, which soaked them up. At that stage it would have been appropriate for world economic harmony, as well as to materially reward Japanese citizens for their productive labor, for Japan to promote domestic growth through structural liberalizations and a revalued yen. Yet the oil shocks rekindled the island nation's sense of its vulnerability to unpredictable, external forces. Each time Japan fought back by sharpening the efficiency of its export machine.

By the early 1980s no extraordinary external force could mask Japan's underlying export supercompetitiveness and the lopsided disparity with its domestic economy. Japan's current account surpluses burst upon the world with astonishing force. Small surpluses in 1981 swelled to 4.3 percent of GNP, or $86 billion, in 1986.

Japan's surpluses were swelled farther by Japan's stringent fiscal consolidation policy aimed at eliminating new government borrowing by the end of the decade.[13] Born from the 1982 alliance between new Prime Minister Yasuhiro Nakasone, big-business men, and the powerful Finance Ministry, deficit elimination was rigorously pursued by MOF officials. Their overriding goal was to halt the growing intrusions of the political pork barreling class into its budget-making domain and to restore fiscal probity after a decade of large borrowing.[14]

Fiscal policy inflexibility put even more responsibility for piloting the economy on monetary policy. The soaring dollar presented the BOJ with a classic internal/external dilemma: raising interest rates to defend the yen would worsen Japan's "growth recession"; lowering them to stimulate growth would weaken the yen, worsen inflation, and whip up U.S. protectionism by boosting Japanese exports.

Maekawa's unofficial compromise, adopted in March 1982 following the final turn of the screw in Volcker's war on inflation, was to shadow U.S. interest rate moves and the yen/dollar exchange rate, even though it meant slower than potential Japanese growth. The yen's nadir of ¥278 was reached in November 1982.[15]

Exports to a rebounding U.S. economy fueled Japan's growth in 1983–84. Japanese firms kept their export earnings in dollars on the speculation of further appreciation. This propelled the superdollar and more U.S. imports. The postwar biases of the U.S. and Japanese economies were perversely being reinforced and fast pushing political protectionist and economic pressures to explosive levels.

"In the latter Maekawa period, monetary policy had to go through a tightrope to defend the yen against the dollar or avoid killing the economy," explains the BOJ's Ogata. "We followed the interest rate differentials. When U.S. rates fell, the BOJ tried to follow. We were fed up with the strong dollar for so long."

Germany too was hit hard by the soaring dollar on top of the second oil shock. Growth fell for two years and was anemic for four. Unemployment hit 8.2 percent, or 2.3 million. Alarming to German leaders was the deterioration in competitiveness of the country's great exporting companies: after thirteen years of surpluses the current account balance plunged into the red for three years. The DM 29 billion ($14 billion) deficit in 1980 was the largest for a nation that size in history. Confidence in the DM was shaken: Germany lost one-third of its foreign exchange reserves futilely intervening to stop a 25 percent DM plunge. A falling DM struck Germany's most sensitive nerve—inflation.

"The Germans are afraid of inflation the way most people are of AIDS," says Swiss central banker Fritz Leutwiler.[16] In 1981 inflation hit 6.3 percent. German governments could fall on such inflation. A 6 percent inflation rate challenged the Bundesbank's very existence. Its reputation as the diehard defender of DM soundness was the source of its independence and power in German society.

Bundesbank independence evolved with an intolerance of inflation from several tragic chapters of German history. Germany's first central bank, the Reichsbank, set up in 1876 as a government-directed institution, wound up presiding over one of world history's greatest hyperinflations in 1923; with prices doubling every hour, Germans needed wheelbarrows of banknotes to go shopping. The experience wiped out the savings of an entire generation and left a scar on the German economic psyche as indelible as the Great Depression had on America's and Britain's.

Germany's inflation angst was reinforced by the memory that the August 1924 reform making the Reichsbank independent of the government failed to prevent Adolf Hitler from seizing control to pursue another bout of inflationary finance.[17] The postwar hyperinflation obliterated the savings of a second German generation.

Bundesbank independence to bolster its commitment to sound money thus became a cornerstone of postwar German reconstruction. It delivered: in its first thirty years of rapid growth Germany's average annual inflation rate of 3.6 percent was lower than in any other rich country except Switzerland, whose central bank was even more independent. The Bundesbank, says ex–Deutsche Bank chief executive Wilfried Guth, "is almost a godlike institution in this country." Its base of popular support was so strong that Hans Tietmeyer, then state secretary at the Finance Ministry (and later Bundesbank president), says: "I would never advise my government to conflict publicly with the Bundesbank—every government will lose. They are perceived by the public as doing the appropriate things to ensure stability even if politically unpopular. Bundesbank independence is a very important element of German economic success."

The Bundesbank's independence was so vaunted that many Germans believed it was part of the constitution. It wasn't. But the 1957 Act of Parliament creating the Bundesbank granted it two legal authorities lacked by the U.S. Fed and coveted by all central bankers. First, it made clear that the central bank's paramount function was currency stability, even ahead of promoting growth. Although the central bank had to support the government's economic policy, it also expressly stated that the Bundesbank "shall be independent of instructions from the Federal Government."[18] That independence was buttressed by strict limitations on the amount of short-term financing the central bank could extend to the government.

The seminal event in the evolution of Bundesbank independence was the collapse of the Bretton Woods fixed parity exchange rate system. Fixed exchange rate targets—like any hard monetary rule, such as the gold standard or monetarism—undercut the practical independence of the central bank. It forced the Bundesbank to manage monetary policy to defend the dollar/DM exchange rate parity negotiated by its government rather than to achieve low domestic inflation. Both goals could be achieved as long as the anchor currency of the Bretton Woods system, the U.S. dollar, was sound. But when U.S. inflation accelerated in the late 1960s, the Bretton Woods system required the Bundesbank to print money and import inflation. Floating exchange rates liberated it to pursue its inflation targets on its own terms—circumscribed by the check on all central banks of having to maintain a high level of support with the democratic electorate and credibility with financial markets.

Under floating exchange rates, the Bundesbank effectively inherited from the government the political power of managing the DM's external value. Its ownership and control of Germany's foreign exchange reserves—in contrast with most other major central banks—enhanced this independence. Thanks to the large impact of inflows and outflows of global capital on Germany's money supply, the exchange rate lever was crucial to control of German monetary policy.

Bundesbank leaders' vow never again to compromise their independence with fixed exchange rate commitments set up a collision with German Chancellor Helmut Schmidt in 1978 when he and French President Valéry Giscard d'Estaing set to create the European Monetary System. The EMS contained an adjustable parity exchange rate mechanism (ERM) for Europe. Schmidt's political vision was to create an island of monetary stability amidst the disruptive volatility of floating exchange rates in order to foster European economic and political integration in which an eventually reunited Germany would be solidly anchored. Schmidt, for whom "monetary policy is also foreign policy," was willing to trade the Bundesbank's monetary dominance in Europe to get it.[19] Yet German "central bankers [who] were not trained to think of foreign policy ends" were not.[20]

The Bundesbank rebuttal was a doomsday vision of being compelled to print inflationary amounts of DM to defend a French franc that was plunging because of unrestrained spending by the French government. "The central bankers argued against the EMS," says Schmidt, who at one point bluffed trying to change the law guaranteeing Bundesbank independence to force them to go along. "They had some valid arguments. But mostly it was the fear of losing influence and slots."[21]

Lacking control in both houses of Parliament, and wary about a bruising public battle with the Bundesbank, Schmidt compromised with Bundesbank President Otmar Emminger. The EMS would be set up as a monetary agreement among central banks instead of with the government. "No one would complain if central bankers created an agreement among themselves," Schmidt explains. "Only their signatures, not foreign secretaries." A letter of understanding between the central bank and government stated that the Bundesbank could withdraw from the EMS's obligation of unlimited intervention to defend its exchange rate bands if doing so was inflationary. A rare visit by Schmidt to the Bundesbank's Frankfurt headquarters assuaged the final dissenters.

In time the DM's credibility as sound money made it the EMS's de facto reserve and transaction currency and the Bundesbank the monetary hegemony of Europe. The Bundesbank was still able to make monetary policy without regard to the economic conditions in the rest of Europe. "The Bundesbank has almost never taken any regard or notice of anybody else," says Professor Charles Goodhart of the London School of Economics. "It has always given overriding, absolute commitment to domestic price stability. The EMS is actually operated by the other central banks deciding whether to realign or to hold on to the Bundesbank."

With lower inflation, economic restructuring, and European integration topping national agendas in the early 1980s, most European governments elected to latch on to the DM and the Bundesbank's anti-inflation credibility; when things got hot politically, the Bundesbank made a convenient scapegoat. In the occulted European political economic bargain, German exporters obtained a small price subsidy equivalent to the inflation differentials between Germany and her European partners between ERM realignments. This produced larger German trade surpluses. Most attractive to German central bankers was that by providing a stable currency zone around Germany accounting for half its trade, the ERM helped the Bundesbank buffer volatility in the dollar—the external monetary force that could most easily knock it off course (and, in fact, did in 1980–81).

Like the BOJ, the Bundesbank responded to the second oil shock with a tighter monetary policy.[22] Like the BOJ, it too had eased in summer 1980 when the worst of the shock seemed over—just as Volcker was relaunching his assault on inflation. "When we eased in the summer of 1980 the dollar started to move up," recounts a high Bundesbank official. "We were not used to that! What we totally failed to realize at the time was the new confidence in the United States after the morale crisis of Vietnam, Watergate, and a weak president—Volcker's strong hand and Reagan's inspiration. With the enormous lead weight taken off, the dollar rose. The dollar *always* has a competitive edge in the world unless you do really bad things to it.

"Volcker and Reagan's supply-side policies were both applauded everywhere. Only when the budget deficits became big did we become critical. The trouble was that Volcker came before Reagan and gave him a present of a stable dollar, and Reagan misused it—only the basic confidence in the dollar allowed Reagan to finance the budget deficits."

From its summer 1980 peak of DM 1.75, the DM plunge gathered force at the start of 1981. Fleeing funds threatened simultaneously to starve Germany of investment capital and to inflate prices. German central bankers "were very worried with the DM at 2.20. At this stage the DM was weak within the EMS. That *really* got us nervous."[23] To the Bundesbank's embarrassment, other EMS central banks bought DM to prevent the DM from falling through the floor of its ERM band.[24]

The attack on the DM was a personal baptism by fire for the Bundesbank's new President, Karl Otto Pöhl. The DM slide began within a few weeks of his taking office in January 1980. Arresting the plunge was crucial to establishing the credibility he needed to be effective. It didn't help that it was well-known that Chancellor Schmidt had wooed someone else and was concerned that the fifty-year-old Pöhl might be too young and undistinguished in monetary affairs for such a big job.

The center of Bundesbank power was the Central Bank Council. Every Thursday fortnight at 9:30 A.M. councilmembers ascended a one-flight spiral staircase to take their seats around the oval oak table in the thirteenth-floor boardroom at the top of the glass-and-concrete Bundesbank headquarters in suburban Frankfurt to make German monetary policy in secret by majority vote. They altered the German discount and Lombard rates, changed reserve requirements, and authorized money market actions—mainly security re-purchase (Repo) agreements—to steer short-term market interest rates.[25]

In contrast with the United States, government ministers had the right to attend Council meetings. The government also possessed the right—though it dared not exercise it—to delay proposed policy changes by two weeks. Summary minutes of Council meetings were made public only after thirty years. Bundesbank leaders were not obligated to testify before the German Parliament. Democratic accountability was left to the Bundesbank's discretion and maintained primarily through regular press conferences and interviews.

Prior to German reunification in 1990, the Central Bank Council had up to twenty-one members, though in practice usually eighteen. Eleven were presidents of the state or *länder* central banks, formally nominated by the Bundesrat (the *länder* house of Parliament) and in practice chosen by the *länder* prime ministers.[26] The rest, including the president and vice president, were members of the executive managing directorate in Frankurt and chosen by the federal government with the directorate's approval.[27]

The resemblance of the directorate and *länder* president structure to the U.S. Federal Reserve System Board of Governors in Washington and twelve regional Reserve Bank presidents was the result of conscious modeling by the Allies, who reformed Germany's currency and financial system after World War II. Yet where the Fed centralized power in the Board through control of the discount rate and majority representation on the FOMC, the *länder* representatives were a voting majority on the Bundesbank Council. Nor did the Bundesbank have the Fed's tradition of looking to the chairman for leadership and none of the absolute powers invested in European governors. Instead the Bundesbank president was primus inter pares. His main task was finding the consensus in an often unwieldy Council. The result was less operational flexibility than most central banks and a bias toward plodding gradualism.

The most important individual to whom new President Pöhl had to prove his mettle was the Bundesbank's inside power and new vice president (and in 1991 Pöhl's successor), Helmut Schlesinger. Tall, erect, white-haired, and blunt-spoken, the personally gentle Schlesinger dominated Bundesbank policy-making mainly by his sheer intellectual force. A career central banker, he was the institution's severest anti-inflation hard-liner; even Paul Volcker's sound money reputation paled next to his. Although domestic critics charged that he was an "economic nationalist" without sensitivity to the international effects of Bundesbank policy, they added respectfully that he was a "first-rate man"—an affection that foreign policymakers, feeling the sting of tight money at the Bundesbank, rarely appreciated. Schlesinger had been an intellectual leader of the Bundesbank's conversion to pragmatic monetarism in the mid-1970s. He continued to orient his monetary policy view on whether the national money supply growth was within its annual target long after most other central bankers had jettisoned monetarist techniques.[28] He retained his staunch suspicion of EMS commitments and was the most formidable Bundesbank opponent of economic and monitary union (EMU).

To quell the storm the Bundesbank needed something drastic, yet flexible enough to respond quickly to developments. On February 19, 1981, Pöhl impressed skeptics by persuading enough *länder* presidents for the Central Bank Council to temporarily delegate to the directorate discretionary power over monetary policy between Council meetings. Lombard lending was suspended and replaced by a special Lombard facility at 12 percent—three percentage points higher—which the directorate could alter as it saw fit. Money market rates zoomed to 30 percent. The DM soon stabilized within the EMS's ERM. Although the DM continued its long slide against the dollar, its anti-inflationary credibility was restored. "Since 1982 I've been in a good position when inflation came down," Pöhl says.

However, Chancellor Schmidt, Pöhl's political mentor, hit the roof when he learned of the Bundesbank's February 19 action. Schmidt, who had "a deep distrust of central bankers, especially the Bundesbank," suspected political subterfuge and institutional blindness by the Bundesbank.[29]

At an April 2 meeting of Germany's top financial officials at his office, Schmidt blasted Pöhl and Schlesinger. The DM had to be defended, he said. But the central bank's move was an overreaction that could turn a recession into a Europe-wide depression. He then stunned all but his closest aides by announcing that he would "repair some of the damage done by Frankfurt" by arranging a small, joint Franco-German capital issue at 2.5 to 3.0 points *below* Bundesbank interest rates.

The sparks flew. Pöhl and Schlesinger stalked out early.

"Schmidt, in spring 1981, was in bad physical shape, overstressed," explains ex–Finance Minister Manfred Lahnstein. "He was rash with Pöhl. Perhaps he gave the Bundesbank representatives the impression that he wanted to counter the Bundesbank's moves. The Bundesbank had overdone it. It had a really lasting effect on growth through the 1980s."[30]

A week later Pöhl and the Bundesbank publicly challenged the government with a detailed criticism of Schmidt's Franco-German issue proposal. German political interests took sides. The influential government Panel of Economic Experts backed the central bank in a special public report. Public opinion sided with the Bundesbank. An embittered Schmidt, who presided over a doubling of German unemployment to two million in the 1981–82 recession, later blamed the Bundesbank for the 1982 fall of his government.

The tempest of 1980–81 was the turning point for German political economic policy in the 1980s. While sensational, the clash over Bundesbank monetary policy was only a side effect of the core German problem of the structural rigidity long developing in its political economy. Extramarket practices underpinning the nation's social democratic capitalist compact—such as rigid labor rules, heavy government subsidies of industry, overtaxation, myriad regulation, the spreading social welfare net—had grown so extensive, they made the economy insufficiently adaptive to technological change and external economic shocks. Other European nations also suffered from this "Eurosclerosis"; "Europessimists" predicted that without radical reform, Europe was foredoomed to competitive decline against U.S. and Japanese capitalisms.

Germany's sclerosis helped drive its federal budget deficit up to 3.7 percent of GNP in 1981. Virtually all government economic targets were being missed. In response, Schmidt enacted severe fiscal austerity. The budget deficit shrank to 3.3 percent of GNP. Schmidt's political time, however, had expired. Economics Minister Otto Lambsdorff, a leader of the Free Democrats allied with Schmidt in the coalition government, declared that it was impossible to pursue the necessary economic policies of fiscal restraint and structural reform within the Schmidt government. In October 1982 the FDP abandoned Schmidt to enter a coalition led by Helmut Kohl's Christian Democrats.

The Kohl government's program promised deficit reduction, followed by tax and structural reform. By the end of the decade fiscal austerity reduced Germany's budget deficit to 1 percent of GNP. But it was so inflexibly pursued, "virtually as a goal, not a policy instrument," that it often aggravated international economic imbalances.[31] Reduced deficits held down German real interest rates and enlarged Germany's excess national savings over investment—much of which flowed into the superdollar. The Bundesbank reacted with a relatively tight monetary policy stance that partly offset DM weakness against the dollar with strength within the ERM and let exports lead Germany's slow growth path to recovery. German current account surpluses swelled to record highs.

Only France's newly elected Socialist Mitterrand government dared challenged the tight monetary harness imposed on all European nations by the Bundesbank's policy. Its expansionary policies, however, backfired. Capital flight rose, and private business investment withered. Following a dramatic Sunday night showdown among factional government leaders in March 1983, Mitterrand capitulated. France stayed in the ERM and imposed the economic austerity that doing so entailed. It was a brutal warning to all political leaders that the regime of global capital made it much harder for any government, whatever its democratic political mandate, to go its own way.

The International Politics of the Dollar

Unable to counteract the "third oil shock" of the global capital rush into the dollar, democratic world leaders pressed President Reagan for joint intervention to sell dollars on currency markets and especially for U.S. action to remedy what they all viewed as the root economic villain behind it, America's outsized budget deficits. Most U.S. presidents had little interest or knowledge about the political economy of the dollar. They usually saw the dollar as a nuisance or as a bargaining chip to be traded for something more important, like military cooperation. Reagan was no exception. "Reagan lacked certain bodies of economic knowledge," says ex–Deputy Treasury Secretary Tim McNamar, who prepped him for many international economic meetings. "He only knew that people called him to bitch about it."

The Reagan administration's retort was that there was nothing wrong with U.S. policies: the strong dollar was a vote of confidence by the free market. The problem of the dollar, rather, lay abroad. If Europe wanted to grow faster, it should adopt U.S. supply-side strategies like deregulation and tax reform to break up its Eurosclerosis. Japan was suffering from a yen that was kept artificially weak by overregulated and incestuous domestic financial markets that created a paucity of internationally attractive investments. The cure was Anglo-Saxon-style financial deregulation.[32]

Shortly upon taking office in 1981, the Reagan team had announced a nonintervention policy to affect the dollar's level; it would intervene only on exceptional occasions to calm disorderly market volatility, such as occurred on March 30, 1981, when a would-be assassin shot Reagan. To many key Reagan officials, government intervention in free-floating exchange markets was an ideological anathema. Others believed that surging global capital flows simply rendered government intervention ineffective.[33] From spring 1981 through January 1985 the United States intervened in only ten periods for a paltry total of $1.1 billion. Foreign central banks spent several tens of billions of dollars in intervention over the same period.[34]

At the 1982 G7 head of state economic summit at the Versailles Palace, France, the United States deflected foreign pressure by agreeing to jointly study the effectiveness of exchange rate intervention. In the spring of 1983 the "Jurgensen Committee" concluded that sterilized intervention—that is, intervention whose net effect on national money supply and interest rates was "sterilized" by offsetting central banker liquidity injections or withdrawals from domestic money markets—had little more than a transitory, "announcement" impact on currency values. Only "unsterilized" intervention—which was the same thing as changing monetary policy—had a lasting effect. Yet for diplomatic purposes, the Europeans, supported by the Fed, fudged the final committee report to appear less negative than they were privately.[35]

Volcker had few illusions about intervention's lack of long-term effectiveness. Nevertheless, he thought it might at least slow the superdollar's ascent by chastening speculators. As a result, "the Fed was on the phone constantly, just begging us to intervene," reports Treasury Secretary Don Regan. "They're little boy traders with someone else's money."[36]

After a couple of years, Volcker pressed less often. "If I did give up," he says, "it was probably from simple hopelessness that anything would be done."[37]

At Basel Volcker argued to his fellow governors that because the dollar was the world's money, it was better in the long run for everyone to accept the stronger dollar as a short-run cost of fighting inflation than to ease U.S. monetary policy prematurely to bring it down. "In central bank circles, very few or none of us criticized Paul Volcker's tight monetary policy," says BOJ Deputy Governor for International Shijuro Ogata.

Adds the late Renaud de la Genière, Bank of France governor in the early 1980s: "The stronger dollar was discussed in the G5. It was a dialogue of the deaf. The [strong] dollar contributed to reduced inflation in the United States and to the speculative capital flow to the United States. There were inflation fears in Europe, so European rates rose to match the dollar to ease the outflows. There was great stagnation in Europe. Volcker was *not* interested. Volcker's policy was to defeat inflation. As long as the budget deficit was what it was, monetary policy in the United States had to be strongly restraining."

The international debate over the superdollar, though couched politely in technical dialogue, was the same international burden-sharing political struggle that ran through the LDC debt strategy: Which nation altered its policies most when there was trouble in the global economy? Who adjusts?

The fallen Bretton Woods fixed exchange rate regime had defined the rules of the game for governing the international economy. Under floating, it was left to markets and ad hoc policy coordination among nations. To bring the dollar back into line with economic fundamentals required restraining U.S. consumption and faster domestic growth abroad. But cutting consumption slowed growth; overstimulation risked reigniting inflation. So the international economic imbalances were left unmanaged by governments, while each side demanded that the other adjust.

Yet it was an asymmetric peculiarity of the international economy that foreign nations suffered the most discomforting consequences of a misaligned dollar before the United States itself.[38] Outside the United States, the powerful economic effects of currency exchange rate values demanded an early political response. This was why for most world central banks, the exchange rate was the paramount monetary policy operating guide for raising or lowering interest rates. Even those few that did not normally target exchange rates, like the Bundesbank and Bank of Japan, often were forced to adjust their monetary stance to rapid and extreme movements in the mighty dollar. In the United States, by contrast, American citizens would be shocked and politicians outraged if the Fed announced it was tightening monetary policy to defend the dollar. This was unlikely if only because most FOMC members gave the dollar only minor weight in policy-making.

As a result, the usual global economic pattern, describes Princeton Professor William Branson, was that "the dollar reacts to domestically oriented shifts in monetary policy, and the others—Germany, Japan, the United Kingdom—react to the dollar."

The dollar originally took off in summer 1980, when Volcker relaunched his tight money campaign against inflation following the lost first year; simultaneously the Bundesbank and Bank of Japan were easing monetary policy. But the really big thrust for the superdollar and global economic imbalances came from the subsequent fiscal policy clash between Reagan's expansive megabudget deficits, which pushed real U.S. interest rates sky high, and contractionary budgetary policies in Japan and Germany. The abrupt cutoff in LDC lending from mid-1982 was another autonomous force that swelled the net U.S. capital inflows lifting the superdollar. One Federal Reserve estimate was that the LDC debt shock accounted for one-third of the U.S. current account deficit. Another one-quarter it attributed to the unleashed competitiveness of newly industrialized countries—Taiwan, South Korea, Hong Kong, Singapore—which had been masked by the weak dollar of the late 1970s.

The unprecedented scale of the global imbalances underlying the superdollar was possible only because of the 1980s birth of the full-fledged regime of global capital. The United Kingdom in 1979, and Japan in 1980, lifted regulatory controls on the outflow of their national financial capital. Soon many continental European nations also yielded gradually to the innovative and deregulatory liberalizing forces footloose in the world's financial markets. The postwar dams restraining restless national capital suddenly burst. Huge volumes of new capital rushed into the global financial marketplace.

The new landscape had a structural slope favoring inflows into the dollar. The dollar enjoyed an inherently greater demand thanks to its role as world money as well as the comparative attractiveness of the U.S.'s liquid, transparent, and politically stable capital markets. There was an especially steep slope running from Japan's less liberalized domestic financial markets to the United States. "By not staying home, the outflows slowed domestic demand in Japan; by going to the United States, they stimulated domestic demand there," explains Nomura Research Institute senior economist Richard Koo.

The United States, in other words, was like a drug addict, mainly but not wholly responsible for its external deficits and its dependency on foreign capital, since it dwelled in an environment of ubiquitous—even directly injected—supply. The Reagan government's policy failure was its inability to "Just Say No" by reducing budget deficit consumption or at least not undertaking policies to direct more of the abundant foreign capital into wealth-enhancing U.S. investments.

"The way major countries have learned to use the international economy to avoid tackling disagreeable domestic problems is unprecedented: the United States has used high interest rates to attract foreign capital and avoid confronting its domestic deficit; the Japanese have pushed exports to maintain employment despite a sluggish domestic economy," comments Peter Drucker. "This politicalization of the international economy is surely also a factor in the extreme volatility and instability of capital flows and exchange rates."[39]

Zeroing In on the Superdollar

That something was askew in international finance was heralded by the dollar bubble of July 1984 to February 1985. Despite slowing U.S. growth and narrowing U.S. and foreign interest rate differentials, the dollar inexplicably surged by 20 percent.

With the blinkered political logic of reelection dominating its 1984 agenda, the Reagan administration failed to recognize the damage being done to the U.S. manufacturing economy. It started to take serious notice only in late 1984, when the lopsided, consumption-led recovery seemed in danger of stalling out and when business and labor lobbying began to sway moderate congressional Republicans to join calls for protectionist trade relief.

The German Bundesbank placed the superdollar high on the international agenda by unilaterally bombarding the foreign exchange markets with $2.7 billion in dollar sales on Black Friday, September 21, 1984, just ahead of a G5 meeting at Washington. The action infuriated unforewarned U.S. officials; furthermore, in a breach of central bank protocol, the unagreed dollar sales were carried out under their very noses in New York.[40] In a single chaotic day the dollar plunged 4 percent to DM 3.04. Yet within three weeks the superdollar had recouped all its lost ground.

At the G5 meeting, Treasury Secretary Don Regan first indicated U.S. readiness to undertake strong budgetary belt-tightening to correct the overshooting dollar. But presidential election politics came first. "When I first came in I remember that there were some things you couldn't do right away due to your national politics," Regan told fellow ministers and governors. "Well, this is something I can't do right away."[41]

Following President Reagan's reelection landslide, German Finance Minister Gerhard Stoltenberg telephoned Regan, since "after the election they promised a strong action on the budget deficit." At the next G5 meeting at Washington on January 17, 1985, amid a blizzard that closed airports and stranded many of the participants the way the soaring dollar was intellectually stranding the apostles of free-floating exchange rates, Regan edged closer toward agreement on cooperative exchange market intervention to stop the superdollar. Nothing specific was agreed. But for the first time Regan indicated some greater readiness to intervene.[42]

A hidden diplomatic antecedent to this first sign of the Reagan administration's imminent about-face from laissez-faire on the dollar was an urgent appeal from U.K. Prime Minister Margaret Thatcher to President Reagan to request action to prevent the pound from plunging to the politically humiliating record level of one dollar. A personal appeal from Thatcher, Reagan's personal friend, ideological soulmate, and staunchest international ally, could not be dismissed.[43]

At the reception following the G5 meeting, the ministers were introduced to White House Chief of Staff James A. Baker III, who was set to soon swap jobs with Regan. Although Baker had no formulated dollar policy, during their hour-long chat they sensed that his political pragmatism made him ready to act jointly. "In early 1985 we began to understand that the United States saw that it was in its own interest to give a signal to the market that we'd like to see a downward movement in the dollar," summarizes Stoltenberg. "Volcker was especially keen on it."

In late January and early February the United States joined in some concerted intervention against the dollar. Yet from DM 3.17 at the G5 meeting, the one-sided market boosted the dollar to a stunning DM 3.47 by late February.

What could be done? The central bankers who gathered in Basel for the February BIS meetings negotiated the modalities of massive, visibly concerted intervention to try to turn expectations in foreign exchange markets that had grown far too large for them to move individually. In hindsight it was a turning point for the dollar. It was a watershed in European monetary politics as well; from that point forward, the Bundesbank formulated its dollar policy in concert with its EMS partners. The collective intervention would be executed through the central bank concertation network, which by the late 1980s included twelve EEC and ten other central banks. Four times daily by teleconference at 9:30 A.M., 11:30 A.M., 2:00 P.M., and 4:00 P.M. European time, they shared information about foreign exchange market developments.[44]

The tactic adopted was that of the respected and feared Bundesbank, to bombard an overshooting market that seemed ripe to turn with large forays that inflicted losses so painful that foreign exchange traders would afterward run whenever rumors spread that it was intervening. The Europeans left it to the Bundesbank to decide when the timing was right to intervene.[45]

The Bundesbank gave the signal on February 26, 1985, when the dollar plummeted to under DM 3.40 within five minutes following Volcker testimony in Congress that recent interventions hadn't been forceful enough. Led by $2.7 billion sales by Germany, the major central banks dumped $4.6 billion on the foreign exchanges between February 27 and March 1 to pound the dollar bulls.[46] "The Bundesbank came in and really beat the Red man—the Russians," remembers Scott Pardee, Yamaichi International chairman who formerly headed the New York Fed's foreign exchange desk, explaining that the Soviet Foreign Trade Bank was a big dollar speculator at the time, with German banks and others through whom they often transacted piling in after them. "Those were the days of the Red man, the Black man—South Africa—and the Yellow man—the Monetary Authority of Singapore [MAS]. You have to turn around the big operators to turn the market."

The dollar turned. The bubble started to deflate.

Foreign monetary authorities, however, were upset at the small scale of the U.S. intervention, only $257 million in DM purchases. The Europeans would "intervene in the morning when Europe opened, and as the sun moved west the Fed would come in with only $50 million, and the market would get the impression it was halfhearted."[47] Part of the incoherence stemmed from unresolved policy conflicts within the transition from the Regan to Baker at Treasury.

European central bankers were also miffed by the lack of Bank of Japan intervention in the yen/dollar market. In fact, the Japanese Establishment had been operating effectively behind the scenes since the January G5 meeting through "administrative guidance." "Until February 1985 we were selling a lot of zero-coupon bonds of good U.S. corporations," reports Yoshio "Terry" Terasawa, then head of Nomura U.S.A. "Japanese investors loved them. This pushed the dollar very high. In January 1985 I was told that the MOF had patted the shoulder of institutional investors to slow down. And they did. And the dollar fell. The MOF also said to us, Nomura Tokyo, 'Take it easy.' "

By mid-April the dollar was down 20 percent against sterling, 15 percent against the European currencies, and 7 percent against the yen. In July it stood at DM 2.90 and ¥240. Crucially, the dollar's fall was sustained by Fed monetary policy easing as the economy and financial system showed weakness.

One heart-stopping plunge, which awakened Volcker's premonitions about a hard landing, occurred on March 19 when the dollar suffered its largest single-day fall, by 2.4 percent, in postwar history. The hair trigger was a run on Ohio's state-insured S&Ls. It was part of a financial chain reaction precipitated by the bankruptcy of a small Florida securities firm, E.S.M. Government Securities. It spread like a brush fire through small, nonbank channels in the new integrated financial system and for a while "came close to putting the whole mortgage-backed securities business in trouble."[48]

Volcker quelled the incipient crisis by extending Fed lender of last resort facilities to the Ohio state S&Ls, even though they neither were regulated by the Fed nor had normal access to the discount window. The episode warned that market jitters about an inflationary bailout of the fragile financial system could clash with engineering a soft landing as the dollar fell. The dollar's record tumble also coincided ominously with the official Commerce Department announcement that the United States had become a net debtor for the first time in seventy years.

Yet in late summer the dollar bottomed out, then started to rise. G5 finance ministers grew anxious that the world recovery would stall and that the protectionist momentum building in the United States would become unstoppable. These fears soon galvanized their celebrated Plaza Accord of September 22, 1985.

The Trouble with Floating

To Paul Volcker and many monetary experts, the unprecedented international economic imbalances, the superdollar, and rising protectionist backlash were symptoms not merely of incompatible national policies, but of a world monetary order itself gone awry. Volcker drew parallels with the world's last sad experience with floating exchange rates in the 1930s when volatile capital movements helped destabilize national banking systems and "beggar thy neighbor" currency devaluations that fed the downward spiral into worldwide depression.

On the eve of the final breakdown of the Bretton Woods fixed exchange rate monetary regime in March 1973, Fed Chairman Arthur Burns, an ardent foe of floating exchange rates, had predicted to MOF Vice Minister for International Takashi Hosomi and his young assistant, Toyoo Gyohten, that "float-ing would surely bring misery to mankind, and that once begun, floating would be hard to end and could last anywhere from a few years to a cen-tury."[49] By the end of the 1970s the jury of expert opinion was still out on the efficacy of floating exchange rates. But by the mid-1980s superdollar, few expert believers were left.[50]

The Reagan government's support for free-floating exchange rates was the necessary complement of its domestic monetarism: floating's hypothe-sized insulation against foreign economic developments—since exchange rates were postulated to adjust quickly and autonomously to levels reflective of the new comparative economic fundamentals—freed it to employ purely domestic monetary targetry. "We now know that those models were pitifully inadequate," writes Princeton Professor Peter Kenen. "The short-run behav-ior of a floating exchange rate is not determined by current-account flows. It is determined mainly by capital-account flows, which reflect the highly volatile views of various asset holders. Exchange rates can change hugely from day to day and week to week, and there can be large cumulative move-ments lasting for three or four years. . . . It can thus influence the level, loca-tion, and composition of economic activity. For this same reason, moreover, floating exchange rates cannot reduce economic interdependence. They can only alter the *form* of interdependence, because monetary and fiscal poli-cies, as well as nonpolicy shocks, impinge directly on the real economy by affecting the real exchange rate."[51]

Compared to its government-run predecessor, the floating exchange rate "nonsystem" was distressingly much more volatile, unpredictable, and mis-aligned.[52] Without an anchor the market expectations driving global capital movements ran wild. Cross-border capital sloshing among major currencies rendered individual money supply targets less meaningful. International money was like domestic money after all. It would not manage itself well. By early 1985 the dollar was at least 40 percent overvalued—twice as much as blew apart the old Bretton Woods fixed parity system.

The monetary disarray was symptomatic of the decaying postwar mar-riage of convenience between markets and governments underpinning the liberal world order. Extreme volatility and misalignment in the dollar cor-rupted the price signals upon which capitalist enterprise relied to make pro-ductive investments. Investment was misdirected to less productive nations and industries. Efficient enterprises were starved of capital and inefficient ones overfinanced. Ultimately, misinvestment engendered slow growth, busi-ness failures, needless unemployment, higher inflation, and financial booms and busts that weakened the financial fabric.

When the competitiveness arduously earned from a 10 percent gain in productivity was overwhelmed by a finance-driven 50 percent swing in the dollar, there was no way to ascertain each nation's theoretical comparative economic advantage—what they did best—underpinning the free trade order.[53] World trade became a political free-for-all. Under floating, free capital movements were imperiling free trade. "It is a paradox of the 1980s that international capital flows have been increasingly liberalized while international trade has been increasingly protected," notes C. Fred Bergsten, director of the Institute for International Economics. "It would be far better to reform the monetary system than to reverse the liberalization of capital flows, but one of these two courses will be necessary to avoid continued movement away from open trade."[54]

Democracy, too, was weakened when governments tried to escape political accountability for the lightning-fast global capital movements dictating key economic conditions of their citizens' lives by blaming the seemingly omniscient invisible hand of free market forces. "Governments are only too happy to blame markets for the ups and downs of their currency," decries Helmut Schmidt. "Poor old Ronald Reagan, who didn't understand any of this, could say, 'It's not me. It's those damned young guys in short sleeves without ties who sleep with computers next to their heads.' "

The visible shortcomings of the privatized, floating nonsystem reawakened calls for world monetary reform. Yet monetary reform was a once- or twice-in-a-lifetime event. Many economic and political conditions had to come into rare alignment. This was why it was often associated with crises— the gold standard was dropped with World War I, and Bretton Woods was born of the Depression and World War II.

Citing market shortcomings did not mean that governments could do better—especially at the close of the Cold War era, when economic and political power was spread more diffusely among nations and the world economy was undergoing profound structural changes from the rise of global capital mobility. Comparative economic advantages too were being shaken up by the information technology revolution and by developing nations moving up the development ladder. It was little wonder that there were huge world current account imbalances. "There are good and bad imbalances," reminds Brookings's international economist Ralph Bryant. "The deep problem is that no one knows how much are good and how much are bad."

This was just the sort of environment in which the thousands of daily decisions that constituted market forces usually fared best. For all its flaws, points out Princeton Professor William Branson, the floating, privatized nonsystem was resilient: "Give the system a smack and it gyrates." Endorses George Shultz, under whose tenure as Treasury secretary the United States adopted generalized floating in 1973: "The system has done very well with all the shocks. I don't know what would work better."

By 1985 the "muddling through" approach was invading political and economic tolerances. Demands were rising to correct misaligned exchange rates and to reassert political control over the international economy. Two alternatives were often proposed: international policy coordination or protectionist autarky.

As U.S. point man for the negotiations surrounding the demise of the Bretton Woods order, Paul Volcker knew firsthand that democratic political leaders had preferred to let the postwar world monetary regime collapse rather than undertake policy coordination—that is, enacting policies by international accord that differed from those they were ready to enact for purely domestic reasons. Yet protectionist autarky meant a jettisoning of the postwar free trade order and a return to the conditions that helped produce the Great Depression. Ominously, a storm of a few hundred protectionist trade bills was gathering force in the U.S. Congress.

Prelude to the Plaza Meeting

Immediately upon taking office, Treasury Secretary James Baker perceived that the superdollar and trade imbalances, by choking growth and firing protectionist backlash, had the makings of a political disaster for Republicans in the 1986 midterm elections. Scion of one of Texas's blue-blood law firms, commerce secretary in the 1970s, and best friend and former campaign manager of Vice President George Bush, Baker was the first to admit that he had never had a course in economics. He took office mainly with a "Texan's aversion to high interest rates and a politician's indifference to longer-term policy effects."[55] He was, however, a quick study—and one of the savviest political operators to scale the heights of Washington power in many years, a "Machiavelli reborn, an adept man who knows his agenda."[56] His trademark was to associate himself with successes and to wipe his fingerprints clean of failures.

Step one was clear to Baker: the dollar had to be made to fall. In April 1985 his chief strategist, Deputy Treasury Secretary Richard Darman, in a private memo, recommended capitalizing upon the political pressure to bring down the superdollar to launch a step-by-step, two-track approach to world monetary reform. The first track, exchange rate management, centered around adjustable target zones. To give a rough idea, he suggested a band that allowed 10–15 percent fluctuation on either side of a central dollar exchange rate. Concerted currency intervention would help guide the dollar within the bands. But the main fulcrum would be the second track: coordination of economic policies by the main countries, guided by an indicator mechanism grounded in economic fundamentals. In time the system could evolve step by step into world monetary reform.[57] Darman's memo articulated all the policy elements of the "G7 process" that Baker would unveil at opportune moments over the next two years.[58]

Baker's first international overture for the new dollar strategy was made to Japanese Finance Minister Noboru Takeshita just prior to the June 22, 1985, Tokyo meeting of the G10.[59] Baker asked: If the United States agreed to joint intervention, later to include Europe, to lower the dollar, would Japan be willing to take measures to stimulate growth in its domestic economy? Domestic demand stimulus by Japan and Germany, he argued, was crucial for increasing U.S. exports, maintaining world growth as U.S. consumption slowed with the falling dollar, and easing trade frictions.

Ever since an April 11, 1985, address by free trader Secretary of State George Shultz urging Japan to reduce its side of the U.S.-Japanese structural imbalances, Japanese leaders had been frantically seeking an expedient way to reduce Japan's huge trade surplus with the United States. Even so, the Ministry of Finance was not willing to accept Baker's suggestion of fiscal stimulus or tax reform, since it might compromise its fiscal consolidation goals. By August 21 the two sides instead agreed to joint intervention in exchange for Japan's promise of a "flexible"—code for lax—monetary policy and implementation of some financial liberalizations it was already undertaking.

Baker then initiated telephone conversations with German Finance Minister Stoltenberg to expand the U.S.-Japan bilateral to the G5. Was Baker genuinely ready to make a public about-face in Reagan's nonintervention policy? Stoltenberg thought so. The summer rebound in the dollar overtook any doubts. It threatened to worsen sluggish German growth and 9 percent unemployment by sucking in more savings from Germany. Stoltenberg agreed to a G5 initiative, but only "provisionally, on an ad hoc basis. Even if we talk of a new system, it is all provisional."

The final preparations were negotiated secretly by the G5 deputy finance ministers, mainly at two London meetings. There was no direct participation of central bankers, largely because of the compressed time frame and doubts until the last minute that it would even come off. At the German Finance Ministry, only the top two officials, Gerhard Stoltenberg and State Secretary Hans Tietmeyer, knew about it. In France, central bank Governor Michel Camdessus was informed by the Finance Ministry about a week before the meeting.[60] The G5 deputies worked from a U.S. draft that was so sensitive that U.S. Assistant Treasury Secretary David Mulford distributed and collected it from each deputy at the start and end of their meeting. At the all-day meeting on September 15, 1985, and unable to resolve some key points, the deputies worked out a nine-page draft—dubbed by them the "nonpaper"—which served as the basis for the G5 meeting at New York's Plaza hotel a week later.[61]

As yet, few in the Reagan government knew what Baker was plotting. Baker's stealth kept at bay the influential laissez-faire factions opposed to managed floating and policy coordination, such as George Shultz, Don Regan, and Beryl Sprinkel. However, Paul Volcker, whose support or at least neutrality was essential, had been briefed at private "kitchen conversations." Volcker had never liked unmanaged floating and had authored one of the several alternative monetary reform proposals floated in the 1970s. Yet better than most he understood the shortcomings of formal obligatory systems. He had never endorsed the target zone concept Baker was proposing.

As a central banker Volcker was keenly cognizant that monetary policy was one of the two main instruments needed to make target zones work. With fiscal policy paralyzed, managed exchange rates could easily become a monetary policy target trap. Volcker also understood the huge political temptation for Baker, or any Treasury secretary, to try to use a weaker dollar to cajole lower central bank interest rates.

Thus when Baker approached Volcker in August and suggested it would be futile to proceed with G5 intervention to lower the dollar if monetary policy were in conflict, Volcker says, "I was cautious about it. My God, it was enormously welcome that he was concerned about exchange rates. He was very cautious about monetary policy—he was not asking for commitments. There was an understanding that he wouldn't go ahead unless monetary policy would support it."

Baker was satisfied with Volcker's reply that the slowing economy and low inflation made any monetary tightening unlikely in the near future. They discussed preliminary plans for G5 intervention. Skeptical to the last that Baker really could deliver, Volcker kept his nightmare of an uncontrolled plunge in the dollar to himself until a few weeks later, when they got down to planning the Plaza strategy in detail.

The uneasy alliance between Volcker and Baker matched two of Washington's champion political operators. By temperament, background, and outlook they were an odd couple. Volcker's style was down-to-earth, even coarse, and full of dark forebodings; Baker was full of grandiosity and panache. After the ideological, bombastic Regan Treasury, Baker's pragmatic preference for quiet negotiation was welcomed by Volcker. Although not personally close, the two men shared a Princeton-shaped worldview and a proclivity for government activism toward markets.

At the August meeting, Volcker wondered: How was Baker going to get his pro-interventionist dollar policy U-turn past administration free marketeers?

That's my problem, Baker answered.

Baker solved it by presenting it privately with a tailored spin to heavyweights like Shultz; then he sprang it only a day or two in advance of the

Plaza—without vetting by usual government planning councils—before his adversaries could rally opposition. Final clearance came from President Reagan, whose contradictory sympathies for the fixity of a gold standard and the laissez-faire of floating were superseded by his strong conviction in the Plaza's political purpose of thwarting protectionism. "The president was reluctant to intervene on the dollar, but he fully supported the G7 policy," notes Howard Baker, who became White House chief of staff in 1986.

Chapter 18

Governments Take a View

Until the Plaza meeting on Sunday, September 22, 1985, G5 meetings had always taken place in deep secrecy in order to protect frank exchange and to limit political posturing. With a single, grand, last minute gesture that caught participants by surprise, Jim Baker overthrew the tradition started on March 25, 1973, when Treasury Secretary George Shultz and Undersecretary Paul Volcker first invited their German, French, and British counterparts to the White House library to secretly discuss world monetary affairs without the Bretton Woods system. The array of television lights and press cameras highlighted that under Jim Baker's orchestration the G5 was embarking on political theater as much as economic policy-making.[1]

When the fifteen finance ministers, their deputies, and central bank governors finished their five-hour meeting convened at 11:30 A.M. in the Plaza Hotel's White and Gold Room, they unveiled the "Plaza Agreement" to the expectant world in a lengthy communiqué. Cutting through the sanitized economic analysis and restatement of each G5 nation's policy intentions was the following compact, intensively negotiated operative language: "[T]hat in view of the present and prospective changes in fundamentals, some further orderly appreciation of the main non-dollar currencies against the dollar is desirable. They stand ready to cooperate more closely to encourage this when to do so would be helpful."

Translated, this communiqué, written in a symbolic code language fraught with esoteric meaning, said: The G5 had reached secret arrangements for concerted intervention to drive down the rebounding superdollar. The secret provisions featured up to six weeks of intervention to initially knock 10–12 percent off the dollar, to settle at roughly ¥214 from the current ¥240, and to arrive at the DM 2.55 level from DM 2.85. Up to $18 billion would be committed to the intervention, divided roughly by thirds among the United States, Japan, and Germany/Europe.[2] All then would be reviewed.

The key political significance of the Plaza statement for most parties was the Reagan government's first public acknowledgment that the superdollar and the external imbalances were a serious problem and that alleviating them required joint currency intervention with coordinated policy changes. For Baker, the activist dollar policy and declarations to fight protectionism provided a welcome political warm-up for Reagan's unveiling next day of the administration's counterprotectionism campaign.

Three of the meeting's five hours were spent negotiating linguistic nuances of the intervention strategy. The G5 accommodated Baker's emphatic domestic political requirement that the objective be framed in terms of appreciation of "nondollar currencies" rather than depreciation of the dollar, and avoidance of the word *intervention* in favor of "cooperate more closely when . . . helpful."[3]

The G5's greatest anxiety was how the meeting's great absent protagonist—global financial markets—would react to it. Yet whereas most finance ministers mainly feared a dollar rise, central bankers' preoccupation was just the *opposite*. Volcker in particular believed that the underlying long-term trend of the dollar was downward, not up, and that too aggressive a signal to markets could cause it to snowball.

Volcker warned that a precipitous dollar fall could scare global dollar buyers and force U.S. interest rates to rise, contrary to G5 goals. Pöhl seconded Volcker.[4] As veteran monetary officials, they fretted that relatively inexperienced and politically motivated finance ministers would rediscover the 1970s lesson that it was relatively easy to get a currency to fall, but much harder to stop it from cascading out of control.

Although the U.S. Treasury dismissed Volcker's fear as the overgloomy imaginings of a central banker institutionally biased toward exchange rate stability, the G5 agreed to insert the word *orderly* into the communiqué. Secretly it endorsed a step-by-step decline, too, so that "[i]nstead of pushing hard on the days that the dollar was declining anyway, intervention should be mainly concentrated on leaning against any tendency for the dollar to rise on particular days."[5] Should the dollar plunge too rapidly, it accepted Pöhl's suggestion that central banks could intervene to support it.

The Bundesbank president's ulterior reason for fearing a rapid dollar fall was that it often caused global capital to rush disproportionately into the DM within the EMS's exchange rate mechanism. This pushed the French franc, Italian lira, and other ERM currencies toward their band floors and the DM to its ceiling. Moreover, this threatened involuntary unlimited intervention, interest rate changes, and unnecessary realignment disruptive to

Bundesbank monetary policy and European growth and integration goals. European G5 members met to discuss this problem before the Plaza.[6]

Even though the Germans privately were prepared for an eventual 30 percent DM appreciation to DM 2.00 and discussed an ultimate goal of DM 2.10–DM 2.20 at the meeting, Bundesbank President Karl Otto Pöhl and German Finance Minister Gerhard Stoltenberg adamantly refused to obligate themselves to the 10–12 percent dollar devaluation target or any specific commitments on intervention amounts. They feared encumbering German monetary policy freedom. Their insistence on the ad hoc, provisional, and nonbinding nature of the understandings was supported vocally by U.K. Exchequer Chancellor Nigel Lawson and quietly by the Japanese and by Volcker. As a result, says Daniel Lebegue, then director of the French Treasury, which even more than the U.S. Treasury sought defined commitments and accented the system-building nature of the process, "[a]t the Plaza we did not really agree on protocols and rules of the game. We discussed the deputies' draft, but we didn't have a formal agreement on terms and weight of intervention as we did [later] at the Louvre. Pöhl was not ready to take specific commitments."

Without admitting targets, the Germans nonetheless argued that the yen should appreciate more than the DM. The superdollar was predominantly a U.S.-Japan problem, they said.[7] Their hidden concern was to blunt an expected marketing assault on Europe from Japan's world-class exporters as the falling dollar made it more difficult for them to penetrate the U.S. market.

The Europeans' immediate worry was alleviated by Minister of Finance Noboru Takeshita's unexpected eagerness for a yen revaluation up to ¥200, or 17 percent. It was an open secret in Tokyo that MOF was ready for an eventual rise to ¥180—the low point reached in the 1978 dollar crisis—in order to correct the huge trade disparity with the United States. MOF Vice Minister Mitsuhide Yamaguichi frequently stressed to MOF Vice Minister for International Tomomitsu Oba that Japan's Plaza strategy was first yen revaluation, then joint international interest rate reduction so that the "main castle [fiscal consolidation policy] would be free from attack."[8]

Baker brought no specific ultimate dollar target levels to the Plaza, even though Treasury officials privately discussed ¥170–¥180 and under DM 2 among themselves. His overriding goal was simply to get it moving down.

Monetary policy was discussed only briefly at the Plaza. Although the G5 deputy finance ministers had discussed the idea of a coordinated interest rate cut in preparing for the Plaza meeting, monetary policy was so sensitive that they left blank the final paragraph of their draft nonpaper, "Implications for Interest Rates," save for the bracketed phrase *to be discussed.*

Independent central bankers like Volcker and Pöhl would not tolerate any substantive discussion about monetary policy in front of finance ministers. Their worry was entrapment in a political commitment to manage money to defend an exchange rate level. It was an iron law of policy-making that at the end of the day one policy tool could hit only one target. If central bankers targeted the dollar, monetary policy could not be used to achieve their primary missions of low inflation growth and financial stability. Floating exchange rates had given statutorily independent central banks a practical taste of freedom to choose their own monetary policy targets that only the Fed had enjoyed under the dollar-centered fixed exchange rate Bretton Woods system. "Central bankers want to avoid any international event of any kind that takes away through the back door the independence they got through the front door," says BIS General Manager Alexandre Lamfalussy.[9]

For their part, finance ministers were politically unwilling to push central bankers too hard for international monetary commitments. "It is ironic in this whole Plaza-Louvre business that monetary policy was hardly discussed," says Volcker. The finance ministers "didn't press on monetary policy at all. Oh, there was some vague statement directed at stability. But Baker didn't want to fight with me on that point. And the German finance minister wanted to profess that he had no influence over monetary policy. Well, Stoltenberg didn't want a clash with the Bundesbank—because in Germany the Bundesbank always wins."[10]

After the Plaza, Volcker reported to the FOMC that no monetary commitments had been made. There was, however, an understanding—the one Volcker had given Baker—that the United States was unlikely to raise interest rates, which would run counter to the G5 concerted intervention.[11] "Monetary policy was not ruled off the table forever at the Plaza," says one deputy minister. "It just wasn't dealt with because there wasn't time. Once we decided to cooperate on exchange rates, we took all the time on that." Instead the G5 decided to take up monetary policy at its next meeting.

The final business at the Plaza was to vow secrecy and consistent answers to the throng of press outside. Should the central bankers—technically invitees to the G5 finance ministers' forum—attend the scheduled photo session and press conference? Baker suggested that the ministers and governors attend both. But the wary governors, led by Pöhl, agreed to appear in the photo only.[12] "Within the G5, we central bankers are not just decorations, but our role is limited," Pöhl explains.[13]

Alone among the governors, Volcker agreed to attend the press conference because "it was a U.S. meeting and a message to the market of a major shift in U.S. policy, and the people you needed there to make that convincing were the secretary of the Treasury and the Federal Reserve Board chairman."[14] Volcker's presence telegraphed to markets that U.S. interest rates were not likely to rise soon.

Market players noted, too, the tension about how far central banker monetary policy would be used to support an international finance ministers agreement, as symbolized by the revealing Plaza photo of a recoiling Paul Volcker, the world's most indomitable central banker, being pushed front and center like a prop for the media cameras and financial markets by Jim Baker.

In the event, the Plaza "announcement effect" was much more powerful than the G5 expected. The dollar was plunging even before the central bank intervention started on Monday. For the day it fell a stunning 4.3 percent. Between September 23 and October 1 the G5 sold $2.7 billion, $1.25 billion by Japan alone.[15] After only one week the dollar was down 12 percent versus the yen and nearly 8 percent against the DM.

Over the next five weeks central bankers continued one of history's largest intervention operations to prevent a dollar rebound. Despite a public outbreak of dissension between the U.S. Treasury and the Bundesbank over the scale of Germany's intervention, the dollar operation exceeded Plaza targets by closing the period down around 13 percent against the yen and 10.5 percent vs. the DM.[16] G5 intervention in the period totaled $8.2 billion, far less than the $18 billion war chest at the ready.[17] To Volcker's relief, the dollar fall was achieved smoothly.

Volcker had grown briefly worried about a cascading dollar fall in late October when the Bank of Japan, without any forewarning to fellow central bankers, tightened monetary policy. Japanese money market interest rates spiked up by two percentage points. The dollar, then rebounding, abruptly plunged to around ¥200. "I thought it [the BOJ action] was stupid," says Volcker. "I probably politely said so to them."[18]

Back in Tokyo, BOJ officials were initially elated with what they maintained was "their operation."[19] MOF, which "had expected a reduction of interest rates," was unpleasantly "very surprised."[20] The chief motivation, it seemed, was *not* to hit the rebounding dollar. "It was a BOJ independence action," explains a BOJ official close to the action. "The Business Department [which conducted money market operations] was angry with the MOF and the [BOJ] internationalists" for using the Plaza to dictate BOJ policy. "So they let MOF-directed intervention wash through [to the money supply] and may have added some to the squeeze. It took two months to unwind."[21]

After October, intervention virtually ceased. Yet the dollar continued to slide. It did so largely because the sudden collapse of oil prices, from over $30 a barrel in late November to $12 in late March, was a greater immediate economic fillip to Japan and Germany, which imported nearly all their oil, than to the oil-producing United States. By the end of January the dollar had depreciated about 20 percent since the Plaza, to ¥191 and DM 2.37.

The Plaza looked like a smashing success of governments managing markets—of supplying the stabilizing rationale private investors sought, but that the free market forces had been at a loss in the short run to provide. But was the success *less* than met the eye? In retrospect many thought so. "If you look at a chart tracking the dollar/DM and dollar/yen, you don't have too easy a time picking out the Plaza Agreement," points out critic George Shultz. "The Plaza Agreement has been misdescribed for so long that it became thought that it produced the change. From that, they [the G5] thought they could influence the market. It is better to let people know the markets are in charge." The dollar market, in this view, was already on a downward trend—just as Paul Volcker had said. The Plaza interventions delivered the coup de grace, accelerating what would have happened anyway.[22]

The perception at the time in markets and in governments, however, was a landslide: The Plaza "was a very successful political show and gave the market a very strong impression of the real clout of the G5."[23]

Campaign for Coordinated Interest Rate Cuts

The greatest political glory covered the Plaza's maestro, Jim Baker. He discovered himself in an unusual position: a finance minister who seemed strong by presiding over a falling currency. The apparent success emboldened him to push forward with his step-by-step strategy to manage the dollar.

At the Plaza, the G5 had concurred that national monetary and fiscal policies had to be coordinated to underpin the dollar decline and a gentle unwinding of the world economic imbalances. All agreed that the United States had to slow its consumption below GNP growth—above all by cutting its budget deficit—and to stimulate exports; Japan and Germany needed to do the opposite. Yet none had been willing to implement new policies to achieve it.

In preparatory meetings for the next G5 meeting at London on January 18 and 19, 1986, Baker pressed his Japanese and German counterparts for both fiscal stimulus and for interest rate cuts. The latter he hoped to coordinate with a cut in U.S. interest rates.[24] Japan and Germany firmly rejected any fiscal stimulus. But Finance Minister Takeshita strongly endorsed a global cut in interest rates that would perk up world growth without altering the yen/dollar exchange rate he now found satisfactory. An international political bandwagon for coordinated interest rate cuts gathered ahead of the London G5 meeting.[25]

At the G5's Saturday night dinner and Sunday meeting at Chancellor Lawson's residence at 11 Downing Street, the case for a joint reduction in interest rates was pressed most forcefully by Japanese and French Finance Ministry men. A written declaration to reduce interest rates "was an important document for Minister Takeshita."[26] It could be used as *gaiatsu,* or foreign pressure, to compel BOJ compliance in the domestic burden-sharing struggle between fiscal and monetary policy. France could not ease without risking a politically humiliating and inflationary franc devaluation in the ERM unless the Bundesbank cut interest rates in tandem.

This helped foster a secret French alliance with Baker. "We tried to move the Bundesbank with the support, intellectually and tactically, of the U.S. administration," reveals French Deputy Minister Daniel Lebegue, who describes frequent phone calls over tactics. "There was progressive improvement of the connivance after the Plaza and becoming more intensive at the end of 1986 and beginning of 1987 in preparation for the Louvre. French interests were the same as the United States' for different reasons."

In one important regard French and U.S. aims differed: The United States wanted more expansive German monetary *and* fiscal policy; France's focus was exclusively on the Bundesbank "because the common line in Europe was to reduce budget deficits." As a result, "the idea was to get from Germany a clear idea on concerted intervention and to support Mr. Stoltenberg in his debate with the Bundesbank. How? You don't do these things publicly. Our line was not to attack the Bundesbank and create divisiveness. Rather, you do it in multilateral meetings or bilateral talks with our counterparts—our Ministry of Finance to press their Ministry of Finance and for central bankers to press their central bank colleagues. Volcker and [Bank of France Governor Jacques] de Larosière have a role to play in discussion with Karl Otto Pöhl."

France supported international policy coordination, and above all exchange rate target zones, to compel the Bundesbank to make monetary policy according to the dollar range set by the G5 under U.S.-Franco influence. It served as a surrogate political lever for French impotency to force the Bundesbank to bend to French interests in the EMS.

Pöhl resisted any such exchange rate commitment precisely for the opposite reason: "We were concerned we could lose control [of monetary policy]. In Europe [the ERM] it is different because there we are number one. But where the United States is the dominant player, it is a danger. We were always being bashed by the French under the headline of international cooperation," grumbles Pöhl.

When Volcker briefly left the G5 meeting room on Sunday morning, MOF's Tomomitsu Oba turned to U.K. Deputy Finance Minister Geoffrey

Littler. "*Now* we can add the words *reduction in interest rates* to the draft communiqué," he said.[27]

When Volcker returned and saw the addition, he said forcefully, "No!"

Volcker recalls, "In a communiqué proposed by the U.S. Treasury, the significance of which I might have underestimated at the time, there was an effort to include a few words about monetary policy that, to my sensitive ears, at least, suggested that monetary policy should or would be eased. The wording was rejected by Karl Otto Pöhl of the Bundesbank as well as myself."[28]

Exchequer Chancellor Nigel Lawson, who controlled U.K. monetary policy, also supported Volcker. "There was a concerted move to bring interest rates down," Lawson says. "Volcker and I would not go along with that. It was not a turf question, but the realization that on the merits it didn't stand up. Why? Because it is quite impossible to have exchange rate stability and interest rate stability. You can't peg both simultaneously."[29]

The London G5 meeting ended with a bland, three-sentence statement. It affirmed satisfaction with the results of their Plaza cooperation and their intention to continue to cooperate—without reference as to how. Although there were no secret agreements, "we noted a disposition to move [interest rates] shortly in parallel. Not formally. It was an unwritten understanding."[30]

Having failed to move the central bankers to lower interest rates within the G5 framework, the finance ministers sought to do so one on one at home. The first to oblige was the Bank of Japan. The fast-rising yen, or *endaka*, was rapidly slowing Japanese growth. Takeshita urged Governor Satoshi Sumita to reduce the BOJ's discount rate—even unilaterally if the Fed and Bundesbank couldn't be brought along. Although governor of the central bank, Sumita had been a career MOF official. In Japan, bureaucratic allegiances were lifelong. MOF officials thus relied upon him to "understand" their interests. He did. On January 30, 1986, for the first time in two years, the BOJ cut its discount rate, from 5 percent to 4.5 percent.

Gloomier growth prospects and spreading financial fragility from the oil price collapse effect on Texas banks and from big bank exposure to LDCs were also building pressures on Volcker to ease. Many Federal Reserve banks for months had been requesting a discount rate cut from the board. Volcker wanted to move, but he was afraid that the dollar would cascade unless the cuts were coordinated with the Bundesbank and BOJ. His worries mounted as the dollar began to slide sharply in the beginning of February, falling through ¥180, the unofficial target threshold of Japan's financial establishment, to its low since the 1978 dollar crisis of ¥177.4 on February 19. The attack then shifted to the DM. By early March the dollar fell to DM

2.19. Since the Plaza five months earlier the dollar had lost about one-quarter of its value; from its February 1985 highs it was down about one-third.

The dollar bears were encouraged by Baker comments *welcoming* the dollar downtrend. On February 18 Baker stated he would "not be displeased" if the dollar fell further. Next day Volcker countered publicly that the dollar "may have fallen enough."[31]

Baker urgently wanted the dollar, and interest rates, down farther. He was growing preoccupied that despite the dollar's sharp fall, economic improvement would arrive too late to help Republican prospects in the 1986 elections. Signs of slow U.S. growth were deepening. Owing to the J curve effect—the lag until rising export volumes overtook the impact of currency depreciation on dollar-denominated trade accounts—a currency normally had to be falling for fifteen months before the dollar trade balance showed visible improvement. But as policymakers' maxim stated: The economist's lag was often the politician's tragedy. "Baker was willing to lower the dollar due to the trade deficit. He was more willing to use interest rates to lower the dollar than to stabilize it," says Treasury Undersecretary George Gould. "Treasury's advice to Baker was that Volcker's fear about a dollar collapse was overblown."

Volcker, meanwhile, flew to Basel for the G10 governors dinner on Sunday to personally urge an immediate joint interest rate cut. He left the next day with only a few central bankers knowing he'd been there. His main target was the Bundesbank's Karl Otto Pöhl. The world's two preeminent central bank chiefs had a "tough argument where Volcker presented the U.S. political position that growth was needed elsewhere to lower U.S. interest rates," recounts Pöhl, who did not appreciate such pressure within the central banker brotherhood. "As a central banker, Paul knew I couldn't live for long with rates that are so low they threatened to undermine my credibility against inflation." Volcker argued that German inflation was low, oil prices were falling, and there was plenty of spare capacity to push for growth to help achieve Germany's own 4 percent forecast without risk of inflation.

At the conclusion, says Pöhl, "[w]e decided on a coordinated cut." But the Bundesbank Central Bank Council, Pöhl advised, was not willing to act right away.

The Palace Coup

Basel central bankers thought they gleaned insight into Volcker's unusual lobbying of them when news leaked out that two new Federal Reserve Board appointees had joined with two previous Reagan appointees on February 24, 1986, to outvote the Fed chairman for a discount rate cut. It was a central banker nightmare: the U.S. government seemed to be seizing political control of the Fed, whose independence was a patron to them all, and bringing the mightiest central banker to political heel.

The "Palace Coup," as it became known, was the most serious political assault upon the independence of the Fed in recent history. While there was much press commentary about the Reagan government's unusual opportunity to appoint a majority of Supreme Court justices, little notice had been taken that the same had happened at the nonpartisan central bank. "We kept appointing people, and eventually we got a majority," says Beryl Sprinkel, then CEA chairman. "Volcker couldn't control it."

The Fed had certain legal, customary, and institutional inoculations against politicalization. Two board retirements, one early, in late 1985 helped overcome the statutory defense provided by staggered fourteen-year terms for the seven governors. The customary rule that gave the Fed chairman the courtesy of vetting prospective board nominees was simply breached. The final inoculation was institutional, developing gradually as new governors imbibed the unique culture of the central bank. Yet the new governors, Manuel Johnson, a thirty-seven-year-old assistant secretary at the Treasury who had won Jim Baker's confidence, and Wayne Angell, a fifty-five-year-old Kansas banker and farmer close to senior Senator Robert Dole (R-Kans.), had been at the Fed barely a few weeks. So they still felt mostly like outsiders.

From the beginning they knew what was expected of them. Angell says, "When I was interviewed for the job by [Don] Regan and [Jim] Baker, among others, no one asked me if I'd be for easier or sound money. The key question was this: 'Wayne, are you really *independent?*' That was a code word for 'Can you stand up to Paul Volcker?' Regan asked me more forcefully than Baker, but both asked."

On the morning of February 24, Johnson and Angell joined ambitious Vice Chairman Preston Martin—who seized the occasion to make a naked bid for Volcker's job—and Martha Seger to push a discount rate cut.

Volcker, caught by surprise, said the weak dollar prevented the Fed from acting without coordinated cuts by Germany and Japan. The Bundesbank, he said, wasn't yet ready to go. Nor was it absolutely clear that the BOJ was, either. But the others didn't share Volcker's preoccupation about a dollar free-fall—not yet.[32]

"The time isn't right yet," Volcker insisted.

"When will it be right?"

"I don't know. A few weeks, maybe."

"That's too long."

They went over and over it for nearly an hour. Volcker's tendency to contemptuously dismiss the concerns of the Reagan-appointed governors, sometimes in front of Fed staff, aggravated the atmosphere. It devolved into a contest of wills and one of the tensest meetings in Fed history. A clearly upset veteran Governor Henry Wallich, dying of cancer and ill from chemotherapy treatments that limited him to just a few hours' work a day, pleaded with the rebels not to be hasty. The senior Fed staff, which sat in the back row of policy-making meetings, "was astounded" at the violence being done to the central bank's collegial traditions.[33]

When it became clear that the "Gang of Four," as the mutineers were dubbed, was going to press the vote, Volcker stormed out of the boardroom in fury. A press release was prepared announcing a discount rate cut from 7.5 percent to 7 percent by a four to three vote. It was to be released to the public at 4:30 P.M.

But the two new Fed governors were shaken. Fed chairmen simply did not appear on the losing side of votes. They had expected Volcker to yield. Fearing the political and economic fallout, they sent word through Volcker's assistant that they really didn't want to force anything on him.

Volcker had gone to a scheduled luncheon with Baker and visiting Mexican Finance Minister Jesus Silva Herzog—the same luncheon at which Silva Herzog first outlined the parlous financial deterioration that led to the second Mexican debt crisis. Volcker pulled Baker aside to inform him privately what had happened. He bluntly warned that "if this was going to be the basis on which things were going to proceed, he might have to resign."[34]

Baker wanted interest rates down. But to get it he wasn't willing to risk the disruption of bond markets, foreign exchange markets, and the increasingly fragile energy and farm banks, not to mention the renewed precariousness of the Mexican and LDC debt menu of that day's discussions, that could result from Volcker's resignation. "Baker didn't want a public confrontation," says the Treasury's Gould. "He was concerned about the perception in international financial markets that U.S. monetary policy would be run from the White House. And also he didn't trust Preston Martin."

Baker discreetly let Volcker know he preferred a compromise.

When Volcker returned to the Fed after lunch, he met with Angell and Martin. "Do you still want me to be chairman?" he asked them. He hinted he was willing to compromise if they agreed to delay the discount rate cut for a limited time while he attempted to persuade the Bundesbank and BOJ to move jointly with them.

Martin, who wanted the chairmanship for himself, said nothing. But Angell indicated he wished to avoid Volcker's resignation.

Angell left to consult with Manley Johnson. Johnson had phoned Baker to alert him to what had happened. They were still talking when Angell entered his office.

Baker indicated to Johnson that he didn't want Volcker to resign.

Angell and Johnson agreed to compromise. That afternoon the board reconvened. Angell switched votes. A few weeks later Martin resigned. Johnson succeeded him as vice chairman.

Volcker contacted his foreign counterparts. "I didn't know he lost the vote," says BOJ Deputy Governor for International Shijuro Ogata. "We just had a negotiation on a rate cut." The Bundesbank needed to hear the Palace Coup story before being persuaded. "We thought Volcker was in trouble," says Central Bank Council member Norbert Kloten. For one of the rare instances in its history, the Bundesbank decided to put an international interest—saving Volcker—ahead of its desired domestic policy.

At the next regular meeting of the Central Bank Council on March 6, the Bundesbank cut its discount rate from 4 percent to 3.5 percent. Japan lowered its discount rate by one-half point on March 7 to 4 percent. Also on March 7, the Fed finally enacted its discount rate cut to 7 percent by a unanimous vote.

Baker was satisfied with the outcome. Yet inside the Fed, Volcker remained furious about the Palace Coup. Fed watchers waited with bated breath for a new blowup. When month after month went by and it didn't come, markets began nervously to conclude that through the political muscle of the Plaza Accord and Palace Coup, Baker had Volcker and Fed independence on a leash. Only months later did markets understand that Volcker "wasn't dead, just wounded."[35] "Paul had to move back and regather his troops," explains Beryl Sprinkel. "But he remained in control because he controlled the information people and most of the [Federal Reserve Bank] presidents."

Campaign for Lower Interest Rates—Round Two

Jim Baker seized his advantage after the Palace Coup to press for a second round of coordinated interest rate cuts. To pressure Japan and Germany, he adopted the risky tactic of coded, verbal "talk-down" of the dollar to yet lower levels. "The dollar decline started at the Plaza as a strategy against protectionism," says George Gould. "Then we fell into it [talk-down] as a tool to get the others to adjust."

Japan and Germany were vulnerable because the rapid yen and DM rise against the dollar threatened them with immediate recession. This strongly motivated them to try to spur growth, even if it meant risking renewed inflation later on. Baker's oft invoked specter of congressional protectionism unless the U.S. trade balance improved dramatically additionally threatened Japan with major unemployment in its export-dependent economy.

It was testimony to Baker's political prowess—as well as to the prevailing ignorance of international economic matters and short memory of the similar dollar talk-down strategy employed by Carter Treasury Secretary Blumenthal less than a decade earlier—that his facile mantra equating a lower dollar and faster growth abroad with improved U.S. exports was swallowed whole by Washington, much of the major media, and, for a while, Wall Street. At the margins, faster foreign growth did help suck in more U.S. exports. But even a huge foreign expansion would translate only into a tiny improvement simply because foreigners spent just a small fraction of their income on U.S.-made goods. An unpublished fall 1986 IMF report found that if Japan and Germany increased growth by 1 percent more over three years, the net improvement in the projected $170 billion U.S. trade deficit would be only $5 billion to $10 billion.[36]

Standard textooks instructed that a major adjustment would result only if U.S. consumption—boosted by the record U.S. $200 billion budget deficit—was cut in tandem with the falling dollar. By focusing attention on slow foreign growth, Baker expediently deflected the political blame from the largest culprit, the Reagan budget deficits, which he was unable to rectify.

Baker clearly signaled his dollar talk-down tactics when he rejected Takeshita's strong personal entreaties to support the dollar verbally or through joint intervention when it plunged again in April 1986. Prime Minister Nakasone too was rebuffed by President Reagan. By this time, recounts MOF Vice Minister for International Toyoo Gyohten, "[a]rguments were raging in Japan that the Plaza Accord had been a mistake or even a failure, because it had started an unstoppable, uncontrollable fall of the dollar or, in other words, an uncontrollable rise of the yen."[37]

Rapid yen appreciation tossed Japan into a "growth recession": for the year, GNP growth was 2.5 percent and unemployment 3 percent, poor by Japanese standards. Uncertainty about the ultimate yen/dollar level caused business investment in Japan's tradables industries to collapse. Export volume fell, corporate profits were down. Consumption also suffered. As the yen soared to ¥171 in May, ¥165 in June, and ¥154 in July, Nakasone, fearing for his political future, implored MOF to restore ¥170 before the upcoming July 1986 elections. MOF ordered BOJ intervention. But with the United States refusing to concert, the dollar bears simply overpowered it. "When the yen appreciated from ¥200 to ¥160, we couldn't stabilize the market. Business did not have time to adjust," says a high MOF official, adding, "That was the *only* major occasion in which the MOF couldn't control the capital flows to slow the flight from the dollar."

To fight recession, the BOJ and MOF argued that the other's policy instrument should be activated. The BOJ said that its earlier monetary easing merely had produced a flood of potentially inflationary liquidity.[38] "Monetary policy is good for restraining excess demand, not stimulating it. We felt fiscal policy should move," explains the BOJ's Shijuro Ogata. But MOF, fixed adamantly on its political goal of fiscal consolidation, "preferred not to touch it."

Reluctantly the BOJ offered to cut its discount rate to a postwar low of 3.5 percent.

But Baker could not similarly move the Bundesbank. Why not? Because Germany's extensive economic links within EMS countries caused its net foreign trade exposure to dollar markets to constitute a much smaller percentage of its GNP than Japan's. "The EMS makes Germany similar to the United States, a large country with a small foreign sector, which is always more favorable under floating exchange rates," explains Italian Professor Giuseppe Tullio. "The DM/dollar exchange rate can fluctuate one hundred percent, but if the weight of the dollar on German trade is low, then it doesn't hurt much. Alone, Germany is like a great battleship, but not big enough. So it is always interested in finding a flotilla of [EMS partner] support ships to float with it.

"The greater vulnerability of Japan to major fluctuations of the dollar is because Japan is like a huge aircraft carrier without the flotilla around it. The Japanese adjust though with greater flexibility in their economy to increase productivity or whatever."[39]

BOJ hopes that the Bundesbank's unwillingness to ease might help them postpone their own discount rate cut were dashed by Volcker. Afraid of stalling U.S. growth, Volcker met with Governor Sumita in Washington on April 10 to suggest that the BOJ and Fed cut their rates jointly, even without the Bundesbank. "In April 1986 we felt it was too hasty to cut the ODR [official discount rate]," grumbles BOJ Executive Director Yoshio Suzuki. "It was quite natural that the Bundesbank was against it."

On April 21 the Fed and BOJ each cut their discount rates by half a percentage point. Major European central banks, other than the Bundesbank, also cut interest rates between April 14 and 25.

International Policy Coordination

Holding the whip international political economic hand, Baker decided to launch the next phase of his step-by-step world monetary reform strategy at the annual economic summit of G7 (G5 plus Italy and Canada) world leaders, to be held in Tokyo on May 4 and 5, 1986: a new mechanism of 10 "objective" economic indicators, including exchange rates, to govern G7 policy coordination.[40] To administer the indicator mechanism, Baker proposed a new peer group of G7 finance ministers and their deputies—central bankers would be excluded.

In its most grandiose vision, Baker's conception was an embryonic world economic directorate. Through linkage to the G7 summits held since 1975, Baker hoped to endow the group with greater political authority over economic policy. The new G7 forum also helped assuage Italian demands for inclusion in the G5, which had become an issue at the head of state level thanks to the publicity generated by the Plaza Agreement and the difficulties it caused for the lira.[41]

Foreign officials were suspicious that Baker's "objective" indicators mechanism was a political artifice to manipulate their policies to suit U.S. needs. Some suspected that it was an incipient exchange rate target zone in disguise. German Deputy Finance Minister Hans Tietmeyer objected vociferously.[42] His Japanese counterpart, Tomomitsu Oba, also stated that Japan "had no interest in indicators."

The finance ministers were willing to employ indicators only to help focus their private, nonbinding, multilateral economic policy reviews. On that basis, deleting the offending word *objective* from the final Tokyo declaration text since it connoted something systemic, indicators for G7 policy coordination were launched. The G7 ministers decided that they alone would conduct the multilateral surveillance. The G5, with invited central bankers, would concentrate on intervention and exchange rate management. Baker instantly hailed international policy coordination as the most significant initiative since the collapse of Bretton Woods.

Despite the anomaly of excluding central bankers who made world monetary policy, most governors didn't mind not attending the G7 economic summits, "where politics and publicity have come to loom large."[43]

Volcker, who contrary to some speculation had nothing at all to do with their design, notes that the indicators were "subject to manipulation" and inadequate even to focus useful economic exchange. "It was a little embarrassing. I thought it was ridiculous. I paid no attention to them. I thought it would fall of its own weight."[44] The Bundesbank's Pöhl combated the new G7 indicators with a public campaign against automatism or "robotization" in policy-making. He "worried that the indicators would be a tool to put pressure on the Bundesbank" for lower interest rates.

Within a week of the Tokyo summit the dollar slipped from ¥165 to under ¥160. Only when the failure to arrest the soaring yen seemed visibly to doom Nakasone's chances for a rare second term as prime minister after the

July 6 elections did Baker, very temporarily, suspend his talk-down tactics. On May 13 he stated that the dollar had recaptured all its earlier appreciation against the yen. Foreign exchange traders promptly bid up the dollar. By June 2 it had rallied to ¥177 and DM 2.34.

Soon, however, it was falling again, with Baker's noticeable acquiescence, in response to the deteriorating health of the U.S. economy and financial system and the persistent failure of the U.S. trade deficit to show any improvement from the depreciated dollar. By the end of July it stood at ¥154 and DM 2.09.

All international policymakers accepted that a soft landing for the world democratic capitalist economies required mastering political as well as economic logics—and that the duo could run for lengthy periods in different trajectories. Yet foreign policymakers increasingly felt Baker's orchestration of the process was myopically serving short-term Republican domestic political goals without tackling the fundamental economic problems, led by the U.S. budget deficit. To Toyoo Gyohten, who became MOF vice minister for international in mid-1986, this represented a perverse decay of the postwar international economic order: "[T]he process was dominated too heavily by American efforts to make a political deal rather than to reach an economically viable conclusion. From the Japanese and German viewpoints, the whole process was frustrating because we thought that the United States was trying to gain political concessions from the surplus countries of Japan and Germany by using the threat of talking down the dollar and the threat of protectionism, knowing that both could really damage the economies of the surplus countries. This was in stark contrast with the economic situation under the Bretton Woods system, when the world order was supported by a credible dollar and an open market. Instead, the credible dollar and the open market were transformed into threats."[45]

Both Japan and Germany feared that the interest rate and tax cuts Baker urged upon them were more likely to reignite inflation than to stimulate growth-inducing consumer spending and business investment. The Bundesbank nervously saw its main money supply gauge expand at nearly double its median target of 4.5 percent. It hadn't missed an annual target since 1978. The BOJ, having been forced into the April discount rate cut, helplessly watched the flood of money pouring into real estate and stocks in the final kickoff to Japan's fantastic late 1980s financial "bubble economy."

World Economy at the Brink

"The world economy is in danger!" Throughout the summer of 1986 Paul Volcker echoed Jim Baker's drumbeats for joint global interest rate cuts at

Basel and to visiting foreign monetary officials. With peers his gruff style remained within international proprieties. But with others he sometimes veered toward indelicate lecturing.

Volcker's rough tone offended Sumita's heir apparent, BOJ Deputy Governor Yasushi Mieno, when Mieno visited the Fed in the summer. So it did too many BOJ officials who read the transcript of Volcker's insistence that the BOJ cut interest rates. "We felt it was the U.S. financial system that was in danger," BOJ Executive Director Yoshio Suzuki comments acidly. "Mr. Volcker was a very good central banker when discussing with the U.S. government, but *not* when discussing with us. Sometimes I got angry. No central banker should talk to us that way. I felt as if Mr. Volcker were trying to persuade us to cause inflation. 'Is he really a central banker?' we asked ourselves. If he were on our side, how would he have felt?"

Twice, on July 11 and August 21, Volcker led the board to unilaterally cut the Fed's discount rate to try to force the BOJ and Bundesbank to follow in what amounted to a global game of chicken with dollar depreciation. Gossip in Washington, Wall Street, and even Basel focused on two theories. The first was that Volcker was "in bed" with Baker because he wanted to be reappointed as Fed chairman the following year. Even Reagan's monetarist CEA Chairman Beryl Sprinkel grew worried that Volcker was going too far as he watched the U.S. monetary supply surge. "Baker doesn't like to see rates going up when his best friend [George Bush] is likely to run for president. Jim [Baker] wanted the dollar down, and the Fed eased up to make it happen. Jim doesn't worry what will happen in two years on inflation." The second, more Machiavellian theory was that Volcker's public reassurances about the dollar following episodes of Baker talk-down was an artful bad cop, good cop routine to guide the dollar lower without a freefall.

Both theories were wrong. The simpler truth was that Volcker was genuinely anguished that Baker's dollar talk-down would end in a tragic flight from the dollar, as it had in 1977–78. The public bad cop, good cop routine was an extension of his private efforts to muzzle Baker: "Every day I talked to him about it. He was less aggressive than he otherwise would have been in talking down the dollar. I was concerned not so much with the substance of the policy, but with the fact that it could so easily get out of hand. You only had to remember [Treasury Secretary Michael] Blumenthal to know it can get out of hand sometimes."

Yet if Volcker was so alarmed about the dangers of a dollar free-fall, why was he willing to risk triggering it by making the two unilateral interest rate cuts in July and August 1986? Although it didn't accord with the simplistic public image of Volcker as a single-minded inflation slayer, Volcker in 1986 pushed the limits of his dollar free-fall nightmare because "I was worried the whole world economy would stall. I could see that we weren't growing and we weren't getting enough growth from abroad."

In summer 1986 the U.S. economy was teetering on the edge of recession. Germany and Japan, he sensed intuitively, were overestimating their likely growth. Mexico, Bank of America, the core Texas banking system, and S&Ls were in extreme distress. U.S. corporate debt loads were building to alarming proportions. Any major fragility could start it all cascading into his long dreaded, catastrophic financial chain reaction. The democratic capitalist world was skirting perilously closer to the chasm of depression than almost everyone realized. "Paul was a very worried man at that time," remembers Treasury Undersecretary George Gould. "It wasn't the political pressure that made Volcker make the interest rate cuts."

In explaining its first unilateral discount rate cut on July 11, from 6.5 percent to 6 percent, the Fed extraordinarily cited slow growth and limited inflation risk in *other* industrialized countries. This was a thinly veiled threat to whip up market speculation that could stampede the Bundesbank and BOJ to follow. The initial pressure was concentrated on the BOJ. BOJ Governor Satoshi Sumita was emboldened to resist when President Pöhl informed him during the July Basel weekend that the Bundesbank would not yield to U.S. pressure for lower German interest rates. During the summer and autumn of 1986 the normally distant relations between the BOJ and Bundesbank drew closer—but not close enough to overcome the independence gap between them: the Bundesbank spurned a BOJ offer to intervene jointly to slow the DM's rise against the falling dollar in part, says a high Bundesbank official, because "a central bank that can't act on its own won't be looked upon as an equal partner."[46]

The BOJ gained some international credibility by holding out against strong MOF pressure to follow the Fed's interest rate cut. Shortly after the Fed's move, the MOF refused the BOJ's request to intervene to support the dollar. Some BOJ officials interpreted this as a naked effort to blackmail the BOJ into an interest rate cut through threat of further yen appreciation.[47] "Since the Plaza Accord, what had fiscal policy done?" says BOJ Deputy Governor for International Takeshi Ohta. "Only monetary policy had moved. Next it's your [MOF's] turn to do something, we said."

In the end, the BOJ escaped immediate monetary easing when a financial boom (reinforced by the LDP's unexpected landslide electoral victory on July 6) began to blunt the strong yen's initial recessionary thrust and when new Finance Minister Kiichi Miyazawa decided to campaign for fiscal stimulus to complement an interest rate cut. This caused Miyazawa, though a MOF graduate, to be resented within the ministry. "In the summer of 1986 Miyazawa tried to activate fiscal policy," says the MOF's Oba. "He didn't succeed in this. He finally succeeded only in summer 1987."

With lower U.S. interest rates causing the dollar to fall toward the DM 2 threshold, Volcker took the occasion of the funeral of ex–Bundesbank President Otmar Emminger to travel to Germany to personally make the case for another round of coordinated interest rate cuts to the Bundesbank. On a pleasant late Sunday afternoon, August 10, Volcker met with President Pöhl and Vice President Helmut Schlesinger in the garden of Pöhl's home in suburban Frankfurt. "I was a little surprised, but of course appreciative, that Paul [Volcker] came over for Emminger's funeral," says Pöhl. "The main reason he came was to talk to us. He came to convince us to lower interest rates. He never would put pressure on us. That would have been bad form among central bankers. Instead we discussed and explored the issue."

To move the Bundesbank, Volcker had to persuade the rigorous, domestic-oriented Schlesinger. Schlesinger presented Volcker an analytical paper arguing that the apparent differences in the U.S. and German savings rates, when adjusted to be properly comparative, weren't as large as national statistics suggested. Nor were Germany's 9 percent unemployment figures, properly defined, as high as seemed.

Volcker wasn't impressed. "Pöhl brought Schlesinger along to give me all the figures about how, when properly adjusted, the German economy was about to take off," he recounts. "They had just had second-quarter GNP numbers, I think, with all the various numbers down to working day adjustments and two different versions of this and that. The conclusion was that, well, if one looked at the numbers cross-eyed, it would be very good indeed."

Despite outcries from German exporters, the Bundesbank was not yet under severe pressure from its government to cut interest rates. The Finance Ministry still believed in Germany's rosy growth forecasts. Yet the rapidly falling dollar was itself putting the Bundesbank in a difficult bind. The large capital flows from dollar to DM assets were swelling German money supply beyond the Bundesbank's capacity to offset it through domestic monetary operations. Raising interest rates to drain money from domestic markets was likely to attract further foreign inflows; lowering interest rates to stop the inflows risked flooding domestic money markets.

In the end Pöhl thus offered Volcker a deal: "I have a majority for a interest rate cut on the Central Bank Council, provided that the United States is ready to intervene—and to *say* it is ready to do so—to stabilize the exchange rate."[48] The deal, of course, was intended for Treasury Secretary Jim Baker. Baker's reply, Pöhl reports, eventually came through "a hint from some channel. Baker said, 'No. We have an election coming, and depreciation of the dollar is welcome for exporters.' "

Gloomily Volcker returned home. Since the July discount rate cut, the dollar had fallen about 5 percent against the yen and DM. Yet neither the

BOJ nor the Bundesbank had blinked in his game of global dollar chicken. The U.S. bond yield curve between short- and long-term interest rates had steepened slightly. He knew there wasn't much margin for another cut in short-term interest rates without risking dollar free-fall.

Nevertheless he recommended to board governors one last unilateral discount rate cut. The most outspoken skeptics, surprisingly, were Palace Coup mutineers Manley Johnson and Wayne Angell. They fretted over budding inflationary signals. But they deferred to Volcker's judgment of the global economic peril and his desire to try to force the monetary hand of the BOJ and Bundesbank. The internal Fed politics from the Palace Coup had been inverted. It was now Volcker leading the others to go out front with unilateral easing moves.

"The last two moves in 1986 had more to do with international issues than domestic, especially the last one, which was to influence the Japanese," says Johnson. "Angell and I thought policy was easy enough for domestic reasons. We were fighting the yield curve. Volcker is very cynical about data. He worked mostly on instinct. He would procrastinate for a long time and then make a signal."

"I didn't feel Paul was sure," adds Angell. "Manley and I were going on vacation. It was the least well discussed and planned of all the discount rate cuts. I wanted to blow the BOJ into another discount rate cut, so I went along."

In hindsight Volcker confessed that the Fed's final half-point discount rate cut to 5.5 percent on August 21, 1986, "may have gone too far. After the July cut, nothing untoward happened to the dollar."

The BOJ and Bundesbank refused to follow the Fed's August discount rate cut. Worse still, markets reacted with a sharp veto: long-term interest rates backed up by over half a percentage point, steepening the yield curve in a clear "no confidence" trajectory. Downward pressure on the dollar intensified. Through the semiotics of financial market discourse, global investors were declaring that if the United States was going to pursue policies that depreciated the dollar, they were going to demand higher long-term yields to keep their money in greenbacks.

"I had an ominous feeling when long bond rates rose after the August cut," says Angell. "Also, gold, silver, and platinum ticked up. That was when I felt the move was wrong." In the midst of the bond and dollar downturn, the New York equity market nosedived by 120 points on September 11 and 12. The plunge was linked to index arbitrage between futures and equities in the newly forming single capital market continuum, a harbinger of the Black Monday crash a year later.

THE CONFIDENCE GAME

More turbulence rocked financial markets just ahead of the G5/G7 and IMF/World Bank annual meetings in Washington in late September. Pöhl declared that the Bundesbank had no intention of lowering interest rates just because the United States wanted it to. "Baker was upset by it," says Pöhl. "It was a bad atmosphere."[49]

On September 18 Baker fired back that the dollar might have to fall farther, "unless there are additional measures to promote higher growth abroad."[50] When the dollar knifed below the German political and psychological market threshold of DM 2 in response, Baker "was delighted."[51] The yen jumped to ¥152.

European finance ministers and central bankers meeting in Gleaneagles, Scotland, on September 20–21, 1986, replied angrily that they intended to fight Baker's talk-down with their own concerted intervention to push up the dollar. In the "spirit of Gleneagles," the Bundesbank, for the first time, volunteered to join in nonobligatory, intramarginal intervention to defend other ERM currency bands.[52]

Buoyed by massive European central bank intervention, the dollar struggled back to over DM 2. On September 24 Volcker stepped into the political fray—on the Europeans' side. The dollar had fallen enough, he declared. Further dollar depreciation without immediate U.S. budget cutting risked renewed inflation in the U.S. and recession abroad without unwinding the global economic imbalances.

Why did Volcker take such an outspoken stand at that time? "I feared all along that things would snowball," he says. "I thought too much emphasis was being placed [by Baker] on dollar decline."

Central banker Volcker, whose job required straddling the unsteady democratic capitalist equilibrium between the economic reality of markets and the political logic of governments, sensed intuitively that a snapping point was at hand. Lack of concrete improvement in the U.S. trade deficit was breeding dangerous sentiments in markets that the dollar might have to fall much farther than it already had to restore balance. By declaring that the dollar had fallen enough, Volcker was sending a strong signal to global investors and the U.S. government that the independent Federal Reserve would take no further chances with monetary policy to try to borrow time for Washington's political budgetary paralysis.

A critical juncture in the global political economy had been reached. From his central banker's perch atop the world financial system, Volcker saw mounting strains in the flow of global capital under the dollar. The steepening yield curve following the Fed's unilateral discount rate cuts was a red alert that the record capital inflows preventing a U.S. hard landing were becoming harder to sustain. Second-quarter 1986 data confirmed the ominous slowdown of net foreign private inflows and its replacement foreign central bank dollar purchases.

The predominant global investors were Japanese. Some one-fifth to two-fifths of U.S. Treasury securities at auction were sold to Japanese buyers. Often when Japanese institutions didn't buy enough U.S. government debt, "we saw a backup in U.S. yields."[53] Virtually alone among foreign investors, Japanese private institutions had continued to buy more and more dollar securities while the dollar fell. Those purchases began to taper off after April 1986. This was when Baker commenced dollar talk-down and the Japanese Establishment was unable to stabilize the dollar at ¥170–¥180. Massive BOJ dollar intervention began to supplant them. Large European intervention kicked in after the Gleaneagles meeting in September. For the year 1986 foreign central bankers bought a record $40 billion of the U.S. currency.

The shift from private market to foreign government financing of the United States also alarmed Nicholas Sargen, director of research at Salomon Brothers. From his Wall Street skyscraper overlooking New York Harbor, Sargen watched, like an electronic age customs house man, the inflows and outflows of global capital in order to anticipate bond, stock, and foreign exchange market trends. He drafted a report entitled "Is a Dollar Crisis Looming?"[54] Like Volcker, Sargen had been long pondering, "Why did the Japanese stay with the dollar when they were losing money hand over fist? The cynical view is that it was a Ponzi scheme, and they didn't figure it out till three years later. But how can you make what they did rational?"

Until mid-1986 many Japanese institutions simply reasoned that if the yields were three percentage points higher than what was available in Japanese paper, then they could withstand a 3 percent-a year devaluation in the dollar versus the yen—or 90 percent over the life of the thirty-year "long" bond—and still come out even at maturity. Years of exchange controls had also built a pent-up desire to diversify out of the yen assets.

Most important, diminishing inflation expectations allowed the Fed to cut U.S. interest rates. Falling interest rates meant substantial bond profits, which partially offset the currency loss. "The dollar fell like a rock, and their [Japanese institutions] loss was only ten percent!" exclaims Nomura Research capital flow specialist Richard Koo. "It was only in 1987 that they lost their shirts."[55] This provided a major cushion under the dollar. As the dollar fell, furthermore, fewer yen needed to be spent to support its lower value.

When the dollar plunged through the expected floor of ¥170–¥180 in spring 1986, however, the calculus changed. Japanese investors began to hedge their dollar investments and to diversify away from the U.S. Treasury market.

Japanese government influence gradually took over to replace private markets. Easier monetary policy, foreign exchange market intervention, relaxed regulatory ceilings on overseas financial portfolio investment, and administrative guidance were all employed to prop up the dollar. Wall Street experts observed a pattern that whenever Japanese investors bought less than 30 percent of a U.S. Treasury auction, the Bank of Japan intervened to buy dollars. It then reinvested them in U.S. Treasury securities.[56] Treasury auctions benefited from MOF's intimate command of Japan's financial environment, since it was "quite normal for the International Finance Bureau [of MOF] to gather information about what the institutions are planning to do."[57]

"When the United States expressed some apprehension that maybe Japanese life insurance companies would not purchase bonds, the MOF high officials telephoned the heads of life insurance companies," recalls Nomura's ex–head of international operations, Yoshio "Terry" Terasawa. "They do not say straightforwardly, 'Please continue to buy.' But they hint, imply gracefully. That's what they do. A life insurance company does not have to follow. But it's very uncomfortable since it has to live with the MOF daily and consult on many matters. Usually they obey."

Yusuke Kashiwagi, the partly Brooklyn-reared Bank of Tokyo chairman who had served as the first MOF vice minister for international, summarizes, "The MOF is very mindful of good relations with the United States, so there is a political pressure they pass on to us. They don't want to see disruptive things happening. Sometimes they use moral suasion. Sometimes they hang a carrot. Over the long run, looking back, it has been very effective, though not at all particular moments, in reducing the fall of the dollar."

Of course, Japan's self-interest in averting high unemployment and recession in its heavily export-oriented economy required doing almost everything to guarantee that the U.S. current account was financed without disruption.

The Japanese Establishment's effort to recycle dollars to the United States was abetted by Japan's political economic structure. This structure produced huge excess savings without enough attractive investments in its tightly regulated financial system or its domestically underdeveloped economy to absorb it. "The leading institutional investors had no alternative to invest their money except in dollar-denominated bonds," explains Kaneo Nakamura, Industrial Bank of Japan chairman. "They had day-to-day inflows. They had to put it somewhere. There was nowhere else. That's why they did so much. It was not a well-made calculation with risk control, though they might not admit it."

The shortage of good Japanese investments at home, in other words, was propelling huge amounts of excess Japanese savings into the global financial marketplace, above all to U.S. government bonds. The surge *exceeded* mere recycling of Japan's current account surpluses. It became a financial speculation of its own, exploiting the opportunities created by access to free international financial markets to feed a growing financial mania. This structural savings-investment imbalance was the symbiotic global counterpart of the U.S.'s overconsumption and deficits. Together they animated many of the 1980s capital flow and trade dynamics in the new global financial landscape: they propelled the superdollar of 1983 and 1984 and, for a time, provided a braking mechanism under it as it fell. Only in periods when dollar confidence was in tatters did the dollar's built-in "investment advantage" give way. But as soon as the dollar seemed ready to stabilize, it reemerged.

"Japan has a lack of domestic investment opportunity on a massive scale," exclaims Nomura Research's Richard Koo. "It is the *major* source of the [global economic] distortion. It's far more important than the U.S. budget deficit. It is causing large short- and long-term movements of hot money."

The U.S. huge democratic political failure to cut its fiscal deficits as the dollar fell, in other words, was complemented by an immense Japanese "democratic deficit" to restructure its domestic economy as the yen appreciated. Japan, quite simply, had outgrown the export-focused, financial "repression" industrial strategy underlying its postwar "relationship" capitalist compact between capital and state. The grand scale of its success produced bizarre results that had grown incompatible with liberal world economic harmony. Japan's political challenge, recognized Finance Minister Kiichi Miyazawa, was "to transform itself from a supercompetitive export machine to a new, more balanced, and affluent society that provides its citizens with quality of life."[58]

Political Failures

Japan knew how to transform itself. In April 1986 the report entitled "Economic Structural Adjustment for International Harmony," under the chairmanship of retired BOJ Governor Haruo Maekawa, provided the blueprint for financial liberalization, internationalization, and opening up the backward and protected sectors of its domestic economy to international norms.[59] Yet even as it was offered internationally by Prime Minister Nakasone to blunt protectionist momentum as evidence that Japan was about to reform itself, the Maekawa report was stillborn.

The drive to restructure Japan's economy was originally launched in

1982. As the new prime minister, Nakasone had assembled an informal Advisory Friends Group from business, banking, and government. He asked one of its members, Takashi Hosomi, an ex–MOF vice minister for international, to map out a strategy for liberalizing the economy and strengthening the yen.

The strategic centerpiece of Hosomi's memorandum was a gradual yen appreciation to ¥170–¥180 per dollar. A strengthening yen, which had always appealed to Nakasone on the nationalistic logic that a strong yen equaled a strong nation and strong leader, would help reduce Japan's trade surpluses and provide the political momentum for the structural transformation from export-led to internal demand-led growth needed to make it durable. "We tried to initiate a high-yen policy to start the changes going and then capitalize politically," explains Hosomi. "The policy was yen appreciation means deflationary pressure that can be offset with strong [domestic] spending."[60]

Hosomi rallied foreign officials to apply external pressure, or *gaiatsu,* on Japanese leaders for Maekawa-type liberalizations. Genuine liberalization, however, threatened too many protected economic sectors, the pork barrel practices of LDP politicians, MOF's control over its bureaucratic empire, and the inviolability of its fiscal consolidation policy. These "domesticists" were willing to countenance some cosmetic liberalizations, and even some recalibration of domestic regulatory methods, to accommodate the new reality of large capital and trade surpluses. But they rallied to block any radical change that threatened their privileged position. Nakasone lacked the political clout and will to fight them.

"The Maekawa report enjoyed a good reputation outside Japan, but not inside, because it is against the established interests—agriculture, distribution, and transportation. The Liberal Democrats relied on these to stop it," says Hosomi. "Only appreciation of the yen has made any adjustment. The political part didn't contribute."

Why didn't the powerful market force of the soaring yen catalyze more political momentum for liberalization as Hosomi had anticipated? In an expression, the bubble economy. Stratospheric real estate and stock prices acted like financial shock absorbers to blunt the painful incentives to make fundamental changes. "In 1986 most manufacturing companies had losses on their normal operations. Yet all could pay dividends. Do you know why?" asks Akira Nambara, executive director at the BOJ. "They sold some of their stock and easily offset losses from operations." Securities trading accounted for all the 1986 profits of car maker Nissan and two-thirds in 1987; nearly 60 percent of the profits at Matsushita Electric, 93 percent at JVC, three-fourths at Sharp, and 134 percent at Sanyo in 1987.[61] Stock prices rose on the back of corporate real estate holdings, where prices catapulted to breathtaking levels. By 1987 one square kilometer of Japanese land was worth one hundred times its U.S. equivalent, even though Japan's GNP per square kilometer was only fifteen times greater.[62]

Inflated financial asset prices made raising capital about five percentage points cheaper than in the United States. This was a huge competitive edge for Japan's *endaka*-shocked international companies and provided borrowed time while they adjusted operations to become competitive at ¥140 or higher. Fast-rising asset prices provided ample booty to be shared with LDP politicians and even some previously incorruptible senior ministry bureaucrats. The strong yen gave long repressed consumers a popular taste of foreign luxuries. The paradoxical combination of cheap, plentiful domestic money and a strong yen allowed Japanese corporations to easily buy up foreign assets and made its financial institutions overnight colossi storming the domineering heights of international finance. The same policies simultaneously slowed the dollar's fall and supported a soft economic landing for Japan's major export market.

Japanese policymakers, at first, had viewed the easy BOJ monetary policy firing up the financial boom as a necessary evil to offset economic stagnation. But as the benefits became more tempting politically, and policymakers grew confident they could manage the financial price inflation without a destructive bust or spillover into goods price inflation, it became the expedient panacea for "domesticists" to resist "internationalist" structural reforms. "In a stable situation it is not necessary to make changes," says Hosomi of the complacency engendered by Japan's bubble economy. "Politics requires special leaders. All enjoy the LDP here. If you behave and are a Liberal Democrat, you know that you will one day become a prime minister, without knowledge. How can we expect major changes by these men?"

At the core of postwar Japanese democratic capitalist society was a "gap . . . between Japan's underdeveloped political capacity and its seemingly uncontrollable economic expansion."[63] Japan's problem was that it was not a conventional modern state, explains analyst Karel G. van Wolferen, but instead a "stateless nation" of overlapping hierarchies of bureaucrats, political cliques, industrialists, and others—without any power center *capable* of establishing new national priorities.[64]

A recessionary halt in economic expansion could overturn cornerstones of Japan's relationship capitalist compact. To Peter Drucker it was a "[s]mall wonder, then, that the Japanese policymaker prefers the almost certain but future losses on the loans made to the U.S. government to the political and social—and immediate—risks of massive unemployment at home."[65]

The financial bubble highlighted Japan's democratic political shortcomings in other ways as well. It jarred Japanese sensibilities of egalitarianism by grossly magnifying the economic gulf between the small percentage of real estate and stock-owning haves and stockless, rentor have-nots. On both sides of the Pacific Ocean many referred to the grotesque political inequity of a system that forced Japanese citizens to work long hours and live in cramped houses to finance Americans who lived in large houses and consumed luxuries beyond their productive means. The long masked schism between privileged Establishment insiders and the mass of politically weak-voiced citizens was unavoidably spotlighted by political scandals of illegal insider stock tip-offs and financial gifts on a scale Japan had never seen before. Financial scandals would bring down two prime ministers in 1989. Yet the speedy rehabilitation, after brief public contrition, of top LDP politicians, begged the question of democratic robustness after decades-long reign by a single political group.[66]

Financial bubbles could not go on forever. But like the 1920s United States, the longer the euphoria went on, the more people believed the proliferating explanation that it was not a bubble at all, but the passage from the American to the Japanese century.

Democratic political shortcomings in Germany also contributed to the distress in the international economy. The central platform of Helmut Kohl's new 1982 coalition government had been elimination of the 3.3 percent of GNP budget deficit over the medium term, followed by structural reform to break up the sclerosis-engendering subsidies, wage and labor inflexibility, and tax burdens that were slowing Germany's potential growth rate. Through the decade, fiscal deficits were doggedly reduced. But "after 1982 Germany didn't do structural reform," notes Deutsche Bank chief economist Norbert Walter. Structural reform failed on the weakness of coalition government and Germany's highly decentralized federal political system in which two-thirds of total national spending discretion was the province of the state *länder* governments.

In the second half of 1986 Bundesbank President Pöhl was privately pressing the Finance Ministry for the same accelerated tax-cutting schedule that Jim Baker was. "Pöhl felt there was more room to move on the tax side," reports Deputy Finance Minister Hans Tietmeyer. "But we needed a majority of the *länder* to do it, and there was no chance for any change. Had we done it, we'd have lost the support of Lower Saxony."

Convinced that a monetary stimulus "can work only when the economy is flexible," the Bundesbank stuck to money supply growth targets consistent with its 2.0–2.5 percent estimate for real German growth potential.[67] Through the DM dominance in the ERM, Germany's slow growth was exported to all Europe—aggravating world economic imbalances.

Countdown to the Louvre Accord

As the G5 and G7 set to meet in Washington on September 26 and 27, 1986, Jim Baker's G7 policy coordination initiative came under media attack as having stalled. Above all, it was foundering on his inability to persuade allies that he could meaningfully trim the U.S.'s 3 percent of GNP structural budget deficit. "[I]t became quite tiresome to hear American representatives tell us that although the government favored measures to reduce the budget deficit, controlling the deficit was really up to Congress, and the government could not control Congress," says Japanese MOF Vice Minister Toyoo Gyohten. "You feel quite hopeless when your counterpart tells you that he does not know whether his commitment will remain valid."[68]

As the time clock ticked down to the November 1986 midterm elections, Baker was increasingly anxious about torpid U.S. growth, the unimproving U.S. trade deficit, and the protectionist legislation gaining force in Congress. For all these reasons he demanded more forcefully than ever greater growth stimulus packages abroad.

Europeans and Japanese in turn demanded dollar stabilization from Baker. The falling dollar was hurting their exports, business confidence, and investment—in short, undermining the very growth that Baker was demanding of them.

"There was tension between the German and American sides," reports tall, square-jawed, fifty-eight-year-old German minister Gerhard Stoltenberg, Baker's blunt interlocutor at the seven-hour G5 meeting at the U.S. Treasury on September 26. "We didn't like 'high U.S. officials' [such as Baker on background] talking down the dollar."

Stoltenberg accused Baker of asking Germany to risk inflation by artificially stimulating its economy. "You're pushing us to grow since you won't take the hard decision to reduce your budget deficit."[69] Baker silently knew Stoltenberg was right, yet he was simply incredulous that the Germans could reject growth measures with their unemployment at 9 percent.

"You are projecting onto us the needs we don't have," Stoltenberg retorted at one of their many discussions of the subject over the year. "We can tolerate a level of unemployment in Germany that would sweep you [Americans] out of office. On the other hand, we're much more sensitive to inflation. Remember our history. Also, we're a no population growth economy, so we have less need of growth."[70]

Although always cordial, Baker bristled privately at Stoltenberg's "arrogant attitude of the old world dealing with the new world: 'You lucked into your riches. You are parvenus.' "[71] For his part, Stoltenberg was frustrated that Baker wouldn't recognize that *medium-term* fiscal consolidation was a domestic political imperative for the Kohl government—and for him personally as a prospective future chancellor. "It was important politically for Stoltenberg not to deviate from our medium-term policy," says Horst Köhler, a top Stoltenberg aide and later deputy finance minister. "We stuck to medium-term policy so as not to have the stop-and-go policies of the past. Our American friends seemed not to be fully aware of the implications of the change in our policy in 1982."

At one point during the September 1986 meetings when Baker's talk-down and U.S. fiscal policies were criticized by the others, the normally cool U.S. Treasury secretary exploded irritably. Although in time this round of bargaining would produce the landmark February 1987 Louvre Accord experiment in managed exchange rates and promises of macroeconomic policy coordination, the meetings broke up with Baker again resorting to dollar talk-down: "[Y]ou're going to resolve those external imbalances in one of two ways. Either we're going to see increased growth abroad or you're going to see a more competitive U.S. dollar."[72]

Baker was willing to be tough with Stoltenberg in part because he and Japanese Finance Minister Kiichi Miyazawa had been secretly negotiating a bilateral deal—dollar stabilization for a Japanese interest rate cut and fiscal stimulus package.

Their originally scheduled first meeting in late August had been postponed until September 6 in San Francisco, when MOF bureaucrats (from whom Miyazawa tried to keep the meeting secret because of their rigid opposition to any fiscal stimulus) found out about it. With MOF Vice Minister for International Affairs Toyoo Gyohten closely watching his English-fluent and economically expert finance minister, Baker and Miyazawa conversed for two and half hours at the penthouse of the Fairmont Hotel.

At the top of Baker's agenda was a discount rate cut from the BOJ to match the unilateral summer easings by the Fed. Next was a fiscal stimulus. "We are going to have a midterm election. I want you to help us now."[73]

Miyazawa, then jockeying within the LDP to become the next prime minister, was already pursuing fiscal and monetary expansion as the centerpiece of his domestic political agenda. But he was not eager to press prematurely for a BOJ discount rate cut since he hoped to use it as a bargaining chip to extract fiscal growth concessions from MOF bureaucrats.

Miyazawa insisted that Baker agree to stop talking down the dollar as quid pro quo for any Japanese concessions. To reduce the U.S. temptation to devalue the dollar, he wanted the Treasury to issue yen-denominated U.S. government bonds.

Baker was willing to stop talking down the dollar, but he ruled out any issue of yen-denominated "Reagan bonds." Their political symbolism was linked too closely to the foreign-currency "Carter bonds" the United States had issued to combat the dollar crisis in the late 1970s, he said.[74]

The ministers agreed to use any deal to press Germany for complementary moves. "To understand the autumn 1986," explains the Treasury's David Mulford, "we were searching how to keep the momentum going. We were being stonewalled by Germany. So we did a G2 with Japan. The San Francisco meeting gave us important leverage. We were showing the Germans we could go along without them. Then they'd get pressures from their European allies to come back."

Back home, "Miyazawa was being undercut by the central bank and his own bureaucracy" in his economic stimulus goals, reports MOF Vice Minister Gyohten. "Gradually he gained influence over them."[75] The BOJ fell into line first. The MOF was able to hold out until spring 1987.

Prior to the G5 meeting on September 26, Baker and Miyazawa met again.[76] They made a mental footnote of that moment's yen–dollar rate—¥154—which was to serve as a stabilization benchmark once a G2 deal was concretized.

Following his unproductive exchanges with Stoltenberg, Baker invited Miyazawa to meet him once more three days later to give the green light for a U.S.-Japan G2. But the BOJ had to cut its discount rate. On October 2 BOJ Governor Satoshi Sumita presented himself at Volcker's office at the Fed to negotiate the terms of a BOJ discount rate cut and dollar stabilization package.

Announcement of the Baker-Miyazawa agreement was delayed until October 31, however, for maximum impact on the U.S. elections. The BOJ's discount rate cut from 3.5 percent to 3 percent, its lowest level since 1945, was the only substantive policy change amid many statements of good fiscal policy intentions.

But at what level had Baker made his first explicit commitment to stabilize the dollar? Just before the announcement, the dollar mysteriously *strengthened*—the Treasury suspected that MOF had purposely leaked a higher dollar level to Tokyo money markets. The impression in Japan was that the United States had agreed to defend ¥160. Convinced there was now a floor under the dollar, Japanese investors returned to buying dollars and removing hedges. The dollar rose comfortably above ¥160.

Baker shattered that belief by refusing to intervene when the dollar fell at the end of December and early January. When the dollar broke through ¥158 on January 13, following an EMS realignment, Japanese investors stampeded to sell the dollar forward in the futures market. Miyazawa and Sumita made it known "that the Japanese central bank would intervene to prevent the dollar from depreciating further, almost regardless of cost."[77] In preceding weeks the BOJ had already spent an estimated $10 billion defending the dollar.

A front-page *New York Times* article the next morning cited an unidenti-
fied senior U.S. official—speculation centered on Baker or Darman—as
stating that the Reagan administration wanted the dollar to fall farther.[78]
Within a few hours the dollar fell more than 3 percent. BOJ intervention was
completely overpowered. By January 19 the dollar plunged through ¥150.
Baker did nothing to arrest it. Volcker was furious at the reversion to talk-
down when the dollar was so vulnerable.

In Tokyo Miyazawa was frantic. His chances to succeed Nakasone as
prime minister hinged on stabilizing the dollar successfully and demonstrating his leverage with the Americans. Another precipitous dollar fall threatened to push the fragile Japanese economy into a downward spiral.[79]

Without warning Baker, Miyazawa rushed to Washington on January 21,
1987. The two finance ministers publicly reaffirmed their October 31 understanding that the current exchange rates were broadly consistent with underlying fundamentals. But now the dollar was at ¥150, not ¥160. Privately
Miyazawa had tried, and failed, to persuade Baker to make substantive commitments to defend ¥150.

To entice Baker, Miyazawa even offered another BOJ discount rate cut.
But Deputy Secretary Dick Darman recommended Miyazawa save his "sou-
venir" for the Louvre package then in the advanced stages of negotiation.[80]
Miyazawa said he was ready to meet with the G7 as early as the following
week. Baker stalled him. The Germans, he said, had not yet agreed to a sufficient expansion package.

Miyazawa returned home virtually empty-handed. The turning point in
the dollar came a week later on January 28, the day before the G5 deputy finance ministers were to meet secretly to negotiate details of the Louvre Accord. The United States intervened jointly with the BOJ to sell yen and buy
dollars to defend ¥150. The amount was tiny, only $50 million, but the psy-
chological "announcement effect" in markets was large: it was the first time
the United States had intervened to stop the dollar from falling.

The day before the G5 and G7 Louvre meetings of February 21 and 22,
the BOJ announced it would again cut its discount rate, effective February
23, to 2.5 percent.

Compelling the Germans to accept the Louvre Accord's core political bargain of foreign growth stimulus for dollar stabilization (and promise of U.S.
budget deficit cutting) was far more difficult than Japan. But in the end it
was the same force that drove them to do so—the plunging dollar. The dollar's decisive descent below DM 2 in late 1986 finally demolished the shield
of the EMS "flotilla." Panicked German corporations froze their business
investment. Confidence vanished. The recovery, which seemed to be on a

satisfactory course to German officials through the autumn, collapsed. Fourth-quarter growth, in hindsight, was negative. Baker's charge that Germany was growing too slowly had become self-fulfilling through dollar talk-down. Recession fears gripped German policymakers.

The dollar plunge below DM 2 also swamped the Bundesbank's monetary control. The October 31 Baker-Miyazawa agreement accelerated the speculative global "hot money" inflows into DM bonds that had been causing the overshooting of money supply targets.[81] Germany's European partners were forced to intervene, and to consider raising interest rates, to defend their ERM parities. Market speculation intensified that an ERM realignment was imminent.

Bundesbank policymakers were hamstrung by a monetary catch-22: they were unable either to raise interest rates for fear of spurring more foreign inflows or to lower them for fear of flooding domestic money markets. Both instances worsened the money supply overshooting. From April to late November 1986 the Repo rate, which was intended to bounce around every day as freely as the U.S. Fed Funds rate, was visibly frozen. "There is an increasing influence of the outside world on monetary policy," says Bundesbank Council member Norbert Kloten.

The Bundesbank's best hope of extrication was a DM revaluation within the ERM. Revaluation would at once ease some of the speculative foreign capital inflows and dampen domestic inflation fears. "If we fail to get a revaluation, we can be in true trouble," says Deutsche Bank chief economist Norbert Walter.

ERM realignment authority, however, resided with governments, not central bankers. Minister Stoltenberg was on the record as opposed to any realignment, especially before the January 25, 1987, national elections. DM revaluation might help the Bundesbank control inflation. But it would hurt the politically important export constituency. Many other key EMS governments—as well as many central bankers—thought that the situation was difficult but did not merit realignment.[82]

Although it lacked legal authority, the Bundesbank was "always in a position to create a situation so that the Ministry of Finance must accept realignment. January 1987 was such a case."[83] In late 1986 the Bundesbank "talked about realignment," reports Kloten. "Could we raise interest rates, and what would the reaction be? Would we get more inflows? was a question. We had overshooting, and it was difficult to explain and understand why. I and others felt it was time to cautiously raise interest rates to see the effect."

During a tense seven-hour Central Bank Council meeting on December 4, Vice President Helmut Schlesinger made the case for provoking a realignment. Most at the table favored a 4.0–4.5 percent DM revaluation. "What turned the 'no' to a 'yes' was that the election was ahead. You can't have it right around the election," says Kloten.

Despite evidence that domestic investment was faltering, the Bundesbank nudged up its Repo rate in baby steps from 4.35 percent to 4.65 percent in late November and early December. In response, speculative capital inflows into Germany accelerated. The DM surged to 1.92 per U.S. dollar by year-end, overwhelming the massive DM sales by EMS countries whose currencies were falling rapidly toward the floor of their target zones.[84] The Bundesbank's small moves, abetted by social unrest in France, had triggered a full-fledged EMS currency crisis.

Infuriated by the absence of voluntary intramarginal intervention by the Bundesbank and the rapid draining of France's national monetary reserves, French Finance Minister Edouard Balladur declared that "France won't defend the EMS against speculators by itself." He then stunned the Bundesbank in late December by ceasing to intervene. The franc soon fell to its ERM floor. Under EMS rules, that triggered *obligatory* and *unlimited* intervention by the Bundesbank. The Bundesbank's mandatory sale of DM 17 billion ($9 billion) in the period caused the already swollen German money supply to balloon, the very *opposite* of the Bundesbank's intention!

"The French reaction was unexpected," acknowledges Kloten. "They just used some of the band and then let it go. We didn't realize their policies had changed."

France's new policy was a "hard franc," which had evolved since its 1983 policy U-turn toward austerity and the EMS. Its central tactic was to resist realignment between the franc and the DM in the ERM, even though doing so meant shadowing Bundesbank interest rate policies that were based exclusively on German economic conditions and usually too growth restrictive for France. Through nonrealignment France effectively imported price stability and sound money credibility from Germany.

Painfully, France had learned that under the new laws of global capital mobility, devaluing nations often had their nominal competitive price advantage negated by anticipatory, inflationary rises in domestic wages and prices, high long-term interest rate "inflation" premiums charged by global investors, and a loss of long-run external discipline to improve productivity. This represented a sea change in world economic politics: low inflation and a strong currency, not currency devaluation and quick export sales, was the path to prosperity. "The game is clear: Be the lowest inflation country and you get the best for your country," says Deputy Finance Minister (later Bank of France Governor) Jean-Claude Trichet. "This has been the German attitude from the beginning of the EMS, and they undoubtedly benefited from that strategy. You never regain competitiveness if it is done with realignment. For us the Bundesbank is the leverage we use to get the lowest inflation possible. Some politicians argue that we are under their power. We don't consider it so. We are catching up by free choice. We want our monetary policy to be as wise and cautious as that of the Bundesbank."

By exerting its monetary hegemony in Europe to force a realignment, the Bundesbank was challenging the credibility of the "hard franc." By letting the franc fall to its ERM floor to compel massive Bundesbank intervention, however, Balladur, a crafty fifty-seven-year old who became prime minister in early 1993, had pulled a trump card.

The Bundesbank had no effective policy answer. Without much hope of success, a "very worried" President Pöhl "urged Stoltenberg to have a realignment."

But there was a wild card in the political equation—the financial markets. If the markets anticipated a realignment after the January 25 German election, the one-sided speculative buildup was likely to become too enormous beforehand to contain. "If you don't do the realignment now, the market could push it on the eve of the election and it'd become a big political problem," Deputy Finance Minister Hans Tietmeyer counseled Stoltenberg. "It's better to show the public a smaller realignment now."[85]

Stoltenberg concurred. Stoltenberg also smelled a political advantage. In a rare turnabout, the powerful Bundesbank stood on bended knee before the government. Stoltenberg could extract concessions from it to spur domestic growth and boost the Kohl government's electoral prospects. He could use the same concessions to win bargaining chips internationally in negotiations with France and with Jim Baker, with whom he was then haggling over Louvre Accord terms.

After talking over the situation with Chancellor Helmut Kohl, he told relieved Bundesbank officials on Friday, January 9, "If you need it, we'll do it—but only under certain conditions": first, that the realignment be small; second, that the Bundesbank cut interest rates *before* the January 25 elections.

The Bundesbank delivered at the next Council meeting on January 22, 1987, by voting to cut its discount and Lombard rates half a point each to 3 percent and 5 percent.

Stoltenberg meanwhile had two long phone conversations with Balladur over the preconditions for holding an EMS realignment meeting. These culminated in thirteen hours of acrimonious bargaining among EMS finance ministers and central bank governors in Brussels over the weekend January 10–11, 1987. In the end, Balladur consented to a 3 percent DM revaluation; the franc would remain unchanged. But this DM/franc realignment would be the last. "I let the franc fall to the floor once," Balladur warned Stoltenberg, "and I'll do it again, if necessary."

With a single bold stroke, Balladur changed forever the political dynamics within the EMS. Soon thereafter he launched the first of several initiatives to diminish the Bundesbank's hegemony over European monetary policy, which reached its culmination in the bid for European monetary union and a single European central bank by the year 2000.[86] That initiative led to the autumn 1987 Basel-Nyborg agreement committing the Bundesbank to more onerous rules for defending ERM parities.[87]

Balladur envisioned the Basel-Nyborg agreement as the complement of the Louvre's DM-dollar target ranges in defense of France's hard franc and EC integration goals. Balladur explains, "The Louvre for France was the front line of defense against a dollar free-fall, since I felt it would take a long time for the United States to overcome its imbalances. Stability in the DM/dollar protected the EMS and the franc from pressure. The insurance policy was Basel-Nyborg. If it were not possible to keep the dollar stable, then the EMS and the franc would be protected from the stress effects."

The January 1987 EMS crisis helped catalyze the Louvre Accord. It delivered Stoltenberg a tangible Bundesbank interest rate cut to offer Baker. It increased the pressure on him to stabilize the dollar in order to avert a full-fledged German recession. Additionally, other European ministers also urged him to do a Louvre deal with Baker since they worried that the dollar might *undershoot* its long-term fundamental value. This would put European exporters at a price disadvantage to their American competitors on world markets. They noted that the last time the U.S. current account was in balance in 1980, the dollar/DM cross rate was about DM 1.80.

By mid-December 1986 Stoltenberg was ready to enter into serious negotiations to halt further dollar decline. A breakthrough was reached on December 14 in Kiel in northern Germany, when Jim Baker and his deputies, Dick Darman and David Mulford, met with Stoltenberg and Hans Tietmeyer. At Kiel the two sides agreed in principle upon the Louvre's two-track framework. The first track was the policy coordination process—gradual U.S. deficit reduction and German (and Japanese) domestic demand stimulus—to create the fundamental conditions for dollar stability over time. The second track were measures for ensuring dollar stability—exchange rate management. But Stoltenberg continued to insist that it was politically impossible for him to commit Germany to any binding currency target zone.

The distance between the two sides narrowed significantly a few weeks later, when Tietmeyer and top Treasury officials meeting in Washington explored dollar/DM ranges and operating techniques around an understanding that the German commitment would be flexible. Yet Baker still felt Germany's interest rate and fiscal expansion concessions were inadequate. The front-page leak in the January 14, 1987, *New York Times* that the Treasury was prepared to see the dollar fall further added pressure on the Germans for more. It was made amid speculation that the previous day's DM ERM revaluation relieved dollar pressure on the Bundesbank.

The Bundesbank's Pöhl responded angrily that Baker was "playing with fire" and inviting a late 1970s-type dollar free-fall crisis. EC President Jacques Delors denounced Baker's tactics as "blackmail."[88] When the United States finally intervened in the yen market on January 28, the dollar stood at DM 1.77.

The G5 deputy finance ministers met in Zurich the next day to begin preparing the draft communiqué and understandings for the Louvre Accord. The major final sticking point was Stoltenberg's resistance to a larger fiscal stimulus. After the January 25 elections, Stoltenberg had offered the small gesture of bringing forward to 1988 DM 5.2 billion ($2.9 billion) of the DM 44 billion ($24.5 billion) tax cut scheduled for 1990.

But Baker wasn't satisfied. In a phone conversation just before the Louvre, he urged Stoltenberg to "move the tax side further to strengthen the [German] recovery." Sufficient substance was necessary for the accord to have credibility with financial markets and to silence domestic U.S. critics of G7 policy coordination, Baker added.[89]

Stoltenberg repeated that doing any more was impossible, given the delicacy of German coalition politics.[90]

In that case, Baker said, he was very reluctant to proceed to the Louvre.

Calling off the Louvre meeting was seriously debated right up until the last moment by top Treasury officials. Baker never fully believed Stoltenberg's assertions that he could not do more to lean on the Bundesbank for lower interest rates or to deliver more fiscal policy stimulus. In the end Baker wondered: Was it better to insist on more concessions up front or to engage Germany in the process and keep working for more substance later? "It was a trade-off for us," Treasury's David Mulford amplifies. "If you wanted a significant change in their policies, then you needed a consensus. In retrospect, we did the Louvre too early and didn't get enough from Germany."

Baker's frustration that his G7 dollar depreciation policy had not yielded much visible improvement in the U.S. trade balance was causing him to reckon that a period of dollar stability, coupled with policies to help correct the underlying fundamental national fiscal and monetary mismatches, might shorten the J curve distortion. This would also make it easier to judge the ultimate "right" level for the dollar.

Also tempting Baker to do the deal was the finance ministers' willingness to accept head of state endorsement of a more institutionalized framework of refined Tokyo indicators at the G7 Venice economic summit in June. This would advance his agenda for step-by-step world monetary reform and his own political reputation as process maestro. "What was very important for James Baker," remembers Daniel Lebegue, deputy finance minister of France, "was to give a clear signal of success of the international economic coordination process before the coming summit."

Yet right until the very end Baker vacillated whether to cancel the meeting. "The Louvre was a deal that just barely made it. It was almost not done," says Mulford.

What finally convinced Baker to go ahead with the Louvre meeting?

Many have speculated that it was the fear of dollar free-fall—concern about not being able to induce sufficient foreign capital inflows. On February 3, 1987, indeed, a rapid dollar skid caused Baker personally to assure Finance and National Economy Minister Mohammed Ali Abalkhail of Saudi Arabia, one of the world's largest dollar asset investors, that the dollar was not in a free-fall.[91]

Yet fear of dollar free-fall per se was *not* Baker's chief motivation. In the latter half of January Baker's Treasury had been talking down the dollar— hardly the behavior reflecting fear of free-fall. "The Treasury never cared so much about the Japanese dollar investment issue because we were ready to take a further depreciation of the dollar," says David Mulford. Only in the spring of 1987 did Baker become genuinely worried about any additional dollar fall.

The decisive factor that convinced Baker to convene the Louvre, rather, was a private warning from Volcker that U.S. interest rates would soon start rising. Volcker explained that downward pressure on the dollar was inflaming inflation expectations and putting upward pressure on bond interest rates—and on the Federal Reserve to tighten. Markets could even overreact, he added, and trigger a stock market crash.

Baker knew that Volcker wasn't bluffing. His main private conduit to the Fed, Vice Chairman Manley Johnson, had advised him personally in January that the internal Fed consensus had tilted toward tightening. In fact, despite sluggish U.S. growth, the Fed nudged up short-term interest rates by one-quarter of a point in January. "Before the Louvre we informed Baker that we would have to raise interest rates due to the reversal in oil prices," says Johnson, who was increasingly hawkish himself. "Baker is a crafty and good politician. He saw there was a shift in Volcker and also in the board. He realized this meant there would be no more dollar depreciation. So he shifted to dollar stabilization within the Louvre ranges as a means to avoid, or at least dampen, the Fed's interest rate increases. G7 intervention to defend the dollar floor would ease pressure on the Fed to raise interest rates; the dollar ceiling would constrain the Fed from raising rates too far and too quickly if the dollar rebounded."

Higher U.S. interest rates were odious to any Treasury secretary and anathema to Baker. They tended to slow U.S. growth. They added stress on the shaky financial system. The day before the Louvre meeting, giant LDC debtor Brazil defiantly announced its unilateral moratorium on interest repayments, while observers worldwide waited with bated breath to see if chunks of the U.S. banking system would collapse. Postwar record corporate debt burdens, amassed during the long period of falling interest rates, faced unknown traumas when interest rates started rising. So did borrowers in the troubled farm, energy, and real estate sectors. On January 23 the skittish stock market reacted to Volcker's comment that the legislative stalemate over bank deregulation could threaten the U.S. banking system with a wild afternoon plunge of 115 points. Rising interest rates were bad news for George Bush's 1988 presidential election prospects. "Baker's preoccupation was U.S. growth," affirms France's Balladur, who spoke frequently with him in preparing the Louvre.

At the Louvre meeting itself, Baker argued vigorously that foreign central banks should keep their interest rates sufficiently below the U.S.'s to act as a floor under the dollar. Baker's effort to finesse dollar stabilization at existing U.S. interest rate levels was the source of one of the most controversial secret understandings—or, in actuality, misunderstandings—among many Louvre participants: the presumption that U.S. interest rates would not be raised and, abroad, possibly lowered.

But attempting to blunt U.S. interest rate increases by building an artificial box around the dollar was a heroic gamble. Economic policy-making gospel said that in a world of free private capital mobility and free trade it was possible to stabilize exchange rates *or* interest rates, but not both at the same time. Altering one was necessary to support the other: EMS countries often moved interest rates to protect their fixed target zones. Baker's optimistic political hope was that through the Louvre Accord he could square the free market circle of holding both interest rates and exchange rates steady—through concerted government statement of intentions, and then policy actions, to unwind the unsustainable global economic imbalances.

The Louvre, in short, was a defensive political strategy to borrow more time before markets revolted. It was another in the series of ad hoc official sector rescue efforts necessitated by governments' failure to undertake the timely domestic policies needed to maintain world monetary and economic order in the new global capital era.

"The Louvre was a respite for the United States to solve its problems," Balladur sums up. "You can be cynical and say that they went to the Louvre to enable them to avoid the unpleasant problem [budget deficit cutting] before the election—U.S. leaders would *never* do that!"

Central bankers approached the Louvre with great caution: any exchange rate commitment impinged monetary policy freedom; one embedded in a rule-bound target zone system and policy coordination process run by fi-

nance ministers threatened to impose political control over them. They were
on especially high alert because of their perception that "the G7 under
Baker became a more political operation" than economic, more form than
substance.[92] "Baker's attitude was, Wherever there is structural progress in
any country, let's call it G7 and package it to make it seem more was happening with coordination than really was," describes the Fed's Manley Johnson. "Baker and Darman ultimately had in mind a new Bretton Woods
agreement. They never got that far. If they had, they might have forced monetary policy's hand."

In contrast with the Plaza, the central bankers received preparatory "nonpapers" and exchanged views with their finance ministers in advance. They
also took counsel among themselves at Basel. Over the February 8–10, 1987,
Basel weekend, they concurred that they "wanted to avoid the possibility,
even the impression, that monetary policy was part of the G7 process," reports Johnson, who attended the Sunday night G10 governors' dinner. "We
didn't want to get pinned down by a tighter intervention arrangement to stabilize the dollar. We *did* get tied down on intervention—there was not much
we could do about it. But our major objective was not to tie monetary policy. And we didn't."

Despite their caution, central bankers strongly supported the Louvre's intent of stabilizing the dollar. Most had been long urging their finance ministers to negotiate to do so, leading one Finance Ministry deputy to complain
that "the central bankers pushed prematurely for stability at the Louvre."
Central bankers' institutional memory of the late 1970s, "when the dollar
got away from us," prevailed over separate analysis by the Fed and the IMF
that the dollar still had to fall well *below* its Louvre target ranges to restore
the U.S. trade account to equilibrium. As a result, central bankers preferred
to "get some adjustment, then wait and see what happens."[93]

Central bankers nonetheless fretted that neophyte finance ministers, ine-
briated from their apparent success at the Plaza, might be under the delusion that they were capable of managing markets through their elaborately
formulated policy coordination mechanisms for target zones, economic indicators, and concerted intervention—without delivering real substantive
policy adjustments. This created "the danger of the G7 being seen [by mar-
kets] as an emperor with no clothes," says Fed international finance chief
Ted Truman.[94] If that happened, central bankers feared, it could set off a currency crisis—dollar free-fall—leaving them to pick up the pieces.

Most central bankers agreed with Pöhl that in an environment of free
global capital movements, unprecedented economic imbalances, and fiscal
policy immobility in the major countries, "it's fantasy to believe we either
have the power or the will to defend a target zone!" Papering over fundamental economic problems with an exchange rate target threatened to over-

burden monetary policy, to the detriment of achieving central bankers' basic goal of low inflation growth. "The exchange rate is the messenger," explains Robert Solomon, guest scholar at Brookings Institution. "You don't change the messenger when you don't like the news. It's kind of fruitless to stabilize exchange rates until you can stabilize the macroeconomic incompatibility [underlying it]. The dilemma for target zones is that fiscal policy is immobilized. If you want target zones or a world EMS, which is essentially the same thing, how do you keep exchange rates within those zones except by using monetary policy? But if you use monetary policy for that purpose, then you have no other instrument to use for domestic stabilization. So the first reform you need is fiscal policy reform. Then we can talk about exchange rate reform."

Of the governors of the three leading central banks entering the Louvre Palace in Paris, the Bundesbank's Karl Otto Pöhl, consistent with the negotiating perameters set out in advance by his Central Bank Council, was the most determined to loudly resist any automatic or mechanistic commitments. Having been arm-twisted by Finance Minister Miyazawa to announce a discount rate cut on the eve of the Louvre, the BOJ's Satoshi Sumita was determined to avoid any further interest rate cuts. The BOJ had in fact sought Fed assurances prior to making its discount rate cut that it would not undermine this goal by cutting interest rates itself.

Most complex was the attitude of Paul Volcker. The Louvre was in one sense his victory—his nightmares of dollar free-fall were at last being treated seriously by Treasury Secretary Baker. Yet he was unwilling to commit Fed monetary policy, intellectually dubious that Louvre target zones and G7 policy coordination would work and cynically "amused and astounded how they [finance ministers] negotiated the communiqué so seriously, using the same phrases over and over again."[95]

The view shortly became prevalent at the highest levels of the Treasury that Volcker had outfoxed Baker into making the Louvre Accord—and then exploited it to achieve his own central banker agenda.

Chapter 19

Who's Managing Whom?

The Louvre was a two-part weekend meeting on February 21 and 22, 1987. The main negotiation was conducted by G5 finance ministers and central bank governors in the Louvre Palace's Salon de Familia on Saturday afternoon and over dinner at the French Ministry of Finance in the evening.[1] The formal G7 meeting on Sunday morning merely ratified the G5. This format provoked a several hour delay when Italian Treasury Minister Giovanni Goria protested at being excluded from the decision-making G5. The Italian delegation stormed out of Paris in protest at dawn Sunday.[2] The Louvre Accord consequently was announced to the world as a G6 communiqué.

The governing logic of what was to become the Louvre Accord's historic bid to manage exchange rates within the international floating monetary nonsystem was that G7 governments could anchor currency market expectations by expressing a common view of fundamental dollar levels that would be backed by concerted intervention until the announced substantive coordinated policy steps began to correct the global imbalances. To stimulate domestic demand growth, Germany pledged to try to move its tax cuts forward; Japan pledged to work for tax reform and stimulatory fiscal spending.[3] The United States pledged to reduce its fiscal 1988 budget deficit to 2.3 percent of GNP, as mandated by the Gramm-Rudman-Hollings budget-balancing law.

Baker's commitment to a specific goal for U.S. budget-deficit reduction was taken against the advice of Volcker. "You know you'll never hit it, and then you'll lose credibility," he argued. "Why not be vague instead and say 'substantial progress'?"

Baker admitted privately that significant budget-deficit reduction was unlikely. But he said that publicly he had to stand by the president's recent budget. Not surprisingly, the United States missed its budget target; the final deficit was 2.9 percent of GNP.[4]

The Louvre's secret accords on managed dollar ranges were encrypted in the last sentence of the long communiqué: "They agreed to cooperate closely to foster stability of exchange rates around current levels." Intense speculation in financial markets and the press created the misconception that the exchange rate guidelines were systematic, precise, and binding. In reality, no effort was ever made to try to define the specific accords too closely, lest the fragile bonds of understanding and degree of commitment come undone. "[N]either the central points nor the ranges were to be set in concrete; the understandings would be reviewed at the next meeting," describes Volcker. "It added up to the mildest possible form of exchange rate targeting—limited, temporary, and unacknowledged."[5]

To accommodate the ad hoc camp of Japan, the United Kingdom, and, most vociferously, Germany, the G5 adopted nomenclature defining dollar stability loosely around present *levels,* instead of the more systematic-sounding *range.* The G5 privately accepted the deputies' draft "nonpaper" proposal that the accord last six weeks until the next G5/G7 meeting in early April. But they dared acknowledge only "for the time being" in the communiqué from fear of speculative attacks from currency markets.

"The Louvre was a short-term agreement on reference ranges, for the six following weeks, with an understanding to continue if all the countries considered the agreement to be working well and if it was welcomed by the market," says French Deputy Finance Minister Daniel Lebegue. "It was not a long-term target zone system, which was the French position."

The discussion about how to ensure dollar stability became very specific over dinner. Host Edouard Balladur proposed to define dollar levels numerically as a specific midpoint bounded within two concentric ranges: currencies would be considered to be at current levels within 5 percent of either side of the midpoint; intervention would presume to begin when the 2.5 percent range was breached. As for the midpoints, Balladur proposed the previous day's exchange rate. The DM was 1.83 per dollar in Europe and DM 1.82 in New York. By splitting the difference across the Atlantic, the DM midpoint ultimately became 1.825. The yen midpoint was ¥153.5. The 5 percent band effectively created a DM/dollar range of about DM 1.74–DM 1.93 and a yen/dollar range of about ¥146–¥161. The concerted intervention ranges were thus DM 1.78 and DM 1.87 and ¥150 and ¥157.3.

A chorus of opposition to Balladur's precise exposition rose around the dinner table. Bundesbank President Pöhl and German Finance Minister Stoltenberg instantly smelled devious French system building to entrap them into target zones. Pöhl's argument to wait and see how the markets responded before discussing any numerical levels was supported by the U.K.'s Nigel Lawson, who worried about giving the markets a range to shoot at.

Japanese Finance Minister Kiichi Miyazawa expressed his opposition by stony silence. It was a political imperative for him that the minimum floor for the dollar be ¥150. At one point he suggested a ¥150–¥170 range. Outraged European ministers retorted that the yen should rise higher. Baker, whom some believed had conspired with Balladur to propose the reference range mechanism, remained quiet, watchful.

The breakthrough came when Bank of France Governor Jacques de Larosière, who had left the IMF only a month earlier, took the floor to "give a brilliant and precise exposition in wonderful English" where the discussion was.[6] The precise mathematics served only as a convenience for managing a loose, nonbinding framework, he stressed. The bands merely expressed presumptions of when intervention might be used. No country was obligated to intervene, nor amounts implied. Participants would simply take "note" of the ranges as a common expression of their intent. Interventions would presumably intensify between 2.5 percent and 5 percent, at which point there would be obligatory consultations among the G5 about what to do next.

In the end Pöhl acquiesced, but only as a nonbinding, working understanding, with daily operating decisions left to central bankers closest to markets. "Let's see how it goes and be aware of the limits. There is not a range or unlimited intervention. We must discuss it."[7]

Miyazawa, however, wouldn't budge off his ¥150 bottom line. Moreover, he was ready to intervene to stop the dollar from falling, but not from rising. U.S. Deputy Treasury Secretary Richard Darman tried unsuccessfully to persuade him with his own exposition emphasizing concerted intervention at the 2.5 percent level.

Jim Baker then got tough. He suggested a ¥140 ceiling. This was well below the 5 percent band and pleasing to the Europeans eager to revalue the yen farther. In doing so, Baker exploited Japan's two Achilles' heels in international negotiations—its lack of allies, save the United States, and its dependence on the dollar and U.S. markets. "The Japanese were very reluctant to accept the lower level," recalls one German participant. "They really had no leverage here. Baker pushed Miyazawa."

France and other ERM countries were "all in favor of the Louvre" because "a rapid fall of the dollar makes the DM too strong in the EMS, and they all have to raise interest rates," says Pöhl. U.K. Exchequer Chancellor Lawson also exploited the Louvre Accord to do through the back door of G5/G7 dollar management what he had been unable to persuade Prime Minister Thatcher to do through the front door by joining the ERM—to peg the British pound to the sturdy DM. He did so, moreover, without informing Thatcher. "When we had a G5 Accord enlarged by one for exchange rate stability, it seemed to me useful to latch on to it and prevent a further depreciation of sterling," he says. "Initially I didn't have any exchange rate in mind. The market took the view of a DM 3 peg, so I went with the grain of the market."

Lawson hoped that by shadowing the DM, he had at last found a reliable anchor for British monetary policy—the Bundesbank. A rotund, fifty-five-year-old former financial journalist with a mop of dark hair and arrogant wit, Lawson was a political meteorite whose laissez-faire instincts drew him originally toward monetarism and free-floating exchange rates. Since the U.K.'s monetarist policies terminated in disarray in 1985 under the influence of financial deregulation and globalization, he had sought stability through the external guide of ERM membership. Few experts believed that exchange rate targets made a suitable anchor for guiding the monetary policy of major countries such as the United States, Japan, and Germany. But for smaller ones with large international trade, the case for doing so strengthened with growing global capital mobility. Impressed that the DM's "credibility is reinforced by, inter alia, the fact that German monetary policy is the responsibility of a statutory independent central bank, charged by law with the task of maintaining monetary stability," Lawson from 1988 also tried (unsuccessfully) to convince Thatcher to upgrade Bank of England independence.[8]

The G5 accepted Baker's proposal that they stand ready to intervene up to $12 billion in the six-week period, $4 billion each among the three main currency blocs, the dollar, DM, and yen. But, as he had at the Plaza, Pöhl insisted that all ERM intervention count, not just DM. This negotiation was tantalizing agony for French officials: they badly wanted to compel the Bundesbank to do more DM/dollar intervention, since as a by-product it protected the franc in the ERM. Yet because of national pride, says a senior German policymaker, chuckling, "[t]hey cannot accept in a formal agreement that they want only DM counted, though they do want more, or else they'll be admitting that the DM is the center of the EMS." The issue remained unsettled.[9]

Volcker was one of the most active figures at the Louvre, especially in describing how supportive dollar intervention could work in practice. In the memory of Louvre participants, his prominence ranked just behind that of Bank of France Governor de Larosière and U.S. Deputy Treasury Secretary Darman. Pöhl, by contrast, was relatively subdued, agreeing, but firmly unsympathetic.

Yet Volcker was cool toward the Louvre's systematic flavor. "Volcker defended the Louvre," recalls French Finance Minister Balladur, "but he was not enthusiastic. Baker was much more so."

Volcker and Pöhl, supported verbally by Lawson and de Larosière, kept shoulder-to-shoulder vigilance against monetary policy commitments. "Noninflationary growth" was the cryptic paean that central bankers insisted on as the accord's overriding objective in order to guarantee their freedom to act.

Interest rate policy was nevertheless the Banquo's ghost at the Louvre dinner table. What would happen if concerted foreign exchange market intervention was insufficient to keep the dollar within its soft-target ranges? Should interest rates be altered to defend it? "The implications for monetary policy were clear at the Louvre," says Volcker. "But it wasn't discussed much."

Baker was reluctant to press for interest rate commitments. If the dollar fell, the other G5 members were likely to insist that U.S. interest rates *rise*— the very opposite of his primary objective for convening the meeting. Instead he tried to finesse a general "understanding" or "spirit." In view of the weak growth projections for the United States and world, the presumption ought to be that interest rates would not rise. He wanted the others to lower their interest rates under the dollar. During this conversation Volcker kept "conspicuously quiet" to avoid undermining the U.S. position.[10]

"It was not a binding obligation, but an *understanding* that the common aim was to lower interest rates, given the poor growth prospects," says German Finance Minister Gerhard Stoltenberg. "There wasn't dynamic growth in Europe, and we didn't want the central banks to be too rigid in monetary policy. Central banks fought rising long-term interest rates in the first part of 1987. In hindsight, the fear at the time that there would be insufficient growth was unjustified."

According to one central bank governor, interpretation of this unwritten understanding "was mainly left to the governors, under the confidentiality rule." Yet not all Louvre participants recalled this unwritten understanding. Some interpreted its duration and spirit differently.

Volcker reported to the FOMC and board immediately after the Louvre that no monetary policy commitments had been made. "Presumably strong pressure on the agreed [Louvre] ranges would imply a reappraisal of monetary policy," Volcker says, "but there was no commitment, implied or otherwise, that monetary policies would necessarily be changed."[11]

The operative word in Volcker's sleight of hand was "changed." Volcker knew very well that Baker's understanding was that interest rates would remain *unchanged*. In the event, Volcker waited until the six weeks had expired before he secretly began to snug up interest rates to combat the weak dollar and rising inflation expectations.

When the dollar came under pressure in spring 1987, Stoltenberg traveled to Frankfurt to urge the Bundesbank policy-making Council to commit itself to the Louvre's spirit: "Now we have this agreement. Will the central bank respect it? If the limits in the accord were reached, will the Bundesbank follow the *geist* [spirit] of the Louvre?"

"He was determined to have a success to bind us," reports Norbert Kloten of the Council, which had been briefed on the accord by Pöhl. "Stoltenberg wanted us to give a certain guarantee to the package, in advance. He is no economist. He believed more and more that politicians can determine the markets. He wanted us to say 'yes' or 'no.' We couldn't say 'yes.' We couldn't bend."[12]

"Stoltenberg," adds Pöhl, "became a supporter of international coopera-tion. I felt isolated."

As political theater, the Louvre received rave reviews in democratic world capitals. But its substance failed to pass muster in global capital's golden tri-angle of Wall Street, the City, and Nihonbashi-Marunouchi. By year-end many of its framers believed it had been premature, overambitious, ill de-fined, and perhaps flawed in concept. The loose nature of the accords and understandings reached at the Louvre dinner table had "left a rather ambigu-ous, blurred agreement," which soon led to private and public squabbles among its framers over what had and had not been agreed. MOF Vice Minis-ter for International Toyoo Gyohten, a participant, saw one "rather obvious contradiction" right in the communiqué that markets also detected: "On the one hand, it endorsed the exchange rates then prevailing as broadly in line with economic fundamentals. But at the same time, the G7 recognized that their external payments were badly out of balance and conceded that this imbalance was unsustainable. But if a payments situation is unsustainable, the exchange rate cannot really be in line with economic fundamentals."[13] That was an open invitation for private speculators to attack the dollar when the policy pledges, such as trimming the U.S. budget deficit, were not achieved.

Market expectations about the parameters and nature of the secret ex-change rate ranges quickly ran far ahead of what its government framers in-tended or could deliver. "At the Louvre they were so anxious to stabilize the exchange rate that they believed if they represented a united front, the mar-kets wouldn't challenge them," Goldman Sachs International Vice Chairman Robert Hormats sums up. "The markets did challenge them. And they weren't prepared."

Testing the Louvre

"Plaza Two": That's how U.K. Minister Lawson characterized the Louvre for reporters. "I see this meeting as the lineal descendant of the Plaza meeting. There we all agreed that the dollar should fall. Now we all agree we need stability."[14]

For the first few weeks it looked as if the G7 had indeed pulled off a "Plaza Two." The dollar not only remained firm, it rose. When on March 11 it surpassed DM 1.87, the Louvre's 2.5 percent intervention point ceiling, the United States even startled foreign exchange market traders by *selling* $30 million against DM. It was the first indication of what became a mechanical devotion to the Louvre range intervention points.

But big trouble erupted in late March. Word had gone through the Japanese Establishment that the Louvre had guaranteed a floor of ¥150. For a while Japanese investor behavior made that self-fulfilling. But when the dollar was driven below the ¥150 Maginot line on March 23, investment houses, corporations, and insurers panicked. Their dollar bearishness peaked with $2 billion in net sales on March 31 alone, the final day of Japan's fiscal year. Total net purchases for March fell to under $1 billion vs. an average of nearly $6 billion in each of the previous two months.

The dollar fall through ¥150 was answered by massive intervention by Japan, the United States, and others.[15] But it failed to beat back the avalanche of market selling. The dollar closed March at ¥147.

The attack on the dollar triggered a stock price plunge in New York, London, and Tokyo and a surge in gold prices. Over the next six weeks the U.S. bond market crashed by 17 percent. A mirror-opposite market reaction occurred in Tokyo: bonds soared, with long-term interest rates falling from 4.5 percent to 2.5 percent, as Japanese capital stayed home. On April 1 BOJ Governor Sumita called an emergency press conference in Tokyo: "The dollar hasn't gone into a free-fall. I'd like to say this strongly."[16]

What set off the dollar plunge below ¥150? One culprit was a March 22 comment on British television by Treasury Secretary Baker that the United States had no target value for the dollar. Confused by the apparent contradiction with the Louvre Accord, and afraid that Baker might be signaling a new round of dollar talk-down, markets stampeded. March 1987 was also a low point for world tolerance of Japan's incompatible trade practices. Prime Minister Thatcher threatened to expel Japanese financial firms from London. Japanese dumping of dollars accelerated after March 27, when the Reagan administration unilaterally slapped $300 million of sanctions on Japanese products for violating their semiconductor agreement.

By the time the G5 convened again in Washington on April 7, the dollar had broken through its yen/dollar bottom of ¥146. Once again Miyazawa was isolated when Baker proposed enlargening the Louvre's yen/dollar bands to 5 percent and 10 percent around the new midpoint ¥146 to reflect the changed market reality. That preserved the Louvre's uppermost boundary of ¥161, with the 5 percent band corresponding to the old ¥153.5 midpoint. But the amended range tolerated dollar depreciation to about ¥139 at 5 percent and ¥132 at 10 percent.

The Europeans were "delighted to have the yen go up in relation to them-selves."[17] The Japanese, however, were quietly furious. They refused to rec-ognize the wider bands. But Baker didn't insist upon their explicit acceptance. The yen/dollar rebasing was enacted "passively": G7 parties simply interpreted the communiqué differently, which again affirmed that "around current levels their currencies are within ranges broadly consistent with economic fundamentals and the basic policy intentions outlined at the Louvre meeting." But now the dollar/yen level was different.

Baker pressed Miyazawa for yet another BOJ interest rate cut to help sup-port the dollar. This inflamed tensions between the Japanese Finance Min-istry and the central bank over whose policy tool should adjust. Top BOJ officials were outraged when MOF International Finance Bureau Director General Makoto Utsumi supported Baker's call. "Utsumi was a dangerous person, quite dangerous," says BOJ Executive Director Yoshio Suzuki. "He knew nothing about the domestic economy. He was behaving in cooperation with the U.S. Treasury. At the time of the April G7 in 1987, BOJ members were carefully watching his behavior. I heard from Mr. [Governor] Sumita that he said officially at the G5/G7 not to listen to Utsumi."

Baker's harshest exchanges at the April meetings, however, were again with the outspoken Germans Stoltenberg and Pöhl. On the surface there was little to argue about: the DM was still within its Louvre range. But Baker, supported by the other Europeans, demanded more expansionary measures to offset Germany's sluggish growth forecasts. To Germans, Baker's pressure seemed tantamount to stabilizing the dollar through German inflation that devalued the DM. "The United States always wants to bail out their inflation with more abroad," says economist Kurt Richebacher.

With the Bundesbank and Finance Ministry both unwilling to budge, Stoltenberg and Pöhl told Baker that fundamental U.S. belt-tightening through cutting the budget deficit—or, if necessary, higher U.S. interest rates—was the proper way to stabilize the dollar and ease the global imbal-ances. But higher U.S. interest rates and slower U.S. growth was precisely what Baker had concocted the Louvre to avoid.

Baker and David Mulford also criticized the tiny share of German foreign exchange intervention since the Louvre. The United States and Japan, each accorded a one-third share of the $12 billion intervention war chest, had ex-pended nearly their entire allotments, while the EMS countries together had bought on the order of only $1 billion. In the future Baker wanted to count only DM intervention by the Bundesbank in the European pole. This was an old gripe, in part political appearance and in part substantive, that had been running unresolved since the first G5 deputies meeting in Paris on Novem-ber 13, 1985, after the Plaza. The Germans, supported by their EMS partners, reiterated that all EMS intervention was the equivalent of Bundesbank intervention; who actually executed it was determined by the inner workings of the EMS. The Americans insisted that foreign exchange markets were more impressed when the Bundesbank itself intervened.[18] The issue remained unresolved.

The G5 agreed on a new intervention war chest of $15 billion—$12 billion in fresh money, plus the "unspent" $3 billion European share—to be divided among the three poles. But the G5 rejected Baker's demand that the war chest funds be explicitly pooled and expensed on a dollar-for-dollar basis, whether the intervention was in dollar/DM or dollar/yen.[19] "It was a typical American flip-flop," says a high Fed official of the Reagan government policy U-turn. "We went from a Treasury policy of nonintervention to a situation in which intervention was everything."

The debate over intervention policies also underscored how much operational success depended on back-room cooperation of central bankers, who actually executed currency interventions. Their closeness to powerful global market forces and technical experience rendered the more remote government finance ministers dependent upon them to make any intervention strategy operational.[20] Throughout the G7 process, Finance Ministries, especially in the United States, harbored suspicions that central bankers exploited this knowledge to surreptitiously pursue their own agendas and "have not been faithful to the big meeting."[21]

Since the Plaza, finance ministers tried to guide the intervention process by giving the governors rough guidelines of how much they could spend on any given day—about $300 million to $400 million—until the war chest was exhausted. Following the April 1987 meeting, central bankers tried to adhere to arithmetically shared proportions. But before 1987 was over they'd abandoned it for traditional Basel club understandings. "We have a clear idea among ourselves informally about who is best able to intervene at any given time," says Bank of England Governor Robin Leigh-Pemberton.

A Brush with Free-Fall

The markets took no regard of the G7 ministers' latest effort at managing the dollar. Speculators promptly attacked it. In the last week in April the dollar tumbled to a low of ¥137 and DM 1.77, despite heavy concerted intervention.

For the first time, Baker became genuinely alarmed about dollar free-fall. "We got nervous around ¥135 to ¥140," says Treasury Undersecretary George Gould. "We definitely didn't want it any lower at that point." On April 15 Baker went before the Japan Society in New York to jawbone *support* for the dollar.

Baker's alarm was acute because it was the first clear emergence of the causal linkage—which remained prominent until the October 19, 1987, stock market crash—between the plunging dollar and rising and more volatile long-term interest rates that Volcker had long warned about. In the late March to mid-May dollar attack, U.S. long-term interest rates spiked from 7.5 percent to nearly 9 percent. This bond market crash was the first loud warning, repeated later at amplified volume on Black Monday, of a hard landing.

The dollar-bond price linkage meant that any force that put pressure on the dollar—such as hints of breakdown in the Louvre Accord, narrowing U.S. real interest rate differentials with Japan and Germany, disappointing U.S. trade data—could swiftly be transmitted into higher U.S. interest rates. Real U.S. economic prospects would become hostage to a single financial factor on which it was only partially dependent; the dollar tail would wag the U.S. economic dog.

"We were afraid of the symbolism linking the falling dollar to rising interest rates. It happened in 1987 for the first time," says Gould. "We were *really* worried that the markets would say that monetary policy is going to be used in defense of the dollar. Then you get a direct correlation: every time the dollar is weak it hits the bond market. The bond market could overreact, and we'd get an unwarranted recession."

Critics charged that Baker himself contributed to the expectational bond-dollar link by the Louvre Accord. "The Louvre signaled intentions of what monetary policy would be" to defend the dollar, notes George Shultz. "It is probably one of the reasons for the [stock market] crash."

The growing influence of the exchange rate and global capital flows on domestic economies was rendering obsolete usual distinctions between the domestic and external economy. Alluding to the U.S.'s continued heavy dependence on foreign borrowing to maintain U.S. growth, Volcker warned on May 11 that the "volatility in exchange rates and interest rates in recent weeks gives a little taste of how vulnerable our own financial markets and our economy have become to what other people think. We are obviously in danger of losing control over our own economic destiny."[22]

Baker's conversion to dollar stability was welcomed by Volcker and Wall Street. But had it come too late? Wall Street expectations fixed anxiously on the mammoth three-day, $29 billion quarterly Treasury auction to refund the U.S. debt commencing May 5. In late April half of the top twenty Japanese investors indicated intentions to scale back their auction purchases because of uncertainty over the dollar. Mitsui Trust and Banking, which alone normally bought about $500 million, said that if the dollar fell below ¥130, it would pull out of the auction altogether.[23]

An auction boycott in retaliation for the March U.S. trade sanctions was reportedly urged, though not adopted, at an early May meeting of cabinet members from the powerful LDP Tanaka faction by Chief Cabinet Secretary Masaharu Gotoda and Ministry of International Trade and Industry (MITI) Minister Hajime Tamura, who said, "Japan's weapon is money. We should let the United States know what would happen if Japan refused to buy U.S. government bonds."[24]

At the Federal Reserve, Paul Volcker listened to the anxieties about dollar depreciation from the growing legions of Japan-interest lobbyists in Washington. In late April, without informing other Fed policymakers, Volcker began to snug up interest rates in the Fed Funds market by nearly half a percentage point. "There was a lot of grumbling and anger about the way Paul engineered the snugging on his own," says one governor. "Rather than go to the FOMC or the board, he let seasonal pressures on reserves build up and then did it on the chairman's prerogative [to manage money supply between FOMC meetings], using unreal factors such as tax period distortion that everyone knew was bullshit. It was a classic Paul Volcker–type approach. I was surprised he tried it, especially because he was well aware that the board had a tendency to tighten at the time."

At the end of April Prime Minister Nakasone visited President Reagan to negotiate an end to America's trade sanctions. Prior to Nakasone's departure, Reagan sent him a personal letter expressing the U.S.'s desire for lower Japanese interest rates in order to "stabilize the currency."[25]

When Volcker learned of Nakasone's favorable reaction, he convened a special telephone conference of the FOMC on April 29 to authorize a second snugging move. On the morning of April 30, 1987, while it was being announced that Nakasone had ordered the Bank of Japan to start operations to guide Japanese money market rates lower, Volcker revealed publicly that he'd been snugging up interest rates to defend the dollar. The Bundesbank, pleased that the United States was following its recommendation, joined in two weeks later by lowering its Repo rate from 3.8 percent to 3.55 percent.

It was an overt case of the kind of cooperative interest rate signaling that central bankers usually kept private. But it was not, by central bankers' reckoning, explicit coordination. "Cooperation on intervention was closer in 1987 than it ever had been, that's all," says Volcker. "There was no interest rate coordination. Everyone had the same objective. We were on the tightening side. It had a good effect on expectations."[26]

The synchronized announcements, abetted by concerted U.S and foreign intervention, rallied the dollar. Bond prices rose; long-term interest rates fell. With the Fed and the BOJ steering U.S. and Japanese short-term interest rates in opposite directions, the big U.S. Treasury refunding got off to a good start with the three-year note auction. But on Wednesday, May 6, Japanese investors stayed away from the ten-year securities. High tension thus prevailed on Wall Street going into the thirty-year "long bond" auction on

Thursday. To everyone's relief, Japanese investors piled in, buying 40 percent to 50 percent of the $9.25 billion auction. The average yield, however, was 8.76 percent—1.25 percentage points higher than the previous auction in February.

The downward pressure on the dollar finally abated only after the Japanese MOF applied strong administrative guidance a week later. On May 13 the heads of ten securities firms, twenty banks, ten insurance companies, and fifteen foreign banks were called in and warned about the repercussions of speculating against the dollar. MITI officials delivered the same message to the chief executives of industrial trading companies.[27] MOF then instituted daily monitoring of their dollar transactions, so it could identify any noncompliance, and notified the press of its actions. In effect, Japan had informally reinstituted currency controls—in direct abrogation of the spirit of liberalization and deregulation it had promised the United States and its international allies after years of negotiation. Yet no American leader dared murmur a protest.

MOF's action succeeded in freezing Japan's securities investment trusts, which, in contrast with the giant life insurers and pension trusts, engaged in aggressive, Western-style hedging and short-selling as the dollar fell. "[T]he world should be grateful that only this group among Japanese investors operated like their Western counterparts," says a sardonic Richard Koo of Nomura Research Institute, noting a close correlation between the dollar trading of the securities investment trusts and movements of the dollar and U.S. interest rates in this period. "For if everyone else in Japan operated like investors in Europe or America by selling dollars when it was coming down from September 1985, what happened in March 1987 would have happened long before then, and the repercussions would have been worse, a lot worse. . . . [The year] 1987 . . . was the closest we have come to a total collapse of the international financial system. For even today, many people, both in private and official circles, are unaware of how close we came to a total breakdown and what measures were necessary to keep all the pieces in place."[28]

In the event, nearly all international policymakers' main tools were employed to assist the dollar's narrow escape in the spring 1987—moral suasion, unprecedented central bank dollar-buying on foreign exchanges equal to the U.S.'s *entire* net foreign borrowing needs, and steerage of the interest rate differentials supporting the dollar from 2.5 percentage points to a huge six percentage points against the yen and to two percentage points against the deutsche mark.

Even these tools would have been ineffective, however, without another necessary, occulted force—markets' faith that Volcker's independent Federal

Reserve would uphold the soundness of America's currency. One could only imagine how global investors of all nationalities might have stampeded if monetary policy had been in the hands of Jim Baker and the same elected politicians responsible for the U.S.'s uncontrolled budget deficits.

The falling dollar and bond market crash, as it was, helped precipitate an "inflation hysteria" on Wall Street. In May Fed policymakers debated what to do about it. Was the dollar-driven bond market overreacting to the genuine inflation threat that more gradual snugging would assuage? Or should the Fed make an emphatic "announcement" of its anti-inflationary resolve by boosting the discount rate? As always, Fed policymakers' gaze was on the likely economic environment six to twenty-four months ahead. The measurable indicators of reality were unclear.[29]

"The spring was one of those white-knuckle periods," remembers then Fed Governor Robert Heller. "You have to make the decision at the margins. If you wait until it [the inflation threat] is clear, you're behind the curve of expectations. It gets away from you."

It was a close call—against. What tipped the balance? Fear of an adverse reaction in the fragile financial system. The April bond market crash compounded financing burdens throughout the overindebted economy. With the Brazilian debt moratorium, and Citibank's May 19 bad-debt provisioning, the LDC debt strategy was at a precarious juncture. "The bond market crash did affect our spring discussion on the discount rate," reports Manley Johnson. "It was generally agreed that the market could overreact, so it was better to do gradual snugging. If we hadn't perceived the financial system as fragile, we would have moved more aggressively."

Despite their trepidations, by the May 19, 1987, FOMC meeting, Volcker and the board decided to raise the discount rate at the *next* sign of serious trouble in the dollar. "In May 1987 we were looking every day to raise the discount rate," says Governor Wayne Angell. "Yet each day the dollar looked better. Every day seemed to be the wrong day to act."

Even though the snugging was enough to stabilize the dollar and calm inflation fears, Volcker came to regret his decision not to raise the discount rate in May. "I felt it was a pretty close call," he mourns, "but I wanted to save it for the next crisis."

By the time the next crisis came, Volcker was no longer Fed chairman.

Volcker's Fall

In reassuring markets that he'd defend the dollar, Volcker irked Reagan officials then debating whether or not to renominate him for a third term as Fed chairman. In 1983 fear of adverse market reaction and Jim Baker's support led to Volcker's reluctant reappointment. Markets, speaking through the tremulous dollar, were still vocal in 1987. But this time Jim Baker switched sides.

Baker was furious when he learned that Volcker had stealthily snugged up interest rates. It violated his "understanding" that the Louvre Accord would prevent the Fed from increasing interest rates. That Volcker had waited out the Louvre's six-week term was merely a devious political cover. "We really felt we'd been *had* a bit by Volcker," says the Treasury's David Mulford. "You see, once he had the dollar stabilization in place, he felt he could tighten. That was *not* agreed."

Baker decided Volcker could not be trusted for the 1988 presidential election. "We should look for our own Fed chairman, our own appointment," he recommended to President Reagan.[30] Reagan was divided. He was very concerned that skittish financial markets might riot if it appeared that Volcker was being pushed out. If Volcker showed he wanted to stay, it would be okay with him, Reagan decided. If not, he was gone.

Rumors swirled that Volcker wanted to retire to private life. Yet there was also informed speculation that he desired another term—but that he wanted to be asked by the president, perhaps even publicly. He was still fuming about the Palace Coup and the Fed board packed with Reagan appointees he hadn't vetted. Things would have to be different in another term.

Through anonymous administration leaks, the press was signaled that Volcker's reappointment was likely. One of the main leakers, White House Chief of Staff and ex-Senator Howard Baker, went to Volcker. He told him that if he wanted to be reappointed, he could be. He suggested he meet with Reagan to resolve the issue. But Baker's between the lines message was that Volcker would have to do the asking, not the president.

On Monday, June 1, 1987, after a reflective weekend of fly-fishing, Paul Volcker met in the White House's third-floor living room with President Reagan and Howard Baker. The men were barely seated when Volcker brought out a letter of resignation.

Without protest, Reagan accepted it.

So ended the career of "the central banker of the decade," one destined for the loftiest pedestal in the Basel club pantheon.[31] Paul Volcker went out as he'd come in, politically independent. At a time when FOMC members, Basel gossipers, Wall Street financiers, and Washington politicians were on highest alert for signs that he was succumbing to the temptation to cozy up to the Reagan government to secure renomination, Volcker had done just the *opposite* by snugging up interest rates.

By such an exit, Volcker reinforced the ideology of the independent central bank that had been gaining democratic credibility but was not yet an established tradition. The mantle of doyen of Basel central bankers passed on to the Bundesbank's Karl Otto Pöhl, who in the same period was renominated for another eight-year term as president by Chancellor Kohl, after some hesitant temptation to choose a political ally. The task of consolidating the gains against inflation, while holding together a fragile and transforming financial system and overindebted economy in the face of Washington fiscal policy paralysis, passed to the new Fed chairman, Alan Greenspan.

Financial markets staged a final salute to Volcker's going: Treasury bonds suffered their worst one-day plunge in five years; the Fed alone spent over $500 million, including an unusual Far East intervention, in concert with G7 central banks to counter heavy dollar selling around the globe.

Central Bankers Start to Disengage

From mid-May to mid-August 1987 the dollar stabilized. The U.S.'s "investment advantage" as the world currency country with deep, liberalized, and politically safe capital markets reappeared. Money shifted from Japan and Europe back to U.S. dollar assets. By mid-August the dollar rallied to ¥152, just below its Louvre midpoint. Notwithstanding concerted G7 dollar selling, it rose through its 2.5 percent inner Louvre upper band to DM 1.90.

The financial imprint of volatile global capital swings was strikingly transparent: as the dollar rallied, U.S. long-term interest rates eased. In contrast, German and Japanese interest rates jumped. Much of the "hot" money fleeing yen for dollars flowed back not to U.S. bond markets, however, but into booming U.S. equities. This fueled the historically wide differential between bond and equity yields that closed so violently on October 19, 1987. By mid-August U.S. stock prices were up 30 percent for the year. Yet it was hard to find any change in U.S. economic fundamentals to warrant newfound bullishness.

On June 9, 1987, Jim Baker garnered the promised endorsement of the Venice economic summit for the Louvre and a refined six-economic-performance-indicator mechanism to govern the G7 process. Baker's distant hope that the endorsement might also inject significant political energy into policy coordination, however, proved hollow. Just prior to the summit conference, Nakasone implored Reagan privately: "Please cut the budget defict, in serious and significant ways. Otherwise the world economy will be in a serious situation."[32] Reagan's response—dead silence—was more resounding than all the communiqués and secret agreements on the dollar at every international meeting since the Plaza.

Nakasone felt able to make this special plea to Reagan because a week earlier Japan had overcome year-long MOF resistance and passed a long awaited ¥6 trillion ($40 billion) supplementary fiscal spending package that was later heralded as the first—and only—sign of genuine policy coordination under the Louvre. Needing something to ease trade tensions at the Venice summit, Nakasone had gotten it at the price of scrapping his tax reform program—a key liberalizing reform—and heavy political pork barrel larding. "There had been quite a strong feeling at the ministry those days— almost a sense of *crisis*—that the fiscal situation was quite serious," describes MOF Vice Minister for International Toyoo Gyohten. "If we gave up the continuing effort to improve it, then we would be thrown back to the late 1970s, when the fiscal deficits coupled with the oil crisis led to serious inflationary pressures. The politicians, of course, wanted big projects requiring large quantities."

MOF's last wall of resistance was overcome when the BOJ leaked to Nakasone that there was likely to be an extra ¥2.4 trillion in revenue that MOF wasn't including in its official projections.[33] This swayed the big-business group Keidanren, a key ally of fiscal austerity. "It was a defensive move," explains the BOJ's Suzuki, "so we shouldn't have pressure to lower the official discount rate. The discount rate cut to 2.5 percent was regarded as too much within the BOJ. It was time for fiscal policy to come into play."

Japanese bond markets, heavily speculated on another BOJ discount rate cut, corrected violently. Interest rates shot up nearly three percentage points by August. The losses claimed its first big *zaiteku* victim, Tateho Chemical, and set off a small panic of future failures. This domestic storm helped propel the flight into dollar assets.

The BOJ's satisfaction with the ¥6 trillion supplemental budget was short-lived. In June it suddenly became evident that the Japanese economy, which had 0 percent recorded growth in the second quarter, was surging out of the *endaka* recession. Annual growth outturn, almost all in the second half, would be 4.6 percent. The ¥6 trillion fiscal stimulus, which would have helped jump-start the economy when Miyazawa was originally pushing for it, now threatened to overheat it.[34] Quite the contrary of a triumph for Louvre policy coordination, it demonstrated the practical perils of democratic governments trying to fine-tune economic growth.

Although measured inflation was still zero, the alarm bells sounded at the central bank's Nihonbashi headquarters. Borrowing zoomed ahead. By June Japan's money supply growth hit double digits.[35] Much of the accelerating money supply was feeding the financial mania pushing up real estate and stock prices. It had not spilled over into goods price inflation thanks to temporary deflationary braking phenomena such as the yen's rise against the dollar and spare Japanese capacity and courtesy of the liberal global capital order, a safety valve that pushed some excess liquidity abroad.

The BOJ tried to keep a lid on inflation expectations "by saying in our forecasts that money growth was at the upper acceptable limit," explains BOJ Executive Director Yoshio Suzuki. "But we weren't satisfied. We wanted to reduce it."[36] When the wholesale price index surged abruptly from -5 percent to 0 percent in mid-1987, BOJ officials decided they had to choose: it was either domestic inflation or the dollar.

Behind the scenes, BOJ inside power Deputy Governor Yasushi Mieno engineered a policy turn toward tightening. "The summer of 1987 was a turning point from an easy monetary policy to soften the shock of the high yen to a more prudent stance," says Mieno, who became governor in late 1989. "Before mid-1987 we looked more closely at the foreign exchange developments in the formulation of our monetary policy; afterward we shifted more to domestic market conditions. This was reflected in money market rates, which rose. Looking back now, I believe it was *still* the right move. It has been said that Japan should be the world's anchor on interest rates. But considering Japan's large share in the world economy, it is proper that our contribution be to noninflationary growth, not to anchor world interest rates."

In addition to permitting call money rates to rise in midsummer, the BOJ issued tighter "window guidance" ceilings on bank's lending growth for the coming three months. "Window guidance" was an administrative monetary control technique that in most democratic capitalist countries had been rendered ineffective by the global financial revolution. But in Japan's guided financial system, it was still a powerful tool.

The BOJ started its tightening moves only under the political cover provided by the Bundesbank, which in late July had started snugging up its Repo rate from 3.55 percent to 3.6 percent. Where the BOJ feared incipient, actual inflation, the Bundesbank's worry was inflation expectations. Measured inflation was practically nonexistent. It wasn't likely to be fired up by Germany's sluggish economic growth. But the money supply was overshooting the Bundesbank's target range for a second consecutive year.

As in Japan, the main culprit behind the overshooting was the wobbly dollar. Global capital inflows from the dollar, low German interest rates, and record central bank dollar support intervention all swelled German money supply.[37] The foreign capital inflows abruptly reversed directions when the dollar stabilized after mid-May.[38] In reaction, long-term German interest rates *rose* by a full percentage point to 6.7 percent by September. The Bundesbank tried to level the steepest slope in the yield curve in twenty years by nudging up German short-term interest rates. But with an inflation-wary eye on the monetary overshooting, domestic German investors stayed short-term.

In one sense the Bundesbank was victim of a rule trap of its own devising: it had so long indoctrinated the market with monetarist symbolism that German investors responded in a Pavlovian manner to the overshooting. When Bundesbank officials tried to explain the mitigating factors of why inflation was not an immediate threat, the market perceived double-talk and steepened the yield curve.

The Bundesbank's anti-inflation credibility was also wounded, in part, by the erroneous market perception that the Louvre had sworn it to defend a rigid dollar range, which was tantamount to a "promise to print more DM."[39] Top Bundesbank officials began to believe that the G7 process had gone too far. One side effect of defending the dollar was a historic explosion in international liquidity that was lifting world real estate, stock and commodity prices—and renewed inflation expectations.

Fresh doubts about the dollar resurfaced as the Bundesbank and Bank of Japan began to turn away from Louvre dollar stabilization in order to fight inflation fears at home. Rising foreign interest rates undercut the dollar's strength. It was becoming evident to markets: either the dollar would have to fall below Louvre levels or U.S. interest rates would have to rise—possibly both.

The prospect of rising U.S. interest rates and a falling dollar haunted the central bankers at the July BIS meetings. In 1986 losses from the falling dollar were partially offset by gains from rising U.S. bond prices. But that Basel weekend BIS chief Alexandre Lamfalussy presented research that warned that if both the dollar and bond prices fell in tandem—as they had in the spring 1987—foreign U.S. bond buyers faced such staggering compounded capital losses that they might flee the dollar. "There was a very uneasy feeling that the long-term interest rate increases and the dollar fall in 1987 was moving us into dangerous territory," Lamfalussy recalls.

The dangerous territory was invaded on August 14, 1987. A much worse than expected $15.7 billion U.S. trade deficit report for June generated market expectations that the international imbalances could not be unwound at Louvre dollar levels. Global investors promptly slashed their purchases of dollar assets: in September Japanese bought only $839 million of U.S. securities, the lowest level since March 1985; in October they were net sellers of $39 million.[40]

Despite large concerted central bank intervention, the dollar fell sharply. At ¥140 and DM 1.79 in early September it was challenging its spring lows. The U.S. bond market also plunged in sympathy. The 8.4 percent 30-year bond started its fateful crash to 10.4 percent, and with it, the high-flying New York stock market began the 500-point slide that preceded its 508-point blow-off on Black Monday.

The bad trade data breaking on top of reviving inflation fears and the shift in central banker priorities to quell it had ignited an incipient market hysteria of a global interest rate spiral. Rising U.S. long-term interest rates as the dollar fell transmitted downward pressure back to the DM and yen, exacerbating inflation fears in Germany and Japan, and adding pressure on their central banks to tighten further. But that would undercut the dollar. The cycle would start anew. When the prospective fear of a global competition in monetary restraint took hold, markets on their own could launch an anticipatory spiral that ratcheted up long-term interest rates beyond central bankers' control. Ominously, in late summer and fall 1987, rising short-term interest rates were pushing up the whole structure of interest rates with it everywhere.

Countdown to Black Monday

Alan Greenspan had been sworn in as Volcker's successor on August 11, only three days before the bad U.S. trade report roiled the markets. Greenspan knew his success as a central banker depended on establishing his sound money credentials with markets. He knew he was slightly suspect because he was a Republican appointed by a Republican White House in the run-up to a presidential election year and that with his appointment the entire Federal Reserve Board of Governors had been chosen by a single president. Too, he had to fill the shoes of a legend whose very name on Wall Street was shorthand for hard currency and indifference to political pressure.

Greenspan was determined to meet his first test with vigor. In early September he urged the board of governors to make its first discount rate hike since spring 1984. "Alan was determined to make a strong statement," says Manley Johnson. "He knew that everyone would compare him to Paul Volcker."

The situation was vexing: the inflation visible in May 1987 had receded. Only one Federal Reserve Bank was requesting a discount rate increase. Market expectations of inflation, Greenspan and his colleagues agreed, were overblown. Most of the anxiety was concentrated on the fragile dollar and the risk of a global interest rate spiral. Yet market expectations had to be treated lest they did tangible economic damage. But would a discount rate hike "announcement" alarm expectations rather than calm them?

Managing such market psychology was what made central banking more art than science: sometimes market expectations were assuaged and gave a more leveraged bang to small central bank tightening moves; other times markets interpreted the same move as a belated endorsement of their fears, driving long-term interest rates higher and requiring central bankers to

sharply swing up interest rates to hurdle the expectations curve—at the risk
of upsetting growth, financial stability, and political sensibilities. With expectations leveraging ever huger volumes of high-speed global capital, central bankers simply had less margin for error than ever before.

Following a turbulent drop in the bond market on Thursday morning,
September 3, the board assented to Greenspan's recommendation for the
half-point discount rate hike to 6 percent. The FOMC doubled up, with a
two-week lag, with a similar boost in the Fed Funds rate to 7.25 percent. In
an effort to dispel any market perception that Fed policy was hostage to the
dollar, the governors drafted a "carefully, though badly written" announcement describing the Fed's motivation as "potential inflationary pressures."[41]

Although Jim Baker privately felt "there was not much justification for
Alan's discount rate move," he too strongly counseled Greenspan to downplay any dollar motive.[42] "Jim was very concerned that the discount rate increase would be perceived as not against inflation, but to defend the dollar,"
explains Treasury Undersecretary George Gould. "I don't think you can ever
really say that monetary policy was used to defend the dollar. But there *appeared* to be a linkage. The trade deficit started to get into the bond market,
and then we got that very rapid rise in interest rates, culminating in the 10.4
percent in the long bond before the crash."

Baker was especially perturbed by Greenspan's refusal to delay the discount rate hike so it could be used as a bargaining chip for interest rate concessions from the Bundesbank and BOJ. Nor did Greenspan, when
introduced by Volcker to the governors at his first "Basel weekend" of September 6–8, 1987, press them for concessions after the fact. Most of the governors applauded Greenspan. They thought a discount rate hike was long
overdue. Yet privately they worried that a half-point move might not be
enough to prop up the dollar.[43]

If the political reaction to Greenspan's debut action was cool, the market
judgment was terrible. The dollar steadied but didn't rebound. Stock prices
retreated. Ominously, bond market interest rates backed up—a thumbs-down
in the symbolic dialogue between markets and central banks. The Fed Funds
rate hike that came through the pipeline two weeks later confused market
players over whether the Fed had tightened again. When Greenspan soon afterward stated that he saw no inflation danger, suspicions mounted that the
Fed's genuine motives had been dissembled. "Greenspan literally popped up
the discount rate without a signal," says David Jones, Aubrey G. Lanston
chief economist. "It shook up the market. It started the clock ticking on the
stock market crash."

Prime culpability for the spiral of events leading to Black Monday seven
weeks away, however, lay with the growing fundamental pressures on the
dollar from the global economic imbalances and renewed inflation fears

pushing up world interest rates. The predominant Fed view was that "if there was a U.S. monetary policy mistake in 1987, it was made in the spring of 1987. We should have been tighter."[44] In the transition between Volcker and Greenspan, the Fed had slipped too far behind the power curve of market expectations to catch up. Volcker, with his credibility, might have been able to hurdle it; Greenspan, an untested new man, could not. "It was not logical that every time the Fed raised interest rates the whole structure of interest rates rose," says Goldman, Sachs International Vice Chairman Robert Hormats. "The reason is that it was seen as part of the effort to keep the dollar from falling."

Over the September 1987 Basel weekend, Greenspan and the Basel governors discussed the danger of a global interest rate spiral as well as the crash potential of the record discrepancy between U.S. stock and bond market yields.[45] "The situation we saw was fragile," reports the Fed's Manley Johnson. "We agreed we had to be incredibly careful on the 'announcement effects' of interest rate moves."

The Basel governors agreed that instead of thunderous discount rate moves, they would try quietly to snug up money market interest rates, on separate schedules, without upsetting the interest rate differentials supporting the dollar. In hindsight many central bankers were not proud of getting caught up in the market-driven juggernaut.

"The only time I felt *helpless* was September to October 19," says Fed Governor Angell. "The whole event [reaction to the discount rate hike] was created by uncertainty in the capital market due to the dollar instability and the lack of official resolve. You can't engineer a crisis any better than that. The long bond rate has credibility and expectational votes. If you're ahead of the curve and you tighten, you keep the long rates in line or lower. The tragedy of monetary policy is when you get behind. When the long bond got to 10.4 percent, I knew our credibility was gone. I felt the jig was up."

By the time of the G5/G7 meetings on September 26, 1987, at Washington, central bankers faced a crossroads: market forces were demanding that interest rates be raised to fight incipient inflation and be relatively highest in the United States to stabilize the dollar. G7 government finance ministers, led by Jim Baker, were demanding dollar stabilization at unchanged interest rate levels.

Central bankers bridled when they reviewed together that the G10 had bought a breathtaking $70 billion since the Louvre to hold up the dollar.[46] Most galling to non-U.S. central bankers was that their intervention was financing *all* the U.S.'s foreign borrowing requirements. In effect they were printing potentially inflationary amounts of domestic money to underwrite the U.S.'s profligate budget deficits. The cardinal principle of central bank independence was freedom from obligation to buy their own government's debt issues. Yet they were doing precisely that for *another* nation's government, the United States!

The G7 dollar defense looked increasingly like a Baker-orchestrated political operation to postpone difficult and possibly recessionary U.S. belt-tightening, through the 1988 presidential elections. Policy coordination had failed in its central economic mission to induce sovereign democratic nations—above all fiscally reprobate America—to adjust their economic policies. More and more it resembled a global equivalent of the U.S.'s Gramm-Rudman-Hollings budget-balancing law—smoke-and-mirror "process" without genuine substance. "We felt that the United States pushed us into a corner to avoid the painful fiscal adjustment. We had no choice but to intervene if we wanted to avoid suffering from overvalued European currencies," explains Fabrizio Saccomanni, head of the Bank of Italy's foreign department.

Volcker being pushed by Baker to the foreground for the Plaza photo now seemed like a prefiguring metaphor of how the G7 process at bottom functioned—finance ministers pushing central bank monetary policy to undertake all the adjustment until it became overburdened. "What we've been asked to do has been against the trend of the market, so it won't work," says Bank of England Governor Robin Leigh-Pemberton. "We felt we'd been asked to take excessive risk, marching like infantry into battle."

"What is problematic in the G5," adds the Bundesbank's Pöhl, "is that politicians have a different set of values—to win elections. They aren't prepared to do the analysis that central bankers are." The dollar appeared destined for a new fall, and that analysis told central bankers in Washington that there were diminishing incentives to go on accumulating depreciating dollars to forestall the market force consequences of governments' failure to fundamentally adjust fiscal and structural policies.

IMF Managing Director Michel Camdessus alerted the G7 finance ministers to the dangers when he presented the IMF's confidential September 23, 1987, "Economic Situation and Outlook" for the indicators exercise. At the Louvre the IMF had assessed that the dollar ranges had been set too high. Now its gloomier view was that world economic "imbalances could be even larger." Inflation "may be reemerging." Rising U.S. interest rates foreboded a potential world recession and a new eruption of the LDC debt crisis. Unless overdue adjustments were implemented right away, "there can be little doubt that exchange market pressures will reemerge, which it would be ineffective or costly to resist through intervention or shifts in monetary policy."[47]

Turbulent global financial markets voiced their own exclamatory warning. On September 24 the newswire of the *Nihon Keizai Shimbun* newspaper reported that the BOJ was imposing much tighter window guidance on bank lending growth as a prelude to a discount rate hike. U.S. Treasury bond prices plunged, driving the thirty-year bond to 9.69 percent from 9.55 percent. The stock market fell, too.

The BOJ's monetary policy intentions were much discussed at the G5 meeting at Washington the next day. The BOJ's new 3.6 percent bank lending growth guidance for October through December implied a further tightening that would add to the sharp rise in Japanese money market rates over the previous weeks. Yet Governor Satoshi Sumita avowed to Baker, "We at the Bank of Japan have no intention of raising the discount rate any time soon."[48]

Sumita's deceptive emphasis was the word *soon*. At the instigation of Deputy Governor Yasushi Mieno, the BOJ was pressing its case to MOF and Establishment leaders for a discount rate increase. "We didn't set the final date, but before the crash we were thinking of doing it in November or December," reports Yoshio Suzuki. "The reason for waiting was that then the rising trend in inflation would be clear to members of the government and MOF. We told the MOF that our estimates in the fourth quarter were for domestic inflation of three to four percent. The MOF said, 'Wait and see.' We believe it would have happened without the October crash and the [subsequent] sharp appreciation of the yen." One key unconvinced person was MOF Minister Miyazawa.

Baker's harshest criticism was against the agent he saw lurking behind the BOJ—the Bundesbank. "The BOJ raising rates was a concern, but we felt the Japanese were following the Bundesbank," explains Treasury Assistant Secretary Charles Dallara. "The Germans were not taking a cooperative approach in the weeks before the crash."

The German central bank was the U.S. Treasury's natural chief adversary in almost all international economic burden-sharing negotiations. This was because of its independence, its opposition to any binding exchange rate commitments, the DM's status as the leading alternative to the dollar, Germany's slow growth potential, and its abhorrence of inflation. The United States had a unique capacity to initiate cooperation. But it could usually go only as far as the Bundesbank could be induced, or compelled, to go.

Baker charged that Bundesbank snugging while projected German growth was only 1.8 percent violated the Louvre's "spirit"—the nuanced "understanding" of lower interest rates and growth orientation. Its fanatical overreaction to the true inflation risk, he criticized, was pressuring the dollar and world interest rates.

Bundesbank President Pöhl stridently rebutted that the Louvre had been a nonbinding accord for the time being only. Besides, there was nothing to complain about: German interest rates were *lower* than the 3.85 percent level they'd been at the Louvre. The DM was still trading within its Louvre ranges. German growth was paced by 4 percent domestic demand. This was precisely the type of growth they all agreed was needed to reduce the external imbalances. Germany had simply reached its limits.

"What you really want us to do is to take a big risk on inflation to help you avoid the hard steps to reduce your budget deficits," Pöhl told Baker.[49] "We are not neurotic on inflation," he added publicly soon after, "but overshooting for a lengthy period increases the risk of affecting credibility, and it is no exaggeration to say that credibility is the capital stock of any central bank."[50]

Pöhl instead proposed another solution: "The United States should have a recession." Recession would reduce the U.S. consumption that the United States had been unable to do through fiscal restraint. In all history, he argued, there'd never been a reversal of trade deficits of the U.S.'s magnitude without a recession.[51]

The suggestion that the United States should "have a recession" infuriated Baker. Treasury officials knew that Pöhl and the G7 chorus were right: the tentacles of the huge U.S. budget deficit *were* strangling the U.S. and world economy. But they had little influence in the stalemate between Congress and White House. That conditioned Baker's response. "You can't say 'Mr. Stoltenberg and Mr. Pöhl, you're right. It is the budget deficit that is the problem.' But we can't mention taxes or the president will throw us out on our ear,' " explains the Treasury's Gould. "So you try to tell them that they've got to grow."

European G7 members nonetheless supported Baker's criticism of the Bundesbank, since they were bridling at the slow growth harness its tight monetary policy imposed on them.[52] As a result, Baker was able to insert a veiled rebuke of Germany in the G7 communiqué, that "growth in domestic demand in surplus countries is picking up, but it is important that it improves further in some countries."

Baker, however, rejected European suggestions to relax the Louvre's dollar/DM range. A stronger DM, the Europeans hoped, would alleviate some of the inflation worries behind the Bundesbank's tightening.[53] Baker likewise rejected appeals from Ministers Stoltenberg and Lawson that the United States defend the dollar with higher interest rates or foreign currency–denominated "Reagan bonds." Baker, in short, demanded dollar stability by one means only—lower foreign interest rates under the dollar.

Stretching market credulity, the G7 communiqué language was nearly identical with the Louvre and others. Once again currencies were "within ranges broadly consistent with underlying economic fundamentals." Again the G7 was committed to stability "around current levels."

"The biggest problem we have, even with our own politicians," laments then Bundesbank Vice President Helmut Schlesinger, "is that one cannot have stable exchange rates if the rates are *wrong*. Men of politics think they can manipulate exchange rates and interest rates in different directions. They don't accept market conditions. It is hard to explain to politicians. They have a short-term view. It goes with the business they're in."

"Being intellectually honest is important for economic policy," agrees the U.S. Treasury's David Mulford. "We were all guilty as we approached that meeting of failing to recognize that we had stabilized too soon and probably the Louvre was too narrow. The nuanced flexibility was lacking. The continuing deterioration of the trade numbers in the summer indicated that the stabilization was inconsistent with the fundamentals. It indicated we were living on borrowed time."

Rupture Between Markets and Governments

The chasm between the G7 political show and economic reality was spotlighted by a pair of surprise speeches at the IMF/World Bank annual meetings on September 30, 1987, by U.S. Treasury Secretary Baker and U.K. Chancellor of the Exchequer Nigel Lawson. To the surprise of most of his G7 partners, Baker unveiled a proposal for a new commodity price indicator, including gold, to help anchor low inflation in the policy coordination process.[54] Many suspected a domestic political motive to woo Reagan supply-siders, several of whom were enamored of commodities and gold, for George Bush's run at the Republican presidential nomination.

Even more startling was Lawson's speech, which divulged much about the secretive nature of the Louvre Accord. Most worrisome to central bankers seeking to disengage their credibility from Louvre target zones was the British minister's advocacy of "a more permanent regime of managed floating" exchange rates. To sensitive central bank ears, this signaled political momentum to make the G7 into a systematic world economic directorate, headed by finance ministers, to control monetary policy. "There was an illusion that the Louvre Accord was a move not just to 'more stability,' but to a fixed but adjustable peg. Even Nigel Lawson in his famous speech at the IMF in 1987, which I didn't like at all, suggested this," complains Bundesbank President Karl Otto Pöhl. "At the G5 just before, we talked of cooperation. Nigel never mentioned he was about to make this speech. I thought that was very uncooperative."

Lawson's initiative was undertaken largely as a surrogate means to anchor Sterling after Lawson came to realize that Prime Minister Margaret Thatcher was inalterably opposed to the British membership in the ERM that he had been advocating. It also stunned the unforewarned Thatcher and many senior U.K. Treasury and Bank of England officials. The only G7 minister Lawson consulted beforehand, it turned out, was Baker. "My thinking and Baker's were very similar," says Lawson. "I worked with Jim Baker."[55]

Lawson's call for a new regime of "managed floating" exchange rates represented the remarkable completion of the round-trip odyssey in government attitudes toward the international monetary order. Freely floating markets had failed to produce medium-term speculators who stabilized currencies around underlying economic fundamentals, Lawson confessed, and instead had produced "wild gyrations" damaging to the real economy of world trade and productive investment.[56] He argued that to anchor volatile expectations, governments had to fill the role of the absent stabilizing speculators. They would do so by providing a medium-term government view of appropriate exchange rates, anchored within a system of target zones and indicators-based policy coordination.

Lawson's speech amounted to a last rites for the laissez-faire Reagan and Thatcher Revolutions and a revival of the mainstream viewpoint, clung to throughout by central bankers, that some government mediation in markets was necessary to save capitalist markets from their inherent tendency to destabilize occasionally. The speech recognized implicitly that democracies had to reassert their political responsibility for currency exchange rates. It was, in essence, a groping to reforge a democratic capitalist compact that incorporated the new force of global capital.

Neither Lawson nor Baker, however, offered a solution to the main obstacle to any new world monetary order: how to politically compel sovereign democratic nations to adjust their macroeconomic and structural policies to support it. But this was soon overshadowed by their even more spectacular failure of timing—on the eve of the Louvre's collapse in the global stock market revolt of Black Monday, October 19.

The first thunderbolt struck on October 6. The Bundesbank announced a small Repo rate increase from 3.65 percent to 3.75 percent. Ten-year bond interest rates ratcheted higher. From the G7 meeting to the October 19 crash, they rose half a point to 7.25 percent.

U.S. short-term interest rates reacted by jumping nearly one-third percentage point. The long bond hit 9 7/8 percent, its highest level since December 1985. Big U.S. banks hiked their prime rate by one-half percentage point. Stock prices tumbled.

Furious, Baker demanded to know what the Bundesbank was doing only a week after the latest G7 consultation about the danger of raising interest rates.

The Bundesbank's snugging, in fact, had been in the pipeline for two weeks. It had been decided at the Central Bank Council meeting on Thursday morning, September 24, by a very slender majority led by Vice President Helmut Schlesinger and over Pöhl's objection that the timing was awful since he was departing a few hours later for the Washington meetings. "You send me to Washington knowing this is in the cards!" a frustrated and shocked Pöhl declared to his fellow Council members.

When Pöhl arrived in Washington he informed an upset Minister Stoltenberg what had happened. Fearing escalation of the acrimonious atmosphere, neither man forewarned Baker, either at Washington or subsequently. Pöhl says he informed fellow central banker Alan Greenspan, but Greenspan "obviously did not pass it on to Baker."

Thus Baker was stunned at the news of it on October 6.

Pöhl tried diplomatically to explain the circumstances of his being outvoted. Much of his trouble lay in the decentralized federal structure of the Bundesbank Central Bank Council. Unlike the Fed's FOMC, which centralized power in the Board and chairman, Council majority voting power lay in the hands of the generally more parochial-minded, and often politically rather than professionally selected, *länder,* or regional state central bank presidents, some of whom "clearly do not know what they are talking about."[57]

"The FOMC is like the Central Bank Council. But the FOMC has only five members from the regions, and here we have all of them," explains Pöhl, who pleaded successfully for consolidation of the *länder* representatives upon German reunification in 1990. "It's absolutely overdone given the size of the nation. Bundesbank decision making is inflexible. There are eighteen people. Only ten have to agree, but it takes a long time to build a consensus."

While Pöhl often sided with the conservative majority around Vice President Schlesinger—the common international perception that he was Schlesinger's main growth-oriented opponent was mistaken—some Council members suspected he was unduly influenced by his large exposure to politics, international and domestic.[58]

"No one understands decision making in the German system," says Norbert Kloten, the *länder* central bank president from Baden-Württemberg. "If Pöhl tells us to do something, we might say 'no.' We may be *more* likely to do so if there is external pressure. Pöhl is an excellent man, but he is more conditioned by internal and external political matters. His strength is not economic analysis."

On September 24 the Council majority judged that Pöhl's appeal was motivated more by political than by economic needs. "We were aware of the sentiments of the Americans," says Kloten. "Nevertheless, the Louvre was no longer in line with the facts. The Louvre was 'for the time being only.' We could not let it be a straitjacket. The Americans always believe our monetary policy is too restrictive."[59]

From the dialogue on the internal politics of the Bundesbank between Deputy Finance Ministers David Mulford and Hans Tietmeyer, Jim Baker knew that Pöhl's problem was genuine. Yet any inclination he had to overlook it vanished on Wednesday, October 14, when the Bundesbank bumped up the Repo rate *another* notch, from 3.75 percent to 3.85 percent.

"It's a little clique headed by Helmut Schlesinger," Baker, described as finger-pointing mad, railed to U.S. colleagues. "They are rigid monetarists bent on zero inflation, no matter what!"[60]

Baker telephoned Stoltenberg. The Bundesbank was again violating the spirit of the September meetings, he protested. He wanted the policy reversed.

"I'm not happy about the Bundesbank interest rate increases, either," Stoltenberg commiserated. But he denied that he had the power to alter them.

Baker informed Stoltenberg that he would be traveling to Sweden the following week to go hunting with the king of Sweden. He proposed that he stop over in Germany en route on Monday, October 19, to discuss the matter.

Stoltenberg suggested, "Let's meet in Frankfurt. Since you and the Bundesbank have a problem, we can include Pöhl."[61]

Baker agreed, but he did not want to meet on Bundesbank turf. So they settled on the Sheraton Hotel at the Frankfurt airport as neutral ground.

Further ominous news that Wednesday was another larger-than-expected U.S. trade deficit for August. The dollar sold off immediately to ¥142.5 and DM 1.805.

Tokyo investors had been primed for a fresh dollar plunge the day before, when Governor Sumita said the BOJ would allow Japanese money market interest rates, already up to 5 percent from 4.25 percent at the start of September, to go on rising. This meant that ten-year bond yields, up from 4.2 percent to 5.9 percent, were likely to continue upward, too.

As Japanese investors raced to dump dollars, the U.S. government thirty-year bond yield broke through the psychological threshold of 10 percent. U.S. bond yields were a record nearly four times higher than equities. Pandemoniac selling of stock index futures in the Chicago futures pits fed back to the New York Stock Exchange, which plunged ninety-five points. Overnight the Tokyo stock market fell, followed by a fall in London.

A Thursday morning stock market rally collapsed after Baker publicly blasted the Bundesbank and suggested that the DM/dollar range under the Louvre could be rebased lower. He unnerved currency markets further with the first public admission, seemingly inadvertent, that the yen/dollar range had been rebased in the spring.

On Friday, October 16, the dollar fell through DM 1.80, which many market players deemed to be a key threshold of the secret Louvre ranges. The stock market suffered one of its worst plummets in history, down 108 points on record volume. In the three days from October 14 to 16, the New York stock market had fallen 250 points. During the day, Baker and Alan Greenspan discussed the market turmoil and whether Baker should postpone his trip to Europe. Baker decided to go.

Baker left on Sunday evening with one parting shot at the Bundesbank and, unintentionally, at markets. While insisting that the Louvre was still operative, Baker warned on the TV show *Meet the Press* that the United States would not sit back and "watch surplus countries jack up their interest rates and squeeze growth worldwide on the expectation that the United States will follow by raising its interest rates."[62]

To markets and policymakers, it sounded like reversion to dollar talk-down. But if the United States didn't raise interest rates, and if G7 cooperation collapsed, market pundits feared, the dollar could plunge far and fast. Dawn rose on Black Monday, in short, with markets entering the jaws of Volcker's dollar free-fall nightmare.

Mark Fitzsimmons of Morgan Stanley's foreign exchange desk remembers the mood: "Just before the crash the market felt U.S. leadership was in disarray. Volcker was out. Reagan was in a cloud over Iran-contra [scandal]. The Bundesbank tightened up just when Baker was screaming for them to loosen. Well, the Germans were a problem. But on the relative scale of things, everyone knew that the United States was a much greater problem. This undermined confidence. There was no G7 coordination. It showed that the policymakers weren't even focusing on the problem, much less coordinating to solve it. So the market asked: 'Who's running the ship?' If no one, then we'd get the inflation of the 1970s again. So the bond market was nervous, and that dropped the dollar. This to me was the cause of the stock market crash."

Still, no one was prepared for the scale of the Wall Street stock market revolt—prices down 22.6 percent on trading volume that nearly doubled Friday's record levels—nor that it would be transmitted worldwide in an awesome unveiling of the extent of the reach of the new regime of global capital.

Baker blamed the Bundesbank, which charged back that "Baker shot at the Bundesbank and hit Wall Street."[63] The Louvre Accord was mauled by critics for trying artificially to stabilize the messenger, the dollar, without addressing the fundamental message of economic imbalances. When governments failed to adjust, global market forces did, and according to its own politically indifferent, economic logic.

The Black Monday crash was the sound of the dollar starting to free-fall from unsustainable imbalances. This converged with the huge volumes of high-speed, volatile, stateless capital and innovations overwhelming financial market "plumbing" structures and regulations designed for an earlier era. At its broadest, the global crash was thus a warning about democratic governments' failure to pool their sovereignty to "civilize" the revolutionary force of global capital altering the nature of democracy and capitalism through new rules, protocols, and understandings.

When Baker and Stoltenberg eventually met at Frankfurt for one hour and then were joined by Pöhl over a two-hour lunch on October 19, none had any inkling of what was dawning on Wall Street. After some talk with Stoltenberg about German banks' participation in managing the LDC debt process, Baker, Stoltenberg, and Pöhl got down to the business of improving relations. Baker's tone was conciliatory. He did not repeat his public criticisms of the prior days.

Baker wanted two things: first, the Bundesbank to roll back its interest rate increase of October 14; second, flexibility to lower the Louvre's dollar/DM range.

"It's my impression that the Central Bank Council is not likely to increase interest rates again in the near future," Pöhl said. "The Council will meet on Thursday and can discuss a rollback in rates then."

"No," Baker replied, making clear he wanted a cut *before* the meeting.

Pöhl finally offered that the seven-man Bundesbank directorate in Frankfurt in charge of daily executive operations might be able to accommodate Baker with a gesture without consulting the full Council.

Baker agreed and left it for Greenspan to follow up. Next day the Bundesbank did a fixed rate tender offer for Repos at 3.8 percent, down a fraction from 3.85 percent.

Baker didn't win Stoltenberg's consent to redefine a lower dollar/DM range, however, because Stoltenberg didn't want to penalize German exporters with a stronger DM or to let Baker out of his Louvre commitments so easily. "It's not a bilateral matter," he told Baker. "We must include the G5."[64]

When the meeting broke up and Baker reboarded his airplane for Sweden, it was still only morning in New York. The stock market was down sharply, but the crash was not yet evident. Pöhl went home to dress for a state dinner for French President François Mitterrand in Bonn. Before leaving, he called Vice President Schlesinger. "I settled it. We've made a 'peace for our time,' " he said, sketching in the details.

When Pöhl left, the Dow was down around 120. A few hours later he was called out of the dinner by a telephone call from Deputy Finance Minister Hans Tietmeyer. "Why are you disturbing me here?" he asked, slightly annoyed.

Tietmeyer was still in his office. "I'm looking at my Reuters monitor. The Dow Jones Index is down five hundred and eight!"

"Don't worry. It's got to be a technical problem with your monitor. It's not possible. Just a few hours ago it was down only a hundred and twenty."

Pöhl says now, "I honestly didn't believe it was possible. I had never heard of such a thing. The next day I got in touch with Alan Greenspan."

When Baker learned of the stock market crash, he quickly called Stoltenberg. "It's terrible," he said.

"Yes, terrible," agreed Stoltenberg.

"Let's make a common statement."

Stoltenberg agreed. The statement, which reached frenzied stock traders in New York over the newswires late Monday afternoon, announced the Baker-Stoltenberg-Pöhl meeting as "very positive." It highlighted: "The parties agreed to continue economic cooperation under the Louvre Agreement and its flexible application including cooperation on exchange rate stability and monetary policies.

"They are consulting with their G7 colleagues and are confident that this will enable them to foster exchange rate stability around current levels."

BOJ Governor Satoshi Sumita, who earlier had stonewalled Fed Vice Chairman Manley Johnson's pleas for a BOJ statement of readiness to supply liquidity paralleling the Fed's own, chose instead next day to endorse the Baker-Stoltenberg statement supporting the Louvre and dollar stability.[65] It was a clear indication of Tokyo's displeasure at Baker's new dollar talk-down and the Fed's unilateral decision to cut interest rates to meet the crisis. Over the next days and weeks the BOJ's main preoccupation was dollar instability, not stock prices.

On Tuesday morning Baker linked up with Dillon Read Chairman Nicholas Brady for the flight home to Washington. Treasury Undersecretary George Gould met them at Dulles Airport. Brady accompanied them directly into an afternoon meeting at the Treasury with Fed Chairman Alan Greenspan, White House Chief of Staff Howard Baker, and Council of Economic Advisers Chairman Beryl Sprinkel.

Although the stock market had begun its Terrible Tuesday rally, the crisis was still at its most dangerous. After agreeing to hold a presidential press conference at which Reagan would announce the Brady Task Force to study the crash, the group tackled the more difficult subject of what of substance could be done to calm markets.

Howard Baker had brought two versions of a draft statement. One stressed only the White House's affirmation of the Louvre Accord and international policy coordination, after the joint Baker-Stoltenberg statement. The second, and more controversial, added the White House's willingness to compromise with Congress on budget-deficit reduction.[66] All knew that the one thing that would most settle markets, and assuage G7 allies, was a major cut in the budget deficit. Calls were pouring into the White House and Treasury from business and financial leaders, urging Reagan to compromise on his intractable no tax increase position to break the five-year impasse with the Congress. Yet this met strong resistance to any tax increase from "ideologues" Budget Director James Miller and Beryl Sprinkel, as well as from Reagan himself.

The "pragmatist" Bakers and Greenspan bet that the crisis offered a rare chance to galvanize meaningful action. They drafted a paragraph for Reagan declaring his readiness to enter budget-deficit negotiations with Congress in which "everything" would be on the table. At 3:45 P.M. the two Bakers, Greenspan, and Sprinkel moved across the Treasury garden to meet the president at the White House residence. Greenspan emphasized that the banking and credit system was the weak link through which the crash could spread into economic disaster. By 4:30 P.M. Reagan acquiesced uneasily. "He was willing to compromise," says Howard Baker, who would chair the "budget summit." "A meaningful negotiation is what he wanted."

After the meeting Reagan walked the the South Grounds of the White House and announced the U.S. and other nations' commitment to the Louvre policy cooperation and the call for a budget summit.

Wall Street reacted with mild favor. But it all had been said too many times before to have much credibility in quelling the immediate panic. At best it was a support prop for the policy actions that mattered most—those of the central bankers.

Chapter 20

Markets Revolt

Alan Greenspan opened channels to the international central bank network on Terrible Tuesday, October 20. He and Karl Otto Pöhl discussed, among much else, the Bundesbank's monetary relaxation gesture promised to Baker the day before.

But as U.S. interest rates fell sharply in response to the Fed's emergency injection of lender of last resort liquidity, world markets and governments' attention turned nervously to Frankfurt on Thursday, October 22. Would the nationally focused Bundesbank Council do more to help contain the unfolding crisis in financial markets beyond its borders?

Before the 9:30 A.M. start of the Central Bank Council meeting, Gerhard Stoltenberg's limousine drove up the long inclined driveway to the squat glass-and-concrete Bundesbank building. Invoking his infrequently exercised prerogative as finance minister, Stoltenberg took the elevator to the thirteenth-floor boardroom to attend the secret deliberations.

The Council meeting opened as usual with comments from Pöhl, who recounted the October 19 meeting with Baker and Stoltenberg. Pöhl explained the directorate's decision to take the exceptional liberty of reducing, on its own, the Repo rate: "Baker caused the crash. We reacted to it."[1] Although he didn't think the crash would effect Germany dramatically, he said, the Bundesbank was under great pressure from the world community and Chancellor Kohl to cooperate with the global crisis-fighting effort.

Next to speak was Vice President Helmut Schlesinger. His analysis of monetary and economic developments framed the policy debate. Strictly in domestic terms, he said, there was no need from the crash to ease policy. But it was still too soon to judge the longer-term recessionary risks.

The meeting proceeded, as usual, with other directors' reports on developments within their purview. Before opening the discussion to statements around the table by Council members, the "guest," Stoltenberg, was invited to speak. Stoltenberg urged, for the sake of international cooperation, an interest rate cut. "The earlier interest rate increases were a mistake." To some he seemed to be supporting Baker and blaming the Bundesbank. "Stoltenberg was shaken by the crash," says Council member Norbert Kloten. "He is no economist. He believed more and more that politicians could determine the markets. He was convinced by the international meetings."

Stoltenberg's call for lower interest rates excited divisions within the Council. Those, like directorate member Claus Köhler, who had opposed the earlier tightening, looked across the boardroom at Schlesinger and pointed fingers. "We told you! You shouldn't have done it! We need this cooperation, and you are the one who raised rates! Now we must cooperate." Others spoke in support of Stoltenberg's plea as well.

"I remember vividly that Köhler was concerned and Stoltenberg was even more concerned than Pöhl," says Wilhelm Nölling, president of the *Länder* Central Bank of Freien and Handestadt at Hamburg, who was one of the most worried about the need to restore confidence. One Council member suggested cutting the discount rate by .25 percent. No one took it up. "We felt strongly," says Kloten. "No more acceptance of agreements such as the Louvre."

"There were those skeptics of cooperation in the Bundesbank who were ready to chime in, 'We always said it wouldn't work,' " recounts Stoltenberg of the morning's debate. "Some were disappointed with the Louvre rates 'forever.' "

Anger at Baker for "bashing" the Bundesbank also hardened the majority against any immediate easing. Hard-liners nevertheless conceded that the psychological uncertainty caused by the crash, and the "responsibility to central bankers internationally," was sufficient to warrant a softer line.[2]

Before voting, Pöhl summed up the issues and policy options. The vote was overwhelmingly to stop nudging up interest and to stand ready to loosen, if necessary. "Even if it were unnecessary from an objective point of view, it would have been a failure not to do it given the high unrest in the markets," explains Schlesinger.

Although Council members felt they had made a concession to cooperation, to the rest of the world "the Bundesbank seemed detached from the international financial crisis, totally in a vacuum," says the Fed's Manley Johnson. "There was a perception that they might even *tighten,* with unforeseen consequences."

Within Germany, conservative supporters also criticized that "it was not an excellent policy of the Bundesbank before or after the crash."[3] The Panel of Economic Experts, which feared the crash would trigger a U.S. recession that would radiate to Germany, also thought "the Bundesbank should have reacted earlier and stronger to increase money volumes."[4]

A roar of international criticism at the Bundesbank's failure to lower rates on October 22 was touched off by a new dollar plunge and fresh EMS currency crisis. To everyone's relief and brief perplexity, the dollar at first had rallied in response to the Fed's aggressive liquidity injections after Black Monday. "I felt it was very strange that the yen was stable after Black Monday—I thought the dollar would go down," says ex–MOF Vice Minister Tomomitsu Oba. "The reason was that U.S. institutional investors sold Japanese equities [and converted the yen proceeds into dollars]—almost two billion dollars a day on average. This was like massive intervention to support the dollar." The dollar also benefited temporarily from being a safe haven as world money.

But when the initial shock wore off, global investors again began focusing on world interest rate differentials. U.S. short- and long-term rates had fallen farthest because of the Fed's last resort lending. The renewed dollar plunge presented the Fed with a dilemma: tighten policy to prevent a dollar free-fall or remain loose to fight financial crisis and recession. This dilemma threatened to become catastrophic in the weeks ahead if the precrash bond-dollar linkage reemerged to drive up bond interest rates.

Picking Up the Pieces

On October 27, with the dollar plunging closer toward its Louvre floor of DM 1.73, Jim Baker and Gerhard Stoltenberg called each other again.

"Let's find ways to cooperate," Baker urged during the long conversation. The postcrash U.S. budget "summit" that Reagan reluctantly endorsed was just convening. Baker hoped to use it to extract expansionary steps from Germany. "The market needs a signal that we have a common position how to handle the situation."

Stoltenberg concurred. But he reiterated that it be done within the G5 and the G7.

"That's fine," said Baker. "But let's do the negotiation at the ministerial level." It would be up to each finance minister to bring along his central banker. Baker, in short, was trying to work around the more reluctant central bankers, especially Pöhl.

Although agreeing, Stoltenberg warned, "Karl Otto Pöhl is skeptical. Without him you know I'm not in a position to make full commitments."[5]

Soon after the conversation, Stoltenberg initiated contact with G7 European finance ministers. Baker later did the same with Japan and Canada.

Stoltenberg's contacts included two secret meetings. The first, a European G5, was at Stoltenberg's home with the U.K's Nigel Lawson, France's Edouard Balladur and their deputies, Geoffrey Littler, Jean-Claude Trichet, and German State Secretary Hans Tietmeyer. The second meeting was held at the time of an EcoFin meeting at Brussels, seat of the EC, and added Finance Minister Giuliano Amato and deputy Mario Sarcinelli of G7 member Italy.

Over the ensuing weeks the main negotiations were conducted by telephone between Baker and Stoltenberg, who represented the European finance ministers, with deputies Mulford and Tietmeyer listening in. Each negotiated separately with their central bankers. Baker brought in Japanese Finance Minister Miyazawa subsequently.

Although they concurred that markets would react badly if G7 policies appeared to be in disarray, none of the European ministers was enthusiastic about a new G7 accord. The Louvre had become a political target for causing the crash. Policy coordination, moreover, had flopped for U.S. allies by failing to discipline the outsized U.S. budget deficits or provide a stout U.S. defense of the dollar. The United States still cooperated only when convenient.

As the dollar fell through its Louvre floor of DM 1.73, with the United States making only perfunctory effort to arrest it and Treasury officials making off-the-record hints that they wished to rebase the dollar at a lower level, Baker again seemed to be unilaterally changing the rules. Balladur told colleagues that after the crash he considered the Louvre to have been broken by the United States.

The dollar's plunge accelerated after an angry October 28 outburst by Jacques Delors, the French president of the EC: "The Louvre agreements are going to suffer very much in the coming days. The Americans, having been unable to get a commitment for more growth in Europe, will be putting pressure on reducing the rate of the dollar. . . . Let us not have any illusions. The Americans are prepared to let it fall to DM 1.60."[6] Delors's comment was in part fomented by strong selling pressure on the French franc as dollar investors fled preferentially into the DM. Despite massive intervention by the Bank of France, the franc slid toward its ERM floor.

To avert a new EMS crisis, both Balladur and Stoltenberg wanted to steady the dollar. Lawson, too, desired a stable dollar now that the U.K.'s monetary policy response to the stock market crisis was constrained by sterling's DM 3 shadow and to stem the U.K.'s huge porfolio losses on the dollar reserves it had amassed previously.

At Stoltenberg's home, the European ministers concurred that if policy coordination were reactivated, they didn't want to repeat past mistakes. It was better not to meet at all than to meet and fail to deliver substance, they agreed. "We said that if we failed within a critical time to deliver after issuing a statement, the credibility of the cooperation process would be finished," says Stoltenberg.

The ministers knew that markets, which were already speculating obsessively about a new G7 action, would surely test them. For this reason Lawson especially was cautious about adopting any inflexible new dollar range. Lawson was likewise the most vociferous in insisting that any new agreement come with a new U.S. policy.

Stoltenberg told Lawson and Balladur he thought that Baker would accept delivery of U.S. budget deficit cuts up front as the precondition for a new G7 accord.

Lawson, however, also wanted a *guarantee* that this time the United States would honor its agreement to defend the dollar. Either he wanted the United States to issue foreign currency–denominated "Reagan bonds"—a reassurance that over the longer run, the United States wouldn't simply inflate away its dollar-denominated foreign debt—or he expected to receive Baker's pledge to raise U.S. interest rates, if necessary. "If they'd had more conviction that we were really going to do something about the deficit, they might have been less vocal about monetary policy," admits Gould. Lawson shared his fellow ministers' criticism of the relatively tight policy stance of the Bundesbank, which he exhorted publicly a week after the crash to "show more obvious awareness" of the dangers.[7]

With Lawson leaning toward a wait-and-see position on a new G7 accord and Balladur favoring more active support, the decisive influence belonged to Stoltenberg.[8] The crash altered Stoltenberg's political calculus by slashing Germany's official growth forecast for 1988 to 1.5 percent; privately he expected only 0.5 percent. The government's cornerstone budget-deficit reduction policy faced a major setback, with projected deficits rising in 1987 and 1988. "Stoltenberg was scared that falling growth meant lower tax revenue and the loss of political credibility," says one ally. "With the impact of the falling dollar on business investment, it could have been a calamity."

Stoltenberg thus favored negotiating with Baker for the G7 to swing into action. With the approval of the the European ministers, he acted expeditiously to do so.

"The Germans became infinitely more cooperative after the crash. Stoltenberg became a very different person. He just became frightened. You *saw* the difference," says Treasury Undersecretary George Gould, adding, "The reason I'm optimistic on cooperation is that they have a self-interest in not having us collapse."[9]

Baker readily accepted Stoltenberg's proposition of a credible U.S. budget deal as a precondition for any new G7 package, though he insisted that Germany deliver some further growth stimulus as well. He vehemently rejected defending the dollar through higher interest rates or Reagan bonds. At one point he told Stoltenberg that if he "tried to put U.S. monetary policy on the agenda, there'd be no G7 meeting."[10] Bundesbank President Pöhl also opposed Stoltenberg's effort "to put U.S. monetary policy on the table because it would effect us, too."

The finance ministers postponed tackling the dollar range rebasing issue until the United States delivered on its budget-deficit reduction pledge. In the meantime, they'd acquiesce to market reality and temporarily suspend the Louvre ranges. They'd simply try to prevent a disorderly fall.

Over the next weeks Baker's energy was consumed by the budget summit negotiations with Congress. He grew excited that for the first time he might have a real political opportunity to do something substantive about the deficit. At a stroke, that could stabilize financial markets, ease world economic imbalances, and underpin growth through the 1988 elections. The "crisis" budget negotiations produced a tentative accord on November 20. Concluding the final pact dragged on another month to December 22. But that pact was swiftly condemned as having been achieved through "accounting tricks . . . and clever maneuvering, not through serious, painful cuts in spending."[11] Nevertheless, Baker believed at the time that he was negotiating deficit reduction that "we actually felt was real, even if it looked in hindsight like a joke."[12]

Over the weeks following Baker and Stoltenberg's October 27 phone call, meanwhile, several versions of draft accords were sent back and forth between Bonn and Washington. Stoltenberg kept Baker apprised of the progress he was making in his negotiations for easier monetary policy from the Bundesbank.

To the annoyance of his fellow ministers, Baker vacillated between expressing support for dollar stability and hinting that he wouldn't mind seeing the greenback fall farther. "Jim Baker tended to be ambivalent," Lawson remembers. "Basically he believed in exchange rate stability. But he wanted to be able to use the threat of depreciation to bring the Germans into line and, to a lesser extent, the Japanese." Lawson kept the pressure on Baker through public jawboning of his own: "It is, indeed, ironic that an apparent unwillingness of the United States to raise interest rates because of an exaggerated fear that this might tip the economy into recession has led to the collapse on Wall Street, whose recessionary threat is very much greater."[13]

But Baker did not relent. Balladur recalls, "Baker said many times on the telephone that we shouldn't do anything that will break U.S. growth, so don't stabilize [the dollar] too quickly. I said, 'Beware! The last time there was a stock market crash a Republican was president, and the Republicans lost power for twenty years.'"

Bringing Along the Central Bankers

The renewal of finance minister negotiations for a new G7 accord returned the spotlight to the central bankers—above all, the Bundesbank. Stoltenberg acted as point man for an intense campaign that finally forced the Bundesbank to trim interest rates.

The first breakthrough came through pressure from France. Balladur viewed the fresh rumors of an impending ERM realignment as a challenge to his cornerstone "hard franc" policy. At one point near the end of October, French authorities were in a "panicked state of mind" around 2:30 P.M. as the market swallowed their reserves as fast as the Bank of France pumped them in to keep the plunging franc within its ERM band. Unexpectedly the pressure broke. But France's currency reserves were badly depleted.[14] By October 29 the dollar was DM 1.72; by November 10, despite concerted G7 intervention, it hit DM 1.65. Against the yen, it fell from ¥145 to ¥133.

Instead of intervening or lowering interest rates to stabilize the ERM, the Bundesbank lent about DM 12 billion ($7.7 billion) to help finance France's intervention.[15] Yet French, and most European, officials were outraged that the Bundesbank hadn't intervened directly or cut interest rates. When the EC Monetary Committee met on October 30 and 31, its members angrily demanded that the Bundesbank undertake a more symmetrical amount of the burden sharing. Even the Dutch, normally stalwart German allies, attacked the Bundesbank's "benign neglect."

The French suspected that the Bundesbank was again trying to force another ERM revaluation of the DM, despite their declaration that the January 1987 realignment would be the last ever. Balladur reminded Stoltenberg of his January 1987 warning to again let the franc fall to the bottom of its ERM margin to compel mandatory Bundesbank intervention if the Bundesbank didn't desist. "He was extremely furious," recalls Deputy Finance Minister Jean-Claude Trichet.

The Bundesbank, which believed that the January 1987 "realignment should have gone 1 percent more than it did," indeed wanted to realign.[16] Unlike January 1987, however, French protests persuaded the German Finance Ministry against revaluation. Deputy Finance Minister Hans Tietmeyer explains, "From a purely German point of view, realignment is the best solution. But I understood the French were not willing because they'd lose credibility with the market with two major effects. One, the import of inflation could undermine their wage policies. Two, interest rate differentials in the EMS would widen again and they'd lose all they gained.

"So I said, 'Should we push their country down again?' Short-term realignment was in our interest. But long term reestablishing the credibility of French policy was in our interest even more. So the government didn't push it."

Balladur was blunter: "The Germans remembered what happened in January 1987. The lesson was learned. The 'stick' had to be used only once."

The final showdown came at one of the most extraordinary Bundesbank Council meetings in history on November 5. Unusually, Stoltenberg attended again for a consecutive time. Unprecedented was the open telephone line to

Paris in a room outside the boardroom over which coordinated interest rate moves were negotiated.

"The uncertainty in European and world financial markets is continuing," Stoltenberg warned Council members. "The risks are more serious and could snowball downward."[17] West Germany faced an emergency: The Bundesbank had to cut interest rates for the sake of good relations with Europe and the United States, to calm markets, and to reduce the threat of recession. He urged the political importance of doing so even if it went against their better economic judgment.

Stoltenberg also alluded to Baker's attack on the "Schlesinger clique" of anti-inflation zealots, which had become public a few days earlier. Oddly for a man of long experience around politics, Schlesinger was personally hurt that neither Pöhl nor Stoltenberg defended him publicly. The German press, in which the story became a sensation (in the United States it went unnoticed), however, rallied to him with nationalistic fervor. "Mr. Baker has made a mistake here," admitted Stoltenberg. "Others, however," he added in pointed reference to Bundesbank hard-liners, "have made mistakes, too."[18] In his opening remarks, Pöhl had called Baker's words "a provocation."

Most of the debate centered on how to halt the capital flows destabilizing the franc's ERM parity. Stoltenberg made it clear that a DM revaluation was out of the question. The rules of the game in the recent Basel-Nyborg agreement called for coordinated interest rate moves once the perimeter defense of short-term financing for intervention was exhausted. But which country should adjust rates? By how much?

In principle, who should adjust depended on whose policies were mainly creating the crisis. Actual adjustment turned on naked power politics. "The French were blaming us for Black Monday," remembers Council member Norbert Kloten. "One of the consequences was that the DM was stronger in the EMS. So they constructed a causality. While the meeting was going on, there was the open phone. The question became 'How much should we lower interest rates?' "

Once a Council consensus had been reached, Stoltenberg and Pöhl negotiated with Governor Jacques de Larosière and Balladur in Paris on the open phone. They agreed that the Bundesbank would reduce its Lombard rate by .25 percent if France increased by .75 percent. The Bundesbank also reduced its Repo rate from 3.8 percent to 3.5 percent. England and Switzerland later enlisted in the coordinated interest rate moves.

French officials were very satisfied, despite having accepted a larger adjustment. November 5 came to be regarded by them as a model of coordinated monetary policy. Just getting the question "Who adjusts?" debated seriously was a victory for France: it helped mitigate the disappointment that the asymmetric investor preference for the DM had reemerged despite

French liberalization and hard franc policies. The fact that France actually got the Bundesbank to cut rates at all suggested that Bundesbank hegemony over the EMS was eroding.

The market was stunned. Expectations were altered. Although the dollar soon again came under severe attack, the ERM remained stable. France had demonstrably gained a point of market credibility at the Bundesbank's expense.

Against the Bundesbank's will, the pace toward European monetary union quickened after November 5. The victory emboldened French Minister Balladur to launch a proposal for European monetary union, which generated an unexpected German political bandwagon led by Foreign Minister Genscher and resulted in the charging of the Delors Committee of central bank governors and "wise men" to map out the blueprint for EMU (economic and monetary union) and the creation of a single European central bank. Eventually this was codified in the Maastricht Treaty.

An unexpected coup d'état of Bundesbank independence was nearly pulled off in January 1988 when French President Mitterrand at the eleventh hour insisted, and German Chancellor Kohl seemed to accept, that the joint Franco-German military and finance council the two nations were negotiating be signed not as a simple intergovernmental agreement, but as a full-fledged treaty—legally superseding the Bundesbank law. The Bundesbank, which was blindsided by the initiative, would be obliged to follow the monetary policy directives of the bilateral finance council on which it had only one of three German seats. Amid recriminations between the Bundesbank and German Foreign and Finance Ministries, and in an atmosphere of political crisis, Bundesbank President Karl Otto Pöhl scrambled to mobilize just enough political support in the Parliament to stall ratification. With more difficulty than expected, a compromise to protect its autonomy was worked out in the autumn 1988.[19]

"Basically, beautiful French tactics terrorized the Bundesbank," sums up S. G. Warburg economist David Mars.

The Bundesbank easing suited all Germany's G7 partners. "French initiatives in Europe serve the useful function of pushing the Germans to their international responsibilities," points out Brookings Institution Guest Scholar Robert Solomon.

The Bundesbank's November 5 easing helped steady the dollar. But it was quickly overtaken by Baker's renewed assertion that the United States wouldn't defend the Louvre ranges at the expense of recession and his blame of the Fed's September monetary tightening for the crash.[20]

Talking down the dollar and scapegoating the Fed may have alleviated the political pressures on Baker in Washington. But they counterproductively constricted Greenspan's narrow margin with markets to steer monetary policy between the Charybdis of recession and the Scylla of dollar free-fall. On November 10 the dreaded triple fall in the dollar, bond prices, and stock prices reemerged for the first time since just before Black Monday. Tokyo stocks plunged below their Black Tuesday lows.

With the world edging closer to renewed financial crisis, the central bankers gathered for their monthly Basel meetings from November 8 to 10. The attention of an unusually large press corps led them on November 9 to issue an exceptional G10 communiqué projecting solidarity and confidence that they had matters under control.

Privately the central bankers weren't so sure. The governors queried Greenspan about his and Baker's attitudes toward the dollar and the G7 negotiations. Greenspan stressed that he personally wanted a strong dollar and stood solidly with the central banker brotherhood against any rigid reference ranges. He did not press Pöhl or Sumita for interest rate cuts to support the dollar. Greenspan said that he believed that market forces would likely stabilize the dollar on its own. But he was alert to the danger that matters could snowball out of control if the bond market-dollar linkage returned or the stock market crashed anew. "At some point the bond market would have sold off in response to the falling dollar," says Fed Vice Chairman Manley Johnson. "Then we would really have been in the soup."

The central bankers also pondered how the stock market crash might alter the international flow of capital. A capital flow interruption could make the dollar free-fall nightmare an instant reality. One worrisome sign was that foreign investors had become large net equity sellers in most countries. Japanese capital was staying home.

Central bankers also discussed whether the crash would lead to another Great Depression. U.S. monetarists were incanting that the dramatic 1987 fall in the M2 aggregate heralded recession. Although the Fed dismissed it as another technical aberration, most other mainstream economic forecasts were also gloomy. Only a few central bankers, led by the BOJ, entertained that the crash might beneficially cool the inflation expectations behind the spiraling autumn interest rates.

Any sanguine view, however, started with arresting the dollar's fall. In their communiqué the governors signaled their willingness to cooperate with the new G7 effort to stabilize the dollar—provided governments went first with fiscal policy. The next morning, November 10, Jim Baker asked Reagan to issue a statement supporting the dollar. Later that day Reagan used democratic governments' highest political pulpit to emphatically declare to rioting financial markets that the United States did not want to see any additional dollar decline. The dollar gained a brief respite. Yet the central bankers departed Basel with an insecure foreboding that a dollar showdown lay ahead.

Over the next several weeks, they eased monetary policy.

• • •

Most significant was another, very grudging, interest rate cut by the Bundesbank. This time the irresistible triumvirate of domestic, European, and worldwide political pressures aligned against it was led by domestic German fears of recession. Soon after the crash and renewed dollar slide, there was a loud chorus of calls for economic stimulus, most notably from Economics Minister Martin Bangemann of the swing Free Democrat Party, Germany's Panel of Economic Experts, and jointly from the five leading economic institutes. This catalyzed one key November meeting, chaired by Bangemann, in Chancellor Kohl's office, at which Germany's top economic policymakers, including Pöhl and Schlesinger, debated: "What can we do to keep the economy growing and to meet the demands of 'some'—French—people? We discussed ideas for a small program."[21]

The problem was political inflexibility. "We talked to Kohl, to the Finance Ministry, and to Otto Schlecht, the strong man at the Economics Ministry," recalls then Economic Expert Helmut Hesse. "They couldn't do very much. Fiscal policy has lost its flexibility; it is not possible in a democracy to change it. You could only reassure the public that all was under control. The only tool left is monetary policy."

Schlesinger spent much time in Bonn to repel pressure on the Bundesbank to go beyond its November 5 cuts. Futilely he insisted that any stimulus package tackle Germany's core structural rigidities and reduce business taxes.

At the November 19 Central Bank Council meeting, Pöhl described the political pressure from Bonn, Paris, and Washington as well as his dissatisfaction with the economic debate in Bonn. In view of the need for flexibility to react to the uncertain environment, he asked the Council to grant unusual, intermeeting discretionary authority to the directorate to lower the Repo rate from 3.5 percent to as low as 3.2 percent. Reluctantly, enough *länder* representatives agreed to muster a narrow majority.

When the tentative U.S. budget summit accord was reached, the Bundesbank directorate on November 24 lowered its Repo rate to 3.25 percent. France and the Netherlands concerted with their own interest rate cuts.

But the political pressure on the Bundesbank did not abate. Stoltenberg was in a double negotiation for a domestic package and with Baker for a new G7 accord. At last a domestic German deal came together: a mostly symbolic DM 21 billion ($12.7 billion), below-market interest rate investment loan program was the centerpiece. The substance came from a Bundesbank discount rate cut to a historic low 2.5 percent.

The December 2 decision to cut the discount rate was as tortured as any the Bundesbank ever made. "There was very much divided opinion for and against," recalls Kloten. "At the time were were still expecting a tough quarter. It was a misprognosis. The feeling was, Should we do something for Black Monday or not? There was political influence." Some came personally from Chancellor Kohl. Nor could the Council ignore the late November outbreak of a new run on the dollar to an all-time low of DM 1.63. U.S. bond and stock markets plunged in sympathy.

Although Pöhl argued in favor of the cut, "I didn't feel comfortable. But we came under heavy political pressure to not be the bad guy."[22] Mindful of having been outvoted in September and about being suspected by council colleagues of bending to political pressure, Pöhl warned Stoltenberg that such an action was his absolute limit. "I can't have a losing vote again in the Council or I'll lose my credibility. Either I defend the Bundesbank, which I have to lead, or I have to resign."

"Don't exaggerate,"[23] Stoltenberg replied. "If the Bundesbank is not ready to continue with reasonable international cooperation, those politicians in Paris and Brussels who want to abolish independent national central banks and transfer the responsibility for monetary policy to a new European institution will be successful."

European central banks quickly followed the Bundesbank's discount rate move with interest rate cuts of their own. The U.S. Treasury, eager to later represent the German stimulus package as part of a new G7 accord, announced its "delight" and highlighted the Bundesbank's discount rate cut. Privately the Treasury, like most German and foreign economists, was tepid. Anticipating that U.S. pressure would switch to Japan, Governor Satoshi Sumita preemptively declared that the BOJ would not follow the Bundesbank in lowering its discount rate.

The December 2 package put in place the German side of the G7 accord. By the beginning of December Baker and Stoltenberg had worked out the basic terms and language. But agreement on new dollar levels was missing. Still undelivered was the final U.S. budget-deficit reduction deal.

Pöhl spent the bargaining chips earned by the Bundesbank's interest rate cuts to shape the G7 negotiation. He had first publicly outlined his basic conditions during a New York speech on November 2. Stressing that the Louvre had completed its exclusively short run mission of stabilizing the dollar in order to help the United States avoid higher interest rates and inflation, and its partners to overcome sluggish growth, Pöhl stated that any future cooperation had to be clearly recognized as a nonbiding, ad hoc "process" that respected the economic policy limitations of each country. This time governments had to deliver on overdue fiscal and structural adjustments *first*. "The capability and willingness of leading central banks to act as firemen when world financial markets start to burn has its limits," he warned. "The fire engines cannot move unless governments cooperate closely on general economic policy."[24]

In private bargaining Pöhl extracted several specific concessions. First, the U.S. Treasury once and for all had to accept the Bundesbank's interpretation that all EMS currency intervention, not Germany's alone, counted in the tripolar burden-sharing accounting. Second, Pöhl wouldn't discuss any new dollar levels without the full participation of Alan Greenspan. Pöhl knew the exchange rate negotiations were going to be hard, and he wanted allies. "Alan is ever cautious and reluctant to say anything, but I'm convinced he has the same view as I have about intervention—that you can use it once in a while, but that it is no substitute for credible fiscal and monetary policy."

Although Baker kept Greenspan informed about the G7 negotiations, the many hours Greenspan spent collaborating with Pöhl enhanced the Fed chairman's leverage in shaping U.S. positions. Greenspan, like Pöhl, was determined to avoid any monetary policy commitment to defend the dollar. He believed the the zero-sum nature of foreign exchange markets meant that the dollar would stabilize on its own, unless U.S. bond or equity prices also crashed in sympathy.[25]

The "Son of Louvre" Accord

Yet an ominous pattern of just such parallel linkages started to develop in late November and early December, when the dollar came under the most serious pressure since Black Monday. The New York Stock Exchange fell to its lowest level since the October 19 crash. London fell 4.4 percent. Most worried of all were Japanese authorities. "The dollar trouble became *really* serious in late November," says MOF Vice Minister for International Toyoo Gyohten. "It affected the stock market."

The dollar attack was exacerbated by the small scale of supportive U.S. intervention and waning market expectations that a G7 meeting would be held before year-end. Another problem was dollar *sales* by the Bank of England. Motivated by a desire to prevent a buoyant sterling from rising through its DM 3 shadow peg as well as to cap the losses on its official dollar holdings, Nigel Lawson decided to diversify into DM reserves. But when bank officials, following EMS protocol, asked the Bundesbank's permission to buy DM, the Bundesbank, annoyed at Lawson for shadowing the DM without joining the ERM, refused. Lawson was furious. Protocol required that approval not be withheld unreasonably. Since there was no threat to the ERM, he ordered the bank, "Go ahead and buy them anyway."[26] Meanwhile Fed officials remonstrated effetely about the U.K.'s dollar sales to the bank, which itself didn't like Lawson's policy.

On December 10 the bottom nearly fell out. Within a few minutes of an announcement that the U.S. trade deficit in October had worsened to a record $17.6 billion, the dollar gapped downward by 2 percent. U.S. long-term interest rates leaped to their highest levels since Black Monday. The stock market plunged. Central banks intervened aggressively; the Bundesbank took the unusual step of confirming it was doing so. Yet by December 14 the dollar had fallen to DM 1.63 and ¥128. Private citizen Paul Volcker spoke up that the dollar had fallen too far—it was threatening new inflation in the United States and renewed recession abroad.

On December 14 Alan Greenspan and Vice Chairman Manley Johnson joined Jim Baker, George Gould, David Mulford, and Assistant Treasury Secretary Charles Dallara in the Treasury Secretary's conference room to review the draft communiqué sentence by sentence and to brainstorm the outstanding issues. Negotiations over exchange rate levels had been going on since early December. Neither the Europeans nor Japanese were willing to accept a permanent dollar rebasing or a new range. The U.S. Treasury, on the other hand, continued to favor numerically elaborated ranges and mechanisms.

To make an accord meaningful, *some* numerical parameters had to be used. The G7 talked around all sorts of numbers and soft range concepts, including widening the DM/dollar range to 5 percent and 10 percent, as the yen/dollar range had been widened in April 1987. They discussed possibilities of countering trends and different zones within which intervention and consultations might occur—nothing hard or binding, simply indications.[27] "The statement had to contain something on exchange rates, but it didn't presuppose numbers," says Geoffrey Littler, U.K. deputy minister.

However soft the numbers, there had to be some consensus of the dollar floor they'd all defend. But the dollar kept falling through each floor they discussed.

On December 14 Greenspan, supported by Johnson, suggested that the language be altered to imply an asymmetrical range in order to help get strength under the dollar. "Markets are so sensitive that even symmetry will be viewed bearishly," he argued. "We don't want it to look like a dollar rescue operation."

Greenspan also insisted, "Asymmetry implies a top." A top level was more controversial because it implied an actual range. Despite doubts that the G7 would go along, U.S. officials adopted Greenspan's recommendation.[28]

The large outstanding item holding up everything was final passage of the U.S. budget summit deficit cuts. "Its fortunes pulsated with the market," recalls Mulford. "If there was a bad day in the markets, Congress acted. On good days they tended away from action. The only way to keep it together was the tremors in the markets."

By this time Baker had persuaded a very unenthusiastic Japanese Finance Minister Kiichi Miyazawa, whom he'd contacted only after the negotiations with the Europeans were well advanced, to support a new G7 accord. Baker's tepid defense of ¥150 had doomed Miyazawa's bid for Japan's prime ministership. His dollar talk-down before and after the crash was a further political humiliation that Miyazawa was not eager to codify in another, probably equally worthless, G7 accord.

Baker enticed Miyazawa with the assurance that Japan's ¥6 trillion fiscal package fulfilled its policy coordination pledges: it need contribute no more save a "flexible"—code word for easy—monetary policy. Miyazawa relented as a temporary expedient against the recessionary shock on Japan of a dollar free-fall. "We went from stability at a certain exchange rate to stability at *any* rate," grumbles MOF Vice Minister for International Toyoo Gyohten.

Greenspan negotiated the details with Governor Satoshi Sumita. Lowering Japanese interest rates to support the dollar was not on the table; many inflation-wary BOJ officials were still uneasy at sacrificing the discount rate hike. They discussed the risk that higher Japanese interest rates could again destabilize Wall Street. Greenspan accepted Sumita's floor for the yen/dollar exchange rate—¥120. But no ceiling level was discussed. Explains one high BOJ official, "The ceiling was very delicate. If there was any admission at that time, it might have been seen by the general public that we were agreeing to a big appreciation of the yen."[29]

The prospective G7 meeting was postponed repeatedly by delays in concluding the U.S. budget summit. The Feds' Johnson recalls, "Baker wanted to issue a G7 statement *badly* before Christmas. Then he could point to the December 2 German discount rate cut and announce to the world that 'I got real substance.' "

An early, substantive statement, Baker hoped, would turn market expectations. Yet Lawson remained cool about issuing a G7 statement because the substance seemed so meager. Only when Baker persuaded Stoltenberg that he needed a statement for domestic political reasons to confirm the U.S. budget accord did Lawson relent. He told U.K. colleagues, "Okay, let's make the best of a bad job, then."[30]

But where and when to meet? In addition to the temporal uncertainty of when the U.S. budget summit would be completed, planning was hindered by G7 ministers' eagerness to get away for the Christmas holidays. Then Miyazawa maintained that it was difficult politically for him to leave Tokyo since the new MOF draft budget was going before the Diet. To G7 participants he seemed to be trying to avoid meeting by invoking a ritual excuse that had not stopped him before.

"How about Anchorage?" Baker finally suggested to Stoltenberg. "It's neutral ground, and it'll be easier for Miyazawa."

Stoltenberg agreed. But Lawson objected. "It's neutral ground all right—equally difficult for us all to get to. This is ridiculous. Let's do a communiqué without a meeting."[31] Greenspan endorsed Lawson's no meeting idea. He hoped it would diminish the fantastically inflated market expectations around G7 meetings since the Plaza—and thus soften the fallout if they weren't fulfilled.

Thus the December 22 (December 23 in Japan) G7 telephone accord came to be. That it was negotiated over the global telecommunications network without a face-to-face meeting suggested that democratic governments were in a small way adapting to the technological realities of the global financial marketplace they wanted to influence. Pundits quickly dubbed it the "Son of Louvre."

Baker rushed the G7 statement to the Treasury press corps as soon as the U.S. budget deal was completed late in the afternoon. This perplexed journalists, who found it an inconvenient hour to meet their morning edition deadlines. Those versed in G7 nomenclature immediately zeroed in on the new communiqué language in paragraph 8 signaling the asymmetry of the dollar exchange rate: "The Ministers and Governors agreed that either excessive fluctuation of exchange rates, a further decline of the dollar, or a rise in the dollar to an extent that becomes destabilizing to the adjustment process could be counterproductive. . . ."

This begged speculation of a new range. The journalists quickly ascertained that there was an explicit understanding to defend an undefined upper limit among at least "some" of the G7. They determined too that the G7 would defend the dollar at a precise floor level. At first they believed the floor was the then current market levels of ¥126.5 and DM1.63. The next day *The Washington Post's* Hobart Rowen learned that there was some undetermined amount of cushion to the floor. This was signaled by the use of the word *could* in lieu of *would*.

In fact, the actual bottom of the range was understood by participants to be ¥120 and DM 1.60. The top was the amended April 1987 G7 midpoints of ¥146 and DM 1.825. Not all, however, attached meaning to the ceiling. Nor was the range the same *kind* as the Louvre: it was expressly looser, with fewer commitments to defend, softer, and flexible. It would bend with market developments and be reviewed periodically.

One of the nonpapers summarizing the agreement describes, "The participants will hold regular consultations on financial market conditions. On the basis of these consultations they will make ad hoc decisions on exchange market interventions at levels which the participants consider appropriate under present circumstances. Intervention should be considered appropriate on the one hand if the dollar had a tendency to fall below present levels and on the other hand if it approached levels prevailing at the time of the April meeting of the Group of Seven in Washington." The nonpaper also specified an intervention war chest of up to $15 billion, divided roughly equally among Japan, United States, and Europe and covering an undefined period.

The use of the April G7 midpoints as the ceiling was a finesse of the Japanese, who never fully accepted the April rebasing. Insists the MOF's Gyohten, "There was no ceiling on December 22. The only time I agreed to a ceiling was at the Louvre. The Germans won't admit it, either."

"The Japanese might not accept a new range concept with an upper limit depending on whom you talk to, but they all agreed then," says a top U.S. Treasury official. "The Japanese had a severe psychological problem with ¥150."

As for Germany, Finance Minister Stoltenberg reports, "We agreed to some soft range parameters. This was a rather flexible notion, not fixed zones as much as trends. There was no real rebasing. We wanted the dollar to stay at DM 1.60 to 1.80. We said we had to reassess the situation from time to time. There was some room for interpretations. This was the last of the understandings on intervention."

"The December agreement was enormously subtle," says Treasury Undersecretary David Mulford. "The language of the communiqué tells the market that the ranges still exist: it kept the *impression* of a range intact. It is the answer to the Louvre, where you want reasonable stability of the exchange rate without threatening monetary policy flexibility. We don't have to agree with Pöhl, and at the same time he's not in a corner."

For the first time, the communiqué had more than a perfunctory clause on monetary policy. Citing the recent easing steps, it stressed that interest rate policy was to be aimed at growth and financial market stability. There were no specific commitments, but an "understanding" by *some* that European interest rates might eventually decline further, depending upon market conditions.

After the December 22 accord, the will for G7 activism dissipated. The U.S. Treasury alone remained earnest. Karl Otto Pöhl spoke for many central bankers when he commented soon afterward, "All we do now is sit around and dream up communiqués that serve U.S. domestic political interests and are excuses for the United States not doing anything about its deficits."[32]

Outside expert judgment was equally damning. "There is an enormous amount of rhetoric about international cooperation," says London School of Economics Professor Charles Goodhart. "But what I think happens is that the authorities in each country, when undertaking an action that they would have undertaken anyhow for their own internal reasons, claim how international-minded they are if it coincides with the perceived need of the international community. When they take action that doesn't coincide, they keep rather quiet. One would have thought that following a 25 percent collapse in equity prices worldwide, the ministers of finance with their central bankers could have agreed a worldwide cut in interest rates of one percent within one week. In practice, it dribbled out, country by country, unconcerted, uncoordinated, and rather slow. It was the reverse of cooperation."

Showdown with Dollar Free-Fall

"The half-life of announcements without policies isn't very long," Paul Volcker had remarked about the Louvre.[33] The half-life of the December 22 accord was so fleeting that it was barely measurable. After a small uptick, the dollar quickly sank. Governments' best effort had had no more than a popgun effect with markets.

A truly perilous situation was created, as market players realized that the G7 no longer stood between them and a fresh round of global crashes. Worse, the collapse of G7 credibility catalyzed fresh downward momentum, as central bankers had long feared. "They are gambling that the trade deficit will improve, that they can stabilize the dollar without raising U.S. interest rates. But that is risky," warned market economist Rimmer de Vries of Morgan Guaranty.[34]

The sinking dollar accelerated into a nosedive after CEA Chairman Beryl Sprinkel called a press conference on December 23 to pronounce that there had been no pledge in the communiqué to stabilize the dollar at a specific level. An ideological monetarist, Sprinkel believed that unless the U.S. increased money supply fast—implying lower interest rates and a lower dollar—the United States was headed for a recession.

Were Sprinkel's comments based on inside information? Not at all. "I read the statement carefully before I made those comments," he says. But they were "only based on my reading of the statement. They [Baker and his Treasury coterie] never shared this information, and I didn't have much information about what was going on."

Baker and the G7 were furious at Sprinkel's jawboning. With George Shultz's support, Baker had Sprinkel muzzled by the White House. But the damage was done.

Believing it was futile to buck a strong market trend, the Bundesbank halted its intervention. Concertation was further marred by the departure of top government officials for the Christmas holiday. As fast as the Fed and the BOJ, under orders from their Finance Ministries, kept pouring money into the foreign exchanges, it disappeared like light into a black hole.[35] Private traders fattened profits. The thin holiday trading before year-end accounting became a headlong one-way market—down. Massive uncovered dollar short positions built up.

By Monday, December 28, the dollar had fallen through the "Son of Louvre" floor of DM 1.60. As the dollar fell through ¥124, steadily sliding Tokyo stocks knifed below the psychologically important 21,000 barrier that it had staved off on Black Tuesday. The New York Stock Exchange plunged nearly fifty-seven points.

The White House rushed out a statement that any further decline in the dollar was counterproductive. The central bankers, with a conspicuous Bundesbank presence, entered the market in force the next day.

But the dollar continued to slide. At year-end it was down to DM 1.57 and ¥121. That was 14 percent and 21 percent below its Louvre levels. From its February 1985 peak, the dollar was down 55 percent against both currencies; trade-weighted, the overall dollar depreciation was 35 percent.[36] The major stock markets were dangling at loose ends close to their post–Black Monday lows. They were poised to crash again.

The world stood eyeball to eyeball with Volcker's dollar free-fall nightmare. At the Treasury, attests George Gould, "[w]e were getting very worried. When you get something going downhill, who the hell knows where it will stop? We became very market-oriented and conscious of the perceptions of the outside world."

"Baker had used the dollar as a club so long, and all of a sudden he got his worst nightmare," observes Wall Street economist David Jones. Japanese leaders too were "getting desperate."

Unless the dollar was turned soon after New Year's, the bottom could fall out.

The world's central bankers spent the New Year holidays working on an emergency action to try to rescue the world from an imminent financial and economic calamity. Their plan: a huge global squeeze of the dollar shorts for Monday, January 4, the first day traders would be back at their desks. As on Black Monday, it was time to put all the cash in the bank-front window to try to halt the dollar run. "In one sense it was defensive," says Fed international finance chief Ted Truman. "If one didn't take a fling at it in the beginning of the year, you would be picking up the pieces on January 15."

The board in Washington, and the Treasury, gave more operating discretion to the foreign exchange trading desk at the New York Fed, the plan's conceiver. The BOJ quickly signed on. Finally the Bundesbank, disgruntled by Washington's ineffective tactics, agreed to throw its prestige behind a concentrated two-day hit. As usual for concerted dollar interventions, it organized Europe.

The key to success was to reverse market expectations. With some $640 billion turning over each day in the world's major foreign exchange markets—enough to absorb all the foreign exchange reserves of the world's central banks in less than a day's trading—interventions of $1 billion to $2 billion couldn't possibly succeed by "leaning against the wind." In trader's imagery, trying to do so was the equivalent of lying down in front of a charging locomotive. However, by using their collective edge of being the largest individual players and armed with insider information on imminent official policy moves, they could, with well-timed interventions, create psychological uncertainty, then outright fear of loss, among dollar bears. By applying sufficient force to the markets' psychological pressure points, the central bankers could leverage market forces to do most of the work on its own.

"As a matter of tactics, we did not want to effect the December 22 dollar levels as much as to generate a significant rise to inspire a covering of short positions," explains New York Fed foreign exchange trading chief Margaret "Gretchen" Greene. "The idea is to force those who sold dollars in December to have to buy them back at a much higher price." Relying on her intuition, anecdotal evidence, and market gossip, Greene calculated what pain thresholds she thought would force dollar shorts to cover.

With the rising volatility and volumes of world foreign exchanges, central bankers had been trying to improve their intervention techniques by thinking and behaving more like market players.[37] Like currency dealers, most now talked to a range of big market players whose stances could converge into a trend.

Central bankers had varying degrees of reliable information about the markets. The Bank of England was privy, on a traditional, confidential basis, to many of the actual orders moving through the markets. The Fed had a pretty good reading on the foreign exchange trading position of banks, its traditionally closest constituency, but less on corporations, insurance firms, and securities houses. The most complete information was possessed by the Bank of Japan. In January 1988 "we knew the shorts. The main speculators were nonresidents."[38]

To rescue the dollar, the central bankers called upon nearly all intervention tools in their arsenal. However, their most potent weapon, higher U.S. interest rates, could *not* be deployed. Doing so could trigger the financial crisis and recession all dreaded. Their task was thus like trying to win a prizefight with only a left jab.

The central banker bear trap was sprung Monday, January 4, when the dollar opened abysmally weak in Sydney, Australia, at ¥120.25 and DM1.5615. In New York, where it was Sunday night, Fed traders were waiting with "the nervous mood of a racehorse at the starting gate, when any little movement gives a sense that the race is on," recalls Gretchen Greene.

As markets opened, Fed traders called banks in Asia, including Tokyo, to ask for price quotes on dollars. Since it was exceptional for the Fed to operate outside U.S. markets, "it scared them. They thought they saw coordinated intervention," says Greene. "It is not what happens that matters, but the perception, the human psychology aspect. The event might have turned out differently if we'd not made the calls."

For two days, January 4 and 5, the Fed, Bundesbank, and BOJ, joined by the central banks of Switzerland, Italy, Canada, and Austria, pounded the markets with high-visibility tactics.[39] Actual central bank intervention was a closely guarded secret. Currency dealers estimated that they bought $2 billion on Monday and $1.5 billion to $2 billion more on Tuesday. The BOJ was rumored to have spent $1 billion, the Bundesbank about $800 million. The Fed later reported that the United States had bought only $685 million, far less than believed.[40] Prominent press coverage amplified the effect. No one in the markets knew, in the confusion of the moment, what was really happening. But with millions of dollars of profits or losses riding on split-second decisions, the effect was powerful. "The market to a man was short of the dollar," recalls Michael Beales, chief London currency dealer at Westpac Banking and ex–Bank of England head trader. "It was very risky to leave it short over a weekend. Then the central banks came in with their big boots. There was a lot of blood in the streets. Four billion dollars is not a lot, but it was well timed for maximum psychological effect when all the dealers were back at their desks [after Christmas]."

The central bankers were unusually aggressive in trying to inflict pain on the dollar shorts. The Fed bought in lot sizes of $25 million instead of its usual $10 million. To make the interventions as "noisy" as possible, it even encouraged one bank trader to publicize its intervention in a TV interview.[41] As the dollar rose, then settled back a little, they also reentered the market at higher and higher levels. Mark Fitzsimmons of Morgan Stanley remembers the action: "They intervened at dollar/yen 120 and drove it up to 122. The market took it up to 124, then decided to sell it down to 122. At this point the Fed came in again. So here is what we saw: The Fed was in first only at 120. Now it was jumping in at 122. Also, ours is a bid/asked market. You can move it in two ways: by going in and making a bid and taking those that 'hit' your bid. Or more aggressively, you can go in and take all offers. The Fed took all offers, even at higher prices. So that ratcheted up the markets to ¥124.7."

To make a big splash on the markets, Fed Vice Chairman Johnson reveals that he, Greenspan, and the New York Fed's Jerry Corrigan and Sam Cross even considered "innovative ideas, such as intervening in the forward market."

The effects of the bear trap were spectacular: by the Tuesday close, the dollar had rebounded to ¥127.8 and 1.63 DM—or up 8.3 percent and 10.4 percent, respectively. U.S. and European financial markets surged. The New

York stock market leaped seventy-six points, or 4 percent, on Monday. Most important, long-term bond prices also rallied.

Crucially, the dollar foreign exchanges supported the dollar largely on their own thereafter until March. Solitary BOJ intervention until mid-January aided briefly, as did an unsourced report on Japanese television that the G7 accord had included a $15 billion intervention pool (accurate) to defend a range of ¥130–¥140 (inaccurate).

Market expectations, in short, had been turned. By risking their credibility, central bankers salvaged some of the tattered credibility of G7 governments. Stability in the dollar gave Greenspan precious added leeway to fight recession.

When asked about their smashing success, however, central bankers were curiously sheepish. When probed, they confessed that their success was as much a surprise to them as it was to the markets.[42]

The New Year's bear trap capped a year of historically unprecedented central banker intervention. Central bankers' substitution for fleeing private global investors helped save the plummeting dollar from Volcker's nightmarish free-fall and hard economic landing. It was empirically impossible to know at what depreciated dollar and higher U.S. interest rate levels free market private investors might have voluntarily returned to the U.S. currency. But it was in the conservative nature of central bankers, urged on by government finance ministers, to lack the sangfroid to risk finding out.

Japanese capital outflows dried up after Black Monday and began flowing again only in February 1988, after the dollar bottomed out. Foreign central bank dollar buying, and a doubling of fourth-quarter international bank lending, helped avert another of economic history's traumatic interruptions of cross-border capital flows.

The unprecedented 1987 central bank dollar intervention amounted to another of the atypical lender of last resort rescues that were becoming more commonplace with the rise of global capital. For all of 1987 central bankers acquired a record $120 billion in dollar assets. Effectively they financed almost two-thirds of the U.S. foreign borrowing needs for the year.[43] Of the secret central bank intervention, roughly $35 billion to $50 billion, or one-third to two-fifths, was concerted through the G7 process. Japan alone did one-third, or nearly $40 billion, of the total. The United Kingdom, pursuing its DM shadowing strategy for sterling in parallel, but outside the Louvre Accord, acquired about $25 billion, or one-sixth.[44]

Central bankers and finance ministers knew that the bear squeeze had done no more than borrow extra time. The dollar's fate hung on fundamental economic forces and financial market psychology. Thus all waited with bated breath for the January 15 release of the U.S. November trade figures on which markets had become singularly fixated. "We had very good luck in the markets in the early days after the bear trap," recalls the Treasury's Mulford. "Then it was a quiet, nervous period of everyone holding their breath. But there was no further attack. Then the fundamentals improved."

In the event, the U.S. trade deficit shrank sharply by 25 percent to $13.2 billion. As soon as "the number" hit Wall Street, dollar-buying pandemonium erupted on world foreign exchange markets. For the first five minutes sellers nearly disappeared completely. At day's end the dollar had soared to ¥131, up nearly 4 percent, and DM 1.69, up 3.5 percent. U.S. stocks jumped forty points, U.S. long-term bond rates fell .25 percent.

At long last the J curve effect seemed to be wearing off: U.S. manufacturing exports, booming in volume terms prior to Black Monday, were growing in dollar terms as well. U.S. consumption growth, too, was moderating. It was a key, early step in the huge resource shift that was needed to softly unwind the world external imbalances. The success of the central banker bear trap had been, for the moment, consolidated.

Trouble in Tokyo

The dollar bear trap helped avert a second, unsuspected global financial shock—a Tokyo stock market crash. The skidding dollar gave the Japanese Establishment "a lot of fear about the future trend of the equity market," says Tsuneo Fujita, director general of MOF's securities bureau. "Miyazawa and I talked about it often."

Also troubling Tokyo was the anticipated impact of regulatory changes to rein in the *zaiteku* frenzy that were to go into effect March 31, 1988. These rules stripped the tax incentives from the special investment trusts, or *tokkin* funds, used by companies to make many of their stock market speculations.[45] In mid-November the Big Four securities firms beseeched Fujita for a special exemption from the rule change. He agreed. But when he asked the MOF banking bureau to suspend the *tokkin* fund reform for financial firms, its "position was clearly 'no'. Since in early 1987 they had issued a ministerial decree, they couldn't change so easily."

To work through Japan's dense bureaucratic politics, Fujita instead sought to persuade the accountants association not to adopt the rule for nonfinancial corporate *tokkins*. The accountants were reluctant. Yet in the end, Fujita says with a bubble of laughter, "[W]e arrived at a 'sophisticated' solution: The rule would apply *after* the financial accounting year, from April 1, 1988, which means effectively one year later. The CPA association issued the rule change but added an explanation that a certain time was necessary to apply it."

Armed with the probable action by the accountants association, Fujita concurrently reapplied to the MOF bureaus responsible for banking and insurance to administer functionally equivilant "guidance" for the financial companies. They agreed.

Fujita's negotiations had begun in mid-December in a race against deteriorating stock market psychology. With panic starting to infect stock market players because of the dollar's Christmas week trouncing, Finance Minister Miyazawa called Fujita at home over the New Year's holiday to urge their rapid completion.

By January 3 Fujita's plan was finally approved by the relevant parties.

On January 4, the first work day of 1988, Fujita assembled with MOF staff at the run-down MOF offices at Kasumigaseki to exchange traditional New Year's greetings. Soon after, he joined Miyazawa, the two vice ministers, and the bureau directors general in a private meeting room. All were formally briefed about the planned dollar bear squeeze. Fujita then explained his plan for the stock market. "Excellent," Miyazawa commended. "I trust you on the timing about when to implement it."[46]

As the success of the bear trap became apparent on January 6, Fujita moved to implement the measures. The stock market celebrated with its second-largest rise in history, up 1,215, or 5.6 percent. A new bull market rally was launched. By mid-April it had surpassed its precrash levels. Within less than two years the Tokyo money machine would lift it to an astounding 39,000. "If the yen had gone on appreciating, I couldn't have done it," says Fujita, for whom grateful security industry executives jokingly suggested erecting a statue in front of the Tokyo Stock Exchange.

The danger to the dollar was not over. At the White House on January 13, 1988, new Japanese Prime Minister Noboru Takeshita alerted President Reagan that unless the dollar closed the Japanese fiscal year on March 31 above ¥127, Japanese insurer losses on dollar investments would exceed the 15 percent threshold for public disclosure. That could trigger a massive dumping of dollars and a new dollar crisis.

The BOJ, Takeshita promised, would adhere to an accommodating monetary policy to support the dollar. But cooperative help from the United States was needed. Reagan agreed to shore up the U.S.'s yen swap lines to insure that the United States had access to sufficient yen to give concerted intervention support to the dollar.

The tone was set for the unusual bilateral diplomacy in 1988 between the Republican administration and the Japanese Establishment to avoid a dollar crisis that could upset a Republican victory in the November 1988 U.S. presidential elections.

Chapter 21

Election of a President

The dollar's narrow escape spurred a two-hour "crisis summit meeting" of top U.S. international financial policymakers at the Treasury Secretary's conference room on the afternoon of January 19, 1988. Attending the meeting were the Treasury's Jim Baker, George Gould, David Mulford, and Charles Dallara, economist Michael Darby, and the Fed's Alan Greenspan, Manley Johnson, and Ted Truman. "The question on the table," reports Gould, "was What is the right or 'natural equilibrium' level for the dollar?"

The prevailing sentiment "was that sustaining the dollar in the face of the trade figures had been a flawed effort that played into the crash. The implicit but clear consensus was that there had been risks to focusing on exchange rate stability that had not been appreciated. The key point was the need to allow the dollar to reflect the fundamentals."[1]

Yet a year after the Louvre, no one had any firm sense of what the "fundamental" value of the dollar was. All they knew for sure was that the Louvre levels had been judged wrong by markets. Imponderable too was whether huge and volatile global financial markets would respect the fundamental value even if it could be ascertained.

Many of the January 19 meeting participants were distressed that the December 22 accord ranges for the dollar had been driven by pure expediency without any theoretical analysis to justify it. Did the improvement in the trade figures four days earlier augur that the dollar was coming into line with fundamentals? they wondered. Or was it caused by something else entirely? "You could never tell," says Gould.

U.S. and G7 policymakers were adrift because even the experts didn't know. Influential ex–Reagan CEA Chairman Martin Feldstein was saying the dollar should head down toward ¥100 and DM 1.2 to reflect America's lost competitiveness and relatively higher inflation. The Fed's analysis concurred that under existing conditions, the dollar probably had to fall below its December 22 floors over time.

Yet thirty-three top economists from thirteen countries who conferred in December believed that the current level of the dollar could be adequate.[2] Still other experts, who based their analysis not on models of what it took to restore U.S. trade to balance, but upon purchasing power parities (PPP), or what it cost people from differing countries to buy the same basket of tradable products, argued that the dollar was way *undervalued!* "Global monetarist" Stanford Professor Ronald McKinnon, whose theory of fixed exchange rates through coordinated management of the de facto world money supply by the Fed, Bundesbank, and BOJ was discussed on January 19, argued the dollar should be worth about 200 yen. Based upon PPP analysis, the German Panel of Economic Experts estimated after the crash that the proper dollar/DM level was between DM 1.90 and 2.0[3]

Some academics puzzled whether the superdollar shock had permanently changed the orientation of the economic system, much like the electromagnetic phenomenon of "hysteresis," so that when the shock was removed with the dollar's fall, the former conditions did not return. Others dared suggest that the global information revolution permitting money and goods to shift rapidly among national markets was so profoundly remaking the world political economy that "there is no longer . . . such a thing as a 'natural' or 'equilibrium' exchange rate."[4]

Most experts agreed on the various supply and demand factors that drove exchange rates.[5] But there was no widely agreed model to explain why any factors predominated at any given time. "The theory of exchange rate determination is today in a shambles," sums up BIS General Manager Alexandre Lamfalussy.[6]

Without a relatively stable dollar that approximated the underlying competitive fundamentals of each nation, the postwar democratic capitalist free trade order degenerated into conceptual economic gibberish and mercantilist confrontation. Without a credible answer to the deceivingly simple question "What is the right level for the dollar?" G7 international policy coordination too was a fantasy.

The senior Treasury and Fed officials reevaluating U.S. dollar policy in January shared the pragmatic consensus that Fed monetary policy should not be geared toward defending the dollar. Baker wanted to give the Greenspan Fed what it too wanted—maximum freedom to pilot the economy away from the much predicted recession. George Bush's presidential quest hinged upon it. Yet the Fed's room to steer interest rates depended much on whether the current dollar levels would hold up. It thus remained imperative to know: What was the right value for the dollar?

The prevailing uncertainty was expressed by the Fed's Manley Johnson as he got up to leave the rambling Treasury discussion. "I think I can summarize what we've all been saying here." He threw up his hands: "Who the hell knows?!"[7]

Dissolution of the G7 Process

Baker had pressed for G7 cooperation when he thought it was consistent with lower or stable U.S. interest rates. As soon as it called for higher U.S. rates, he quietly backed away from it. This further soured foreign finance ministers on the G7 process.

"There was strong frustration in the December G7 statement," says a high Japanese MOF official. "People here are willing to take a lower standard of living to cure deficits. That is *not* accepted by people in the United States."

Agrees French Finance Minister Edouard Balladur, "We haven't solved any problems with the Louvre system." In early 1988 Balladur wrote to his G7 colleagues, urging a review to go beyond the Louvre to reform the "financial anarchy brought about by international speculative capital flows" and to create "a true international monetary system with a standard unit of value, automatic mechanisms, and sanctions that would be beyond the control of the countries involved."[8] He expounds, "We have $500 billion in foreign exchange market transactions each day, when $20 billion would be enough for industrial needs. I'm afraid there can be such disorder that the central banks are not able to control the situation. The question is, Is money a commodity like any other? If it is, let the markets play. If not, we need a system."

How did the G7 react? "I got a response of general indifference. There is a lot of complacency in the world," he laments. "It was a cry in the desert."

Baker easily deflected Balladur's call for small study group on the international monetary system at the April 1988 G7 meeting. It became a narrow study on the working of exchange rate ranges, intervention tactics, and intervention's effect on international reserves headed by the G7 Finance Ministry deputies—a group Baker could control. Putting the central bankers in charge, as some in the G7 proposed, was rejected because "the Treasury would never accede to the Fed or the Bundesbank." Instead central bank deputies were invited to the meetings on "an ad hoc basis. It was *not* implied they'd attend future meetings."[9]

Curiously, the secret meetings held in the Louvre library in September and December 1988 were hailed by participants as the most edifying of the entire G7 process. The G7 deputies reached a consensus about how best to make the ranges work. They delineated a concept of secret, flexible, soft ranges bounded by gray and black zones where concerted intervention could take place depending on market conditions, as opposed to the more rigid Louvre formula.[10] Yet the G7 deputies' consensus was not effectively translated into practice. "A consensus and a conclusion was arrived at, but *only* in that room, as it turned out," grumbles one participant. "There was backsliding on our understandings on the exchange market, by the Germans."[11]

The Greenspan Fed also disengaged from G7 dollar management. In a flip-flop, by the end of the decade it was the Treasury pressing intervention upon a reluctant Fed. "The Fed probably is less convinced of the effectiveness of intervention than the Treasury," says David Mulford. "But it is not clear if this is an intellectual difference or a concern by them on the infringement on interest rate policy."

In the wake of Black Monday and the near collapse of the dollar at year-end, Baker's G7 process evaporated into another one of the periodic ad hoc episodes of coordination from the July 1927 Long Island central bankers' meeting to relieve pressure on British gold to the 1978 Bonn summit's fiscal "locomotive." Enthusiasm remained high chiefly among a tiny band of Finance Ministry deputies.

G7 policymakers had been stumped by democratic government's political inability to adjust domestic policies for the international good. Fiscal immobility was the most obvious problem. But, over time, G7 policymakers became increasingly cognizant that the even more politically intractable microeconomic incompatibilities embedded in the structure of each major nation's political economy also had to be redressed. Assistant U.S. Treasury Secretary Chuck Dallara reviews the evolution of G7 perceptions: "Going to the Plaza, we all recognized that there had to be an emphasis on the fundamentals beyond the exchange rate. The exchange rate itself became the focus for a while. We used the period up to the Louvre to address Japan's and Germany's fundamental problems, and we got some commitments from Japan that produced their fiscal package and some smaller tax cuts from Germany. In 1987, as we developed detailed indicators, we recognized that given the inherent difficulty of all governments to adjust fiscal policy in the short term, if we wanted to avoid dangerous undue pressure on monetary policy, we needed to look at the underlying rigidities. You had to give greater weight to the structural factors.

"There was a recognition that the imbalances were in part structural. The labor markets in Europe were weighing heavily on their exchange rates. So were Japan's distribution system and its inefficient capital markets. Land use was a major handicap. Also, the *keiretsu* corporate structure added to the capital imbalance. It became increasingly obvious that we won't find a lasting solution to the current account imbalances without looking at the macro and the structural policies."

At the 1988 Toronto G7 economic summit, U.S. officials tried to insert language in the communiqué calling for redressing the structural incompatibilities. But the leaders had no political appetite for it. Instead the G7 nations turned to other avenues to pursue their political economic agendas.

"Having lost the battle for [dollar] target zones that they saw as a way to reduce Bundesbank hegemony, the French have left the question of the dollar and shifted all their political attention to European unification," notes Bank of Italy Deputy Governor Lamberto Dini. Chancellor of the Exchequer Nigel Lawson stepped up his private campaign to persuade Margaret Thatcher to bring the United Kingdom into the ERM and to underpin sterling's credibility with upgraded Bank of England independence.

Jim Baker and Kiichi Miyazawa turned toward each other. Through a U.S.-Japanese G2, they pursued their common political interest of tranquillity in the dollar and Republican George Bush in the White House. Attainment of their goals depended foremost upon the cooperative action of their central bankers.

The Soft Landing Strategy

In early 1988 the Greenspan Fed sought to balance the risks of economic depression and a new dollar crisis by adopting a "soft landing" strategy. This meant holding interest rates low enough to avoid recession and further financial fragility, yet high enough to attract just enough foreign savings into dollar assets.

When Fed policymakers thought they detected signs of economic weakness shortly after the January 19 meeting, they nudged interest rates down farther from their postcrash emergency levels. Taking this insurance was informed by the historical memory that the 1929–30 Fed had also aggressively injected liquidity following the Great Crash and that the crash had been followed by several months of recovery.[12]

In early 1988 most prognosticators believed the U.S. economy was teetering. The index of leading indicators was falling for the fourth month from October; three successive declines usually heralded recession. The monetarist Cassandras were led by Reagan CEA Chairman Beryl Sprinkel, who explains, "When I came back from vacation in August, interest rates had gone up and the money supply was tighter than hell. In trying to stabilize the dollar, they were too tight. Ultimately they changed those damned policies, but not until after the crash. After the crash the Fed played it exactly right. We avoided a recession, which is a miracle, maybe." Recalls Manley Johnson, "The monetarists and others were saying that we were in a recession and that we'd caused it. We weren't confident of the situation until the end of January."

Two days after the January 19 dollar summit meeting, and just prior to February Fed policy meeting to set the new annual money supply targets for

1988, Treasury monetarist Michael Darby sent an unusual letter to FOMC members exhorting faster money growth. When the letter was leaked, Democratic Washington and Wall Street howled. Greenspan protested privately to Baker, then parried publicly, "The only thing I hope does not happen is that the concern of our responding to political pressures gets so extraordinary that we will feel the necessity to do precisely the opposite. . . ."[13]

Yet February's economic signals were buoyant. Growth held up, led by the long awaited jump in exports. Money supply growth rebounded. In March market fears of inflationary overheating began to supersede concerns about recession. Bond market interest rates rose. This coincided with the collapse and government rescue of two huge financial institutions, First RepublicBank and Financial Corporation of America, the parent of America's largest S&L, which had nearly failed just before Black Monday. Pressure on the dollar returned.

The attack on the dollar was set off on March 7, when the United Kingdom allowed the pound sterling to rise above DM 3 without intervening.[14] Currency traders wrongly assumed that the sterling/DM 3 defense line was part of the G7 accord. When it was breached, their anxiety of disintegrating G7 cooperation was transmitted to the dollar.

Dollar markets were also unsettled by credible rumors that Japanese investors planned to dump the dollar if it started to fall. Staggering losses had transformed their investment psychology from shunning purchase of new dollar bonds to unloading them actively. Japanese investors had paid dearly for their education in becoming the world's banker; they didn't want to pay twice.

In late March, notwithstanding a good U.S. trade report, an intense attack drove the dollar below the danger threshold of ¥127 about which Takeshita had warned Reagan. Market speculation mounted nervously: Would Japanese investors dump their dollar assets ahead of the fiscal year end March 31?

MOF technocrats obviated the risk by modifying the rules. Instead of the March 31 spot exchange rate, the March average would be applied. The dollar would have to fall below ¥123 for the month's remaining few days to breach the ¥127 average.

Yet, ominously, the dollar continued to fall, hitting ¥125 on March 25. U.S. bond and stock prices plunged in response. Market players commented that the atmosphere felt just like before Black Monday. The U.S. and Japanese central banks intervened jointly on the foreign exchange markets on March 25, 28, and 29. BOJ Governor Satoshi Sumita and MOF officials publicly admonished Japanese investors against unwarranted dollar speculation. More important, the BOJ began collecting data from Japanese banks to identify which of their clients were speculating against the dollar. It was tantamount to what the MOF had done to stop the dollar run in the spring 1987—an unofficial reimposition of currency controls.[15]

Again it worked. Again Reagan free marketeers didn't protest. The dollar closed Japan's fiscal year at ¥124.5, just above the danger line.

The falling dollar and bond markets loomed large in the minds of FOMC members when they convened in the Fed boardroom at Washington on March 29 to plot the course of monetary policy for the coming six weeks. Although encouraged by the apparent robustness of the U.S. economy, the FOMC remained hesitant to push up interest rates for fear of destabilizing the fragile Texas banking system, the S&Ls, and the stock market. Nonetheless they voted to modestly tighten reserve conditions to guide the Fed Funds interest rates up from 6.6 percent to about 7 percent.

In the event, the monetarist warnings about imminent recession proved totally wrong. The economy was booming in the first quarter at a 3.9 percent annual rate. The conservative *Wall Street Journal* editorial page led the backlash with a scathing last rites of monetarism as a practical policy prescription: "The Fed's 1987 monetary policy has occurred simultaneously with a plunge in the value of the dollar and a pre-crash, nine-month run-up in the price of gold from $400 to $475. This is a 'tight' policy only if you never venture outside the M temple."[16]

Yet it wasn't just monetarists who misjudged the strength of the economy. Nearly all economists, in nearly all countries, got it wrong. Even the BOJ, which in hindsight stood out as the accurate exception in fearing overheating, underestimated the explosive force of Japan's 11.3 percent expansion in the first quarter of 1988. In the United States, Japan, and Germany, 1988 was one of the decade's growth banner years.

The market signals of rising long-term interest rates in 1987 had proven to be more accurate indicators than the experts after all. Why were the experts so wrong? The answer lay in the poorly understood workings of the changing global economy.[17] Very few had foreseen the onset of the severe 1981–82 U.S. recession or how close the world economy came to stagnation in 1986. The world economy was undergoing multiple revolutions driven by large-scale capital mobility, new technologies, the rise of poor countries up the development ladder, loosening links between the commodities and industrial production, and a loosening bond between production and employment within the industrial economies. Most economists, including central bankers, had been trained to view the economy through models that were simply obsolete.

The upheaval of basic economic relationships left central bankers without a reliable objective policy guide to discipline themselves, anchor market expectations, and make themselves clearly accountable to the democratic public. As a result, they were forced back to the seat-of-the-pants approach that had failed in the 1970s.

In early 1988 Basel central bankers began to worry that saving the dollar had pushed them too far toward monetary laxity. At the BIS on January 10 and 11 they nervously pondered whether the record 1987 explosion of international liquidity—world central bank reserves jumped 42 percent—portended a new burst of global inflation.[18] Instead of foreboding recession, they began to realize "the stock market crash was a lucky blow-off of financial asset inflation before the wealth effects spilled over into inflation generally."[19] It was nonetheless a perilously violent, market-driven way to obtain economic and expectational adjustment that deadlocked governments might have achieved more smoothly by changing policy.

One silver lining was to break the autumn 1987 interest rate spiral hysteria. This gave central bankers a second chance to stay ahead of the power curve of market inflation expectations. "We got the ball back with the crash," says Fed Governor Wayne Angell.

Another silver lining was that Greenspan's acclaimed performance baptized him as a credible successor to Paul Volcker. This gave him the opportunity to meet what he considered to be the great challenge of his chairmanship—to complete Volcker's war against inflation. "One difficulty with inflation is that you have to kick it twice," he explains. "Having a single period like the one in which Paul Volcker put the screws on runaway inflation never quite kills it, in the expectational sense."

Greenspan's March 1988 tightening launched a steady, year-long march that lifted short-term interest rates by three percentage points to almost 10 percent. "Inflation unwound in the 1980s until 1986, then started to rebound again and accelerate, especially through 1988 and 1989," says Greenspan. "We saw it quite clearly. We were leaning against it."

The Greenspan Fed moved in small, swift steps. It aimed at slow growth just below U.S. potential of about 2.5 percent. The small steps could be easily reversed if the financial system showed severe signs of distress. "What we can do within the constraints of financial fragility is gradualism," explains Vice Chairman Manley Johnson. "We can't afford extreme steps. It's too dangerous."

Greenspan's gradual tightening helped stabilize, then strengthen, the dollar. The gap with market-driven long-term rates narrowed. The flattened yield curve was a sign that the Fed was at last ahead of the inflation expectations power curve. By moving interest rates over three points, Greenspan reassured markets and established precedent for political tolerance of wide, swift swings in interest rates necessary for effective monetary policy in the global capital era. "In 1988 many felt Greenspan would be a wimp, worrying too much about the election or debt," says Aubrey Lanston Fedwatcher David Jones. "But he tightened three points in the funds rate, at a time of high real interest rates. He proved he was no wimp. He got more bang for the buck."

Wall Street was especially impressed by the coup de grace, a hike in the discount rate from 6 percent to 6.5 percent on August 9, 1988, just days before the Republican national convention nominated George Bush for president. FOMC hawks and doves had been arguing for months over the extent of the inflationary threat. The air was thick with a suspicion of partisan political intrigue. By August, nine of the twelve mostly hawkish Federal Reserve Banks, controlled by private-sector board members, were requesting increases in the discount rate. The Republican-chosen board in Washington had been turning them down for months. During the FOMC telephone conference on Friday, August 5, the Reserve Bank presidents vociferously demanded action from the board. Siding with the hawks, Greenspan persuaded the reluctant board members to go along. Their six to zero vote sent a strong signal to the bond markets that the Fed wasn't going to take chances with inflation to help Bush's election.

What Wall Street cheered, however, made Republican Washington furious. Jim Baker, about to become Bush's campaign manager, spoke to Greenspan, but there was little he could do to change the vote of the independent central bank.

Rising worldwide inflation worries also put pressure on the Bundesbank and the Bank of Japan to tighten. To avert a rerun of their simultaneous autumn 1987 effort to fight inflation, which fueled the global interest rates spiral, central bankers shared a consensus that it was "better that we move on separate schedules" and "to let call money move first and the discount rate move with a lag."

But which central bank would refrain from raising rates? The Fed couldn't. The Bundesbank wouldn't. Facing overshooting of its monetary targets for a record third straight year, the Bundesbank at the April 1988 G5 meeting petitioned unsuccessfully for a concerted defense of a DM 1.70 dollar ceiling.[20] Denied help, it dumped over $4 billion, much disguised through execution by the anonymous BIS. "The Bundesbank intervention was not supported by the others," reports a European central banker. "It was so mad that it ceased to intervene in the summer."[21] From late June the Bundesbank started rapidly pushing up German short-term interest rates from 3.5 percent to 5 percent. In early July it hiked its discount rate from 2.5 percent to 3 percent.

The United States joined the Bundesbank intervention on the foreign exchange markets on June 27 to try to cap the dollar at the December 22 ceiling, DM 1.825. But against a weakened DM, the dollar kept rebounding. On August 10, a day after the Fed raised the U.S. discount rate, the dollar burst through its old Louvre ceiling to DM 1.925.

At this point the Bundesbank ceased intervening, in part, states its president, Karl Otto Pöhl, "to demonstrate that there were was no [G7] range."

U.S. Treasury Undersecretary David Mulford flew to Frankfurt and lunched at the Bundesbank with Pöhl, Vice President Helmut Schlesinger, and Deputy Finance Minister Hans Tietmeyer—a visit that raised some eyebrows because it violated normal protocol (increasingly honored in the breach) of communication among institutional counterparts. Concerted intervention soon resumed. On August 25 the Bundesbank, in concert with other European central banks, boosted its discount rate to 3.5 percent.

That halted the dollar. Because these actions occurred with the dollar testing its previous highs of DM 1.925, foreign exchange traders erroneously concluded that the G7 dollar/DM band was now DM 1.72 to DM 1.925, which closely overlapped its old Louvre range. This faith was self-fulfilling over the next few months.

With the Fed and Bundesbank both raising interest rates, it was the BOJ that reluctantly risked inflation at home to anchor world interest rates and financial markets. "The United States is highly dependent on money from Japan, so if interest rates are higher here, then U.S. interest rates have to be higher, too," says BOJ Executive Director Akira Nambara. "That's why we must be careful not to raise our ODR [official discount rate] too sharply. It would trigger a war of interest rates in the world." One big worry of BOJ leaders in 1988 was a new U.S. stock market crash: "We didn't raise the discount rate in 1988 from the fear of fragility in the U.S. markets, not Japan," says the BOJ's Yoshio Suzuki. "That's why it then became too late for us to take liquidity out of the market. We had a too expansionary policy."

Fed officials consulted regularly with the BOJ about the most propitious timing for US interest rate hikes. "We knew what our options were," says Greenspan.

Conspiracy Theory

Many financial market players were convinced that more than ordinary Basel cooperation was at work behind the dollar rebound. Ever since the June 21 G7 world economic summit at Toronto, market rumors circulated that on the sidelines Baker and Miyazawa had struck another bilateral bargain: to help elect George Bush in November 1988, Japan would be careful to avoid actions, above all an increase in Japanese interest rates, that could disrupt the U.S. economy or the dollar.

Markets were always neurotic with rumor. But this one had a lasting ring of veracity. Although no smoking gun ever emerged, the circumstantial evidence supported it. Most germane, financial markets took it as gospel. Its self-fullfilling actions were more effective than truth. "The dollar was supported until the election by the conspiracy theory," says Salomon Brothers analyst Nick Sargen.

Both Baker and Miyazawa had motives. Baker couldn't stop the Fed from pushing up interest rates to fight inflation. But he could, through the existing conveyance of dollar policy cooperation, alleviate Japanese pressure on U.S. interest rates. Miyazawa was eager to hold Japanese interest rates down to encourage expansion and a stronger dollar to repair his political reputation and assist the powerful exporters that anchored the Japanese economy.

There was also no doubt that Japanese, like most foreign officials, preferred Republican Bush over Democrat Michael Dukakis. The Democrats tended to be more protectionist. Though it would have been considered vulgar for central bankers to argue their preferences among each other, Manley Johnson says, "You could sense that in Europe and Japan they were pulling for Bush. You knew that was whom they wanted. But if they acted on it, they did not share it with us."

An explicit deal between Baker and Miyazawa need not have been struck to consummate an "understanding." "Normally you wouldn't have to say anything, because there is a protocol that you don't do anything that could affect someone else's elections," explains Dan Crippen, an aide to White House Chief of Staff Howard Baker.

Such a deal had been already presaged by Prime Minister Takeshita's January 1988 pledge to Reagan not to raise Japanese interest rates in order to support the dollar. Takeshita's commitment had incensed BOJ officials. But lacking the independent power of the Bundesbank or the Fed, and its leverage diminished by engagement in the G7 process of managing exchange rates (where MOF's authority was undisputedly supreme), the BOJ could not resist. If Miyazawa chose to target the U.S. presidential elections for political reasons, the BOJ had to go along.

In the event, the BOJ in fact *did* target the dollar, against its better judgment. The BOJ tolerated low interest rates "to encourage outflows of capital," confirms BOJ Executive Director Yoshio Suzuki. "In mid-1988 we aimed at influencing the exchange rate." In addition, reports BOJ Deputy Governor for International Mikio Wakatsuki, "[w]e asked the life insurance companies to continue to buy U.S. bonds. There was a lot of administrative guidance."[22] The rapid growth in Japan's money supply fed market speculation that a discount rate hike was imminent. But the BOJ never moved.

The BOJ campaign to anchor dollar interest and exchange rates reached extraordinary lengths in the summer. Inflationary expectations were causing money to leak away from Japan's domestic money markets, where interest rates were held artificially low through unofficial BOJ "whispers" to *tanshi,* or money brokers. Instead the funds shifted to the recently established, deregulated offshore open money markets. Short-term interest rates offshore surged to over 4.5 percent versus the tiny premium above the 2.5 percent discount rate onshore. Because Japan's money markets were highly regulated, no arbitrage was possible to bring the two prices into line. As a result, the domestic interbank markets dried up. For a three-day stretch in the summer, not a single transaction was done. To no avail, the BOJ offered larger dollops of discount window funds at the below-market rate of 2.5 percent to banks that shunned the offshore markets. The BOJ let itself lose control of the ability to steer short-term domestic money market rates rather than raise them.[23]

The BOJ ultimately repaired the situation with a major deregulatory reform that injected more market forces into the onshore money market and made Japanese interest rates less rigidly linked to the official discount rate. It was a reform the BOJ had wanted to do for years, in part to give itself more institutional freedom from MOF, whose influence over the politically visible discount rate was greater than it was over BOJ money market operations. Onshore interest rates promptly shot up to offshore levels. When was this reform instituted? In November—when the U.S. presidential election was safely decided.

The Fed's surprise discount rate increase of August 9, and the European hikes two weeks later, intensified pressure on the BOJ to follow. By September 2 the dollar surpassed ¥137. Japan's yield curve was in a very steep, "no-confidence" trajectory.

Finance Minister Miyazawa intervened with an extraordinary, headline-making declaration: The BOJ would *not* raise its discount rate. BOJ Governor Satoshi Sumita, who normally made the declarations about the BOJ's intentions, lost face. "In September 1988 the MOF's judgment on the economic situation was different [from the BOJ's]," reports Tomomitsu Oba, then special adviser to the finance minister. "I thought the Federal Reserve feared inflation, but that the BOJ feared the fear of inflation. The MOF feared the BOJ, which feared the fear of inflation. Someone told this joke to Sumita. He was very upset."

There were several plausible explanations why Japanese authorities might have chosen not to raise domestic interest rates. One was that "inflation took a different form. Not wholesale prices, but prices of financial assets, which don't show up in the indices."[24] Inflationary bottlenecks in the overheated construction sector were also alleviated by cheap Korean imports. According to Mark Farrington of MMS International, the BOJ ultimately escaped a discount rate increase when lower than expected U.S. employment figures released on September 2 weakened the dollar. Japan's booming money supply growth, too, cooled slightly.[25]

The final reason the BOJ may not have pushed harder for a discount rate hike was that its hawkish deputy governor, Yasushi Mieno, had been purportedly put on notice that another "mistake" like the increases he'd engineered that ended in the global stock market crash might jeopardize his long groomed ascendancy to the governorship. Mieno squelched his resentment to fight again another day.

The dollar peaked in September. In October it skidded. It hit bottom just days before the U.S. presidential election, at ¥124.5 and DM 1.76.

Instead of the celebratory dollar rally after Bush's victory, there was a dollar sell-off requiring central bank intervention support. To what did analysts attribute this paradoxical market reaction? Anticipatory selling ahead of the end of the alleged Baker-Miyazawa deal.

Bequeathments

Whether or not the Baker-Miyazawa dollar conspiracy was apocryphal, the larger significance was that the election of a U.S. president, and his subsequent policy options, were profoundly affected by decisions taken in Japan. Japanese investors, and the bureaucrats who influenced them, acted like a large fifty-first state, and solidly Republican. "Our networks could give similar intellectual uplift to this year's election campaign by organizing a panel of Japanese life insurance portfolio managers to address the American people on the policy changes they will demand before putting new funds into the U.S. securities markets next year," wrote Kemper Financial Services Chief Economist David Hale in 1988. "Such a program probably would give American voters more information about the direction of economic policy after 1988 than they appear likely to get from the candidates themselves."[26]

By failing to adjust their domestic economic policies, U.S. and Japanese leaders had struck a historical political Faustian bargain to allow Americans in the 1980s to live beyond their means on borrowed Japanese money against the promise that America's unborn would labor effectively on behalf of Japan's large pensioner generation tomorrow. But would America's children be willing to make the material sacrifices their parents wouldn't and live below their means in order to honor this legacy of indebtedness? Or would they succumb to the temptation to exploit America's unique, residual hegemonic privilege of having all its foreign debt in its own currency to inflate as soon as paying back seemed too politically and economically onerous?

"The United States hates to adopt any kind of stringent monetary policy. The so-called floating rate system is best for the United States to issue whatever amount of currency it wants without any responsibility to pay back," laments ex–MOF Vice Minister for International Takashi Hosomi.

"There are two polar views of how the situation [of America's debt to Japan] will work out," says Princeton Professor William Branson. "One view says that the Japanese are in deep trouble since all their investment is in the United States and the U.S will inflate it away. The other view is that the Japanese are gaining a dominant position in the U.S. economy and will eventually control the politicians—buy a congressman."[27]

The lopsided interdependencies between the U.S. and Japanese political economies also exacerbated trade tensions that threatened to sink the international free trade order. "I think we run an increasing risk of an impasse with the Japanese," warns Paul Volcker. "We see a big deficit with Japan and we say, 'Goddamn it, you Japanese better open up your markets,' when their markets are more open now than they were ten years ago, however much they are in absolute terms. It's kind of an escape for us from dealing with our budget deficits and other things. And the Japanese now are turning around and saying, 'The days when we could liberalize are over, politically, and we're going to be much more aggressive about telling the Americans to do the things they don't want to do.' So both sides are getting more aggressive about telling each other to do things that we each consider politically impossible."[28]

When a trade reciprocity bill was introduced in the U.S. Senate in the winter 1990–91 to open Japan's financing markets, MOF Vice Minister for International Affairs Makoto Utsumi warned bellicosely that Japan might deploy its "money weapon" if the sanctions were enacted—it might cut off the capital flows to which America was addicted to live beyond its means. This, he warned, would create a "very, very harmful situation."[29]

With the United States borrowing more savings from abroad than the total personal savings generated by Americans between 1987 and 1989, the recessionary risk of any sudden capital cutoff from Japan was obvious. But if America went down, Japan's export-dependent economy was all but doomed to follow in what would be the economic equivalent of a nuclear World War III. Thus, hearing the money weapon threat from a top official of Japan's elite MOF boded ominously about how long reason could prevail in the face of prolonged external imbalances.

Despite the obvious centricity of Japanese capital recycling to the well-being of the U.S. and international economy, the subject was never discussed by the G7.[30] The U.S.-Japanese tensions were symptomatic of a unique juncture in world economic history. For the first time the world's reserve currency country was also its largest debtor. Simultaneously, the world's largest

creditor nation, Japan, produced a currency that was internationally scarce
and hostage to a strongly guided, illiberal financial system. America's postwar hegemony over the international economy had all but vanished. Yet
there was no single candidate able or willing to supersede it. The post–Cold
War environment thus resembled the unhappy post–World War I era when
no nation took political charge and the world monetary and economic order
decayed into destabilizing international capital flows, spiraling trade protectionism, and depression. Today a robust, open world trade order depended
on cooperative, if not coordinated, fiscal and monetary policies, among at
least the United States, Japan, and Germany. The experience of the G7
process gave a taste of the formidable difficulties of doing so at a time of
great economic imbalances. When the disequilibria departed for cyclic reasons, so did the political motivation to coordinate.

Is joint decision making "even conceivable," Peter Drucker wonders bleakly,
"except perhaps in the event of worldwide financial collapse? . . . Have we
come to the end of the three-hundred-year-old attempt to regulate and stabilize money on which, after all, both the modern nation-state and the international system are largely based?"[31]

The unanchored, volatile, floating monetary nonsystem and unredressed
economic imbalances announced themselves again in 1989, when a new market stampede created a minireplay of the dollar's painful 1980s round trip.
Overpowering $75 billion in central bank intervention, and a narrowing of
interest rate differentials, the dollar rebounded some 25 percent from its
1988 lows and through its asymmetric "Son of Louvre" ceilings. It tested its
old Louvre ceiling of ¥161 and smashed through DM 2. All the experts had
expected the collapse of the dollar, not its rise, to break the G7 bands. When
market sentiment turned in 1990–91, the dollar abruptly plunged again to
new historic lows of DM 1.45 and ¥109. By that time the unusual global "balance sheet recession" of the early 1990s had begun.

Global capital could serve as a healthy disciplining force on democratic
government profligacy and a boon to capitalist productivity. But its propensity to extreme volatility and occasional self-destructiveness, as well as the
clash between its single-minded profit logic and the broader political goals
of liberal democratic nations, argued that for it to do so required updating
and enforcing new rules of the game for governing the international democratic capitalist economy. In the absence of such reform, the weighty task of
delivering growth and economic order in an increasingly politicized environment was left to unelected central bankers.

In the late 1980s the central bankers, almost unnoticed, made one historic
political breakthrough toward rebuilding those international rules—the
world's first common standards for bank capital adequacy.

PART FIVE

GLOBAL STANDARDS FOR STATELESS MONEY

Chapter 22

The World's First Capital Standards

On September 2, 1986, the fine cutlery was laid once again at the Bank of England governor's official residence at New Change, site of some of the secret dinners that helped launched the LDC debt strategy four years earlier. The occasion was an impromptu visit from Paul Volcker, en route home from Europe. When the Fed chairman sat down with Governor Robin Leigh-Pemberton and three senior BOE officials, the topic he raised was bank capital. He discussed his political difficulty in upgrading its adequacy for U.S. banks as well as perilous incompatibility of standards internationally.[1]

Adequate capital—the bank's buffer against bankrupting loss—was the keystone of a central banker's mission to uphold financial system safety and soundness. It was the banks' capital inadequacy that made LDC overindebtedness so grave a threat; upgrading U.S. bank capital was the second leg of Volcker's strategy to extricate the world financial system from that crisis.

In late summer 1986 Paul Volcker was a worried central banker: U.S. and world economic growth was sputtering. The global economic imbalances threatened a dollar free-fall. Mexico was in its second debt crisis. Texas banks were collapsing. Bank of America was at the precipice. Other U.S. money center banks, farm belt banks, and S&Ls were fragile. Corporations were historically overleveraged. The explosion of untested, new "securitized" and off balance sheet financial instruments posed unknown risks. The Fed's room to ease monetary policy had reached its limit with the adverse market reaction to its unilateral August discount rate cut. Volcker feared that his nightmare of a "catastrophic chain reaction" in the fully floating, volatile, integrated U.S. financial system might be at hand. The likely outcome was depression or, as the Fed tried to stave it off with massive injections of liquidity, a resurgence of inflation.

Volcker knew that the Bank of England was also trying to upgrade U.K. bank capital adequacy rules. Why not see if they could move in tandem in overlapping areas? Parallel upgrading of standards in the two main world financial centers might help break through the opposition each faced from their own bankers and give a badly needed shot in the arm to the development of compatible worldwide standards. Since both the Fed and BOE were struggling to incorporate "off balance sheet" items, such as swaps, options, financial futures, and credit guarantees, into their separate risk-weighted bank capital models, Volcker recommended that their collaboration start there.

Specifically Volcker endorsed the initiative of New York Fed President Jerry Corrigan. Corrigan had been discussing the supervisory implications of rapidly innovating global financial markets over the previous months with Leigh-Pemberton and inside BOE power Deputy Governor George Blunden. Their expert staff were talking and were to make presentations to Corrigan and Leigh-Pemberton at the BOE a month hence, on October 6 and 7.

"Certainly frustration was building up that there was something less than a great deal of enthusiasm for a risk-based capital system just for the United States. We, the Fed as an institution, had moved farther and faster on that issue than others might have liked," says Corrigan. "This was the driving force of the London meetings."

The quandary confronting central bankers, and all financial supervisors, was that "we face a global problem trying to oversee markets and institutions that have gone international, while still being regulated on a national level."[2] Widely disparate financial industry structures and regulatory concepts and standards had evolved within nations through the postwar era when finance was nationally segregated. When the sovereign barriers were washed away by the explosion of freewheeling, stateless capital, supervisors faced the large challenge of bolstering their financial defenses with upgraded standards and by constructing a gapless, safe, and undistorted circuit for international finance from the tangle of incompatible national regulations. This required makeshift bridges and eventually universal rules and standards.

The collapse of national and sectoral barriers, and the disparate regulations, left behind a competitively lumpy global playing field among banks of different nationalities and between banks and their capital market competitors. U.S. and U.K. bankers argued persuasively that upgrading their capital requirements would worsen their competitive regulatory disadvantage against foreign banks and securities firms with lax or no capital requirements. Rather than enhancing their stability, the more onerous regulations would undermine them! By moving in tandem with the United Kingdom, Volcker hoped to assuage their complaints.

Over dinner with Leigh-Pemberton, Volcker observed, "If we process official bank capital standards, we're both going to get a lot of complaints about Japan and the level playing field."[3]

Japan was the most prominent regulatory lump in the 1980s global financial landscape. Where a U.S. bank had to raise $6 of capital for every $100 loan it made, its Japanese competitor was required to hold only $2 or $3. Armed with this huge cost advantage, Japanese banks' share of international banking business catapulted from 17 percent to 38 percent from 1983 to 1988. U.S. banks' share fell from over 26 percent to under 15 percent. National banking markets were invaded, too: by the end of the 1980s Japanese banks controlled one-eighth of all U.S. bank assets—about half the total foreign share—up from zero in the mid-1980s. Japanese owned four of the ten largest California banks and 25 percent of all California banking assets. U.S. bank assets in Japan's highly protected and profitable home markets, by contrast, were neglible. Degrees varied, but Japanese "overpresence" existed in major European markets, too.

Japanese banks could operate safely on lower capital ratios because the Japanese government had never let any major bank fail since World War II.[4] The rapid yen appreciation exaggerated the force of Japan's financial thrust abroad. Overnight it transformed Japanese banks into leviathans while reducing America's once world-dominant banks to mere minnows: by the late 1980s the world's seven largest banks and fourteen of the top twenty were Japanese; only one U.S. bank ranked among the top twenty. What Japanese banks couldn't win through competition, they could buy up. In large measure Japan's astonishing assault on the domineering heights of world finance was the flip side of recycling its record current account surpluses.[5]

The U.S.-U.K. Bilateral Agreement

Between the Fed and BOE there was a tradition of close collaboration dating to the 1920s between New York Fed President Benjamin Strong and BOE Governor Montagu Norman and renewed by Volcker and Gordon Richardson in the 1980s on LDC debt. Volcker and Leigh-Pemberton didn't share the same central bankers' mutual affinity. An amateur gentleman beekeeper and commercial banker of winning, egoless charm, Leigh-Pemberton bore the reputational cross of managing monetary policy on a short political leash controlled by Prime Minister Thatcher. Yet the BOE retained

an independent authority in supervisory matters that was respected in the
Basel club. By 1986 relations were close enough that Volcker stayed
overnight at Leigh-Pemberton's country home and even once invited him
along on a fly-fishing excursion.[6]

At dinner that evening Leigh-Pemberton responded positively to Volcker's
overture. The Bank of England had some additional, British reasons for
wishing to collaborate. For decades the Old Lady of Threadneedle Street
had supervised banking and finance in the City through informal use of the
governor's winks, nods, and arched eyebrows among a club of "gentlemen."
But the volatility, dimensions, and sheer competitiveness of globalized finance, with its Euromarket heart in London, was effecting a transformation
to a written, rule-based prudential system for "players." At the time, the
BOE was gearing up for the uncertainties of the all-at-once, systemic "big
bang" deregulation on October 27, 1986. The U.K. Treasury was then drafting its 1987 banking act, which included regulations for capital adequacy.
This act was to rectify the flaws in the heavily BOE-influenced 1979 law.
The BOE's credentials and future role as bank supervisor were in the balance. At one point Exchequer Chancellor Nigel Lawson contemplated stripping the BOE of its supervisory authority entirely.[7]

But the BOE's spring 1986 proposal to incorporate banks' exploding off
balance sheet activities into its risk-weighted model of bank capital adequacy was being impeded by U.K. bank opposition. "We couldn't get it
moving," says Executive Director Brian Quinn. "Then Volcker and the governor came together."

At dinner the governors' hopes had been modest: to find areas of sufficient
convergence of goals and regulatory concepts to achieve separate but parallel upgrading moves. "We were *not* talking about the same standards,"
stresses BOE Deputy Governor George Blunden.

Yet the momentum it galvanized for the October sessions between the
Corrigan-led Fed team and top BOE officials produced the unanticipated
breakthrough of a fully articulated, common bank capital adequacy regime
for the United States and United Kingdom. This in turn catalyzed one of the
1980s' most remarkable diplomatic achievements—the first worldwide protocol on the definitions, framework, and minimum standards for the capital
adequacy of internationally active banks. It became one of those rare instances when years of tedious negotiation were suddenly rewarded by a fortuitous alignment of conditions that broke through all remaining opposition.
"Even Volcker was extremely skeptical that we'd be able to get any international standard," says Corrigan.

Exploratory staff meetings held in Washington on September 24–26,

1986, revealed that the U.S.'s and U.K.'s bank capital regulatory conceptions were not as distant relatives as first appeared. Instead of seeking limited regions of convergence, the four-man U.S. team headed by Fed Board staff chief for supervision Bill Taylor and the three-man British team under his BOE counterpart, Brian Quinn, began to wonder excitedly: Might it be possible to do the whole thing—common definition, regulatory framework, and standards?[8] "Sometimes it is more expensive to do renovation than to build a new building," says Quinn.

They literally wiped the blackboard clean, then explored designing a new risk-weighted capital adequacy regime for both countries. They resumed in London just ahead of Corrigan's October 6–7 visit. At their Saturday morning presentations to Corrigan and Leigh-Pemberton, describes Corrigan, "It was as if all the lights suddenly went on! We just kind of looked at each other. We said, 'We're so close as it is, why not have our technical people put it under the microscope?' This they did over the next two weeks. At that point it became *very* apparent how close we really were."

At that point "we set the objective to get convergence by the end of the year," says Deputy Governor George Blunden, adding, "We didn't actually believe we could get it by then." Over the next three months of "terrific, marvelous fun," the supervisory experts worked on almost nothing else.[9] By December they had an articulated, bilateral bank credit capital adequacy regime: it included a common definition of capital and was based on a five-category framework of risk-weighted assets—0 percent, 10 percent, 25 percent, 50 percent, and 100 percent—for on and off balance sheet activities. It required banks to hold the full capital standard against the highest-risk loans, half the standard for the second riskiest category, a quarter for the middle category, and so on to zero capital for assets, such as government securities, without meaningful risk of credit default. The specific minimum standard was unspecified, but their common understanding was that it would be higher than the U.S.'s existing 6 percent ratio.

One of Volcker's unsung central banker–type accomplishments had been to arrest the slow deterioration of U.S. bank capital adequacy that had been spurred by the same revolutionary financial forces that helped fuel the late 1970s double-digit inflation. When Volcker became Fed chairman in 1979, there had been no formal capital adequacy guidelines. Prudential supervision was guided by identification of outliers among the banking herd. But it failed because the standards of the entire herd were drifting downward. "The weakest link in the chain was the banking system," Volcker remembers. "They are the ones you have to have be the *most* prudent and historically had been. This was frustrating to me, to say the least."

In December 1981, at Volcker's behest and over strong banker resistance, America's first minimum numerical federal capital adequacy ratios—5 percent for primary, or highest quality, and 5.5 percent for total capital to assets—were imposed. But the seventeen big multinational banks were exempted. Why? The official rationale was that they commanded more liquidity and confidence and thus needed less capital. "The real reason the seventeen were excluded," says Kenneth McLean, then Senate Banking Committee chief staffer, "was that they couldn't meet the standard."

The big banks were finally included in June 1983 in the congressional backlash at the bankers' folly in the LDC debt crisis. Through the Fed-drafted International Lending Supervision Act (ILSA) that was attached to the November 1983 legislation that augmented IMF funding, the Fed effectively arranged for itself a congressional mandate to raise capital further. In April 1985 the numerical capital-asset minimums were bumped up to 5.5 percent for primary and 6 percent for total capital.

The May 1984 collapse of Continental Illinois Bank, which had a relatively high 5.8 percent capital-asset ratio, had delivered a shuddering signal that simple numerical ratios alone weren't enough. Instead of adding safety, higher capital ratios perversely induced some "go-go" banks to take on riskier business to try to boost profitability. "People were selling off quality assets," recalls J. P. Morgan Chairman Lewis Preston. "The Volcker [numerical ratio] formula was counterproductive."

The Continental failure prompted Volcker to call together the Fed's supervisory brain trust. "Let's look at what we've been doing wrong," Volcker charged a group headed by Corrigan, Bill Taylor, Volcker special assistant Steven Roberts, and New York Fed executives Steve Thieke and Fred Schadrack. "How did Continental happen?"[10]

Several studies were launched. One led to the January 15, 1986, issuance of a proposal to supplement numerical capital adequacy requirements with risk weighting of assets.[11] By requiring banks to hold more capital for riskier loans and other assets, regulators hoped to steer the banks away from excessive risk.

A second led to a closer examination of the financial stability and monetary policy implications of the explosion in innovative, fee-generating activities not booked on bank balance sheets—notably currency and interest rate swaps, options, foreign exchange forwards, standby commitments, and letters of credit—which were generating a rapidly rising share of bank profits as bankers lost their traditional business to the neighboring capital markets.[12] Being off balance sheet, these activities escaped inclusion in the numerical ratios. Simply, they were not regulated. The Basel central bankers working under the aegis of the New York Fed's Sam Cross, concluded that bankers were probably underpricing them given their novelty, complexity, and volatility and the competitiveness of global financial markets.[13] "The Cross Report told us that there was a whole other banking system out there that had to be taken into account," says Steven Roberts.

Volcker was dubious that bank managements understood the risk of such innovations better than he did. This prompted him to incorporate off balance sheet activities into the U.S.'s proposed risk-weighted framework—the antecedent of his overture to Governor Leigh-Pemberton to unite forces. But what was really needed to ensure systemic safety and soundness was worldwide standards.

Basel central bankers had been discussing bank capital adequacy ever since the 1974 collapse of Germany's Herstatt Bank revealed the dangerous absence of supervision and regulation of the mushrooming sector of international banking. To try to catch up, the G10 governors created the Committee on Banking Regulation and Supervision Practices.[14] The Basel supervisors committee worked along three tracks. First was the who-does-what accord of home and host country central bankers to define supervisory responsibilities for banks' international activities; it was codified in the two Basel Concordats of 1975 and 1983. The second track yielded the 1978 consolidated worldwide financial reporting agreement. The third track was capital adequacy.

But no significant progress was made. By April 15, 1980, the BIS governors were sufficiently worried by the worldwide erosion of bank capital-asset ratios through the aggressive use of innovative practices to issue one of their rare communiqués. They "noted" (between the lines one read "askance") the 25 percent-a-year growth in international lending and stressed the "cardinal importance" they attached to capital adequacy. The Basel committee began systematically to monitor the capital ratios of leading international banks. By March 1982 it reported confidentially to the governors that the deterioration of capital ratios had to stop. The governors took note "in their usual deadpan way."[15] The eruption of the LDC debt crisis a few months later fully exposed the system-threatening scale of the failings of internal bank risk management and of external central bank and government supervision. But still no progress was made.

In March 1984 Volcker injected fresh urgency and political leadership. During one of his infrequent visits to Basel, he informed the G10 governors at dinner that he "wanted to talk about a major concern" of his: he wanted to devise a method to compare disparate national regimes of capital adequacy according to a test of "functional equivalence." Over time he wanted to establish an international minimum standard. "I don't care what the levels are," Volcker told them. "That's a picayune detail. The key thing is the agreement."[16]

Volcker was acting under the Fed's November 1983 ILSA mandate, which admonished supervisors to attain fair competition and capital adequacy from foreign banks as they raised U.S. bank capital adequacy standards. "Paul brought the congressional proposal to the group," recalls then BOJ Deputy Governor for International Shijuro Ogata. The Basel governors responded by giving an unusual personal mandate to Basel supervisors committee chairman Peter Cooke to report within a year on how international convergence could be achieved.

Convergence depended upon three elements: a common definition, a common framework for assessing capital adequacy, and, finally, a common standard. The technical task alone was formidable. Japan's formal regulatory regime, for instance, was based on "a totally different concept" from its Western counterparts. "Our system is based on total liabilities, not assets," says a BOJ official. "How do we measure Japanese banks' capital adequacy if they don't accord to our standards and rules?" Cooke wonders. "You can't quantity the differences."

The most insuperable problem was the most basic—attaining a common *definition* of capital. Agreement began and ended that shareholders equity and retained earnings constituted "pure" capital. After that, Cooke's Basel committee identified four broad categories of "dirty" or second-rate capital that some countries recognized. The United States counted a bank's loan loss provisions—the money earmarked to cover bad debts—in primary capital, something almost no other countries would countenance. Japan alone counted as capital the unrealized capital gains on banks' equity portfolio. The Germans adhered to a pristine view: they believed only in pure capital—everything else should be excluded.

No one was ready voluntarily to incur the national political tempests and large economic costs of rewriting national computer programs, accounting codes, and regulations for the sake of an international norm. In early 1986 Volcker returned to the Basel governors to urge faster action on convergence.

The only area in which Cooke made headway was on the framework. Seven of the twelve G10 governors were members of the EC, which since the late 1970s had been advancing its own common framework of risk-weighted capital ratios. In January 1986 the United States joined the train. In February 1986 Cooke was able to recommend that the Basel governors encourage convergence around the risk-weighted framework, based primarily on a pure capital definition. In May 1986 the MOF's international finance bureau reluctantly gave administrative guidance that banks should maintain a capital-asset ratio of 6 percent (the U.S. regulatory minimum) at their foreign branches. MOF also accepted the risk-weighting framework and a 4 percent standard for the international activity of their onshore banks, although the method for realizing it remained enigmatic. "The Japanese, feeling the hot breath of international consensus down their necks, said they'd do risk weighting for their banks' international business," relates Peter Cooke. "Frankly, I don't know how the Japanese managed to make the distinction between the domestic and international part of a bank's book—but you are thankful for what you get. Crumbs are better than nothing."

The international bandwagon toward the risk-weighting framework climaxed in October 1986, when bank supervisors from some eighty countries meeting in Amsterdam endorsed it. By that time, however, the U.S. and U.K. central bank supervisors were secretly light-years ahead of them on the road to total bilateral convergence.

Once Volcker and Leigh-Pemberton realized that Fed and BOE experts could actually achieve a common bilateral regime for bank capital adequacy, they asked themselves: Would they dare implement it?

To do so was an audacious political choice disguised as a technical regulatory matter. It was tantamount to a ganging up by the two leading international financial centers. The implicit threat was that other nations would either submit to the U.S.-U.K. capital definitions and standards or face exclusion of their banks from London and New York. In one bound it bypassed the multilateral negotiations going on within Peter Cooke's G10 Basel supervisors committee as well as within the EC. Such high-handedness was bound to provoke fury from Tokyo to Brussels.

Volcker and Leigh-Pemberton hoped to use bilateral convergence as a political lever to spur an international accord—especially with Japan. But they vowed to each other to forge ahead bilaterally, if necessary. "We felt it could be expanded at least to Tokyo and were convinced that sooner or later you'd get a pan-G10 agreement to make it universal," says Leigh-Pemberton. Of the sharp resentment the United Kingdom could expect for apparently sabotaging the EC negotiation for rules for a single European banking market, he adds, "I felt we could ride out that storm."[17]

For the United States the political calculation was much simpler. Explains Corrigan, "My overriding consideration was this: Would a joint initiative by the United States and United Kingdom harm or help in getting other countries on board? It could only help. I was especially sensitive to two problems. One, could we bring the Japanese along? And two, would U.K. relations with Europe be so soured by this initiative that it would be counterproductive to bring them along? It was a very courageous position on Leigh-Pemberton's part."

"Volcker was very shrewd," says BIS chief Alexandre Lamfalussy.

"When he felt a multilateral approach was not as effective as a bilateral agreement with the United Kingdom or Japan, he'd operate bilaterally. Later, when he felt the bilateral approach no longer served his purposes better, he would again go multilaterally."

Bringing Japan along in the autumn 1986 had mounting political urgency. Congressional backlash at headine-making Japanese financial takeovers and the perception that the dollar's fate was hostage to Japanese investors were producing protectionist legislative proposals that pressed the Fed to use its regulatory authority to exclude new foreign—read "Japanese"—firms from entering U.S. financial markets unless U.S. firms had reciprocal access. "The question here was: How can we let the Japanese banks expand when they have no capital?" recalls the Fed's Bill Taylor.

The Fed was in the political hot seat because it had to decide whether to grant the applications of Japan's Big Four securities firms to become primary dealers for Treasury auctions and whether to permit Sumitomo Bank to buy into the heart of Wall Street through a $500 million minority stake in Goldman Sachs. "The Japanese promised that if that happened, they'd open their markets," remembers Treasury Undersecretary George Gould, who was lobbied by big U.S. financial firms to approve it. "If not, it would be harder for the Morgans, etc., to get what they wanted."

From the outset of their October decision to pursue a common regime, U.S. and U.K. central bankers agreed that it would be the Fed's job to bring along Japan. The BOE would manage the Europeans. Out of fear of sabotaging leaks, they also decided to keep their bilateral negotiations secret, including from their central banker brethren. Awkwardly, Peter Cooke was deliberately kept in the dark by his BOE colleagues, even as the bilateral convergence work went on around him, "since it would have compromised his position as head of the [Basel] standing committee."[18]

Shijuro Ogata and Takeshi Ohta, his successor as BOJ deputy governor for international, were informed in advance by Corrigan about his October meeting with Leigh-Pemberton and what it was generally to be about. Then the curtain of silence dropped until the final common U.S.-U.K. bilateral standards were ready in December.

Unveiling the U.S.-U.K. Accord

In mid-December 1986 MOF Vice Minister for International Toyoo Gyohten visited the New York Fed for Jerry Corrigan's personal unveiling of the U.S.-U.K. capital adequacy accord. Accompanying him into the tenth-floor boardroom were three men from the MOF banking, international finance, and securities bureaus and a BOJ observer. "We told them what we and the British had done," says a U.S. participant. "They were hanging out of their chairs."

That Gyohten brought along the three MOF bureau representatives offered a rare window into MOF's internal politics and that of U.S.-Japanese financial diplomacy. At first blush the securities bureau man seemed extraneous in a banking agreement. Yet "any issue of commercial banks or of security firms couldn't but affect the other group. The balance between these two groups is an issue all the time," explains Gyohten. This competition was reflected in the deep-seated rivalry between the two bureaus that regulated them.[19]

MOF's predominantly domestically blinkered technocrats had little sensitivity to the large international importance their policies suddenly took on in the 1980s. Thus it was to expose them to it that Gyohten brought along his juniors. After listening to Corrigan's explanation of the level global playing field intent of the U.S.-U.K. accord, Gyohten says, "They really recognized the importance of the issues." Increasingly, "internationalist" Japanese policymakers employed such *gaiatsu,* or foreign pressure, to shortcut Japan's slow, bottom-up consensus-building policy process to try to stave off political blowups harmful to Japan. Gyohten, fifty-six, was then negotiating informal financial market access understandings to prevent Japan's "overpresent" financial firms from being thrown out of European marketplaces. He knew that a common bank capital adequacy standard was likely to influence the outcome in the United States.

Posturing as the "good cop," Corrigan greeted his MOF guests in December 1986 with a few regulatory carrots—though noticeably withholding others. In November the Fed approved Sumitomo's buying into Goldman Sachs. On December 11 it granted two of the four primary dealership applications by Japan's Big Four.

An unspoken quid pro quo was Japan's joining the bank capital accord. Corrigan made it plain that the United States wanted to move fast: initially, U.S. and British central bankers talked about implementing their bilateral accord within six months.

The Anglo-American accord placed enormous pressure on MOF officials. They left the New York Fed meeting with accommodating words but questioning the timetable with which it could be applied to Japan. This masked their deeper reservations about whether MOF bureaucrats and Japanese bankers would—or should—accept it. The U.S.-U.K. definition of capital seemed punitive: it excluded Japan's largest component of capital—the unrealized capital gains on bank's shareholdings—and subtracted cross-equity holdings among banks. International Japanese bank expansion would be stopped dead in its tracks overnight and possibly forced to retreat.

"Japanese banks were not interested," recounts one member of the MOF team. "The banking bureau was not sure if the capital rule was a good idea. It was still trying to figure out how to regulate banks, given deregulation and internationalization—with a general rule or by guidance. We were sure Japanese banks were healthy, but we didn't want to see discrimination against them."

More comprehensive follow-up talks were held at the Bank of Japan on January 8 and 9, 1987, when Corrigan and a U.S. team visited Tokyo coincident with the simultaneous U.S. and U.K. public announcement of the accord. In addition to Gyohten, Corrigan conferred with BOJ Governor Satoshi Sumita and Deputy Governor for International Takeshi Ohta.[20] Finance Minister Kiichi Miyazawa, as well as Gyohten and some top BOJ officials, were the most ready to compromise because "they realize it is in their longer-term interest to be viewed as a cooperative member of the international community."[21] But most of the MOF and BOJ cadre remained unswayed.

. At a social function Corrigan personally took the pulse of Japanese bankers as he chatted about off balance sheet activities, risk management, and Japan's comparatively low levels of capital. The reception was cold. Says Industrial Bank of Japan Chairman Kaneo Nakamura, one of the few to welcome the chance to reduce political friction through world rules, "When the capital adequacy discussions started, some in the banking community were saying that it was more 'Japan bashing.' "

Before Corrigan departed, however, Gyohten agreed secretly to work toward a global bank capital adequacy agreement "in principle, but couldn't yet say so."[22] The biggest obstacle was a formula that would permit Japanese banks to meet the eventual standard. No national bank regulator would sign on to an agreement that unduly penalized his banking system. "I anticipated difficulties," says Gyohten. "I was overly cautious in hindsight."[23] The realpolitik bottom line, notes Bank of England Deputy Governor Blunden, was that "once we proved that the [U.S.-U.K.] agreement was possible, then for Japan a multilateral agreement was far better."

At that early juncture it was uncertain whether the U.S.-U.K. proposal, like so many global initiatives, might not fall of its own weight. By agreeing to cooperate in principle, Gyohten was also playing for time. On Friday evening he and Corrigan flew together to Amsterdam. Gyohten was en route to conference on the LDC debt crisis. Corrigan was headed for Basel and a crucial test of support from central bankers.

. . .

The governors had received advance briefing of the U.S-U.K. accord at the December BIS meetings. Soon thereafter, the Bank of England's Brian Quinn unveiled it to the European members of the Cooke committee and to the European commission in Brussels during an eight-country, two-day whirlwind trip. The Fed informed the Bank of Canada. "After January 1987 everyone realized that something had happened," relates a European central banker. "The United States and United Kingdom made it very clear that they were going to do it. They made it clear that they would apply it to any subsidiary operating in the United States and United Kingdom." But they stressed their preference to trade their accord for a G10 agreement of the Basel supervisors committee.

Initial reactions were pretty much as expected. Irate EC officials "felt it was anti-*Communitaire* and even suggested it was illegal," says BOE Governor Robin Leigh-Pemberton, who was upbraided by them. "It isn't." British central bankers explained that the U.S.–U.K. agreement evolved almost accidentally. It was as yet merely a proposal and therefore couldn't violate any European legal obligations.[24]

The governors at the Basel club on the weekend of January 11 were more understanding. "My worst fear—that they felt we had usurped the Cooke committee multilateral process—did not materialize," says Jerry Corrigan. "They mostly recognized that the United States and United Kingdom had provided a catalyst, though not all, of course. It shows the value of the central banker network, the long close relationships. That was what carried the day." Some who publicly condemned the accord supported it in private as a necessary shot in the arm.

The sourest greeting was from Bundesbank President Karl Otto Pöhl. Pöhl objected to any deviation from the German national definition of "pure" capital—that which "is really at the disposal of the bank."[25] He bridled at prospective capital adequacy levels of 8 percent; German banks couldn't meet that standard using only "pure" capital. He later counterproposed a 6 percent all-pure capital standard—which no banking system but Germany's could meet.

Pöhl's trenchant objections were informed by a delicate domestic political problem: the legal banking regulator in Germany was not the Bundesbank, but the Federal Banking Supervisory Office in Berlin, an arm of the Bonn government. "This was a clear decision by the Bundestag because it wanted to make clear that monetary policy should not be influenced by regulatory things," explains Hans Tietmeyer, deputy finance minister. "This is different from most other countries."[26] The German Finance Ministry objected strongly to having the Bundesbank nose into this domain of political power. Such a Basel agreement on bank capital conflicted with the painstakingly negotiated German banking reform of January 1, 1985. The government didn't want to expend any of its political capital until the next bruising banking reform battle that would come after Europe harmonized its banking laws around 1992.[27]

Pöhl eventually tried to finesse the political clash by acknowledging the supreme authority of the Berlin supervisory office while justifying his participation in the Basel negotiations on his capacity as chairman of the G10 governors. As a result, he paradoxically asserted a formal reservation against the legal validity of any G10 agreement all the while he negotiated it actively. Although the governors accorded the supervisory office representative the courtesies of a quasi-central banker at the Basel meetings, Pöhl and Finance Minister Gerhard Stoltenberg clashed over the negotiations, and the matter was taken up in the politically charged environment all central bankers strived to avoid: parliamentary discussion.

The Germans' outspoken criticism contrasted with the quiet opposition of the Japanese. "Japan normally doesn't make any critical comments whether or not related to us," says one Japanese official. "We don't engage in theoretical criticisms. That's a big difference between us and the Germans."

German and Japanese positions defined the opposite poles of the world negotiating spectrum. The Germans favored the most formal, theoretically consistent and purist rule-based postures—too rigorous for any other country. The Japanese represented the most informal, antilegalistic, situationally adaptable positions. Thus despite their common interests, the Germans and Japanese could rarely ally themselves politically in international negotiations. The center of gravity remained Anglo-American: flexible law-based pragmatism, punctuated with occasional policy flip-flops when circumstances made it advantageous to do so.

In their isolated ways, the Germans and Japanese each tried to derail the momentum the Anglo-American proposal gave to the international capital adequacy agreement: the Germans head-on; the Japanese by agreeing in principle while playing for time to apply it. Both failed. "We tried to put on the brakes," admits a Bundesbank official. "We were not successful."

Faced with the Anglo-American fait accompli, the Basel governors followed the pragmatic course. They agreed that Peter Cooke's G10 supervisors committee should explore whether there was enough common ground for a multilateral alternative. At a special committee meeting Fed and BOE officials proposed a six-month deadline before implementing their bilateral standards. They compromised on a twelve-month deadline to year-end 1987.

For the first months Cooke's main job "was to turn the wrath of the Europeans aside."[28] It took until the meetings of April 15 and 16 at Gercensee,

Switzerland, for the committee to agree in principle to actually try to achieve multilateral convergence. "This could be one of our last chances for an international agreement," Cooke warned them at the time. "Otherwise countries could go off on their own."[29]

"The Cooke meeting in Gercensee was very good," reports U.S. representative Bill Taylor. "All the differences came out." The biggest stumbling block continued to be definitions. "Common equity was the *only* thing no one disputed as good capital."

Cooke put aside the U.S.–U.K. definitions and returned to his committee's own six broad elements of capital. From the start it was clear that to reach an agreement, "you simply *had* to accept a degree of fuzziness at the edges," Cooke says. "I once described it as trying to push fog through a keyhole with a fork to produce something with a clear-cut shape. It is easy to attack the guidelines for logical inconsistencies. But we needed something realizable. It was also clear to pretty well everybody that you wouldn't have a useful agreement unless the Japanese were on board."

Japan Gets on Board

While work was proceeding on the multilateral track of the Basel supervisors committee, the Anglo-American teams continued to goad them. They met in February, May, and September, coordinating bilateral positions for supervisors meetings, reviewing the multilateral progress, and taking stock of banker and political moods.

Their priority was to get Japan to join their agreement. Delivering Tokyo, thereby closing the final corner of the world's golden financial triangle, would be a virtually irresistible spur to the G10 supervisors committee. At the same stroke it would subdue U.S. and British banks' opposition to the upgraded capital standards.

At Gercensee the Japanese position was still that it "would take ages" for it to comply with any global agreement.[30] Foreign central bankers reasonably argued for the exclusion of the unrealized stock appreciation, on the grounds that it was likely to vanish quickly if stock prices fell sharply— which was also precisely when capital would be most needed. Without the unrealized stock gains, Japanese bank capital ratios were only about 3 percent. Given Japan's virtually seamless government-bank compact, however, Japanese supervisors were supremely confident of their ability to maintain banking system stability. To placate foreign pressure to exclude Japanese firms from foreign financial markets, they offered to allow for falling share prices by taking a "haircut" of 30 percent on unrealized equity gains. The

BOE's Brian Quinn counterproposed inverting the Japanese formula—admitting 30 percent into capital for a 70 percent haircut. "The Japanese," recalls one committee member, "had a strong negative reaction."

Counting stock market gains as capital was further politicized because of the stratospheric stock prices driven by Japan's speculative financial bubble. Japanese banks benefited doubly: first, by being able to raise huge amounts of common equity as their own stock prices tripled from 1984–86; second, by counting the inflated value of their stockholding portfolios as capital. The effect was to magnify their cost of capital advantage over foreign competitors. This allowed them to price their international loans aggressively, while creating the illusion, in Western-style capitalism terms, of a huge capital cushion. Since a major motive of the exercise was to level the world competitive playing field, central bankers' bottom line was a haircut that effectively slowed Japan's aggressive expansion abroad.

Jerry Corrigan and Robin Leigh-Pemberton sent Japan a doubled-barreled signal that the status quo was intolerable in dual addresses to the Overseas Bankers Club at London on February 2, 1987. Before many senior Japanese bank officers and government guests, they highlighted the U.S.-U.K. agreement and urged other international financial center countries to get on board "with emerging international norms." Leigh-Pemberton maintained that their capital adequacy accord created "opportunity to level out some of the bumpy playing fields that now prevail in many of our international banking and capital markets."[31] Failure to act, Corrigan warned, would feed the gathering momentum for punitive financial protectionism.

Their message was received loud and clear. "The Overseas Bankers Club dinner was a very striking thing for me," remembers Tatsuya Tamura, then London representative of the Bank of Japan. "I took all the texts of the Leigh-Pemberton and Corrigan speeches. The Japanese banks were very unhappy. At the time they did not seriously think that they themselves would be subject to that kind of rule."

Even more pointed was Corrigan's early March 1987 request to five Japanese banks, with long-pending applications to open New York subsidiaries, to supply more information about their capital structures consonant with the U.S.-U.K. proposal—notably the difference between the book and market values of their shareholdings.

Corrigan's request was also taken with an eye on the mounting political furor over Japanese "overpresence." During his January 1987 trip to Tokyo, Corrigan had indicated to Gyohten that no further primary dealerships would be granted to Japanese applicants until more American financial firms were allowed into Tokyo markets. "There was lots of pressure from Congress to use primary dealerships in a persuasive way," says Federal Reserve Board Chief Counsel Michael Bradfield. "They *were* used. Corrigan believes in carrots as well as sticks." Chuckling, he adds, "Congress, [Rep. Charles] Schumer [D-N.Y.] still takes credit for giving us teeth."

In March MOF responded by granting approval for four U.S. banks to establish securities' subsidiaries. In the ensuing weeks MOF likewise tried to mollify the Europeans by admitting more firms. In all cases, however, MOF stopped short of satisfying foreigners' greatest desire for seats on the Tokyo Stock Exchange and entry into other core sectors with significant direct intermediation of Japan's huge savings.

The tensions over Japanese financial "overpresence," as well as its trade surplus counterpart, were starting to escalate out of the hands of central bank and Finance Ministry technocrats into the highest political levels—where they were close to breaking out into an international trade war. On March 26 no less an ardent free trader than U.K. Prime Minister Thatcher threatened to eject some ninety-six Japanese financial firms from London within a month unless more than thirteen U.K. financial firms were immediately given market access in Japan. The Reagan government imposed trade sanctions. EC Commissioner Willy de Clercq bellicosely threatened to do so. These political missiles helped trigger the dollar's late March plunge below the ¥150 threshold and ensuing panicked dollar sell-off by Japanese investors that ignited the U.S.'s spring 1987 bond market crash. While Corrigan was testifying to Congress that the contemplated financial protectionist legislation against Japan could disrupt economically vital foreign capital inflows, Japanese investors were staying on the sidelines on the second day of the May 1987 U.S. Treasury quarterly auction.

By late spring 1987 the central bankers and MOF technocrats were in danger of failing to perform one of their unspoken filtering functions in democratic capitalist society—to quietly resolve financial market problems before they fomented procrustean political solutions. In early June a worried Fed International Finance Division staff chief, Ted Truman, who was in Tokyo for a BOJ conference, separately warned BOJ Governor Sumita and the MOF's Gyohten "that if something doesn't happen at the technical level, it will be a major political trade issue. You have to settle it."

Momentum toward a financial trade war was also building in global markets. In June U.S. credit-rating agency Moody's Investors Service announced it might downgrade four big Japanese banks because of insufficient capital. Bank of Tokyo Chairman Yusuke Kashiwagi retorted in the press that if 70 percent of the Bank of Tokyo's equity gains were counted, its capital-asset ratio "would be more than 9 percent. Why pick on us? What about the Europeans?"[32]

Most Japanese bankers vigorously rejected Gyohten's appeal "that due to Japan's importance in the global economy, Japan had to compromise with the Cooke committee."[33] Most, who had never before had any reason to think of their impact beyond the Japanese archipelago and "don't have any idea of the kind of devastation they can cause if they put Citibank or Paribas under," smelled mainly "Japan bashing."[34] Their view was expressed in an unusual four-page letter on May 12, 1987, from Mitsui Bank President Kenichi Kamiya in his capacity as chairman of the Federation of Bankers Association, to the Fed and the BOE. Citing the uniqueness of Japan's financial system, it emphasized: "It is impossible for different countries to devise identical regulations which ignore the distinctiveness of each nation." The letter appealed for unrealized capital gains and cross shareholdings among banks to be counted in primary capital in order to facilitate convergence. Off balance sheet activities should be omitted entirely from the risk-weighting framework.[35]

Soon thereafter a consortium of twenty-three Japanese banks flexed its muscles in protest by delaying for several months a $250 million investment to prop up teetering Bank of America. "It's our major concern," said one of the bankers, referring to the U.S.-U.K. guidelines excluding stakes in other banks from capital. "If we accept this proposal from the Bank of America, it will seriously affect our primary capital."[36]

It was in this confrontational atmosphere on June 8 and 9, 1987, that four Fed officials headed by Bill Taylor, and a dozen and half MOF men and BOJ observers, sat down secretly in Tokyo for another round of negotiations. They met away from the rumor mill of the MOF building, in a guest house near the Okura Hotel. Simultaneous interpreters worked from a glass booth. French wine and food was served. Soon after presentation of technical position briefs, Fed officials began to sense that the outsized number of Japanese were "negotiating among themselves as much as with us."[37]

The negotiations bogged down on the size of the "haircut" on unrealized shareholding gains. Then in the last half hour there was a sudden breakthrough. MOF officials capitulated on the general range of the haircut—agreeing on 45–50 percent—as well as on other disputed matters. "There was a sense of drama," remembers one Fed participant. "It was one of these down-to-the-wire discussions. We knew we would be able to get close to an agreement."

Why did the MOF men suddenly yield? First was a consensual awareness that international political tensions had reached the exploding point. Most important, they calculated that the 45–50 percent haircut level provided sufficient leeway for Japanese banks to hurdle the minimum capital standards.[38]

News that Japan had agreed in principle to the international bank capital accord was promptly leaked by MOF to the press. This caused some consternation for Fed officials, since U.S. bankers were unaware they were in

Tokyo. Why was the leak made? "Our local bankers were the audience," explains MOF's Gyohten. "We decided as a policy objective this is now our set goal. We announced that we would do it rather than leave it unclear. We made it clear that this is *not* an issue that could be repealed."

The change in Japan's position became evident to all at the next Cooke G10 Basel supervisors committee meeting on June 23 and 24 in Brussels.

Breakthrough to a Global Standard

The Brussels meeting also ratified the decisive, elegantly simple conceptual breakthrough that paved the way for the multilateral accord: a leveraged, two-tier formula for assessing capital adequacy—Tier 2, or "dirty," capital could be counted only to the extent that the bank had an equal amount of the Tier 1, or best quality, capital. Thus, under the final agreement, Tier 1 and Tier 2 had to total 8 percent of assets. But Tier 1 had to comprise at least 4 percent. This went a long way to assuaging German and Swiss objections that their banks were being penalized by having to fill the 8 percent quota with the best and most expensive capital while others could fill it with "dirty capital" their law didn't even recognize. It also helped solve the Japanese problem, since unrealized capital gains fit less controversially into Tier 2 capital. The Tier 1/Tier 2 concept, in short, worked because it was rigorous enough to upgrade capital standards while offering sufficient ways to do so without disrupting any country's regulatory regime.

The Brussels breakthrough was the product of private brainstorming sessions Peter Cooke conducted in his quest for a pan-G10 formula. The key creative session was an impromptu one-on-one meeting with Jerry Corrigan at the New York Fed.

Corrigan's enthusiasm for the leveraged Tier 1/Tier 2 concept increased the odds that the United States would trade its bilateral accord with Britain for a multilateral agreement. At Brussels, U.S. and U.K. representatives discussed doing so.

Brussels participants also tackled a new problem raised by Citibank's May 19 $3 billion loan loss reserves increase to cover LDC debt. Under U.S. accounting rules—as well as under the U.S.-U.K. bilateral proposal—Citi's shareholder equity fell; but because loan loss reserves qualified as capital, its total capital *increased* by $500 million. Yet if those reserves were used to offset LDC debt losses, surely common sense dictated that they should not be counted in capital?[39] The problem was that many U.S. banks couldn't meet the proposed 8 percent minimum standards without them.

Many tittered at the United States wriggling in the artifice it had contrived to compel involuntary adjustment by others. The Brussels meeting adjourned without resolving it.

Prospects for any multilateral agreement came close to unraveling when Japan began to backslide on its 45–50 percent haircut agreement at a meeting at the New York Fed on August 24 and 25, 1987. Corrigan arrested it by getting very tough at a dinner he hosted for MOF delegation leader and banking bureau director general Tadao Chino. Corrigan bluntly informed his guests that there was much anti-Japanese political sentiment in the United States from which he was shielding them. It would be more difficult for him to maintain a nonpoliticized, free market "national treatment" decision-making process if his credibility were undercut by the failure to deliver an agreement. The sheer size and international presence of Japan's financial institutions, he added, obligated them to live up to global responsibilities. "The Americans are quite capable of heavy-handed tactics with the Japanese," notes a European central banker. "Not bully boy tactics, but putting financial pressure on them."

Chino appeared visibly shaken as he left the dinner. The next day, after presumably conferring with Tokyo, he capitulated to the 50 percent haircut.

By late summer 1987 central bankers were close to achieving the international agreement that had eluded them for so many years. They hoped to resolve their outstanding differences when Peter Cooke convened the next supervisors committee meeting at Basel on September 17 and 18.

In preparation, U.S., U.K., and Japanese bank supervisors, headed by the Fed's Bill Taylor, the BOE's Brian Quinn, and the MOF's Tadao Chino, met for a series of bilateral and then trilateral meetings at London from Friday, September 11, through Sunday, September 13.[40] The teams further narrowed differences among them. They negotiated transition periods and the interim treatment of contentious elements of capital. "The three of us agreed to stick together," says one participant. "Once we got to Basel we had most of it worked out. It was hard for Germany to challenge us. France and Italy couldn't. As each country's turn to comment on each issue came up around the table, we each took the same positions. Chino all the time was saying that Japan agreed. Everyone of course noticed it."[41]

BOE's Brian Quinn qualifies, "It was not a wholly cooked package. We thrashed out what would be acceptable to each of us. It was to understand what the problems were going into the Cooke committee meeting later in the week."

• • •

When the roughly thirty members from the twelve G10 countries of the Basel supervisors committee convened on Thursday, September 17, about a dozen issues still divided them.[42] Still contentious was the size of the Japanese haircut. Some were still reluctant to allow these hidden gains in capital at all. After long discussion, however, most were willing to accept the 50 percent haircut compromise negotiated by Japan and the United States. But Brian Quinn was not. "Our [U.K.] bankers won't go along with that," he said. "They'll say that the deal is not worth the paper it's written on." The German representatives from the Berlin Federal Banking Supervisory Office and the Bundesbank also protested that 50 percent was not enough.

After huddling with his team, Chino agreed to a final compromise: Japan would shave off another 5 percent to bring the haircut to 55 percent. Henceforth 45 percent of the unrealized capital gains of shareholdings would be counted in capital.

Treatment of general loan loss reserves had become the main American issue, since its weakness was exposed by Citibank's LDC debt provisioning. Throughout the summer the United States held out that 2 percent of the 8 percent capital risk assets should be admitted—at least as Tier 2 "dirty" capital. But to Quinn 2 percent was a deal breaker.

In the event, the preparatory negotiations at London paved the way for the final compromise at Basel: the reserves temporarily would be allowed in Tier 2, but up to no more than 1.25 percent when the final agreement took effect in 1992. It was the U.S.'s Taylor who proposed this solution. "If you are suspicious that we will use the loan losses to help us make the [8 percent] guidelines, then we will prove to you that this is not our intent by putting a ceiling on it," he said.[43]

Another difficult debate was over how long the transition period to compliance should be and which elements of capital could be counted in Tier 1 and Tier 2 during it. The original goal was to reach an 8 percent capital to asset ratio—half Tier 1—by the end of 1990. The United Kingdom pressed for this short and stringent transition, since "all our banks were 8 percent and above and suffering from unfair competition for years and years."

But too many other countries feared that the deadline might be too tough for them to meet.[44] As a result, a transitional standard was set of 7.25 percent by year-end 1990 during which some Tier 2 elements of capital could be counted in Tier 1. The 8 percent minimum, with a more stringent Tier 1 capital definition, was set for year-end 1992. The Japanese got an extra three months, until the end of their fiscal year, March 1993.

The final meeting dragged on hour after hour. Dinner was brought in. Midnight bells tolled. Finally Peter Cooke drew the half a dozen remaining issues on the blackboard and proposed a global compromise for all. When the exhausted members accepted it, the world's first universal bank capital adequacy accord, save for a few politically sensitive issues that would be left for the governors, was attained.

The governors prepared to consider the committee's draft report at the November 1987 BIS meetings. But the October 19 global stock market crash forced a one-month postponement. Over the December Basel weekend the governors tackled three main issues. First was the politely labeled "club question": Which countries' debt instruments would be rewarded with the lowest risk weighting? The LDC debt crisis demanded that sovereign debt be risk weighted. Yet it was politically sensitive and could even upset international capital flows—the plunging dollar was paramount in all their minds at that moment—to rate one country's debt a higher risk than another's. This was just the sort of political judgment central bankers studiously avoided to make. The supervisors committee didn't dare address it. The governors had to.

In the end, the governors accorded 0 percent risk weighting to all twenty four governments of the OECD, plus those countries that had concluded special lending arrangements with the IMF through the General Agreements to Borrow (GAB). The GAB was merely a contrivance "to finesse Saudi Arabia," since all other GAB members were part of the OECD.[45] Possessing enough oil wealth to move global financial markets, the Saudis had become a shadow member of the inner club of world finance. The OECD definition had some financially untidy corners, such as inclusion of troubled debtor Turkey. But it angered few with sufficient political clout to matter.

The second problem was the "German question." For domestic political tranquillity, Bundesbank President Karl Otto Pöhl regularly lodged pro forma dissents on any definition that included "dirty" capital not recognized under German law, as well as any perceived commitment to alter German regulations in advance of the legally binding EC-wide 1992 bank regulatory reform. To accommodate Pöhl, the governors included the German exception in every draft—that all countries but one agreed. In exchange, Pöhl gave his fellow governors a gentleman's wink of support. "We realized we did have to help Pöhl, so we added the "except for one country" phrase," says Bank of England Governor Leigh-Pemberton. "The country wasn't specified, but everyone understood it was Germany. Pöhl had a difficult constitutional problem. We were all sympathetic to his position. It all could have foundered at some stage on technicalities, and we are grateful that he accepted."

An unexpected third problem was a demand by Banque de France Governor Jacques de Larosière that the general loan loss provisions attributable as capital be boosted from 1.25 percent to 2 percent.[46] At the September Cooke committee meeting, France's representatives had agreed to the 1.25 percent. In the intervening period, says a British central banker, "they went away to do their sums and realized it didn't add up for them." French banks probably couldn't reach the minimum standards without relief.

Countries that wouldn't count such provisions as capital, such as Germany and the United Kingdom, were outraged. But with "the French holding out longer than anyone, as usual," the governors finally relented. In addition they allowed that at each nation's discretion until 1992, some of the general loan loss reserves in diminishing amounts could be counted as Tier 1 capital.[47]

"The meeting was a horse-trading session," says one central banker. "The haggling went on through the year. It was good-natured except for one or two occasions." In December 1987 the governors issued a six-month consultative paper outlining the proposals. In July 1988 they endorsed the final agreement.

The final accord called for minimum capital at internationally active banks worth 8 percent of risk-weighted assets, half of which had to be Tier 1, or "pure" capital.[48] There were five risk-weighting categories: 0 percent, 10 percent, 20 percent, 50 percent, and 100 percent. Off balance sheet activities were included. Each country could apply its national criteria within these minimums. Some intended to be more stringent than the Basel standards.

The endorsement and publicity of the bank capital accords required several rare procedures for Basel central bankers accustomed to osmotic communication and informal consensus. "There was no vote in the sense of raising your hands, but there was a decision," says Leigh-Pemberton. "It was also unusual in that it was announced. It normally would have been referred back to the Cooke committee. But there was no method to publicize a decision of the G10 governors."

Although legally nonbinding—and adopted without any democratic national legislative vote—the central banker club code of honor made it as good as law. "It is not an international treaty, but if you sign up to something like that, it must be taken very seriously," says Bank of Canada Governor John Crow. "It's a commitment to live up to the spirit. There is no limit to the imagination of people to invent hybrid instruments that might count as capital. Now they must submit to peer review."

Chapter 23

Catch-up

The awesome global dimensions of the Black Monday stock market crash rallied a bandwagon of support for the Basel capital accord within governments and markets. Within six months it was endorsed by ninety national bank supervisors and implemented by the United States, United Kingdom, and Japan. The EC adopted most of it by December 1989.[1] When the Bush administration, eager to escape blame for the early 1990s credit crunch and economic downturn, sought to relax the Basel standards, central bankers, says Alan Greenspan, responded "as a group that it was not subject to negotiation and that it would be counterproductive if it were relaxed." Bush backed off.

Financial markets seemed to heave a great sigh of relief at the added protective capital cushion it built into a world banking industry under its greatest stress in half a century from structural revolution and an economic environment of record indebtedness and world imbalances. It was as though the central bankers struck a psychological nerve by supplying something desperately desired that market forces themselves were unable to provide. Financial penalties began to be imposed spontaneously by the marketplace on weakly capitalized banks, forcing them to raise capital or seek merger partners. Bank executives stifled their particular grievances and supported the Basel accord because of its universality.

The most important market reaction was that banks all over the world began raising massive amounts of capital. From 1988 through September 1992 U.S. banks alone added $77 billion to their equity capital, helping them to survive $123 billion in bad loan write-offs. Bank executives reoriented their strategic emphasis away from the unrestrained credit growth encouraged by the globalization of finance and back to basic profit margins. By the 1992 implementation date most major world banks defied pessimistic predictions and met the 8 percent minimum risk-weighted capital-to-asset ratio.

The bank capital accord even galvanized a market movement to extend the Basel guidelines into comprehensive harmonized global rules and oversight for *all* financial firms. American Express Chairman James Robinson set the pace in June 1988 by calling for parallel rules on his own securities sector.

At first blush the sight of market leaders calling for governments to regulate them clashed with the stereotype. But with the fates of a handful of global financial giants, banks as well as securities firms, increasingly bound together through huge trading and large payments systems exposures to one another around the world, it made sense. "Banks and investment banks will *want* to have the central oversight because it is the counterparty risk that can bring us all down," explains ex–J. P. Morgan Chairman Lewis Preston. "Once the rules are set and the [market] mechanisms are in place, then anybody can fail—but first you have to do the regulatory things."

The mutual interests of the political democratic and capitalist economic realms converged on building a seamless, transparent safe circuit for the new high-speed volatile, interlinked, and fully floating nonsystem of global finance. From the start the central bankers envisioned their bank capital accord as the basic building block for doing so. "The first and most important line of defense of financial system stability," says New York Fed's Jerry Corrigan, "is the capital of individual institutions."

The thickened cushion of bank capital alleviated some anxieties that major failures in the United States and world banking system would drag down many others with them. It added some margin of safety against nervous-making financial asset price volatility, huge and high-speed changes in international and intermarket capital movements, large risk concentrations and homogeneous herd behavior by big players, hard-to-assess risks in explosively growing innovative products like off balance sheet derivatives, and the opacity of which entities were holding what ultimate financial risks in an interlinked global financial network with supervisory gaps and regulatory disharmonies.

Central bankers, nevertheless, remained far behind the curve in a game of supervisory catch-up. The Basel bank capital adequacy accord "covers basically only credit or counterpart risk," acknowledges Peter Cooke. "It does not set out to cover many other very important risks—interest rate risk in particular, position risk or trading risk, foreign exchange risk, and liquidity risk."[2] It took until 1993 for the Basel supervisors to propose global standards for banks' risk from foreign exchange, securities, and derivatives trading and from interest rate fluctuations.

Central bankers' top priority after the Basel Accord was improving the robustness of the world's strained and expanding cross-border bank clearance, settlements, and payments network. With surging financial turnover, intraday payment exposures among counterparties often reached many times the capital base of the largest banks. An inability of a big bank to settle payments, perhaps due to an unexpected crisis of a large client during the day, could still cause many other payment system participants to be unable to meet their payment obligations. Major payment defaults and clearinghouse failures could quickly cascade across markets and national borders.

Central bankers had been losing sleep over the risk posed by settlement of different legs of foreign exchange transactions in different continental time zones since the 1974 failure of Germany's Herstatt Bank left a huge volume of half-completed trades and commensurate uncertainty in the international payments system pipeline. To reduce the danger of a systemic cataclysm, a G10 committee headed by BIS General Manager Lamfalussy in November 1990 issued "best practices" guidelines for multilateral, cross-border payment netting operations, such as CHIPS. The Basel supervisors committee, under the new chairmanship of Jerry Corrigan, followed up with complementary capital adequacy guidelines.[3] The highlights were to minimize credit risk exposures through "netting" of amounts owed, standardized, short settlement periods, and assurance of final settlement by obligating all clearinghouse members to stand behind any troubled sister through legally binding loss-sharing arrangements.[4] The eventual goal was a "real-time" settlement system, which would eliminate dangerous exposure buildup because of time lags in payment.

The central bank governors also agreed in principle to assign responsibility among themselves for supervising such cross-border netting operations—a thinly veiled demarcation of lender of last resort responsibilities. A new concordat, piggybacked upon its predecessors, was informally agreed upon, although formal adoption got snagged on incompatible national bankruptcy laws.[5]

The Black Monday crash also highlighted the global peril of inadequate and incompatible national capital market clearing and settlement plumbing—illiquidity in one market caused liquidity drains on others via intermarket linkages and world-straddling players. This problem headed the discussion at the meeting of the New York Fed's international advisory committee of top international bank and capital market executives on Friday, October 23, 1987, only four days after the crash.

Central bankers worked around the awkward fact that their domain usually did not encompass capital markets, even though systemic disruptions could originate there, by pulling strings backstage. They did so through the shadowy, private nonprofit club of financial leaders known as the Group of Thirty. The chief puppeteer behind the G30 was retired Bank of England Governor Gordon Richardson. He acted in concert with the New York Fed's Corrigan, who "thought it was important that the initiative take place in the private sector." Under G30 auspices Richardson orchestrated a three-panel meeting of one hundred top world financial executives and regulators in London on March 8, 1988. Corrigan delivered the luncheon address. The end result months later were nine "best practices" recommendations, with a monitoring secretariat and (ultimately too ambitious) timetables to upgrade and harmonize national securities' clearing and settlements systems. "From the start it was clear that we couldn't just move to a brand-new global clearing system," explains Richardson. "So we had to work to make the national systems more compatible and better. Many national systems were inadequate. If a system is inadequate nationally, then it is certainly inadequate internationally."

To make the first world bank capital standard for banks effective, the Basel governors knew that they had to extend parallel rules to the big security firms that competed with them across integrated world markets. Carrying expensive physical branch networks in an age of electronic money transfer, and hemmed into a declining market segment by obsolete and onerous industry regulations, banks were losing badly. In the first half of the 1980s securities' market share of international lending soared from one-quarter to nine-tenths. Banks' share of domestic U.S. lending declined steadily from 55 percent in the mid-1970s to only 36 percent by early 1993. Unless applied to securities firms doing similar business, the Basel standards perversely would hasten the banking industry's decline. "Take foreign exchange as an example," says Corrigan. "It makes *no* sense at all to impose different capital standards." Bush Treasury Secretary Nicholas Brady concurs, "It is hard to argue that commercial banks should be overseen by a Federal Reserve System but that the securities industry should function far more autonomously."[6] As banks' financial market share declined, so did the effectiveness of central bankers' main lever for executing monetary policy and protecting financial system stability.

But how could central bankers extend the Basel standards to security firms? Central bankers did not supervise them. Securities regulators were at least fifteen years behind central bankers in coming to grips with the global financial revolution. Some securities firms had completely unregulated affiliates. There was no Basel Concordat counterpart defining home and host country responsibilities for problems arising from international capital markets. National capital markets supervision was generally oriented toward fair transactions and smoothly functioning markets—not the systemic stability concerns of central bankers. Not only was there was no supranational BIS-type club for world securities regulators, but few talked often to each other. During the 1987 crash U.S. SEC Chairman David Ruder and Tsuneo Fujita, MOF director general of the securities bureau, exchanged home phone numbers and vowed to have frequent consultations in future. After the crisis faded, however, "[W]e did talk, but *not* so frequently," says Fujita.

Basel committee central bankers' solution was to undertake to identify and organize international securities regulators with whom they could negotiate common capital standards in areas where banking and security activities overlapped. Within a year of the bank capital agreement, bank and securities regulators had met twice.[7] Progress, however, proved to be very slow.

As financial markets integrated further, the necessity for worldwide convergence with big insurers and corporate financial services firms, which also competed increasingly with banks, loomed on the horizon. The Basel committee took the first step by meeting with the highly fragmented insurance regulators in December 1990.[8]

Despite central bankers' supervisory and regulatory gains, there were many places that the new integrated global financial landscape was running far ahead of them. Central bankers were especially worried about the multiple opaque risks in the $8 trillion derivatives markets that were overwhelmingly concentrated in a handful of global banking giants seeking to compensate for the loss of their traditional lending business to securities markets. Nervous-making too was the payments default risk and financial volatility generated by the trading practices of highly leveraged hedge funds, many of which were domiciled in effectively unregulated "offshore" financial centers. Complex and opaque derivative product linkages made systemic financial contagion harder for central bankers to assess and contain. Since final (and presently poorly reported) risk positions were held across national borders, it was possible that a monetary policy tightening move by the Fed aimed at the United States, for example, could have its largest restraining impact in Europe or Japan. Such changes in the new financial landscape exemplified why global standards for financial disclosure were becoming a complementary necessity of minimum prudential standards for central bankers in the future to fulfill their twin financial stability and monetary policy goals.[9] In 1994, central bankers took a step forward with a refined proposal for covering derivatives in its basic bank capital adequacy framework for credit risk.

The immediate political test of the Basel Accord for capital adequacy was to fulfill its tacit promise to arrest the "latter-day Japan Inc. assault on world financial markets" by neutralizing Japanese banks' pricing advantage through Japan's lax capital regulatory requirements.[10] To meet the new Basel standards, Japanese banks had to add huge amounts of capital or sharply scale down their international lending. In 1987 and early 1988 most Japanese and foreigners believed it was impossible for them to raise sufficient additional capital. Trying to do so, some MOF officials feared, could even knock the prop out from under Japan's *zaiteku*-crazed stock market.

They were wrong. "We didn't know the market would keep soaring as it did," says MOF's Toyoo Gyohten. Unique among the world's major equity markets, the Tokyo Stock Exchange resumed its surge in early 1988, nearly doubling to 38,916 by December 1989. Instead of dragging down the stock market, "bank stocks were pushed on capital adequacy."[11] Bank shares traded at several times book value, while U.S. banks languished at book value or below.

The boom enabled Japanese banks to boost Tier 1 capital by an astonishing ¥7.8 trillion ($60 billion) through virtually costless issues of fresh equity and retained *zaiteku* profits. Tier 2 capital swelled from the doubling of their equity portfolios. By 1989 all city banks were comfortably above the final ratios required for March 1993.

Instead of disciplining Japanese banks, the Basel capital guidelines had armed them with a political license to besiege world financial markets. "The BIS ratios were directed to point to the weakness of Japanese banks," notes Bank of Tokyo Chairman Yusuke Kashiwagi. "But they just clarified our strength in the end."

The central bankers had embarrassingly miscalculated. "The Japanese cost of capital is lower," says J. P. Morgan Chairman Lewis Preston. "I don't think Cooke or Corrigan understood it." While waiting vainly for market forces to break the Tokyo stock market fever perverting the intent of the Basel standards, Jerry Corrigan alerted Japanese bankers and industrialists at a luncheon at the Keidanren in October 1989 that the international inequality in capital costs arising from Japan's highly controlled financial environment and *zaiteku* was threatening U.S. protectionist sanctions.

The following month Treasury Undersecretary for International Affairs David Mulford publicly put Japanese leaders on notice that their continued foot dragging in liberalizing Japan's financial system to international norms "invites congressional action and risks exhausting the U.S. Treasury's patience. . . ."[12] Mulford elaborates, "In the last year or two [1988–89], the momentum for liberalization has not been there. They think the job is done. But Japanese banks are profitable in part because they are subsidized at home with a cheap deposit base and other things. They have fourteen percent of our market; we have 1 percent of theirs. Asset inflation is giving them a cost of capital advantage. Is it fair? If they're clever enough to have a system that produces cheaper capital, then yes. But if the regulatory system is helping produce the advantage, then it will be seen as political."

The intent of the Basel Accord to level the financial competitive playing field was being defeated by the same entrenched Establishment forces that blocked Japan's internationalists from using rapid yen appreciation as the wedge for restructuring Japan's lopsided and internationally incompatible political economy. Confides a high BOJ official, "I didn't believe the capital adequacy guidelines alone could stop Japanese banks' behavior. I think opening the market domestically is more important."

In late 1989 Japan was at the apex of its intoxicating "bubble economy." Fueled by the speculative *zaiteku* euphoria associated with Japan's sudden leap to economic superpower status, financial asset prices were rocketing off the charts. Banks and businesses were raising almost unlimited amounts of capital several times more inexpensively than anywhere else in the world. All cylinders of the economy were thundering ahead at breakneck speed. Finance was visibly driving the real economy out of line with sustainable fundamentals.

To meet the unslakable demand from frenzied domestic financial speculators, Japanese firms borrowed tens of billions of additional short-term dollars from unregulated international financial markets. At the same time, low domestic interest rates helped export Japanese long-term capital abroad in amounts far exceeding the huge surpluses it earned from international trade. One consequence of the "overrecycling" was to prolong the world economic imbalances. Another was the foreign "overpresence" of the Japanese banks and securities firms that intermediated most of this business. A political bureaucratic stalemate over reforming the domestic regulatory barriers restraining bank and securities competition at home further deflected pent-up Japanese financial competition into new markets abroad. "MOF thought it could liberalize banking and securities by mutual entry outside Japan and keep them divided at home," explains ex–BOJ Deputy Governor for International Shijuro Ogata. "Overpresence in London is due to regulatory arbitrage."

Simply, the guided financial system that worked so effectively when Japan was a capital-short, small world player had to be adapted to a new environment of abundant, globalized finance and a Japan that generated huge structural capital surpluses that exerted strong gravity on the world political economy. Rather than reform its financial system along the Anglo-Saxon free market model, the Japanese Establishment elected instead to profess its intention to liberalize and to tinker with controlled admission of market forces and token foreign firm presence in order to achieve a new guided equilibrium that didn't upset traditional interests yet was tolerable to its trading partners. As a result, the MOF and BOJ were slowly evolving from "high priests" into "franchisers" that oversaw a financial system of "franchisees." A blatant form of control was being substituted for a subtler one. Many illiberal practices were eliminated formally but continued informally through the myriad incestuous interconnections between regulators and regulated.[13]

One paradoxical result of the interaction of Japan's "repressed" financial system and export-lopsided political economic structure with the liberal financial world order was that for a prolonged period Japan had a strong external yen while overproducing yen domestically to help levitate financial asset values. "Insofar as Japan is enjoying surpluses, it need not pay back substantial money with real assets, so those assets like securities and land can be too high versus those in other countries," explained former MOF Vice Minister for International Takashi Hosomi at the peak of the stock and real estate boom. "I'm not sure if it can continue forever or not. We are waiting for economic rationality to work. The real problem is that people have such a huge amount of savings and no other way to deposit it. Japanese financial institutions are very slow or incapable of producing new products, and regulations forbid it. Is it national policy? I'm still thinking about it, I'm not sure. There is a lack of political will. In the meantime Japanese paper money is strong enough to buy anything."

Central bankers' capital ratios finally began to deliver its intended restraint only after Yasushi Mieno became governor of the Bank of Japan in late December 1989. Mieno, a career central banker, had been appalled by the financial bubble and its potential for inflationary spillover. He promptly boosted the discount rate from 3.75 percent to 6 percent over half a year and imposed strong window guidance against real estate lending. Long-term rates rose four percentage points.

Equity prices went into a slow-motion nosedive; with a lag, real estate prices peaked out. From 38,916, the Tokyo Stock Exchange plummeted to 20,221 by October 1990. After rallying in 1991, it crashed again to its August 1992 bottom of 14,309—a total fall of 63 percent. After having gained nearly $4 trillion from 1985 to 1989, equity values lost back nearly $3 trillion. It was yet another example of economically fruitless financial volatility unhinged from economic fundamentals.

The effect was as if the central limousine in the Japanese convoy, which had been zooming along the international economic highway at 120 miles an hour, abruptly slammed on its brakes. With the cost of capital suddenly risen to world levels, Japan's capital spending explosion went bust. The economy became stagnant. Business failures and bad debts mounted. Japanese banks, which looked so invincible in the 1980s, suddenly faced their worst crisis in postwar history.

It was on top of this treacherous asset bubble deflation that the Basel capital-to-asset ratios were finally biting. As stock prices collapsed, so did the unrealized capital gains in bank portfolios—far in excess of the 55 percent haircut provision of the Basel Accord. The illusion that puffed up Japan's bank capital cushion was suddenly deflating. Japanese banks, it turned out, were even more undercapitalized than the Basel central bank negotiators had believed. A cottage industry sprouted up in predicting at what stock market level the leading banks would fall below the BIS minimums. Around 17,000 looked to be the key threshold for clearing Tier 2. Meanwhile, banks' total capital faced a massive write-down from loan losses in the Japanese real estate bust as well as from their overseas misadventures in property and leveraged buyout lending.

Since raising fresh equity was impossible, the banks shrank assets at home and abroad. Talk began to circulate in Tokyo that the implementation date of the Basel capital hurdles might have to be extended for Japanese banks to clear them. Central bankers were loath to do so formally. Yet they weren't going to make an issue of compliance—there were no automatic sanctions anyway—when compliance was likely to impart a further deflationary squeeze to Japan and the foreign capital–dependent United States.

With government assistance the stock market rallied just enough, big banks' *keiretsu* family companies bought just enough of their subordinated debentures, and Japanese regulators took a sanguine enough—baldly fictitious, commented many—view of the quality of Japanese banks' troubled loan portfolios that all big Japanese banks cleared the Basel hurdle, on paper, by early 1993.

Political Limits

The difficulty extending the Basel capital standards to neighboring financial sectors, and in leveling out the playing field with Japanese banks, highlighted that central bankers could no more guarantee a safe and sound international circuit for the huge, volatile volumes of global capital while national financial industry structures and supervisory regimes were obsolete and globally incompatible than their monetary policy could consistently deliver robust growth in an economy of imbalanced savings and investment. The two, in fact, were closely related: disharmonious national financial systems helped drive the cross-border capital flows, exchange rates, national savings levels, and money supplies that influenced trade and growth. Financial fragility was a sword of Damocles threatening monetary policy with disruption of credit flows to the economy, inflationary bailouts, and insidious moral hazard effects.

Beyond the foundational structural changes required in Japan, the U.S.'s egregiously overdue renovation of its 1930s compartmentalized financial architecture had created a fragmented, fragile, and peculiarly accident-prone industry. What was required was comprehensive deregulation of the obsolete barriers of the financial system, accompanied by enhanced controls and disclosure requirements over freewheeling neighboring sectors—and then international harmonization of definitions, regulatory framework, and standards. Yet periodic efforts at comprehensive reform were stymied by special-interest-group lobbying and the personal vanities of a few key legislators. The outcome was democratic ungovernability that everyone knew was deleterious to capitalist and democratic well-being. CONGRESS FAILS; WILL BANKS? was *The New York Times'* concise editorial headline to one such legislative failure in 1991.[14] Even after the stock market crash warning, the Brady Task Force's modest recommendation to assign oversight responsibility for intermarket risks to one institution—its preference was the Fed—had stalemated in Washington turf wars.

Ironically it was the central bankers so worried about moral hazard who themselves were often the first to press for early and comprehensive rescues across markets and internationally to head off potential crises in the interlinked financial landscape. New York Fed President Jerry Corrigan explains the dilemma: "Are the statistical probabilities of a major and systemic financial shock higher or lower than they once were? I'd say they are lower. But widespread damage would flow from a problem. As a central banker, you have to assume that the risks are greater." Despite Alan Greenspan's effort to perpetuate a chastening ambiguity, market and political leaders took it for granted that the Fed stood behind capital market firms over which it had no prudential oversight. Any lingering doubts were erased during the 190-point "minicrash" of the stock market on Friday, October 13, 1989. Instead of waiting to act until Monday as in October 1987, the Fed over the weekend informed market leaders and overseas policymakers that it was prepared to pump money into the financial system. FED PREPARES TO PROP UP MARKETS was the reassuring *Financial Times* headline greeting market players when they arrived at work Monday morning.[15]

Democratic government gridlock was also inducing central bankers to run greater political risks by compensating with regulatory fiat. In 1989, and then again in September 1990, Greenspan made two bold forays across the U.S. political Rubicon by permitting J. P. Morgan's holding company to do corporate securities underwriting by a liberal regulatory interpretation of the 1933 Glass-Steagall Act. Although politicians attacked the hubris of unelected central bank technocrats, Greenspan was merely bowing to the market reality that Washington was denying. "Global finance creates mechanisms that can deregulate a domestic economy," explains a Fed official. "The Fed lets banks underwrite securities because they're doing it already in the international markets and the Fed can't stop them."

That the strongly capitalized J. P. Morgan received the coveted regulatory passport to the domestic securities business was also significant. It was a message from Greenspan that he would wield the Fed's profit-influencing regulatory powers to reward banks that complied with the spirit of the Basel Accord—and use the stick of forced capital-building actions, against those which did not.

An industry shakeout and consolidation was occurring under the competitive pressures of the global financial revolution. Without overdue systemic reform, the inevitable messiness ran the heightened risk of spillover into a financial and economic crisis and diminished central banker capacity to counteract it. "The financial fragility will be with us for some time," says BIS General Manager Lamfalussy. "This gives central bankers a task—and considerable responsibility."

A Faint Beacon

In establishing the first worldwide financial standards, central bankers were fulfilling their peculiar role in democratic capitalist society as unspoken arbiters of the unsteady marriage between nation-state governments and financial markets that had gone global. "It is not necessarily wisdom that has made central bankers the ones to make the international rules first," says Lamfalussy. "They are in the forefront because they had to deal with the internationalization of banking in their policies."

Central bankers *could* act—and in a speedy and a depoliticizing manner—thanks to their independence, their regulatory authority, and the existence of the supranational BIS. "Central bank independence was critical in the capital adequacy negotiations," argues the Fed's Manley Johnson. "With independence we can pursue the smooth flow of capital to the United States even while the politicians rail that Japan is not opening its markets. A channel with that flexibility is terribly important."

The growing danger that a financial crisis arising anywhere in the world could spill rapidly and with complexity throughout integrated global financial markets indeed argued for *extending* central bankers' supervisory reach to major nonbank players and to encompass public disclosure and transparency. "Scarcely a singe regulatory issue that formerly was viewed solely a domestic matter can now be intelligently discussed without reference to international flows of funds and the regulatory environments in foreign countries," points out Brookings Senior Fellow Ralph Bryant.

Yet the arcane technical nature of international finance meant that "[p]ublic opinion is not likely to force the underlying issues onto the agendas of government policymakers. . . . It may take a major economic or financial crisis to catalyze a widespread awareness of the underlying trends."[16] The way forward, suggests ex–Senator William Proxmire (D-Wisc.) was "international regulations, mutual consultation. Congress—*fortunately*—doesn't play much of a role in the process. It must be done by the administration and the Fed—not the other regulators so much."

The Basel Accord was a landmark political policy disguised in the technical jargon of money and finance and the studied, apolitical demeanor of central bankers. For the first time a supranational political discipline was imposed on the mushrooming privatized, floating global financial "nonsystem" that so often diverged from economic fundamentals, spread systemic financial fragility, and increasingly dictated the policy options of democratic polities. Through the Basel Accord, nations effectively pooled their sovereignty to win back from markets some of the control that was slipping away from each individually. By bringing one of the forces shaping the political and economic rules of the game by which wealth was produced and allocated within and among nations a little bit more under the influence of elected representatives, the accord promoted capitalist stability and the long-term transposition of the liberal national democratic political ideals to the changed world economy driven by stateless capital. Encouraged by central bankers and other regulators, financial market institutions were frequently themselves tabling self-regulatory proposals that benefited financial order and headed off more restrictive, possibly distortion-producing external regulations.

At superficial glance, the fact that an international political accord was made by unelected central bankers without public debate or legislative vote might seem to constitute an unacceptable lack of democratic accountability. Yet through private dialogue with their Finance Ministries and key legislators, central bankers received signals that they were safely in tune with political currents. "Congress was kept generally informed," says Ken McLean, then Senate Banking Committee staff chief. "We knew that something was afloat, and [we understood] the general concept of Tier One and Tier Two. We didn't know the numbers. Congressional approval was not needed. But it was favorably received."

The central bankers' universal bank capital adequacy accord was politically significant in other ways. It marked the turning point from the "go-go" laissez-faire deregulation trend that swept world financial markets from the mid-1970s to the start of a reregulatory counterrevolution. Like the G7's dollar management experiment, it was an example of how democratic governments were trying to discourage disruptive overtrading in global financial markets by giving—in this case, imposing—their view(s).

Most significant was the accord's risk-weighting framework. By raising or lowering risk weights on categories of assets, central bankers could influence the flow of credit to preferred economic sectors or away from frothy ones. By assigning a 0 percent risk weighting to U.S. government debt, for instance, the governors quietly supported—indirectly subsidized—the then plunging dollar at the expense of businesses that had a 100 percent risk weighting. "I think these international financial regulations are in some sense new instruments," observes Princeton Professor William Branson.[17]

Yet if risk weighting offered a potential new tool for exerting leverage over global financial markets, it also elevated the moral and political hazards by making the central bankers more responsible for bank lending allocation decisions. Inauspiciously, public sector track records were worse than capitalist free markets in allocating investments most productively. For these reasons Volcker only reluctantly had endorsed the risk-weighted framework in 1986 as a least bad option. "The one thing Volcker hoped to avoid was dictating the credit allocation decision," says his then special assistant, Steven Roberts. "It was not the central bank's role to allocate."

Risk weighting had to be monitored carefully to avoid creating its own financial distortions, political abuses, and inequities. Politicians would be sorely tempted to relax standards for electoral goals. Governments generally might try to tilt the risk-weighting scales so much in its favor to facilitate financing of the government deficits that it could prejudice lending to private enterprises. Central bankers—provided they were independent—had an institutional self-interest in being vigilant, however: having fought for their monetary independence through a front-door "divorce" from the obligation to monetize their governments' fiscal deficits, they didn't want to lose it through back-door entrapment in the mix of risk-weighting incentives or charges of partisan political pandering.

The Basel Accord, and the global financial forces involuntarily expanding central bankers' supervisory vistas generally, accentuated the paradoxes inherent in central banks' dual regulatory and monetary functions. Critics saw a conflict of interest. Most central bankers, however, saw synergy: regulatory powers enhanced their leverage over private bank policies at pivotal moments. This helped uphold financial system stability needed for monetary policy to work. It also provided useful intelligence on business conditions that informed monetary policy decisions. In this view, the monetary purity of the Bundesbank, with its puny regulatory powers, put it at risk of becoming an ivory tower and afflicting it with myopia in recognizing threats to global financial system stability.[18] The Bundesbank's absence of regulatory powers was a hindrance in the negotiation of the universal Basel bank capital agreement.

The global financial market arguments favoring an expansion of central bankers' supervisory roles gathered additional force when one considered that the practical alternative was partisan political control of regulation— and, with it, influence over money. To foresee the dangers, one had only to recall the U.S. Office of the Comptroller's narrow partisan disregard for systemic safety and soundness in the near failure of First Options during the October 1987 stock market crash.

From the mid-1980s Paul Volcker warned privately and almost obsessively that the unholy orgy of debt, consumption, and financial speculative behavior unleashed in the global financial revolution might end in a catastrophic chain reaction of financial and business failures. Volcker forestalled the chain reaction on his watch by maintaining growth, firefighting crises, and slowly upgrading banks' capital adequacy. The true test, he warned in 1989, would come in the next recession.[19]

That test arrived in 1990, with Alan Greenspan at the helm.

PART SIX

DENOUEMENT—A CONTAINED DEPRESSION

Chapter 24

Financial Dunkirk

On December 19, 1991, Fed Chairman Alan Greenspan took his boldest move since Black Monday: a full one-percentage-point cut in the discount rate to 3.5 percent. The move surprised Wall Street and many Fed insiders. At the FOMC meeting just three days earlier, no Federal Reserve Bank had requested more than a half-point discount rate cut. By tradition, the Board of Governors never changed the discount rate without such a request. The December 19 action came after five half-point cuts in twelve months that slashed the discount rate to its lowest level since the early 1960s. At under 4 percent, the Fed Funds rate too was at a quarter-century low.

Greenspan's bold move reflected his growing alarm at the unusual nature of the U.S. downturn that started in mid-1990—a "balance sheet" recession, akin in nature to the sort that had resulted in the Great Depression. It was, says Greenspan, "a situation utterly without precedent in the post–World War II period."

The 1980s credit explosion had turned into the financial bust of the 1990s. The Black Monday October 1987 stock market crash had been a warning shot about the unsustainable global economic imbalances, record indebtedness, and speculative financial euphorias spawned by the financial revolution. The failure of government leaders to heed it was resulting in the denouement—a free market force adjustment. Would it be Volcker's long dreaded hard landing?

Since late 1990 Greenspan had been quietly gearing Fed monetary policy to ferry the infirmed U.S. banking system away from a near 1930s-type collapse and a reprise of all central banker's worst nightmare, depression. He thought he'd succeeded when a cyclic economic recovery started to take hold in spring 1991. But when the spark was extinguished in the summer by the "fifty-mile-an-hour headwind" of an overstretched national balance sheet, Greenspan saw the economy start to slide into a rare "double dip" downturn.

"During the last five years we've experienced an extraordinary debt buildup followed by a decline in the value of the assets used to collateralize it," Greenspan explained in early 1992. "To repair balance sheets means that instead of consumption and investment, people are paying off their debts. Since it'll take a long time to get back to equilibrium, the economy can't move forward."

Overindebted businesses and households were frantically retrenching to reduce leverage. An overexposed banking system was not lending. Despite the low interest rates, money supply growth was anemic—a condition that had characterized the early slide to the Great Depression.

Most worrisome to Greenspan was that market-determined long-term interest rates had not fallen much as the Fed guided down short-term rates. They had actually *risen* after the Fed's last discount rate cut of November 6—an effective market veto. The yield curve sloped in an extremely steep, "no confidence" trajectory; the 3.45-point differential between three-month and thirty-year government securities was almost twice as steep as the average yield curve in the previous twenty years. High real long-term interest rates, another feature of the Great Depression, added a crushing deflationary burden to the overindebted economy. It crippled the Fed's capacity to spur a recovery.

Three major forces were at work. One was tighter supply and demand conditions for the global savings on which the United States had become so dependent. Germany and Japan were now consuming their national savings surpluses in the traumatic adjustments of reunification and bubble economy deflation, respectively. Second, higher real interest rates were demanded by global investors as protection against the interest rate volatility of the new financial landscape. The third force, according to the Fed's mathematical analysis of the yield curve, was stubbornly high dollar inflation expectations among global investors. Why? First and foremost, the U.S. budget deficit was ballooning toward a projected world-class embarrassment of 6.5 percent of GNP, or $400 billion, in 1992. Second was trepidation among "inflation vigilantes" on Wall Street that Greenspan would succumb to the political duress for easy money from a Bush government fearful of facing the 1992 presidential elections in a recession.

"As we moved down, we did not alter inflation expectations," says Greenspan. He was particularly troubled by the deteriorating confidence, which was so essential to firing a strong recovery. "Fully half the decline in the recession has been recovered so far. But the perception is of a continued decline!" Unless the psychology was reversed soon, he feared, the recession could spiral away into depression.

The deflationary gloom caused some FOMC members to fret at the December 17, 1991, meeting that a further interest rate cut might ineffectually "push on a string." Greenspan, however, thought he detected signs in the Fed's yield curve analysis that inflation expectations might be at last abating. In congressional hearings the next day, December 18, Greenspan was confronted with the rising chorus from prominent economists, in particular Nobel Laureate James Tobin and Wall Street graybeard Henry Kaufman, that the Fed was being too timid for a dire economic situation.

Greenspan decided, as he had on Black Monday, that the time had come to bet the central bank's preciously guarded credibility. He'd try decisively to turn market expectations with a big discount rate cut "announcement."

That same day, while in Chicago, Greenspan persuaded Chicago Reserve Bank President Silas Keehn to request a 1 percent cut. New York Fed President Jerry Corrigan agreed to make the same request. At an unusual dinner meeting on December 19, the Board of Governors voted for the 1 percent discount rate cut.

Anxiously the central bankers watched Wall Street for the initial verdict. So many circumstances were novel that it was hard to know what to expect: the huge structural federal budget deficits and strained state and local budgets meant that for the first time in postwar history the fiscal tool could not be used to assist Fed monetary policy in pump-priming the economy. The huge military economy was being trimmed for the post–Cold War era. For the first time the United States was a net foreign debtor dependent upon foreign nations' policies and capital. Abnormally, the recession had started when U.S. interest rates were *falling*—it was anything but a typical Fed-induced recession. By late 1991 Japan and Europe were slowing down, adding international momentum to the forces of deflation. The real estate values that collateralized much of the nation's debt was falling and facing the unprecedented test of the government's $350 billion operation to bail out and liquidate the real estate properties of failed S&Ls. Another large rescue was shoring up the bankrupt Federal Deposit Insurance Fund that backstopped the nation's troubled banking system against depositor runs.

With the benefit of hindsight, economic data revealed that the United States had been indeed at the edge of the economic precipice in December 1991. Greenspan's big move contained an imminent depression: Long-term interest rates fell. Equity prices rose. Confidence and economic growth revived.

Greenspan's strategy for slowly repairing balance sheets to shepherd America out of its most fragile economic condition since the 1930s began to take hold from that point forward. "This is the first balance sheet recession of the postwar period," he says. "But this occurred quite often in the nineteenth century, when it led to a short but sharp economic adjustment and huge financial liquidation. In effect, wealth moved into other hands. We can't socially and politically accept such a solution today. We have automatic stabilizers that put a floor under the economic activity levels. But we can't eliminate the need to reduce the imbalances. So we try to unwind them without a sharp contraction. But nonetheless this creates slow economic growth."

Borrowed Time Runs Out

The slide into the contained depression started with the danger Paul Volcker had repeatedly warned about: that the falling dollar alone was not enough to correct the global economic imbalances; the U.S. budget deficit also had to be slashed. The failure to do so set off an inflationary clash for scarce economic resources as the devalued dollar finally sparked the long awaited U.S. export boom in 1988 that lifted the U.S. economy to near full operating capacity and 4.5 percent growth.

Once Greenspan realized in spring 1988 that inflation had overtaken depression as the greater post–Black Monday threat, the Fed pursued a "soft landing" strategy for the imbalanced economy that aimed implicitly for growth at only half the U.S.'s estimated 2.5 percent potential. Greenspan's signature style was "gradualism"—frequent small steps that swung interest rates over a spectrum wide enough to stay ahead of market inflation expectations but could be quickly reversed if the economy started to stall or if vital pillars of the fragile financial system began to totter. In less than a year the Fed Funds rate rose three percentage points to 9.5 percent.

Gradualism sounded good in theory, but it was notoriously difficult to implement. Long and variable lag times, and the collapse in the financial revolution of predictable relationships between central bank monetary policy, credit creation by the financial system, and real economic activity, made an accurate, early reading of economic trends more elusive. Inflation expectations were hard to rein in when so many Americans maintained money market instruments that caused their spendable income to rise almost as fast as interest rates and when businesses could keep on borrowing at floating interest rates and from so many sources other than central bank–regulated banks. The absence of any objective policy "anchor" in the postmonetarist era made it harder for central bankers to convince the public that they were on a noninflationary track.

As forcefully as Greenspan leaned against inflation, inflation pressures mounted even faster. In winter 1988–89 core U.S. inflation zoomed in successive months at a double-digit pace—en route to an annual 5 percent, the worst rate since 1981.

Reignited inflation psychology was aggravating the economically rooted inflation. Volcker's anti-inflation war had beaten back inflation psychology but hadn't extinguished it. That required modern democratic capitalist society to demonstrate its sustained determination to contain it. Greenspan's stated goal was to reduce inflation to the level at which it no longer entered into business or consumer spending plans.

Inflation expectations in early 1989 were exacerbated by new chicanery in Bush administration fiscal assumptions to meet legislated budget guidelines.[1] Inflation psychology was compounded too by the morally hazardous perception that the Fed's fear of financial fragility was imparting an inflationary bias to monetary policy. The Black Monday stock crash, the early 1988 government rescues of First RepublicBank and Financial Corporation of America, and the February 1989 revelation by the Bush administration that the S&L debacle was much worse than previously admitted helped translate financial market anxieties into higher real long-term interest rates.

In February 1989 Greenspan sided with Fed hawks, mainly Volcker-era Reserve Bank presidents, by advocating a discount rate hike from 6.5 percent to 7 percent. The doves, who predominated on the Reagan-selected Board of Governors, saw signs that growth was faltering and feared triggering massive real estate liquidations by the imploding S&L industry. As an alternative, Vice Chairman Manley Johnson proposed a one-quarter-percentage-point hike.

But Greenspan wanted to make a stronger "announcement" of anti-inflationary resolve. On February 24, 1989, with most dissenters voting with Greenspan in the interests of institutional solidarity, the Fed boosted the discount rate by half a percentage point. The Fed Funds rate was nudged up one-quarter point to its peak of 97/8 percent. Doves retrospectively viewed the Fed's move as a policy mistake. Clear signs of economic weakness caused Greenspan to start to backpedal in June. Throughout the year the Fed eased interest rates in quarter-percentage-point baby steps to 8.25 percent.

The rebounding dollar in 1989 charted the path to recession. The dollar's initial thrust came as the Fed raised interst rates to contain inflation. Its second thrust—another episode of overshooting global currency markets—came after mid-1989 from a global institutional investor bandwagon even though U.S. interest rates were declining against those of Germany and Japan. The rising dollar curtailed the U.S. export boom with the massive international economic imbalances still outstanding. The main growth engine of the over-leveraged, imbalanced U.S. economy was sputtering.

The combination of slowing growth, continuing inflation pressures, twin budget and current account deficits, and the scale of the unfolding S&L debacle triggered a financial market reassessment of the rosy asset price and economic assumptions underlying the 1980s debt explosion that caused overall U.S. debt-to-income ratio to break from its stable 1953–80 average of about $136 of debt per $100 of GNP to $180 by the end of the 1980s—greater than in any period of the century save 1932–35.[2] The celebrated government

deficits accounted for only one-third of the increase. Another third was corporate: businesses massively substituting equity for debt in one of the greatest
asset-reshuffling speculations in U.S. history. Debt growing faster than corporate tangible assets in plant and equipment caused total U.S. corporate net
worth to fall from 95.4 percent of GNP in 1980 to 74.3 percent in 1988. When
those assets failed to generate substantially more productivity and profits,
debt service-to-earnings burdens doubled. Businesses failed and defaulted on
their debts at a rate two and a half times greater than their 1953–80 average.

"It is now clear," said Greenspan in 1991, "that a significant fraction of
the credit extended during those years should not have been extended."[3] U.K.
Exchequer Chancellor Nigel Lawson noted that all Anglo-Saxon countries
that had taken deregulation farthest "experienced a particularly virulent
form of the credit cycle."[4]

As financial markets began to take a soberer view of future economic
prospects in 1989, the U.S. debt bubble began to deflate. Plunging commercial real estate prices set the pace. The highly leveraged transactions mania
climaxed with the $24.7 billion buyout of RJR Nabisco; in October the mar-
ket collapsed with the failure of a leveraged buyout for UAL. Immediately
the stock market, which had been riding high on the takeover wave, suffered
the October 13, 1989, 190-point minicrash. In February 1990 junk bond king
Drexel Burnham Lambert went under, causing the $200 billion junk bond
market to seize up; clearing and settlement in the $1 trillion mortgage-
backed securities market narrowly averted a major disruption.[5]

The combination of financial asset deflation and economic slowdown, in
turn, excited fears about a banking system crisis. By 1990 big banks' troubles in
commercial real estate and highly leveraged transactions, on top of their continuing LDC exposure, put them in their most woeful condition since the 1930s.

In 1990 signs of stagflation were pronounced: 1 percent growth, 5.4 percent inflation, rising unemployment. Fed policymakers were confused and
divided: the board had requests from Federal Reserve Banks for both discount rate increases and cuts. When the dollar finally fell in early 1990, core
inflation and inflation expectations again accelerated. Following the Fed's
easing on December 20, 1989, Governors Manley Johnson and Wayne Angell, sensing that the balance of risks in the "soft landing" strategy had
tipped back to inflation, abandoned the dovish FOMC majority. In the first
half of 1990 Fed policy remained unchanged—to the many retrospective
critics, paralyzed—while the overleveraged economy and fragile financial
system swooned into the credit crunch that foreboded the recession.

Greenspan might yet have succeeded in averting the downturn had not
Fed policy been rocked by four shocks, three foreign and one domestic: the
Iraqi invasion of Kuwait, German reunification, deflation of Japan's bubble
economy, and intense political pressure from the Bush administration.

•   •   •

From the outset Alan Greenspan made the controversial decision to collaborate closely with the new Bush administration. In contrast with Volcker, who behaved almost as an independent sovereign power toward the Carter and Reagan governments, Greenspan consulted and socialized so regularly with President Bush, Treasury Secretary Nicholas Brady, and CEA Chairman Michael Boskin that he sometimes seemed to be part of the administration. The strategy backfired. It compromised his credibility with financial markets and with Fed policymakers—the other two in the trinity of relationships any Fed chairman needed to master—and even failed in its main aim to blunt White House political pressure.

By protracting the partisan gridlock over fiscal policy with his celebrated "Read my lips—no new taxes!" campaign pledge, Bush was left with little way to govern the economy other than pushing the Fed. Relations got off on the wrong foot almost from the start. The Bush team was angered by the Fed's tightening from spring 1988 to early 1989. In contrast with Reagan, who rarely rebuked the Fed personally, Bush himself set the tone by publicly criticizing the Fed's February 24, 1989, discount rate hike. Treasury Secretary Nick Brady expressed his concern that the Fed wasn't lowering interest rates at his weekly breakfast meeting with Greenspan. Still not satisfied in the spring of 1989 that his message was getting through, he arranged a pair of unusual private luncheon meetings with Greenspan and Governors Manley Johnson and Wayne Angell in the chairman's dining room at the Fed. The meetings were a disaster.

"Brady is almost incapable of articulating his position. He couldn't say why," recounts Johnson. "The feeling in the room among us was almost embarrassment" when Brady misinterpreted an interest rate chart. "We tried politely to discourage him. It was a delicate meeting. But I'm sure he felt patronized." Adds Angell, "I remember Brady in effect saying, 'We're trying to get a balanced budget. Please give us more money!' He saw a balanced budget as a means to get inflation down, without realizing that inflation is a monetary process. I felt sorry. He was out of his league with three central bankers who were in such close agreement."

After the meetings Brady grew increasingly antagonistic toward Greenspan. This tension remained submerged while the Fed was cutting interest rates in the second half of 1989, but it surfaced when the Fed stood pat throughout the sagging first half of 1990. Relations soured so badly that their Thursday morning breakfast meetings lapsed—interrupting the tradition maintained by Volcker even during his stormy periods with the Regan Treasury. Between exhortations for lower interest rates, Brady talked openly in official circles about not reappointing Greenspan when his term expired in mid-1991. "It was terrible," recalls a senior Fed official. "Brady threatened not to reappoint Greenspan. He said he was uncomfortable with Alan. He expressed it over and over." Brady's pressure climaxed in July 1991 when he dangled reappointment for Greenspan's pledge to hold interest rates low enough to achieve 3 percent growth for the 1992 election. Mistakenly, Brady thought Greenspan had assented, then reneged.

The overt calls for lower interest rates from Brady and President Bush satiated political needs; but they bred suspicions on Wall Street that every Fed easing was a response to political pressure. This undermined their intentions—and Greenspan's. The Fed said its motivation for its first easing move in 1990, on July 13, was the spreading bank credit crunch. Markets, however, focused on Brady's public criticism of July 9 and Bush's July 11 call for lower interest rates at the G7 economic summit in Houston. Although subsequently released FOMC summary minutes confirmed that the decision to ease indeed had been taken on July 2–3, the perceptual damage had been done. The yield curve steepened.

Bush's pressure also weakened Greenspan's leadership of the Fed. Many Fed policymakers, an eclectic, independent group, harbored suspicions that "Greenspan had to manage the politics, so he wanted to ease more than the others."[6] Especially disturbing to many was Greenspan's active role in the summer 1990 White House–Congress budget-deficit reduction negotiations for which Bush was later pilloried for compromising his "no new taxes" pledge. "Many of the governors and presidents were uncomfortable that Greenspan worked so closely on the budget agreement with the administration and that he had virtually promised to cut interest rates when they got a compromise," says Fed Vice Chairman Manley Johnson, who quit the board in 1990. "Then they got that watered-down and ineffective compromise."

This political fissure erupted at the October 2, 1990, FOMC meeting at the climax of the budget negotiations. The U.S. economy was slumping, although the economic statistics didn't yet clearly confirm it. But core inflation was also high. Greenspan, siding with the doves, proposed two separately timed interest rate cuts of one-quarter point each. The hawks rebelled. After a contentious debate, the FOMC compromised on a single one-quarter-point cut—to be implemented only after budget negotiations were complete. Accordingly the Fed guided interest rates down from 8 percent to 7.75 percent on October 29.

The financial markets' reaction to the political odor was immediate—and allergic. The yield curve steepened. One consequence was that Greenspan postponed an imminent Fed easing move by several days to avoid looking as though he were bowing to President Bush's pointed demand in his January 29, 1991, State of the Union address for lower interest rates "now."[7]

Nevertheless the Fed discount rate cut from 6 percent to 5.5 percent on April 30, 1991, was soundly repudiated by financial markets. It came on the heels of a G7 finance ministers' meeting, highlighted by an ineffective public campaign by Brady for the Bundesbank to disregard the inflation pressures of German reunification to take part in a world interest rate cut. "Everyone was embarrassed," says Johnson. "No one thought it made any sense for Germany to cut interest rates at that time."

When Germany refused, Japan showed no interest, and the Fed was cool, the joke circulated in financial circles that Brady's bid for a G3 coordinated cut had turned into a G-zero. To save face, Brady redoubled pressure on Greenspan. Greenspan told him that the Fed balance hung on two wavering governors, John LaWare and Edward Kelley. Brady took the highly unusual step of lobbying them personally.[8]

It worked. "Greenspan knew he was under pressure to come through," says Manley Johnson. "But the way in which it occurred right after the G7 made it look like Brady pressure—and it *was*. Two weeks earlier the market would have accepted it. But not after."

Market anxiety at Bush political pressure was a significant reason long-term interest rates stayed so persistently high as the Fed battled the balance sheet downturn in 1991. The coup de grace came when long-term interest rates *rose* following the Fed's half-point discount rate cut on November 6, 1991. On Wall Street it became known as the "Thornburgh cut," since it followed the upset loss of ex–Bush Attorney General Richard Thornburgh for a vacant Pennsylvania Senate seat.

"There has not been a single instance we've taken action due to politics," Greenspan insists. "We failed to get the administration to keep quiet on what we do. But they had no effect." However, he admitted his frustration: "If the market gets concerned and long-term interest rates go twenty to fifty basis points higher, it's counterproductive."

At first blush it seemed odd that Nicholas Brady, a Wall Street man, would aggravate a situation he knew worked against the administration's growth goals by continuously jawboning the Fed for lower interest rates. But as a central banker, Greenspan comprehended well that it reflected the asymptotic logic of markets and governments. "There is a blind spot," he says softly. "Or, rather, the politics of being able to beat on the central bank is worth more than the adverse economic effects."

The Saddam Shock

The decisive event that sent the overindebted and imbalanced U.S. economy tumbling ineluctably into recession occurred on August 2, 1990, in the sands of the Persian Gulf. Iraq invaded Kuwait, giving dictator Saddam Hussein control of Kuwait's oil riches in his bid for regional nuclear superpowerdom. The Saddam shock registered immediately in world financial markets. Oil prices leaped from $18 to almost $30 a barrel. Bond prices plunged—yields on thirty-year Treasuries backed up from 8.5 percent to nearly 9 percent. In two days the New York stock market fell 148 points.

By simultaneously slowing growth and heating up inflation, the Saddam shock had the economic impact of a mini–third oil shock. The Fed faced a no-win dilemma: if it cut interest rates to fight recession, it would permanently ratify the one- to two-percentage-point increase in inflation added by the oil price rise. Yet if it tightened to fight inflation, it was likely to knock the very weak economy into a recession that could cause whole chunks of the fragile financial system to collapse. Save for its budget-related October move, the Fed froze.

But the die had already been cast by Main Street. In a sudden self-fulfilling expectational shift wholly unanticipated by Washington, Wall Street, and central bankers, consumer and business confidence collapsed. In anticipation of a downturn, businesses slashed inventories, cut spending, and fired employees. Borrowers stopped demanding new loans and began repaying what they owed. Banks retrenched lending even as demand was falling.

The sudden zapping of the "animal spirits" of American capitalism reflected an elevated sense of vulnerability. Overindebted businesses and consumers did not dare wait to see whether the adverse history of the first two oil shocks would repeat itself. Nor could bankers with thin capital cushions and huge loan exposures to such borrowers with collateral whose value was already falling wait to see whether a downturn would break their clients— and themselves. The economy slid into the unusual balance sheet recession. Bankruptcies and bad debts soared to post-Depression record rates. "It looked unlike any other recession," says Manley Johnson. "Usually there are rising interest rates, weak orders, and involuntary inventory buildup. This time expectations of weakness caused *anticipatory* cuts in orders and inventories."

The unexpected response to the Saddam shock had been foreshadowed by a subterranean tightening of credit conditions and anemic lending activity in 1990—the bank credit crunch. Fed policymakers had been slow to recognize it. In summer 1990 they debated the significance of the mostly anecdotal evidence, but, reports Johnson, "there were mixed views on how serious it was." In hindsight, loans fell 3.6 percent during the first three quarters following the 1990 business cycle peak. This was unprecedented: in the previous five recessions, lending had always grown strongly.[9]

Particularly difficult for Fed policymakers wielding a blunt, national monetary brake/accelerator was that the credit crunch was concentrated in hard-hit economic regions with fragile banks. Banks in New England, which from

1988 to 1990 had suffered loan losses that wiped out one-quarter of their capital, slashed lending by 13.6 percent. New England citizens paid dearly for America's obsolete interstate banking prohibitions, which prevented healthier banks outside the region from picking up the slack.

The Bush administration was quick to blame the bank credit crunch for the sagging economy in 1990. The true culprits were "overzealous" bank regulators, who, it charged, were overcompensating for their previous laxity in supervising the reckless lending binges of the 1980s.

Greenspan and the other politically savvy U.S. bank regulators went through the motions of taking President Bush's charges seriously. On May 10, 1990, the heads of the three main federal bank regulatory agencies, Fed, FDIC, and Comptroller, assured top U.S. bankers that their regulators would not be too quick to classify as "nonperforming" prudent lending to sound borrowers that became questionable because of the poor economy. The bankers stoutly insisted that the main trouble was not their unwillingness to lend, but the reduction in credit demand by borrowers. The day after Bush bluntly called for sound banks to be "making more sound loans, now," in his State of the Union speech on January 29, 1991, Greenspan met again with his federal regulator counterparts to brainstorm regulatory interpretations that could be implemented to encourage bank lending.

The Basel bank capital adequacy standards were also singled out for blame. While most major U.S. banks met the interim 1990 standards on paper, analysts argued that if the true bad debts were subtracted from their balance sheets, they might have to slash their lending by a strongly recessionary $356 billion.[10]

Although Greenspan agreed that supervisor overzealousness was real, and that the Basel capital adequacy ratios contributed to the credit crunch, he believed they were swamped by a far more potent market force: "Almost all of it was explained by the uncertainty of bankers about the degree of their nonperforming loans. What concerned them was that their book value data were unrealistic."[11] Simply, bankers faced a huge shakeout from the financial excesses and economic imbalances of the 1980s and their weakened capacity to survive the resultant big losses. States Greenspan, "[Bank] fragility . . . in fact was the cause of the credit crunch."[12]

Saving the Banking System

Just how close the U.S. banking system came to collapsing in 1990–91 was necessarily conjectural, since it depended much on developments in the economy. But there was little doubt that the wildfire spread of market fear of major bank collapses nearly became a self-fulfilling disaster that the Fed helped narrowly to avert. On September 13, 1990, Greenspan himself made the startlingly candid admission for a central banker bound to ultraconservatism in every utterance that there were "all too many problems in the banking system, problems that have been growing of late as many banks, including many larger banks, have been experiencing a deterioration in the quality of their loan portfolios. . . ."[13]

Several days earlier the less restrained head of the U.S. General Accounting Office told Congress that some thirty-five major banks were in immediate danger of failing. Independent experts estimated that 25 percent of U.S. banks, controlling over $750 billion in assets, including some of the nation's backbone institutions, were essentially dead in the water and couldn't extend loans even if there was booming demand.[14] To forestall a crisis, the Fed and FDIC had been pursuing a morally hazardous, ad hoc bailout policy since the 1984 Continental Illinois nationalization that protected nearly all depositors, not just those insured by the FDIC. In the second half of the 1980s the Fed extended unpublicized discount window loans to over 350 banks that later failed. These loans gave time for depositors to flee. When the banks later failed, the FDIC reimbursed the Fed for the loans.[15] This reached its apogee in the spring of 1990, when the Treasury took over the Fed's discount lending role by depositing $1.8 billion in the faltering $22 billion asset Bank of New England. This gave cover to big and foreign depositors to exit. At Greenspan's request, the Bank of England used its moral suasion to help the New England Bank maintain access to international money markets while its foreign exchange book was unwound. When the Bank of New England finally experienced a fatal $1 billion run by depositors in winter 1990–91, the U.S. government stepped in with a $2.3 billion bailout to prevent a devastating regional failure.

Incipient market panic began to infect the U.S. banking system in 1990. Bank share prices fell far below book value. This made it virtually impossible for them to raise new equity capital. Many big bank credit ratings plunged to double-B levels and below—undermining the quintessential banking service of being able to pass along its traditional capacity to raise funds more cheaply than its borrowers.

Most terrifying was the silent, slow-motion, global wholesale money market flight from America's largest banks. Interest rate premiums began to be demanded of troubled money centers selling their certificates of deposit to fund their banking operations. In the first nine months of 1990 Japanese investors cut their U.S. bank CD holdings by nearly $20 billion. Taiwanese investors fled by $7 billion. Large U.S. corporate treasurers trimmed back their exposures with the credit downgradings.[16]

The crisis zone was entered in autumn 1990 soon after the Saddam shock.

Chase Manhattan experienced a near run in September; Citibank and other giants came under attack, too. The core U.S. banks responded with unprecedented draconian cuts in operations to husband their capital. In September Chase set aside $850 million to cover bad loans, announced it would lay off five thousand employees, and broke a long-standing taboo by slashing its dividend in half. Chemical Bank took similar steps. Under Fed duress in the winter of 1990–91, Citicorp launched a survival strategy by slashing its dividends to zero, selling off prized businesses, and chopping its payroll by eleven thousand. All retrenched their lending, in the United States and abroad. The U.S. banking system was in full retreat. Partly in panic and partly because they were undergoing a crisis of their own, Japanese banks failed to take up the lending slack.[17] Neither did distressed insurers and other neighboring financial sectors, whose own deep troubles added to the deteriorating market psychology of impending systemic financial crisis.

Statistics later showed that while half a million U.S. soldiers faced off against Saddam's Iraqi troops in the sands of the Kuwait–Saudi Arabian border in the late fall and winter of 1990–91, the U.S. economy was nosediving at a nearly 4 percent annual rate. Unless America's core banking system was stabilized, the United States faced a financial crisis and hard economic landing.

Nightmare images of the Great Depression began to haunt top Fed policymakers, who had "continual conversations about this period and the 1930s," when all the main money supply indicators suddenly collapsed in autumn 1990.[18] A similar pattern had occurred in late 1930, when a year of abundant money supply and cheap credit was overwhelmed by forces of economic deflation and midwestern and southern banking failures. In 1930 an unpredicted shift in velocity, or the rate at which money was spent, helped throw the Fed tragically off course.[19] Portentously, Fed policymakers discovered that money demand had again collapsed unpredictably. The Fed was tighter than it thought.

Frightened Fed policymakers swung into action. On November 5, 1990, alarmed by the "widespread perception of relatively fragile financial conditions," the FOMC voted to ease interest rates in order to "provide some insurance against a deep and prolonged recession."[20] In December the Fed deployed all three of its main monetary policy tools. It lowered the Fed Funds rate through open market operations in two steps from 7.5 percent to 7 percent. It also cut the discount rate for the first time in nearly two years from 7 percent to 6.5 percent. Most unusually, it eliminated the 3 percent reserve requirement banks had to hold in non-interest-bearing deposits at the Fed on its short-term CDs. These easings were followed up in early 1991 by Fed Fund rate reductions on January 8, February 1, March 6, and April 30 and discount rate cuts on February 1 and April 30. In six months the cost of

Fed Funds was lowered from 8 percent to 5.75 percent; from December to April the discount rate fell from 7 percent to 5.5 percent.

"We all know we have to be accountable in a democracy," explains Governor Wayne Angell. "The Fed doesn't ever want to be blamed like the Fed in the 1930s and lose its freedom over a monetary policy mistake."

Yet in winter 1990–91 the economy did not respond. As in the last balance sheet downturn, the Great Depression, the Fed was fecklessly pushing on a string of unconfident, fragile borrowers and lenders. The *Financial Times* observed "that a heavily indebted economy with big financial problems is much less responsive to relaxations in monetary policy than expected."[21]

In late 1990 the focus of Federal Reserve policy shifted subtly to containing a depression by engineering a Dunkirk rescue for the infirmed U.S. banking system. The electronic wholesale market run on core U.S. banks receded as a threat. Bank stock prices soared, allowing banks to heal themselves more quickly by raising huge amounts of fresh equity capital. A crisis flash point, possibly comparable to the panic-inducing December 1930 failure of the Bank of the United States, had been averted.

The decisive psychological action, in retrospect, was cutting the CD reserve requirements. "For reasons that were never obvious to us, the price of bank stocks took off when we lifted the reserve requirements on CDs," says Greenspan. "The market bid up stock prices beyond any conceivable immediate relation to future earnings."

Several crisis-containment operations underpinned the abrupt turn in market psychology. These featured the January 1991, $2.3 billion bailout of the Bank of New England and, in late 1991, Congress's $70 billion emergency refinancing of the functionally insolvent FDIC bank deposit insurance fund, the safety net created to prevent Depression era–type banking runs. Most spectacular of all was the secret two-and-a-half-year rescue of the U.S.'s largest bank, $213 billion–asset Citibank.

The Citibank saga started the day before Thanksgiving 1990, when Citibank Chairman John Reed and President Richard Braddock were summoned to the New York Fed to meet with its president, Jerry Corrigan, and board bank supervision division chief Bill Taylor.[23] Citibank, and with it the entire U.S. banking system, the central bankers informed them, was headed for big problems unless they took drastic, immediate steps to add $5 billion to Citi's capital base. Corrigan and Taylor said they were worried that Citibank, which had one of the lowest capital-to-asset ratios and highest non-performing loan ratios among big banks, didn't have sufficient capital to survive the huge losses that were coming on its $30 billion commercial real estate portfolio. Loan losses in regions of the country where the real estate bubble had burst were running fifteen to twenty times the amount Citi was anticipating.

Taylor enumerated the painful options to raise the $5 billion: selling profitable parts of its business, trimming staff, selling more stock even though it watered down existing shareholders, and cutting dividends. The other troubled money center banks were biting the bullet. Citibank had to also.[24]

Corrigan and Taylor didn't order Reed to act; they didn't have to. Reed understood the coded moral suasion message as if he'd been clubbed over the head: unless he obeyed, the Fed and Comptroller would use their regulatory powers to make him—or more likely his successor—do it their way.

In his eagerness to escape the frying pan of LDC debt, Reed had unwittingly launched Citbank headlong into the fire of the commercial real estate bubble. At the time, Reed and Citibank brass were not yet fully cognizant of the debacle they were heading into. They did not anticipate that 1991 would produce Citibank's first annual loss, some $457 million, since the Great Depression.

Faced with the humiliating dressing-down from his central bank regulators, John Reed got into line. Within weeks he produced a drastic five-part plan to restore Citibank's health. The dividend was eliminated. Massive layoffs were made. Streamlining saved $1 billion in operating expenses. Some $4 billion in new capital was raised from stock issues and business sell-offs. Citibank also announced a 25 percent scale-back in lending to improve its deficient capital-to-asset ratio. Dutifully Reed traveled every month to Washington to report updates to the Fed and Comptroller. The regulators cleared every major decision he made.

For well over a year Citibank's fate hung in the balance. Perhaps the darkest moment came in December 1991, just as Greenspan was contemplating his bold one-point cut in the discount rate. Citibank shares plunged to only $8.50. Regulators put Citibank on the nation's list of 1,071 "problem" banks that were most likely to fail. The Fed, meanwhile, reviewed the contingency plans for a lender of last resort rescue it had worked out with foreign central bankers. At the depth of the banking crisis in 1991, U.S. regulators closed 125 banks with a record-shattering $65 billion in assets. For 1992 the FDIC bleakly forecast 200 bank collapses with $85 billion in assets.

In the event, the Fed's Dunkirk rescue staved off disaster. Bank industry profits nearly doubled in 1992. Capital was rebuilt. Even Citibank climbed above the Basel minimums; by spring 1993 its stock price had rebounded to $30.[25] A series of megabank mergers began to rationalize the industry for global competition. Under Fed guidance the banking industry gained temporary respite from its structural woes. "It [the bank trouble] never got to the point where we feared it would unravel," Greenspan postures now with a central banker's reassurance. "It was overblown in the press."

• • •

Yet in early 1991 Greenspan was anything but confident. On January 30 he declared that the economy was in "the most confidence-sensitive cycle I've seen in decades." A deep recession might be unavoidable, he warned, unless there was an early end to the two-week-old Persian Gulf War.[26]

The overwhelming Allied victory against Iraq on February 27, 1991, sparked the turnaround. Greenspan had witnessed auspicious signs on his computer monitor the night the Allied air attacks on Iraq commenced on January 16, 1991. As the perception of their success spread, "you could basically see not only the price of oil coming down very sharply across the world, but the effects minute by minute in the exchange markets, in the interest rate markets, in the gold markets, all arbitraged across and around the world."[27]

With victory, consumer and business confidence surged back as quickly as it had disappeared. Money supply rebounded. Pressure on long-term interest rates eased, buoyed by international cash payments from Allies for fighting the war—enough to turn a $23 billion balance-of-payment deficit into a $10 billion surplus over the six months from October 1990.[28] "Unanticipated and surprising was the quick surge back in confidence to prewar levels," says Manley Johnson. "Oil prices fell back. All the predictions were for a pickup in consumer demand. Companies had kept inventories lean, so there'd have to be increases in inventory production. It looked like a classic recovery. Everyone built it into their forecasts."

Following easing moves at the end of April, the Fed stood pat and watched. By mid-July Greenspan publicly declared his optimism that the recovery was under way. Relieved, President Bush renominated him to a second term as chairman. Looking back, the recession had been scary, but shallow and brief: three negative growth quarters, with unemployment peaking at 6.8 percent.

Double Dip

But it wasn't over.

Against almost all predictions, the recovery began to stall. Employment growth was lethargic. Consumer and business spending turned cautious again. Then industrial production peaked out. The M2 money stock actually began to shrink—reducing debt was still Americans' major preoccupation. The post–Gulf War surge in confidence began to wane. America swooned toward a rare double-dip downturn.

The Fed was slow to believe it was happening. On August 6, 1991, it nudged the economy by trimming the Fed Funds rate from 5.75 percent to

5.5 percent. On September 13 it pushed more vigorously to 5.25 percent and cut the discount rate from 5.5 percent to 5 percent.

But still there was little demand for credit and little willingness to lend.

By late October Greenspan declared pessimistically that because of a huge balance sheet adjustment, the economy was struggling against "a fifty-mile-an-hour headwind." Shortly thereafter the Fed moved twice more, on October 30 and November 6. The Fed Funds rate was lowered to 4.75 percent. The discount rate was slashed by another half point to 4.5 percent. On December 6, following an unexpectedly sharp fall in November payroll employment released that day, Greenspan instructed the open market desk in New York to inject sufficient liquidity to lower the Fed Funds rates to 4.5 percent.

Yet as the Fed lowered short-term interest rates, long-term interest rates fell much less. This created record steepness in the yield curve. Businesses and individuals, who borrowed mostly at the intermediate-term maturities, were getting little relief—and the Fed was almost powerless to help.

The negative trends accelerated toward year-end: confidence plunging to a seventeen-year low, growth stalling out, Europe and Japan sliding into downturn, financial institutions teetering on the verge of collapse, Wall Street petrified by politicians' talk of an election-year stimulus that would cause the budget deficit to spiral hopelessly out of control. The Fed, too, was "very confused," says Manley Johnson. "They all thought the smaller steps would have solved it. Yet the economy didn't take hold."

Greenspan began to mull over the need for a startling policy move to break the psychological doom on Wall Street and Main Street that was threatening to turn the unprecedented balance sheet downturn into a full-fledged depression. A big "announcement effect" move was discussed at the November 5, 1991, FOMC meeting and again at the December 17 meeting. Support was only lukewarm.

Then, on December 19, Greenspan orchestrated the full one-point cut in the discount rate.

The reaction was terrific: long-term bond interest rates fell sharply. The stock market rallied. Equity and bond financings surged, fostering major repairs in corporate and personal balance sheets. A ray of optimism broke through the gloom. America inched away from the economic precipice.

On February 18, 1992, the Fed trimmed the reserve requirement for deposits on checking and other transactions accounts from 12 percent to 10 percent. That freed another $8 billion for banks to lend or to invest in government securities. On April 9 Greenspan pushed down the Fed Funds rate from 4 percent to 3.75 percent. At midyear he proposed "buying some insurance" by lowering the discount rate to an emergency low-level 3 percent.

Other Fed policymakers protested that was too much of a long-term inflation risk, given the historical political pressure against raising rates. "You won't be able to take it up fast enough," they argued.

"Yes, we will," Greenspan insisted.[29]

The discount rate was cut to 3 percent and the Fed Funds guided down toward that floor benchmark. Market-determined long-term interest rates followed the Fed's lead. Each one-tenth-point fall in interest rates, Greenspan estimated, was the equivalent of a $10 billion boost to the economy. Slowly America began to pull out of its first postwar balance sheet recession.

How long was it likely to take?

In early 1992 Greenspan was unsure. "There have been very heavy offerings in the equity and bond markets that is restructuring balance sheets quickly. But there is a long way to go to get to square one at the start of the 1980s. We're holding our own now." With echoes of the "malaise" described by President Jimmy Carter in 1979, he mused, "More fundamentally, I suspect that what troubles consumers, and indeed everyone, is that the current pause in activity may be underscoring a sense of retardation in the growth of living standards over the long run . . . and whether the current generation will live as well as previous ones. . . . The record of the past decade provides ample reason for concern."[30]

Inflation, which in 1979 was the most visible drain on America's economic vigor, had been brought under control. But now the malaise was rooted in America's net debtor status, outsized structural budget and trade deficits, inadequate national savings, chronic underinvestment and overconsumption, and the apparent paralysis of the U.S. democratic political institutions to cope with the challenges of global capital and the changed global political economy. Ironically, the equilibrium so unsatisfactory to voters in 1980 had come to be regarded as the halcyon yardstick by economists.

Greenspan and Fed central bankers fighting the U.S.'s unusual balance sheet downturn without the assistance, for the first time in sixty years, of a fiscal stimulus, experienced the terrible lesson of the Great Depression that "[i]t was not sufficient to make money abundant and cheap; one also had to improve creditworthiness by reversing the outlook."[31]

In early 1992 that outlook had improved but not been reversed. America's recovery was more conditioned by what happened abroad than at any time since World War II. Japan and Europe were slumping. "Given all the financial fragilities around the world," warned C. Fred Bergsten, director of the Institute for International Economics, "we could easily be tipped into a world recession."[32]

Chapter 25

The Global Downturn

A dramatic shift in the supply-and-demand conditions in the reservoir of foreign savings from late 1989 already had much to do with America's slide into recession. German reunification, the deflation of Japan's "bubble economy," and the Gulf War's costs for Arab oil producers sharply reduced the world's surplus savings supply. Demand also jumped from leaner LDCs and ex-communist Eastern-bloc countries. As a result, world, and with it U.S., real interest rates ratcheted higher—just as the Fed was trying to moderate monetary conditions for a soft landing.

Japan and Germany had begun raising interest rates in the spring of 1989 to contain the added inflationary pressures caused by the rebounding dollar. The Bundesbank led the way on April 20, 1989, by lifting its discount rate by half a point to 4.5 percent. The move startled Basel governors, who just had been signaled at their April BIS meetings by Bundesbank President Karl Otto Pöhl that no tightening move was imminent. At the May G 10 Basel governors dinner, attended by IMF Managing Director Michel Camdessus, Pöhl explained that he and the directorate were outvoted in a mutiny of the eleven *Länder* bank presidents on the Central Bank Council.[1]

In late May the BOJ boosted its discount rate for the first time in nine years, by .75 percent, to 3.25 percent. In June the Bundesbank pushed up its key rates by half a point again. Over the summer the BOJ permitted market-driven short-term interest rates to rise sharply.

When the aberrantly soaring dollar began rebounding after a big concerted G7 dollar-selling intervention in late September, the Bundesbank soon boosted its discount and Lombard rates by a full point more, to 6 percent and 8 percent, respectively.

Foreign exchange markets promptly vetoed Japanese monetary authorities' declaration that they wouldn't follow. The yen plummeted against the dollar. In disarray the seven-man BOJ policy board gathered on October 11 between 11:00 A.M. and 12:45 P.M. to vote a half-point increase in the discount rate to 3.75 percent. They announced it immediately, stunning Japanese financial markets accustomed to announcements made after local markets closings at 4 P.M. and well leaked in advance to give time to market players to unwind positions without big losses.

Within forty-eight hours of the BOJ's surprise discount rate increase, Japanese banks began heeding MOF's previous warnings against excessive exposure to the U.S. leveraged buyout market . Their pulling out of the financing syndicate for UAL contributed to the deal's collapse. Immediately the New York Stock Exchange plunged into its October 13, 1989, minicrash, feeding a major market reassessment of all loftily valued U.S. financial assets.

Then, in November 1989, the Berlin Wall fell. German long-term interest rates leaped nearly two percentage points to 9 percent, and the DM soared. For separate reasons the Japanese bond market crashed soon thereafter, propelling Japanese long-term bond yields from 5.5 percent to 7.4 percent. This quantum jump in international interest rates was transmitted to U.S. capital markets, where ten-year U.S. bond rates backed up from 7 7/8 percent to over 9 percent by April 1990. With market forces driving long-term interest rates up and the dollar down, the Fed had little leverage to counteract it.

In one movement all the stimulus earned by the Fed's easing moves from mid- to December 1989 was wiped out. A new, back-breaking burden was added to the overleveraged, imbalanced U.S. economy, which began to stagger under the strains of its credit crunch toward its midsummer rendezvous with the Saddam shock.

"Real interest rates worldwide moved up perceptibly with the problems in Eastern Europe, German unification, and the prospective credit requirements of the Soviet Union," comments Fed Chairman Alan Greenspan. By early 1990 the entire world economy was struggling uphill against historically high real long-term interest rates of about 6 percent in Germany, 4.5 percent in Japan, and 4 percent in the United States.

German Reunification

In retrospect, global financial markets were justified in their initial gloomy reaction to the fall of the Berlin Wall and its portent of reuniting Germany for the first time since Hitler. Eager to make reunification politically unstoppable, and desperate to stem the spontaneous flight into West Germany from economic collapse of tens of thousands of East Germans, Chancellor Helmut Kohl conceived of an accelerated timetable on popular terms for monetary union between the two Germanys (GMU). The DM, and behind it the historical sound money reputation built up by the Bundesbank, was to be the vehicle of the effective political takeover of East Germany. Anticipating opposition from the conservative Bundesbank about the popular terms for digesting the largest monetary, economic, and social shock experienced by any major democratic capitalist country since World War II, Kohl purposely excluded its leaders from the inner councils formulating the policy.

On Monday, February 5, 1990, Bundesbank President Pöhl, who was to travel the next day to East Berlin for monetary talks, received his first telephone call from Kohl since the fall of the wall. Kohl probed him on his views about monetary union. But he never mentioned that his GMU policy had been already formulated.

After his February 6 meetings Pöhl declared that it would be "fantasy" for monetary union "to come anytime soon."[2] A few hours later Kohl stunned him, and even his own Foreign Ministry, by calling for immediate negotiations on monetary union. Pöhl briefly considered resigning. Instead he vented his anger at a stormy Bonn cabinet meeting. Through gritted teeth he endorsed the government's initiative to the press, adding pointedly, "This is a political decision by the federal government for which the federal government bears responsibility."[3]

Most private German economists argued that the appropriate exchange rate for converting East German marks into West German marks was between two-to-one and five-to-one (versus seven-to-one on foreign exchange markets). At a heated April 5, 1990, Bundesbank Council meeting that lasted three times longer than usual and was attended by Finance Minister Theo Waigel, the Bundesbank voted in favor of a two-to-one conversion rate with implementation in October. Waigel endorsed it.

Leak of the Bundesbank's two-to-one conversion plan triggered a political uproar in the East, where leaders charged it would impoverish them. A few days later Kohl rejected it outright. Instead he chose a sugar-coated exchange rate of one-to-one on July 1, 1990. He also accepted wage parity between East and West German workers.

The Kohl government's dash to GMU confiscated wealth from West Germans and gave it to East Germans, who went on a short-lived spending spree. But their effective 35 percent wage increase far outstripped their productivity gains. East German firms soon collapsed. East German unemployment soared to depression levels, fomenting xenophobic violence by neo-Nazis.

Kohl's insistence on extending government welfare parity to the East and his rejection of tax increases or spending cuts to pay for it undid a decade of budgetary consolidation. A 1989 fiscal surplus turned into a deficit of over 5.5 percent of GNP by 1991. Government borrowing exploded. The one-to-one conversion rate led to a one-time, 15 percent increase in total German money supply. Inflation jumped to an annualized 4.5 percent rate by early 1992 from the 1 percent level of the late 1980s. Labor strife broke out in the West for higher wages to recoup lost buying power, raising the specter of an inflationary wage-price spiral. In March 1991 Pöhl labeled monetary union a "disaster," infuriating Kohl and contributing to his resignation several months later. In July 1991 Kohl was forced to confess for the first time that he had underestimated the difficulties of reunification.

Kohl's mess shifted the main fulcrum of German economic policymaking to the Bundesbank. It faced the classic central banker dilemma on an epic scale: What to do when government policy was irresponsible?

The Bundesbank's answer was to take away the punch bowl—austerity. It clamped down on the money supply needed to nourish inflation. Short-term interest rates leaped way above long-term rates. The most inverted yield curve in postwar German history was as strong a recessionary message as a central bank could deliver. Its condition for easing was a reunification "solidarity pact" by the government that contained wage settlements, restored fiscal probity, and trimmed the industrial and unemployment subsidies making the economy sclerotic.

Kohl, however, delivered little. As a result, tight monetary policy in the face of large budget deficits re-created on a smaller scale the effects of the titanic clash between Volcker's disinflationary monetary policy and Reagan's record budget deficits—real German interests shot up. Capital was sucked into Germany from abroad. The DM soared. The current account swung from a DM 77 billion ($48 billion) surplus in 1990 to a DM 34 billion ($21 billion) deficit in 1991. Germany, a large net world lender in the 1980s had suddenly became a net borrower to help pay for the costs of reunification.

It was against this backround that the Greenspan Fed launched its contained depression strategy to save the U.S. banking system in winter 1990–91. U.S. Treasury Secretary Nicholas Brady, desperate for lower U.S. interest rates, tried to pave the way on January 20, 1991, by attempting to revive G7 coordination for lower global interest rates. Just ten days later, however, the Bundesbank *boosted* its discount rate by one-half point to 6.5 percent. When the Fed moved in the opposite direction the next day, the dollar started its plunge to a new record low of DM 1.4475 while U.S. long-term interest rates remained high. At U.S. behest, central bankers rushed in with the first concerted intervention in almost a year to stabilize the dollar.

In the euphoria of the Gulf War victory, the dollar rebounded to DM 1.77. This alarmed the Bundesbank, already worried about an inflationary upsurge from German wage pressure. This was why Brady's lobbying in Germany in April 1991 for a G3 interest rate cut was rejected as nothing more than a nakedly self-serving attempt to bail out the political fortunes of the Bush administration with higher inflation in Germany. A few months later the Bundesbank hiked its discount rate a full percentage point. The Bundesbank's discipline succeeded in moderating the inflation expectations of reunification. German long-term rates edged downward. But they remained at a high level that was transmitted throughout Europe and the world.

German reunification thundered again on December 19, 1991—the same day Greenspan cut the discount rate by a full percentage point—when the Bundesbank ratcheted up its discount rate by another half point to 8 percent.[4] The heaviest brunt fell on Germany's European partners in the EMS's exchange rate mechanism. ERM members faced an odious choice: either they raised interest rates to maintain their ERM parities at the probable cost of recession or they risked a European monetary crisis that could upset their aspiration for European economic and monetary union (EMU). "The Bundesbank has now pushed Europe to the edge of a cliff," said a U.S. central banker at the time. "Can it take a recession? France is hanging on."

In the event, the Europeans chose to relentlessly pursue the Bundesbank.

The Bundesbank's December tightening underscored why many Europeans wanted monetary union. Under the status quo, the Bundesbank made monetary policy based exclusively on domestic considerations—now strongly conditioned by the shock of reunification—and was politically accountable only to German citizens. Yet free capital mobility and the Bundesbank's supreme credibility radiated its policy to all Europeans, whose democratic political voice in shaping it was faint.

Europeans were further upset by the December tightening because many suspected that the German central bankers were thumbing their noses at the landmark treaty for monetary and political union agreed by European leaders at Maastricht, Holland, only a week earlier. The EMU component of the Maastricht Treaty called for the creation in three stages of a pan-European central bank and a single currency by 1999. The Bundesbank and DM hegemony over Europe would be ended.

Through monetary union, and convergence of fiscal and other national economic policies, European leaders hoped to reconcile free international capital mobility with stable, realistically valued exchange rates. Such stability was essential to Europe's goal of creating an integrated, internal economic zone. The realpolitik linchpin of Maastricht was Germany's willingness to surrender the Bundesbank's monetary hegemony for political concessions over the governance and defense of an integrated Europe into which a reunited Germany would be anchored.

"Germany can't work for cooperation and simultaneously insist on [monetary] independence," says Edouard Balladur, who became French prime minister in 1993. "That's the core of the issue," agrees the Bundesbank's Karl Otto Pöhl. "Monetary union is at conflict with Bundesbank independence."

Over Bundesbank obstruction, German leaders, with occasional wavering, chose to join the bandwagon that formed for European monetary union in the wake of the October 1987 stock market crash and near collapse of the dollar. At the Hannover European summit on June 27 and 28, 1988, the German government blindsided the Bundesbank when it itself instigated the commission of a seventeen-person study group to report on feasible paths to economic and monetary union. In April 1989 the Delors committee, composed of the twelve EC central bank governors, five outside experts, and EC President Jacques Delors, outlined a three-step evolution of increasing monetary cooperation and economic convergence culminating in currency union and a single federally structured European central bank. This served as the blueprint for the Maastricht Treaty.

Early on, the Delors committee capitulated to the conditions set down by Pöhl to earn his endorsement.[5] The single European central bank was to share the Bundesbank's primary commitment to price stability. It was to be independent of the EC and national governments. Existing European central banks were to become independent first. The committee also stipulated convergence preconditions, including national ceilings for budget deficits, debt, and inflation, before monetary union could advance, in order to limit economic disruptions when exchange rate flexibility was lost.

On many difficult details, including actual mechanics and convergence standards, the committee was intentionally vague.[6] Pöhl calculated that this was a poisoned chalice that would either force elected leaders to take responsibility for the hard political decisions or immobilize them—and EMU. "It is easy to describe paradise," he explains. "But it is very difficult to get from A to B."

The sudden onset of German reunification, however, catalyzed urgent political momentum for EMU. Europeans petrified of a German superstate able to dominate Europe without shared decision making, and German leaders suffering from East German digestion, stunned Pöhl and the Bundesbank by consenting to the terms for central bank independence and thrashing out the details and timetables the Delors Report had left blank in the December 1991 Maastricht Treaty.[7] What was more, the political leaders made monetary union *obligatory* in 1999 for all signee nations that met the stiff convergence targets. They envisioned a single Europe-wide monetary policy and currency managed by a single central bank whose policy-making council would comprise six directors and the presidents of the European national central banks. In effect, it was a U.S.-type Federal Reserve System for Europe.

Yet the Maastricht conference—with an assist from the Bundesbank's mighty PR—also awakened German public consciousness to the fact that EMU meant abolition of Bundesbank independence and the DM. The intra-German political battle for Europe had been joined.

EMS in Crisis

By summer 1992 the clash between the Bundesbank's tough monetary response to reunification and its recessionary impact on the rest of Europe exploded in the worst currency crisis in EMS history. The instability started when the interaction of Fed easing and Bundesbank tightening sent the dollar tumbling from May. By late August it reached a new all-time low of DM 1.40. Danish voters' unexpected rejection of the Maastricht Treaty in June set off attacks against weaker ERM currencies. Speculation grew of a big realignment, or even collapse, of the ERM, if France voted "*non*" in its national Maastricht referendum on September 20.

Runs broke out against the Italian lira and the British pound—the United Kingdom had joined the ERM at DM 2.95 in October 1990, six weeks prior to Thatcher's removal as prime minister—and other currencies that speculators judged to be overvalued. The attacks overwhelmed huge concerted central bank intervention, including vast amounts executed through the supranational facade of the BIS, forcing the Bank of Italy to raise interest rates on September 4 to defend the lira's ERM parity.

U.K. officials, supported by France, categorically rejected either raising British interest rates to defend the sterling or an ERM devaluation as politically unacceptable when the EC finance ministers and central bank governors met in Bath, England, on September 4 and 5. They were counting on a strong "oui" vote in France's September 20 referendum to break the speculative fever. Instead they demanded immediate German interest rate cuts. U.K. Exchequer Chancellor Norman Lamont was so vociferous that new Bundesbank President Helmut Schlesinger had to be restrained from stalking out by Finance Minister Theo Waigel. The contentious meeting broke up with a public declaration that there'd be no realignment.

Currency markets rioted. Fueled by the highly leveraged bets of hedge funds and other innovative vehicles of the changed global financial landscape, speculators pounded sterling and the lira. Massive intramarginal intervention by the Bank of Italy and Bundesbank failed to prevent the lira from falling below its ERM floor on Friday, September 11. Bank of Italy Governor Carlo Ciampi and the Bundesbank's Schlesinger agreed that lira devaluation was inevitable. Schlesinger informed the German government that intervention—which in September soared to an astronomical DM 92 billion ($60 billion)—in support of weaker currencies had surpassed manageable proportions. The Bundesbank would invoke its right to opt out of ERM's unlimited intervention obligations under the 1978 letter between the Bundesbank and the government.[8]

Chancellor Kohl and Finance Minister Waigel secretly visited the Bundesbank to propose a deal to trim interest rates for an ERM realignment. Bundesbank officials agreed. The size of their interest rate cut would depend on how many countries realigned. Finance Ministry officials were dispatched to Rome via Paris to negotiate a lira and a broader realignment. Through a combination of mix-up and French opposition, however, a broader realignment was never discussed.[9] Italian Prime Minister Giulliano Amato received a frosty "No" when he asked U.K. Prime Minister John Major for sterling to join the lira's 7 percent devaluation. At a special council meeting at 9 A.M. on Monday, September 14, the Bundesbank cut its floor discount rate by one-half point and its ceiling Lombard rate by one-quarter point.

That the Bundesbank had seemingly bowed to political pressure at all stirred a sensation in Germany. In contrast, other ERM members, and currency markets, were unimpressed by the small size of the cuts. The currency attacks resumed. A full-fledged run on sterling erupted following publication of a report that President Schlesinger had said that a broader realignment would have eased the crisis. British leaders later accused him of deliberately trying to incite an attack on sterling.

The next day, "Black Wednesday," September 16, opened with massive sterling purchases by the Bank of England, Bundesbank, and Bank of France against a one-way avalanche of sellers. British foreign exchange reserves dwindled with astonishing speed. At 11 A.M. the government announced it would boost short-term rates from 10 percent to 12 percent. After a brief pause the speculative attack resumed. Just after 2 P.M. interest rates were boosted again to 15 percent.

But the selling pressure only *increased*. Finally, at 4 P.M., having exhausted half its roughly $40 billion reserves of foreign exchange, the government told the Bank of England to stop intervening. The pound plunged through its ERM floor.

At 7:45 P.M. Britain announced it would pull out of the ERM and float the pound, which promptly plunged. The Italian lira and Spanish peseta were also forced below their ERM floors. At midnight the European Monetary Committee convened an emergency meeting. By dawn they agreed that the lira too would be temporarily suspended from the ERM. The peseta was devalued by 5 percent.

The devaluations and ERM exits excited an attack against the French franc, just days ahead of its Maastricht referendum. Yet France's underlying economic fundamentals were as good as or better than Germany's; not even the Bundesbank believed the franc should be devalued. But if the franc didn't hold its parity, what remained of the ERM and any realistic hope of EMU would be blown away. In the event, the franc scraped the bottom of its ERM floor but survived the rest of the week's onslaught with extraordinary assistance from the Bundesbank. On September 20, by official tally, French citizens approved the Maastricht Treaty by the slenderest of margins. The French currency crisis abated temporarily.

The September 1992 ERM currency crisis, in retrospect, marked the turning point from Bundesbank austerity. But German interest rates dribbled down in 1993 with painful slowness, both for Germany, which was then contracting at an unexpectedly severe 3 percent annual pace with four million unemployed, and for France.[10]

Currency speculators mounted another assault against the franc in the summer of 1993 when they sensed weakening French political resolve to keep interest rates high enough to stick with the DM as French unemployment soared past three million. When the Bundesbank Council failed to cut its discount rate from 6.75 percent on July 29, 1993, as markets and French leaders had expected, the attack on the franc turned ferocious. Top French and German monetary officials hastily arranged to meet the next morning at the French Finance Ministry in Paris.[11]

Even as they met, up-to-the-minute reports apprised them of the staggering loss of French reserves that would become the largest and most futile daily total in history—in all, France expended some FFr 300 billion ($50 billion), leaving the Bank of France with a net reserve deficit of FFr 180 billion ($30 billion) at day's end. Bank of France Governor Jacques de Larosière led the French negotiators; Finance Minister Edmond Alphandéry's tactless public demands a month earlier for lower German interest rates made him persona non grata to the Bundesbank. De Larosière asked Schlesinger and his successor-designate, Hans Tietmeyer, to cut the Bundesbank Repo rate. He also pressed for unlimited intervention support to defend the franc's ERM floor.

The Germans hardly had time to refuse both requests when word came that the franc had already hit its floor. This triggered mandatory unlimited intervention by both central banks. Facing its longtime inflationary nightmare scenario, the Bundesbank men proposed suspending the intervention obligation, and with it the ERM, for the afternoon. Even though France was losing reserves at a prodigious rate—at one point $100 million a *minute*—French officials refused to accept what would be a humiliating political defeat of the "hard franc" policy it had defended at high recessionary cost.

The next day, July 31, the twelve finance ministers and central bankers of the EC Monetary Committee gathered at commission headquarters in Brussels for an emergency weekend session. Deputy Finance Minister Jean-Claude Trichet repeated French demands for unconditional Bundesbank intervention and interest rate cuts. He was interrupted by Hans Tietmeyer, who observed acidly that he had left out one item—that Germany abandon the DM and its monetary sovereignty.[12] He suggested that instead the franc's ERM range be widened from 2.25 percent to a more flexible 6 percent to 8 percent.

France countered that Germany should temporarily pull out of the ERM—and acknowledge implicitly that its reunification policies were the crisis's source. But unbeknownst to France, Germany had agreed in advance with Holland to keep the DM and guilder firmly bound together, whatever happened. France was checkmated. It had no answer for the Bundesbank's readiness to let the ERM dissolve into floating exchange rates rather than defend the franc with inflationary unlimited intervention.

In a crushing defeat for its political monetary aspirations, France capitulated around midnight Sunday. By phone, de Larosière and Balladur agreed upon a wider 15 percent band, so as not to give speculators another easy target to shoot at. Thus in the wee hours Monday, August 2, 1993, just before the opening of Asian currency markets, all ERM currencies save the DM and guilder adopted a 15 percent fluctuation band.

The currency crises of 1992 and 1993 left Europe staggering toward EMU and its single-market goals. It left the ERM shorn of two of its four main currencies, 15 percent target zones for most of the others, and lasting enmity among monetary officials.

The EMS crises were awesome demonstrations of the diminishing power of governments to guide their currencies, and thus their economic destinies, amid the oceanic tides of global capital. Their most determined intervention efforts in world history were no match for the $1 trillion a day that was turning over the world's foreign exchanges by 1992—twice the total foreign exchange reserves of all world central banks. Governments' rigid political commitments not to realign caused the currencies of Italy, the United Kingdom, and Spain to become unsustainably overvalued. Yet the overwhelming attack on the soundly valued French franc demonstrated the inherent propensity of floating currency markets to snowball. That the crisis erupted among a homogeneous economic group of nations guided by a fully articulated exchange rate regime made the G7's target zone effort to manage the dollar look even more forlorn in retrospect.

Ironically, EMS countries spent the 1980s eliminating the regulatory controls that dammed up the intra-European and global flows of capital that, in the end, made the ERM harder to operate and finally overwhelmed it. The lesson, concludes two leading monetary scholars, is that "open capital markets are incompatible with pegged exchange rates, pure and simple."[13]

Not trusting to democratic referendum with pro-Bundesbank sentiment strong in the national polls, Germany, by parliamentary vote, became the final EC country to ratify the Maastricht Treaty. Its constitutional court, however, ruled that any transfer of Bundesbank monetary powers was contingent upon a supranational European central bank meeting German democratic standards of transparency and accountability, as well as treaty criteria—which in 1994 most countries, Germany included, did not yet meet. This was a fine irony since other Europeans often charged that the Bundesbank itself was not democratically accountable enough for their liking.

In the crises' aftermath, some EMU partisans called for reinstituting capital controls to try to bottle up, or at least reduce, economically and politically disequilibrating capital flows. Others called for a blind early leap to pool monetary sovereignty among an inner core of nations with the others to follow later—a "two-speed" Europe. A late 1994 poll showed why, above all, EMV partisans wanted to act without giving European citizens any more opportunities to vote: only one in four Germans, and one in three British, said they would vote in favor of a single European currency if given the chance. France, the most ardent advocate of an early monetary union, sought to bolster global investors' confidence in the franc and to get into line with the Bundesbank's terms for EMU, by finally granting political independence to the long subservient Bank of France. Oddly, perhaps the riskiest path to EMU was the most politically conservative one of sticking to Maastricht's evolutionary timetable and hoping that market forces cooperated.

One decisive variable would be how credible financial markets judged the newly independent national central banks would be in upholding the soundness of their currencies and in offsetting any political moves, such as those discussed in 1994, to relax the Maastricht convergence criteria so that more countries could qualify for monetary union.

Deflating Japan's Bubble Economy

Another of the big foreign shocks that forced America's borrowed economic time to run out occurred in Tokyo on December 17, 1989—the day that Yasushi Mieno succeeded Satoshi Sumita as governor at the Bank of Japan. Mieno came to office with a mission: to restore Japan's economic house to order by puncturing the *zaiteku*-driven financial bubble. Mieno's relentless drive to "take away the punch bowl" came to so thoroughly dominate the Japanese political economy that *The Economist* wrote, "Mr. Mieno could claim to have been the most important person in Japan over the past two years, with his determination to bring down land, property, and share prices and to cool Japan's overheating economy."[14] In the process he closed the final chapter on the G7 dollar management enterprise and ushered in the consequences it had postponed at home and abroad.

Japan in 1989 was possessed by the same type of financial euphoria and myopic sense of economic invincibility that gripped the United States in the Roaring Twenties before the Great Crash of 1929. Already astronomical stock prices had doubled within three years. Ever-rising land values, the cornerstone of the financial speculation, was such an article of faith that even Masaru Yoshitomi, director of Japan's Economic Planning Agency, said, "Land prices are a bubble, they say. But for over twenty years it never collapses. If it is a bubble, it's a leather bubble."

Mieno disagreed. Being a quintessentially conservative central banker, he feared that sooner or later it would lead to an inflationary blowout, systemic financial trauma, and debasement of the BOJ. Evoking Paul Volcker's puritanical moralism, he added, "The bubble hurt the soundness and stability of Japanese society. The efforts of labor, which is to work with sweat on your forehead, had been weakened. Morale was reduced, and there was unfairness in the distribution of wealth."[15]

Although cursed within the Establishment for the losses he inflicted on land and stock speculators as "Oniehi," a legendary samurai avenger who severely punished his enemies, Mieno became something of a folk hero for ordinary Japanese who hadn't shared in the financial spoils. In the process he struck a blow for greater BOJ independence from its big brother, the Ministry of Finance.

A man of medium height, unpretentious demeanor, and slightly bucked teeth, his eyes hidden behind plain dark-rimmed eyeglasses, Yasushi Mieno blended in unnoticed among the nondescript rank of bureaucrats. He was born in Manchuria in 1924, the son of a banker who lost all during World War II. While in high school he sold soap and butter and lived in a sumo stable, serving the wrestlers. After graduation from the elite Tokyo University Law Department, which stocked the upper ranks of the Japanese financial technocracy, he joined the BOJ in 1947. As a central banker he still frequented the stores and markets unrecognized to get a firsthand smell of price developments. Although he spoke no English and had little international experience, Mieno was thoroughly imbibed in the Basel credos of sound money and central bank independence. As deputy governor he had not been well-known abroad. When he became governor, his presence was felt right away.

By the time Mieno took office, measured inflation was picking up from 1 percent to 3 percent and money supply growth was rocketing at 12 percent.

Most worrisome was the heating up of inflation expectations, reflected in the 13.6 percent trade-weighted slide of the yen in 1989, which had continued even after the DM rebounded after the fall of the Berlin Wall. MOF had been sufficiently concerned to go along with a two-step hike in the discount rate in 1989, from the "emergency level" 2.5 percent to 3.25 percent. In October the ODR was boosted again to 3.75 percent.

With Mieno's ascension, the MOF and Japanese Establishment accepted that the time had come to engineer a managed collapse of the Japanese bubble economy. But they were not altogether prepared for Mieno's swiftness and vigor. Within eight days, delayed by a leak and vehement denial by Finance Minister Ryutaro Hashimoto, which required going through the motions of a ritual review, the BOJ boosted its discount rate to 4.25 percent. Bankers noted as well that Mieno's BOJ became "more orally discouraging of real estate lending than before."[16]

Bond prices started their biggest crash in half a decade. The equity market plunged. MOF intervened to buy bonds, and the BOJ offered lender of last resort liquidity support to banks to keep the correction orderly.

Concerned that the yen was still falling, Mieno made a secret visit to Greenspan in Washington in February 1990. He sought and received the Fed chairman's "moral support" for a large one-percentage-point discount rate hike.[17] On March 7, 1990, with the yen at ¥151, Mieno flew to Europe to gain support, as the BOJ routinely did before major moves, from Basel central bankers.

On March 20, 1990, the BOJ boosted the discount rate to 5.25 percent. The Tokyo stock market fell sharply, requiring MOF and BOJ support.

When the yen continued to weakened further, MOF Minister Hashimoto appealed to the U.S. Treasury and G7 for help. But Secretary Nick Brady, supported by the Europeans, wasn't interested. At its April 7, 1990, meeting at Paris, the G7 agreed only to term the decline of the yen to ¥160 "undesirable" and to offer some mild supportive intervention.

International capital finally began to turn in favor of the yen only after mid-May, when signs of a U.S. slowdown instilled expectations of lower U.S. interest rates. Since its 1989 peak the differentials between dollar and yen bond interest rates had narrowed from 4.5 to only 1.5 percentage points. The Tokyo stock market, down a quarter since December 1989, bottomed out.

Then came the unexpected stagflationary Saddam shock—the August 2, 1990, invasion of Kuwait. Long-term interest rates lurched upward worldwide, but farthest in Japan because of its oil dependence. Tokyo stocks tumbled anew. The Mieno BOJ reacted by hiking the discount rate another three-quarters of a point to 6 percent on August 30, 1990, to show its anti-inflationary resolve. In mid-September Mieno shocked the Japanese financial community by asserting he would welcome an orderly 20 percent fall in still lofty land values. Two weeks later the BOJ issued its toughest window guidance on lending growth to city banks since 1974 to see that it happened.

Tokyo stock market selling grew frantic. The Nikkei closed at 20,221 on October 1, 1990, down 35 percent since the Saddam shock and 50 percent below its peak. Bankruptcy rumors abounded. Fear of panic-driven share dumping was ubiquitous.

When the market knifed below 20,000 during its October 1 fall, the MOF mounted a furious emergency defense, including actions not taken since the near crash at the start of 1988. The next day the stock market turned in a record single-day gain of 13 percent. Over the next months the market stabilized. Real estate prices cooled. Money supply growth eased. The storm had been weathered.

Mieno held down the monetary brakes until July 1, 1991, when the BOJ cut its discount rate by half a point to 5.5 percent. The world's greatest financial bubble had been deflated. There'd been a lot of outcries of financial pain, many revelations of stock and political scandals, but amazingly little economic trauma. A wave of self-congratulation embraced the Japanese Establishment for having managed financial asset markets up and down almost as an economic policy tool. It vindicated the efficacy, even the superiority, of Japan's relationship capitalist model before free market critics calling on Japan to change.

But the story wasn't finished.

One consequence of rising Japanese real interest rates to deflate its financial bubble was that Japanese investors kept their money at home. A decision of small import in Tokyo, however, imparted significant shocks on economies abroad, above all on the foreign capital-dependent United States.

The drying up of Japanese capital outflows in autumn 1990—registered in the 15 percent fall of the dollar from ¥150 to ¥128—worsened the U.S. credit crunch and the flight from U.S. bank CDs just as the United States was tipping into recession. The most painful impact was in battered California, where Japanese banks accounted for one-quarter of commercial lending. The sharp retreat of Japanese investors who bought some $70 billion in U.S. real estate from 1985 to 1990 helped knock the legs out from under the U.S. commercial real state bubble and added to the deflation in the collapsing U.K. property market.

From being the world's largest exporter of capital with over $130 billion in net long-term capital outflows in each year between 1986 and 1988, Japan in 1991 actually had a net investment inflow of almost $40 billion. In the first eighteen months of Mieno's tenure Japan retrenched its international lending by an astounding $100 billion, tightening credit conditions worldwide. The United States was left to finance its stuttering economy from its paltry national savings. This reinforced the upward pressure on U.S. real long-term interest rates associated initially with the fall of the Berlin Wall. "The Japanese have withdrawn from the world," commented a senior Fed official.[18]

Sharp global financial displacements were commonplace before the creation of the postwar Bretton Woods world monetary regime and had had a prominent role in spreading the Great Depression. Under the floating privatized global monetary nonsystem, it had reemerged in a more volatile, high-speed, large volume form.

The Mieno BOJ's easing policy from July 1991, on the other hand, gave the Greenspan Fed more latitude to reduce U.S. interest rates to fight the second dip of the U.S. recession. From mid-1991 to January 1992 Japanese and U.S. interest rates danced a monetary minuet: short-term interest rates in Japan fell by 2.5 percentage points and 2.0 points in the United States; ten-year rates eased by 1.25 points in both countries. Without Mieno's easing, the outcome of Greenspan's bold December 19, 1991, discount rate cut gamble might have been very different.

By the winter of 1991–92 it became evident that something was wrong with Japan's economy. Deflation was taking on an unforseen momentum. In 1992 growth was less than 1 percent; in 1993 it was zero. Japan was sinking into its worst economic period since World War II. What happened?

Depressionary momentum was emanating from both the production and financial circuits of the imploding bubble economy. First there was a bust of the late 1980s capital spending boom that had expanded capacity in Japan's structurally maturing industries at a pace that could be sustained only by the most wildly optimistic assumptions of future demand and international political tolerances. In 1990 capital spending reached 22 percent of GNP, or $660 billion—30 percent more than the United States, with an economy twice as large. When Mieno's deflationary squeeze pushed up capital costs toward world levels for the first time in half a decade, the boom collapsed. The auto industry alone had overcapacity equal to the entire French car market. Despite wishful predictions by Japanese leaders, demand in Japan's underdeveloped and unreformed domestic economy did not pick up the slack.[19]

Once again the old pattern emerged: Japanese prosperity depended overwhelmingly on export growth. Exports rose 8 percent; imports fell 4 percent. The bilateral deficit with the United States grew for the first time in five years. When the overindebted U.S. economy fell back into the second dip of its downturn in late 1991, Japanese business confidence and growth slumped, too. With its external surpluses rising, the yen appreciated 30 percent in trade-weighted terms from mid-1992 to the end of 1993. This imparted another deflationary jolt, further crippling export profits. Unlike the high yen shock of 1985–87, this time there was no financial boom to soften the blow. Japan had finally been trapped by its failure to reform the lopsidedness and international incompatibilities of its political economy.

Government policymakers, second, also misjudged the effects of financial asset price deflation—a phenomenon never before seen in postwar Japan. The real economic indicators on which they had always relied, explained the Economic Planning Agency's Masaru Yoshitomi, didn't look nearly as bad as the financial.[20]

Some $3 trillion in land values and $3 trillion more in equity values had disappeared in the bubble deflation by late 1993—six times more than the amount lost in New York on Black Monday and twelve times more in proportion to the size of the Japanese economy. At the center of the deflationary spiral were the main banks, which were caught between two closing scissor blades. On the one side, they faced large defaults on loans now inadequately collateralized with land that was plunging in value. On the other side, falling stock values were obliterating their "hidden" capital cushions against bankrupting loss. "Inflated stock and real estate prices created the illusion that Japanese banks rested on a sizable capital cushion," explains Akio Mikuni, president of a Japanese credit-rating agency.[21]

Uncertainty over how far prices would fall and how great their losses would be brought bank lending growth to a halt in 1991. Corporations laden with overcapacity had no interest in borrowing. Confidence was eroded. Stock prices fell toward the 20,000 threshold touched in October 1990. The narrow, closely guided Japanese financial system, anchored in the main banks, had given the Japanese authorities great leverage to inflate the system. Now its lack of diversity and self-balancing free market forces were concentrating the momentum of its fall.

Mieno was besieged by political demands for further interest rate cuts. MOF bureaucrats, opposed to any major domestic fiscal action that would compromise the 1980s budgetary consolidation, seconded them. In February 1992 LDP power broker Shin Kanemaru threatened publicly to "sack" Mieno and curtail the BOJ's modest independence: "They say that the Bank of Japan governor has the authority on the official discount rate, but the prime minister is almighty."[22] Even the supportive *Financial Times* warned, "The Bank of Japan has overplayed its waiting game; monetary policy has remained too tight for too long. The desire of its governor, Mr. Yasushi Mieno, to appear independent of political influence has prevented the interest rate cuts needed to boost confidence and revive Japan's ailing economy. . . . An independent central banker is better than a politically compliant one, but there is no merit in being independently wrong."[23]

What was really needed, Mieno countered vainly, was for Japan to promote domestic demand through greater economic deregulation and market accessibility and transparency.[24] But such structural reform was still hostage to the "Japan problem"—the lack of a political power center capable of leading fundamental reform.

Mieno finally cut the discount rate by three-quarters of a point, to 3.75 percent, on April 1, 1992, a day after the government announced a mostly cosmetic fiscal stimulus package. He announced it would be the BOJ's final easing.

Japanese markets reacted disastrously. Long-term interest rates rose. The stock market plunged in a funk. Led by panic selling by insurers, who raced against each other to dump shares to raise cash to cover policy payments, it crashed 20 percent in ten days to only 16,598. At one point the fall infected U.S. and European bourses.

The great preoccupation in the markets was that losses, real and anticipated, would cause banks to sell shares and liquidate real estate collateral to limit their downside exposures. That could foment a race to sell among all financial institutions, with an inexorable, catastrophic conclusion. Plunging prices would trigger a downward spiral of bank credit retrenchment, economic contraction, business and bank failures—and a new round of asset dumping. Some regional banks and finance companies were already selling to alleviate their critical capital shortages.

Market speculation was acute: How vulnerable were the main banks?

The MOF technocrats who guided the Japanese financial system routinely kept serious problems secret until opportune moments for resolution arose, so as not to spook the public. But in early 1992 the lack of transparency for what everyone knew to be the most serious banking crisis in half a century caused market players to assume the worst. Nor were anxieties assuaged by Finance Minister Hashimoto's declaration to international bank chairmen at the June 1991 International Monetary Conference in Osaka that Japan's government would never let a major bank fail.

As a result, MOF took the unprecedented action of publicly estimating the problem loans of the leading twenty-one banks. No one believed them. A promptly leaked BOJ document estimated the problem as three and half times larger. The figures being whispered in Tokyo financial circles of ¥30 trillion ($275 billion) to ¥75 trillion ($680 billion) were four to ten times greater—some 8–20 percent of their total loans.[25] If actual loan losses at the top twenty-one banks ultimately reached the ¥10 trillion ($90 billion), some bankers calculated, it would wipe out half their total equity capital.

Led by panicky selling of bank shares, the Tokyo stock market nosedived to ¥15,400 by July 1992. With virtually every leading financial and economic indicator pointing downward, the BOJ cut its discount rate cut on July 27,

1992, from 3.75 percent to 3.25 percent. Again Governor Mieno declared it would be the last.

But with LDP politicians and MOF bureaucrats still dickering over a fiscal stimulus package, the market continued to plunge. It hit bottom in August at 14,309. Finally the government announced what would be the first of three emergency spending packages in the next twelve months. The stimulus package accompanied a plan to rescue Japan's banking system. It amounted to a Japanese Establishment version of a "contained depression" strategy.

When the government revealed its intention to supply public funds to help liquidate banks' bad loans, however, there was an unexpected, furious public backlash. The bank bailout promise was hastily retracted. To average Japanese citizens, the banks were the epitome of the bubble economy's greed and inequities; they were now suffering their just desserts.

With a direct bank bailout blocked, Japanese authorities launched an indirect, preemptive, unusual lender of last resort type rescue. It featured a well-leaked "price-keeping operation" (PKO), a pun on the U.N.'s "peace-keeping operations," to put a floor under real estate and stock prices by government buying. Some ¥4 trillion ($36 billion) was spent buying stocks in 1992 and even more in 1993.[26] Major institutions received stern MOF guidance against opportunistic selling.

The main banks were told to prevent their troubled nonbank affiliates from collapsing and to tow along troubled borrowers with interest rate concessions and repayment relief. Eventually asset price stabilization and brightened growth prospects would make their problem loans good. In the meantime MOF would orchestrate a gradual schedule for writing off the hopeless debts that every bank could meet without disturbing its competitive position in the industry pecking order.[27]

The MOF-led bank rescue amounted to an old Japan Inc.–style industrial cartel convoy, which traveled at the speed of the slowest and leakiest ship. All would make it safely to shore—or none. The strategy could work if all maintained enough discipline and confidence in the pilots to stick together. If any major bank liquidated equity or land assets ahead of the pack, or if one of the stronger banks followed competitive market incentives to write off its loans faster than its troubled competitors were able, it could trigger a panicked chain reaction throughout the financial system and a full-fledged economic depression.

"There's almost been a nationalization of the financial system," says ex–BOJ Deputy Governor for International Mikio Wakatsuki.[28]

At first the covert convoy rescue was a smashing success. The stock market rebounded within weeks by 25 percent to nearly 19,000. Bears, many of them foreigners, were chastened. The danger of panic selling abated. Bank balance sheets were strengthened, on paper, by the rise in "hidden" capital from unrealized share gains.

But trading volume stayed low. Lending and borrowing in the real economy also remained moribund. Industrial production and business confidence plunged. BOJ officials figured that money supply normally had to grow at 6 percent to support 3.5 percent annual growth. Instead money supply growth turned *negative* for the first time in history. Contracting money supply was the hallmark of the U.S. path to the Great Depression of 1930–31. Economic historian Charles Kindleberger approvingly cites his monetarist adversary Milton Friedman: "Whatever happens in a stock market, it cannot lead to a great depression unless it produces or is accompanied by a monetary collapse."[29] In early 1993 Nissan and NTT shook economic spirits and Japan's vaunted lifetime employment guarantee by announcing they would lay off thirty-five thousand workers over the next three years through "compulsory" early retirement.

Heavy political pressure built for still another BOJ interest rate cut. Behind the scenes, Mieno held out for further fiscal stimulus. Extraordinary rumors spread in creditable circles that ex-MOF officials in top positions of industry and government were plotting to depose Mieno and install a less independent governor.

Mieno finally yielded in early February 1993. The BOJ cut its discount rate by three-quarters of a point to 2.5 percent, the historically low "emergency level" at which BOJ officials had bridled several years earlier. The emergency then had been to save the U.S. dollar and stock market. Now it was to contain a financial collapse and depression in Japan. Mieno pointedly did *not* declare that this cut would be the last. Shortly thereafter the government unveiled its second emergency stimulus package.

Again financial markets rallied, then sagged when the economy did not revive. In September 1993 the coalition government, which had recently broken the LDP's long monopoly on power, passed a third emergency stimulus package. A week later Mieno's BOJ cut the discount rate again to its lowest level in history—1.75 percent. Still the BOJ was pushing on a string of unconfident borrowers beset with overcapacity and unwilling, overexposed lenders.

It grew increasingly evident that the government convoy rescue was not confronting the core problems of asset price deflation and industrial overcapacity. The MOF's price-keeping operation of government purchases and *dictakt* was geared to stabilizing the Tokyo stock market at 20,000, then waiting for a spontaneous rise to enable banks to build capital through share sales and to then write off their bad debts so they could start to lend again. On the economic front the strategy was similarly to stretch out the adjustment process until capitalist animal spirits revived or Japan was lifted by exports in a cyclical global economic recovery.

However, the artificially of government-managed markets also prolonged financial players' uncertainty about what land and share price levels were ultimately sustainable. This inhibited spontaneous buying. The extremely slow pace of the bank cartel convoy—analysts estimated that it would take three to five years to work off its problem debts—starved Japan of the credit needed to fuel any incipient economic recovery. Hostage to financial fragility, monetary policy lost its potency.

By winter 1993–94 the deflationary momentum, assisted by the sharp 25 percent rise of the yen to ¥105 per U.S. $1, was causing Japanese inflation to fall toward zero or even below, to outright price deflation. This meant that real long-term interest rates—the difference between inflation and the 3.8 percent ten-year bond yield—were actually *rising!* This left Japan closer to a depression-era scenario than any other country. The best the BOJ could do, as Greenspan had done in the United States, was to hold bank funding rates so low that banks could build profits and capital by reinvesting in higher-yielding government bonds until their balance sheets improved.

The slow pace of the convoy opened a rift between the Mieno BOJ and the MOF. Mieno openly urged the stronger Japanese banks to "escape from the conventional management stance of doing the same to its competitors" and emulate their U.S. and U.K. counterparts in aggressively writing off bad loans, even if they had to show losses, in order to get the problem behind them quickly.[30] He and many market players recommended tax incentives and the securitization, or bundling and sale, of bad loans in security form, on open markets. But the rigidly conservative MOF bureaucrats, jealous of their tax revenue and leery of any innovation that could dilute their financial system control, blocked substantive action.

Years of failure to reform its lopsided political economic structure left Japan's recovery still highly dependent upon export growth, especially to the United States. Yet the overindebteded United States could not provide the same strong locomotive for a Japan that had become an economic giant. "The problem is very simple," assessed MIT Professor Lester Thurow. "Japan does not know how to engineer an economic recovery without such an export surge; the United States will not have a domestic recovery if such a Japanese export surge were to occur."[31]

As the old structural pattern of Japan's large current account surpluses and U.S. deficits reemerged with the cyclic U.S. recovery, the Clinton administration, in winter 1993–94, stepped up its threats of protectionist reprisals. The yen rose toward ¥100 to the U.S. dollar—further squeezing Japanese exporters and adding depressionary impetus. The flaw in Japan's economic policies of the 1980s was now revealed: like most economic fixes that dealt with symptoms and not fundamental causes, forestalling one problem created others—the financial bubble, which when burst, left Japan dependent upon an uncontrollable, external force that could knock it into a full-fledged depression. The United States would likely be injured by the reverberations.

The very fabric of Japan's "relationship capitalism," and its underlying organizing focus on very rapid economic expansion through a guided financial system and cartelized industries, was under stress. The long downturn reinforced the pleas of reformers. Yet by 1994, the combination of Japanese business's remarkable resiliency and world economic recovery was finally lifting Japan towards recovery. "I wish the recesssion could go on for one more year," confided one prominent reform-minded Japanese commentator sadly. Once again the sheer inertia of entrenched Establishment interests and habits seemed immovable without a full-fledged crisis. Likewise, the United States and European democracies faced formidable fundamental adjustments for a crisis-free transition to the new post–Cold War economic society driven by global capital flows.

A Glimpse Ahead

By 1993 it was clear that the Greenspan Fed had single-handedly engineered a sustained, if modest, recovery of the overindebted and imbalanced U.S. economy. Criticism that it had acted too slowly faded against the achievement. For the first time since the Depression, the United States recovered without a fiscal stimulus. It occurred, too, in an economy undergoing structural transformation from the third major technological revolution in a century, the downsizing of its military economy, and competition from emerging LDCs. "We've had a sector-by-sector depression in the last ten years—energy, farm, real estate, and now defense. It they'd hit all at once, we couldn't have contained it," confesses Fed Governor Wayne Angell.

The recovery came too late to help George Bush win reelection as president in November 1992. The new president, Bill Clinton, entered office on the promise of overcoming Washington's decade-long fiscal gridlock and revitalizing America's economic fortunes. Benefiting from one of the rare times in recent U.S. politics that a single party controlled the White House and both houses of Congress, Clinton managed to deliver a significant down payment in cutting the budget deficit.

Yet even if achieved, by the Clinton administration's own calculations the deficit would be reduced only to 2.7 percent of 1997 GNP. It would still absorb *half* the nation's meager savings. To the extent that the deficit expenditures were used for current rather than capital spending (U.S. government accounting conventions didn't differentiate, as businesses did), the United States was being drained of its main resource to finance wealth-producing investment. After 1997, moreover, the deficit would resume its uncontrolled growth.

America's economic homework remained truly daunting. To reverse its major long-term problem—sluggish productivity growth—required net business investment in plant and equipment not merely better than the dismal 2.6 percent of GNP average of the 1980s, but significantly more than the 3.6 percent of GNP achieved in the 1960s and 1970s. A necessary condition was to boost its national savings, the lowest of all G7 nations for two decades. Americans had to do what its postwar political economic structure made unnatural: consume less, save more. Eliminating the large dissavings of the structural budget deficit, which in the 1980s consumed two-thirds of U.S. business and household net savings, was the surest way to do so. Time was no longer on America's side. With the government increasing its indebtedness faster than the economy's capacity to produce wealth in the 1980s for the first time in peacetime U.S. history, government debt rose from 26 percent to 53 percent of GNP. America stood at the maximum safe debt limit among nations that markets judged to be fiscally secure.

A foretaste of the dangers came in the first half of 1994. With the spread of the U.S. recovery internationally, the 1980s pattern of huge world current account imbalances returned. When the Greenspan Fed nudged up short-term interest rates by a gentle .25 percent in February 1994, startled U.S. and foreign bond markets fell sharply. Abetted by global investor anxiety that a unified Democratic Party government would restrain the Greenspan Fed from lifting record low real interest rates fast enough to contain an inflationary upsurge, and more attractive real bond yields in Germany and Japan, the U.S.'s mammoth foreign borrowing needs caused the alarming bond-dollar price linkage of 1987 to reemerge. Once again Japanese investor shunning of dollar assets, following mild Clinton administration dollar talk-down at its frustration to open Japan's domestic markets, charted the trend. By midyear speculative attacks drove the dollar definitively below the ¥100 threshold and toward its postwar DM lows. In six months U.S. long-term interest rates backed up nearly two percentage points. The thirty-year long bond stalked the 8 percent level last experienced under the Bush government.

To most observers, U.S. interest rate levels had seemed appropriate to foster a sustainable U.S. domestic recovery. But it was investors in the "Court of World Savings," not the Fed or U.S. government, who were dictating the financial, and ultimately economic and political, environment under the regime of stateless capital. With currency intervention ineffective, the Fed faced the unhappy political prospect of having to boost interest rates for what appeared to be a financial market overreaction and, to all but the cognoscenti, a strictly international one at that[32].

The sharp upswing in U.S. interest rates necessary to assuage the expectations of financial market "inflation vigilantes" inflicted heavy losses upon large, heavily leveraged speculators in complex derivatives, including Proctor & Gamble and Orange County, California, as well as upon their financial intermediaries. Orange County, which lost an estimated $2 to $3 billion and had been one of the highest-rated public borrowers, declared bankruptcy when its panicked financiers began liquidating its securities they held as collateral. Leading the liquidation charge were a number of banks beyond the Fed's regulatory reach. As a result, the Fed was all but powerless to head off the destructive panic, or to prevent the purely finance-caused economic trauma to the Southern California economy. Once again, the Fed's monetary policy and financial system stability goals had collided violently.

Global financial market integration meanwhile transmitted the sharply higher U.S. interest rates worldwide. German long-term rates jumped nearly two percentage points; elsewhere in Europe, the backup in rates was even steeper. In recession-weary Japan, long-term interest rates also rose over one and a half points.[32] This helped set off the 1994–95 Mexican crisis.

As the world headed into another imbalanced economic cycle, political tolerance fuses were likely to be shorter. The reaction could lead to curtailment of central bank independence in a futile effort to boost growth through lower interest rates, or to trade protectionism. Either could abort the world recovery prematurely and possibly topple the faltering world economic and monetary order.

Given the flailing performance of elected national leaders before the revolutionary impact of stateless capital, government of the world economy was likely to continue to lurch precariously from crisis to crisis under the ad hoc leadership of publicly little known central bankers. The 1980s had been a golden era for central bankers: they reversed runaway inflation, contained serious financial crises, helped generate an unusually long period of growth, and finally contained the balance sheet depression. Could they do it again through the 1990s?

It would be harder. The task of productively channeling stateless capital flows to the economy through monetary policy was becoming more difficult to control; financial system disruptions often intruded. As central bankers' prominence in governing the world economy grew, meanwhile, so did the political constraints.

During the U.S. presidential election debate on October 11, 1992, Democratic candidate Bill Clinton was asked: "Governor Clinton, when a president running for the first time gets into the office and wants to do something about the economy, he finds in Washington there's a person who has much more power over the economy than he does: the chairman of the Federal Reserve Board, accountable to no one. That being the case, would you go along with proposals made by Treasury Secretary Brady and Congressman Lee Hamilton to make the Federal Reserve Board chairman somehow more accountable to elected officials?"

Clinton paused before answering. "Well, let me say that I think that we ought to review the terms and the way it works, but frankly, I don't think that's the problem today. We have low interest rates today. . . ."[33]

As challenger, of course, Clinton had no incentive to deflect blame for the woeful economy from President Bush to the Federal Reserve. As president-elect, however, he wasted no time in letting Alan Greenspan know that he was counting on low interest rates to underpin his economic program and his presidency. In contrast with the Bush government, Clinton sent his signals softly. In part, this was the result of a keener sensitivity that the U.S. central bank had a powerful invisible political patron—the investors in the "Court of World Savings"—that was likely to react to high-profile political pressure by bidding real long-term interest rates counterproductively higher. In part, too, it was knowledge that behind him he had the big stick of a Democratic congressional majority boisterously threatening to enact legislation to trim the Fed's independence if it dared to interfere with the Democrats' golden governing opportunity.

The Republican landslide victory in the 1994 midterm elections, of course, disarmed any potential Democratic threat to Fed independence. But it came with a return to divided government and the prospect of renewed political paralysis over fiscal policy.

Perilous, perhaps catastrophically disruptive clashes between global markets and national governments lay ahead. How well central bankers managed through them depended much on their independence—which in turn hinged upon their perceived accountability to the interests of the democratic society that appointed, but did not elect, them.

PART SEVEN

EPILOGUE

Chapter 26

Independence and Accountability

The proper role of a central bank, notes ex–German Chancellor Helmut Schmidt, "depends upon the monetary system of the world."

The world monetary system—or, more accurately, nonsystem—today was a shambles. Volatile torrents of stateless money rushed in and out of national financial markets without any political regulation and unhinged for long periods from underlying fundamentals of the real economy. These uncontrolled capital flows increased international economic interdependence. Increasingly, democratic nations' economic destinies were being shaped by private shifts in global demand for different monies and financial crises originating beyond their sovereign borders and control.

In this unprecedented setting, central bankers' success in the 1980s was being translated into a surprising landslide worldwide trend toward upgrading central bank independence. Meaningful independence in the 1980s was confined chiefly to the federal democracies, the United States, Germany, and Switzerland, and a few unitary democracies where the government was chronically weak or a strong central bank governor commanded extraordinary public prestige. By the mid-1990s statutory independence modeled on Bundesbank standards was the norm throughout continental Western Europe as an intermediate step toward the creation of a single, politically independent European federal central bank system, akin to the U.S. Federal Reserve, within the decade.

Autonomy was granted to the long subservient Bank of France, founded at Napoleon's instigation in 1800 as a private bank but soon taken over by France's *dirigiste* public managers. The central bank independence vogue was coming full circle in Tory England, where after a decade of close political control, successive Conservative chancellors of the exchequer since 1988 had secretly lobbied their reluctant prime ministers to buttress sterling's shaky credibility by relinquishing monetary policy to an independent Bank of England. The crescendo reached a high point in late 1993 with the endorsement of an expert panel of British luminaries.

From Chile to Mexico, independent central banks were springing up as linchpins of a new, hard currency free market Latin American model of economic development. New Zealand was the pioneer of central bank independence in commonwealth nations. South Africa adopted central bank independence to reassure foreign and domestic investors about the transition to black majority rule. Central bank independence and hard currency policies in some states of the former Soviet Union were setting the pace for new Western-style central banks to anchor privatized financial systems in ex-communist Eastern Europe. A Chinese-IMF workshop in September 1993 urged the adoption of a politically independent central bank as vital to China's financial reform. Pakistan, Zambia, and Turkey flirted with central bank independence. In Japan, Canada, and Israel, central bankers were operating with more de facto independence than ever before.

What happened? The overriding common denominator was that governments were bowing to the demands of the revolutionary political force of "stateless" capital. First and foremost, to attract globally mobile savings, governments were trying to allay capitalists' historical fear of the state's inflationary propensity. Second, an independent central bank reassured global investors of the safety and soundness of a nation's financial and payments system.

But was accommodating democratic capitalism's increasingly potent, invisible second electorate by granting more independent political authority to unelected central bankers likewise best for democracy's primary voting political citizenry?

In a word: Yes. In the absence of politically set new rules of the road for this global, floating monetary nonsystem, the balance of best interests for both democratic polity and prosperous capitalist markets lay in delegating monetary policy and financial system soundness to a cadre of independent, nonpartisan central bankers dedicated to sound money and financial system order and who enjoyed greater credibility than most elected officials to influence the powerful trends in global financial markets.

Yet there was one important caveat: it was no long-run substitution for the urgent political reforms that were needed to anchor stateless money within global democratic society. Central bankers were above all managers of existing systems. They had neither the institutional mandate, capability, nor outlook to govern indefinitely in lieu of decaying ones. Unless democracy's elected leaders took action, even independent central bankers would eventually fail to hold back stateless money's self-destructive propensities.

Independence

The running, often bitter debate over central bank independence was not so much decisively won in the 1980s by the arguments marshaled in favor as it was lost by those opposing it. The crudest "democratic deficit" argument that "the country's economy is too important to be decided by invisible officials who work behind closed doors without any accountability" had always been belied by the fact that the Fed and Bundesbank owed their autonomy to legislative acts that could be rescinded or altered by simple majority vote.[1] Fed officials were obliged to explain themselves in frequent public testimony before Congress. The very fact that no majority in these democratically elected, representative bodies had risen up to strip their independence was itself evidence that central banks' policies were not clamorously offensive to the democratic mainstream. The speciousness of the unaccountability charge was demonstrated time and again by the broad U.S. middle-class tolerance of Volcker's painful war on inflation, by Germans' support of Bundesbank austerity after reunification, by Governor Mieno's popular deflation of Japan's financial bubble, and by the 1990s electoral success of hard currency policies in Latin America. Volcker showed sensitivity to democratic accountability by seeking White House approval for the Big Three plus Yugoslavia LDC debt strategy when the problem spread beyond Mexico. He obtained a legislative mandate to raise U.S. bank capital standards and negotiated the first international standard with broad support from elected leaders. Central bankers were political agents maneuvering to further their agendas like others in democratic society. But they were in all cases independent within their government, not of it.

The U.S.'s political paralysis to control its record budget deficits, and the rigid pursuit of fiscal consolidation in Japan and Germany in the 1980s, also undercut the contention that government-run monetary policy would be as competent as one administered by an independent central bank.[2] The continuity, technical competence, and the flexibility to adapt to changing conditions necessary for effective monetary policy-making was something that the ebb and flow of the democratic policy-making process couldn't always reliably provide. Sound monetary policy also required the discipline not to subordinate economic logic to short-run political temptations, especially at election time. "Why central banks are separate institutions is intriguing," says a senior European Treasury official. "The right to mint money belongs to the government. But it abuses it. Governments have a huge appetite for money, especially where the government is rarely in surplus. Over time there is a growing awareness that for a system of checks and balances in the public sector you need to separate supply and demand."[3]

After several years of running monetary policy, U.K. Chancellor of the

Exchequer Nigel Lawson became an advocate of an independent Bank of England that could "be seen locking in an anti-inflationary force into the system, as a counterweight to the strong inflationary pressures which are always lurking and to depoliticize interest rate changes."[4] Even an anti-inflationist politician like Mrs. Thatcher, he noted, had a "profound hostility to raising interest rates [and] never objected to lower interest rates."[5] Simply, no government could ever attain as much of the market credibility needed to make monetary policy less difficult as an independent central bank.

The 1980s experience also weakened the argument that an independent central bank threatened economic policy incoherence for which no one held clear democratic accountability. "An independent Fed, with its ear to the bankers and its fingers twitching every time a hint of inflation pulses through the economy, makes such coherent economic management impossible," argues New School Professor David Gordon. "Paul Volcker and his colleagues should not run our lives. We should defrock the delphic priests and take responsibility for our own economic destinies."[6]

Improved coherence was a worthy, badly needed goal. Yet in practice government policy rarely was conceived or implemented from a comprehensive, coherent blueprint. Rather it was molded from the inconsistent push-pull of competing factional, ideological, and special interests. Reagan fiscal policy, as Budget Director David Stockman has testified, was an internally inconsistent Frankenstein of clashing viewpoints among administration supply-siders, monetarists, and conservative mainstream economists before it was ever subjected to the paralyzing partisan divisions of Congress. The never-ending buck passing between president and Congress over responsibility for the 1980s budgetary fiasco for which no one was definably accountable at the polls showed that democratic accountability was a systemic problem transcending the fiscal/monetary divide. If anything, the independent Fed's refusal to monetize those deficits exerted a disinflationary checks and balances counterforce that enhanced political accountability to the democratic electorate.

Implicit and explicit among many critics was that central bankers were biased to sacrifice maximum growth and employment in pursuit of their "hard money" mission. This critique was destroyed with the conceptual collapse of the Phillips curve—the alleged trade-off between inflation and unemployment—that had been a gospel of postwar Keynesian economic policymaking. The experience of the 1970s and 1980s demonstrated that while faster money growth could lift unemployment and spur growth in the short run, the long-run result could be permanently higher inflation without any lasting employment and growth gains.[7]

Monetarist critics of central bank independence had never believed the Phillips curve trade-off between inflation and unemployment. But their arguments for a rule-based monetary alternative too lost force as the short- and medium-term relationships between money and the economy proved unpredictable. That left pragmatic central banker judgment as the last fighter standing.

Because of global financial integration, any democratic government that tried to pursue expansionary monetary policies that global investors considered excessive often found its intentions promptly vetoed as capital fled its national borders. This could shrink money supply despite lower interest rates. Nor was export growth always stimulated by a falling nominal exchange rate. Anticipatory inflation expectations often quickly bid up domestic wages and prices, which, with higher import costs, cancelled out the competitive benefit of any currency depreciation; the *real* exchange rate didn't change. A sound, credible monetary policy, on the other hand, stimulated greater global capital inflows. In appropriate proportion this expanded the domestic money supply, kept inflation in check, strengthened the currency, and gave industry positive incentives to enhance its international competitiveness through productivity gains. This sea change in the world political economy meant that currency hardening, rather than devaluation, was the best strategy for augmenting national wealth. The most credible anchor of a hard money policy was an independent central bank.

The traditional economic and political arguments favoring central bank independence had better withstood the experience of the 1980s global financial revolution. International comparisions were necessarily approximative. But a 1991 study indicated that countries with independent central banks tended to have lower and less volatile inflation rates, while real economic growth was about the same.[8]

A separate, independent central bank that functioned as a "supreme court" over money was still democratic capitalist society's most pragmatic political means of depoliticizing the partisan struggle for the control of money and for providing the long-term monetary soundness necessary to maximizing economic wealth production. Its checks and balances function was dramatically revalidated when Russian President Boris Yeltsin pushed through a constitutional reform that made the central bank independent of both the executive and a Parliament that had been employing its previous control to undermine Yeltsin's economic reforms through a hyperinflationary monetary policy.

But by far the most persuasive case for central bank independence was the rise of stateless money and global financial market integration. Broadly put, in a landscape in which tears anywhere in the interwoven financial fabric or abrupt alteration in the direction or size of international capital flows could disrupt prosperity across borders, it served the enlightened self-interest of citizens and capitalists everywhere to pool their sovereignty through the upgraded independence of all central bankers.

Lender of last resort rescues were never uniform. They required fast, situational judgments in fluid circumstances. Often there was no time for political consultation, even within single nations. It was simply more prudent to rely upon central bankers' natural second allegiance to world monetary order than upon a network of nationally blinkered politicians to act judiciously and expeditiously in a crisis. "[I]nternational financial cooperation is likely to be very much easier among independent central banks, all charged wth the same task, than it is among governments with different domestic electorates to appease," U.K. finance minister Nigel Lawson argued in pressing his case for Bank of England independence to Prime Minister Thatcher in November 1988.[9] Congress's fumbling of the 1994–95 Mexican crisis bore recent witness.

Central bankers' depoliticized financial international diplomacy likewise helped avert disputes that could spill over into trade protectionism and interruptions in cross-border capital flows. It was the independence of central bankers that facilitated the Basel club's development of world bank capital rules.

Independent central bankers were also better placed to collectively manage the de facto world money supply. Monetary policy changes in major currency countries rippled abroad, affecting economic prospects and citizens' lives far beyond its own borders; indeed, with risk positions spread opaquely throughout global markets the effects could sometimes be larger abroad than domestically. Fed independence was the best available check against America's temptation to inflate away its roughly $600 billion net foreign-dollar debt, as the full economic burden of the debt of its unborn to Japanese pensioners and other foreigners was comprehended; if America inflated, the fallout from the collapsing dollar could unhinge the entire world economy.

The most compelling immediate incentive for most countries to make their central bankers independent, however, was to avoid the practical costs imposed by global investors if they didn't. Despite a sounder economic performance than Germany since the mid-1980s, French citizens were penalized with relatively higher real long-term interest rates in part because of France's long delay in institutionalizing its credibility gains with Bank of France independence; British citizens were still paying for their government's determination to swim against the tide of informed opinion advocating Bank of England independence.[10] The independent Bundesbank's monetary hegemony in Europe, by contrast, benefited German citizens with lower interest rates and a strong political bargaining chip used by its leaders in European negotiations over EMU and defense.

• • •

All central bank independence ultimately rested on national public support for its goals and methods and on political leaders' perception of the same. Several statutory and customary cornerstone principles, variably expressed within different national political cultures, made it practicable. These started with freedom to set interest rates, reserve requirements, and other tools of monetary control. Unrecallable, long terms of office for the governor and policy board supported it. Another sine qua non of independence was a "divorce" from any obligation to finance its government's deficits. De facto budgetary autonomy helped; self-financing through seigniorage profits freed central bankers from political control through the purse strings.

A statutory mandate that put price stability clearly ahead of growth and other monetary goals further shielded central bankers from political attacks by spelling out the terms of its democratic accountability. Price stability primacy, in fact, was being widely adopted by nations that were upgrading central bank independence. An aging of populations in industrialized countries, and the spread of the discovery of the political popularity of sound money policies to LDCs in the 1990s, reinforced the trend. In Europe the definition of price stability was left to central banker discretion. In the New Zealand experiment, the government set the central bank's inflation target. By doing so publicly, however, it made itself accountable to the electorate and global financial markets. This effectively tied its own hands against later political interference.

With their victory in the 1994 midterm elections, Republicans began a call for the United States to catch up with the world trend by proposing a sole inflation target for the Fed. Although it was unclear whether this was merely a political ploy to ensure slow growth for the 1996 presidential elections to assist Republicans' aspirations to the White House, if enacted it would serve the capitalist construct and democratic justice goals of making money to be worth what it appeared to be worth on the surface.

Government leaders transferred monetary control to an independent central bank only with extreme reluctance. Prime Minister Thatcher unyieldingly rejected Bank of England independence in part because it carried the tacit admission that her government was unable to control inflation. Furthermore, "[s]he seemed quite incapable of accepting the possibility that there might be another government someday" and that "[w]hile she was there, she was not going to give up the levers of power."[11]

Financial globalization itself was opening new frontiers in the evolution of central bank independence. Should the government or the central bank control national foreign exchange policy? International capital movements and monetary policy were part of a single continuum. Both affected the national money supply and interest rate levels. For smaller countries the distinction between monetary and foreign exchange policy was academic; it was the reason smaller nations still had little practical monetary independence under the floating currency regime. Even for the Bundesbank, the large impact of inflows and outflows of global capital made the exchange rate lever crucial to control of Germany's overall monetary policy.[12] Yet in most countries exchange rate policy was still legally vested in government Finance Ministries. Central bankers were thus wary about governments reasserting their authority through a fixed exchange rate peg or target zone in order to surreptitiously manipulate monetary policy. Yet the exchange rate was such a key price of economic government, that ultimate political authority was also indispensable; the important EMU initiative might not have been possible without it, for example. Ideally the tension could be managed through close consultation between a government and an independent central bank with a clear price stability priority mandate. On intervention, government could set broad guidelines and leave daily operating discretion to central bankers.

A second frontier was central bankers' regulatory authority. With systemic risks arising outside of banks and national borders, central bankers needed broader, and more internationally parallel, supervisory mandates to cover all major financial institutions and activities capable of threatening the safety of the global capital circuit.[13] Yet governments were loath to grant it. The central banker–dominated Delors committee in 1989 recommended more central bank authority for prudential supervision than the political framers of the Maastricht Treaty ultimately gave them. One illogical consequence was a greater risk of a financial fragility constraint on central bank monetary policy. Also anachronistic was the U.S. Clinton administration's 1993–94 effort to strip the Fed of its regulatory powers, as the Reagan administration had tried but failed to do a decade earlier, and to concentrate them in its own Comptroller of the Currency. Disarming the Fed of its regulatory powers removed powerful carrots and sticks that the central banker used to influence banks' behavior at pivotal moments, such as during the LDC debt crisis. It would also have denuded the Fed of the authority it used to launch the Basel capital adequacy standards initiative. A sound informing of monetary policy too was safeguarded when central bankers had direct regulatory access to information unpolluted by possible government political adulteration.

Why did governments resist delegating supervisory powers to central bankers? Simply, it was part of the age-old naked power struggle to exert political control over money. Wielding regulatory carrots and sticks, setting bank capital and reserve requirements, and admonishing bank examiners to be more or less rigorous granted enormous power over a bank's profit level and economic fortunes—and thus influence over its lending behavior. One had only to recall President Bush's bashing of "overzealous" bank examiners in the credit crunch ahead of the 1992 presidential election to understand the enormous temptation of any government to try to influence the regulation of money for partisan political advantage. By stripping the Fed of its powers over small banks, whose survival and failure posed little systemic risk, Clinton's reform proposal was a subtle political assault on the Fed's monetary independence as well. In the U.S. political culture, small bankers wielded disproportionate political clout in Congress; their political support was an important shield against attacks on Fed independence.

The dual pressure on nation-states to fragment into smaller regional states or to federate into larger entities was abetting the trend to central bank independence. The independence of the envisioned single federal European central bank was likely to be enhanced by the fact that central bank independence was historically greater in federal democracies than in unitary states. Its independence would be reinforced by the protection of an international treaty and, even more, its symbolic identification with European unity.

Financial globalization and the emergence of an effective world money supply meant that the independence of major central banks was increasingly interlinked. The global trend toward upgraded statutory independence was noticeably lagging in Japan, notwithstanding the prominence that the strong governorship of Yasushi Mieno had brought to the Bank of Japan in the early 1990s. The BOJ was in part a special case because its master, the Ministry of Finance, was also politically independent. MOF's rigid fixation with fiscal consolidation and dollar stability nevertheless compelled the BOJ to adjust with an overlax monetary policy that fueled Japan's financial bubble economy, when fiscal and structural action was really needed. BOJ independence was likely to grow more internationally significant if, as many experts believed, the democratic capitalist world was evolving toward a tripartite economic and currency bloc regime—a European zone anchored in the basket of European currencies known as the ECU (European Currency Unit) or DM; a U.S. dollar–based American zone; and, though least defined, an Asian zone centered around the yen.

Accountability and Transparency

With greater power came greater obligations of democratic accountability and transparency—more than to which most central banks were accustomed. Ironically, the political clamor was loudest in the nation that already had the world's most transparent and scrutinized central bank, the United States.[14]

Following Democrats' 1992 sweep of the White House and both houses of Congress, congressional Democrats demanded that FOMC seats be reserved for women, minorities, and union members and that the Fed immediately release videotapes of FOMC meetings. The most popular legislative call was for stripping the FOMC voting privileges of the regional Federal Reserve Bank presidents, who, denounces Joint Economic Committee Chairman Paul Sarbannes (D-Md.), "are accountable not to the people or their elected representatives, but to their boards of directors, which are dominated by commercial banks."[15] In early 1993 Democratic legislators summoned the twelve Federal Reserve Bank presidents before the Senate Banking Committee. Squeezed together in a row, they listened to Chairman Donald Riegle (D-Mich.) admonish them on the need for monetary and fiscal teamwork and declare that President Clinton's election signified that the nation was expecting "more accountability from everybody."[16]

After departing the Fed, Volcker said in its defense: "The organizational characteristics of the Federal Reserve are seemingly odd, but it somehow, in its peculiar way, reflects a pretty good balance. You get some continuity, professionalism, and insulation from politics. And the way the presidents are selected contributes to all of these things."[17]

Not all of the congressional roughness was partisan posturing to intimidate the Fed into a compliant monetary policy while the Democrats held power. Amid the blunderbuss was the healthy, ongoing accountability process of democratic oversight at work, whereby elected officials communicated their concerns to their technocratic monetary policy deputies.

Outside the United States, the trend to greater central bank independence was outpacing attention on accountability and transparency. In most of the world, central banking was still inexcusably almost as secretive as national security. Many central banks remained free to decide what little to disclose about their operations and had no obligation to testify before elected representatives.

The gap between independence and accountability in Europe was glaring. For the first time in history currency union and monetary policy run by an independent 'Eurofed,' directly answerable to no counterpart political body, was being given responsibility to provide the external discipline for economic and political integration. Even central bankers worried that this scheme might be quixotic and fretted about the huge expectations being placed upon them. "Is it politically and economically realistic to have a central bank that springs out of Zeus' head like Athene? Can you set up something that answers to a political vacuum?" wonders a veteran European monetary official.

The inherent danger of undefined political accountability was double-edged: it made the central bank more susceptible to falling captive to special interests; at the same time it gave greater leash to elected leaders to scapegoat central bankers to cover up their own undisciplined management of economic policies. In the end, poor fiscal and other policies overburdened and defeated any monetary policy.

Central bankers "who normally wouldn't talk about" political account-ability tackled aspects of the subject during their Delors committee discussions.[18] To sober unachievably high political expectations and to reduce external economic pressures that would swamp even the best monetary policy, they emphasized the importance of convergence and coordination of various national economic policies and financial burdens as preconditions for EMU. The ill-managed German monetary union soon exclaimed their point. Yet if, as seemed likely, few European countries achieved the Maastricht Treaty convergence criteria by 1999, central bankers feared that leaders would move the goal posts closer and leap to monetary union anyway—leaving them with a technically nightmarish task.

Another widening gap was between acceptable domestic and international standards of accountability. It no longer sufficed for each central bank to cultivate its own garden exclusively and to explain itself solely in domestic terms. Some minimum world standards of accountability were needed, just as they were in financial regulations. Accountability would be improved, too, if the three leading central banks disclosed their policy goals, gave a meaningful, timely account of their operations, and testified before the legislatures of the other two countries, according to the present standards of the U.S. Federal Reserve. In addition to giving its central bank a primary sound money mandate, governments could abet accountability by presenting their own, nonbinding views of acceptable ranges for inflation, nominal GNP, and government policy variables, such as budget-deficit size, which shaped the monetary policy environment.

There was no solution on the horizon for another serious accountability gap created by the collapse of national monetary targetry as a viable policy anchor. With no other satisfactory objective replacement method to explain and measure monetary policy goals and performance, central bankers were forced to rely on seat of the pants judgment. Moreover, it compelled them to appeal for support from the democratic public and financial markets on an inherently unsatisfactory "Trust Me" basis. This incited both partisan political and market suspicions that worked against the credibility any central bank policy needed to succeed.[19]

Democratic accountability was also being undermined by the steady stretching of the central bankers' field of action in the changed global financial landscape. Should central bankers try to dampen excessive financial volatility or snowballing? Should they head off financial crises before they happened, even though doing so might require bailing out nonbanks with different implicit democratic capitalist compacts and responsibilities? What were their international responsibilities? *Could* central bankers even be held accountable for low inflation growth and financial system stability when the core banking system through which their policies mainly acted held an increasingly shrinking share of financings and when innovation constantly altered the channels and impact of their policy actions? Most of these questions hadn't been answered.

At the end of the day central bank accountability—as well as their success or failure in attaining their low inflation growth and financial stability goals—depended on how well democratic capitalist society politically "civilized" stateless money's supranational mobility and volatility. One risk was that instead of being used as a tool to achieving a larger political end, upgraded central bank independence would become a political narcotic for governments to avoid facing this epochal challenge. In that event, even the most independent central bank couldn't prevent monetary policy from becoming fatally overburdened by financial fragility and trying to compensate for fiscal policy failures. " 'When fiscal policy is not working, should monetary policy act?' After both Volcker and I had retired, we discussed this. We agreed, 'Yes, it should.' This is the sad part of central banking," says ex–BOJ executive Shijuro Ogata.

I started upon this journalistic inquiry several years ago with a perception of central bankers' heightened prominence in governing the world economy as my guide. I possessed only a general grasp, gleaned from fifteen years' experience as an economic journalist, of the historical underlying force that was propelling them to the front policy-making ranks.

At the end the inquiry, informed by a deeper and more detailed understanding, I am frankly alarmed by what I have found out. The uncontrolled, high-speed gyrations of stateless money unhinged from economic fundamentals or national economic policies has transformed the international monetary system from a smooth adjustment-facilitating mechanism that anchors a harmonious world political and economic order into a fully floating, private nonsystem driven by the roller-coaster shifts in focus and manias of the collective herd of global financial investors. Such financial caprice promotes abrupt economic adjustments, long-term misinvestment, and trade conflicts. To be sure, there are positives in the new landscape. Global capital mobility offers a welcome long-run check on governments' temptation to pursue expedient and confiscatory economic policies. Overall, the "nonsystem" has been remarkably resilient in the face of large economic shocks. But these are far outweighed by perils of endogenous arrhythmia and frequent shocks in the financial heart of the economy. As competent as central bankers have been, I find it frightful the extent to which we are relying for the prosperity of the free world economy—and ultimately the stability of democratic society—on the judgment of a handful of expert technocrats who, to tell the truth, are often caught by surprise like the rest of us about the transformations occurring in the economy and financial system.

We are living at a watershed moment in world history. Communism's demise means that capitalism is the only viable economic system on the horizon. The free market economic model, and with it democracy, has an unprecedented opportunity for a long, worldwide rule. Yet ironically, in its moment of triumph, it is threatened from within by its one of its well-known, occasional self-destructive tendencies.

All models of democratic capitalism—Anglo-Saxon laissez faire, European social welfare, Japanese relationship, and all other variants—are in distress because of the new phenomenon of uncontrolled stateless money. No country can solve the challenge singly. Nor can any country cut itself off to escape its effects. The fates of all democratic capitalist nations are dependent upon how well we can collectively civilize stateless money within a new international compact of world monetary rules, norms, and policy actions that reduces its excessive volatility, grounds its trends in economic fundamentals, weds the global horizon of its wealth-building capacities to democratic concepts bred in nation-states, and reconciles its lightning fast, purely profit-seeking mobility with slower-adapting and more broadly motivated individual human lives.

Many experts believe that the world political economy functions best when a single, dominant nation sets and enforces the international monetary and trade rules. Great Britain, as the world's leading manufacturing and creditor nation, executed this task for about sixty years from 1860. After the tragic lapse of leadership in the interwar period, the United States assumed the hegemonic mantle in the postwar era. But by the late 1980s the United States became the world's largest debtor. It can no longer perform the hegemonic function. Yet neither Japan nor a unified Europe can replace it.

Previous wars this century demarked the rise or fall of global hegemons and monetary regimes. The post–Cold War environment eerily resembles that at the end of World War I when the absence of a hegemon contributed to the ensuing monetary disorder and world depression. The overarching struggle of the present era is similar to that of the interwar years: economic nationalism and closing off with protected trade regions vs. economic integration through policy coordination and economic convergence at a loss of some national sovereign autonomy.

Many experts envision the eventual, long-term evolution to a single world monetary policy, based on a single or few freely interchangeable world reserve currencies, managed by a supranational central bank. But how to get there from here? Veteran international monetary policymakers forlornly cite the paradox that the political motivation to undertake fundamental reform awakens only in a crisis when the conditions for reform are wrong; when the crisis passes and conditions are more auspicious, the political will dissipates into renewed complacency and conservatism to not rock an economic boat that still sails. This is a reason why so many are pessimistic that a sound new world monetary order can be born without the catalyst of an economic trauma.

The road map for civilizing stateless money has three interrelated dimensions. One urgent task, as warned in the July 1994 report of the Bretton Woods Commission co-chaired by Paul Volcker, is international monetary reform to reduce large exchange rate volatility and misalignments so that signals of underlying economic fundamentals can clearly set the pace for world savings, investment, and trade. To make international monetary reform effective, second, requires the leading nations to coordinate their national economic policies and to restructure relationships in their political economies that have become globally incompatible. The third dimension is to construct a sound, safe, and transparent financial circuit for stateless money. This requires overhauling and then internationally harmonizing incompatible, and often inadequate, national banking and financial market structures, regulations, and supervisory regimes.

There are numerous proposals to achieve this formidable agenda. Sadly, a sober assessment reveals that most face insuperable practical impediments.

Heading many people's list for international monetary reform is exchange rate "target zones," as tried by the G7 in its Louvre Accord experiment and, with more rigor and in a more conducive environment, by European nations in their ERM. Yet experience reveals that even target zones grounded in economic fundamentals can be overwhelmed by the speculative snowballing to which free capital movements are wont. Target zones also require a political will to subordinate national economic policies to international exchange rate targets that simply doesn't exist. Fiscal policy is so politically inflexible that if governments did target their exchange rates, the practical burden was likely to fall heavily on monetary policy. But if monetary policy were targeted on the exchange rate, then it couldn't simultaneously be used to stabilize domestic prices and growth. Thus fiscal and structural reforms are a precondition for target zones. A third problem, as the G7 experience shows, is that not even experts are sure what the right exchange rate levels should be for the major currencies. Finally, even if a target zone system can be made to work, it provides no solution to the lack of world monetary anchor to prevent the system as a whole from being excessively inflationary or deflationary. Nevertheless, modest experiments with very flexible target zones that built upon current IMF macroeconomic surveillance are probably useful, if only to promote dialogue and better understanding among national policymakers about economic interdependence.

Many of the insuperable problems with target zones also beset other world monetary reform proposals. This is the case with that of the "world monetarists" who advocate cooperative or supranational management of the de facto world money supply—dollars, DM, and yen—to keep overall supply and demand for world money in target. Frustration with the absence of a world monetary anchor has encouraged a vocal minority to call again for a return to some form of the gold standard. But they have yet to devise a workable proposal that most experts seriously think can overcome the gold standard's mechanical rigidity and its other historical failings.

An intriguing, achievable (though administratively difficult) half step toward monetary reform is financial "speed limit" proposals to slow down purely speculative currency movements through actual or implied taxes. One of the oldest is a uniform transactions tax of .5 percent on all spot market foreign exchange transactions, including deliveries on futures contracts and options.[20] Its main design is to throw sand in the wheels of currency speculation by raising its short-term cost (but much less so investments held for the longer term) so that currency markets might better reflect long-term fundamentals. A second purpose is to re-create part of the Bretton Woods buffer mechanism so that nations could regain more flexibility to pursue divergent monetary policies. Such a tax might net some $13 trillion a year—twenty-five times more than all the foreign exchange reserves held by world central banks. Such great sums could be used to pay the cost of administering new financial regulations. Some could be turned over to the Basel club to pursue interventions to stabilize currencies and to carry out lender of last resort missions. Some could finance the World Bank for economic development, or an IMF that might be restructured to evolve into a world central bank and seat of a genuine world economic directorate. Another "speed limit" proposal requires financial institutions buying foreign exchange with its national currency to make a non-interest-bearing deposit with its central bank.[21] This implicit tax could be justified as a prudential measure against foreign exchange risk and possibly incorporated within the expanding scope of central bankers' Basel minimum standards. There is one catch to any speed limit proposal, however: to be effective, it must be imposed worldwide.

Most reforms to make fiscal and structural policies more flexible have to be thrashed out politically within individual nations. Europe, in its bid for economic and monetary union, has established some continentalwide guidelines to help discipline national processes. The urgent need for U.S. fiscal reform has produced sunset and legislative supermajority voting proposals to discipline spending. But these modest reforms haven't generated a bandwagon. The success of central bankers begged wondering whether their politically insulated independence might serve as a model for fiscal reform. A Federal Budget Review Board of twelve prominent and technically competent persons, for instance, might use moral and some statutory authority to set medium-term fiscal policy parameters to take some of the disagreeable decisions that all knew to be overdue but found too politically onerous to take.

The most promising area for incremental progress is in increasing the transparency and safety of integrated global financial markets. Both financial firms and governments share an interest in standards that promote a stable financial environment. Worldwide industry standards are also terribly important to alleviate some of the regulatory distortions that drive capital flows and exchange rates and to peel away one of the veils obscuring central bankers' view of the size and direction of international capital flows and where the ultimate risks are being held. Yet given the rapid pace of financial product innovation, and the continued inaction of the United States and Japan in overhauling obsolete industry structures, the question remains open whether the current movement toward government and industry self-regulation can keep from falling tragically behind market developments.

For the foreseeable future, the best that can be realistically hoped for to contain the self-destructive potential of stateless capital is for democratic governments to reinforce the authority of their central bankers. Upgraded independence, with commensurate political accountability, is the essential starting point. Governments can enhance their central banker's public and market credibility by declaring that sound money is the central bank's primary task and by injecting more anti-inflationary discipline into their own fiscal operations through the issue of inflation-indexed bonds. Convergence around low inflation rates in the major countries would do more than any single viable action to reduce excessive currency volatility. G7 leaders could provide important support for central bank and other financial regulators by giving them a collective political mandate to negotiate world financial harmonization.

But there should be no delusion. Upgrading central bank independence is little more than a stopgap. It is only a matter of time before even independent central bankers' effectiveness will be inundated by the uncontrolled, revolutionary political force of stateless money.

The truly important message in central bankers' heightened prominence in governing the changed world economy is the fundamental failure of democratic society's primary governing mechanism to meet the historical challenge. If we can civilize stateless money, capitalism and democracy can be in for a long, prosperous reign. But if we continue apathetically to allow our economic and political destinies to be shaped by the unanchored supranational mobility and volatility of stateless money, there will be many more events like Black Monday and Terrible Tuesday—one of which may end in a catastrophe that even central bankers can't contain.

Appendix

Chronology

1944

July   Bretton Woods conference establishes the International Monetary Fund (IMF), the World Bank, and the fixed but adjustable exchange rate monetary system. A par dollar value is established for many currencies; the U.S. promises to convert the dollar into gold at $35 per ounce.

1958

January   The European Economic Community (EEC) is born.
December   Ten European countries make their currencies convertible.

1960

November   U.S. and seven other central banks begin to sell gold in London markets to counteract its price rise through $35 an ounce. The U.S. takes measures to try to reduce its balance of payments deficits. It is the start of a decade of ever-growing strains in the Bretton Woods international monetary order.

MID-TO-LATE 1960S

U.S. inflation accelerates.

1971

May   Germany lets the DM float, following failed efforts to stem the speculative capital movements from the dollar to the DM. U.S. declares that it will not devalue the dollar.
August 15   Nixon suspends the convertibility of the dollar into gold.
December 17–18   Smithsonian Agreement by G-10 to realign Bretton Woods currencies, featuring a dollar devaluation.

1972

March   EEC nations create forerunner of the EMS, the "snake" in the Smithsonian "tunnel," to try to stabilize their currencies against the dollar.

1973

February   Dollar in crisis. Treasury undersecretary Paul Volcker makes a secret, round-the-globe trip to world capitals to try to salvage the world monetary order. The U.S. devalues the dollar by 10 percent. The yen is floated.

March   Massive speculation against the dollar causes EEC nations to announce a joint float of their currencies. The breakup of the Bretton Woods system into generalized floating exchange rates soon begins.

May   Forerunner of the G5 meets in the White House library to informally discuss international monetary matters under floating exchange rates.

October–December   The OPEC oil embargo causes the price of oil to quadruple, stoking inflation and creating huge balance of payments imbalances that end all hopes of a return to fixed exchange rates.

1974

June   Germany's Herstatt Bank collapses, causing international foreign exchange and interbank transactions to freeze up in panic.

September   Basel central bankers declare their readiness to act as lenders of last resort to the unregulated Euromarkets. The panic ebbs. The effort to supervise international banking yields the first Basel Concordat in 1975.

1975

November   First economic summit of six world leaders, soon to become the G7, is held in Rambouillet, France.

1977

June   U.S. Treasury Secretary Blumenthal "talks down" the dollar. The dollar soon cascades into its 1977–1979 crisis.

1978

July 6–7   European governments decide to create the European Monetary System (EMS) to be a zone of monetary stability.

July 16–17   At the G7 head of state economic summit in Bonn, Germany and Japan agree to stimulatory policies to act as world economic "locomotive" in exchange for anti-inflation and dollar defense measures by the U.S.

November 1   The U.S. announces extraordinary dollar defense measures.

December   Start of the second oil shock following the onset of the Iranian revolution. The major countries respond with austere monetary policies.

1979

March 13   The EMS begins to operate.

August 6   Paul Volcker becomes Federal Reserve Board chairman, succeeding

G. William Miller, in the Carter cabinet shakeup following Carter's "malaise" speech. U.S. inflation is 14 percent.

October 6   The Fed announces its experimental conversion to practical monetarist operating procedures. Interest rates begin to rise sharply. Volcker's war on inflation has begun. By April 1980, banks' prime interest rates will surpass 20 percent.

1980

January   Peak of the gold and silver bubbles. Inflation is running at 17 percent. Inflationary speculation is at a frenzy.

March 14   U.S. credit controls imposed. The U.S. economy abruptly collapses.

March 27   Silver prices crash. When the bursting silver bubble threatens to bring down the Hunts' empire, and with it some leading banks, Volcker soon helps engineer a rescue.

May   Volcker begins to reverse the dramatic easing in Fed monetary policy that has inadvertently re-created negative real interest rates and a new money supply explosion.

June   Credit controls lifted.

Summer   When the Fed tightens and the Bank of Japan and Bundesbank ease, the dollar begins its 1980s takeoff. Over the year, it surges 34 percent. The rising dollar is the first breakthrough in the war on inflation.

December   Japan liberalizes its foreign exchange controls.

1981

February 19   In response to a crisis in the DM and German balance of payments, the Bundesbank hikes interest rates by three percentage points. The DM stabilizes, but the action leads to a political confrontation with the Schmidt government.

April   The new Reagan Administration announces its nonintervention policy in currency markets.

May   The Fed tightens sharply. The combination of massive budget deficits and tight monetary policy produces record high real interest rates. It is the decisive turn in the anti-inflation war.

December   Eastern European debt crisis erupts.

1982

Winter   The recession becomes the deepest since the Great Depression.

March   Mexican government officials begin secretly visiting Washington to discuss Mexico's large financial troubles.

July 4   Penn Square Bank collapses. It sets off a chain reaction that threatens to topple giant Continental Illinois and other major banks. At the same time, the $80 billion Mexican debt crisis has become imminent.

July   Fed starts a series of major easing steps. The war on inflation is over—in 1983, inflation will be only 3.2 percent. Yet the economy is alarmingly slow to revive.

August 13–15   The "Mexican weekend." To avert a debt renunciation by Mexico, the U.S. arranges a $2 billion emergency financing package for Mexico. World central bank governors agree in principal over the phone to a $1.5 billion bridge loan. The plan is to get Mexico through its presidential transition of power into an IMF economic adjustment program.

August 19   Mexico seeks a ninety-day moratorium on its debt repayments from its private bankers.

Mid-August   Wall Street rally kicks off a five-year global bull market.

September 1   Outgoing President Lopez Portillo unexpectedly nationalizes Mexico's banks and castigates the IMF, unsettling the Mexican rescue strategy.

September 6–9   The full dimensions of the LDC debt crisis unfold during the Toronto IMF/World Bank annual meetings. The problems of other large Latin American debtors are revealed. A potentially catastrophic run in the international interbank market is barely contained. The central bankers assume crisis management leadership.

October   Private bankers, secretly working on a private bridge loan for Brazil, discover the parlous state of Brazil's national finances and alert Volcker.

October   Schmidt government falls in Germany. Kohl coalition government replaces it.

Late October   Volcker secretly gains White House approval for an IMF-centered debt strategy that focuses on the big three Latin debtors: Mexico, Brazil, and Argentina, plus Yugoslavia.

October 29   Volcker wins the endorsement for the big three plus Yugoslavia from Bank of England governor Richardson and Swiss National Bank president Leutwiler at a secret dinner in London.

November   Yen hits its nadir against the dollar, ¥278. The Bank of Japan has adopted a policy of shadowing U.S. monetary policy in order to prevent further yen depreciation and a possible trade war.

November 10   Mexico signs a Letter of Intent for an IMF adjustment program.

November 16   IMF managing director de Larosière announces that IMF financing for the debt crisis will be contingent upon prior commitment of new private bank loans. He gives bankers one month to raise $5 billion in commitments for Mexico. Volcker announces that U.S. bank regulators will treat new loans with leniency. The essential structure of the "buying time" debt strategy is now in place.

November 22   Bank of England's Gordon Richardson hosts a private dinner for leading bankers to persuade them to cooperate with the debt strategy.

December   U.S. unemployment rate hits a postwar high of 10.7 percent. Little sign of U.S. and world economic recovery.

December 1   Miguel de la Madrid sworn in as Mexican president, facilitating the negotiations of the financial terms of the rescue package for Mexico. U.S. announces a $1.23 billion loan to Brazil. Brazilian banks suffer a continuing run in the international interbank market.

December 9   The G5, meeting in Germany, ratifies the big three plus Yugoslavia political focus, as well as support for the strategy of IMF conditionality. They consider a U.S. compromise of a smaller IMF quota increase in exchange for a tripling to $20 billion of funds available to the IMF through the G10's General Agreement to Borrow. Two months later IMF members agree to boost IMF lending resources by nearly 50 percent, or $32 billion, to meet the debt crisis.

December   BIS bridge loans are negotiated, and in the coming weeks granted, for Brazil, Argentina, and Yugoslavia.

December 20   Brazil makes a "take it or leave it" demand to 125 international bankers for a huge refinancing package. It calls for their agreement in principle before year-end.

December 23   Declaring victory in the private bank campaign for new loans for Mexico, IMF managing director de Larosière approves a large Fund drawing by Mexico.

1983

Late January   IMF approves a $2.18 billion loan to Argentina.

February 28   When private banks commit to lend $4.4 billion in 1983 and to roll over existing debt, the IMF approves a $5.4 billion loan to Brazil.

March   France decides to remain in the EMS. The Socialist government adopts austerity policies and negotiates an EMS realignment that devalues the franc.

Mid-April   It is clear the Brazilian rescue has failed. Riots break out in Brazil, which is nonetheless missing its IMF-agreed economic targets. The interbank run on Brazil reaches critical proportions.

Spring   U.S. economy begins to show clear signs of recovery.

May 28–30   G7 world economic summit at Williamsburg. European leaders complain that the rush of foreign capital into dollar assets is depriving them of the savings they need to fuel a recovery at home. They press the U.S. for joint action to halt the surging dollar.

May 31   Brazil's advisory committee is restructured at Volcker's intervention. The IMF and private bankers suspend new funds for Brazil until it adopts austerity measures.

June   Reagan Administration reluctantly renominates Volcker for another term as Fed chairman.

June   Fearing the inflationary stimulus of the impending $200 billion budget deficit and Reagan Administration tax cuts, the Fed tightens interest rates.

September   The summer standoff between creditors and Brazil is finally resolved.

November 18   After weeks of delay and suspense, the U.S. Congress narrowly ratifies the U.S.'s $8.4 billion share of the IMF quota increase needed to meet the debt crisis.

1984

March   Facing a policy dilemma between signs of an overheating economic recovery that is pushing up inflation to 6.5 percent on the one hand, and widespread financial fragility and an overshooting dollar that is killing the U.S. manufacturing economy on the other, the Fed raises interest rates. Furious Reagan officials, focused on the 1984 elections, attack Volcker.

March 31   U.S. and Latin borrowers arrange an artificial loan to enable Argentina to make its overdue quarterly interest payments to U.S. banks, thus averting classification of Argentine debt under U.S. accounting rules. A similar package is arranged at the end of June. The action angers Continental European bankers, who are growing fed up with the U.S. bank-tilted debt process.

May   Continental Illinois collapses. The contagion begins to spread to other money-center banks and some large S&Ls. A bailout package for Continental is created, culminating in the bank's effective nationalization in July.

Early June   European and U.S. big bank creditors clash at the International Monetary Conference. The bank creditors' cartel narrowly holds together. Bankers accept in principle a multiyear rescheduling package for Mexico.

June 21   Ministers from eleven Latin debtors meet conspicuously in Cartagena, Colombia, to spread speculation about the formulation of a debtors' cartel.

August   The Fed begins to ease.

Summer   The dollar inexplicably *continues* to surge. As it does, the U.S. current account deficit heads toward a record $100 billion in 1984. Record Japanese surpluses are also registered.

September   Premature optimism at the IMF/World Bank annual meetings about prospects for ending the LDC debt crisis as the economic recovery deepens worldwide. Europeans press U.S. for action on the dollar.

1985

January 17   At a G5 meeting, the U.S. gives its first sign of willingness to intervene to bring down the superdollar.

February 26–March 1   Massive concerted intervention, including U.S. participation, causes the superdollar to depreciate from peaks of DM 3.47 and ¥263. The fall continues in the next months as the Federal Reserve eases monetary policy.

Early to mid-year   Gloom, missed targets by debtors, and "debt fatigue" begin to jeopardize the debt strategy. By summer, U.S. officials are anxiously exploring ways to revitalize the debt process.

Summer   The Baker Treasury initiates exploratory talks with Japanese and, later, German officials about stimulatory policy moves in those nations in exchange for cooperative U.S. currency market intervention to bring down the dollar. Demands for protectionist trade legislation are rampant in Congress.

September 22   Plaza Accord on concerted intervention to drive down the dollar. The dollar immediately plunges 10 percent in one week.

October 8–11   The "Baker Plan" for re-energizing the debt process is unveiled at the IMF/World Bank meeting in Seoul.

1986

Early   World economic slowdown and oil price plunge of 40 percent drives Mexico toward its second debt crisis. Dollar fall gathers force.

January 18–19   G5, meeting in London, fails to agree on coordinated interest rate cuts.

February 24   The Federal Reserve Board "palace coup" against Volcker. The event catalyzes a coordinated interest rate cut by the U.S., Germany, and Japan.

February–May   Mexican officials press for debt relief from U.S. officials.

April 21   U.S. and Japan cut interest rates. Japanese leaders are alarmed about the rapid appreciation of the yen and U.S. unwillingness to support the dollar. Private Japanese investor purchases of dollar securities decline markedly.

May 4–5   G7 Tokyo economic summit leaders agree to a U.S. Treasury plan for an economic indicators and policy coordination process run by G7 finance ministers in cooperation with the IMF.

Early June   Mexican debt default is averted when Volcker rushes secretly to Mexico City and proposes to work for additional relief.

July 6   Surprisingly large victory for Japan's LDP in national elections.

July 22   IMF reaches a standby agreement with Mexico on considerably easier terms. It gives bankers until September 29 to reach a financing accord with Mexico on $7.7 billion in new loans.

Summer   Fed unilaterally lowers discount rate in July and August. Volcker fears a U.S. and world recession. The market repudiates the last easing, placing dollar stability in jeopardy.

September 2   Volcker and Bank of England governor Leigh-Pemberton privately agree to strive for a parallel upgrading of each nation's bank capital adequacy rules.

September 20–21   European monetary officials meeting at Gleneagles prior to the G5/G7 and IMF annual meetings agree to resist further dollar decline through concerted currency market intervention.

End September   When the bankers and Mexico fail to agree on terms for the new loan, Volcker and de Larosière summon bank chairmen to an extraordinary "armtwisting" meeting at which the bankers are effectively ordered to make the loans at a term set by Volcker. Getting commitments from bankers will require six difficult months.

October 31   The Baker-Miyazawa Accord, negotiated more than a month earlier, to stabilize the dollar is revealed.

November 4   U.S. midterm elections. Democrats gain control of the Senate.

December   Fed and Bank of England attain a fully articulated, bilateral regime for bank capital adequacy. They use the threat of implementing it to try to spur negotiations with Japan and Continental European nations to develop world standards.

December   Bundesbank tightens, helping trigger an EMS crisis. U.S. and German treasury officials negotiate the outlines of a dollar stabilization for German economic stimulus deal as dollar falls anew.

1987

January 11 EMS realignment. France swears it will be the last time the DM's value will appreciate relative to the franc.

January 21 Baker and Miyazawa reaffirm their agreement for dollar–yen stability, although the yen has appreciated since their October 31 statement.

January 23 Bundesbank lowers German interest rates two days ahead of the German national elections.

January 28 U.S. intervenes on the yen market to support the dollar for the first time.

February 20 Brazil announces a unilateral interest repayment moratorium on its $81 billion debt.

February 22 G6 Louvre Accord on target zones for the dollar and coordinated policy actions to reduce the global economic imbalances.

March 20 Mexico's bankers finally sign commitments to lend it $7.7 billion.

Late March Dollar knifes below ¥150, triggering heavy Japanese investor selling and a six-week U.S. bond market crash. The selling accelerates when the U.S. retaliates against Japan's failure to live up to their bilateral semiconductor trade accord by imposing a large tariff on Japanese electronic products.

April 7–8 The G5/G7 informally rebases the yen–dollar exchange rate by widening its reference range around a new midpoint.

April 30 In synchronization with easing steps by the Bank of Japan, Volcker reveals that the Fed has tightened monetary policy to brake the dollar's fall. Renewed inflation fears also stalk the bond market.

May 19 Citicorp increases its reserves by $3 billion to 25 percent of its total LDC loans.

May 29 Japan approves a ¥6 trillion fiscal stimulus program.

June 2 Volcker announces his retirement as Fed chairman.

June 9–10 G7 economic summit at Venice endorses a modified economic indicator system to govern the G7 process.

June Breakthrough with Japan in the bank capital adequacy standards negotiations is followed by multilateral acceptance of a new conceptual mechanism in the basic risk-weighted framework.

Summer Fearing renewed inflationary momentum, the Bundesbank and Bank of Japan begin to tighten monetary policy.

August 14 A large U.S. trade deficit report triggers a dollar sell-off and bond market crash. The U.S. stock market begins to slide.

September 3 Greenspan Fed raises its discount rate. The move inadvertently feeds an upward spiral of rising worldwide interest rates.

September 17, 18 Basel Supervisors' Committee attains basic accord for the first worldwide bank capital adequacy standards.

End September Contentious G5/G7 meetings. At the IMF/World Bank annual meetings, Baker and Lawson make proposals to add formality to the Louvre's skeletal system of managed floating.

October 19 "Black Monday" global stock market crash. Baker, Stoltenberg, and Pöhl meet in Frankfurt.

November 5 The Bundesbank eases monetary policy.

December 2 Bundesbank votes to cut its discount rate.

Early December Central bank governors issue a six-month consultative paper outlining the proposed worldwide bank capital adequacy accord.

December 22 The G7 "Son of Louvre" telephone accord of new, loose asymmetric ranges is announced. The dollar nosedives.

1988

January 4, 5   Concerted central banker global dollar bear trap saves the dollar, and world financial markets, from crashing. Dollar rebounds from its bottom of ¥120 and DM 1.56.

Late March   Japanese ministry of finance emergency actions save the dollar from a renewed plunge. The Federal Reserve begins to reverse its crisis liquidity injections from Black Monday. In the next few months it will raise interest rates by three percentage points.

June 21   G7 world economic summit in Toronto. Rumors take hold in currency markets that Baker and Miyazawa have secretly agreed to try to stabilize the dollar through the U.S. presidential elections.

July   G10 central bank governors endorse the worldwide risk-weighted bank capital adequacy accord.

November   Bush elected U.S. president.

1989

February   Bush Administration reveals that the S&L debacle is much worse than thought.

March   The Brady Plan for reducing LDC debt is launched.

April   Delors Committee Report outlines a three-step evolution to European monetary union, a single currency, and a pan-European central bank.

Spring   Rebounding dollar starts to elicit foreign interest rate increases.

October 13   U.S. "mini" stock market crash of 190 points marks the bursting of the late 1980s credit bubble and the onset of a darker view of U.S. economic prospects.

November 9   Berlin Wall falls. German interest rates leap, propelling world interest rates higher.

December 17   Yasushi Mieno becomes Bank of Japan governor. He promptly acts to deflate Japan's "bubble economy" through a severe monetary squeeze. The stock market plunges nearly 50 percent in ten months. Overinflated real estate prices also plunge. The bursting bubble sends Japan into a prolonged downturn. Japanese capital outflows dry up, pushing up interest rates worldwide.

1990

February   Drexel Burnham Lambert fails, causing the junk-bond market to seize up. U.S. banking system is in its worst condition since the 1930s.

February 6   German Chancellor Kohl calls for immediate negotiations on German monetary union.

Spring   The Bank of New England falls into crisis, requiring Treasury and Fed support.

Mid-1990   Bush Administration blames the sagging economy on a bank-induced credit crunch.

July 1   German monetary reunification at the sugarcoated 1-to-1 exchange rate for East and West marks.

August 2   Iraq invades Kuwait. Oil prices leap, U.S. bond and stock prices plunge. Consumer and business confidence collapses. The U.S. economy, teetering between a weak economy and rising inflation, is tipped over into its "balance sheet" recession.

September   Runs break out on giant U.S. banks in international interbank markets. U.S. General Accounting Office estimates that thirty-five major U.S. banks are in immediate danger of failing. Chase, Chemical, and others take drastic survival measures.

October 1   Tokyo stock market falls below 20,000, prompting the Ministry of Finance to enact emergency measures to prop it up.

October 2   Financial markets, sensing a political deal to cooperate with the White House–Congressional budget compromise, react adversely to the Fed's monetary policy easing.

October 3   German political reunification.

October 6   The U.K. joins the EMS's exchange rate mechanism.

November   Under regulator duress, Citibank implements a survival strategy. For more than a year, Citibank's survival hangs in the balance.

November   G10 central bankers issue "best practices" guidelines for multilateral, cross-border payment netting operations.

December   Fed cuts interest rates and eases reserve requirements. Over the next four months, it cuts interest rates sharply.

1991

January   U.S. regulators engineer a bailout when the Bank of New England fails.

January 16   Allied attack on Iraq sparks recovery in oil and financial markets worldwide. Consumer and business confidence surges back with victory on February 27, underpinning an economic recovery.

January 29   Bush demands lower interest rates "now." Fed lowers interest rates soon thereafter.

January 30   Bundesbank raises the German discount rate to combat the inflationary pressures of German reunification. The dollar falls toward a new record low of DM 1.4475.

Mid-year   The U.S. economy shows evidence of recovery. Greenspan nominated for a second term by Bush.

July   Bank of Japan ends its monetary squeeze.

Autumn   Fed cuts interest rates as U.S. economy swoons into double-dip downturn.

December   European leaders approve Maastricht Treaty.

December 19   Fed cuts its discount rate one percentage point to its lowest level since the early 1960s. Bundesbank raises its discount rate half a point.

1992

Spring   Tokyo stock market crashes again. Panic surfaces about the health of Japan's banking system.

August   Tokyo stock market plunges to its lowest level in six years, 14,309. Japanese authorities launch an emergency rescue plan that features maintaining a floor price for stocks and an informal promise to protect all major financial institutions.

September   EMS currency crisis drives the U.K.'s sterling and the Italian lira out of the ERM. Other ERM currencies are forced to devalue. A devaluation of the French franc is barely averted. The crisis foreshadows another severe speculative attack in the summer of 1993, which forces the franc to widen its fluctuation band.

November   Bill Clinton elected U.S. president. The U.S. is finally emerging from recession. Europe and Japan are in economic downturns.

Notes

CHAPTER ONE: BLACK MONDAY

All unsourced quotes are from author interviews with the person cited in the text.

1 Drucker, Peter F., "The Changed World Economy," *Foreign Affairs,* Spring 1986, pp. 781–782.
2 Volcker, Paul, interview by author, August 8, 1989, New York, and interviews with Fed officials.
3 Editorial, *Wall Street Journal,* October 23, 1987.
4 Author interview of high Fed official.
5 The crisis team consisted of Johnson and senior Federal Reserve staffers, including Donald Kohn, Greenspan's young chief of staff; Edwin "Ted" Truman, the head of the international finance division; chief counsel Michael Bradfield; and bank supervision chief William Taylor.
6 Conversation recalled by Howard Baker in interview by author, January 10, 1990, Washington, D.C.
7 Topping Baker's list of U.S. leaders were William Schreyer of Merrill Lynch; John Gutfreund of Salomon Brothers; Goldman, Sachs's John Weinberg; Roger Smith of General Motors; and John Phelan of the NYSE.
8 Report of the Presidential Task Force on Market Mechanisms U.S. (hereafter "Brady Report"), Study III, Government Printing Office, Washington, D.C., January 1988, p. 20.
9 Editorial, *Wall Street Journal,* October 21, 1987.
10 Phelan, John, quoted in Randall Smith, Steve Swartz, and George Anders, "Markets' Weak Links Caused Sell-Off to Run Wild on Black Monday," *Wall Street Journal,* December 16, 1987.
11 Gould, George, interview by author, August 4, 1989, New York.
12 In the event, Reagan was never asked to sign the executive order closing the NYSE.
13 "White House Statement," *New York Times,* October 20, 1987.
14 Apple Jr., R. W., "Washington Quiet as Wall St. Panics," *New York Times,* October 20, 1987.
15 Foley, Thomas, quoted in Tim Metz, Alan Murray, Thomas E. Ricks, and Beatrice E. Garcia, "Stocks Plunge 508 Amid Panicky Selling," *Wall Street Journal,* October 20, 1987.

CHAPTER TWO: BETWEEN MARKETS AND GOVERNMENTS

1 Volcker, Paul, in Tobias, Andrew, "A Talk with Paul Volcker," *New York Times Magazine,* September 19, 1982.

2 Hamilton, Lee, "Sarbanes and Hamilton Introduce Bills to Make Fed Board Solely Responsible for Monetary Policy," Joint Economic Committee Press Release, August 1, 1991.

3 Adenauer, Konrad, speech to the Federation of German Industry, Cologne, May 23, 1956, cited in Marsh, David, *The Most Powerful Bank,* Times Books, U.S.A., 1992, p. 45.

4 See Woodward, Bob, *The Agenda,* Simon & Schuster, New York, 1994.

5 Leutwiler, Fritz, cited in Epstein, Edward Jay, "Ruling the World of Money," *Harper's,* November 1983.

6 This was a third again more than the U.S. gold held at Fort Knox, Kentucky.

7 Burns, Arthur, quoted in Kettl, Donald F., *Leadership at the Fed,* Yale University Press, New Haven and London, 1986, p. 6. Governor Teeters soon agreed that Burns had been right.

8 Wojnilower, Albert M., "The Volcker Era," First Boston mimeograph, December 28, 1988.

9 Keynes, John Maynard, cited in Harrod, Roy, *The Life of John Maynard Keynes,* W. W. Norton, New York and London, 1951, p. 273.

10 Adenauer, Konrad, quoted in Marsh, *The Most Powerful Bank,* p. 22.

11 See Gilpin, Robert, *The Political Economy of International Relations,* Princeton University Press, Princeton, N.J., 1987, p. 4; Heilbroner, Robert, *The Nature and Logic of Capitalism,* W. W. Norton & Co., New York and London, 1985; and Braudel, Fernand, *Afterthoughts on Material Civilization and Capitalism,* The Johns Hopkins University Press, Baltimore and London, 1977, p. 64.

12 To economic historian Fernand Braudel, the market economy had two layers: a lower one, characterized by ordinary business conditions; and a "domineering" one, associated with the control of capital and reaching its highest development in finance. See *Afterthoughts on Material Civilization and Capitalism,* pp. 62, 64.

13 Kindleberger, Charles P., *Manias, Panics, and Crashes,* Basic Books, New York, 1978, p. 77.

14 *The Papers of Woodrow Wilson,* cited in *Leadership at the Fed,* p. 24.

15 "[T]he Bundesbank appears to be a fourth constitutional power besides the legislative, executive, and judicial branches of government," writes Professor Carl-Ludwig Holtfrerich in "Relations between Monetary Authorities and Governmental Institutions: The Case of Germany from the Nineteenth Century to the Present," mimeograph, p. 46. In the political idiom of the United Kingdom, central banks were likened to a House of Lords, with the similar function of providing a check on the monetary excesses of democratic governments.

16 Through sufficient monetary policy stringency, however, the central bank could eventually curtail lending.

17 Wriston, Walter, quoted in Neikirk, William R., *Volcker,* Congden & Weed, New York and Chicago, 1987, p. 203.

18 Previously, actual FOMC minutes were published with a five-year lag. Fearing forced disclosure under the Freedom of Information Act, Chairman Arthur Burns in 1975 replaced the minutes with more politically antiseptic summaries.

19 The bank's freedom gained impetus from Italy's effort in the 1980s to arrest spiraling inflation and fiscal profligacy. This started with its commitment to the EMS's exchange rate mechanism. A 1981 "divorce" from the Treasury began the process, completed in the early 1990s, of freeing the bank from the obligation to underwrite the Treasury's financial needs. Full legal control, to match its effective authority, was also granted over the discount rate. The Bank of Italy's independence and stature was reinforced by the long tenures of its governors, who were appointed for indefinite terms by a board of directors selected by the bank's shareholders, mostly banks and financial institutions, with approval by the Italian government.

20 Gyohten, Toyoo, in Volcker, Paul, and Gyohten,Toyoo, *Changing Fortunes,* Times Books, New York and Toronto, 1992, p. 253.
21 Heilbroner, Robert L. *The Nature and Logic of Capitalism,* p. 172.
22 Shultz, George P., "My Final Word," *International Economy,* January/February 1989.
23 Wriston, Walter, "In Search of a Money Standard, We Have One: It Comes in a Tube," *Wall Street Journal,* November 12, 1985.
24 Crook, Clive, "Fear of Finance," *The Economist,* World Economy Survey, September 19, 1992, pp. 6–9.
25 BIS, *Sixty-second Annual Report,* Basel, June 15, 1992, p. 198.
26 BIS, *Sixty-second Annual Report,* pp. 192–193.
27 Lamfalussy, Alexandre, "The Changing Environment of Central Bank Policy," *American Economic Association Papers and Proceedings,* Vol. 75, No. 2, May 1985, p. 411.
28 Drucker, "The Changed World Economy," p. 768.
29 Drucker, Peter F., "From World Trade to World Investment," *Wall Street Journal,* May 26, 1987.
30 "When the capital development of a country becomes a by-product of the activities of a casino," warned John Maynard Keynes in 1936, "the job is likely to be ill done." Cited in Bianco, Anthony, "Playing with Fire," *Business Week,* September 16, 1985.
31 The rise of the yen in the late 1980s exceeded that of the dollar in 1980–85.
32 Friedman, Benjamin M., "Implications of Increasing Corporate Indebtedness for Monetary Policy," Group of Thirty, Occasional Papers No. 29, New York and London, 1990.
33 Other bursting financial bubbles were junk bonds, highly leveraged transactions, and energy and farm loans.
34 Solomon, Robert, interview by author, March 15, 1988, Washington, D.C.
35 The U.S. Fed was free by virtue of the dollar's solar role in the Bretton Woods system.
36 Leutwiler, Fritz, interview by author, March 15, 1989, Baden.
37 Volcker, Paul A., "The Triumph of Central Banking?" Per Jacobssen Lecture mimeograph, September 23, 1990, Washington, D.C.
38 Examples included the alleged Keynesian trade-off between inflation and employment, the neoclassicists' predicted stability of floating exchange rates around levels reflective of the underlying economic fundamentals, and the reliability of monetarist-posited relationships between money and the economy.

CHAPTER THREE: ACCIDENT WAITING TO HAPPEN

1 Greenspan, Alan, "Testimony before the Committee on Banking, Housing, and Urban Affairs," United States Senate, February 2, 1988.
2 The Pink Book detailed what kind of crisis team would be assembled, which other agencies should be contacted and when, how to monitor the financial system, what implications there were for banks and other financial institutions, and what the Fed's options for action were in each case.
3 "Brady Report," Study I, p. 1. In the first nine months of 1987, Japanese investors bought $15 billion of U.S. equities.
4 The first and still largest futures stock index contract was the Standard & Poor's 500 on the CME.
5 Options markets traded stock and futures options, as opposed to actual cash equity transactions or contractual obligations to buy or sell in the future.
6 Greenspan, Alan, in "Nominee Alan Greenspan on the U.S. Economy, Global Policy, and the Fed," *Washington Post,* June 7, 1987.
7 Macrae, Norman, "Sweaty Brows, Slippery Fingers," *The Economist,* September 8, 1990.
8 Ibid.

9 These included currency and interest rate swaps, futures, and options.
10 Proxmire, William, interview by author, December 18, 1989, Washington, D.C.
11 Friedman, Benjamin M., *Implications of Increasing Corporate Indebtedness for Monetary Policy,* Group of Thirty, New York and London, 1990, pp. 16, 17.
12 The bailout came two years later. By 1994, the estimated ultimate cost of the cleanup burden on the beleaguered U.S. government finances was about $140 billion before interest payments.
13 Volcker's reference was to the LDC debt crisis, but he adds, "There is the same dilemma now in other areas."
14 Ford Motor Co., among others, demanded unacceptable large government subsidies to ride to the rescue.
15 Crippen's informant was Makoto Utsumi, director general of the International Finance Bureau of the Ministry of Finance, during telephone calls to the United States on Sunday night and Tokyo Monday morning.
16 Portfolio insurance was intended to limit losses by selling quickly when prices fell and maximize profits by quickly buying the stock index futures when prices were headed up. Their natural trading partners were the program traders, who simultaneously bought futures contracts and sold the underlying basket of shares, or vice versa, to profit from the small price discrepancies that normally arose between the two markets during a trading day.

CHAPTER FOUR: THE LAST RESORT

1 Kindleberger, *Manias, Panics and Crashes,* p. 6.
2 Bagehot, Walter, *Lombard Street,* Hyperion Press, Westport, Conn., 1979. Reprint of 1962 edition, Richard D. Irwin Inc., Homewood, Ill., pp. 31, 32.
3 Kindleberger, *Manias, Panics and Crashes,* p. 77. The Fed was born largely from the Panic of 1907 that Wall Street colossus J. P. Morgan and his cronies tried and were unable to contain.
4 Greenspan comment as recalled by high Fed official.
5 "With the broadening scope of activity of financial institutions, the Fed's responsibility for liquidity spreads enormously," agrees Princeton University Professor Peter Kenen. "A very large part of the money stock—the liquidity of the system—is lodged with money market funds of brokerage firms. Is the Fed lender of last resort over institutions it can't regulate and whose fortunes it can't control? What happens if Merrill Lynch or some other brokerage closes its doors? There are money market funds, but no deposit insurance or lender of last resort commitments." The Fed went beyond banking to help stabilize conditions in the corporate commercial paper market following the 1970 bankruptcy of Penn Central Railroad; in the 1980 Hunt brothers silver market crisis; in the 1982 government securities industry crisis when small Drysdale Government Securities Inc. defaulted, and again in 1985, when E.S.M. Government Securities collapsed; during New York City's mid-1970s financial crisis; when the Farm Credit System was running out of money; and during the 1985 Ohio and Maryland S&L crises. Charles P. Kindleberger argues that the international rescues from the LDC debt crisis and the plunging dollar in 1987 qualified as international lender of last resort operations in *The International Economic Order,* MIT Press, Cambridge, Mass., 1988, pp. 10, 24.
6 "Central bankers don't like to regard themselves as having to provide liquidity through the whole system—only through the banks," points out BIS General Manager Alexandre Lamfalussy. "But to the extent that the relative size of banks has diminished, banks can't so easily perform the liquidity buffer function."
7 Phelan, John, quoted in Richard E. Rustin and Thomas E. Ricks, "Stocks' Plunge Brings Calls for the Overhaul of Financial Markets," *Wall Street Journal,* October 28, 1987.

8 Corrigan, E. Gerald, "Statement before the Committee on Banking, Housing, and Urban Affairs," U.S. Senate, May 3, 1990, pp. 29, 30, 17, 22, 24.
9 The Fed often injected funds earlier than its usual 11:30 to 11:35 A.M. "Fedtime." On days when the market was especially nervous, the Fed took the extraordinary steps of doing Repos two times or announcing in the afternoon that a special operation would be done next day.
10 Long-term interest rates fell from over 10 percent to 8.8 percent during the crash and stayed there until early 1988.
11 "Brady Report," Study . . . , p. 53.
12 Baker, Howard, interview by author, January 10, 1990, Washington, D.C.
13 Comment as recalled by Howard Baker.
14 At all times he was accompanied by two senior officials, usually Manley Johnson and his chief of staff, Donald Kohn, who could take over if obligations called him away. Each weekday at 4:30 P.M. between October 20 and 31, he convened special telephone conference call meetings of the FOMC to share information and find out what was happening in regional markets.

CHAPTER FIVE: IN THE MARKETS

1 Corrigan, Gerald, interview by author, June 19, 1989, New York.
2 Corrigan got an edifying glimpse of how fast trouble could cascade on November 21 and 22, 1985, when a computer software failure at the Bank of New York (BONY) prevented BONY from clearing and rendering final payment on the huge volume of government security transactions it handled each day. At first, to keep liquidity flowing while the computer technicians tried to repair the glitch, Corrigan was forced to authorize at 2:15 A.M. a staggering $23.6 billion BONY loan from the Fed's discount window—twenty-three times BONY's capital. When the computers were still down next day, Corrigan ran an experiment: he stopped allowing BONY to accept and make Fedwire payments for the securities it was receiving. Trading in the government securities markets quickly began to break down, as key market participants expecting to receive payments from BONY found themselves without sufficient cash to meet their obligations.
3 The problems included (1) the absence of a mechanism to net out winners' and losers' payments across the different markets in order to vastly reduce overall financing needs for settlement; (2) timing differences in settlement—five days for stocks and one day for futures and options; (3) different margining standards—four times lower in futures than in stocks—which undercut the more prudent stock market leveraging standards; (4) the capacity of thinly capitalized market makers, such as NYSE "specialists" and futures' market "locals," to absorb the huge volumes being dumped across the intermarket spectrum.
4 Futures and options feedback had been in the middle of the equity market turmoil of September 11 and 12, 1986, as well as in the spring 1987 bond market crash. Corrigan had been concerned enough to set up a special interdisciplinary team, the International Credit and Capital Controls group, to improve the Fed's oversight of the evolving linkages between securities markets, banking, and payments systems. In early 1987 he also launched an international advisory board of securities and banking executives to stimulate senior-level international policy thinking about it.
5 Phelan, John, cited in Metz, Tim, Black Monday, William Morrow & Co. Inc., New York, 1988, p. 159.
6 SEC, The October 1987 Market Break, February 1988, pp. 5–23, 24, 30, 31.
7 Corrigan did not know that Vice Chairman Manley Johnson had called the Bank of Japan and the Bundesbank the prior evening. Johnson also called Blunden.
8 Crow, John, interview by author, September 27, 1989, Washington, D.C.

9 Sanford, Charles, in Meyers, Mike, "Corrigan Kept a Cool Grip on Black Monday Events," *Minneapolis Star Tribune,* January 5, 1988.

10 Federal Reserve data as reported in SEC, *The October 1987 Market Break,* pp. 5–25.

11 Some "naked" investors, who had written unhedged put options, did indeed fail. But their size was not enough to drag down clearinghouse mechanisms.

12 In the end Goldman lost $111 million, Shearson $93 million, and all U.S. underwriters combined $400 million.

13 "Brady Report," Study VI, p. 71.

14 Upstairs people were the big block traders.

15 Story recollected by Howard Baker, interview by author, January 10, 1990, Washington, D.C.

16 "Brady Report," Study . . . , p. 41.

17 Corporations could reissue the shares later on at a much higher price and thus realize a large profit. Simply being able to stanch the decline when the rest of the market fell would boost their attractiveness to investors when normal conditions returned.

18 Fed Counsel Mike Bradfield says, "There's an internal memo [at Continental] that says, 'Let's not ask the Fed. They wouldn't approve it.' "

19 U.S. bank supervision featured three overlapping main federal regulators—the Fed for bank holding companies, the Comptroller for nationally chartered banks, and the FDIC for the thousands of state banks—fifty state regulators and separate regulators for thrifts. Capital markets supervision was an even more incoherent maze of private regulatory fiefdoms without any consolidated intermarket oversight.

20 SEC, *The October 1987 Market Break,* pp. 5–44; and "Volatility in Global Securities Markets," hearing before the Subcommittee on Oversight and Investigations of the Committee on Energy and Commerce, House of Representatives, February 3, 1988, p. 3. See also pp. 8, 16, 17, 85.

21 The firewall limited unsecured loans from the bank to First Options to 15 percent of the bank's capital.

22 Story as recounted by Johnson, Manuel, interview by author, November 17, 1989, Washington, D.C.

23 On Friday, October 23, clients pulled out $39 million more from First Options; on Monday, October 26, an additional $9 million.

24 In the event, a redoubled postcrash drive for financial reform failed anyway.

25 In 1991, Continental sold First Options, which continues to operate without incident as a major player in the options business.

26 Rawls, S. Waite III, telephone interview by author, October 24, 1989, Chicago.

27 Author interview of a source close to the meeting.

CHAPTER SIX: IN THE REALM OF THE ESTABLISHMENT

1 "Hold harmless" was a legal term defining blamelessness for a contractual party.

2 Story recollection of Gould, George, interview by author, July 25, 1989, New York.

3 Because of extensive cross-holdings, its float was much smaller, however.

4 Chiba, Futoshi, in Meyer, Michael, with Takayama, Hideko, "Zaitech for the People," *Newsweek,* November 23, 1987.

5 Tabuchi, Setsuya, quoted in Metz, *Black Monday,* p. 161.

6 A further protection were rules that halted trading in stocks when markets became too one-sided or when shares fell about 15 percent a day. In the event, trading in nearly half of Tokyo's listed stocks was halted when they hit their preset "circuit breaker" limits.

7 Aderhold, Robert; Cumming, Christine; and Harwood, Alison, "International Link-

ages among Equities Markets and the October 1987 Market Break," *Federal Reserve Bank of New York Quarterly Review,* Summer 1988, p. 40.

8 Fujita adds, "On foreign exchange intervention it [consensus] is more difficult since our interests are different."

9 Fujita kept Makoto Utsumi, director general of the International Finance Bureau, apprised of what was being done. Utsumi and his superior, Vice Minister International Toyoo Gyohten, informed the international community.

10 Unlike those in most other democratic capitalist societies, the securities firms had deposits and credit facilities with the central bank.

11 The executive board's members were the governor, senior deputy governor, deputy governor for international relations, and at least three of the six executive directors.

12 The other 55 percent of BOJ shares was in the hands of the government.

13 See van Wolferen, Karel, *The Enigma of Japanese Power,* Macmillan, London, 1989.

14 Window guidance and moral suasion were most effective when the BOJ wanted to restrain credit growth.

15 Mikuni, Akio, "Occasional Paper No. 2," derived from speech "Evaluating Japanese Banks," made before the International Banking Conference in February 1987, p. 11.

16 "Announcement by Governor Sumita," Bank of Japan mimeograph, October 20, 1987.

17 For the week, individuals bought ¥650 billion, or $5 billion. Institutional investors were net buyers of ¥309 billion, or $2.5 billion.

18 In May 1965 it extended a large, several years' unsecured financing to the forerunner of Yamaichi to prevent its collapse and major damage to the stock market.

19 van Wolferen, Karel G., "The Japan Problem," *Foreign Affairs,* Winter 1986–87.

CHAPTER SEVEN: WHEN MARKETS AND GOVERNMENTS COLLIDE

1 *Report of the International Stock Exchange on the Stock Market Crash,* March 1988, p. 10. Much of the data in this chapter comes from this report as well as the Brady Report and the SEC reports.

2 Instead he consulted daily with Blunden from U.K. embassies.

3 This eased monetary stance was maintained too long. It fed spurting inflation in 1988.

4 Leigh-Pemberton, Robin, "Convergence of Capital Standards and the Lessons of the Market Crash," speech at Overseas Bankers Club, February 1, 1988, in *Bank of England Quarterly Bulletin,* May 1988, p. 221.

5 Aderhold, Robert; Cumming, Christine; and Harwood, Alison, "International Linkages among Equities Markets and the October 1987 Market Break," *Federal Reserve Bank of New York Quarterly Review,* Summer 1988.

6 Edwards, Franklin R., "Policies to Curb Stock Market Volatility," in *Financial Market Volatility,* symposium sponsored by the Federal Reserve Bank of Kansas City, Jackson Hole, Wyo., August 17–19, 1988, p. 164.

7 David Lascelles's excellent three-part account of the BP privatization in the *Financial Times,* November 14, 16, 18, 1988, supplemented by personal reporting, form the basis for this narrative.

8 Internal memo from a G7 central bank.

9 "Force majeure" was defined in the underwriting agreement as follows: "Any adverse change in national or international financial, political, industrial, or economic conditions or currency exchange rates or exchange controls . . . which is of such magnitude and severity as to be material . . . and which should not, in the reasonable opinion of a majority in number of the underwriters be regarded as proper underwriting risk. . . ."

10 Peston, Robert and Bruce, Peter, "KIO, BP and the $5bn Shell Game," *Financial Times,* September 24, 1993.

CHAPTER EIGHT: WHY THE CRASH?

1 Tabuchi, Setsuya, interview by author, January 31, 1990, Tokyo; Terasawa, Yoshio, interview by author, October 24, 1989, Washington, D.C.
2 "Brady Report," Study . . . . , p. 67.
3 Volcker, Paul, quoted in Silk, Leonard, "Volcker on the Crash," *New York Times Magazine,* November 8, 1987.
4 Recounted by Tabuchi, Setsuya, interview by author, January 31, 1990, Tokyo.
5 Data from MOF, in Koo, Richard, "Japanese Investment in Dollar Securities after the Plaza Accord," mimeograph statement submitted to the Joint Economic Committee of the U.S. Congress, October 17, 1988.
6 Cited in Burstein, Daniel, *Yen!* Simon & Schuster, New York, 1988, pp. 163–164, from Ricks, Thomas E., "Task Force's Brady Says Japanese Sales of U.S. Bonds Touched Off October 19 Crash," *Wall Street Journal,* April 22, 1988.
7 The final straw was a large outflow of dollars to Germany at the start of the 1970s, when the Fed lowered interest rates to spur growth—and, some charged, to serve Chairman Burns's desire to help reelect President Nixon—and the Bundesbank tightened to restrain inflation; when the Bundesbank redeposited those dollars in the Euromarkets, the Eurocurrency banks were awash with liquidity. See Kindleberger, *The International Economic Order,* p. 35.
8 Volcker, Paul, quoted in Silk, "Volcker on the Crash."

CHAPTER NINE: INTERNATIONAL FREEMASONS

1 The original G10 nations—Belgium, Canada, France, Holland, Italy, Japan, Sweden, West Germany, United Kingdom, and United States—were really twelve, since Switzerland and Luxembourg joined later, and sometimes thirteen, since the Saudi Arabian Monetary Authority (SAMA) was included unofficially. The G10 was founded to create the 1962 General Arrangements to Borrow (GAB) to supplement IMF funding to bolster the Bretton Woods monetary system.
2 Greenspan, Alan, "The Crash of October 1987 Fourteen Months Later," remarks before a joint meeting of the American Economic Association and the American Finance Association mimeograph, December 28, 1988, New York, p. 1.
3 Thirty-three member central banks owned 84 percent of BIS shares. A thirteen-member central banker board elected a chairman, who usually also served as BIS president. Had it been a normal bank, its $75 billion in assets in the late 1980s would've ranked it among the largest fifty banks in the world, on par with J. P. Morgan, Lloyds, and Credit Suisse.
4 America's shares were sold to registered individuals, who automatically delegated Citibank's forerunner as trustee; Citibank, in turn, delegated BIS executives to represent them. On September 13, 1994, Federal Reserve Board Chairman Alan Greenspan and New York Fed President William McDonough took up the two U.S. board seats at the BIS. Also taking their long-vacant board seats were the governors of the Bank of Japan and Bank of Canada.
5 Three to six members of each central bank usually attended the Basel weekend. A supersecret G4 "currency mafia" of central bankers from the United States, Germany, Japan, and Switzerland sometimes used to meet before the G10 dinner in the later 1970s and early 1980s.
6 Coombs, Charles, *The Arena of International Finance,* John Wiley, New York, 1976, p. 26.
7 Author interview of senior European monetary official.
8 See Goodhart, Charles, *The Evolution of Central Banks,* MIT Press, Cambridge, Mass., 1988.

9 The Bank of England was born out of the reluctance of British capitalists to lend to King William III to finance his war against France, in part from the memory that an earlier king had confiscated private bankers' gold deposited at the Exchequer for safe-keeping. The bank was founded to raise £1.2 million for the Crown at the then modest interest rate of 8 percent in return for becoming the government's exclusive banker with a privileged (and eventually sole) right to print banknotes. See Bagehot, *Lombard Street,* pp. 45–49.

10 Goodhart, Charles, "Why Do We Need a Central Bank?" mimeograph, p. 23, published in "Temi di discussione," Banca D'Italia, No. 57, Gennaio, 1986. In the event, foreigners became sharp net sellers of stocks in every country, and capital market financing slowed abruptly. Fortunately this was partly offset by a doubling of bank lending in the fourth quarter; central bankers facilitated international recycling through massive dollar buying on foreign exchange markets.

11 Some argued that the cutbacks were likely to be small since the upsurge in stock prices had been so recent that investors hadn't really incorporated it into their spending habits. Central bankers also entertained whether the crash might not fortuitously cool inflation expectations and break the autumn interest rate spiral. Central bankers from Japan, where the economy was booming, were most sanguine on this point.

12 Volcker, Paul, in Silk, "Volcker on the Crash."

13 Interview of central banker present at the time.

14 Since they didn't want to say so publicly, they at first leaked it to the press. But when hot money continued to flee into the world's largest banks on the supposition that they were the most likely to be protected by national lenders of last resort, they had to go public. See Spero, Joan, *The Failure of Franklin National Bank,* Columbia University Press, New York, 1980, p. 154.

15 Two other contemporary central bankers, including Bank of Italy Governor Guido Carli, confirm.

16 Dale, Richard, "Bank Supervision around the World," Group of Thirty, New York, 1982, p. 71.

17 The United Kingdom reversed the original eleven-to-one preference for the host country to take all solvency responsibilities by suggesting that if it were stuck with all the responsibility for London's many foreign banks, it would be likely to impose stiffer qualifications for market access.

18 In Germany and Luxembourg in the mid-1970s, for instance, there was no official lender of last resort.

19 Luxembourg's secrecy laws prevented Italian supervisors from examining Ambrosiano's activities there; its own supervisory capacities were also notoriously weak.

20 Central Bank G10 Study Group (chairman: Sam Y. Cross), *Recent Innovations in International Banking,* Bank for International Settlements, Basel, 1986.

21 Corrigan, E. Gerald, quoted in Bartlett, Sarah, "The Fed Nightmare," *New York Times,* February 14, 1990.

22 The Fed's "Pink Book" of contingencies for financial crises dedicated three of its eight sections to payments systems—CHIPS, SWIFT, and Chase Tokyo.

23 There were many non-U.S.-originating international crises that could have threatened world banking and financial system stability. The BOE organized a £1 billion financial lifeboat, with the main British clearing banks, to contain the 1973–74 U.K. "fringe" banking crisis in largely unregulated, unlicensed banks. A decade later, in a poorly handled affair, it contained the potential fallout by purchasing for £1 Johnson Matthey Bankers. In Germany, Bundesbank President Karl Otto Pöhl had to do "great moral suasion, almost a papal decree," in order to swiftly organize the main German banks to rescue Schröder Munchmeyer Hengst in 1983. "The fear we had was that if SMH was not handled quickly, it would be Herstatt all over again," recounts Wilfried Guth, chairperson of Deutsche Bank. In the early 1990s the Japanese rescued their

entire core banking systems from the effects of asset price deflation. In 1994 the French government had to bail out giant Crédit Lyonnais.

24 The 1991 shutdown by world monetary authorities of the $20 billion rogue Bank of Credit and Commerce International (BCCI), colloquially known as the Bank of Crooks and Criminals International, gave a sample of what unscrupulous financiers could do in the future. Exploiting the self-styled moniker of Third World Muslim Bank, BCCI was structured by its Pakistani chairman using a Luxembourg holding company and a Cayman Islands subsidiary precisely to defeat consolidated supervision and rigorous regulation by the industrialized democracies' watchdogs. International supervisors set up a college of regulators in May 1988, but it was too late. The Fed excluded BCCI from operating in the United States because of its suspicious structure (although, through a front bank with prominent American shareholders including Clark Clifford, BCCI effectively entered the United States on a small scale). But the United Kingdom, jealous of London's lucrative bridge to the Muslim world, admitted it.

25 "Statement on Meeting," *New York Times,* November 10, 1987.

CHAPTER TEN: THE WAR ON INFLATION

1 The EMS was a modified version of the Bretton Woods fixed exchange rate system, with the dollar reference replaced by a basket of European currencies.

2 Wallich, Henry, "Honest Money," mimeograph of remarks at Fordham Graduate School of Business, June 28, 1978.

3 Burns, Arthur, "The Anguish of Central Banking," September 30, 1979, Belgrade, Per Jacobssen Foundation, p. 7. The following quotes are from this source.

4 Comment recalled by Bundesbank official.

5 Emminger, Otmar, *Dollar, D-Mark Währungskrisen,* Deutsche Verlags-Anstalt, Stuttgart, 1986, p. 397.

6 Quoted in Reich, Cary, "Inside the Fed," *Institutional Investor,* May 1984.

7 Volcker, Paul, quoted in Gelman, Eric, "America's Money Master," *Newsweek,* February 24, 1986.

8 These included Jerry Corrigan, Mike Bradfield, special Fed adviser and former Treasury official Ed Yeo, Ted Truman, New York Fed executive Sam Cross, Fed monetary policy chief Stephen Axilrod, Fed public affairs officer Joseph Coyne, and personal aides Steven Roberts, Neil Soss, and Richard Syron.

9 The November 1, 1978, package was backed up by a $30 billion war chest, the issuance of $10 billion in foreign currency–denominated U.S. government securities, and a 1 percent hike in the discount rate—the largest jump in forty-five years.

10 Martin, William McChesney, "Nomination of William McChesney Martin Jr.," U.S. Senate Committee on Banking and Currency, 84th Congress, 2nd session, 1956, in Kettl, Donald F., *Leadership at the Fed,* Yale University Press, New Haven and London, 1986, p. 83.

11 See William Greider, *Secrets of the Temple,* Simon & Schuster, New York, 1987, for more on the connections between money and religion, money and human psychology, and money and central banking, especially pp. 53–54; 227–242.

12 Heilbroner, Robert, *The Nature and Logic of Capitalism,* W. W. Norton, New York, 1985, chapter 2.

13 Many, but not all central banks—the Bank of England, for example—employed minimum reserve requirement techniques of monetary control.

14 The 12 percent reserve requirement meant that the initial bank could lend out eighty-eight cents on each dollar. When the borrower spent the eighty-eight cents, it was redeposited at another bank, which, after holding back 12 percent, could on-lend seventy-seven cents to a new borrower—in effect, newly created money. When the

seventy-seven cents was redeposited, it allowed another bank to lend up to sixty-eight cents more, and so on, for a maximum $8.33.

15 Volcker, Paul, in *Changing Fortunes,* p. 166.

16 Greenberger, Robert S., "Fed Takes Strong Steps to Restrain Inflation, Shifts Monetary Tactic," *Wall Street Journal,* October 8, 1979.

17 Levich, Richard, and Walter, Ingo, "The Regulation of Global Financial Markets," in Noyelle, Thierry, ed., *New York's Financial Markets: The Challenges of Globalization,* Westview Press, Boulder, Colo., 1989, p. 55, in Barnet, Richard J., and Cavanagh, John, *Global Dreams,* Simon & Schuster, New York, 1994, p. 395.

18 The Bundesbank, with the understanding of Chancellor Helmut Schmidt, originally adopted monetary targeting in 1974 with the conscious political motive of signaling strident unions that they should cool their wage demands because inflation soon would be under control, says close Schmidt aide Manfred Lahnstein. This is confirmed by Olaf Sivert, chairman of the Panel of Experts, which recommended the adoption of monetary aggregate targetry at the time. Lahnstein adds that afterward the Bundesbank, led by Helmut Schlesinger, used money supply targetry "for general policy and to strengthen Bundesbank independence."

19 The monetarists thought the monetary rule would help impose austerity and reduce inflation. The populists favored the monetary rule to bring the Fed under closer political control in order to end its imagined high interest rate bias from a nefarious influence by big bankers.

20 The Fed also monitored less liquid money supply aggregates, M2, M3, and L. M2 included M1 plus savings accounts, money market deposit accounts, certain money market mutual funds, small (under $100,000) savings and time deposits at banks, S&Ls, or credit unions, and overnight repurchase agreements by commercial banks. M3 consisted of M2 plus such items as large time deposits like CDs, usually held for at least three months, certain longer-term Eurodollar deposits of U.S. residents, and term repurchase agreements. L, which stood for "total liquidity," attempted to measure all financial assets that could one day be redeemed into cash.

21 Nonborrowed reserve demand could be altered by discount rate changes and the sum of borrowed reserve availability. It retained flexibility to modify nonborrowed reserves' target paths and included secret interest rate bands to blunt excessive volatility. See Goodhart, Charles, "The Conduct of Monetary Policy," *The Economic Journal,* June 1989, galley copy, pp. 32, 33.

22 Friedman, Milton, quoted in Kaletsky, Anatole, "Freedom Rules, OK?" *Financial Times,* February 23, 1987.

23 "What is the meaning of the monetary target?" Schlesinger asks rhetorically. "Is it more information for ourselves or for the public? The latter is true."

24 Treasury Undersecretary Tony Solomon had arranged the meeting in the presence of Chancellor Helmut Schmidt in the hope of bringing political pressure on Bundesbank President Otmar Emminger to do more and better supportive coordinated intervention. The U.S. side also proposed an idea of Volcker's to set and defend an unofficial floor for the dollar—in effect, a minimum DM-dollar parity.

25 Emminger, *Dollar, D-Mark Währungskrisen,* pp. 395, 396.

26 The Bundesbank officials were the only central bankers to whom he talked so explicitly. Others, including Haruo "Mike" Maekawa of the Bank of Japan, derived an elliptical sense of his thinking.

27 Conversation as recollected by Solomon, Anthony, interview by author, July 12, 1989, New York.

28 The Federal Reserve Bank presidents were scattered in different hotels. No "Blue Book" was sent out.

29 Coyne, Joseph, in Reich, Cary, "Inside the Fed," *Institutional Investor,* May 1984.

30 Emminger, *Dollar, D-Mark Währungskrisen,* p. 397. Volcker confirms.

31 Conversation as recalled by Ogata, Shijuro, interview by author, April 27, 1989, Tokyo.
32 Kaufman, Henry, in Morgello, Clem, *Institutional Investor,* June 1987.
33 Volcker, Paul, "The Triumph of Central Banking?" The 1990 Per Jacobsson Lecture mimeograph, p. 8.
34 Volcker, Paul, interview by author, November 21, 1989, Princeton.
35 Jones, David, interview by author, June 29, 1989, New York.
36 Volcker, Paul, in Tobias, Andrew, "A Talk with Paul Volcker," *New York Times Magazine,* September 19, 1982.
37 Stockman, David, in Greider, *Secrets of the Temple,* p. 367.
38 BIS, *Fifty-third Annual Report,* Basel, June 13, 1983, p. 55.
39 Conversations as recalled by Leutwiler, Fritz, interview by author, March 15, 1989, Baden.
40 Neikirk, *Volcker,* p. 130.

CHAPTER ELEVEN: ESCAPE FROM THE ABYSS

1 Axilrod, Stephen, interview by author, June 29, 1989, New York.
2 Baker, Howard, quoted in *Secrets of the Temple,* p. 426.
3 Stockman, David, *The Triumph of Politics,* Avon Books, New York, 1986, p. 325.
4 Samuelson, Robert, "The Return of the Living Fed," *The New Republic,* February 22, 1988.
5 Volcker, Paul, in *Changing Fortunes,* p. 175.
6 Reagan, for instance, espoused the contradictory virtues of free-floating exchange rates and the fixed gold standard simultaneously.
7 From October 1980 through April 1981 the money supply grew at an average annual rate of 9.4 percent. From May 1981 through October 1981 it fell to zero. The following three months it shot up at 14 percent, then rose only 3 percent in the next six. Yet over the entire twenty-two-month period it was within the Fed's target range, growing about 5.8 percent.
8 In response, Regan says, Volcker gave him a cartoon drawing on a piece of cardboard done by his daughter of a single par four golf hole with many sand traps and money swamps. He describes, "The first shot slices on the right off the fairway. The next shot punches from the right into a deep rough on the left. The next shot lands in a sand trap near the green. From the sand trap he holes out. When asked how he did, he says, 'Par four, naturally.' But never once was he on the fairway."
9 Friedman, Milton, "Monetarism in Rhetoric and in Practice," keynote paper presented at the First International Conference of the Institute for Monetary and Economic Studies, Bank of Japan, June 22, 1983, published in *BOJ Monetary and Economic Studies,* October 1983, p. 15.
10 *National Journal,* October 8, 1983, p. 2084; cited in *Leadership at the Fed,* p. 192.
11 It became an emergency acquisition of Bank of America.
12 Volcker, Paul, in *Changing Fortunes,* p. 180.
13 "Green Book," December 15, 1982, 1-1.
14 "Who Runs America?" *U.S. News & World Report,* May 10, 1982.
15 Samuelson, Robert J., "The Man of the Year Is Not the Computer," *Washington Post,* December 28, 1982.
16 Stockman, *The Triumph of Politics,* pp. 409–410.
17 Thatcher took an avid interest in monetary policy, frequently called on Volcker at the Fed when visiting Washington—a fact jealously noted at the Treasury. "We mostly talked about the monetary policy of England," says Volcker. "She preferred talking to foreign central bankers other than her own."
18 They included Martin Feldstein, chairman of Reagan's Council of Economic Advisers; Budget Director David Stockman; and Republican Senators Howard Baker

(Tenn.), Robert Dole (Kans.), and Jake Garn (Utah). Reagan's conservative friend Senator Paul Laxalt (Nev.) also endorsed Volcker.

19 A. Becker Paribas, "Decision-Makers Poll," June 2, 1983, *Leadership at the Fed*, p. 187.

20 Cited in Reich, Cary, "Inside the Fed," *Institutional Investor*, May 1984.

21 Akhtar, M. A., "Adjustment of U.S. External Imbalance," *Federal Reserve Bank of New York Annual Report 1988*, April 27, 1989.

22 Bergsten, C. Fred, "Economic Imbalances and World Politics," *Foreign Affairs*, Spring 1987, p. 776.

23 Volcker, Paul, quoted in "Volcker's View of Deficits," *New York Times*, February 8, 1984.

24 Nor did Volcker believe foreigners would be lending much more to enable the dollar to rise much farther.

25 Cited in *Secrets of the Temple*, p. 620.

26 See Murphy, R. Taggart, "Power without Purpose: The Crisis of Japan's Global Financial Dominance," *Harvard Business Review*, March/April 1989. Account confirmed by author interview with one principal.

27 See Kilborn, Peter; Williams, Winston; Bennett, Robert, "Harrowing Week-Long Race to Rescue Continental Bank," *New York Times*, May 21, 1984. Author interviews confirm this general approach.

28 Greenspan, Alan, quoted in Berry, John M., "Banks in Turmoil: Can the System Sustain Shocks?" *Washington Post*, May 27, 1984.

29 Specifically, the four-part rescue included (1) a capital infusion by the FDIC of $1.5 billion in subordinated notes and $500 million more by seven large U.S. banks; (2) a commitment by the Federal Reserve to keep lending huge sums from the discount window as lender of last resort; (3) an increase in the private bank credit line to $5.5 billion and enlargement of the participation to twenty-eight banks; (4) an FDIC guarantee to protect all Continental's depositors and general creditors. See Wolfson, Martin H., *Financial Crises*, M. E. Sharpe, Armonk and London, 1986, pp. 108–113.

30 Volcker, Paul, interview by author, August 8, 1989, New York.

CHAPTER TWELVE: A NEW GLOBAL FINANCIAL LANDSCAPE

1 Frankel, Jeffrey, "Flexible Exchange Rates: Experience Versus Theory," *The Journal of Portfolio Management*, Winter 1989, p. 50.

2 BIS, *Annual Report*, 1985, p. 97.

3 Feldstein, Martin S., "Adjusting the Dollar," *New York Times*, June 2, 1983.

4 "Demystifying Money's Explosive Growth," *Morgan Economic Quarterly*, March 1986; "M1 Revisited: Financial Transactions and Money Growth," *Morgan Economic Quarterly*, September 1986.

5 "Credit Markets in 1986," *Morgan Economic Quarterly*, December 1985. See also Friedman, Benjamin M., *Implications of Increasing Corporate Indebtedness for Monetary Policy*, Group of Thirty, New York and London, 1990.

6 Volcker, Paul, cited in McGinley, Laurie, "Volcker Says Recent Sharp Rise in Debt Is Incompatible with a Stable Economy," *Wall Street Journal*, November 22, 1985. "We have changed from a world in which the commercial bank was the center of the world—banknote issues, time deposits, site deposits," adds BIS General Manager Alexandre Lamfalussy. "It was a simple world to understand intellectually for monetary policy and from the safety side. It is now disappearing in the securitized world."

7 Regan says dismissively of Volcker's protests, "Central bankers have been constantly surprised—I won't say astonished—at the ingenuity of bankers and investment bankers to come up with innovative products. It is not something central bankers like.

The net of it is that all their careful plans have to be altered due to changing market conditions."

8 Blunden, George, quoted in Muehring, Kevin, "Can the Bank of England Regain Its Clout?" *Institutional Investor,* May 1987.

9 Ideally, "you want to be the wild card," says a high Fed official. "When there is a crisis that no one can solve, you'll figure it out."

10 The following quotes are from Volcker, Paul, "Address before the Harvard University Alumni Association," mimeograph, Cambridge, Mass., June 6, 1985.

11 The richest 1 percent of households increased their share of national wealth from 31 percent to 37 percent between 1983 and 1989. See Nasar, Sylvia, "Fed Gives New Evidence of 80's Gains by Richest," *New York Times,* April 21, 1992.

12 For the $600 billion estimate, see Magnus, George A., "Too Many Dollars, Not Enough Cents," *Financial Times,* May 26, 1994. "The fact that [current] investment goes on doesn't mean that future generations aren't worse off," points out Nobel Prize–winning economist and savings behavior expert MIT Professor Franco Modigliani. "The new investments belong to foreigners, not to us. So we lose the income anyway. We have to pay the interest and principal to foreign lenders." Quoted in Solomon, Steven, "Forum on the Future," *Best of Business Quarterly,* Spring 1986, Volume 8, No. 1.

13 This was true of the model single European central bank, the newly independent Bank of France, and the Bank of New Zealand, for instance.

14 Hoffmeyer, Erik, in Marsh, David, "Something Agnostic in the State of Denmark," *Financial Times,* July 16, 1993.

15 Hamilton, Lee, and Kemp, Jack, in Murray, Alan, "Fed Independence: Worse Storms Ahead?" *Wall Street Journal,* July 8, 1985.

16 Volcker, Paul A., "The Triumph of Central Banking?" The 1990 Per Jacobssen Lecture mimeograph, September 23, 1990, Washington, D.C.

CHAPTER THIRTEEN: FINANCIAL ARMAGEDDON

1 Obtaining reliable debt figures, particularly for short-term obligations, was a chronic irritant for LDC debt crisis management. Those in this section were derived from IMF, *World Economic Outlook,* October 1988, Washington, D.C., pp. 123–126; IMF, *World Economic Outlook,* May 1991, Washington, D.C., pp. 193–197; *International Banking and Financial Market Developments,* BIS, Basel, May 1989, and BIS, *Fifty-third Annual Report,* Basel, June 13, 1983, pp. 118–122.

2 Estimates from Palmer, Jay, and others, "The Debt-Bomb Threat," *Time,* January 10, 1983.

3 Cohen, Benjamin J., *In Whose Interest?* Yale University Press, New Haven, London, 1986, p. 37.

4 For supporting data, see Lever, Harold, and Huhne, Christopher, *Debt and Danger,* Atlantic Monthly Press, Boston, New York, 1985, p. 20.

5 Japanese banks had interpreted the administrative guidance from the MOF's International Finance Bureau to keep their single-country exposure to below 20 percent of total bank capital and reserves to cover only long- and medium-term lending. Short-term exposures were huge.

6 Kato, Takashi, interview by author, February 1, 1990, Tokyo.

7 Mikuni, Akio, interview by author, April 12, 1989, Tokyo.

8 Non-U.S. banks also faced a potential dollar liquidity squeeze because their LDC lending was in not easily obtained dollars.

9 Stevenson, Merril, "A Game of Skill as Well: Survey of International Banking," *The Economist,* March 21, 1987, p. 18.

10 Major Latin American nations had repudiated their debts in 1890 and the 1930s.

11 BIS, *Fifty-third Annual Report,* p. 118.

12 Estimate by J. P. Morgan, cited in Stevenson, Merril, "A Game of Skill as Well: Survey of International Banking," p. 23.

13 Wriston, Walter, in Reich, Cary, ed., "Walter Wriston," *Institutional Investor,* June 1987, p. 20.

14 In 1976, Burns called bank chairmen to Washington to warn them not to overdo the petrodollar recycling to LDCs. Still concerned that bankers weren't asking themselves the right prudential questions about credit standards in the explosion of international lending, Burns instigated the "checklist" exercise. In September 1977 two senior BIS officials began visiting fifty-five banks in seven countries to ask them to respond voluntarily to a checklist of questions and to furnish data. The results, recalls Alexandre Lamfalussy, were "disastrous! We were told to mind our own business, especially by the big banks, who said, 'We've been dealing with these countries for years and are far better in assessing creditworthiness than you are.' " The Burns checklist died quietly. Central bankers retreated until April 1980, when the G10 governors, eyeing the alarming buildup of LDC debt from the end 1978 in BIS data, issued their communiqué to warn, in their understated, deadpan style, of the need for better monitoring of international lending risks.

15 Volcker's main effort, taken in conjunction with the U.S. Comptroller, was to relax regulatory interpretations so that the 10 percent lending ceiling to any single borrower did not apply to an entire LDC nation, while slowly trying to enlarge bank's capital cushions. An in-house briefing given to the Board by the Fed's international finance division at the time concluded that LDC debt loads would be manageable as long as world economic growth held up.

16 Schmidt "used pressure" to overcome the "reluctance of Karl Otto" Pöhl, "and the Bundesbank contributed" to the bridge loan, says Leutwiler.

17 Interview of senior banker.

18 Three short-term Hungarian bridge loans worth $510 million in 1982 helped Hungary weather the financial squeeze. The BIS itself took a tranche, says Leutwiler, though "absolutely involuntarily."

19 Truman, Edwin, interview by author, January 19, 1990, Washington, D.C.

20 Silva Herzog, Jesus, interview by author, February 23, 1990, El Paso, Texas.

21 Volcker, Paul, cited in Delamaide, Darrell, *Debt Shock,* Anchor Books, Garden City, N.Y., 1985, p. 3.

22 Interview of European central bank governor.

23 Pöhl, Karl Otto, quoted in Shirreff, David, "Profile: Poehl," *Joint Annual Meeting News,* September 25, 1989. Wilfried Guth and Fritz Leutwiler confirm this.

24 Interview of European governor.

25 Walter, Norbert, interview by author, May 8, 1989, Frankfurt.

26 Recalled by Leutwiler, Fritz, interview with author, May 14, 1990, Washington, D.C.

27 The additional $350 million came when Spain wished to show special solidarity for Mexico with a $175 million contribution, which the United States matched.

28 Solomon, Anthony, interview by author, August 7, 1989, New York.

29 Bennett, Robert A., "Bankers Pressured to Assist Mexico," *New York Times,* August 21, 1982.

30 Subcommittees were also formed to define which of the twenty-five types of debt should be included in the refinancing, to report on Mexican macroeconomic developments, and to manage the interbank debt. A worldwide communications chain of regional subcommittees was established to implement advisory committee decisions.

31 Wriston, Walter, cited in Joseph Kraft's excellent *The Mexican Rescue,* Group of Thirty, New York, June 1984, p. 40.

32 Soon after the Toronto meetings Wriston says he expressed similar sentiments privately when President Reagan telephoned. "What do you think will happen?" the U.S.

president wanted to know. "People are saying there'll be blood in the streets." Wriston assured him, "It won't happen."

33 "When the LDC crisis broke there was no machinery to deal with it," elaborates Bank of England Deputy Governor George Blunden. "Volcker, and Richardson next, and de Larosière worked with fellow governors in establishing the machinery. They helped bankers create the organizations. Subsequently they came in when there was an apparant breakdown."

34 Volcker, Paul, interview by author, November 21, 1989, Princeton, N.J.

35 Conversation recalled by Silva Herzog, Jesus, and Leutwiler, Fritz, interviews by author.

36 By early 1990 CHIPS members exchanged average gross daily payments of $870 billion, which after netting out self-balancing froth required about $6.7 billion a day in fund settlement transfers.

37 Leutwiler, Fritz, interview by author, Baden, March 15, 1989.

CHAPTER FOURTEEN: BUYING TIME

1 Volcker, Paul A., "Sustainable Recovery: Setting the Stage," remarks before the 58th Annual Meeting of the New England Council, Boston, November 16, 1982.

2 Volcker, Paul, interview by author, November 21, 1989, Princeton, N.J.

3 Volcker, Paul, in *Changing Fortunes*, p. 204.

4 Richardson, Gordon, interview by author, February 21, 1989, London.

5 Ex–German Chancellor Helmut Schmidt says, "Governments were interested in the recycling of petrodollars. Some did and some didn't [encourage the banks]. The British government under Callahan encouraged lending. The U.S. government, too." Seconds ex–U.S. Treasury Secretary and Secretary of State George Shultz, "I always advised that we shouldn't ask them [the banks] to put themselves on the line to serve the public interest. I'm sure there was some armpushing afterward." See also *Debt and Danger,* pp. 47–49, for examples of tacit government signals to bankers.

6 Reconstructed from the recollections of McNamar, R. T., interview by author, October 20, 1989, Washington, D.C., and confirmed by other meeting attendees.

7 Interview of senior Fed official.

8 Interview of Fed official.

9 Kraft, *The Mexican Rescue,* p. 42.

10 In every category there were exceptions: J. P. Morgan was much less at risk than Citibank, Chemical, Manufacturers Hanover, BankAmerica, and other money centers; Dresdner Bank in Germany and Bank of Tokyo in Japan as well as Lloyds and Midland in the United Kingdom had threatening concentrations.

11 The rogue Monetary Authority of Singapore (MAS) stood out as one that pointedly did *not* cooperate. "Our banks behaved prudently," they retorted on one occasion when the Bank of England asked for their help. "They just took pieces of loans made by others. We won't do anything." Interview with Bank of England official.

12 Especially so for the Federal Reserve, which operated in the U.S.'s characteristically legalistic and litigious environment, where strong moral suasion could invite lawsuits.

13 Kraft, *The Mexican Rescue,* p. 27.

14 The Fed, worried about its legal exposure from arm-twisting banks to roll over their interbank debts, was inclined not to fight hard to prevent it.

15 Other sources confirm this. Tim McNamar adds, "At one time we discussed how much liquidity you can provide the system before you have to go back to Congress. Of course, that's the death knell of everything. The answer was $148 billion. That was a good number to start with, I thought."

16 By September 21 the U.S. ambassador to Brazil relayed the alarming news to the State Department that "Japanese banks are out of the market, European banks are scared,

regional U.S. banks don't want to hear about Brazil, and major U.S. banks are proceeding with extreme caution" in interbank lending to Brazil. See Motley, Langhorne cable, cited in Witcher, S. Karene, "How Brazil Struggled to Refinance Its Debt but Met Early Failure," *Wall Street Journal,* August 30, 1983.

17 This was the first inkling of what was to become a chronic problem. "We never got honest statistics out of Brazil. Every time we'd get one finance minister broken in, he'd be replaced," explains a senior U.S. official.

18 Without comfort from Volcker, the private bankers were loath to grant the bridge loan.

19 One unsettling occasion was Volcker's visit to National Security Adviser William Clark, who, says Volcker, "didn't want to know [about the problem]." Further evidence of the White House's wishful ignorance about the debt crisis surfaced in a twenty-eight-page classified interagency study known as National Security Directive Three and entitled "Approach to the International Debt Situation—A Policy Overview," which Clark delivered to President Reagan in April 1983. It concluded that the debt problem was likely to be solved by economic recovery in the industrial countries. It recommended no contingency planning.

20 Deputy Secretary of State John Whitehead also assisted when Volcker wanted diplomatic help.

21 Truman, Edwin, interview by author, January 9, 1990, Washington, D.C.

22 "McNamar was indispensable to me," says Volcker. "(A) he understood what we were doing and agreed with it, and (B) he was an operator—in the good sense. He knew how to do things in a Treasury filled with ideologues who had never made a deal in their lives."

23 Bankers often complained that the Treasury never sent observers to their meetings, as the Fed did.

24 Bank of England Executive Director for International Anthony Loehnis joined them.

25 Regan, Donald, interview by author, December 21, 1989, Alexandria, Va. The Germans preferred to bite the bullet through write-offs, capitalization of interest, or conversion of debt to a semi-aid institution.

26 GAB lending eligibility would be expanded beyond the G10 countries to all 146 IMF members in order to encompass the LDCs. The GAB mechanism also freed up a large contribution by the Saudis. The enlarged GAB plan was planted originally by Fed Governor Henry Wallich, who had tabled the concept at a May 1982 meeting of the U.S. interagency International Monetary Group, according to NSC member Norman Bailey. Treasury's Beryl Sprinkel adopted it a few months later.

27 Brazil got $1.2 billion from the BIS, of which $500 million was from the United States, in December 1982. This was soon topped up by another $250 million by the Saudi Arabia Monetary Authority (SAMA), an unofficial member of the Basel club; Argentina (with the Bank of England abstaining) and Yugoslavia got $500 million each. Argentina's loan was less than the $750 million requested. Disbursement of the second tranche of $200 million of the Yugoslav loan was delayed several months because of legal obstacles blocking the BIS's insistence on Yugoslav gold (held at the vaults of the Swiss National Bank in Bern) as collateral.

28 The Fed's Ted Truman accompanied Volcker.

29 The IMF's international stamp muted international banker grumbles about the American domination of the process. Likewise, as odious as the IMF was to debtors, it was more politically digestible than a patently U.S.-led debt rescue.

30 He adds, "But we were conscious we were also ceding some authority to the Fund. There was always the danger that if you built it up too much, it'll get too big for its britches and you'll live to regret it."

31 The other U.S. bank regulators, under Volcker's persuasion, soon endorsed these supervisory parameters.

32 Volcker, Paul A., "Sustainable Recovery: Setting the Stage," remarks before the 58th

Annual Meeting of the New England Council, mimeograph, Boston, November 16, 1982, p. 17.

33 Volcker elaborates, "We didn't want the new money to exceed some combination of the dollar inflation rate and their [the debtors'] real growth rate."

34 Kindleberger, *The International Economic Order,* p. 56. See also p. 26, where Kindleberger argues that the LDC debt strategy was an international lender of last resort operation. The international bank creditors' cartel likewise paralleled the reliance on the inner-core banking club to stand with central banker lenders of last resort in domestic financial crises.

35 Regan's idea, a political anathema at the White House, went nowhere.

36 Guth, Wilfried, interview by author, September 1, 1989, Frankfurt. Lloyds' Jeremy Morse often acted as personal go-between when matters between them needed smoothing out.

37 Leutwiler Fritz, interview by author, May 14, 1990, Washington, D.C. He adds, "It was the bankers who insisted on extremely tight conditionality for the debtors—not the Fund, though it was later blamed for it."

38 A brief revolt headed by Bankers Trust to reject the IMF forced lending approach on the grounds that its numbers and adjustment program were politically sanitized and economically bogus was thwarted by Citibank.

39 Characterization by Fed official.

40 de Larosière, Jacques, "Telex of December 1, 1982, to the Bank Advisory Group for Mexico and the International Banking Community," mimeograph.

41 Finch, David, interview by author, October 6, 1989, Washington, D.C.

42 Delamaide, *Debt Shock,* pp. 112–113.

43 Author interview with senior U.S. bank regulator.

44 Quoted in *The Mexican Rescue,* p. 53.

45 Wriston, Walter, quoted in *The Mexican Rescue,* p. 54.

46 They were not consulted on Langoni's declaration of readiness to suspend principal repayments, although they accepted it as a logical step.

47 Interview of banker close to Project IV.

48 See Atkinson, Caroline, and Rowe Jr., James L., "Smaller Banks Slash Loans, Complicating Brazil Rescue," *Washington Post,* February 23, 1983; Truell, Peter, "Brazil Releases List of Banks Cutting Deposits," *Wall Street Journal,* February 24, 1983.

49 Witcher, S. Karene, "How Brazil Struggled to Refinance Its Debt but Met Early Failure," *Wall Street Journal,* August 30, 1983.

50 On one such occasion, recalls one banker, "we had the wires open to all the central banks—the Fed, Tokyo, the Bank of England. We were told it would be greatly appreciated if the [topping up] payments were made. A decision was taken at the highest level [of the bank] to do so."

51 Wriston recalls caustically, "Preston never said a word throughout the whole meeting. Not a single, solitary word. It was typical of him."

52 Preston, Lewis, interview by author, February 27, 1990.

53 "Volcker was terribly concerned because he had no control over ICERC," recalls McNamar. "ICERC had its own independent power, and tampering with it was a fast way to end up on the front page of *The Washington Post.*"

54 When Tim McNamar asked him what they would do if something they were then trying didn't work, Volcker answered, "I don't know." McNamar thought to himself, Oh, shit. If Paul Volcker doesn't know, then we are in real trouble. Then no one knows. McNamar describes, "It was one of those moments where you think: Where have all the grown-ups gone?"

55 The situation was especially desperate for Citibank. Its $4.9 billion exposure to Brazil was far greater than any other bank's and enough to wipe out about 80 percent of its shareholder equity.

56 With Brazil Leutwiler tried to "play a little bit of poker." At one Basel weekend the
    Brazilian television press asked him, "What do you think the chances are of your
    Brazilian credit being repaid?"
    "Brazil will pay, be *sure* of it!" Leutwiler replied with a stone-faced bluff. "Can you
    imagine what would happen to Brazil's credit standing if it defaulted?" He added that
    the BIS expected Brazil's full repayment by July 15 and would not roll over its bridge
    again.
    Just prior to the Brazilian TV interview, about half Brazil's overdue $400 million
    had arrived unexpectedly at the BIS's account at the New York Fed. It was soon fol-
    lowed by a long telex from Brazilian central banker Langoni, declaring that the pay-
    ment had been sent in error. He wanted it back.
    "Forget it, we keep it," Leutwiler told the furious Langoni over the telephone.
57 Leutwiler, Fritz, interview in *Tages-Anzeiger*, August 20, 1983, from "Dr. Leutwiler's
    Outburst," *International Currency Review*, Vol. 15, September 1983, p. 45, cited in
    Makin, John H., *The Global Debt Crisis*, Basic Books, New York, 1984, p. 199.
58 Volcker, Paul, cited in "Volcker Sees Long-Lasting Fiscal Ills," *Washington Times*,
    October 11, 1983.
59 Interview with a central bank governor.
60 Author interviews with parties close to the discussion.

CHAPTER FIFTEEN: DEBT FATIGUE

1 Mexico, Venezuela, Brazil, and Colombia loaned a total of $300 million to Argentina
   with the informal backing of the U.S. Treasury, which itself agreed to loan $300 mil-
   lion to Argentina once an IMF accord was reached that would repay it. Argentina contributed $100 million itself. Finally, Argentina's eleven major bank creditors loaned
   $100 million at the concessional interest rate of 1/8 percent above LIBOR after the
   Federal Reserve Bank of New York effectively promised to guarantee it against $100
   million it held in a special Argentine account.
2 Interview with senior banker.
3 A few months later Volcker acted out further financial theater of the absurd by insisting during the Continental Illinois bailout that its $1 billion–plus LDC loan portfolio
   be valued at 100 percent.
4 By early 1984 Swiss and German banks' total LDC exposure was only half their equity. U.K. banks' exposure was about equal to equity. U.S. banks still had twice their
   equity at risk with troubled LDCs. Estimates from Standard & Poor's. Cited in Sesit,
   Michael R., "U.S., European Banks Split on Terms for Debtors," *Wall Street Journal*,
   April 9, 1984.
5 Leigh-Pemberton, Robin, quoted in Pennant-Rea, Rupert, "Reluctantly at the Helm,"
   The Economist, September 22, 1984.
6 Guth, Wilfried, "The Role of Commercial Banks," speech before the International
   Monetary Conference, mimeograph, Philadelphia, June 4, 1984.
7 They didn't want to lend longer term than the IMF for fear of holding the bag when it
   came time for repayment. And they bridled at the increasingly easier—less profitable—interest rate terms.
8 At a New York Fed brainstorming meeting in May 1984, Tony Solomon, with Volcker's
   support, offered Europeans the olive branch of an interest rate cap that would, in one
   variant, capitalize interest payments above a ceiling interest rate. But Solomon's and
   Volcker's primary concern at the time was that the Fed's spring 1984 tightening might
   make LDC's debt service burden unbearable. Volcker took up the idea in Basel that
   month. The "cap" died when bankers rebelled, and falling interest rates soon made it
   moot.
9 The MYRA rescheduled $48.6 billion Mexican debt falling due between 1985 and

1990—half the country's total—was rescheduled over fourteen years with few fees and at the thin spread of only 1 1/8 points over LIBOR.

10 Kristof, Nicholas D., "Debt Crisis Seen as Ending," *New York Times,* February 4, 1985.

11 Hector, Gary, "Third World Debt: The Bomb Is Defused," *Fortune,* February 18, 1985.

12 Nyerere, Julius, cited in "Africa's Hungry Mice," *The Economist,* August 31, 1985.

13 Interview of high Treasury official.

14 The prototype global debt plan was put forth in 1983 by Princeton Professor Peter Kenen. Many others, including Senator Bill Bradley (D-N.J.), New York investment banker Felix Rohatyn, and American Express chief James Robinson, proposed variants.

15 Baker, James, quoted in *Changing Fortunes,* p. 213.

16 Mulford, David, interview by author, January 3, 1990, Washington, D.C.

17 The late change and Volcker's terrible handwriting infuriated the sleep-deprived Treasury staffers. After retyping, the Treasury rewrote it one last time. "It was a difficult speech to write," says a high Fed official who worked on it. "It had to be sensitive to the [World] Bank and Fund tension, debtor and creditor tensions, and the different interest of national creditors and of money center and regional banks."

18 Baker later regretted having adopted the Fed's hard $20 billion new lending target— "a balance between what is needed and what's realistic"—to give meat and specificity to the goals," says a high Treasury official, when the failure to achieve it provided irrefutable proof of the plan's failure.

19 Silva Herzog, Jesus, interview by author, February 23, 1990, El Paso, Texas. Some G5 governments saw the promotion of the World Bank as a bald U.S. effort to rob the coffers of that U.S.-dominated institution to avoid paying any more itself.

20 Half a dozen top American bankers had been briefed on the impending Baker Plan by Baker and Volcker on October 1; on Thursday morning, October 17, senior U.S. bankers were again summoned to Washington to listen to their appeal for contributions.

21 Interview with source close to the dinner.

22 A related motive for the meeting was to dissuade invited guest Swiss Bank Corp.'s Franz Lutolf from pressing his interest capitalization scheme.

CHAPTER SIXTEEN: FROM BUYING TIME TO DEBT RELIEF

1 Interview with senior banker.

2 De la Madrid reprimanded Silva Herzog for the leak, and it contributed to Silva's imminent political downfall.

3 Volcker had been closely tracking the darkening political mood in Mexico City through the back channel of his friend Ed Yeo, a former Treasury undersecretary who'd been shuttling to Mexico every couple of weeks to meet with Silva Herzog and other senior Mexican officials he'd known since the mid-1970s.

4 Volcker, Paul, interview by author, August 8, 1989, New York.

5 The reconstruction of this meeting comes principally from recollections of Jesus Silva Herzog, Paul Volcker, and Gustavo Petricioli.

6 In contrast, says a senior Mexican official, "Jim Baker was new to this. He didn't have prestige. His image was that of a political appointee."

7 "When I went down there I had an idea of the order of magnitude of their need," Volcker confirms.

8 Petricioli also met with de Larosière and New York bankers. Over the next months Petricioli "kept Baker and Volcker informed almost every day of developments. I knew the banks were talking to them."

9 Soon after the Mexican compromise, Jacques de Larosière announced his early resignation from the IMF for early 1987 to become governor of the Bank of France. In

what amounted to an effective job swap, his position was filled by Bank of France Governor Michel Camdessus.

10 Description by high Bank of Japan official.

11 Interview with senior banker.

12 "Why that magic number?" adds Petricioli. "To tell the truth, there is a certain point in any negotiation where you have to say 'This is it and nothing else.' You *decide*. We were all tired. We were discussing it again and again and again. Both sides felt it was not worth any more days."

13 Bankers Marc Viénot of Société Générale and Guido Hanselmann of Swiss Bank Corp. stormed out during the meeting.

14 The banker points out it was Reed's and Herrhausen's first really tough meeting.

15 Acknowledges one Fed official retrospectively, "The 1986–87 Mexican deal broke the mold. The bitterness that remained has affected all debt negotiations that have gone on since."

16 Author interview of Fed official.

17 Interview of advisory committee banker.

18 Interview of senior Mexican official. Diplomatic and informal political channels were also employed.

19 Preston, Lewis, interview by author, February 27, 1990, New York.

20 Japanese bankers were also upset by the campaign of the Fed and Bank of England for global minimum bank capital standards, told in Part Six, which they rightly perceived to be targeted partly at them.

21 Preston, Lewis, interview by author, February 27, 1990, New York.

22 The secretive Paris Club was a juridically nonexistent body without a telephone number or full-time staff, although it had been meeting under the chairmanship of the French Treasury since 1956 at the old Hotel Majestic in Paris.

23 See Mendelsohn, M. S., "Wrong Way to Tackle Debt," *The Banker,* March 1987. Baker intervention confirmed by several sources, including Volcker.

24 Whitelaw, John, "Volcker, Eyeing Debt Talks with Brazil, Urges Action on Other Negotiations," *American Banker,* February 24, 1987.

25 Recounted by Preston, Lewis, interview.

26 Interview of senior banker.

27 This generational transformation begged the question of how well the LDC debt crisis could have been managed if young Turks like Reed, Deutsche's Alfred Herrhausen, and IBJ's Kurosawa had been their country's banking leaders at the time.

28 In addition to taking the initiative away from Volcker to impose any more Mexican-type settlements, it allowed Citibank's suddenly enlarged loan loss reserves to be counted as primary capital at a time when sentiment was growing to exclude loan loss reserves from capital among world bank regulators then negotiating a common global capital adequacy regime.

29 Among those present were George Gould and David Mulford of the Treasury, Fed Vice Chairman Manley Johnson, bank supervision chief Bill Taylor, international finance chief Ted Truman, William Seidman from the FDIC, and U.S. Comptroller of the Currency Robert Clarke.

30 Bradfield, Michael, interview by author, August 14, 1989, Washington, D.C.

31 The Brady Plan's main intellectual architect was Treasury Undersecretary David Mulford. Its genesis was a series of cabinet-level meetings starting in October 1988 that included Treasury Secretary Nicholas Brady, then Bush campaign chief James Baker, Fed Chairman Alan Greenspan, Secretary of State George Shultz, National Security Adviser Colin Powell, and their respective successors. Its debt reduction principles were agreed upon among the G7 deputies by February 1989.

32 "As far as the banks were concerned, new money was already dead as a doornail," counters David Mulford. Interview with author, January 3, 1990, Washington, D.C. Af-

ter the initial abstemiousness that greeted the Brady Plan, private financing gradually began to pour into Latin America. This financing (very little of it bank loans) was partly whetted by the liquidity of the secondary market which developed around "Brady debt."

33 IMF, *World Economic Outlook,* May 1991, Washington, D.C., pp. 196–197. These figures exclude liabilities to the IMF itself; for all troubled debtors the government-to-bank ratio changed from 30 percent/70 percent to 50 percent/50 percent.

34 Monro-Davies, Robin, "There Is No Alternative to Forgiveness," *Financial Times,* January 4, 1989; data from IBCA Banking Analysis.

35 Taylor, William, "Testimony Before the Subcommittee on International Development, Finance, Trade, and Monetary Policy of the Committee on Banking, Finance, and Urban Affairs, U.S. House of Representatives," mimeograph, June 27, 1989, pp. 1, 2. For the largest twenty-two U.S. banks, net LDC exposure at end 1988 was $65 billion vs. primary capital that had been built up from $40 billion at end 1982 to $74 billion.

36 One wondered, too, whether the outcome would have been less happy if Volcker, Richardson, Leutwiler, Maekawa, and de Larosière had been less personally compatible or, like their successor generation, less internationally activist by inclination.

37 Hoffmeyer, Erik, "The Real Solution to the Debt Crisis," address at *Financial Times'* Tenth World Banking Conference, mimeograph, London, December 1984.

CHAPTER SEVENTEEN: OVERSHOOTING MARKETS

1 The balance of payments on current account—the balance of trade in goods and services plus investment and other transfer income—had to be financed through corresponding net cross-border capital flows plus net change in national reserves. The current account deficit therefore closely mirrored a nation's foreign borrowing. Both current and capital account balances, by definition, also equaled the balance between national savings and national investment. This tripartite identity said nothing about causality, which ran in all directions at any given time.

2 Volcker, Paul, statement before the Senate Committee on Banking, Housing, and Urban Affairs, mimeograph, February 20, 1985, p. 7.

3 One prominent analysis suggested that foreign capital inflows had kept U.S. interest rates as much as five percentage points lower than otherwise during 1983–84. Marris, Stephen, *Deficits and the Dollar,* Institute for International Economics, Washington, D.C., 1985, revised, August 1987, p. 44.

4 Interview with Fed official. "We have reached a rather uncertain equilibrium with a large budget deficit and a large current account deficit, both financed in large part by borrowing overseas," described an internal draft Fed memo prepared in early 1984 by Sam Cross with Ted Truman's assistance. "Two elements of the triad, the budget deficit and a large current account deficit, are not easily changed, but the third, the capital inflow, can shift very quickly if confidence in the dollar should diminish." Quoted in *Changing Fortunes,* p. 239.

5 For example, closed export factories had to reopen, business contracts to expire and be revised, consumer brand loyalties to shift back, skilled workers to be reassembled, and the aggressive market share holding strategies of foreign competitors to be overcome.

6 See Bergsten, Fred, "Economic Imbalances and Politics," *Foreign Affairs,* Spring 1987, p. 78.

7 About three-quarters of world's reserves were held in dollars, and most international trade transacted in dollars, despite the fact that the U.S. share of OECD exports was only 17 percent in 1989.

8 This was the description of Jacques Delors, Socialist finance minister under François Mitterrand, and later EC president.

9 The fiscal restraint generated huge net national savings surpluses and lower real interest rates abroad rather than in the United States.

10 The ODR had been lifted by Maekawa's predecessor from 3.5 percent to 6 percent in 1979.

11 It also gave backbone to the early March 1980 yen defense package among the secret G4 "currency mafia"—the United States, Japan, Switzerland, and Germany.

12 Suzuki, Yoshio, interview by author, April 24, 1989, Tokyo.

13 Smaller budget deficits increased Japan's surplus of domestic savings over investment.

14 Until the mid-1960s Japan had adhered to a balanced budget principle. But from that period, and especially during the 1970s under the influence of the master pork barrel LDP power broker Kakuei Tanaka and single-issue interest "zoku" or policy tribes who favored fiscal stimulus programs in order to feed their patronage networks, the budget deficits and public debt swelled beyond MOF's control.

15 Thereafter the yen sharply parted company with the DM, which continued to fall sharply. In all, from 1980 to 1985 the dollar doubled against the DM but rose only one-fifth against the yen.

16 Leutwiler, Fritz, quoted in Koenig, Peter, "Seven Men on the Twelfth Floor," *Euromoney*, March 1988.

17 The Reichsbank's formal legal autonomy of May 1922 was undermined by its obligation to finance government debt issues. This was lifted only on November 15, 1923. The episode culminated in a letter from all Reichsbank senior directors, accusing the Führer's government of inflationary financing, and their January 1939 forced mass resignation, including its renowned President Hjalmar Schacht, who had restored order following the 1923 hyperinflation.

18 *The Deutsche Bundesbank,* Special Series No. 7, 2nd edition, Deutsche Bundesbank, Frankfurt, October 1987, p. 110.

19 Schmidt, Helmut, "How to Repair the Anglo-German Rift," *Financial Times,* October 9, 1992.

20 Schmidt, Helmut, interview by author, September 13, 1989, Hamburg.

21 Schmidt's threat was a bluff because changing the Bundesbank law required going to Parliament, where he lacked control of both houses. Schmidt protégé Manfred Lahnstein, who "disagreed with Schmidt" in believing that central bank "independence is more than a gimmick," says he suggested they respond to the Bundesbank by proposing "a European central bank system with independence for all central banks."

   "Nice idea, but romantic," Schmidt shot down. "The French will never give in."

   "In that case, we must side with the Bundesbank," answered Lahnstein, who says he was exhorted privately by his Dutch and Belgian counterparts to fight for the independence of the Bundesbank as the only hope for controlling European inflation. "It's the only way to win the battle at home."

22 From 1979 through spring 1980 it boosted its discount rate from 3 percent to 7.5 percent and its Lombard rate from 3.5 percent to 9.5 percent.

23 Author interview of high Bundesbank official.

24 This was the start of intramarginal intervention in the EMS.

25 The discount rate and Lombard rates formed the lower and upper corridors within which the Bundesbank guided its key Repo rate.

26 Following reunification, *länder* representatives were capped at nine (shared among sixteen *länder*). With the seven-man directorate, the new total was sixteen members.

27 From the long corridor of suites on the twelfth floor, each director exercised executive responsibility for central bank functions such as monetary policy and economic research, banking supervision, and international.

28 The Bundesbank chief money supply guide was its M3. Growth targets were set in December for the forthcoming year.

29 Lahnstein, Manfred, interview by author, September 12, 1989, Guetersloh. "The Bundesbank is ideologically fixed into two quasi-philosophical lines of prejudice," Schmidt criticizes. "One is the alleged psychopathic fear of the German nation of inflation. The Bundesbank itself spreads this idea. Once a week they have the journalists in to sit on their laps. The second is not so obvious and not publicly expressed and maybe even unconscious, a Colbertist idea of producing surpluses on the current account. But they don't see the political consequences of their surpluses. Previously [under the Bretton Woods system] it wasn't necessary to understand. Now they must."

30 Schmidt allies maintain that the Franco-German capital issue, done under an old postwar European program, was mainly a bilateral political maneuver to help French President Valéry Giscard d'Estaing in his upcoming spring elections.

31 Solomon, Robert, interview by author, March 15, 1988, Washington, D.C.

32 This viewpoint informed the bilateral U.S.-Japanese yen-dollar committee process, which from 1984 negotiated specific Japanese deregulatory actions that were intended to open the MOF-guided Japanese financial system to the global forces of financial liberalization in general and to U.S. financial institutions in particular. The U.S. counterarguments to Japan and Europe fulfilled two necessary domestic political tests: it shifted the blame for domestic economic problems created by the superdollar to Japan and Europe; and it did so in a way that affirmed its laissez-faire credo. What they *didn't* do was solve the problem of growing global economic imbalances.

33 Deputy Treasury Secretary Tim McNamar says monetarist Treasury Undersecretary for Monetary Affairs Beryl "Sprinkel's view was ideological. [Treasury Secretary Don] Regan had a nose for the market. He said, 'We've got global trading twenty-four hours a day. We're smaller players, and we're losing influence.' We figured out before the Fed did that we couldn't prevent the dollar from going up. Deregulation changed the game."

34 Destler, I. M., and Henning C. Randall, *Dollar Politics,* Institute for International Economics, Washington, D.C., 1989, p. 23.

35 Volcker and Gyohten, *Changing Fortunes,* p. 237.

36 In practice, U.S. currency intervention policy functioned as a mutual veto system— neither the Treasury nor the Fed was willing to intervene over the other's strong objections. The Treasury's veto came from its undisputed primacy in setting foreign exchange intervention policy under 1934 legislation creating its Exchange Stabilization Fund, affirmed by a secret letter of understanding in the early 1970s from Fed Chairman Arthur Burns to Treasury Secretary George Shultz, to which Volcker was privy as then Undersecretary for Monetary Affairs. The Fed's authority was more elliptical and derived from interpretations of the Federal Reserve Act. Volcker nevertheless maintained that the Fed retained the legal right to intervene without Treasury approval from its own funds. But he never dared test it throughout the dollar's long rise.

37 Volcker never was willing to make a public cause out of intervention policy, however. He didn't want another political battle with the administration. Nor was he willing to ease monetary policy through unsterilized intervention for the dollar's sake.

38 This was the result of their smaller size and greater exposure to foreign trade than the United States and because the dollar's unsubstitutability as world money gave the United States the privilege of being able to finance rather than adjust for longer periods of time.

39 Drucker, "The Changed World Economy," p. 703.

40 Advance warning was given to France.

41 Regan, Donald, interview by author, December 21, 1989, Alexandria.

42 Regan upset staunch Reagan free market ideologues by conceding to intervene not just when markets were "disorderly," but also, following the language of the G7 Williamsburg communiqué, when it would be "helpful."

43 Another sign of the creeping apostasy toward laissez-faire among its Anglo-Saxon re-

vivalists was Thatcher's abandonment of a monetarist monetary policy in 1985. In winter 1984–85 position papers also were being drafted by the Regan Treasury to justify more government intervention; implementation was hampered by the opposition of free market ideologues like Sprinkel.

44 Countries in other time zones, notably the United States, Canada, and Japan, normally participated actively in the concertation that overlapped with their business hours, unless a major intervention operation was in train. They were kept informed of the concertations they missed by telex or telefax. Swap networks—in effect, credit lines to borrow local currency from their counterpart central banks—developed since the early 1960s ensured they had sufficient foreign exchange availability to execute joint interventions. In 1987 the Fed had $30 billion in swap lines with fourteen other central banks and the BIS.

45 The central bankers revealed their bias toward moderation, however, by rejecting the even more aggressive tactic advocated by BIS chief Alexandre Lamfalussy to sustain the heavy intervention over a long period to inflict big losses.

46 Dudler, Hermann-Josef, "Monetary Policy and Exchange Market Management in Germany," in BIS, *Exchange Market Intervention and Monetary Policy,* Basel, March 1988, p. 69.

47 Interview of European central banker.

48 Interview of senior Fed official. The ESM failure threatened to bankrupt Ohio's Home State Savings Bank, which had many dealings with it. When Home State's bankruptcy in turn seemed likely to bankrupt Ohio's S&L deposit insurance fund, the run was on among depositors to withdraw their funds first.

49 Gyohten, Toyoo, in *Changing Fortunes,* p. 130.

50 "Nobody in his right mind could honestly regard as economically sound—and therefore requiring "no major institutional change"—an international monetary system under which the anchor currency of the world, the U.S. dollar, fluctuates as wildly vis-à-vis other major currencies as it has under the present floating," writes the late Professor Robert Triffin, the international monetary expert renowned for positing the "Triffin dilemma," which unmasked the hidden structural weakness in the Bretton Woods system a decade before it collapsed. Triffin, Robert, "Correcting the World Monetary Scandal," *Challenge,* January–February 1986. The 1960 "Triffin dilemma" posited that the United States had to run continuous balance of payments deficits in order to supply dollars for world liquidity, but that such deficits eventually would result in a dollar glut that would undermine confidence in the dollar. At the time, experts most feared an international dollar shortage.

51 Kenen, Peter B., *Managing Exchange Rates,* The Royal Institute of International Affairs, published by the Council on Foreign Relations Press, New York, 1988, p. 8.

52 Frankel, Jeffrey, "Flexible Exchange Rates: Experience Versus Theory," *The Journal of Portfolio Management,* Winter 1989, pp. 45–54.

53 Observes Paul Volcker, "The economic case for an open economic order rests, after all, largely on the idea that the world will be better off if international trade and investment follow patterns of comparative advantage; that countries and regions concentrate on producing what they can do relatively efficiently, taking account of their different resources, the supply and skills of their labor, and the availability of capital. But it is hard to see how business can effectively calculate where lasting comparative advantage lies when relative costs and prices among countries are subject to exchange rate swings of 25 to 50 percent or more. There is no sure or costless way of hedging against all uncertainties." *Changing Fortunes,* p. 293.

54 Bergsten, C. Fred, "Economic Imbalances and World Politics," *Foreign Affairs,* Spring 1987, p. 785.

55 Niskanen, William A., *Reaganomics: An Insider's Account of the Politics and the People,* Oxford University Press, New York, 1988, p. 173.

56 Interview of senior Fed official.

57 The underlying credo of managed floating was that governments could provide the anchor for volatile and snowballing market expectations that foreign exchange traders desperately sought, but that free market forces were unable to supply themselves. This did not deny the reality that the markets dictated the long-term fundamentals; instead it tried to cope with the problem that markets occasionally behaved irrationally and were less likely to do so when stabilized by an external force for the public good. One rub—fatal, as it turned out—was that the "government view" had to genuinely and credibly adjust to the logic of market fundamentals, not just of politics.

58 Funabashi, Yoichi, *Managing the Dollar: From the Plaza to the Louvre,* Institute for International Economics, Washington, D.C., 1988, p. 200. Throughout this section I have had the advantage of being able to draw upon the outstanding reporting in this book to supplement my interviews.

59 Ironically, the G10 meeting accepted its deputies' report, which concluded that "floating was here to stay," summarizes G10 Deputy Chairman and Bank of Italy Director General (and later Italian Treasury Minister) Lamberto Dini. "We all found the dollar to be unsustainable and recognized the volatility that for a long time could be inconsistent with the fundamentals. But at the same time, there was affirmation of having an exchange rate system flexible enough to accommodate the divergent economic policies of the major industrial countries." The main problem was that the large democracies were unwilling, and often politically unable, to subordinate national economic policies for a coordinated effort to keep the dollar within a stable target range. "The decision-making processes are divided among Parliaments, administrations, the market, and central banks. The markets cannot be forced to behave in any given way, only persuaded through credible policy action." The June 1985 "Dini Report," officially entitled "The Functioning of the International Monetary System," concluded that the most that could be realistically accomplished was greater informal policy coordination by the major countries supported by stronger multilateral surveillance by the IMF. Jim Baker's G7 process would provide, in effect, an empirical test of the Dini Report's conclusions. In the end, it verified them.

60 The absence of forewarning to the Bundesbank made President Karl Otto Pöhl more suspicious about it. Explains a top Finance Ministry official, "Pöhl was not involved in the negotiating process leading up to the Plaza because in part we weren't sure it would happen."

61 Funabashi, *Managing the Dollar,* pp. 12–17.

CHAPTER EIGHTEEN: GOVERNMENTS TAKE A VIEW

1 Baker had rejected Volcker's offer to hold the meeting within the seclusion of the New York Fed on Wall Street.

2 By most accounts, the United States and Japan were committed to 30 percent each. The European share was more problematic. The share of non-ERM member Britain was 5 percent. The United States wished to get a 25 percent share intervention commitment from Germany and 10 percent from France. The French and Germans, however, insisted that their combined 35 percent share be pooled among all ERM countries, according to internal ERM mechanics, regardless of which country did the actual intervention. Whether the presumption was Germany alone or EMS countries together would be disputed for two years and resolved in favor of the latter only with the December 22, 1987, G7 Accord.

3 Highlighting the semantic linkage of "helpful" to the Williamsburg summit enabled Treasury officials to misleadingly claim to journalists that the Plaza Agreement did not represent a fundamental change in U.S. intervention policy. Baker's unwillingness

to use "intervention" aroused foreign doubts about the firmness of the U.S.'s policy U-turn.

4 Pohl and Volcker were by far the most internationally experienced officials at the Plaza. Pöhl had attended the original 1973 "library group" meeting in the White House as Volcker's German counterpart. Both lived through the collapse of sterling in 1976 and the dollar crisis of 1978.

5 Volcker, Paul, in *Changing Fortunes* p. 244.

6 Pöhl took the lead in coordinating European intervention strategy with Bank of Italy Governor Carlo Ciampi following the Plaza meeting. Italy eventually sold about half of Europe's total $4 billion intervention.

7 German policymakers differentiated their trade surpluses from Japan's: Japan ran trade surpluses with *every* industrialized country; German exports covered the full gamut of modern industrial products with a vigorous, open, two-way trade in each, while Japan's were concentrated in a few categories in which trade was overwhelmingly one-sided; one third of Japan's exports went to the United States vs. only 10 percent of Germany's. Taken as a whole, Europe, Germany's main export market, was pretty much in trade balance with the rest of the world.

8 Quoted in *Managing the Dollar,* p. 40.

9 To parry finance ministers' overtures for interest rate actions—with general, not total, success—Volcker and Pöhl used the somewhat disingenuous excuse that they did not have the power to commit their monetary policy boards.

10 All but monetary policy homilies about price stability and growth were excluded from G5/G7 communiqués until the final December 22, 1987, accord.

11 Yet according to Volcker, "In the post-Plaza period, as a result [of his dollar free-fall fears], monetary policy was *tighter* than it otherwise would have been."

12 "It is not the role of the central bankers to participate in the press conference," Pöhl declared. Recalled by Lebegue, Daniel, interview by author, September 8, 1989, Paris. The central bankers, however, attended the press conference after the Louvre meeting, which was prepared with them extensively in advance.

13 Central bankers had not even been invited to the original library group. Their customary attendance started when Fed Chairman Arthur Burns insisted to his old protégé, Treasury Secretary Shultz, that he be invited; after that every other country insisted on the presence of its central bank chief.

14 Mulford, David, interview by author, November 27, 1989, Washington, D.C.

15 Gyohten, Toyoo, in *Changing Fortunes,* p. 255.

16 Soon after Bundesbank President Pöhl said on October 8 that the dollar, then down 7 percent, had already fallen to an acceptable level, Treasury Assistant Secretary David Mulford publicly scored the minuscule Bundesbank interventions. In private his criticism was much harsher. At the G5 deputies' first post-Plaza meeting in Paris on November 13, Mulford also scored the United Kingdom for briefly *buying* dollars to alleviate pressure on the pound. "I don't understand what the Bank of England is doing—it's counterproductive!" he said. Interview with meeting participants.

17 Total concerted intervention was roughly $12.8 billion: $3.2 billion by the United States, $3 billion by Japan, $2 billion by France, Germany, and the United Kingdom. The rest of the G10, principally Italy, sold another $2 billion. Other concertation network central banks sold an additional $2.6 billion. Author estimates on the composition based on various sources, especially *Federal Reserve Bank of New York Quarterly Review,* 10, Winter 1985–86, p. 47, and BIS, *Exchange Market Intervention and Monetary Policy,* Basel, March 1988, p. 83.

18 He was also critical because the monetary tightening slowed domestic growth and thus worked against reducing Japan's external surpluses.

19 Pardee, Scott, interview by author, June 29, 1989, New York. Pardee was present at the time.

20 Oba, Tomomitsu, interview by author, April 20, 1989, Tokyo.

21 BOJ domesticists were also upset that the heavy, Plaza-inspired speculation by the Big Four Japanese securities houses was pushing it toward an interest rate cut. The strong market reaction, which startled senior BOJ officials, may also have been influenced by the coincident opening of Japan's new bond futures market.

22 Free market critics still had to debunk the apparent market reality that a well-timed government intervention, later supported by monetary easing, helped turn the dollar in February 1985.

23 Gyohten, Toyoo, in *Changing Fortunes,* p. 256.

24 Baker optimistically assessed that the much disparaged new Gramm-Rudman-Hollings (GRH) automatized budget ceiling bill would help reduce the U.S. budget deficit.

25 On December 18, 1985, Japanese Prime Minister Yasuhiro Nakasone upset BOJ officials by making an unusual public call for joint interest rate cuts. The French Socialist government wanted lower interest rates to help with an upcoming spring election. On January 15, 1986, German Economics Minister Martin Bangemann emerged from a meeting with Baker to tell reporters that Baker wanted concerted interest rate cuts "to be discussed and, if possible, decided" at the London G5 meeting. Baker denied it. Cited in Rowen, Hobart, "Treasury Official Contradicts Minister," *Washington Post,* January 16, 1986.

26 Oba, Tomomitsu, interview by author, January 22, 1990, Tokyo.

27 Oba, Tomomitsu, interview by author, April 19, 1989, Tokyo.

28 Volcker, Paul, in *Changing Fortunes,* p. 273.

29 At the time, Lawson faced the likelihood of having to raise interest rates to defend sterling, which was under pressure because of the oil price collapse effect on the U.K.'s North Sea oil economy. He couldn't therefore commit himself to lowering interest rate jointly. To alleviate Britain's internal/external dilemma, Lawson launched a private campaign in fall 1985 to persuade Prime Minister Thatcher to adopt a fixed exchange rate monetary policy anchor for Britain by taking sterling into the ERM at DM 3.75. Thatcher firmly refused to accept such a blatant subjugation of U.K. economic sovereignty.

30 Author interview of participant.

31 Volcker's comment, plus MOF relaxation of Japan's rules on foreign investment, helped break the dollar slide against the yen.

32 The "Palace Coup" story is constructed from interviews of principals, Fed watchers, and outside accounts.

33 Interview of Fed staffer.

34 Quoted in Smith, Hedrick, *The Power Game,* Ballantine Books, New York, 1988, p. 52. Volcker confirms.

35 Jones, David, interview by author, June 29, 1989, New York.

36 Rowen, Hobart, "Japan, W. German Rate Cuts Urged," *Washington Post,* September 30, 1986.

37 Gyohten, Toyoo, in *Changing Fortunes,* p. 256.

38 In one humorous incident, when the BOJ's Shijuro Ogata was gesticulating to describe this overliquidity to central bankers in Basel, he accidentally knocked over his glass, spilling water across the table.

39 The relatively larger impact of the dollar fall on Japan than on Germany was summarized in the trade-weighted exchange rate appreciation of each currency from late February 1985 to mid-May 1986—35 percent for the yen vs. 19 percent for the DM. Some dollar pressure on the Bundesbank was also offset by a 3 percent devaluation of the French franc and a 3 percent revaluation of the DM within the ERM on April 6, 1986, which reduced speculative capital inflows that were overswelling the money supply and pushing up the DM.

40 The ten indicators were GNP growth, inflation, interest rates, unemployment, government budget balances, current account balances, trade balances, money supply growth, national reserves, and currency exchange rates. At the Venice Summit of June 10, 1987, these were reduced to six: GNP growth, inflation, trade balances, government budget balances, monetary conditions, and currency exchange rates.

41 The G5 had discussed the Italian membership problem at length in London, but "we didn't want to give up the G5," says one finance minister. "So we invented the G7." President Reagan's keenness to satisfy Italian Prime Minister Bettino Craxi because of Italy's support during the then current U.S. conflict with Libya was influential in deciding the issue.

42 Tietmeyer's suspicions were aroused by Baker and Dick Darman's stealthiness in unveiling the scheme. Actually Baker sent a "nonpaper" outlining the indicator proposal to the home of German Finance Minister Gerhard Stoltenberg ten days before the summit. But Stoltenberg was away in China, so Germany didn't receive it until the eve of the summit.

43 *Changing Fortunes* p. 127.

44 However, when the potential for substantive exchange improved by trimming the number of indicators the next year, he allows, "[i]t got more sensible."

45 Gyohten, Toyoo, in *Changing Fortunes,* p. 263.

46 Germans frequently bridled that "Japan is always hiding behind others at international conferences, so the Germans are blamed more." Kloten, Norbert, interview by author, September 1, 1989, Stuttgart.

47 MOF officials deny this was their intention. The incident also coincided with a switch in MOF tactics to slow the yen's rise from largely futile foreign exchange market intervention to administrative guidance and relaxation of Japanese foreign financial investment ceilings to encourage capital outflows.

48 Pöhl communicated the same offer at the time to Richard Burt, America's ambassador to Germany.

49 Pöhl adds, "This was the overture for the Louvre. It took a couple more months for him to agree."

50 Cited in Sesit, Michael R., "Baker's Drive for Rate Cuts by Germany, Japan Pushes Dollar Below Two Marks," *Wall Street Journal,* September 19, 1986.

51 Author interview of senior Treasury official, who adds that the Treasury "had no internal targets. Nonetheless there was disagreement about what the right level was."

52 The "spirit of Gleaneagles" later soured over a dispute whether the Bundesbank's commitment had been just for a few days to enhance Europe's bargaining position for the G5/G7 meetings, as the Germans claimed, or whether it had been a permanent tactic, as top French politicians alleged.

53 Sargen, Nicholas, interview by author, April 6, 1989, New York.

54 Sargen's boss, Henry Kaufman (AKA Dr. Gloom), downplayed the conclusion and changed the title to "The U.S. Dollar: Obstacles to Stabilization."

55 Between 1986 and 1988 the seven largest insurers lost an estimated $25 billion from the falling dollar.

56 Based on advance information about foreign central bank orders placed with the New York Fed, the Treasury included special add-on tranches to auction issues. The Treasury tried to gauge private Japanese investor interest through confidential information the New York Fed received from the Japanese firms, which became primary dealers for the first time from late 1986. The primary dealers' need to handle a large volume of orders during their trial period also helped prop up the dollar in 1987.

57 Fujita, Tsuneo, interview by author, February 1, 1990, Tokyo.

58 Miyazawa, Kiichi, "Japan Needs a Born-Again Economy," *International Economy,* October / November 1987.

59 A second "Maekawa Report" was issued a year later.

60 Hosomi adds, "Nakasone was always eager to make some change to be named after Nakasone—a real politician. He himself did not have much knowledge about industry and finance. But he admired Mr. Reagan and Mrs. Thatcher as politicians who liberalized the economy, and he wanted to behave like them."

61 Emmott, Bill, *The Sun Also Sets,* Times Books, New York, 1989, p. 132.

62 Sterling, William P., "The Leveraging of Japan," *The International Economy,* May/June 1989.

63 Funabashi, Yoichi, "Japan and the New World Order," *Foreign Affairs,* Winter 1991–92, p. 59.

64 Wolferen, Karel G. van, "The Japan Problem," *Foreign Affairs,* Winter 1986–87, and Wolferen, Karel G. van, *The Enigma of Japanese Power,* Knopf, New York, 1989. This spiderweb entangled foreign governments that negotiated liberalization with Japan and increasingly goaded them toward procrustean, protectionist solutions.

65 Drucker, Peter F., "American-Japanese Realities," *Wall Street Journal,* October 11, 1985.

66 The core LDP finally lost government control in 1993.

67 Hesse, Helmut, interview by author, September 12, 1989, Hannover.

68 Gyohten, Toyoo, in *Changing Fortunes,* p. 309.

69 Stoltenberg, Gerhard, cited in transcript, *MacNeil/Lehrer NewsHour,* October 3, 1986.

70 Stoltenberg comments as recalled by senior U.S. official. On another occasion Stoltenberg told Baker that he was overestimating the trade gains that would accrue from the lower dollar because of German attachment to quality and relationships: "I don't care how cheap Delco batteries are! You'll never find one in a Mercedes-Benz. German companies have suppliers with relationships going back two, three, and four generations. To them, price is not everything."

71 Author interview of senior U.S. Treasury official.

72 Baker, James A. III, cited in transcript, *MacNeil/Lehrer NewsHour,* October 3, 1986.

73 Baker, James A. III, quoted in Funabashi, Yoichi, *Managing the Dollar,* Institute for International Economics, Washington, D.C., 1988, p. 157.

74 Privately Baker did not wish to surrender the convenience of issuing foreign debt in the U.S. currency. Nor was the Treasury keen to enhance the international use of the yen—even though this was the U.S.'s official position in the yen-dollar committee—because it could eventually reduce Japan's dependency on the dollar standard and thus reduce U.S. political leverage.

75 Gyohten, Toyoo, in *Changing Fortunes,* p. 265.

76 Miyazawa talked up the ¥3.6 trillion ($23 billion) supplementary budget in train in the Diet, even though he knew it was "essentially cosmetic since much of the money was in the process of being spent anyway." Gyohten, Toyoo, in *Changing Fortunes,* p. 265.

77 "Treasury and Federal Reserve Foreign Exchange Operations: November 1986–January 1987," *Federal Reserve Bank of New York Quarterly Review,* Spring 1987, p. 5.

78 One motive for Baker's reversion to talk-down was the passage two weeks earlier of a less expansionary Japanese budget than he'd expected. Another was defiant words from Germany following the EMS realignment.

79 In hindsight, the Japanese economy bottomed out in November 1986.

80 Funabashi, *Managing the Dollar,* pp. 56, 178.

81 In 1986 German central bank money stock grew 7.75 percent—2.25 percentage points faster than the top of its target corridor.

82 "The possibility to realign is a useful component of the mechanism of an adjustment process to the extent it is balanced by a reluctance to realign," explains one central banker of the paradox that lay at the heart of managing an adjustable, fixed exchange rate system like the EMS, Bretton Woods, and Louvre target zone mechanism. Ultimately the reluctance to realign became so politically rigid in the face of the great

economic divergence between the reunified Germany and the rest of Europe that it partly blew apart the ERM in speculative attacks of September 1992 and August 1993.

83 Sivert, Olaf, interview by author, May 9, 1989, Saarbrücken.

84 Intramarginal intervention by ERM countries, almost all by central banks other than the Bundesbank, totaled DM 44 billion between July 8, 1986, and January 9, 1987, and was concentrated most heavily in this period. Dudler, Hermann-Josef, "Monetary Policy and Exchange Market Management in Germany," in BIS, "Exchange Market Intervention and Monetary Policy," Basel, March 1988, p. 72.

85 Author interview of senior German official.

86 The January 1987 EMS crisis persuaded Basel central bankers that the EMS was becoming more difficult to manage because of the increased volume of intra-European capital flows resulting from the liberalization of capital controls in France, Italy, and elsewhere and to the increased political reluctance of France and other higher-inflation countries to devalue within the ERM. This prompted Bundesbank President Karl Otto Pöhl to query fellow governors whether they should seek the power to settle "small" realignments without finance ministers in order to depoliticize the ERM. In a revealing episode of the hidden dynamics of international monetary politics between central banks and governments, few of Pöhl's fellow governors were in favor. Erik Hoffmeyer, the long-serving governor of the Danish central bank, explained why: Political responsibility for realignment imposed a useful discipline on governments to undertake economic adjustment. If governors had independent responsibility, finance ministers and prime ministers would be sorely tempted to wash their hands of hard adjustments. Central bankers would be left to realign exchange rates—and to take the political blame. EMS exchange rate stability and economic convergence through policy adjustment would decay into a lazy, crawling peg system of frequent realignments and perhaps back into the political economic indiscipline of floating exchange rates. When the same proposal was floated two years later by Danish monetary expert Niels Thygesen during the discussions of the Delors committee, which laid out the blueprint for monetary union and a single central bank, Pöhl was among those against it.

87 The Basel-Nyborg agreement committed central banks to finance intramarginal intervention of their EMS partners and to accept repayment partially in Ecu, the synthetic basket currency despised by the Bundesbank and which France hoped would fulfill its original purpose of supplanting the DM to become Europe's future single currency.

88 Quotes cited in Lewis, Paul, "Europe and Japan Show New Declines in Their Economies," *New York Times,* February 22, 1987. Even after the Bundesbank finally cut its discount and Lombard rates on January 23, Baker didn't act to arrest the dollar's slide. Because the Bundesbank's easing was partially offset by an increase in reserve requirements and other actions to mop up some of the liquidity injected into the German money supply by the obligatory DM 17 billion interventions before realignment, the U.S. Treasury regarded much of it as a trick. Yet as the scale of the German investment bust became more evident in subsequent weeks, the Bundesbank steered its "Repo" rate down sharply from 4.6 percent to 3.8 percent.

89 Interview of senior German official.

90 In the event, "the extra DM 5 billion of tax relief of the Louvre was very hard for Stoltenberg to deliver," says a top Finance Ministry official.

91 "Baker Reassures Saudis Dollar Not in Free-Fall," *Journal of Commerce,* February 4, 1987. From 1987 Baker also included Treasury Undersecretary for Domestic Finance George Gould in G7 issues because the dollar had visibly begun to impinge U.S. financial markets.

92 Interview of U.S. central banker.

93 Truman, Edwin, interview by author, December 27, 1989, Washington, D.C.

94 Like so many Candides, central bankers ritually commiserated that the world econ-

omy would be better off if each nation well cultivated its own garden so there would be little need for international policy coordination managed by politicians.

95 Rejoins U.K. Chancellor of the Exchequer Nigel Lawson, "I think the central bankers enjoy a great luxury. If all goes well, then they all say how wonderful it was. When it is a period when the process is broken down, they blame the finance ministers."

CHAPTER NINETEEN: WHO'S MANAGING WHOM?

1 A series of preparatory bilateral meetings among finance ministers, and separately among central bankers, preceded the Saturday afternoon G5.

2 This was a new outbreak of the political dispute that had presumably been settled at the Tokyo summit in May 1986. It was later resolved by including all G7 nations in the preparatory meetings. Further time was spent by the G5 working out a common position on the unilateral debt repayment moratorium declared by Brazil the previous day.

3 In the event, Germany's small anticipatory tax cut failed to provide much of a lift. Japan's tax reform was never enacted. Only Japan's ¥6 trillion ($40 billion) spending program added a significant, though counterproductively mistimed, boost.

4 Conversation from author interview of high Fed official. Any remaining illusion that U.S. political leaders were serious about tackling the budget deficit evaporated in August 1987, when Congress postponed the GRH target year for balancing the budget from 1991 to 1993.

5 Volcker, Paul, in *Changing Fortunes,* p. 282. "These G7 operations were based on cooperative understandings and pieces of draft communiqués," adds U.K. Deputy Treasury Secretary Geoffrey Littler. "It was all less systematic than the tidy mind would like."

6 Author interview of participant.

7 Interview of participant, reading from meeting notes.

8 Lawson, Nigel, "No Quick-Fix Solution to Economic Problems," *Financial Times,* October 8, 1990.

9 Tactically it was agreed that most operations would be conducted in the home country's currency market. Pöhl, however, adamantly "opposed being dragged into defending the yen/dollar ranges," says Daniel Lebegue.

10 Funabashi, *Managing the Dollar,* p. 209. Finance ministers were also loath to push monetary policy discussions because "in the effort to fix exchange rate ranges central bankers can feel threatened—we finance ministers are smarter than that," says a senior Finance Ministry official.

11 Volcker, Paul, in *Changing Fortunes,* p. 282.

12 "It was very much in our minds: if they subjected us to rigid bands, then we couldn't control monetary developments," explains another Council member.

13 Gyohten, Toyoo, in *Changing Fortunes,* pp. 267, 268.

14 Lawson, Nigel, in Kilborn, Peter T., "U.S. and 5 Allies Promise to Seek Dollar Stability," *New York Times,* February 23, 1987.

15 The United States bought over $3 billion between March 23 and April 6. It was its first big dollar defense operation since the late 1970s.

16 Sumita, Satoshi, in "Sumita Says 'Dollar Hasn't Gone into a Free-Fall,' " DJ wire, April 1, 1987.

17 Interview with high Fed official.

18 The argument digressed into the esoteric cul-de-sac of what constituted "cooperative" intervention under the Louvre and which intervention was "voluntary." Additionally, some central banks, led by the United Kingdom for its new DM shadowing policy, were voluntarily purchasing falling dollars in huge quantities to rebuild their national foreign exchange reserves.

19 Privately German participants ridiculed Baker's pool as "crazy," "unrealistic," "unprofessional," and "legalistic."

20 "When it got to discussion on numbers, they [the G5 ministers] listened and relied a lot on Volcker and Pöhl," says U.K. Second Permanent Secretary Geoffrey Littler. "At nearly every meeting we concluded that the central bankers would work out the precise details."

21 Interview of central banker. Recalls one European deputy finance minister, "Mulford was very suspicious of the Fed. Once he even went to Basel [to check on them for himself]."

22 Volcker, Paul, quoted in Blustein, Paul, "Dollar Looms Bigger in the Fed's Decisions, at Risk of a Recession," *Wall Street Journal,* May 19, 1987.

23 Rapoport, Carla, "Japanese Institutions Shun U.S. Treasuries," *Financial Times,* April 22, 1987.

24 "Don't Buy Any More Treasuries," *Tokyo Business Today,* July 1987.

25 Funabashi, *Managing the Dollar,* p. 60.

26 A top BOJ official adds, "We knew what Volcker was saying. He'd know what we wanted. We knew what Nakasone would say. Sumita and Nakasone met on it."

27 Rodger, Ian, "Japan Urges Restraints on Currency Speculation," *Financial Times,* May 14, 1987.

28 Koo, Richard, "Capital Flows and Structural Adjustment—A New Challenge," mimeograph, April 1989, p. 6,8.

29 Inflation had jumped from 2.5 percent in fourth-quarter 1986 to 6.2 percent in the first quarter 1987; but that could be ascribed to a onetime adjustment from higher oil prices and other commodities. Money supply growth too had picked up in April but was still below the Fed's annual targets. Economic growth was lackluster. But the falling dollar was raising imported goods prices and inciting inflation expectations that could induce businessmen and labor unions to bid up wages and prices in anticipation. And Volcker was mindful that inflationary pressure was lagging somewhere in the pipeline from the resource competition between growing export investments and the government's failure to cut its budget deficit.

30 James Baker quote, as related by Baker, Howard, interview by author, January 10, 1990, Washington, D.C.

31 Characterization by a European central banker.

32 Nakasone, Yasuhiro, quoted in Funabashi, *Managing the Dollar,* p. 1.

33 The BOJ leaked the information through the offices of Nomura Research Institute President Yukitsugu Nakagawa, a former top BOJ official and old navy friend of Nakasone's.

34 The supplemental fiscal spending was concentrated in the booming construction sector, where there were already inflation bottlenecks.

35 The BOJ's main money supply measure was M2 plus certificates of deposits.

36 The BOJ's "forecasts" were quite different from the annual monetary targets used by the Fed, Bank of England, or Bundesbank. They were projections of how money supply growth was likely to turn out—and formulated at midyear with six months' history already known to enhance their accuracy.

37 German central bankers were also aware that their most closely watched monetary aggregate was being distorted by an increased underground holding of DM banknotes throughout Eastern Europe—an early sign of the economic crumbling that led to the spectacular domino collapse of its communist regimes two years later. Such currency would never be spent in Germany and thus couldn't add to German inflation. But it was hard to reliably estimate its amount.

38 In the first five months of 1987 Germany was inundated with foreign capital inflows of DM 17 billion ($9.5 billion). In June through September foreigners pulled out DM 20.5 billion ($11.5 billion).

39 Interview of high Bank of Italy official.

40 Koo, Richard C., "Japanese Investment in Dollar Securities after the Plaza Accord: Statement Submitted to the Joint Economic Committee of the U.S. Congress," mimeograph, October 17, 1988, pp. 8,9.

41 Interview of Fed governor.

42 Author interview of senior Treasury official.

43 To signal Greenspan that not coordinating with him had a political price, Baker leaked their difference over the discount rate hike to the press. See Rowen, Hobart, "When Baker and Greenspan Don't See Eye to Eye," *Washington Post,* October 1, 1987.

44 Author interview of senior Fed official.

45 Some privately were more worried about a collapse of the even more stratospheric Tokyo stock market.

46 Some two-fifths of the $70 billion dollar-buying intervention was done by the Bank of Japan. The Bank of England, mainly to finance the U.K.'s DM shadowing, and to a lesser degree Spain, to pave its entry into the ERM, together did another two-fifths. Italy, France, Germany, and Sweden did most of the rest. At least half of the intervention was done independently of the concerted G7 dollar ranges.

47 "Economic Situation and Outlook: Note by Managing Director," mimeograph, September 23, 1987, pp. 1–3.

48 Sumita, Satoshi, quoted in Mossberg, Walter S., "Seven Nations Reaffirm Plan for Currencies," *Wall Street Journal,* September 28, 1987.

49 Author interview of G7 participants.

50 Pöhl, Karl Otto, "Cooperation—A Keystone for the Stability of the International Monetary System," First Arthur Burns Memorial Lecture at the American Council on Germany, mimeograph, New York, November 2, 1987, p. 8.

51 Pöhl's proposal that the United States take a recession was made bluntly at the many private discussions around the G5/G7 meeting, though only politely suggested at the official gathering. "Japan, Germany, and the United Kingdom accept a recession for reducing overconsumption," endorsed one high MOF official later. "Why must the United States be the exception?"

52 Bank of Italy officials remonstrated privately to the Bundesbank in the summer about its snugging.

53 Rebasing contained two practical dilemmas for government-managed exchange rate targetry: first, how to justify why previous ranges were in error or became wrong; second and more difficult, how to credibly demonstrate that the rebasing was made voluntarily and not simply because market forces pushed them to it.

54 While the search for a policy anchor addressed a major weakness in the world monetary system, few mainstream economists believed commodity prices were reliable enough indicators to be the answer. The inclusion of gold—Keynes's "barbarous relic" that, to the satisfaction of most experts, had been demonetized since President Nixon ended dollar-gold convertibility by fiat on August 15, 1971—mystified most observers. Proposals for a commodities-based anchor had been floating around the Treasury since just after the Plaza.

55 Lawson's speech aggravated the Bundesbank's irritation with the U.K.'s DM shadow policy. The Anglo-German tension was evident during the 1986 IMF/World Bank Annual Meetings when Lawson, in an effort to bolster the beleaguered sterling, had gone to Stoltenberg's hotel room at the Four Seasons to personally request a DM-sterling swap facility to help the United Kingdom acquire DM for intervention from Stoltenberg and Pöhl. Previous requests from the Bank of England had been stonewalled by the Bundesbank. The Germans granted the facility, though not on the friendliest terms, and "Lawson came back with his head all red," recalls a Bank of England official. In the months subsequent to Lawson's "managed floating" speech, the Bundesbank-Lawson feud over DM shadowing turned nastier: when Pöhl refused a U.K. request to buy DM in late 1987, Lawson vollied back in 1988 with a U.K. debt

issue in high-DM-content Ecu, which the Bundesbank loathed. The feud promoted the strange political alliance between U.K. Prime Minister Thatcher and Pöhl to impede those foreign and British forces promoting European monetary union and a single European central bank. In February 1989, Thatcher made an extraordinary helicopter landing at the Bundesbank to meet with Pöhl, top Bundesbank officials, and the chairmen of Deutsche Bank and Commerzbank, Alfred Herrhausen and Walter Seipp, respectively. (Wolfgang Röller of Dresdner Bank fell ill and couldn't attend.) According to an eyewitness, Pöhl tried to persuade Thatcher to bring the United Kingdom into the ERM so she could influence the course of the EMU debate. Thatcher expressed her suspicion of the French influence on the EC government in Brussels and warned Pöhl to be careful in the Delors committee negotiations. "The French are masters at drafting agreements to hide some facts," she said. In emotional terms she tried to convince her German hosts that the Latin European countries had less monetary discipline than northern countries. "We must be careful they don't put their fingers in our pockets," she said. "When Turkey joins the EC," she added, "it will be the end of Europe."

56 Lawson, Nigel, "Statement by the Rt. Hon. Nigel Lawson MP, Chancellor of the Exchequer, at the Joint Annual Meetings," mimeograph, September 30, 1987, p. 7.

57 Lahnstein, Manfred, interview by author, September 12, 1989, Guetersloh. About half at the time were considered political appointees.

58 Schlesinger's main ideological adversary was directorate member Claus Köhler. Major splits during the 1980s most often occurred when there were differences between Schlesinger and directorate member Leonhard Gleske. Gleske tempered Schlesinger's strong attachment to the monetary aggregates by giving more weight to real economic signals; he was also more of an internationalist, especially on European monetary cooperation. One key Pöhl task was to mediate when Schlesinger and Gleske disagreed.

59 An ancillary motive for tightening was increasingly sour relations with Stoltenberg. Bundesbankers resented that Stoltenberg's rigid commitment to fiscal consolidation was deflecting the international political pressure onto them; some suspected that he was doing so *purposely* to pressure them to ease. Relations were further strained in early October, when Stoltenberg and Chancellor Kohl, petrified that the planned tax 1988 cuts would reverse progress in their deficit-reduction program, instituted a 10 percent withholding tax on interest income on German securities over strong Bundesbank opposition.

60 "Newsweek Says Baker Blames Ger," Reuters report of *Newsweek International* story, November 1, 1987.

61 Story reconstructed mainly from Stoltenberg, Gerhard, interview by author, September 20, 1989, Bonn.

62 Baker III, James A., transcript, *Meet the Press*, NBC News, October 18, 1987.

63 Author interview of high Bundesbank official.

64 Reconstruction of the meeting is based also on interviews with participants and their aides.

65 Sumita's statement concluded: "I highly evaluate yesterday's meeting between U.S. Treasury Secretary James Baker III and German Finance Minister Gerhard Stoltenberg and President Karl Otto Pöhl of the Bundesbank, in which they reconfirmed the importance and the necessity of the maintenance of the cooperative framework of 'the Louvre Agreement.' "

66 See Murray, Alan, and Seib, Gerald F., "Reagan's Reversal: Stock Market's Crash Makes Budget Accord, Tax Rise More Likely," *Wall Street Journal,* October 23, 1987.

CHAPTER TWENTY: MARKETS REVOLT

1 Account of October 22 council meeting is from author interviews of participants.

2 Kloten, Norbert, interview by author, September 1, 1989, Stuttgart.

3 Sivert, Olaf, interview by author, May 9, 1989, Saarbrücken.

4 Hesse, Helmut, interview by author, September 12, 1989, Hannover.

5 Conversation recalled by Stoltenberg, Gerhard, interview by author, September 20, 1989, Bonn.

6 Quoted in Kilborn, Peter T., "Central Bankers Permit the Dollar to Slide Further," *New York Times,* October 29, 1987. U.S. Treasury officials publicly and privately denied they had any internal target.

7 Lawson, Nigel, in O'Boyle, Thomas F., "Risk-Averse Western Germans Retain Calm in a World Shaken by Stock Market Crash," *Wall Street Journal,* October 28, 1987.

8 Balladur's support was influenced by the French presidential elections in spring 1988. The chances of his close ally, Gaullist Prime Minister Jacques Chirac, to unseat Socialist President Mitterrand could have been adversely affected by a currency crisis or recession.

9 Gould's comment strikingly echoed the realpolitik assessment of the dollar's pivotal international monetary role, expressed in Treasury Secretary John Connally's celebrated, undiplomatic comment during the negotiations to modify the crumbling Bretton Woods regime: "The dollar may be our currency, but it's your problem."

10 Interview of senior U.S. official.

11 Editorial, "Another Budget Horror Show," *Chicago Tribune,* December 23, 1987.

12 Gould, George, interview by author, July 25, 1989, New York.

13 Lawson, Nigel, Mansion House speech, mimeograph, November 4, 1987.

14 Interview with European monetary official.

15 The figure comes from two Bundesbank Central Bank Council members. It helped finance French intervention under its reluctant concession to lend DM intramarginally under the recent Basel-Nyborg agreement that the governors would initial at the BIS on November 11. When France exhausted the agreement's borrowing limits, the Bundesbank voluntarily lent it more.

16 Kloten, Norbert, interview by author, September 1, 1989, Stuttgart.

17 Stoltenberg comment based on recollection of Council member.

18 Recollection of Council member.

19 Free Democrat Foreign Affairs Minister Hans-Dietrich Genscher defeated the Bundesbank's preferred compromise of inserting a qualifying preamble to the treaty, proposed by his FDP rival Otto Lambsdorff. Instead Pöhl was forced to settle for a qualifying explanation in the reasoning bill accompanying the treaty. It blunted the importance of the joint Franco-German Council, whose meetings were described by insiders as almost comical: the French side laid out well-prepared positions, while the fractious German side, represented by the Bundesbank, Finance Ministry, and Economics Ministry, argued more among themselves than with their French counterparts.

20 Murray, Alan, and Mossberg, Walter, "James Baker Stresses Holding Down Rates Even if Dollar Suffers," *Wall Street Journal,* November 5, 1987.

21 Author interview of meeting participant.

22 Author interview of meeting participant.

23 Conversation retold by a top Bundesbank official.

24 Pöhl, Karl Otto, "Cooperation—A Keystone for the Stability of the International Monetary System," Arthur Burns Memorial Lecture American Council on Germany, mimeograph, New York, November 2, 1987.

25 Since there were no net winners or losers in foreign exchange markets, a dollar run, by itself, could not continue indefinitely.

26 Lawson, Nigel, interview by author, September 19, 1989, London. The Bundesbank also unsuccessfully resisted the acquisition of DM by Spain. Between them the United Kingdom and Spain acquired on the order of DM 17 billion (about $10 billion) in 1987. The United Kingdom took the lion's share. See Holberton, Simon, "Mr. Pöhl's Warning Proves Justified," *Financial Times,* July 11, 1988.

27 Some European and U.S. officials concurred that they didn't want any dollar rebound to get far into the DM 1.90–DM 2.00 zone.
28 The December 14 meeting is reconstructed from interviews of participants.
29 The central bankers did not discuss the financial tremors in Tokyo.
30 Interview of senior U.K. Treasury official.
31 Conversation reconstructed from interviews with senior U.S., U.K., and German officials.
32 Interview with international monetary official.
33 Volcker, Paul, quoted in Wilson, Stanley, "Where Does the Fed Go from Here?" *Institutional Investor,* May 1987.
34 De Vries, Rimmer, quoted in Mossberg, Walter S., "Group of Seven Move Sparks Rally in Stocks, Bonds, but Battle Is Seen," *Wall Street Journal,* December 24, 1987.
35 In the second half of December the United States bought $1.7 billion worth of dollars, half against DM and half against yen; BOJ intervention was thought to be even larger. "Treasury and Federal Reserve Foreign Exchange Operations: November 1987–January 1988," *Federal Reserve Bank of New York Quarterly Review,* Winter, 1987–88.
36 Japan's trade-weighted appreciation was an enormous 75 percent versus 20 percent for Germany since February 1985.
37 Central banks had differing reputations that they carried into battle in the foreign exchange markets. "The Bundesbank has a great reputation in the foreign exchange market—always the best," says one currency trader, gazing out at the controlled chaos of the foreign exchange floor. Traders sat in front of long rows of computer monitors, telephone jammed to one ear while they madly scribbled notes on bits of paper and every few moments glanced up at the overhead electronic newswire monitor that spanned the trading room. "The Bank of England has gotten extremely good in the last few years. The Fed never had a great reputation, but since their last foray [January 4–5, 1988] you'd have to say they're pretty good. The worst is the Bank of Japan. They backstop the yen/dollar rate. This gives their corporations time to unwind their dollar positions first without a loss. They have such a consensus economy that this happens, and the bank-corporation relationship is so tight."
38 Suzuki, Yoshio, interview with author, April 24, 1989, Tokyo. The rise of global capital also prompted major central banks to open intelligence-gathering representative offices in major foreign markets. The Bundesbank opened offices in New York and Tokyo (but pointedly *not* in rival London), as had the Bank of Italy. The BOJ, where time zone gaps hindered telephone communication, had offices in New York, London, and Frankfurt.
39 The Bank of England was notable by its invisibility. This generated speculation that Lawson was expressing his displeasure that the United States wouldn't raise interest rates to defend the dollar.
40 "Treasury and Federal Reserve Foreign Exchange Operations November 1987–January 1988," *Federal Reserve Bank of New York Quarterly Review,* Winter, 1987–88.
41 Interventions could be "noisy" or "silent" depending whether the central bank wanted to be visible or was trying to finesse markets into believing that market forces alone were at work. Orders made through securities houses tended to get spread around the market and thus were "noisy." Trades through big domestic banks tended to "silent."
42 "I have my doubts whether the [central bank] foreign exchange people had the right nose for what was happening," says the BIS's Alexandre Lamfalussy. Interview by author, May 18, 1989, New York. Gretchen Greene confirms.
43 BIS, *Fifty-eighth Annual Report,* Basel, June 13, 1988, p. 188.
44 It was a gray area what should qualify as concerted for the process. Most U.K. intervention was guided voluntarily by its DM shadow policy. Much dollar intervention was related to EMS tensions. One European central banker estimated that Italian dollar intervention was "under $10 billion, France somewhat less than that, and Germany

even less." Nigel Lawson, in his memoir *The View From No. 11* (p. 790), reveals that the United Kingdom acquired $25 billion since the Louvre Accord, and Germany "under $3 billion." Taiwan, which pegged its currency to the dollar, acquired $30 billion in 1987. The United States expended $8.6 billion of its foreign exchange reserve defending the dollar.

45 These *tokkin* funds, which held ¥119 trillion ($133 billion), would in future have to offset unrealized losses with realized gains before paying dividends. Unrealized gains also would be taxed at the lower of acquisition or market value.

46 Conversation as recalled by Fujita, Tsuneo, interview by author, February 1, 1990, Tokyo.

CHAPTER TWENTY-ONE: ELECTION OF A PRESIDENT

1 Dallara, Charles, interview by author, February 14, 1990, Washington.

2 Their caveat was that the United States slash domestic demand and imports via eliminating its budget deficit by $40 billion a year while Japan and Germany increased imports through domestic-led growth.

3 Hesse, Helmut, interview by author, September 12, 1989, Hannover.

4 Bressand, Albert, "Currency Chaos—The Newest Strategic Tool," *International Economy,* October/November 1987.

5 Among them were inflation and real interest rate differentials, current account balance changes, different rates of national money supply growth, expectations about future exchange rates, relative domestic growth rates, financial portfolio shifts due to political upheaval, market bandwagon fads, different financial system regulations and structural attributes, capital or trade controls, and direct investment.

6 Lamfalussy, Alexandre, "International Central Bank Co-operation: What It Can—and Cannot—Achieve," speech Jubilee Robert Triffen, Brussels, BIS mimeograph, December 8, 9, 1988.

7 Recollection by meeting participant.

8 Balladur, Edouard, "Rebuilding an International Monetary System," *Wall Street Journal,* February 23, 1988.

9 Interview of senior U.S. Treasury official.

10 Intervention could be effective only if the exchange rate was temporarily out of the soft range in the "gray zone." "But if it has been out of the range for a long time, say, a month," explains one participant of the contrasting "black zone," "intervention probably won't be effective. Then consultations are needed on underlying fundamental policies."

11 At first the G7 intervened visibly and simultaneously in order to demonstrate their solidarity to private traders—as well as to each other. Because New York and European market hours overlapped for only three hours, a pattern developed in early 1989 for central bankers to intervene around 10:30 A.M. in New York and 4:30 P.M. in Europe and then disappear. After a while traders caught on. They bought cheapened dollars from central bankers in the morning and sold them back in the afternoon as the market bid the dollar higher. As a result, G7 intervention ceased to be effective and private traders fattened profits. Disgusted, the Bundesbank dropped out of the concerted interventions between mid-June and mid-August 1989. Some credibility was restored briefly after a September 23, 1989, G7 communiqué signaling dissatisfaction with the strong dollar, when the central bankers modified tactics over several weeks of large concerted interventions.

12 During the week of the crash New York Fed President George Harrison exceeded the $25 million ceiling given him by his system colleagues and bought $160 million worth of government securities. The Fed also lowered the discount rate steadily from 5 percent in October 1929 to 4.5 percent in November and to 1.5 percent by early 1931. The catastrophic bank collapses and spiral into depression didn't strike until one to two

years after the crash. Short-term interest rates fell from 4.5 percent in 1929 to 0.5 percent in the summer 1931. There was still a lively academic debate over the role of the crash, if any, and Federal Reserve policy, in causing the Great Depression. Celebrated monetarist historians Milton Friedman and Anna Schwartz found incompetent monetary policy to be primarily culpable for the Depression and the crash as largely unrelated to it. Professor Charles Kindleberger led an opposing group that tracked a chain reaction of financial and economic consequences set off by the crash that led to the Depression and blamed Fed monetary policy only peripherally. (There were also nonmonetary contributors, such as the protectionist Smoot-Hawley legislation.) The key monetary problems were the failure of long-term interest rates to fall below 3 percent—thus increasing real interest rates—and the Fed's overly restrictive policies later in the face of a weak economy and European banking crisis in mid-1931.

13 Cited in Kilborn, Peter T., "Greenspan Resisting Pressure," *New York Times,* February 25, 1988.

14 Earlier Lawson won a public row with Thatcher to defend the shadow 3 DM peg by cutting British interest rates. He watched with dismay later as an overlax monetary policy fed an inflationary resurgence that soured the Thatcher "miracle" and contributed to the "Iron Lady's" political demise in late 1990.

15 Wagstyl, Stefan, "Dumping Dollars Too Publicly Earns Official Displeasure in Tokyo," *Financial Times,* March 31, 1988.

16 Editorial, "Economic Olympiad," *Wall Street Journal,* February 23, 1988. "The failure of the monetarists is to take international developments into account," explains Stanford international monetarist Ronald McKinnon. "The St. Louis M1 model broke down with floating exchange rates."

17 In hindsight many economists agreed that they misjudged the delayed pass-through effects of the "oil dividend" from plunging oil prices in early 1986. "People went around trying to figure out how they got it so wrong," says a Fed economist. "The lags are a joke."

18 The concentration of 60 percent of the reserve growth in just four countries—Japan, Taiwan, Germany, and the United Kingdom—reduced the multiplier effect dangers, they judged.

19 Interview of central bank economist.

20 Many Europeans were sympathetic since they feared that otherwise the Bundesbank was likely to raise interest rates. This would be transmitted to them through the ERM. But the U.S.'s concern about getting strength under the dollar prevailed.

21 An angry Fed got retribution by calling public attention to the fact that from late May through mid-June German foreign exchange reserves, the best public proxy for intervention, fell DM 7.4 billion ($4.4 billion). "Treasury and Federal Reserve Foreign Exchange Operations: May–July 1988," *Federal Reserve Bank of New York Quarterly Review,* Autumn 1988.

22 Wakatsuki, Mikio, quoted in Sterngold, James, "The $6 Trillion Hole in Japan's Pocket," *New York Times,* January 21, 1994. In February 1988 the BOJ research department proposed lifting the "emergency" level discount rate of 2.5 percent. But it was told by a senior BOJ official to back off because of pressure from the Americans.

23 See Sender, Henny, "The Bank of Japan under Siege," *Institutional Investor,* November 1988.

24 Author interview of high BOJ official.

25 Farrington, Mark, "How the BOJ Escaped a Discount Rate Hike," *MMS International Report,* undated mimeograph, and Farrington, Mark, interview by author, April 24, 1989, Tokyo.

26 Hale, David, "Accounting for the Dollar Glut," *Wall Street Journal,* April 18, 1988.

27 See Pat Choate's recent book, *Agents of Influence,* documenting the growing Japanese influence in American politics.

28 Volcker, Paul, in Reich, Cary, "The Privatization of Paul Volcker," *Institutional Investor,* December 1989.
29 Utsumi, Makoto, quoted in Farnsworth, Clyde H., "Japan's Stern Warning on Trade Sanctions," *New York Times,* January 29, 1991. Utsumi's threat to manipulate Japanese capital flows in retribution against U.S. trade sanctions was a rare public expression of Japanese technocrats' own supreme confidence that they possessed the capacity to manage powerful market forces. Ironically it implicitly confirmed that MOF officials concurred with Japan critics that the value of the yen, and Japanese financial markets, were rigged.
30 Nor was it on the agenda of the bilateral Japan-U.S. Yen-Dollar Committee "since we [the United States] don't want them to be able to ask us for favors. Recycling is in their interest, too," says a senior U.S. Treasury official. Such politically delicate monetary issues, rather, were handled through indirect diplomacy. The global capital imbalances "mean that when you take counsel you better include the people who have the money," says ex–Secretary of State George Shultz. "We included the Saudi Arabians [during the OPEC recycling of the 1970s], more so than they are included today. It's also the Willie Sutton principle with Japan. It registers itself formally in requests for larger voting shares at the IMF."
31 Drucker, "The Changed World Economy," pp. 790–791.

CHAPTER TWENTY-TWO: THE WORLD'S FIRST CAPITAL STANDARDS

1 The three were David Walker and Rodney Galpin, executive directors for city affairs and bank supervision, respectively, and Economic Adviser John Flemming.
2 Cooke, Peter, quoted in Lim, Quek Peck, coordinator, "Re-Regulation," *Euromoney,* June 1986.
3 Volcker comment as recalled by a senior BOE official.
4 France's nationalized banks, which also operated on significantly lower capital ratios than other international Western banks, were similarly backstopped from failure by a tacit government guarantee.
5 There was also a further "overrecycling" of the surpluses driven by an arbitrage between Japan's highly controlled financial environment and unregulated world financial markets, to feed the growing speculative frenzy of the *zaiteku* bubble economy.
6 Though flattered, the British governor declined.
7 The 1979 law tried to marry tradition and present reality by making a statutory distinction between an upper tier of "recognized banks"—gentlemen—who would be mostly supervised in the traditional way and a second tier of "licensed deposit takers"—players—who were more closely supervised according to statute. But matters went awry with Johnson Matthey Bankers, a blue-blood gentleman of the gold bullion club, which ignored BOE guidelines on loan concentration when it expanded outside its traditional bullion business. Nor did JMB do the gentlemanly thing and bring its problems to the bank's attention—indeed, it may have misinformed it intentionally. Credulous BOE supervisors, for their part, were slow in recognizing the problem. When a hastily prepared private rescue orchestrated by the BOE collapsed, the bank, fearing psychological contagion effects, decided to buy JMB itself. The JMB affair disgraced the BOE and embarrassed the government. The 1987 act abolished the two-tier system.
8 The U.S. team included two men from the U.S. Comptroller's Office.
9 Interview of participant.
10 Volcker comment as recalled by Roberts, Steven, interview by author, October 20, 1989, Washington, D.C. Confirmed by Volcker.
11 Under the proposal banks had to maintain zero capital for riskless assets like cash, 30 percent of the numerical ratio for liquid, low credit risk assets like security repurchase

agreements, 60 percent for higher-risk assets like state bonds, and 100 percent for standard risks like loans to LDCs and commercial businesses.

12 At the eleven U.S. money center banks off balance sheet activities rocketed from almost zero to twice balance sheet assets by 1986—and over four times by the end of the decade. Revenue from these activities increased from 30 percent to 45 percent of banks' total. See Corrigan E. Gerald, "Statement before U.S. Senate Committee on Banking, Housing, and Urban Affairs," appendix VI, "Financial Condition of the U.S. Money Center Bank Holding Companies in the 1980s," May 3, 1990.

13 Central Bank G10 Study Group (chairman: Cross, Sam Y.), *Recent Innovations In International Banking,* BIS, Basel, April 1986.

14 Prior to the Basel supervisors committee, international bank supervisor meetings were infrequent and usually bilateral. The EC since 1969 had a *groupe de contact* that met periodically.

15 Interview of high European central banker.

16 Interview of Basel central bankers.

17 Leigh-Pemberton was careful to keep the U.K. Treasury informally apprised and on board. By doing the U.S. bilateral, the United Kingdom could as well outflank its EC negotiating partners, who were tilting toward accommodation of the small German mortgage banks.

18 Blunden, George, interview by author, February 24, 1989, London.

19 "There is no MOF, only bureaus," MOF technocrats were the first to declare. The MOF was a grouping of seven quasi-autonomous fiefdoms, each commanding its own fierce loyalties. The banking and securities bureaus rivalry was the heart of Japanese financial industry policy-making. The international finance bureau, whose responsibilities overlapped both, floated between them depending upon the issue. In addition, says Takehiro Sagami, an ex–MOF vice minister for international affairs. "The MOF is divided between domesticists and the international side. But the domesticists are still in power. The three very strong bureaus are budget, tax, and finance."

20 "We let the Fed people know what the *real* issues were," asserts a senior BOJ official. Corrigan and Gyohten also spent much time discussing topics related to the dollar and the prospective Louvre Accord.

21 Author interview of senior Fed official.

22 Gyohten, Toyoo, interview by author, January 22, 1990, Tokyo.

23 Gyohten also worried that antagonism on bank capital standards might impede Japanese bank cooperation in the new money drive for the troubled second Mexican rescue. IBJ was campaigning for rebellion.

24 Dutch pique was sharpened by the irrelevance it made of the much touted Amsterdam endorsement of the risk-based framework in October.

25 Interview with senior Bundesbank official. "By admitting 'dirty' capital, you are cheating yourself, creating a false impression of stability," argues a high Bundesbank official. While conceding that "pure" capital was irreplaceable, most governors "thought it was daft" that the German definition of purity excluded unencumbered hidden reserves—above all since German banks themselves had a great deal of it, says a European central banker.

26 The Bundesbank informally vetted supervisory office regulations, since financial stability was a prerequisite for an effective monetary policy. The political sensitivity was aggravated because the head of the German bank supervisory office in Berlin was away when Quinn unveiled the U.S.-U.K. accord in Germany.

27 The 1985 banking reform, which at long last included the consolidated reporting endorsed by the Basel supervisors' committee in 1978, was the belated response to the 1974 collapse of Herstatt. Patchwork changes had been made in May 1976, most notably a lender of last resort facility. Its shortcomings were revealed by the 1983 failure of Schröder, Munchmeyer, Hengst (SMH), which exploited lack of German consoli-

dated reporting to hide lending in excess of legal limits by spreading it among subsidiaries, especially its little supervised Luxembourg Euromarket arm. Disruption to the German and world interbank markets was averted when SMH received emergency funding of DM 630 million ($230 million) from a consortium of twenty German banks in November 1983. The main force behind the scenes was not the Berlin office, but Bundesbank President Pöhl.

28 Author interview of European central banker. Most committee members were incredulous that he'd been as ignorant as they of the U.S.-U.K. negotiation. One diplomatic gain by the amiable and dogged Cooke was to persuade the EC to send an observer to his meetings so that EC negotiations could proceed in parallel.

29 Cooke comment as recalled by a central bank participant.

30 Interview of committee member.

31 Leigh-Pemberton, Robin, "Speech at Annual Banquet of the Overseas Bankers Club," mimeograph, London, February 2, 1987.

32 Kashiwagi, Yusuke, quoted in Bruce, Peter, "Tokyo Unruffled by Moody's Move," *Financial Times,* June 19, 1987.

33 Nakamura, Kaneo interview by author, January 24, 1990.

34 Loughran, John, interview by author, July 21, 1989, New City.

35 Kamiya, Kenichi, "Letter to Office of the Secretary Board of Governors of the Federal Reserve System," mimeograph, May 12, 1987.

36 Gibb, Robin, "Old School Ties May Tie the Knot," *Euromoney,* September 1987. Agreement on the Bank of America investment was reached only in late August, after the international capital adequacy breakthrough had been made.

37 Interview of participant.

38 In spring 1987 the supervisors committee realized that conservative Japanese accounting had caused it to underestimate the size of Japan's hidden capital gains. That "shook everybody slightly," says an international monetary official.

39 The U.S.-U.K. proposal expressed the intention of phasing out from capital such general loan losses that were in fact earmarked for specific doubtful debts.

40 Most meetings were held at the Bank of England or at London hotels. Often Taylor, Quinn, and Chino met alone. On Friday and again on Saturday morning, Quinn met with Chino and the London MOF and BOJ representatives. The United States and Japanese got together Saturday afternoon. On Sunday morning U.S. and U.K. officials met at the Bank of England. The trilaterals started thereafter.

41 Taylor also met bilaterally to work out some problems with the Italians and Swedes in advance of the meeting.

42 Most countries had two members; the United States had four because of its fragmented regulatory regime.

43 Interview of Basel committee members. Admitting general loan loss reserves as capital up to 1.25 percent, Taylor argued, would be in line with the historical provisioning level of U.S. banks before the big LDC reserving triggered by Citibank's action.

44 The Japanese were still holding out for a long transition period. The Germans were worried that they might not have ample Tier 2 "dirty" capital. The French were in the early stages of privatizing the banks they had nationalized at the start of the decade and were way behind everyone else in raising sufficient capital. The United States was worried about accounting for the loan loss reserves.

45 Author interview of senior central banker. In 1994 OECD membership was expanded to twenty-five with the inclusion of Mexico.

46 Later he also wanted at least some of the general loan losses to count as Tier 1, or pure capital.

47 Author interview with European central banker. They would revisit the general loan loss issue by the end of 1990. In February 1991, with French banks having attained the Basel standards, the governors agreed to apply the earlier 1.25 percent cap.

48 The United States was able to get several billion dollars of quasi-equity called "perpetual preferred stock" included in Tier 1.

CHAPTER TWENTY-THREE: CATCH-UP

1 One notable EC exclusion was unrealized capital gains on equity holdings so important for Japanese banks.
2 Cooke, Peter, "Financial Innovations and Risks," mimeograph, remarks before the International Monetary Conference Chicago, June 5–8, 1988.
3 Some nations, including the United States, adopted the G10 guidelines through regulation and law.
4 One benefit was to help close the constant threat posed by lack of final settlement in CHIPS throughout the LDC debt crisis.
5 Under the new, informal concordat, the host country central bank in which the payment system was operating held primary supervisory responsibility for ensuring its stable functioning; the country whose currency was involved, however, shared responsibility with the host country to determine the adequacy of the settlement arrangements. If deemed inadequate, "a central bank should discourage use of the system by institutions subject to its authority." *Report of the Committee on Interbank Netting Schemes of the Central Banks of the Group of Ten Countries,* Bank for International Settlements, Basel, November 1990, p. 7. The major bankruptcy law snags were in France and Belgium.
6 Brady, Nicholas F., "One Marketplace, Indivisible," *New York Times,* February 17, 1988. "The crash of 1987 revealed the capital ratios of brokers—none at all!" adds veteran French monetary official André de Lattre.
7 The bid for parallel world capital standards for securities activities proceeded along three tracks: First, the Basel supervisors committee was working up standards to apply to banks' securities activities. Second, it sought common standards with the International Organization of Securities Commissions (IOSCO), a securities market body. The third track was the EC's work on a directive for a single European passport for all securities firms.
8 "Looking at insurance companies in Germany, you might not be able to distinguish their activities from deposit taking—unless you are a local fiscal authority," quips one capital markets expert.
9 In 1993 BIS General Manager Alexandre Lamfalussy called for international standards on risk disclosure for derivatives dealing by banks. Figuring self-regulation was better than the government regulation that would eventually come from inaction, the Institute for International Finance, representing over 170 member banks from forty countries, responded by drafting a framework disclosure proposal in the spring 1994.
10 Mikuni, Akio, "Occasional Paper No. 2," mimeograph, December 1987, p. 10.
11 Zielinski, Robert, interview by author, April 19, 1989, Tokyo.
12 Mulford, David, "Needed: Bolder Steps Towards Freer Access," *Financial Times,* November 29, 1989.
13 Hence the Bank of Japan formally instructed the *tanshi* money brokers to let market forces guide short-term money market rates in a November 1988 reform, yet the following year a senior Japanese banker reveals that "someone whispers a certain figure—still. The domestic money market is isolated from the world." On June 28, 1991, Yoshihisa "Little" Tabuchi, Nomura's president, made the extraordinary denunciation that the MOF had known about, and implicitly condoned, the illegal practice of offsetting compensatory payments for selected clients by the Big Four security oligopoly even *after* it had formally ordered Normura to stop paying them in December 1989.
14 "Congress Fails, Will Banks?" *New York Times,* December 2, 1991.
15 Barber, Lionel, "Fed prepares to prop up markets," *Financial Times,* October 16, 1989.

16 Bryant, Ralph C., International Financial Intermediation, Brookings Institution, Washington, D.C., 1987, p. 129; pp. 152–153.

17 The risk-weighted bank capital standard provided, moreover, an exceedingly welcome *nonprice, direct administrative* control instrument at a time when most such direct instruments had been rendered ineffective by the financial revolution.

18 Indeed, the Bundesbank was initially blind to the world systemic risk with the 1974 Herstatt failure and slow to grasp the global dangers of the LDC debt crisis and even the October 1987 stock market crash.

19 Volcker, Paul, interview by author, November 21, 1989, Princeton.

CHAPTER TWENTY-FOUR: FINANCIAL DUNKIRK

1 Bush forecast average interest rates on Treasury bills of 8.3 percent and 3.5 percent GNP growth. But T-bills were already nearly 10 percent. The Fed's money growth targets, moreover, were aimed at a growth only half the administration's forecasts.

2 Friedman, Benjamin, "Implications of Increasing Corporate Indebtedness for Monetary Policy," Group of Thirty, New York and London, 1990.

3 Greenspan, Alan, "1991 Monetary Policy Objectives—Testimony," mimeograph, July 16, 1991, p. 7.

4 Lawson, Nigel, "Side Effects of Deregulation," *Financial Times,* January 27, 1992.

5 Drexel's principals played poker by daring the Fed and Treasury not to bail them out. In a significant exception to the unofficial extension of lender of last resort rescues to nearly all major players, they didn't.

6 Author interview of senior Fed official.

7 Murray, Alan, "Democracy Comes to the Central Bank, Curbing Chief's Power," *Wall Street Journal,* April 5, 1991.

8 Jones, David M., "The Contemporary Federal Reserve Policy Process," mimeograph, January 13, 1992, p. 10.

9 Prowse, Michael, "The Credit Crunch Scapegoat," *Financial Times,* November 18, 1991. Based on study by Ben Bernanke of Princeton and Cara Lown of the New York Fed.

10 See Silk, Leonard, "Protecting Banks in a Severe Slump," *New York Times,* November 20, 1990.

11 This view was supported by the fact that credit unions, which were not subject to the Basel standards, also scaled down their ending in similar proportion to banks.

12 Greenspan, Alan, quoted in Rosenbaum, David E., "Greenspan Warns of a Deep Recession If War Lasts," *New York Times,* January 31, 1991.

13 Greenspan, Alan, quoted in Riddell, Peter, "U.S. Banks Increase in Insurance Premiums from Banks," *Financial Times,* September 14, 1990.

14 See Lowell, Bryan, of McKinsey & Co., in *Bankrupt,* Harper Business, 1991.

15 Uchitelle, Louis, "Taxpayer's Role in Bank Bailouts," *New York Times,* August 13, 1991.

16 Lohr, Steve, "One Bank's Expression of Failure: U.S. Presence Sooths the Fearful," *New York Times,* February 18, 1991.

17 Canadian and other foreign banks, however, increased their U.S. market share by continuing to lend through most of the downturn.

18 Interview of senior Fed official.

19 Kindleberger, *The World in Depression,* p. 137. Velocity fell 13 percent vs. normal declines of 4–5 percent in previous depressions.

20 Board of Governors, "FOMC Policy Actions: Meeting Held on November 5, 1990," *77th Annual Report 1990,* Federal Reserve System, Washington, D.C., pp. 148, 149.

21 Leader, "Propping up Japan Inc.," *Financial Times,* March 20, 1992.

22 Prowse, Michael, "Greenspan Faces Monetary Test," *Financial Times,* September 20, 1993.

23 Much of this account is based on Fromson, Brett D., and Knight, Jerry, "The Saving of Citibank," *Washington Post,* May 16, 1993.
24 Earlier in the year Citi had angered regulators by *raising* its dividends in an implicit, morally hazardous "go for broke" strategy to attract capital.
25 The written reprimand—called a "memorandum of understanding"—issued to Citibank by the U.S. Office of the Comptroller in August 1992 was verbally lifted in January 1993.
26 Greenspan, Alan, quoted in Rosenbaum, "Greenspan Warns of a Deep Recession If War Lasts."
27 Greenspan, Alan, "Humphrey-Hawkins Testimony," February 20, 1991, quoted in Jones, David, *The Politics of Money,* New York Institute of Finance, New York, p. 5.
28 The United States in all received $54 billion in cash, materials, and goods as payment for the Gulf War. See Silk, Leonard, "The Broad Impact of the Gulf War," *New York Times,* August 16, 1991.
29 Conversation as recalled by a senior Fed official.
30 Greenspan, Alan, "Testimony before the Committee on the Budget U.S. House of Representatives," mimeograph, February 4, 1992, pp. 3, 4, 5.
31 Kindleberger, *The World in Depression,* p. 138.
32 Bergsten, C. Fred, quoted in "IMF Official Is Optimistic," *New York Times,* April 20, 1992.

CHAPTER TWENTY-FIVE: THE GLOBAL DOWNTURN

1 "You can't do this, I'll lose face," Pöhl had implored the Council, recalls member Helmut Hesse. "I said one thing on Monday in Basel, so we can't change on Thursday. It's against all the rules of international cooperation!" The Bundesbank political intrigue was actually more complex: "That story [the *lände* mutiny] was put out for consumption of *some,*" reveals Norbert Kloten, president of the Land Central Bank in Baden-Württemberg at Stuttgart, implying the complicity of at least "one or two" directorate members. Vice President Helmut Schlesinger, says another Bundesbanker, "didn't mind to be overruled." The "some" were Bonn government leaders. Pöhl had wanted to delay the interest rate hike as a courtesy to Theo Waigel, who had just taken office as finance minister.
2 Pöhl, Karl Otto, quoted in Muehring, Kevin, "The ordeal of Karl Otto Pöhl," *Institutional Investor,* June 1990.
3 Ibid. For a broader, excellent account of GMU, see Marsh, David, *The Most Powerful Bank,* chapter 8.
4 Once again the Länder presidents overrode the call of new President Helmut Schlesinger and Vice President Hans Tietmeyer for a moderate one-quarter-point move.
5 Reporting on the secret deliberations of the Delors committee is based on author interview with members. Nine of the meetings were held on Tuesday afternoons at the conclusion of the central bankers' monthly Basel weekends.
6 Proposed timetables for completion of each of the three stages was removed at the insistence of Bank of England Governor Robin Leigh-Pemberton because Thatcher did not yet accept the principle of monetary union; Leigh-Pemberton's support for the independence conditions for the single central bank and the prerequirement for ERM membership to participate in the process pleasantly surprised committee members. Germany wanted the United Kingdom in the ERM since it felt the United Kingdom was a philosophical ally against France; ironically France wanted the United Kingdom in the ERM as a counterbalance to Germany's economic dominance.
7 Under the Maastricht Treaty, EMU's first stage, during which EMS nations agreed to coordinate monetary policies, began on July 1, 1990. Stage two, scheduled to begin on

January 1, 1994, would make currency realignments an adjustment mechanism of last resort and inaugurate the European Monetary Institute (of undefined responsibilities) that would eventually be transformed into a single central bank. The earliest possible date for the final stage three EMU was January 1, 1997. If a majority of the twelve states met the economic convergence criteria, then a two-thirds majority vote would allow the formation of a single currency and central bank. If those conditions were not met, then the single currency would nonetheless be created on January 1, 1999, and a single central bank six months earlier. At that point countries meeting the convergence criteria would join the monetary union. The convergence criteria highlights were public debt not above 60 percent of GDP; government budget deficit not above 3 percent of GDP; an inflation rate no more than 1.5 percentage points above the three lowest EC inflation countries; long-term government bond interest rate no more than two percentage points higher than that in the three lowest EC inflation countries; two years in the ERM without initiating a devaluation of its currency.

8 Norman, Peter, "Learning from September's currency crisis," *Financial Times*, November 16, 1992; and Brittan, Samuel, "Black Wednesday's Bill," *Financial Times*, November 30, 1992.

9 For still murky reasons influenced in part by France's overwhelming desire to avoid a realignment only a week before its Maastricht Treaty referendum, the chairman of the European Monetary Committee, French Treasury Director Jean-Claude Trichet, did not formally raise the subject when he telephoned other ERM members over the weekend for their approval of a 7 percent lira devaluation. See the excellent account of these events, and those surrounding the September crisis generally, in Norman, Peter, and Barber, Lionel, "The Monetary Tragedy of Errors that Led to Currency Chaos," *Financial Times*, December 11, 1992.

10 The Bundesbank underestimated the severity of the German decline, in part because of distortions in its M3 guidepost.

11 Much of this account comes from Marsh, David, "Faultlines Show in Franco-German Unity," *Financial Times*, December 23, 1993.

12 Norman, Peter, "An Eerie Calm as New Realities of the ERM Sink In," *Financial Times*, August 31, 1993.

13 Eichengreen, Barry, and Wyokosz, "EMS: Time for Some Strong Medicine," *Financial Times*, September 17, 1993.

14 "The Rewards of Independence," *Economist*, January 25, 1992.

15 Mieno, Yasushi, quoted in Lambert, Richard, and Leadbeater, Charles, "Disciplinarian with a Vision," *Financial Times*, June 21, 1993.

16 Kashiwagi, Yusuke, interview by author, February 2, 1990, Tokyo.

17 Contrary to some speculation, he did not ask the Fed to cut U.S. rates.

18 From being a net purchaser of over $25 billion in U.S. Treasury securities in 1989, Japanese investors were net sellers in 1990 by $20 billion.

19 Nor could booming Asian markets that some Japanese had been counting on to "outflank" Japan's dependence on U.S. markets.

20 See Butler, Steven, "Little Cause for Comfort," *Financial Times*, September 1, 1992.

21 Mikuni, Akio, "Behind Japan's Economic Crisis," *New York Times*, February 1, 1993.

22 Kanemaru, Shin, quoted in Wagstyl, Stefan, "Japan Rate Cut Urged by LDP Elder Statesman," *Financial Times*, February 28, 1992.

23 "New Challenges for Mr. Mieno," *Financial Times*, April 1, 1992.

24 Mieno, Yasushi, interview in Wagstyl, Stefan, "Mr. Triple Trouble Fights His Corner," *Financial Times*, February 7, 1992.

25 The huge disparity was due to the market's more comprehensive inclusion criteria and to less rosy projections about economic growth and asset prices.

26 "Dawn Chorus," *The Economist*, April 10, 1993.

27 A collective company was set up by bankers to buy their bad loans and property collateral, with the encouragement of modest MOF tax incentives; MOF also took the

opportunity to rationalize its banking system through forced mergers and entry into some parts of the securities industry.

28 Wakatsuki, Mikio, quoted in Hardey, Quentin, "Japan's Banks, Dogged By Loans Gone Bad, Lose Out on New Ones," *Wall Street Journal,* December 27, 1993.

29 Friedman, Milton, *Newsweek,* May 25, 1970, p. 78. Quoted in Kindleberger, Charles P., *The World in Depression 1929–1939,* University of California Press, Berkeley and Los Angeles, 1973, p. 120.

30 Mieno, Yasushi, quoted in Thomson, Robert, "Japan's Banks Count the Cost of Bad Loans," *Financial Times,* May 28, 1993.

31 Thurow, Lester, "Why U.S. Locomotive Should Decouple," *Financial Times,* March 10, 1993.

32 With U.S. real long-term interest rates at low 2 percent levels, global capital had begun to flood out of the United States toward the 4 percent real rates available abroad in 1993. The rise in U.S. long-bond rates, and downward pressure on the dollar, accelerated visibly in February 1994, when bond markets took fright that the Greenspan Fed's first effort to raise interest rates would be insufficient to prevent inflation from reemerging. Japanese investors abruptly became net dollar investment sellers when the Clinton administration adopted dollar talk-down language at the failure of bilateral U.S.-Japanese trade talks to produce satisfactory results. In contrast with 1987, the unwillingness or inability of the Japanese Establishment to use its administrative guidance to arrest the flows caused the pressures on dollar currency and U.S. bond markets to build. Recognizing the adverse impact on bond markets, the Clinton government desisted from its jawboning campaigns against Japan and the Fed's tightening policy. A new dollar attack erupted in mid-June following a Bundesbank announcement that the German recession was ending and, with it, its easing stance. At that point real U.S. interest rates (based on likely future inflation) were too low to attract sufficient world savings to finance the U.S.'s huge and growing external deficits. The currency attacks, and mirror-opposite bond market reactions, resumed in mid-July, when the G7 head of state economic summit in Naples, Italy, failed to produce any concerted dollar defense.

33 "Transcript of First TV Debate Among Bush, Clinton, and Perot," *New York Times,* October 12, 1992.

CHAPTER TWENTY-SIX: INDEPENDENCE AND ACCOUNTABILITY

1 Melcher, John, in Clark Jr., Lindley H., "The Federal Reserve May Be Living Outside the Law," *Wall Street Journal,* July 22, 1986.

2 "If the president is competent enough to have his finger on the nuclear button, he is competent enough to control the money supply," argued Lester Thurow in the *Zero-Sum Solution.* "If the Congress is competent enough to control taxes and expenditures, it is competent enough to approve changes in the rate of growth of the money supply," quoted in Gordon, David, "Reining In on the Federal Reserve," *Los Angeles Times,* September 30, 1986.

3 Management experts add further that bureaucracies function best when they have a single mission.

4 Lawson, Nigel, in *The View from Number 11,* Doubleday: New York, London, Toronto, Sydney, Auckland, 1993, p. 868.

5 Lawson, Nigel, quoted in Jay, Peter, "Ardent Author of a Revolution," *Financial Times,* November 6, 1992.

6 Gordon, David, "Reining In on the Federal Reserve," *Los Angeles Times,* September 30, 1986.

7 A recent Fed study provides evidence suggesting that low inflation may also promote faster productivity growth.

8 See Alesina, A; and Summers, L., "Central Bank Independence and Macroeconomic

Performance: Some Comparative Evidence," Harvard Institute of Economic Research Discussion Paper 1,496, cited in Balls, Edward, "A (Modest) Case for an Independent Central Bank," *Financial Times,* October 28, 1991. Causality was less clear: did independence produce lower inflation, or was it an expression of a political economic climate that produced the low inflation result? Common sense suggested it was a mutually reinforcing combination of both.

9 Lawson, Nigel, *The View from No. 11,* p. 868.

10 Venezuela felt the financial sting of disappointing the "court of world savings" in April 1994, when a new government's political pressure on the newly independent central bank prompted the resignation of its chief, Ruth de Krivoy. Within seven business days the bolivar fell 9.6 percent, the stock market fell 4.4 percent, and the nation's foreign exchange reserves plunged. The country was left in economic and political crisis.

11 Lawson, Nigel, *The View from No. 11,* p. 871.

12 Only in the United States, with its huge, international dollar-based money supply, and to a lesser degree Japan, could the impact of international capital movements on the money supply be sterilized effectively.

13 With the permutations of financial innovation, and outright fraud, outracing external regulatory capacities, those enhanced powers increasingly had to include standardized and minimum disclosure requirements and vetting of market self-regulatory arrangements. The Reserve Bank of New Zealand took the lead in experimenting with a system of increased market self-regulation by fuller disclosure, which transformed the central bank's role from onerous hands-on regulation to more indirect oversight.

14 A major reason for this anomaly was that political awareness of the strict policy constraints imposed by global capital was least developed in the United States because of its greater international insulation from the dollar's world money role and the hugeness of its domestic economy.

15 Sarbanes, Paul, "Sarbannes and Hamilton Introduce Bills to Make Fed Board Solely Responsible for Monetary Policy," Joint Economic Committee Press Release, August 1, 1991. Sarbannes cosponsored this proposal with Senate Banking Committee Chairman Donald Riegle (D-Mich.). It was supported by influential Senator Jim Sasser (D-Tenn.) and Representatives Lee Hamilton (D-Ind.) and David Obey (D-Wisc.). House Banking Committee Chairman Henry Gonzalez (D-Tex.), longtime populist Fed critic, championed even more radical restrictions on the Fed's autonomy.

16 Riegle, Donald, cited in Prowse, Michael, "A Subtle Battle of Monetary Wills," *Financial Times,* March 15, 1993.

17 Volcker, Paul, in Murray, Alan, "Fed Banks' President Hold Private Positions But Major Public Role," *Wall Street Journal,* August 1, 1991.

18 Interview of Delors committee member.

19 The Greenspan Fed came closest to publicly annunciating the seat-of-the-pants guide that many central bankers actually used, namely tightening up when economic growth seemed to exceed its estimate of "potential growth" on a regular basis. But "potential growth" was an inherently subjective, and politically explosive, judgment. Some experts advocated nominal GNP growth as a target central bankers could reasonably hope to achieve. Other, more ambitious experts favored an actual inflation target, even though inflation was caused by more than simply the money supply growth that central bankers could control.

20 This was known colloquially as the "Tobin tax," after its originator, Yale Professor James Tobin.

21 Such a proposal has been made by Professor Charles Wyplosz of INSEAD business school and Professor Barry Eichengreen of the University of California at Berkeley.

Selected
Bibliography

NOTE ON SOURCES

Interviews with some 250 principals and experts provided the main source material for this book. Supporting published sources included several thousand newspaper and magazine articles, speeches, conference transcripts, and governmental reports and testimony, as well as a prodigious number of published and unpublished technical papers, studies, and annual and special reports produced by the major national central banks, university academics, the International Monetary Fund, the Bank for International Settlements, the O.E.C.D., the Group of Thirty, private nonprofit think tanks, and the research staff of private financial market institutions. Their sheer volume makes it unreasonable to list them all. The main journalistic sources were the *Financial Times, Wall Street Journal, The Economist, New York Times, Washington Post, Institutional Investor, Euromoney, IMF Survey,* and *International Economy.*

SUGGESTED READING

With a few exceptions, the following list is limited to sources of at least essay depth that are readily accessible to general readers and that the author found to be especially enlightening. In no sense does it purport to be a comprehensive survey of leading literature in the field. For readers seeking a more academic understanding of international monetary economic issues, the author recommends researching the citations, among others, of Bergsten, Branson, Bryant, Cooper, Dornbusch, Eichengreen, Frankel, Giovannini, Goodhart, Hale, Kindleberger, Koo, McKinnon, Shigehara, R. Solomon, Thygesen, Triffen, Williamson, and Yoshitomi. Senior central bankers whose speeches and papers the author has often found enlightening include Blunden, Corrigan, Gleske, Greenspan, Hoffmeyer, Johnson, Lamfalussy, Pöhl, Schlesinger, Tietmeyer, Volcker, and Wallich. The annual Per Jacobsson lectures, among speeches at other key fora such as the International Monetary Conference and England's Overseas Bankers club dinner, are also often especially rewarding.

Akhtar, M.A., "Adjustment of U.S. External Imbalances," *Federal Reserve Bank of New York Seventy-fourth Annual Report,* New York, 1988.

Bagehot, Walter, *Lombard Street,* Westport, Connecticut: Hyperion, 1979. Reprint of 1962 edition, Homewood, Illinois: Richard D. Irwin Inc.

Bank for International Settlements, *Annual Reports,* Basel. Reports from 1 April 1978 through 13 June 1994 (49th–64th Annual Report).

Bergsten, C. Fred, "Economic Imbalances and World Politics," *Foreign Affairs,* Spring 1987, pp. 770–94.

Bernstein, Peter L., *A Primer on Money, Banking and Gold,* second edition, New York: Random House, 1965, 1968.

Boyle, Andrew, *Montagu Norman,* New York: Weybright and Talley, 1967.

Brady, Nicholas F., chairman, *Report of the Presidential Task Force on Market Mechanisms,* Washington D.C.: U.S. Government Printing Office, January 1988.

Braudel, Fernand, *Afterthoughts on Material Civilization and Capitalism,* Baltimore and London: Johns Hopkins University Press, 1977.

Braudel, Fernand, *Civilization and Capitalism,* Volumes 1, 2, 3, New York, Cambridge, Philadelphia, San Francisco, London, Mexico City, Sao Paulo, Singapore, Sydney: Harper & Row, 1979.

Bryant, Ralph C., *International Financial Intermediation,* Washington, D.C.: Brookings Institution, 1987.

Burns, Arthur F., *The Anguish of Central Banking,* Per Jacobsson Lecture, Per Jacobsson Foundation, September 30, 1979.

Chandler, Lester V., *Benjamin Strong, Central Banker,* U.S.A.: Brookings Institution, 1958.

Ciocca, Pierluigi, ed., *Money and the Economy: Central Bankers' Views,* New York: St. Martin's Press, 1983, 1987.

Clarke, Stephen V.O., *Central Bank Cooperation 1924–31,* Federal Reserve Bank of New York, 1967.

Cohen, Benjamin J., *In Whose Interest?* New Haven and London: Yale University Press, 1986.

Cooke, Peter, "International Convergence of Capital Adequacy Measurement and Standards," an essay prepared for publication as a chapter in a book, mimeo.

Coombs, Charles, *The Arena of International Finance,* New York: John Wiley, 1976.

Corrigan, E. Gerald, *Financial Market Structure: A Longer View,* New York: Federal Reserve Bank of New York, January 1987.

Crook, Clive, "The Limits to Cooperation," Survey of the World Economy, *The Economist,* September 26, 1987.

Delamaide, Darrell, *Debt Shock,* Garden City: Anchor Books, 1985.

Destler, I.M., and Henning, C. Randall, *Dollar Politics,* Washington, D.C.: Institute for International Economics, 1989.

Drucker, Peter F., *Post-Capitalist Society,* New York: HarperBusiness, 1993.

Drucker, Peter F., "The Changed World Economy," *Foreign Affairs,* Spring 1986.

Emminger, Otmar, *Dollar, D-Mark Währungskrisen,* Stuttgart: Deutsche Verlags-Anstalt, 1986.

Emmott, Bill, *The Sun Also Sets,* New York: Times Books, 1989.

Fay, Stephen, *Portrait of an Old Lady,* New York: Viking, 1987.

Feldstein, Martin, ed., *International Economic Cooperation, NBER Summary Report,* Cambridge, Massachusetts: National Bureau of Economic Research, April 1987.

Frankel, Jeffrey, "Flexible Exchange Rates: Experience versus Theory," *The Journal of Portfolio Management,* Winter 1989.

Friedman, Benjamin, *Implications of Increasing Corporate Indebtedness for Monetary Policy,* New York and London: Group of Thirty, 1990.

Friedman, Milton, *Bright Promises, Dismal Performance,* San Diego and New York: Harcourt Brace Jovanovich, 1983.

Funabashi, Yoichi, "Japan and the New World Order," *Foreign Affairs,* Winter 1991/92.

Funabashi, Yoichi, *Managing the Dollar: From the Plaza to the Louvre,* Washington, D.C.: Institute for International Economics, 1988.

Galbraith, John Kenneth, *The Great Crash 1929,* Boston: Houghton Mifflin, 1954, 1955, 1961.

Galbraith, John Kenneth, *Money,* United States and Canada: Bantam Books, 1975, 1976.

Gilpin, Robert, *The Political Economy of International Relations,* Princeton, New Jersey: Princeton University Press, 1987.

Goodhart, Charles, *The Evolution of Central Banks,* Cambridge, Massachusetts, and London: MIT Press, 1988.

Goodhart, Charles, "Why Do We Need a Central Bank?" *Temi di discussione del Servizio Studi della Banca d'Italia,* N. 57, January 1986 mimeo.

Greider, William, *Secrets of the Temple,* New York: Simon & Schuster, 1987.

Group of Thirty, *The Problem of Exchange Rates, A Policy Statement,* New York: Group of Thirty, 1982.

Harrod, Roy, *The Life of John Maynard Keynes,* New York and London: W. W. Norton, 1951.

Hawtrey, R. G., *The Art of Central Banking,* London: Frank Cass, 1962.

Hearing before the Subcommittee on Financial Institutions Supervision, Regulation and Insurance of the Committee on Banking, Finance and Urban Affairs, House of Representatives, *Globalization of Financial Markets and Related International Banking and Supervision Issues,* Serial No. 100–31, Washington, D.C.: U.S. Government Printing Office, July 30, 1987.

Heilbroner, Robert L., *The Nature and Logic of Capitalism,* New York and London: W. W. Norton, 1985.

Heilbroner, Robert L., *The Worldly Philosophers,* 5th edition, New York: Touchstone/ Simon & Schuster, 1953, 1980.

Hoffmann, Stanley, "Goodbye to a United Europe?" *New York Review of Books,* May 27, 1993.

Hormats, Robert D., "The World Economy Under Stress," *Foreign Affairs,* America and the World Economy, 1985.

Jacobsson, Erin E., *A Life for Sound Money,* Per Jacobsson Lecture, Oxford: Clarendon Press, 1979.

Jones, David M., *Fed Watching and Interest Rate Projections,* second edition, New York: New York Institute of Finance, 1989.

Jones, David M., *The Politics of Money,* New York: New York Institute of Finance, 1991.

Kashiwagi, Yusuke, *The Emergence of Global Finance,* Per Jacobsson Lecture, Per Jacobsson Foundation, September 28, 1986.

Kenen, Peter B., *Managing Exchange Rates,* New York: Council of Foreign Relations Press for the Royal Institute of International Affairs, 1988.

Kettl, Donald F., *Leadership at the Fed,* New Haven and London: Yale University Press, 1986.

Kindleberger, Charles P., *Manias, Panics and Crashes,* New York: Basic Books, 1978.

Kindleberger, Charles P., *The International Economic Order,* Cambridge, Massachusetts: MIT Press, 1988.

Kindleberger, Charles P., *The World in Depression 1929–1939,* Berkeley and Los Angeles: University of California Press, 1973.

Kraft, Joseph, *The Mexican Rescue,* New York: Group of Thirty, 1984.

Krugman, Paul, "Competitiveness: A Dangerous Obsession," *Foreign Affairs,* March/ April 1994.

Lamfalussy, Alexandre, "Is Change Our Ally?" *The Banker,* September 1986.

Lawson, Nigel, *The View from No. 11,* New York: Doubleday, 1993.

Lever, Harold, and Huhne, Christopher, *Debt and Danger,* Boston and New York: Atlantic Monthly Press, 1985, 1986.

Makin, John H., *The Global Debt Crisis*, New York: Basic Books, 1984.

Marris, Stephen, *Deficits and the Dollar*, updated edition, Washington, D.C.: Institute for International Economics, 1987.

Marsh, David, *The Most Powerful Bank*, New York: Times Books, 1992.

Mayer, Martin, *The Fate of the Dollar*, New York: Times Books, 1980.

Meulendyke, Ann-Marie, *U.S. Monetary Policy and Financial Markets*, New York: Federal Reserve Bank of New York, 1989.

Mendelsohn, M. S., *Money on the Move*, New York: McGraw-Hill, 1980.

Metz, Tim, *Black Monday*, New York: William Morrow, 1988.

Moffitt, Michael, *The World's Money*, New York: Touchstone/Simon & Schuster, 1983.

Morse, Jeremy, *Do We Know Where We're Going?* Per Jacobsson Lecture, Per Jacobsson Foundation, October 6, 1985.

Murphy, R. Taggart, "Power Without Purpose: The Crisis of Japan's Global Financial Dominance," *Harvard Business Review,* March/April 1989.

Neikirk, William R., *Volcker*, New York: Congdon & Weed, 1987.

Ogata, Shijuro, Cooper, Richard N., Schulmann, Horst, *International Financial Integration: The Policy Challenges*—A task force report to the Trilateral Commission, New York, Tokyo, Paris: The Trilateral Commission, 1989.

Padoa-Schioppa, Tommaso, *Toward a New Adjustable Peg?* Per Jacobsson Lecture, Per Jacobsson Foundation, June 12, 1988.

Pennant-Rea, Rupert, "Everybody's Business," International Monetary Reform Survey, *The Economist,* October 5, 1985.

Pennant-Rea, Rupert, "Reluctantly at the Helm," Central Banking Survey, *The Economist,* September 22, 1984.

Peterson, Peter G., *Economic Nationalism and International Interdependence*, Per Jacobsson Lecture, Per Jacobsson Foundation, September 23, 1984.

Posen, Adam S., "Why Central Bank Independence Does Not Cause Low Inflation," *Central Banking*, Volume IV, No. 2, Autumn 1993.

Reid, Margaret, *All-Change in the City*, Houndsmills, Basingstoke, Hampshire, and London: Macmillan Press, 1988.

Sampson, Anthony, *The Money Lenders*, U.S.A.: Penguin, 1983.

Silk, Leonard, "Dangers of Slow Growth," *Foreign Affairs,* America and the World, 1992/93.

Solomon, Anthony, *The Dollar, Debt, and the Trade Deficit*, New York and London: New York University Press, 1987.

Solomon, Robert, *The International Monetary System 1945–1976*, New York, Hagerstown, San Francisco, London: Harper & Row, 1977.

Solomon, Steven, "Forum on The Future," *Best of Business Quarterly,* Volume 8, No. 1, Spring 1986.

Spero, Joan, *The Failure of Franklin National Bank*, New York: Columbia University Press, 1980.

Sprague, Irvine H., *Bailout*, New York: Basic Books, 1986.

Stein, Herbert, *Presidential Economics,* New York: Touchstone/Simon & Schuster, 1984, 1985.

Stockman, David A., *The Triumph of Politics*, New York: Avon Books, 1986, 1987.

Suzuki, Yoshio, *Japan's Economic Performance and International Role*, Japan: University of Tokyo Press, 1989.

The Editors of *Institutional Investor, The Way It Was: An Oral History of Finance 1967–1987*, New York: William Morrow, 1988.

van Wolferen, Karel, *The Enigma of Japanese Power*, London: Macmillan, 1989.

van Wolferen, Karel, "The Japan Problem," *Foreign Affairs,* Winter 1986–1987, pp. 288–303.

Volcker, Paul, "The Political Economy of the Dollar," *Federal Reserve Bank of New York Quarterly Review,* Winter 1978–79.

Volcker, Paul, "The Triumph of Central Banking?" Per Jacobssen Lecture, September 23, 1990, mimeo.

Volcker, Paul, and Toyoo Gyohten, *Changing Fortunes*, New York and Toronto: Times Books, 1992.

Walter, Norbert, "Development of a New Economic Policy Paradigm in West Germany in the '80s?" mimeo of paper to be published in *Rivista di Politica Economica*, April 11, 1989.

Wolfson, Martin H., *Financial Crises*, Armonk and London: M. E. Sharpe, 1986.

Wriston, Walter B., *Risk and Other Four-Letter Words,* New York: Harper & Row, 1986.

Acronyms
and Abbreviations

BIS	Bank for International Settlements
BOE	Bank of England
BP	British Petroleum
BOJ	Bank of Japan
CBOE	Chicago Board Options Exchange
CBOT	Chicago Board of Trade
CD	Certificate of Deposit
CEA	Council of Economic Advisers
CFTC	Commodity Futures Trading Commission
CHIPS	Clearinghouse Interbank Payment System
CME	Chicago Mercantile Exchange
DM	Deutsche Mark
EC	European Community
Ecu	European currency unit
EMS	European Monetary System
ERM	Exchange Rate Mechanism
EMU	Economic and Monetary Union (Europe)
FDIC	Federal Deposit Insurance Corporation
Fed	Federal Reserve System
FOMC	Federal Open Market Committee
GDP	Gross Domestic Product
GNP	Gross National Product
G5	Group of Five
G7	Group of Seven
G10	Group of Ten
IBJ	Industrial Bank of Japan
ILSA	International Lending Supervision Act
IMC	International Monetary Conference
IMF	International Monetary Fund
LDC	Less developed countries
LDP	Liberal Democratic Party (Japan)
Libor	London Interbank Offered Rate
Merc	Chicago Mercantile Exchange
MOF	Ministry of Finance (Japan)
MYRA	Multiyear Restructuring Agreement
NTT	Nippon Telegraph and Telephone
NYSE	New York Stock Exchange
OCC	Options Clearing Corporation
O.E.C.D.	Organization for Economic Cooperation and Development
ODR	Official Discount Rate (Japan)
OPEC	Organization of Petroleum Exporting Countries
Repo	Repurchase agreement
SEC	Securities and Exchange Commission

Persons Interviewed

The reporting for this book was primarily based on interviews, many on multiple occasions, with some 250 individuals. The text respects the anonymity of the minority who cooperated on a nonattribution basis. On the other hand, there was not room in the text to cite everyone who provided helpful information. In the interest of documentary completeness, an alphabetical list of all persons interviewed follows.*

M. Akbar Akhtar, assistant director of research Federal Reserve Bank of New York
Wayne Angell, governor Federal Reserve Board of Governors
Stephen Axilrod, staff director for monetary policy at the Federal Reserve Board
Paolo Baffi, governor of the Bank of Italy
Norman Bailey, senior director at the Reagan National Security Council
Howard Baker, U.S. senator, Reagan White House chief of staff
Peter Bakstansky, vice president of public information Federal Reserve Bank of New York
Edouard Balladur, French finance minister, prime minister
Michael Beales, chief currency dealer at the Bank of England, chief manager of European financial markets at Westpac Banking
Jürgen Becker, Bundesbank director, supervision department
Andrew Bevan, first vice president Drexel Burnham Lambert (London)
Robert Binney, senior vice president Chase Manhattan Bank (London)
George Blunden, deputy governor of the Bank of England
Paul Blustein, *Washington Post*
Horst Bockelmann, head of monetary and economic department at the Bank for International Studies
Michael Bradfield, chief counsel Federal Reserve Board
William Branson, professor of economics and international affairs at Princeton University's Woodrow Wilson School
Chip Brown, Bankers Trust
Ralph Bryant, senior fellow at the Brookings Institution
Hubert Calloud, director, cabinet of the governor Bank of France
Guido Carli, governor of the Bank of Italy, Italian treasury minister
Nigel Carter, personal assistant to IMF managing director, manager at Bank of England financial division
Terrence Checki, vice president Foreign Relations department Federal Reserve Bank of New York

*Positions are listed according to those that are most germane to the book. If more than one position is listed, the most recent comes last.

Carlo Azeglio Ciampi, governor of the Bank of Italy, later Italian prime minister
Pierluigi Ciocca, central manager for central bank operations Bank of Italy
Peter Cooke, chairman of the G10 Committee on Banking Regulations and Supervisory Practices and Bank of England associate director
C. Todd Conover, comptroller of the currency in the Reagan Administration
E. Gerald Corrigan, president of the Federal Reserve Bank of New York
Kenneth Courtis, senior economist DB Capital Markets (Asia) Ltd
Joseph Coyne, director of public information Federal Reserve Board
Dan Crippen, economics aide to White House chief of staff Howard Baker
Sam Cross, executive vice president foreign group Federal Reserve Bank of New York
John Crow, governor of the Bank of Canada
Charles Dallara, assistant U.S. treasury secretary
Michael Dealtry, deputy head of monetary and economic department, Bank for International Settlements
Renaud de la Genière, governor of the Bank of France in early 1980s
Darrell Delamaide, freelance journalist, author of *Debt Shock*
Jacques de Larosière, IMF managing director, governor of the Bank of France
Andre de Lattre, deputy governor Bank of France
Lamberto Dini, deputy governor Bank of Italy, later Italian Treasury Secretary, later Prime Minister
Rudiger Dornbusch, professor at Massachusetts Institute of Technology
Hermann-Josef Dudler, Bundesbank director monetary policy department
Mark Farrington, economist MMS International Tokyo
David Finch, IMF director of exchange and trade relations 1982 to 1987
Mark Fitzsimmons, foreign exchange sales manager Morgan Stanley
Werner Flandorffer, German economics ministry
Charles Freeland, Basel Supervisors' Committee staff, Bank for International Settlements
Heiner Flassbeck, head of Deutsches Institute für Wirtschaftsforschung (DIW)
Tsuneo Fujita, director general, securities bureau of the Japanese ministry of finance
Yoichi Funabashi, economics editor *Asahi Shimbun*, author of *Managing the Dollar*
Alberto Giovannini, associate professor Columbia School of Business
Leonhard Gleske, member of directorate of Bundesbank
Charles Goodhart, professor, London School of Economics
George Gould, undersecretary for finance, U.S. Treasury
Margaret Greene, head of foreign exchange trading, senior vice president Federal Reserve Bank of New York
Alan Greenspan, chairman Federal Reserve Board
Wilfried Guth, speaker of managing board, Deutsche Bank
Toyoo Gyohten, Japanese finance vice minister for international affairs
R. T. P. Hall, assistant general manager Bank for International Settlements
Gert Haller, state secretary German ministry of finance
Richard Hanson, editor and publisher *Japan Financial Report*
Hellmut Hartmann, head of public affairs International Monetary Fund
Jon Hartzell, financial attaché U.S. Treasury (Tokyo)
Robert Heilbroner, professor at New School for Social Research
Robert Heller, governor at Federal Reserve Board
C. Randall Henning, research associate Institute for International Economics
Jesus Silva Herzog, finance minister of Mexico
Helmut Hesse, Bundesbank central bank council member, Land central bank president in Lower Saxony
Erik Hoffmeyer, chairman Denmark National Bank
Yusuke Horiguchi, economist International Monetary Fund
Robert Hormats, vice chairman Goldman Sachs International

J. Paul Horne, managing director Smith Barney (Paris)
Takashi Hosomi, Japanese vice minister of finance for international affairs
Friederich Hoyos, Credit Suisse First Boston (Frankfurt)
Herbert Kazmierzak, chairman of Hessische Landesbank (Frankfurt)
Kengo Inoue, economist Bank of Japan
Masahiko Ishizuka, editor *The Japan Economic Journal*
Paul Jansen, special assistant to German finance minister
Karen Johnson, Federal Reserve Board, assistant director international finance division
Manuel Johnson Jr., former vice chairman Federal Reserve Board of Governors
Robert Johnson, chief economist Senate Banking committee, managing director at Quantum Fund
David Jones, chief economist Aubrey G. Lanston & Co. Inc.
Yusuke Kashiwagi, chairman Bank of Tokyo
Yoshiaki Kaneko, Japanese Ministry of Finance, managing director Tokyo stock exchange
Takashi Kato, Ministry of Finance, director general Yamaichi Research Institute
Peter Kenen, professor of economics and international finance Princeton University
Richard Ketchum, Securities and Exchange Commission director of market regulation division
Peter Kilborn, *New York Times*
Shigyo Kimura, manager capital market division, Bank of Japan
Norbert Kloten, Bundesbank central bank council member, president of Land central bank in Baden-Württemberg
Michael Kogon, vice director Bank for International Settlements
Horst Köhler, state secretary German ministry of finance
Donald Kohn, director of division of monetary affairs Federal Reserve Board
Richard Koo, senior economist Nomura Research Institute
Manfred Körber, head of information division Bundesbank
Willem Kortekaas, Algemene Bank Nederland N.V. general manager (Tokyo)
Doug Kruse, U.S. Treasury department
Isao Kubota, Japanese ministry of finance, director of foreign exchange and money market division of the international finance bureau
Yoh Kurosawa, president Industrial Bank of Japan
Manfred Lahnstein, German finance minister
Alexandre Lamfalussy, general manager Bank for International Settlements
Nigel Lawson, U.K. Chancellor of the Exchequer
Daniel Lebegue, director of French treasury, ministry of finance
Robin Leigh-Pemberton, governor of the Bank of England
Fritz Leutwiler, president Swiss National Bank
Geoffrey Littler, second permanent secretary of the U.K. Treasury
Leslie Lipschitz, economist International Monetary Fund
Anthony Loehnis, Bank of England executive director for overseas
Bonnie Loopesko, economist international finance division Federal Reserve Board
John Loughran, head of J. P. Morgan Securities Asia Ltd. (Tokyo)
Charles Lucas, head of international capital markets division, Federal Reserve Bank of New York
David Mars, economist S. G. Warburg (London)
Donato Maschiandaro, London School of Economics
Ranier Masera, Bank of Italy and chairman of Istituto Mobiliare Italiano
Rei Masunaga, Bank of Japan director of foreign department
Michiya Matsukawa, Ministry of Finance, senior adviser to the president Nikko Securities Co. Ltd.
James McGroarty, vice president Discount Corporation of New York
Ronald McKinnon, Stanford University

James McGroarty, vice president Discount Corporation of New York
Ronald McKinnon, Stanford University
Kenneth McLean, chief of staff U.S. Senate Banking Committee
R. T. (Tim) McNamar, U.S. deputy treasury secretary
Yasushi Mieno, governor Bank of Japan
Akio Mikuni, president Mikuni & Co.
Paolo Miurin, manager governor's secretariat Bank of Italy
Richard Smith, *International Herald Tribune*
Gianpietro Morelli, secretary general Bank for International Settlements
Jeremy Morse, chairman Lloyds Bank Plc
Alfred Mudge, attorney Shearman & Sterling
David Mulford, U.S. Treasury undersecretary for international affairs
Takashi Murakami, BOJ deputy chief representative in the Americas (New York)
R. Taggert Murphy, Chase Manhattan Limited in Tokyo
Bill Milam, U.S. assistant deputy undersecretary of state for international finance and de-
     velopment
Yuichiro Nagatomi, president institute of fiscal and monetary policy at Japan's ministry
     of finance
Kaneo Nakamura, president Industrial Bank of Japan
Akira Nambara, executive director Bank of Japan
Graham Newman, International Monetary Fund
Wilhelm Nölling, Bundesbank central bank council member and president of the Land
     Central Bank in Freien and Hansetadt
Peter Norman, *Financial Times*
Tomomitsu Oba, Vice Minister for International Affairs Japanese ministry of finance
Shijuro Ogata, Bank of Japan deputy governor for international relations
Takeshi Ohta, Bank of Japan deputy governor for international relations
Hirohiko Okumura, chief economist Nomura Research Institute, Ltd.
James Oltman, first vice president Federal Reserve Bank of New York
Klaus Päben, Bundesbank head representative Tokyo office
Scott E. Pardee, chairman Yamaichi International, ex-head of foreign exchange trading
     Federal Reserve System
Gustavo Petriocioli, finance minister of Mexico, Mexican ambassador to the U.S.
Dr. Pieske, German finance ministry
Samuel Pizer, consultant to the managing director of the IMF
Karl Otto Pöhl, former president of the Bundesbank
Reinhard Pohl, Deutsches Institute für Wirtschaftsforschung (DIW)
Ignacio Ponce de Leon, assistant vice president Bankers Trust
Lewis Preston, chairman J. P. Morgan, later president of the World Bank
Larry Promisel, senior associate director of the division of international finance, Federal
     Reserve Board
William Proxmire, U.S. senator
Brian Quinn, executive director in charge of supervision Bank of England
Ulrich Ramm, chief economist Commerzbank
S. Waite Rawls III, vice chairman Continental Illinois
Robert Raymond, director general of studies Bank of France and chairman of Basel mon-
     etary committee
Donald Regan, U.S. Treasury Secretary and White House chief of staff
William Rhodes, vice chairman Citicorp
Gordon Richardson, governor of the Bank of England
Kurt Richebacher, chief economist Dresdner Bank
Wolfgang Rieke, head of international department Bundesbank
Steven Roberts, special assistant to Federal Reserve Board chairman Volcker 1983–1987

Massimo Russo, head of European division International Monetary Fund
Fabrizio Saccomanni, head of the foreign department Bank of Italy
Takehiro Sagami, Japanese vice minister of finance for international affairs
Eisuke Sakakibara, director, government debt division, finance bureau, Japanese ministry
of finance
Mario Sarcinelli, director general of Italian Treasury
Nicholas Sargen, director of research Salomon Brothers
Tomasso Padoa-Schioppa, vice director general Bank of Italy
Louis Schirano, Bankers Trust and First Interstate
Helmut Schlesinger, vice president and president of the Bundesbank
Helmut Schmidt, chancellor German Federal Republic
Kermit Schoenholtz, vice president bond market research Salomon Brothers Asia Ltd
Russell Scholl, chief of private capital branch of U.S. balance of payments division, U.S.
Bureau of Economic Analysis
Peter-W. Schlüter, director at Bundesbank, international department
Stephan Schünberg, head representative Bundesbank office in New York
Horst Seidler, head of Deutsches Institute für Wirtschaftsforschung (DIW)
Walter Seipp, chairman Commerzbank
Takehiko Sekine, bank supervision department of foreign department, Bank of Japan
Henny Sender, Asia bureau chief, *Institutional Investor*
Jeffrey Shafer, deputy director general economics branch O.E.C.D., assistant secretary
for international U.S. Treasury
Kumiharu Shigehara, chief economist O.E.C.D.
Masaaki Shirakawa, manager domestic research division, research and statistics depart-
ment Bank of Japan
Horst Schulmann, managing director Institute for International Finance
George Shultz, U.S. secretary of state
Olaf Sivert, chairman German panel of experts 1976–1985, professor University of Saarbrüken
Diethard Simmert, senior vice president Commerzbank
Ralph Smith, assistant director international finance division Federal Reserve Board
Richard Smith, *International Herald Tribune*
Anthony Solomon, undersecretary of the U.S. Treasury for monetary affairs and presi-
dent of Federal Reserve Bank of New York
Robert Solomon, guest scholar Brookings Institution
Neal Soss, special assistant to Federal Reserve chairman Volcker 1982–1983, chief econo-
mist First Boston
J. Andrew Spindler, vice president banking studies and analysis, Federal Reserve Bank of
New York
Beryl Sprinkel, undersecretary of the U.S. Treasury for monetary affairs, chairman White
House council of economic advisers
William Sterling, manager of international economics, Merrill Lynch Capital Markets
Gerhard Stoltenberg, German minister of finance
Yoshio Suzuki, executive director Bank of Japan
Setsuya Tabuchi, chairman Nomura Securities Co.
William Taylor, director division of banking supervision and regulation, Federal Reserve
Board
Yoshio Terasawa, head of international business at Nomura Securities
Stephen Thieke, executive vice president Federal Reserve Bank of New York
Christopher Thompson, secretary, Basel Supervisors' Committee, Bank for International
Settlements
Niels Thygesen, professor of economics, University of Copenhagen
Hans Tietmeyer, state secretary German finance ministry, president of the Bundesbank
Jean-Claude Trichet, director of French treasury, governor of the Bank of France

Edwin Truman, director, division of international finance, Federal Reserve Board
Giuseppe Tullio, economist Bank of Italy
Paul Volcker, chairman Federal Reserve Board
Norbert Walter, chief economist Deutsche Bank
Tetsuya Tamura, chief representative in Europe (London), and director, policy planning department Bank of Japan
Philip Warland, head of press department, Bank of England
Adolph Joseph Warner, economist Deutsche Bank (New York)
Mikio Wakatsuki, deputy governor for international relations Bank of Japan
Tatsuru Watanabe, president Accari/Foote, Cone & Belding (Tokyo)
Maxwell Watson, chief of international capital markets division of the exchange and trade relations department, International Monetary Fund
Manfred Weber, head of the office of the deputy governor, Bundesbank
Helene Williamson, Bankers Trust
Karel van Wolferen, author of *The Enigma of Japanese Power*
Walter Wriston, chairman Citicorp
Izumi Yamashita, chief representative of Frankfurt office, Bank of Japan
Jai Yang, J. P. Morgan
Edwin Yeo, Volcker friend and adviser
Masaru Yoshitomi, director general Japanese Economic Planning Agency
Robert Zielinski, analyst Jardine Fleming Securities, Tokyo branch

Index

savings and loan crisis, 44, 52–53, 457,
526n
moral hazard dilemma and, 58
Schacht, Hjalmar, 545n
Schadrack, Fred, 418
Schlecht, Otto, 382
Schlesinger, Helmut, 30, 102–3, 140, 318,
331, 364, 366, 367, 373, 382, 405,
477–78, 533n, 557n
Bundesbank and, 284–85
1992 currency crisis and, 477–78
monetary policy of, 284–85
Schmidt, Helmut, 27, 28, 43, 120, 140, 197,
234, 295, 497, 533n, 537n, 538n,
545n, 546n
EMS and, 282
Franco-German issue proposal of,
285–86
Schröder Munchmeyer Hengst (SMH),
531n, 563n–64n
Schulmann, Horst, 235
Schultze, Charles, 140, 141
Schumer, Charles, 429
Seattle First National Bank, 159, 160
Second Bank of the United States, 163
Securities and Exchange Commission
(SEC), 21, 68, 74, 75, 77, 97, 98
Seger, Martha, 309
Seidman, William, 543n
Seipp, Walter, 557n
Senate, U.S., 63, 224, 409
Banking Committee of, 153, 506
"settlement" (fund transfer), 65
Sharp, 324
Shearson Lehman, 67, 72, 75, 97, 98, 528n
Shigehara, Kumiharu, 108
Shultz, George, 22, 39, 154, 225, 255, 257,
266, 270, 295, 297, 298, 300, 305, 349,
389, 538n, 543n, 546n, 549n, 562n
Silva Herzog, Jesus, 193, 200, 201, 202, 203,
205, 206, 207, 208, 209, 210, 214, 217,
219, 222, 237, 248, 249, 252, 310, 542n
silver, 125, 135
speculation in, 144–45, 526n
Singapore, 289
Sivert, Olaf, 533n
"sleeping board," 86
Smith, Adam, 31, 38
Social Security Reform, Commission on, 56
Société Générale, 240
soft landing strategy, 400–405, 456
Solidarity, 198

Solomon, Anthony, 139, 140, 141, 143, 146,
154, 166, 173, 205, 206, 213, 215, 242,
243, 533n, 541n
Solomon, Robert, 37, 339, 380
"Son of Louvre" Accord, 384–89, 410
Soss, Neal, 152, 532n
South Africa, 36, 292, 498
Soviet Foreign Trade Bank, 292
Soviet Union, 36, 161, 198, 498
Spain, 480, 537n, 558n
"speed limit" proposals, 511
Sprinkel, Beryl, 61, 175, 298, 309, 311, 316,
370, 371, 389, 400, 546n
stagflation, 458
State Department, U.S., 203, 538n
stateless money, 14, 37, 119, 414, 492, 493, 508
capitalism and, 509
central bankers' independence and, 498,
501–2, 512
emergence of, 20–21, 92
monetary reform and, 510–12
1987 crash and, 20–21
Stockman, David, 149, 153, 158, 163, 203,
224, 500, 534n
stock market crash of 1929, 20, 23, 24, 64,
103, 110, 482
see also Great Depression
stock market crash of 1987, 14, 15, 19–123,
403, 438
Bankers Trust and, 68, 71
Bank of England and, 93–95
bond market and, 47–49, 50, 106
BP privatization and, 72, 96–102
Brady Task Force findings on, 104–5
causes of, 104–22, 368
CBC meeting on, 372–73
Corrigan and, 64–65, 68, 69–70, 72,
75–76
democracy-capitalism conflict and, 37
dollar free-fall and, 368–69
end of, 79
First Options episode in, 76–78
futures market and, 49–50, 53–54,
66–68, 71–73
German banking system and, 102–3
global imbalance and, 106–8
Greenspan and, 19–22, 24, 48–53, 54,
55–61, 62, 69, 110, 372, 403–4, 405
"group" meeting on, 21–22
Hong Kong market and, 102
Japanese banks and, 68–69
Japanese capital flow and, 105–7

DATE DUE

The Library Store   #47-0106